Communication *for* Management *and* Business

Fifth Edition

Communication *for* Management *and* Business

Fifth Edition

Norman B. Sigband
University of Southern California

Arthur H. Bell
Georgetown University

Scott, Foresman and Company
Glenview, Illinois   London, England

Credits

Cover photo © Roger Appleton

Credits continue on page I–15, a legal extension of the copyright page.

Library of Congress Cataloging-in-Publication Data

Sigband, Norman B.
  Communication for management and business.

  Includes bibliographies and index.
  1. Business communication.   I. Bell, Arthur H.
(Arthur Henry),   II. Title.
HF5718.S53   1989   658.4′5   88–29679
ISBN 0–673–38322–9

  23456—RRC—9392919089

Norm dedicates with love his efforts on this book to his wife, Joan.

Art dedicates his work affectionately to his parents, Arthur and Dorothy Bell, and to his new family, Owen, Hinda, and Louis Smith.

Preface

We have approached this revision of *Communication for Management and Business* by listening to instructors, students, and the business community. We heard them asking for a textbook that breaks new ground without excluding traditional topics. In addition, we heard their urgent request for practical supplemental materials, including a resource guide, test bank, lecture transparencies, computer software, and a classroom management system. In this, the fifth edition of *Communication for Management and Business*, we attempt to respond creatively, thoroughly, and responsibly to what *you* have told us.

First, this edition expands its treatment of the revolution in electronic communication. We extended the discussion of new communication technologies to include desktop publishing, FAX, and other new tools. Just as important, we included instruction on how these technologies can be used by individuals and organizations for improved communication. Special emphasis is given to the importance of computer graphics in business documents and presentations, as highlighted in the new state-of-the-art color portfolio at the heart of the text.

Second, this new edition casts a wider net to catch up several more forms of contemporary business communication. We added major sections on writing proposals, business plans, annual reports, and instructional materials. New types of memos, letters, reports, presentations, and interviews have been added to those included in previous editions.

Third, this edition uses cases and examples drawn from today's business concerns. Seven new cases were added on such contemporary topics as health maintenance, computer security, and mergers. We emphasized the importance of legal hazards and sensitivities in business communication with seven strategically placed supplements on business communication law and precedents. And we recognized the new wave of international and intercultural business opportunities and challenges with an entirely new chapter on intercultural communication. This chapter focuses on not only our major trading partners but also on the diverse cultures of our own society.

We offer you a text that practices the stylistic lessons it preaches. Virtually every sentence of this new edition was scrutinized for style, coherence, and meaning. New end-of-chapter questions were added for fresh, motivating assignments. High-interest boxed passages appear throughout the text. New photos, illustrations, and drawings are included to clarify and emphasize major points.

The fifth edition, furthermore, continues the tradition of *Communication for Management and Business* as "three books in one":

- a textbook that covers every major and many minor topics in both written and oral interpersonal and organizational communication.
- a casebook that offers challenging problems based on realistic business situations. These cases provide the bases for classroom analysis and discussion, role playing, as well as exercises for interviewing, meetings, memos, letters, proposals, and reports.
- a book of readings that serves as an important resource for students and instructors. These articles offer various points of view on major communication topics and save time that might have been involved in library research.

The fifth edition of *Communication for Management and Business* represents the best efforts of a committed team of authors, editors, and production staff. We welcome your review and use of the entire text package.

SUPPLEMENTS

The new edition appears with a powerful and complete package of ancillaries.

- The *Resource Guide* now includes advice on using word-processing, desktop publishing, computer graphics, and tutorial software in the business communication curriculum. An overview of principles and methods of business-communication instruction is provided for new teachers or those in transition. A carefully designed writing diagnostic examination tells both instructor and student what writing skills should be studied. In addition, true-false and essay tests are provided for each chapter.
- The updated *Test Bank* is available in a printed booklet and on computer disk, with a test generator. The computerized test bank is part of DIPLOMA, a complete classroom-management program.
- The larger package of *color transparencies* includes "before" and "after" examples of business documents as well as other materials related to every part of the textbook.
- Three ancillaries on *computer disk* provide students with diagnosis of their writing skills and with writing practice. One of these programs is new with this edition, and the other two are thoroughly revised.
- Business communication *videotapes* and *films* are available for use by book adopters.

ACKNOWLEDGMENTS

Many professors, students, and business professionals contributed suggestions, criticisms, and ideas for the fifth edition. We acknowledge a debt to them and extend our sincere thanks: Dean John A. Biles, Associate Dean Phillip Oppenheimer, Administrative Assistant Rachel Pearson, and Professors Ben Enis, Tom Housel, Carol Shuherk, Eric Skopec, and Jim Stevenson, all of the University of Southern California; Professors Tom Klammer, Mohsen Mirshafiei, Joe Sawicki, and John White, all of California State University at Fullerton; Professors James C. Bennett and Kevin F. Mulcahy, both of California State University at Northridge; Professor Lois Bachman, Community College of Philadelphia; Professor David Bateman, Southern Illinois University; Professor Joel Bowman, Western Michigan University; Professor Robert Gieselman, University of Illinois; Professor Annette Shelby, Georgetown University. We also thank Robert Bell, President, Robert Bell and Associates; Tom Boone, Senior Vice President, Countrywide Credit Industries; Davre Davidson, Chairman Emeritus, ARA Services; Ted File, Vice President, Food Marketing Institute; Cherie Kester, Director of Training, Lucky Stores; Diane Lancon, Director of Training, Countrywide Credit Industries; Ron Malanosky, Plant Director, McDonnell Douglas Astronautics; Abe Mirza, Director of Accounting, Ralphs Grocery Company; Phillip Rice, Vice President, Baker Hughes Corporation; Devon Scheer, Director of Training, TRW; and Ellen Siler, Director of Business Credit, TRW.

We also want to thank the many people at Scott, Foresman who have encouraged and helped us with the fifth edition: Jim Sitlington, editorial vice president; Jane Steinmann, developmental editor; Andrea Coens, project editor; Russell Schneck, designer; and Mary-Jo Kovach, market manager.

Once again, we want to acknowledge our families, from whom so much time was taken, for their support, encouragement, and good humor. For Art Bell, special thanks go to his wife, Dr. Dayle M. Bell, and son, Arthur James. And for Norm Sigband, special thanks go to his wife, Joan, as well as to his daughters Robin Gotz, Shelley Wilkerson, and Betsy Seamans; to his son-in-law, Glenn Gotz, and to two of the world's outstanding grandchildren, Tami and Laura.

Norman B. Sigband
Arthur H. Bell

Contents

Part Three

Research and Reports   160

Part Six

Business Correspondence   520

Part Seven

Cases   *C–1*

Part Eight

Readings   *R–1*

Communication *for* Management *and* Business

Fifth Edition

Part One

Aspects of
Communication

1 An Overview of Communication

The greatest illusion in communication is to assume it always takes place effectively.

Today we are all deeply involved in the Information Age. In fact, it might be more accurate to say, as does Alvin Toffler in his book *The Third Wave*, that we are in a communication revolution.

We are inundated with an explosion of information. The daily newspaper that once was 12 pages long is now 210 pages; the single magazine that came to our home weekly is now replaced by five magazines and dozens of catalogs, brochures, and booklets. Two or three movies or books were once released daily; now there are a dozen of each, plus any number of video and audio cassettes. And only a generation ago, the giant complex computer was found only in major corporations. Today we commonly find a desk-top version in the home (often with capacity equal to the very large 1970 unit), plus dozens of computers in almost every organization in this country and abroad.

Add to these the fact that many companies are getting larger; mergers are increasing, and activities within organizations are more specialized. More communication is needed to keep the wheels turning. And we are doing it! A recent survey concluded that Chief Executive Officers (CEOs) spend 78 percent of their time in oral communication, while third-level managers devote 87 percent of their time to all types of communication. Second-level managers devote 81 percent of their time similarly, and supervisors spend an almost unbelievable 74 percent of their time in the same activity![1]

[1]H. Mintzberg, *The Nature of Managerial Work,* Englewood Cliffs, NJ: Prentice-Hall, 1980, pp. 38–39.

But these figures should not surprise you. Just look at your own activities. Note how your academic activities compare with those of students fifty years ago. The routine of attending six lecture classes in a row has largely disappeared. You are frequently involved in discussion groups and in giving presentations in your classes. Social activities are much more communication-oriented. Distances are shorter—traveling by car is easy, and traveling by plane is far more common and often less expensive than it was even as little as 20 years ago. Also, local and long-distance phone calls are used far more frequently.

But communicating more—at home, at work, at play—does not mean we are doing it better or even as well as we did fifty years ago. And yet the importance of effective communication is recognized today as never before. In fact, a textbook in the field lists no fewer than eighteen published research studies attesting to the value of effective communication in business.[2] One study listed the ability to communicate as the most vital attribute in promotability, ahead of such skills as decision-making, motivating others, delegating authority, flexibility, and educational background. In other research, questionnaires that were sent to thousands of executives and business school graduates asked respondents to name the most valuable subject they studied in college. All three leading answers were aspects of business communication: oral reporting, report writing, and written communication. In addition, an impressive number of executives and managers often emphasize the significant role effective communication skills play in their own advancement and promotion.

Early in the 1980s, 1000 executives rated the business communication course "very important" more often than any other course in the business curriculum.[3] And in 1984, a nationwide executive search firm conducted a survey of top-level human resource executives to determine what they believed would be "pressure points" in 1985. Twenty-four issues were ranked on a one-to-ten scale. The first choice of the majority of respondents was controlling the costs of employee benefits programs. The second choice, significantly, was employee communications, reflecting management's concern for establishing a positive, participative, and supportive employee relations environment. As organizations have become more complex and more dependent on cooperative interaction of management and labor, effective communication has become—and will continue to be—increasingly important.[4]

---

[2]H. A. Murphy and C. E. Peck, *Effective Business Communications*, New York: McGraw-Hill, 1980, p. 8.

[3]H. Hildebrandt et al., "An Executive Appraisal of Courses Which Best Prepare One for General Management," *Journal of Business Communication*, Winter 1980, pp. 49–51.

[4]Survey conducted by Fleming Associates. Reported in *Training News Update*, Oct. 1984, p. 5.

COMMUNICATION AND THE ORGANIZATION

In every organization, communication occurs constantly. If we walk from the third to the sixth floor of the Marquette Corporation, for example, we will see staff preparing reports, letters, memoranda, proposals, and studies. Executives and managers are involved in meetings, interviews, and presentations. Dozens of others are having telephone conversations, participating in teleconferences, and carrying through negotiations. Almost every desk has a display terminal; a printer is nearby. The word processing center is humming, electronic mail is being dispatched, and many other human and electronic communication activities, using various media, are taking place.

These are examples of **formal channels of communication.** However, there are also unofficial or **informal channels of communication.** These are the ones that are used when an individual's need to know is not satisfied—when questions have been left unanswered. Employees at the Marquette Corporation, for example, have heard that the West End work force may be cut and 300 employees transferred to the Merryville facility some forty miles north. Nothing has been said officially by management concerning this possibility; employees are understandably upset. The result? The grapevine, or unofficial communication channel, takes over to explain the change.

Of course, any competent manager makes every effort to listen to the grapevine. In this case, he or she will probably distribute a memo setting the record straight to all concerned employees as soon as possible.

What we have seen in our bird's-eye view of the Marquette Corporation are examples based on the behavioral theory of communication. Let's first discuss this theory and its implications. Later, in Chapter 4 (in connection with the "office of the future"), we will examine the mathematical theory.

FIGURE 1-1

Flow chart depicting the process of communication

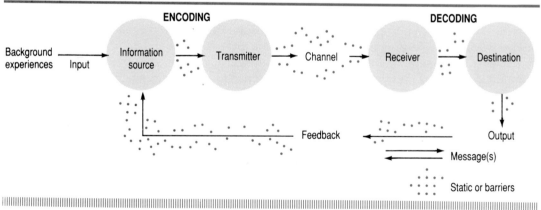

The similarities between these theories will be easy to recognize using the simple chart shown in Figure 1–1.

Let's begin our discussion by defining some terms:

Background experiences are bits of information in human or computer memory that we bring to *(input into)* a communication or a message.

The **message** is made up of bits of information that can be transmitted.

Encoding is the selection and formulation of bits of information to be transmitted as a message in an understandable language.

The **transmitter** is the unit (person or machine) that sends the message to the decoder or receiver.

The **channel** is the means of conveying the message. It may be through print, sound, touch, air, or other channels.

Decoding is the interpretation of the message by the receiver.

Feedback is the receiver's response, which gives the transmitter some indication of how the original message was received.

Input is stored information (in a brain or computer) composed of background experiences. Input is used when communication takes place.

Output is the communication of information from the information source to the transmitter.

Often present in the channels of communication is static, or barriers to effective communication that interfere with the sending or receiving of the basic message. These may be distractions, emotions, bias, or a dozen others. (See discussion of barriers later in this chapter.) Let us now look at two examples of communication: one machine, the other human.

In a computer-assisted manufacturing process (CAM), an automobile manufacturing line may stop automatically because a car chassis is not properly balanced on the conveyor mechanism. The instrument that is "tripped" because of the imbalance is the information source. The message it sends to the computer is selected from various pieces of stored information such as "too heavy," "not balanced," or "backward." The information selected fits the situation and is encoded and sent to the radio transmitter, which in turn transmits the message over a designated channel to a receiver. The message now goes to a computer to be decoded. Because all the systems are programmed similarly, the message is properly decoded "not balanced," and the conveyor mechanism automatically stops. The instrument that was originally tripped is programmed to allow up to four seconds for the conveyor to stop. The halt of the conveyor is the feedback. However, had the wrong feedback been received (no stop after four seconds), an alarm bell would have sounded and the next step in the program brought into play: termination of electric power to the conveyor belt.

A similar situation exists when manager Watkins says to staff assistant Butterfield, "Then, we're all set. You will submit a brief progress report tomorrow on the Jupiter Project to the executive vice-president. I told him he would have it quite early." Here we have encoders, decoders, a message, and a channel. There would seem to be no problem.

However, in this case the experience and semantic backgrounds of the encoder and decoder are different. To the executive vice-president and the manager, "quite early" means *in the morning* and *prior to 9:00* A.M. To staff assistant Butterfield, who is not programmed the same way, "quite early" means *before 2:00* P.M.

When the executive vice-president receives feedback the next day, which is no report by 9:00 A.M., he calls manager Watkins and almost shouts, "You said 'quite early' but I still don't have it!" Watkins now recognizes that his experience (information source) was not the same as Butterfield's, and feedback to Butterfield was necessary.

Thus, it is easy to see how barriers, noise, or static can cause breakdowns in human or machine communications. A related fact is also obvious: although computers can be programmed with similar bits of information to react similarly, this is not possible with people. Because our experiences are different, we may attribute very different meanings to the same verbal and nonverbal signals. When we do, communications (or decoding) between sender and receiver may suffer.

HUMAN OR BEHAVIORAL THEORY OF COMMUNICATION

When we examine an organization, we see many examples of verbal and nonverbal behavior. Some communication specialists believe that these and almost all other forms of behavior are really means of communication. And, conversely, all forms of communication reflect the behavior of individuals.

People who are concerned with human communication do not focus on precisely what we say or write, but on how the persons involved *perceive and think about* the message. Experts working in the behavioral sciences and related areas have contributed a great deal in recent years to the field of communication. For example, valuable work on theories of human communication has been done by psychiatrist Jurgen Ruesch.[5] Much of this chapter, concerned with the pathways and barriers in human communication, is closely associated with this behavioral theory. Dr. Ruesch identifies various communication networks as follows:

---

[5]J. Ruesch, "Psychiatry and the Challenge of Communication," *Psychiatry,* XVII, 1954.

The *intrapersonal* network is entirely within the individual and involves thinking and feeling.

The *interpersonal* communication network links two or more persons.

The *group* interaction network links groups of people. Because of the number of people involved, it is usually difficult to achieve effective communication with everybody.

The final network is *cultural.* Here there is no specific originator or receiver of the message. Certain symbols in our society—cars, clothing, homes, morals, and the like—are part of our cultural network. It is almost impossible to correct or change the system because of its powerful and pervasive nature.

Thus, we see the importance of communication to managers. In an effort to attain organizational goals, they use communication to persuade, inform, and motivate people who play key roles in getting things done. Managers almost always get their jobs done through other people. They may be skilled controllers, production supervisors or directors of engineering, but they need people to help them achieve their objectives. The only way to get other people to do what the manager thinks should be done is through communication. Research indicates that monetary rewards and fear may be effective motivators, but they rarely work on a long-term basis. Communication, which often fulfills basic social and egoistic needs, can and does work as a positive motivator. And spoken words of praise or recognition or a look that reflects encouragement or approval may prove to be just as effective a means of communication as any written memorandum.[6]

THE PROCESS OF HUMAN COMMUNICATION

The complex process of human communication involves senses, experiences, and feelings.[7] It is more than just letters, reports, telegrams, telephone conversations, and interviews. It is the action of people talking, listening, seeing, feeling, and reacting to each other, their experiences, and their environment.

When one person speaks, writes, listens, or gestures to another, there is constant action and reaction between the two. We not only interpret the words we hear; we also listen to and interpret voice inflections and facial

[6]See David K. Berlo, *The Process of Communication*, New York: Holt, Rinehart and Winston, 1960. Berlo's well-known SMCR Model (Source, Message, Channel, and Receiver) is based on human behavior also.

[7]The mathematical process of communication and its association with electronic communication will be discussed in Chapter 4.

expressions, the cast of the eyes, the drumming of fingers, and the nervous tapping of a foot on the floor. Added to these perceptions are our own internal stimuli: our emotions, feelings, experiences, interests, and other contributing factors that cause us to perceive actions and words in specific ways.

When Mr. Able talks or writes to Ms. Baker, they are doing more than simply exchanging words. Let's listen to and observe a conversation.

Able and Baker have been examining and discussing some construction plans for the past three hours. Finally Baker leans back, stretches, and says to Able, "My head is so loaded with figures and statistics that it's going in circles. Besides, the air is hot in here; what do you say we go out for a bite to eat and a cup of coffee?"

Baker has put some specific feelings into words (encoded them). Able, whose mind is still deeply involved with the building plans, listens (completely or partially) and must now receive and understand (decode) Baker's message. But will he decode the message as Baker intended?

Baker is tired, not quite clear about the plans, and hungry. But Able is enthusiastic and wants to get the job done. As a matter of fact, he may be offended by Baker's apparent implication that he confused her. He may think that is why Baker's head is "going in circles." As for the "hot air" Baker mentions, Able's interpretation of that—in his mood—is unmistakable.

Yet Baker made a simple, sincere statement whose meaning seemed obvious to her. Why, then, does Able suddenly seem angry and irritated with Baker's casual comment?

Able, of course, decoded or interpreted Baker's message on the basis of his feelings, experiences, thoughts, and perhaps even his desires; he interpreted not only Baker's words but also her gestures, actions, tone of voice, and their relationship. No matter that the interpretation may not be what Baker intended; as far as Able is concerned, it *is* what Baker intended.

The lesson here is frequently overlooked in the process of communication. We are often victims of the illusion that we have communicated effectively when we have not. The apparent solution to this problem is to check the effectiveness of our communication (whether it is a statement, a memo, a report, a letter, or a speech) through feedback. But how valid is the feedback we receive?

Feedback

In electronic communication, feedback is usually more reliable than it is in human communication. We press the power button and the screen lights up; we turn the switch and the motor begins to turn; we release the lever and the ten-ton press begins to rise. Feedback is *immediate* and reliable.

In 1961, Norbert Wiener's book *Cybernetics* drew attention to feedback as an aspect of communication. Cybernetics is a branch of science that deals with the theory of such systems as the nerve networks in animals, electronic pathways in computing machines, servo systems for the automatic control of machinery, and other information processing, transmission, and control systems.

In cybernetics, *feedback* refers to the ability of man and some machines to detect an error or deviation from what is desired in an operation and to *feed back* that error to a control mechanism, which then makes the necessary correction. If a satellite destined for a point in space moves off course, the deviation is noted and fed back to the controlling mechanism for correction. A home thermostat records a temperature too low and feeds back a signal to the furnace, which then operates to make a correction. Or a person's body temperature goes lower than normal; this information is fed back, and his or her physiological control mechanism makes the muscles shiver.

Thus, a common feature of a control system is that the output produces an effect on the input. In communication engineering this effect is called feedback. A control-systems engineer refers to it as a *closed-loop system.*

The similarities of feedback in this technical concept to that in interpersonal communication are immediately apparent. We even have a common expression, "Have you closed the loop?" It asks whether the communicator (encoder) has secured a satisfactory response (feedback) from the communicatee (decoder) and thus satisfactorily closed the loop and secured understanding.

The popular meaning of the term **feedback** is the verbal or nonverbal response received from the individual to whom a message is directed. It may be a series of words; it may be a raised eyebrow, an angry expression, or a smile; it may be no response at all (which is a response indicating that the message was not heard, not understood, or not accepted). But it is only through the feedback we receive that we can know whether we have communicated our ideas.

If we ask our daughter to open the window and she does it, we know we have communicated successfully. However, if she opens the door, that incorrect response or feedback tells us that communication has broken down.

When we write for our superiors, our subordinates, our colleagues, our teachers, or our students and they do not understand what we have written, they will ask us for a further interpretation. Their questions (or feedback) tell us how successful we have been in exchanging ideas. But here again, we have a question of accuracy.

A boss may quickly explain a new procedure to his subordinate and then conclude with, "Now, Mike, do you see how that works?" Almost invariably the "Mikes," or subordinates of the world, will say, "Yes, I do."

Why do we so often say, "Yes, I understand," when we really do not? The answer is complex. Sometimes we really think we understand but we do not. In most cases, however, our egos or our emotions force us to say, "Yes, I understand," when we really don't. Who wishes to be thought a fool?

Thus the feedback is not accurate. However, the manager often accepts

WHAT ABOUT THE POLLUTION OF OUR LANGUAGE?[1]

There is much discussion these days of pollution—pollution of the water, pollution of the air, pollution of foods, pollution of crops. What about pollution of our language? It seems to me that our language is being polluted these days to an extent that may prove as harmful to us as polluted water or polluted air.

It is often said that concepts and ideas are first conceived in words. And then words are used to transfer that knowledge. And that knowledge results in new knowledge—all expressed in words. But if words are the currency of our thought and we debase the currency, can we continue to initiate ideas with words and then transfer those ideas with other words?

Let's look at the three areas where it seems to me most of the "pollution" takes place. The first is in the use of nonwords for words; the second is using inexact words; and the third is the growing use of profanity and obscenities.

Listen to the radio or watch TV. If the speaker is not a professional announcer, speaker, or moderator, count the number of times phrases such as "you know," "in other words," and "dig it," are used. The statement often starts acceptably with "My reaction was" and then gets derailed when the speaker can't find the words and concludes with "you know." Now what in the world does "my reaction was . . . you know" mean?

But the casual observer is more confounded when the serious reply to that statement is "Well sure, man, I feel, you know—the same way." So statements are incomplete, thoughts are left in midair, and ideas are often not expressed. Why do so many today have such a shortage of words? Perhaps we don't read enough and so can't add new words to our vocabulary; perhaps students are not required to write as much as they should—where a "you know" is not acceptable. Perhaps we listen too much to other language polluters.

The problem is compounded when we choose words carelessly, and often do not say precisely what we mean. We use *farther* for *further*, *anxious* for *eager*, *disorganize* for *unorganize*,

it as reliable. Perhaps this is an ego problem also. What manager wants to hear that his or her communication was *not* clear?

On other occasions, we receive no feedback at all—or receive it too late. Take, for example, a letter that has gone to Pittsburgh, a report to New York, a Christmas speech to 3,000 assembled employees, or a lecture to 38 students. Such communications can seem to disappear into a vacuum.

In the case of the report, let's say that three weeks have passed since it was submitted. McKenzie, the author of the report, learns the company president needs additional information that was not included in the report. Yet when McKenzie offers to supply it, the president says, "I got it myself," or "I made do without it." Thus the feedback has come too late to be of value to McKenzie.

Or, in the case of the lecture, the professor may read the final exam (the feedback) only to discover that fully 80 percent of the class didn't understand concept ABC. It is too late to bring them together and review it.

Thus, we are in a dilemma. We say on the one hand, "Check the feedback to determine how effectively you have communicated." But on the other *continual* for *continuous*. And meaning is further polluted. The word disinterest, for example, has a very precise meaning: objective, neutral, unbiased. It is correct to say, "The disinterested judge rendered his verdict." But if enough of us say, "Joe was completely disinterested in going to the game," then meaning is eroded. The result of having a word like *disinterest* used for *uninterest* is that we will eventually lose the meaning of the word *disinterest*. And that is a pity because the loss of words or the use of diluted words may make the expression of ideas difficult or imprecise.

Most disturbing is the pollution of our language in the last ten years by casual and frequent use of profanity and obscenity. Stand in any elevator, sit in any office, shop in any store and listen to the conversation. Whether it's two casually dressed teenagers, two tennis-outfitted young adults, or three vested business types, you are likely to hear a whole string of "foul" words.

During my years in World War II service, and before and since, I certainly have contributed. But somehow it's different when I listen during the intermission to the three attractive teenagers sitting behind me in the theater discussing their plans for the summer. They lose some of their attractiveness as they casually use words that are more commonly associated with our excretory and sexual systems. Sure, I know that words have no meanings: only people have meanings. And I know too that ugliness is in the mind of the beholder. But I can't help thinking that language pollution needs clearing up as much as our air and water . . . for the benefit of us all.

Who was the ancient philosopher who said, "Speak that I may know you"?

[1]Adapted from "What About the Pollution of Our Language" by Norman B. Sigband in *Journal of Business Communication*, Vol. 18, No. 1, Winter 1981. Copyright © 1981 by Norman B. Sigband. Reprinted by permission.

hand we also say, "Feedback may not be reliable." The answer seems to be that we must become sensitive to all the forms of feedback at our disposal—and must, at times, *provide* feedback by self-evaluation and playing "devil's advocate" to our own ideas. In these ways we have a chance to make important adjustments in our communications before we sign the letter, initial the report, or sit down after a speech.

Such unsparing openness to self-evaluation and self-improvement in communication takes courage, patience, and insight. Communicators at all levels, from the beginner to the expert, face the challenge of putting aside pet notions and assumptions to really *hear* the other side of the story.

That same openness must extend to nonhuman sources of information. Computers have a great deal to "tell" business people: data printouts, statistical summaries, computer-managed logs, and even—with the advent of artificial intelligence—reasoned advice. We cannot let "computer anxiety," a somewhat natural response to a new and powerful technology, prevent us from hearing what we need to hear from computers. Training programs and reading materials for the lay person can help allay such anxiety.

In the final analysis, as we communicate we must keep in mind the following points about feedback received from the world around us:

1. It is necessary to secure it.
2. It may not be accurate.
3. It may come too late to correct the communication.
4. It can reach us by nonverbal and verbal ways (often both).

But to assume that communication always takes place effectively may be the greatest illusion of all.

OBJECTIVES OF COMMUNICATION

We communicate for a purpose, and our basic objectives in communication are generally these:

1. To be understood exactly as we intended.
2. To secure the desired response to our message.
3. To maintain favorable relations with those with whom we communicate.

Whenever we communicate with others, *some* understanding (or misunderstanding) will take place. What we wish to secure, however, is for the decoder to understand the message as *we* understand the message. That is why the last three words in objective 1 are so important. As for objective 2, any response—positive, negative, or noncommittal—tells the encoder something. Of course, the encoder usually hopes the decoder's response (or feedback) will be positive. Finally, because we work, live, and exist in a world of associates, we hope to secure objective 3.

It is apparent that an encoder can write or talk to a decoder and fail to achieve any of the objectives. Or it is possible to achieve the first objective but not the second (favorable response) or third. It is even possible to send a message in such a way as to secure objectives 1 and 2 (favorable response) but to antagonize the decoder and not achieve objective 3. Our goal in *all* types of communication, however, should be to attain all of these objectives.

BARRIERS TO COMMUNICATION

Nonverbal Barriers

It is no exaggeration to say that approximately 60 percent of our communication is nonverbal. The way we stand, walk, shrug our shoulders, furrow our brows, and shake our heads all convey ideas to others. But we need not always perform an action for nonverbal communication to take place. We also communicate by the clothes we wear, the car we drive, or the office we occupy. It is true that what is communicated may not be accurate, but ideas of some kind *are* communicated.

Nonverbal external and internal stimuli play an important role in our interpretation of words. Sometimes these stimuli are so strong that we interpret them instead of the words directed to us. When these factors sway our understanding to a degree that does not harmonize at all with the meaning intended by the communicator, they become *barriers* to the clear interpretation of ideas. This, of course, is what happened to our friends Mr. Able and Ms. Baker. If we become more aware of what these barriers are, maybe we can cope with them better.

Perhaps a good analogy is the physician-patient relationship. It isn't enough for the physician to state, "The patient is sick." If the patient is to be cured, the physician must pinpoint the trouble and treat it appropriately. The same is true of the encoder who has failed to communicate effectively. That individual must determine the specific barrier(s) that caused the communication breakdown and then attempt to alleviate or eliminate it. If the encoder has an idea of some of the barriers that occur, it will be easier to diagnose the case and remedy the problems.

Differences in perception of a situation may cause ineffective communication. Our previous experiences largely determine how we will react to specific stimuli. Viewing the same thing, individuals of different ages, cultural backgrounds, and national origins often have different perceptions. They use their knowledge, their culture, and their experiences to interpret what they see. Not only does each of us see things differently, but when two of us hear a statement, we may also interpret (hear or perceive) it differently.

Let us look at Line Foreman Anderson, his supervisor, Assistant Plant Supervisor Benton, and Development Engineer Carleton. They have just come from lunch and are walking back to their shop area. Forty feet ahead of them are seven or eight production workers who work directly under Anderson and in Benton's department. As the three walk past, the circle of workers suddenly breaks into laughter and backslapping.

How did the foreman, assistant plant supervisor, and engineer each perceive this? Anderson, who has been having trouble securing cooperation from several of the production-line workers, hears derisive and insulting laughter. Benton, who prides herself on "running a tight ship with high morale," hears good-natured steam being let off. Carleton, who works as an engineer with dozens of different shop groups from week to week, doesn't even hear the laughter, which has come at the precise instant when he has reached the high point of the story *he* is telling Anderson and Benton.

Or consider the reaction of three employees to the sight of a large new machine being moved into the shop area. Worker Fenton perceives it as a threat to his job—a replacement for his skills. Production Supervisor Gable views it as an asset that will help her achieve higher production levels and thus secure her bonus. Treasurer Holcomb perceives it as a further drain on the company's limited resources.

The point in both examples is that effective communication cannot take place among persons when each perceives something different. Because they visualize different situations, they *discuss* different situations.

Of course, we can't hope to perceive *every* situation as the other person does, but if we make an honest effort to appreciate his or her point of view, we improve the possibility of achieving effective communication. It is important to understand that we don't have to *agree*. As a visual example of conflicting perceptions, notice how the shapes in Figure 1–2 can be perceived in at least two ways.

Lack of interest in the subject matter, on the part of either the speaker or the listener, can seriously deter the reception of ideas. There are several ways of arousing interest in readers and listeners. One way is to use an attention-catching opening or a statement so provocative or unexpected that the members of the audience must sit up and take notice. But such gimmick devices are, at best, short-term in their overall appeal. At the other extreme, it is possible to *order* people to be interested. "I'll expect that report to be completed and submitted by 4 P.M. *today*. If it isn't, don't bother to come in to work tomorrow!" Certainly a statement like that arouses the interest of the listener; in addition, of course, it arouses his or her animosity and antagonism,

FIGURE 1–2
Perception sketches

and we have lost one of our objectives of good communication: maintaining favorable relationships.

However, the most effective way to secure the readers' or listeners' interest is to motivate them to *want* to pay attention. And the best way to accomplish this is to build the message around the benefits they will receive if they carry through what the speaker or writer suggests. For example, to gain the interest of a group of foremen, a plant manager may point out how production will rise if they follow his or her suggestions. This increase in production will in turn result in higher pay or recognition for the foremen. Because most of the foremen are concerned with increased pay, they probably will be interested in the communication.

Lack of fundamental knowledge can be a third barrier to the clear communication of ideas. How can you intelligently discuss a problem with those who do not have the background to understand what is being said? Certainly there will be a breakdown in communication if a nuclear physicist attempts to explain quantum mechanics to someone with only a high school education. Conversely, it is conceivable that the speaker's or writer's knowledge of his or her subject is superficial. This also becomes a barrier, for it is always apparent to us when someone is, as the saying goes, only one chapter ahead of the class.

Sometimes the communicator's knowledge in a field is so thorough that the other person can't follow. The communicator may assume that the listener has adequate background or fundamental knowledge and then try to proceed on the basis of this false premise. To overcome this barrier, determine how much knowledge of the subject the recipient of the message possesses before you speak or write.

That is not always easy to do. As was indicated earlier, we usually depend on some type of verbal or nonverbal response to indicate understanding or lack of understanding. But the response from the recipient of our message may not always be accurate.

The **emotions** of either the sender or the receiver can be another obstacle in communication. We have all been in situations in which the atmosphere became so emotionally charged that reasonable discussion broke down. When we have deep emotional reactions—love, hate, fear, anger—we find it almost impossible to communicate coherently anything but that emotion. The lesson here is obvious: calm down before you send or receive ideas.

On the other hand, sometimes emotions can be a help in communicating. A person who is emotionally charged up or enthusiastic often finds this quality an asset in helping get a message across.

The **personalities** of those involved can be another barrier to communication. We are often so strongly influenced by the personality of the speaker or the writer that we may either accept or reject what is said without good reason. Personality is not confined to an individual, however. Sometimes an audience seems to react if it were one person; many speakers will attest that some group or other was hostile, friendly, apathetic, or understanding. Of course, our recognition of the personalities of others is often tempered by our own, and perhaps when we feel that communication has broken down because of personality, we should first examine our own—difficult as this task is—and attempt to make changes that improve understanding.

The **appearance** of the communicator or the instrument he or she uses to communicate, such as a letter or report, can prove to be another critical factor. A speaker whose jacket is awry, whose collar is askew, and whose general appearance is poor is not likely to arouse a favorable response in the listeners. The same is true of a business letter or a report that is typed in heavy block paragraphs, is jammed on the page from side to side and from top to bottom, and has a jagged margin and messy erasures and, in the case of a report, few topic headings. The unkempt attire of a speaker or the careless and negligent appearance of a written message may prove to be a serious barrier to the communication of ideas. The solution here is simply correction of the fault. If the appearance of a report is poor, the business executive should have no compunction about sending it back to be retyped. The reader may be a thousand miles away from the company, and his or her image of the firm may be entirely based on that sheet of paper.

Prejudice can also seriously impede the transmission of ideas. An unreasonable bias rejects ideas without consideration. Although we usually relate prejudice to race, religion, and color, most of us encounter it in a dozen other ways. It may be a simple but strongly held viewpoint (or perception) on the part of the chief executive, or it may be the classic statement of the foreman: "Well, I've been here twenty-eight years; we never tried it before, and I'm sure it won't work now."

Of all the barriers to the clear communication of ideas, bias and prejudice are probably the most difficult to eliminate. The usual answer is education, but that is a lengthy and sometimes frustrating job. Perhaps a better way to overcome deep bias is to show people how they will benefit by following a specific course of action. People can adjust their prejudices surprisingly fast when their self-interest is at stake.

Distractions can prove to be another disturbing factor in communication. Clattering printers, noisy punch presses, inadequate illumination, hissing ventilation, or uncomfortable room temperature may be deterrents to the communication of ideas. It is most difficult for production-line workers to understand what the foreman wants when they have to shout to one another over the noise of pounding machinery. Any upsetting factor that impinges upon any of our senses—visual, auditory, olfactory, or others—may prevent the clear transmission and reception of ideas.

Poor organization of ideas may be a serious barrier to communication. Even when ideas are clearly and logically presented, it is still not always easy to assimilate them. The difficulties are compounded when thoughts are presented in a confused manner. No contractor lays a brick and no engineer positions a steel beam without first looking at the blueprint; a surgeon makes no move without examining the laboratory reports and the X rays; an attorney would never file an important case without first drawing up a careful brief; but often we begin to write or speak without bothering to organize our thoughts.

Whether the organizational framework of our message is jotted down on a sheet of scratch paper or carefully typed up as a formal outline, we should not attempt to communicate without knowing precisely where we are going. If listeners or readers cannot follow you easily and logically, they will simply close their minds. A three-minute oral presentation, a fifteen-line letter, a half-hour speech, or a thirty-page report should all be planned before they are carried through. There is almost nothing we do, from an evening's recreation to the construction of a twenty-story building, that we do not plan, except, all too often, our speaking and writing.

Poor listening is one of the most serious barriers to the communication of ideas. We often think of communication as concerned with reading, writing, and speaking. But in fact about 60 percent of our time is spent listening.

Poor listening is often a natural result of the disparity in the time it takes to tell ideas and the time required to assimilate them. Most of us speak at the rate of about 140 words a minute, but we can assimilate approximately 500 words a minute. It is no wonder, therefore, that the listener's mind tends to wander as it moves further and further ahead of the speaker's ideas.

Often listeners are thinking of what they are going to say next, after the speaker has finished. Or perhaps their preconceptions are screening out much of what the speaker is saying. Listening requires effort. If we try, we can learn to listen actively, to concentrate on what is being said, to hear the ideas beyond the words, and to appreciate the desires and needs of the speaker.

Supervisors or executives *must* listen carefully. That's part of their job. They should know that it isn't necessary to agree with subordinates' statements or requests. But it is necessary to show that they understand and appreciate why the employees say what they say. Effective listening helps administrators control many of the activities under their jurisdiction.

The **competition for attention** in our busy society presents still another barrier. With dozens of communication media bombarding us throughout the day, we have, of necessity, become selective. Our grandparents lived with an eight-page newspaper, limited circle of friends, and static-filled radio receiver. In contrast, we live in a veritable torrent of sound and printed words. Sixty- and eighty-page newspapers, weekly news magazines, technical journals, and dozens of reports must be read by each of us, and if we do not get to them we somehow feel guilty. Then there are meetings we must attend, friends to visit, the radio to listen to, television shows to watch, and movies to see. The result is that we become perceptually selective; we hear and do not listen; we see and do not assimilate. This wall of defense serves us to good advantage, for there is too much communication in our world for us to take it all in. We must choose—or have someone else choose for us.

Because of our busy society, communicators must recognize that they are constantly competing for the attention of listeners or readers. They must make their messages so excellent, so clear, so concise, so interesting, and so compelling that the listeners or readers will *want* to assimilate them.

Verbal Barriers

Language itself is probably the most common barrier to effective communication.[8] Among the problems in the use of language for communication are *differences in interpretation of statements.* We have all said things that we thought were perfectly clear and simple, only to have them completely misconstrued. This happens for various reasons. Sometimes it is simply the result of misunderstanding, or it may be due to an unconscious desire not to carry out someone's request. Or perhaps the speaker has chosen a word that conveys a meaning different from that intended. Although *fee, salary, wages, payment, stipend,* and *emolument* are listed in the dictionary as synonymous, each has a different connotation. We would never pay a surgeon "wages" for an operation or a ditchdigger weekly "fees" for his labor. As Mark Twain said, "There is as much difference between the right word and the almost-right word as between lightning and the lightning bug."

Then, too, a specific word may evoke different symbols or pictures in the minds of people whose backgrounds and experiences are different. What does the word *pig* conjure up in the mind of a steelworker, as compared with that of a farmer or a college student? What symbol does the word evoke when it is hurled in anger at a person?

Language uses words to convey ideas, facts, and feelings. Sometimes semantic problems arise in the interpretation of words because the meanings are not in the words but in the minds of the people who receive them. Meanings of concrete words do not vary too much from one person to another. There is little possibility for confusion when we speak of pencil or paper or book. But as words become more abstract (democracy, honesty, happiness), they are more likely to be misunderstood. This is also true of words that carry emotional overtones in a specific society. What *liberal, radical, virtue, morality,* and *integrity* mean to the speaker or writer may not agree at all with the listener's or reader's concept of the same word.

Another verbal barrier is *inadequate vocabulary.* If our stock of words is poor, forcing us to fumble and bumble as we attempt to express our ideas, our ability to communicate will be limited. It is important to build up our

---

[8]See movie, *Communication: Barriers and Pathways,* 1980 (Color, 18 minutes). Paramount Communications, advisor N. B. Sigband. Available from AIMS Media, Inc., 6901 Woodley Ave., Van Nuys, CA 91406.

vocabularies so that we can express our ideas clearly, forcefully, and easily rather than with second-choice words.

We should also make every effort to avoid *errors* in speaking and writing. Whether it is in spelling, diction, grammar, or pronunciation, an error immediately forces the reader or listener to focus on the mistake. You know how errors can jump out of the page you are reading or the statement to which you are listening. Never minimize or rationalize an error, regardless of how minor; make every effort to make your language choice as correct as possible.

Remember also to choose the *proper level* of language when you communicate with others. To speak or write above their heads or down to them condescendingly is to invite misinterpretation, irritation, and confusion. A classic story illustrating this problem is of the plumber who wrote to the Bureau of Standards in Washington, stating that he used hydrochloric acid for cleaning out clogged drains. The bureau wrote him: "The efficacy of hydrochloric acid is indisputable, but the corrosive residue is incompatible with metallic permanence." The plumber replied that he was glad the bureau agreed. The bureau tried again, this time writing, "We cannot assume responsibility for the production of noxious and toxic residue with hydrochloric acid and suggest you use an alternative procedure." The plumber again replied that he was pleased that the bureau agreed with his findings. Finally the bureau awoke to the fact that it was not writing at this plumber's level. Thereupon the plumber received a note which said, "Don't use hydrochloric acid. It eats hell out of the pipes."

CONFLICT BETWEEN VERBAL AND NONVERBAL COMMUNICATION

An interesting fact about communication is that two messages may be transmitted simultaneously. Quite often a verbal message is conveyed with a nonverbal one. Someone may greet us with a great show of enthusiasm: "How are you? Good to see you. Come on into my office and chew the fat, you old son of a gun"; but the nonverbal communication, consisting of a surreptitious but pained glance at the clock, says something else. We all know the guest who says, "Of course we want to see your slides of Europe," as he stifles a yawn and sprawls in the chair. Then there is the employee who tries to sound relaxed and comfortable when he talks to the boss, while his toe tapping the floor tells a different story.

Interestingly enough, whenever the meaning of the nonverbal message conflicts with that of the verbal one, the receiver is most likely to find the former more believable. The alert receiver will almost always be able to determine when a problem exists. Most of us can discern the fearful person behind the good-humored, back-slapping, joke-telling facade. We somehow know quite well how dismally Betty and Joe's marriage is progressing, even though their protestations of undying love for one another are voiced loudly and clearly. The nonverbal message is usually obvious, and if it does not agree with the verbal one, the receiver quickly and almost invariably recognizes the one that is true.

Most of the nonverbal messages that we receive come to us visually. We are quick to see the hurt in someone's eyes or another person's triumphant smile. We notice the twisting, nervous fingers in a lap and the confidence in a posture. We also decode the message of a sudden, frightened tug at our arm when we cross in heavy traffic or the subtle touching of fingers of two people in love.

Our nose also plays an important role in nonverbal communication. What a wonderful message we decode when we walk into the cozy comfort of a home where a Thanksgiving dinner is about to be served. The aromas of a roasting turkey, dressing, and pumpkin pie require no words to transmit a message.

All in all, any message—verbal or nonverbal, formal or informal— received and decoded by one of our senses is communication.

QUESTIONS FOR STUDY

1. Is it possible to achieve communication objective 1 (to be understood exactly as intended) without achieving objectives 2 (to secure the desired response) and 3 (to maintain favorable relations)? Explain.
2. Why is it difficult to give yourself feedback on the effectiveness of your own verbal and nonverbal communications to others?
3. Of the following three barriers to communication, which one is likely to prove most difficult to overcome for Americans traveling in the Near and Far East: 1) distractions, 2) lack of interest, or 3) differences in perception? Explain.
4. Why is the nonverbal communication of a member of a foreign culture more difficult to interpret than the nonverbal communication of another American? Explain.
5. Will "competition for the attention of the decoder" become a smaller or a greater barrier to encoders in the late 1990s than it is today? Explain.
6. Why do many decoders respond with a "Yes, I understand you," when in fact they do not?
7. Why do many encoders accept the "Yes, I understand you," quickly and happily?
8. Differentiate between formal and informal communication.
9. It is often said that we should check feedback to determine the effectiveness of our communication. Is that a valid statement? Explain.

10. Why have most of us become selective listeners in recent years?
11. Define and differentiate encoding and decoding.
12. How do learning, culture, and experience influence perception? Explain each.
13. Is it possible for a person's verbal and nonverbal communication to be incongruent with each other even when they occur simultaneously? Explain and give an example to support your answer.
14. Is it possible for emotions to be a help or a hindrance, or both, to effective communication? Explain.
15. Can architecture (in different ages and in different cultures) be an example of nonverbal communication? Explain.
16. What percentage of your own communication experience is spent in listening? List ways in which you have learned your listening habits. Discuss how listening could be taught in formal schooling.
17. In what ways can language itself prove to be a barrier to communication? Give an example for each way you discuss.

EXERCISES

18. Select friends or business associates who are members of two different minorities. Observe their nonverbal communication for two weeks. Prepare and present a report (oral or written) on the many differences you have observed. Organize your report in whichever manner you feel is most logical.
19. Cut an advertisement out of a magazine or newspaper and submit it to your instructor with your analysis of the nonverbal communication that you feel the advertiser intended to convey. This message may extend beyond the obvious verbal communication.
20. Examine a corporate headquarters office arrangement. Discuss various aspects of nonverbal communication that are evident to you.
21. Several of the following quotations are taken from the writings of various authors. Select three and explain the meaning of each in a brief series of statements:

    (a) "To say that we know what a word means in advance of its use is nonsense."
    (b) "Meaning is relative to experience."
    (c) "Never mind what the words mean. What did the speaker mean?"
    (d) "Some companies believe management can exercise 'stop-go' control over information which employees receive."
    (e) "Speak in order that I may know you."
    (f) "Time talks; space speaks."
    (g) "Speakers are prisoners of their vocabularies."

      (h) "It's what and how you communicate or don't communicate that makes you what you are to others."

      (i) "Words in a communication can cause friendliness, humor, or happiness; used incorrectly, they can cause hatred, hostility, and even death."

22. Find a speaker (perhaps a political speaker or religious speaker) on television. Turn the volume off to observe his or her nonverbal messages. Make a list of your impressions of these messages. Then turn up the volume to see if the speaker's nonverbal messages concur with the verbal message. Write a short analysis of the similarities and differences between your nonverbal and verbal impressions.

23. Choose two classmates who, together with you, have attended a presentation or lecture. List your own perceptions of what you have seen and heard (for example, "monotone voice"). Then ask your chosen classmates to draw up a similar list (without showing it to you or one another). Finally, compare lists and write a brief analysis of how different people form different impressions of the same event.

24. This exercise should reflect a real situation in which you are now involved. Visualize a person with whom you do not communicate effectively. Now record the following on paper:

      (a) Identify the individual (wife, boss, subordinate, boyfriend, instructor, father, neighbor, mother-in-law, mother, etc.).

      (b) State as specifically as possible the barrier(s) that make communication difficult. Also, note on whose part (encoder-decoder) the barrier(s) arise.

      (c) Indicate the possible solution(s) and the specific ways you intend to implement them.

25. Copy a quotation from a recent newspaper or magazine article and cite the source. This may be a statement (or a series of statements) from a world leader, political officer, public figure, corporate director, or private citizen. Analyze the quotation from a semantic point of view in an attempt to substantiate events resulting from it.

26. What are the primary barriers to effective learning in your classes? What are your suggestions for removing them?

27. What are the primary barriers to increased productivity in your present place of employment? What are your suggestions for removing them?

Communication in Organizations

2

There is no vacuum in communication. If something is going on, it will be communicated. If the formal channel is closed or unreceptive, the message will be communicated on the informal one.

Whether in the public sector or the private one, organizations are complex. Obviously, the six-person company is easier to manage than the 60,000-employee organization. But in both cases, communications are used to inform, to persuade, to compare, and to motivate. How effectively communication takes place, both internally and externally, will largely determine whether or not the organization achieves its goals.[1] Naturally, it is much easier to communicate and to manage in a small organization where the owner and the machine operator can quickly discuss a common problem. The task becomes more difficult when a single division numbers 5700 employees. When the production line employee has a problem that may affect the entire division, how long will it take for the message to be communicated all the way up to the division manager? Or, conversely, how successful will the head of the division be if he must send a message down through seven levels to foreman Wilson?

It is immediately apparent that there is much involved when sending a

[1]Some of the worthwhile books dealing with organizational communication are: C. Reuss and D. Silvis (eds.) *Inside Organization Communication,* New York: Longman, 1981; L. Micheli, F. W. Cespedes, D. Byker, T. Raymond, *Managerial Communication,* Glenview, IL.: Scott, Foresman, 1984; S. O'Connell, *The Manager as Communicator,* San Francisco: Harper and Row, 1979; R. K. Allen, *Organizational Management Through Communication,* New York: Harper and Row, 1977; R. W. Pace, *Organizational Communication,* Englewood Cliffs, N.J.: Prentice-Hall, 1983; H. Cummings, L. Long, M. Lewis, *Managing Communication in Organizations,* Dubuque, IA.: Gorsuch Scarisbrick, 1983; J. Wofford, E. Gerloff, R. Cummins, *Organizational Communication,* New York: McGraw-Hill, 1977; G. M. Goldhaber, *Organizational Communication,* Dubuque, IA.: Wm. C. Brown, 1974.

message up or down, for it must go through the lead person, foreman, supervisor, section head, department head, group leader, assistant division leader, and division manager. We need not contemplate what will happen to the accuracy of that original message as it travels through these gatekeepers, even under the best of conditions. What about the other obstacles it will encounter in its journey? It may be affected by such intangibles as empire building, social status, lack of time, and level of trust, as well as many of the barriers listed in Chapter 1. But as difficult as this task appears to be, communication *must* flow up, down, and laterally in an organization if it is to achieve its goals.

The omnipresence of the computer has been both a blessing and a problem in efforts to achieve effective upward, downward, and lateral communication. On one hand, at the effortless press of a key a message stored in the computer can be sent anywhere—or everywhere—in the corporation. In 1987, more than 500 million messages were sent in that fashion. But that ease of sending and receiving also can be a problem. Some messages aren't meant for all eyes in the company, yet can be accessed nonetheless from computer terminals throughout the business. To protect the security of messages, companies have turned to special forms of electronic mail and encryption devices (mathematical encoding) to make sure that messages are read only by their intended audiences.

THE DIRECTIONS OF COMMUNICATION

In most organizations, the largest percentage of vertical communication flows downward. These communications may be orders, directives, memos, policies, bulletins, or dozens of other possibilities. Unfortunately, these are usually one-way communications, based on many managers' assumption that what is sent down is always understood and received. Infrequently, the manager may request a response. But here again we may encounter the difficulties of feedback: the employee too often responds (upward communication) with what he or she believes the manager wishes to hear.

Downward communication can take several forms:

- Printed materials (bulletins, memos, orientation manuals, annual reports to employees, and policy manuals)
- Typed materials (memos, letters, and reports)
- Interview situations (appraisal, informative, counseling, and disciplinary)
- Presentations to groups
- Computer "bulletin boards" and message centers

You, the manager, are cautioned to monitor carefully the feedback received from downward communication. If you assume that you have communicated effectively simply because you gave a speech, sent out a memo, issued a report, distributed an employee manual, held an interview, or carried through some other method of communicating to employees, you may be making a grievous error.

Well-known management consultant Peter Drucker says flatly:

> *For centuries managers have attempted communications "downward." This cannot work no matter how intelligently they try. It cannot work, first, because it focuses on what the manager wants to say. . . . All that can be communicated downwards are commands . . .*[2]

However, Drucker states that downward communication will work if the manager first permits communication to come up.

The point is that managers must recognize that one-way communication may simply amount to whistling in the dark. For that reason we will look carefully at ways to get downward communication to work. One way, of course, is to secure effective upward communication first. The manager who listens carefully to upward communication from employees and assesses correctly what has been said will then be better able to select the topics, the tone, and the time for effective *downward* communication.

DOWNWARD COMMUNICATION

One of our important needs is the need to know. Employees want to know where the organization is going. Was the big contract secured or not? Why was the company's proposal to the Air Force rejected? Is there a reason for the drop in the stock's price? What is this we hear about a possible merger? How will a merger affect the work force? What were the results of the long-range planning meeting? And on and on.

Did employees fifty years ago make such demands for information? The answer is probably "no." At that time, employees certainly wanted to know about the company's plans and progress, but they were essentially concerned with their income. They were often content to "let the boss be boss." Today, by contrast, with well over 50 percent of our work force made up of two-income families, the physical need for more money is no longer the sole driving force. As a result, employees' social, egoistic, self-actualization, and information needs have become more demanding.

Certainly the need to know differs from employee to employee. For some, the job and everything associated with it is their life. For others, whose primary interests may be "outside the job" in a sports, church, or rec-

---

[2]See P. Drucker, "What Communication Means," in the Readings section of this book.

reational activity, the job is simply a source to satisfy their economic need. However, this latter group is invariably a small part of any work force.

An analysis of employees' "need to know" shows that these needs usually fall into one of two categories. The first involves information about the job itself. All employees want to know what their tasks are, how they are to be performed, how they interrelate with other areas to achieve the organization's goals, where and when they are to be performed. They also want to know what their specific duties are, what freedom they have within those limits, and how their superiors view their performance.

The second area concerns the employee's relationships with the organization and the organization's relationship with the world. Employees want to know what the firm's goals and objectives are; what its short- and long-range plans are; what the company's response will be to the union's new request and why; what will the closing of the Bellville plant mean to the overall work force; whether there is any truth to the rumor concerning a possible merger; how the firm has reacted to the various equal-opportunity rulings; and a dozen other things. The organization that does not recognize this second need and build upon it for its own benefit surely will miss a magnificent opportunity to improve morale and increase productivity.

Managers in more and more modern organizations recognize the vital role of internal organizational communication. As a result, some have developed communications plans; others have structured communication policies.[3] An example of a set of communication policies is the "Communication Plan" issued by the Operations and Support Group of the TRW Corporation. The covering memo for the plan itself was signed by the general manager of the group. In part, the memo to employees states:

> *Attached is the Operations and Support Group Communications Plan . . . I am sending you a copy so that you are aware of my objectives and plans for communicating to our employees and customers. . . . It is my intent to raise the level of emphasis on communication with O & SG . . .*[4]

Mr. Hugh Brady, TRW vice-president and general manager, had this to say about a policy of communication:

> *. . . every organization must develop an explicit plan of action to assure that its philosophy of communication is built into the management structure. I have learned through experience that simply recognizing the importance of communi-*

---

[3]See Norman B. Sigband, "Needed: Corporate Policies on Communication," *Advanced Management Journal*, Apr. 1969; Norman B. Sigband, "Face to Face: Employee Communications," *Communicator's Journal*, May/June 1983 (see Readings section); and Norman B. Sigband, "Policies of Communication for a Turbulent Society," *Conference Highlights*, London, 1987, International Association of Business Communicators.

[4]TRW Operations and Support Group, Interoffice Correspondence, O & SG Communication Plan, memo from H. Brady, March 16, 1983. Used by permission.

*cation does not necessarily lead to the translation of good intentions into sus-
tained action. Any shortcomings in meeting our established communication
standards are not due to a lack of willingness to comply; it is, instead, a result
of the fact that every month, week, and day—even every hour—our priorities
shift. Previous secondary priorities suddenly demand immediate attention and
full involvement, particularly for "action-oriented decision makers." The less
urgent, less action-oriented activities (such as those requiring a proactive posture toward communication) tend to slip into the background of our concerns.*

*Unless I demonstrate through consistent behavior my own commitment and
explicit expectations in this regard, our managers will follow other signals dictating what and how much to communicate and to whom. Having a plan with
specific objectives, a detailed schedule of activities, minimum expectations, and
so forth provides a firm basis for managing the communication needs of the
organization with the same fervor as the other important responsibilities we
have.*

*An action plan goes a long way to assuring that our communication activities
are followed through. While it does not guarantee that all communication-
related needs of the organization will be satisfied without fail, it does help to
indicate where and how our communication network needs improvement.[5]*

While TRW understands the need for downward communication, other
companies have not been as perceptive. The International Association of
Business Communicators, in conjunction with a commercial communication
company, has surveyed a large number of employees of various companies
every two years since 1980. The respondents' views on downward communication have become more negative since the initial survey in 1980. Less
than half the respondents felt their companies were candid and accurate, and
more than two thirds felt their companies' downward communication did
not "tell the full story."[6]

Forms of Downward Communication

There are several types of internal organizational communication. First is the
category needed to get the job done each day: memos, directives, policies,
orders, bulletins, interviews, meetings, presentations, and the like. These
are all used to facilitate order processing and shipment, manufacturing and
production, sales and services, income and expenditures, recruiting and hiring, and a dozen other daily activities needed to keep the operation in a
healthy state.

---

[5]Letter from Hugh Brady, vice-president and general manager, Operations and Support
Group, TRW, Oct. 4, 1984. Used by permission.

[6]K. Rosenberg, "What Employees Think of Communication: 1984 Update," *Communication
World*, May 1985, p. 47.

Another important category is creating the feeling among employees that the company is *their* company. Communication downward on certain topics will set the climate for employees to accept and cooperate with the orders, memos, directives, and policies noted above. Following are some of these topics:

Wage and salary structures: how they are established and revised; how they compare with industry standards.

Benefit programs: percentage of salary; who pays what percentage for what benefits; retirement programs; and educational opportunities.

Company products or subproducts: who uses them? How? Are they used by consumers? Manufacturers? Do they play a role in defense? What countries buy them? How are the products utilized?

Company growth and profits: how does the company's income compare with that of others in the industry? Number of employees; expansion and growth contemplated; joint ventures.

Company plans: both long-range and short-range. Where does the company expect to be in five, ten, fifteen years? What impact will that have on personnel numbers? Product mix? Facility locations?

Management-employee relationship: union requests and management's response; what is the viewpoint of each? Why?

Social issues: the employee mix by gender and ethnic background. What company-community projects (educational, cultural, social) are in operation? Cost? Degree of success? What about environmental issues and the company? Waste disposal?

Company organization: plant locations, numbers of employees, organizational structure, subsidiary holdings; structure of the product line, sales distribution, withdrawn products.

Research and development: what areas are being investigated? Why? What products are being developed? Potential?

Existing rumors: reply with facts either correcting or substantiating such unofficial communications.

Litigation: what suits is the company involved in? Results of litigation?

Presenting Information

Effective downward communication covering such topics as those listed above must be planned. Inserting occasional stories in the employee magazine concerning company dividends and plant relocation serves little purpose if they are lost among the items on retirements, new hires, and births.

If you don't keep people informed, you get one of three things: rumor, apathy, or revolution.

Thomas Jefferson

Management must communicate seriously on significant issues. Its viewpoints must be presented consistently, clearly, and honestly. To do this, there must be a stated policy of communication and a series of communication media that are of such quality that they command attention and respect.

Modern managers are now exploring the relative effectiveness of computer information services, including electronic bulletin boards, for downward communication. Although most computers don't offer the advantages of photography, as found in a company publication, the electronic communication link allows employees to talk back to the management and to each other. This feedback can take the simple form of answering an electronic questionnaire or the more complex form of an employee round table discussion, all by computer.

Policies of Downward Communication

In every organization, communications about a variety of activites are transmitted to employees in almost a constant flow. However, some firms do not share information about controversial or sensitive issues. Of course, everyone recognizes that not *all* information can be shared with all employees. Some situations are simply confidential.

When specific information cannot be communicated, many problems can be avoided simply by telling employees that you understand their position and appreciate their desire to know, but "it just isn't possible at this time. And here's the reason for not discussing the details." Such a frank admission is far more acceptable than some obvious hokum that insults an employee's intelligence. Nothing will erode employee loyalty and diligence more rapidly than dishonesty or manipulation of information.

Management must recognize that if something significant is transpiring, employees will be communicating about it. If the communication doesn't take place through formal channels (downward communication), it will surely take place by means of informal ones (grapevine). Remember that there is no such thing as a vacuum in communication. If facts are not supplied by management concerning an ongoing problem or activity, employees will cultivate their own "facts."

The way to make sure that all managers communicate downward is to establish policies of communication for the organization. A carefully conceived set of policies will list the organization's overall communication goals. Among these might be the following:

- To inform concerned groups, such as employees, community members, customers, and vendors, of ongoing activities and/or problems that affect specific parties
- To indicate to employees future company plans, directions, and goals
- To encourage, foster, and build a steady flow of two-way communication
- To communicate to employees, as quickly as possible, information about important events and situations
- To allocate sufficient funds and company time to implement company policies of communication

Beyond these overall corporate policies, a set of statements, none more than a few subpoints in depth, are needed for specific communication activities within the organization. These include interviewing, meetings, handling the media and special interest groups, external written communication, and external oral presentations.

Media for Downward Communication

In addition to the memos, reports, directives, bulletins, orders, and other items that employees frequently receive and use in carrying out their day-to-day responsibilities, there are several other types of media. Among these are employee magazines, orientation manuals, handbooks, annual reports, letters to employees, and bulletin boards (including computer bulletin boards and message centers). If these are composed imaginatively and creatively, are completely honest, and recognize the employees' need to know, they will help increase productivity and improve morale. Such media can be used in attaining the following communication objectives:

- To inform employees about company activities, problems, expansion, markets, mergers, personnel, labor relations, profits, sales, market share, new products, diversification plans, and finance
- To emphasize the firm's dependence on the efforts, creativity, and loyalty of the employees
- To discuss employees' responsibilities, achievements, and status in the firm
- To examine the variety of benefits that employees receive and to recognize the dollar value of such benefits as a significant segment of the employees' income
- To examine relevant social issues and responsibilities, government activities, and political affairs

- To examine company contributions to social welfare, cultural improvements, and educational advancements
- To inform employees' families of company contributions in an effort to build awareness and loyalty
- To examine in detail, from time to time, specific areas of company operations so that employees are informed of activities in areas other than their own
- To encourage employees to use company publications as a forum for expressing ideas

A firm's various employee publications can attempt to achieve any or all of these objectives. Certainly the messages can be emphasized most effectively if the organization issues many publications frequently. On the other hand, a company that can afford only a modest quarterly magazine can achieve similar goals if it is produced in a spirit of integrity and with a clear desire to fulfill the employees' need to know.

FIGURE 2-1

Examples of employee magazines

FIGURE 2-2

Example of tabloid-style employee publication

Company Magazines   It is almost foolhardy to estimate the number of organizational magazines published today, as the quantity has grown enormously. It is safe to assume that every organization of a few hundred or more employees publishes some type of internal magazine. As a matter of fact, there is a professional association comprising individuals in the field of communications who are editors, editorial or production assistants, graphic artists, photographers, and so on. The International Association of Business Communicators has a membership of over 14,000, with dozens of chapters throughout the United States and Canada. Sister associations with huge active memberships exist in England, Europe, and Japan.

Many organizations employ an employee-publications editor and an assistant or two, as well as a photographer and an artist. In smaller firms, these positions may all be held by one individual. Frequently that person has additional responsibilities in the personnel or industrial relations department. Other companies use a communications consulting firm or advertising agency to design and write their employee publication.

Company magazines range from slick, sophisticated four-color publications printed on high-quality stock to modest eight-page affairs that have been run off on the office copier and stapled together. Most employee magazines have one of the following three formats:

Magazine Format.   The most popular of the three, it usually includes several articles on various aspects of the concerned industry, news about contract awards and shipments, as well as listings of employee achievements, promotions, retirements, marriages, births, deaths, educational attainments, sports activities, and so forth.

Tabloid Format.   This type of publication, usually about half the size of a newspaper, has a daily newspaper format. It carries much of the same material as a magazine-type publication and often includes an extended classified ad section of items for sale, rides to share, personal notices, and so on.

Journal Format.   This type of publication usually includes either general articles or highly technical papers. Usually, it lacks news of employee activities. Such periodicals usually are printed on high-grade paper and are illustrated with beautiful photographs or professional technical drawings. Examples of such magazines are Hughes Aircraft Company's *Vectors* and Lockheed's *Lockheed Horizons*.

With regard to the magazine format and the tabloid format, in recent years there has been a strong trend to omit much of the trivia (birthdays, retirements, marriage announcements, and the like) to make room for more substantive topics. These include company growth and decline, the securing or loss of contracts, legal issues, labor problems, social and community situations, and sales, production, and compensation discussions.

One enterprising service to companies with such publications is the "shell" magazine industry. For a fee, these publishers provide a company with a slick, well-designed magazine, including stories provided by the company and other items of general reader interest. Typically, the company will provide for each issue several pages of in-house news, including highlights of new products, production techniques, employee benefits, convention news, and—yes—bowling scores. Typeset along with the rest of the maga-

FIGURE 2–3

Example of journal-type company publication

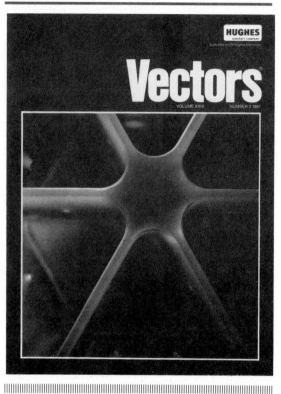

zine, these stories help employees feel the magazine is their "own" even though many of the surrounding pages are not generated by the company itself. Such "shell" publications allow companies to take pride in distributing a professional magazine while avoiding the high cost of in-house publishing.

In 1987 a number of companies added magazines directed to consumers to their marketing strategies. *The Morris Report*, a quarterly, is sent to cat owners by Star-Kist Foods, Inc. In July 1987, Federal Express sent out 220,000 copies of *Express* to its customers and potential clients. Procter & Gamble has *Southern Style* for women, and Johnson & Johnson sends out *GO!* ("Girls Only!").

Corporate sponsored publications are not new; what is new, however, is that many have a paid subscription base as well as advertisements for noncompetitive products. The nation's largest company magazine, the *Philip Morris Magazine*, has over 7 million subscribers.[7]

[7]*Insight,* October 26, 1987, p. 48.

There is probably no medium that can better carry company information to workers than employee magazines. Because their circulation probably exceeds that of all commercial magazines, they can be an immensely persuasive force, not only in the concerned industry, but in the nation as well.

Employee Orientation Manuals   Every firm has dozens of policies regarding such matters as work hours, promotions, vacation periods, days off, educational benefits, transfers, time off, and retirements. These, along with regulations on insurance plans and health benefits, constitute a formidable catalogue of information. Although these matters may well be reviewed and discussed at a new employee orientation session, it is still vital to have them documented. Employee orientation manuals basically serve three purposes:

- To provide an accurate, definitive source of information for all employees.
- To save time. Employees need not crowd the personnel office with a constant series of questions: "Who pays for safety shoes?" "Am I eligible for time off for . . . ?" "Does my policy cover elective surgery?" "What about time off for voting?" "Can I get paid for vacation time not used?"
- To take the supervisor off the hook, save his or her time, and, most important, ensure that all employees receive the same answer to the same question.

Because the employee orientation manual is such a useful reference, it should be carefully organized, clearly written, and easy to read. Some of the areas covered by the typical manual are as follows:

Absences	Community relations	I.D. procedures
Accidents (prevention, reporting, forms)	Contributions	Illness
	Counseling	Insurance
Advance pay	Credit union	Job openings
After-hours rules	Dining	Job performance
Attendance	Discharge	Jury duty
Benefits	Education	Labor relations
Health	Employment	Leaves
Insurance	opportunities	Lost and Found
Retirement	Equal opportunity	Loans
Sick leave	regulations	Overtime
Savings	Job evaluation	Pay and pay days
Profit sharing	Fire protection	Promotion policy
Vacations	First aid	Purchasing policy
Care of equipment	Gifts to employees	Recommendations
Cars	Grievance procedure	Ride sharing
Parking	Holidays	Tuition refunds
Insurance	Hours of working	Use of telephone
Computer Services	Housekeeping	

Organization of the Orientation Manual   A typical organizational plan for an orientation manual might begin with a brief explanation of the company's history, a summation of its organizational philosophy, a listing of company policies, a rundown of short- and long-term goals, and a detailed section on benefits, procedures, and rules.

The overall goals of the employee manual are to give each employee a feeling of unity with the company based on printed policies and philosophies and to permit every worker to find answers to questions quickly and easily. Therefore, the writing level and layout of the orientation manual should be determined with great care. Easy readability should be of key importance. Illustrative material, including drawings, completed sample forms, and photographs should be used generously. Sentences should be short and words chosen carefully. Section dividers and topic headings should be used generously to help employees find needed information easily. Some thought should be given to having a second-language edition if the composition of the work force warrants this.

It is wise to use a spiral binder or notebook for the employee manual. In this way, whenever a change takes place, it will not be necessary to issue and distribute a new booklet. All that must be done is to have a new page or pages printed and sent to employees with the appropriate instruction: "page 34 to

FIGURE 2–4
Examples of employee orientation manuals

be destroyed and the enclosed new page 34 inserted in your employee manual.''

Annual Reports to Employees   Some years ago, a small percentage of companies issued annual reports to employees. These were usually less expensive than the stockholders' report: black and white rather than color, fewer pages, inexpensive paper stock, and distribution from the plant rather than by mail.

However, problems sometimes resulted. Employees wanted to know why they didn't receive the same report as shareholders; what was in the shareholders' that wasn't in theirs; why they were being treated as second-class citizens, and so forth. In the long run, organizations have found it wiser to offer the corporate annual report to employees who wish a copy or to distribute an employee bulletin periodically. Most modern organizations now rely on employee publications and employee bulletins to communicate about ongoing company activities.

Letters to Employees   More and more firms are using letters to employees to communicate about vital issues, unusual problems, and other subjects. There are several reasons for the increased use of letters, not the least of which is the automated office. Typewriters can now be programmed to send the same letter—or four or five different ones—to the various levels of employees. Each letter can use an employee's name and address as well as a personal salutation. In addition, the letter has value because it is a personal message to the employee from, perhaps, the company president. The letter may be read by the employee's spouse; it may even be addressed to both. As such, it becomes an item for dinner-table discussion. What better way to build family loyalty to the firm than through a device such as this?

The letter can cover wide-ranging subject matter, but it should not cover topics that can be discussed equally well in printed employee publications. A welcome to new employees; discussion of new products; explanation of a merger, an acquisition, company profits; a commendation; labor problems (if such discussion is legal); and employee cutbacks are all likely topics for such a letter.

Because the personal letters addressed to employees usually come from the president or some other high-ranking person, they should be worded especially carefully. The tone must be friendly and sincere—definitely not condescending, pompous, or dictatorial. All letters of this nature that are sent to employees' homes should be personally signed in ink. Figure 2–5 shows two good examples of such letters.

Pay Envelope Inserts   The pay envelope insert, used judiciously, is a guaranteed communication device. A message printed on a card or small sheet of paper and attached to employees' paychecks is sure to receive attention.

FIGURE 2-5

Example of letter sent to employees by management

```
Personal Name
Address
City-State
Dear (Employee's name):

Welcome to the Karton and Martin Company.  We are sincerely happy
to have you join our _____Division.  Certainly the
members of that Division, as well as the rest of us here at
Karton and Martin, will do everything possible to make your stay
with us challenging, enjoyable, and happy in the years to come.

You are now joining a family of 12,500 employees working in three
plants in the Chicago area.  And as your know, we are not
newcomers to the field of electronics.  Our first office was
opened almost thirty years ago.  Our growth has been steady and
profitable.  You are now part of that team, and we will be happy
to have you share our achievements in the years to come.

I'm happy to tell you that our salary plan is probably the
highest in the industry.  Added to that you will be able to take
advantage of our profit sharing plan, health benefit program,
insurance coverage, major medical, stock buying privilege, paid
vacations, and other benefits that will add materially to your
compensation package.  These are only some of the items; there
are others which you will learn about from your supervisor or at
your orientation program.

But these are only some of the benefits you will receive as an
employee of Karton and Martin.  There are paid holidays, time off
for personal affairs, an excellent company medical system, file
recreational programs, and wonderful people to work with.  I
hope, too, that you won't hesitate to give the company the
benefit of your suggestions.  We need your help and advice.  Just
walk in and talk to your supervisor or me.

Good luck to you.  We all join together in saying, "Welcome to
Karton and Martin; may your stay be a happy one."

Cordially yours,

Thomas Caxton
Thomas Caxton
President
```

However, the message should be of some significance. If the communication is concerned with a routine topic or, even worse, a bit of trivia, the insert will not be effective. Use such inserts on an occasional basis only. If every paycheck is accompanied by an insert (or two or three), some employees will give them no attention or, at most, a cursory inspection.

The same computer that generates paychecks is, in many cases, also capable of printing short messages onto blank areas of the pay stub. While such messages are certainly easier and less expensive to produce than messages hand-stuffed into envelopes, the computer messages may be read less and, therefore, may be less effective. Some companies have programmed their payroll computers to personalize a message on each check: "Frank, your check contains a bonus this month. Keep up the good work."

Employee Bulletin Boards   Bulletin boards are among the least expensive of all organizational communication media and, if properly maintained, can be among the most effective sources of information. In most companies, they are used for a variety of purposes. The following are perhaps the three most common:

- To announce matters of general interest, such as approaching holidays, meetings, or recognition of outstanding employees.
- To announce matters of specific interest, such as availability of discount tickets for recreational events, personal items for sale or wanted, or announcements of meetings of employee clubs.
- To announce changes in company policies, rules, or regulations.

All displayed notices should carry a stamped message from the office manager: "O.K. for posting until May __ , 19__ ." On the date indicated, that announcement should be removed. Nothing will halt readership of bulletin boards more quickly than outdated layers of announcements. Bulletin boards will prove to be effective communication devices only if they are supervised carefully. One person should be in charge of them to be sure that company policies are followed.

Bulletin boards should be strategically placed to secure maximum attention. Good locations are in cafeterias and locker rooms, near vending machines, or in the employee lounge or recreational room. They should be well-lighted, neat, uncluttered, attractive, and, often, locked. Headings such as "Official Company News" and "Employee Announcements" should be used.

Because locations convenient for all employees are harder and harder to find in modern office layouts, companies are turning increasingly to electronic bulletin boards. These function just as traditional bulletin boards, but with the advantage that employees can access information from the nearest computer terminal. A "message queue" is displayed from which individual items can be retrieved one at a time. Many bulletin boards allow any company employee to add a message. In this way, the electronic bulletin board can provide management not only with an information channel to employees but also with a feedback device.

Management and Supervisory Bulletins For management personnel, a controlled system of bulletins can be an excellent way to announce changes in policies, procedures, or regulations; to convey information; and to ensure that an important message is transmitted in the same way to all individuals at similar levels of authority. Figure 2–6 shows an example of such a bulletin.

Bulletins may also assist the supervisor in communications with subordinates. If all supervisors at a specific level receive the same bulletin, they can then disseminate the same information down. In this way, there is some assurance that all employees will receive essentially the same information at

---

FIGURE 2-6

Examples of management/supervisory bulletin and newsletter

the same time. Such a procedure strengthens the supervisor's authority and emphasizes the position as a source of official information.

It is easy for a firm to become "bulletin happy," with announcements printed on six different colors of paper, emanating from a dozen offices, and spewing from copy machines or reproduction equipment in a never-ending cascade. The remedy, as in the case of bulletin boards, is control. Bulletins or management letters should originate only with authorized persons in specific positions. Because bulletins may announce changes in or amendments to policies or procedures, they should be carefully numbered and dated. It is also wise to three-hole punch them so they can be filed for future reference by the sender and receiver. Some companies give their bulletins added distinction by using different headings or colored stripes to designate, for example, "Manufacturing," "Production," or "Engineering."

LATERAL COMMUNICATION

Of all the directions in which communications move in an organization, lateral or horizontal movement probably is the least efficient because there is rarely pressure to communicate in that direction. It isn't vital that the marketing department know what is going on in production; and the transportation department need not know the details of research to carry on its own activities. However, organizations do need a system for lateral communication simply to keep concerned personnel apprised of companywide activities and to avoid expensive and needless duplication of effort.

But lateral communication must be carefully controlled. Department heads can easily bury each other in a blizzard of paper. One hope for ending the blizzard lies in **electronic mail.** In theory, at least, messages can be sent and received on computer screen without the time-consuming and expensive routine of hand-delivered pieces of paper throughout the company. In fact, however, users of electronic mail have expressed surprise at just how much printer paper is still used for messaging. Many managers still prefer to print out important messages—the so-called "hard copy" of the message—for easy transport and reference.

More perplexing is the electronic blizzard that has replaced the paper blizzard in many offices. Messages stack up one upon another in the computer, all waiting to be read. "Where," one manager has asked in frustration, "are they all coming from?" The answer lies in the technology of electronic mail itself. Once a sender generates a message on the screen, he or she can send it to an individual electronic mail box or to all electronic mail boxes in the company at the press of a key. The burden of photocopying and addressing no longer acts as a bottleneck to keep word-happy executives from publishing their opinions to all employees.

The answer to the electronic blizzard lies in effective managerial decisions, rather than in the electronic mail system itself. Management should determine who is to be informed of which department's activities, the amount of detail to be contained in such reporting, and the medium to be used. A knowledgeable corporate communication director can be of great help in making decisions on who should receive what.

Sometimes unexpected problems arise. Take, for example, an empire-building manager. This person usually has a predictable reaction to lateral communication, first sending bulletins about department activities to almost everyone above, below, and at the same level to convey the idea of extreme productivity. No matter that the bulletins are terribly inflated: the recipients know the source and will discount the content of the announcements by 50 percent anyway.

In addition, the empire builder requests almost everyone in the company to provide copies of their communication ". . . so I may better support your activities . . ." The result of all this is a desk buried in a mountain of paper—a problem the effective communicator tries to avoid. The solution? With a company-wide communication policy and an alert corporate director of communication, the paper proclivities of the empire builder can be effectively curbed.

At the other end of the scale are department heads who communicate nothing on the mistaken assumption that knowledge is power or ". . . if they don't know what I'm doing, they may feel I'm indispensable." But any competent and successful manager is well aware of how important it is for department heads to be aware of each others' activities. He or she can accomplish good intracompany communication in two different but effective ways. First, supervisors can be called together periodically for the purpose of giving and receiving information on current activities. This helps build a climate of cooperative participation. There is no doubt that intelligent supervisors appreciate knowing what is being achieved in related departments. This knowledge often can result in suggestions leading to more efficient production, better economics, and more efficient use of manpower. Second, communication of information from one department to another can also be accomplished through periodic reports, summaries, digests, or abstracts. Such methods are valuable in that a record is made that can be used for future reference.

UPWARD COMMUNICATION

For years organizations have struggled with the question of how to achieve successful and effective upward communication. Although there are such devices as suggestion boxes, forms to complete, group meetings, council meetings, and quality circle sessions, none will prove highly effective without an atmosphere of *trust*. It is difficult, however, to build a climate of trust between management and the work force. The problems are similar, regardless of the field, in all supervisor-subordinate relationships: owner and employees, senior engineer and technicians, doctor and nurses, and so on. Developing trust takes time, effort, and integrity. It is a very fragile quality that can be destroyed through a single careless act. And when it must be rebuilt, an enormous amount of time and effort is required.[8] Figure 2–7 illustrates different forms of upward communication.

Suggestion Systems

One of the most popular methods of securing upward communication is through some type of suggestion box. Based on the premise (usually accurate) that no one knows how to do the job better than the person doing it, management turned to workers for ideas as early as the late 1800s. However, it was during World War II that suggestion systems received their greatest impetus. Workers' suggestions for methods to secure increased productivity were sought and rewarded.

Many companies still solicit suggestions from workers. A monetary award usually is made when the idea is used. Often the sum offered is equal

FIGURE 2–7

Examples of vehicles for upward communication

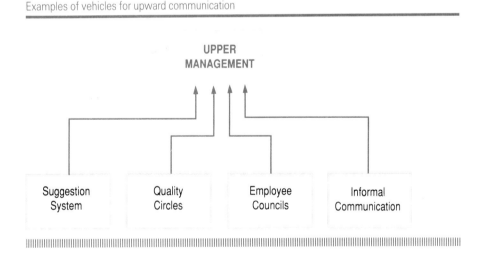

[8]See also Jay Jackson, "The Organization and Its Communications Problems," *Advanced Management Journal*, Feb. 1959.

to 10 percent of the first year's savings resulting from the suggestion. Millions of dollars have been saved by companies as a result of employee suggestions. And employees have benefitted psychologically from participating in the company's efforts. However, problems have caused many organizations to abandon their programs.

First, many employees feel the award they receive is not adequate. Obviously, this has an effect not only on an employee's morale and productivity, but also on those of fellow workers. Next, there are always suggestions that have no merit and must be rejected. Employees often resent being turned down. However, sending a token check to every employee who submits a suggestion is out of the question. Doing so would make a mockery of the entire program.

There is also the problem of the envious supervisor who resents a subordinate's suggestion that has been accepted. The supervisor may feel that the idea rightfully should have come to him (or her) first. Finally, management may prematurely implement some suggestions without careful consideration of the impact on employee morale, the potential for possible employee resentment, or even the possibility of union problems.

Despite the possible problems, managers in many firms conclude that suggestion systems are worthwhile.[9] They do promote upward communication and often lead to improved production and procedures.

Quality Circles

As everyone knows, the idea of quality circles took industry by storm in the '70s and '80s. The concept originated in Japan and continues to be deeply held in Japanese industrial culture. An enormous number of journal and magazine articles describe and evaluate quality circles in depth.

Basically, quality circles involve managers and workers sitting together and *listening* to each other's suggestions.[10] There is neither pressure nor understanding that the ideas proposed will be implemented; they may or may not be. However, discussion flourishes up, down, and laterally, usually with a minimum of negative evaluation, in the full spirit of participative interaction.

In the United States, organizations have had varied experiences with quality circles, ranging from eminent success to dismal failure. When man-

---

[9]There is a wide body of reading available on the topic.

[10]Among the best recent articles on quality circles are "Quality Circles—the Latest Fad or a Real Winner?" *Business Horizons* (May/June, 1984), p. 48ff.; "Quality Circles After the Fad," *Harvard Business Review* (Jan./Feb., 1985), p. 64ff.; "Quality Circles Raise Efficiency," *Coal Age* (Jan. 1983), p. 80ff.; and "Is Quality Circular?" *San Diego Business Journal* (May 14, 1984), p. 1ff.

agers anticipate meetings in a negative or mechanical fashion, expressed by "Well, it's the fourth Tuesday of the month. I guess I'll have to go to that 2:00 P.M. quality circle and listen to those guys bitch," the session is sure to fail. On the other hand, when managers feel that "Here is an opportunity to pick up new ideas and explain our point of view," the potential for success is much greater.

Employee Councils

Employee councils are another valuable means of upward communication. Every company department or division elects a representative to serve on the council. All employee representatives meet with management representatives on a periodic basis—usually once each month. Employees present the questions and suggestions of their department members at the meetings. Because representatives usually are speaking on behalf of anonymous members of their work groups, they will not hesitate to speak out.

For council meetings to succeed, follow several ground rules:[11]

1. Hold meetings in an informal setting—preferably after work hours—with food and beverages available.

2. Hold meetings not more than once each month. Almost any organization has more than enough topics to keep a monthly meeting lively. Also, some persons would have trouble clearing their calendars for more frequent sessions.

3. Choose a skilled meeting leader, one who is tactful, impersonal, and unbiased. He or she may well come from the work force rather than management. This person should serve as motivator, coordinator, or facilitator, not just "talker."

4. Select discussion topics carefully, and draw up an agenda. Meetings should not be dominated by workers' complaints, management's problems, or trivia. Cultivate a positive mental attitude and allow the question "How can we improve?" to serve as a framework for discussion.

5. Allow the work group to decide how it wishes to select its representatives, and build in a method for rotation of representatives.

6. Be sure a record of the meeting proceedings is available to all employees. This can be accomplished by distributing a set of minutes, posting bulletin board announcements, or playing a videotape of the meeting during the noon hour in the cafeteria.

---

[11]See also Norman B. Sigband, "Face to Face," *Communicator's Journal*, May/June 1983, pp. 56–59; and Norman B. Sigband, "Proaction—Not Reaction—for Effective Employee Communications," *Personnel Journal*, March 1982.

When someone complains, "Well, we tried those council sessions, but after five meetings, there just wasn't much left to talk about," hidden factors are probably involved. Perhaps the meeting was dominated by management, or trust was eroded or lost at an earlier session because of heavy criticism of an idea. Other possible reasons are faulty leadership, a poor agenda (or no agenda), or inadequate preparation.

There are dozens of other methods of securing upward communication.[12] Meetings are one common method: ROI (Return on Involvement) sessions, Coffee Sessions, the President's Quiet Hour, Let's Talk It Over, and so forth. Printed methods include forms headed "Spike That Rumor," "Open Line" (used at Northrup), the Q and A Column (in the Southern California Edison employee newspaper), "Speak Up" (at IBM), "Talk Up" (at Bank of America), and "Ideas in Action" (at IBM).

Regardless of the method or format used, it is absolutely vital that management respects anonymity when desired and reinforces the quality of trust constantly.

THE INFORMAL CHANNEL OF COMMUNICATION

Another medium of communication in every organization is the grapevine. It is informal, follows no set pattern or direction, moves in and out of all communication networks, and is part of the social organization of employees. Defined briefly, the **grapevine** is the communication system of the informal organization. It is pervasive and exists at all levels of an organization, from top to bottom.

In 1984, a survey of 10,000 employees in ten companies attempted to determine employees' views of communication in their organizations. The study covered several aspects of communication but perhaps the most startling findings concerned the grapevine.

When asked "What are your major *current sources* of organizational information?" the respondents listed their "immediate supervisor" first and "the grapevine" second out of fifteen listed categories! When the same subjects were asked "What are your major *preferred sources* of organizational communication?" they listed "immediate supervisor" first and "the grapevine" fourteenth out of fifteen listed categories![13] These data tell us that the grape-

---

[12]See also Norman B. Sigband, "Proaction—Not Reaction—for Effective Employee Communications," *Personnel Journal*, March 1982, pp. 190–92.

[13]K. Rosenberg, "What Employees Think of Communication: 1984 Update," *Communication World*, May 1984, p. 49. Similar surveys were conducted in 1980 and 1982, all studies conducted by the International Association of Business Communicators and Towers, Perrin, Forster and Crosby.

vine must be given much more attention by management than it has in the past.

There are strong and conflicting opinions among management about the grapevine. Some managers view it as a positive force in that it acts as a safety valve for employees to blow off steam. It also fulfills a need to know on the part of some recipients and, in some cases, an ego need on the part of the message sender. Other managers perceive the grapevine as a problem: something that spreads rumors, upsets morale, undermines authority, initiates untruths, and most certainly challenges authority. Regardless of what managers think about the grapevine, one fact is certain: it is an integral part of the communication network of every organization. Therefore, you should be familiar with it and try to use it to your advantage.

Unlike formal methods of communication, which proceed precisely and predictably in the organization (up, down, laterally and almost always through "proper" channels), the grapevine jumps around. A message may begin with a supervisor on the second level, go to a line worker, be transmitted to the worker's brother-in-law who happens to be a division manager, hop to one of the organization's five vice presidents, and stop there. Or it may start in the office of the Chief Executive Officer; the secretary transmits it to the division manager and it will stop there . . . or go on to a supervisor and a foreman, both of whom are in the same car pool.

A grapevine thrives primarily through a *liaison individual*. This person hears messages on the informal channel and passes them on to anyone who has a need to know or is simply curious. The liaison individual often receives some ego satisfaction from his or her role because "he (she) knows and no one else does. He (she) must have connections!" By contrast, *dead-enders* may hear messages, but because they have no interest in the topic, no need to know, and little desire for ego satisfaction, they do not pass them on. Finally, there are the *isolates*. At one time they may have been dead-enders, but because they apparently did not relay messages or perhaps did not even listen, they were removed from the informal communication network. They (the isolates) now hear nothing. (See Figure 2–8.)

Why the Grapevine Starts

Because the grapevine involves people and their complex needs, it can be difficult to explain and trace. Certainly it begins, however, in an effort to fill the vacuum created when the formal channel of communication is not working. People have a need to know, and they turn to the grapevine.

When there are changes in an organization (like terminations, plant closures, a dramatic drop in sales, elimination of products or departments, acquisitions, mergers, legal problems, social issues), employees will want to know what is happening and how the change will affect them. If there is no response, an inadequate response, or an obviously false response on the for-

FIGURE 2–8
How the grapevine works

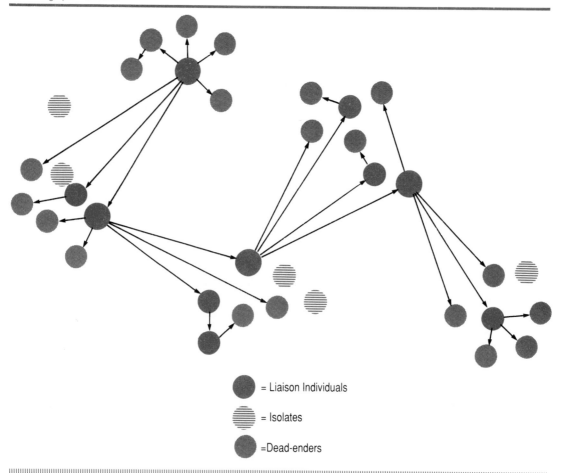

= Liaison Individuals

= Isolates

=Dead-enders

mal channel, employees will turn to the informal channel. As long as their
need to know exists, levels of fear, uncertainty, and frustration will continue
to rise. At some point, employees' feelings will become antagonistic and even
hostile. The grapevine—good, bad, or indifferent—will always exist to fill
the information vacuum.

Management must keep in mind that there is no such thing as a vacuum
in communication; if the formal channel doesn't work, the informal one will
take over. That is why this book repeatedly emphasizes the need to keep
employees informed on the formal network. All channels—upward, downward, and lateral—must be open and available at all times.

Characteristics of the Grapevine

Many people have engaged in research on the subject of the grapevine.[14] As a result, a good deal is known about its functions and attributes. Obviously, it is most active when change is taking place and when individuals' need to know or fear level is rising. Second, it is highly selective; some people hear everything on the grapevine; others hear absolutely nothing. Third, it operates more frequently in the work locale than in a social situation. Fourth, it travels rapidly. Finally, and most importantly, it is a normal part of the communication activities of an organization.

Handling the Grapevine[15]

If the grapevine is a normal part of every organization, the obvious course of action for managers to take is as follows:

- Be aware of it; tune in
- Listen to it; learn from it
- Counteract false, malicious, or harmful facts by feedback through *formal* channels

Listening to the Grapevine

Managers must tune in to the grapevine, although doing so may not always be simple. Certainly a manager cannot ask an employee about the "current word." However, if a feeling of trust exists between a manager and his or her subordinates, the manager need only ask, "What do you hear these days that I should know about?" Obviously, a question like this is much better posed in an informal atmosphere rather than from behind the boss's desk. If the manager wants to know what is on the informal channel, he or she should use that channel to inquire. Other methods of tuning in have been mentioned earlier: "Spike that Rumor" forms, "Speak Up" and "Talk Up" forms, the "Rumor" column in the company newspaper, employee council meetings, "Tuesday Get-Togethers," and others.

If the rumors are never voiced at council sessions or on any of the forms, managers may begin to wonder about the trust level between management and work force.

---

[14]K. Davis, "The Care and Cultivation of the Corporate Grapevine," *Dun's Business Month,* July, 1973. K. Davis, "Management Communications and the Grapevine," *Harvard Business Review,* Sept./Oct., 1953.

[15]N. Sigband, "Communication: The Company Grapevine," AIMS Media, Inc., 6901 Woodley Ave., Van Nuys, CA 91406–4878, color, 16 mm, 26 minutes. This movie is based on The Sun Fresh Case, in the Cases section of this book.

Responding to Rumors

In most cases, if a rumor is responded to, it should be done on the formal channel. Some organizations accomplish this through the use of a signed reply to each inquiry in the rumor column of the employee newspaper; a signed response note to the statement on a "Speak Up," "Talk Up," or "Spike that Rumor" form; an article in the company newspaper; or a meeting conducted by the company president. Other methods include managers meeting on a one-to-one basis with subordinates; an announcement on the "squawk box" by a company officer; or a special bulletin or letter distributed to each employee or mailed to his or her home.

The critical thing, regardless of how it is accomplished, is to make a response.

QUESTIONS FOR STUDY

1. Over the last 20 years, what factors in society have influenced the demand by employees for more vital information about company activities such as profits, contracts, goals, community relations, and so on?
2. Is there any correlation between the level of productivity and the employee's knowledge of company financial, social, sales, and community activities? Explain.
3. Why is it advisable to bind the employee orientation manual in a ring notebook rather than the usual glue or staple binding?
4. Is a pay-envelope insert superior or inferior to a general employee bulletin announcing an important change in company policy? Explain.
5. Is it wise to mail to each employee's home a copy of the company annual report? Explain.
6. Many individuals feel that "quality circles" are not as effective in the United States as they are in Japan. Explain from a *cultural* point of view.
7. Many managers attempt to ignore the grapevine. Is this wise? Explain.
8. In most organizations, is there typically more downward than upward communication?
9. Why do dead-enders on the grapevine usually turn into isolates?
10. Name the four types of communication networks. Which one permits the greatest opportunity for open communication? Explain.
11. Why do some organizations publish several different types of employee publications?
12. Why are an increasing number of firms eliminating the traditional 2 ft. × 4 ft. bulletin board?

13. How has the electronic communication revolution influenced communication within the corporation, particularly between employer and employee?
14. What is the *paper blizzard?* What do you forecast regarding the amount of reading for most executives in the near future?
15. What options does a small company have that wishes to produce an in-house magazine, but cannot afford in-house publishing equipment and personnel?
16. Discuss the usefulness of the suggestion box. What necessary conditions must exist to make it a success?

EXERCISES

17. Draft what you feel would be an effective "Policy of Communication for the College Classroom." This should include policies governing both in- and out-of-classroom communications between faculty members and students, and between students and other students.
18. Some managers believe that the more communication they send to their subordinates, the better. Soon subordinates are receiving various kinds of written, verbal, and nonverbal data from the manager; receiving routine information from upper levels; exchanging all kinds of ideas horizontally; and attempting to keep in touch with the grapevine. These subordinates are excellent candidates for communication overload. Being very specific, identify three things the manager can do to reduce the dangers of this phenomenon.
19. It is said that probably 80 percent of vertical communication in a company is downward and usually is quite ineffective. Make two specific suggestions to improve upward communication in most organizations.
20. Determine the date of publication of the employee publication (newspaper or magazine) for a nearby plant. Visit that organization the day after an issue is published and conduct a survey among "white" and "blue" collar workers as they leave the plant. Your objective is to measure readership of the topics in the publication and determine if there are significant differences in reading interests among the two groups of employees.
21. Design a set of "Communication Policies" for this class. Explain the rationale for each of your policies to your instructor and classmates.
22. Think of a work group of which you have been a part. First, draw an organizational chart of that work group. Then make a diagram of the communication network of that work group.
23. Imagine a magazine for a student organization to which you belong.

What would be included? Create a specific list of regular features and suggestions for several special topics that would be of interest to readers.

24. Obtain employee newsletters or magazines from two different companies. Do an informal content analysis of each. How much space is devoted to personal news (such as retirements, marriages, and bowling scores) and how much to company business (such as profits, contracts, grants, goals, and competitors). In light of each company, its employees, and its products, which publication is more effective and why?

25. Interview an employee publications editor. Determine if he or she follows a specific policy of communication for the publication. What is it and who designed it?

26. Find a small group—a campus office, a secretarial pool, the executive meeting of a student group—where you will be able to study the communication flow. Observe and study how information is transmitted. Watch carefully for verbal and nonverbal communications. After observing the network in action, (1) prepare a written description of what you observed; (2) clearly identify the type of network you observed; (3) ask the leader of the group to describe the network from her or his perspective; compare the leader's analysis to yours.

27. There is probably a close correlation between how a person interacts with others on an interpersonal level and how he or she creates trust. Find a leader of a group, department, or organization who you feel has the trust of his or her subordinates. Observe how this person interacts with people. Identify the characteristics of this leader's managerial approach. Be as specific as possible.

Intercultural Business Communication

3

To maintain a leadership position in any one developed country a business—whether large or small—increasingly has to attain and hold leadership positions in all developed markets worldwide. It has to be able to do research, to design, to develop, to engineer and to manufacture in any part of the developed world, and to export from any developed country to any other. It has to go transnational.[1]

Companies in developed countries such as the United States must engage in international business transactions or lose an important competitive advantage. Such firms have not only found tremendous commercial opportunities a thousand or ten thousand miles from their plants, but they have also found cooperative partnerships because of a "community of interest."[2]

A small U.S. manufacturer may find a German or British firm better able to design, produce, or manufacture a particular portion of the U.S. firm's major product. A "community of interest" has been found and exploited to the advantage of both. A firm in Japan finds an American company with excellent marketing and distribution background ready to cooperate to sell a product highly desired in Western Europe. Another community of interest has been found. General Motors has an enormous plant in Fremont, California, but it is managed by the Japanese who assemble both Toyota and GM cars in the facility. Again, a community of interest has been found. This is happening worldwide with both big and small firms who sell, manufacture, package, or distribute insurance, foodstuffs, banking, publishing, cars and thousands of other products and services.

And how is all this possible? The answers are complex, but undoubtedly one factor is that the worldwide level of technology is about equal. Or as Drucker has said:

All developed countries are equally capable of doing everything, doing it equally well and doing it equally fast.[3]

---

[1] Peter Drucker, "The Transnational Economy," *The Wall Street Journal*, August 25, 1987.

[2] Drucker, "The Transnational Economy."

[3] Drucker, "The Transnational Economy."

The second factor is the ability for developed countries to share information almost instantaneously—information can be communicated anywhere, at any time, in fractions of minutes. Thus the globe has become a village and, like a village, its citizens can communicate with one another quickly and easily. But if that is so, why then do we encounter communication problems from one nation to another?

The answer is simple: worldwide we share much of the same information and technology, but not the same *cultures*. Dr. Werner Krause in Frankfurt may share the same detailed knowledge of computers as his Cleveland counterpart, Emily Westin, but he doesn't share the same culture. Their family, recreational, financial and other values are different. These values spring from their experiences, expectations, habits—their cultures. And yet they both speak English and/or German. The same types of cultural differences are true of Emily Westin and Togo Nakasone, or Ignacia Sanchez or Mohammed Kassabian.

Technological advances in the last 100 to 200 years have spread and been adopted and refined worldwide. But cultures based on thousands of years of development are slow to change. And perhaps they should not change, for these cultural differences among the different societies and nations give individual identity to each group. This persistent diversity of cultures has made our world an exciting place. But it has also created barriers that constitute a major challenge for communicators. Even with the advancements in the transmission of information, when words and actions are not understood in the same way because of differences, communication can suffer. And that is the key to remember when dealing with different cultures: verbal and nonverbal communication may have different meanings to different cultures.

It is true that *some* cultures are fairly easily understood, accepted, and integrated by other groups, but such understanding is not usual. For example, the possibility that various facets of the Oriental or Near Eastern cultures' being thoroughly understood and integrated into the Western culture—and vice versa—is slim indeed, at least for this century.

The answer to better communication among the peoples of the world is knowledge, appreciation, and understanding of cultural differences rather than acceptance or integration. And that is what this chapter is all about: increasing *your* knowledge, understanding, and awareness of other cultures so that you may communicate more effectively with your business counterparts everywhere . . . both in this country and in the rest of the world.

CULTURES IN THE UNITED STATES

What about cultural differences in the United States? Have you noticed how enormous these differences are—especially in the last ten years? Many of the major changes are taking place in urban centers. Most immigrants to the U.S.

go to urban areas because of economic opportunities—jobs and the possibilities for opening business firms. Let's look at a few statistics.

National Changes

Today the United States has a population of 236 million; just ten years ago, the figure stood at 215 million. The demographic changes in those ten years are quite startling. For example, in 1975 there were 24 million blacks in the United States; ten years later, the figure had changed to 29 million. The percentage increase for Asians and Hispanics in the same period is even greater. In 1975 the United States population of Asians was 2 million, but by 1987 this number was up to 6 million, triple the number of 10 years earlier. And the Hispanic population, which was 10 million in 1975, jumped to 17 million by 1987. In contrast, the Caucasian population in the U.S. was 180 million in 1975 but by 1987 had increased only a relatively static 10 million.

Demographic Changes in Urban Centers

Let's bring our microscope into sharper focus and look at a representative major urban center in the United States. We'll choose Los Angeles, although the picture would probably be similar for New York, Chicago, or Boston. In Los Angeles, Asians constituted 3 percent of the city's population in 1975, but by 1987, that percentage had jumped to 8.5 percent. And Hispanics made up 25 percent of the city's population in 1975, but increased to 32 percent by 1987. However, the black population remained almost static, with 9 percent in 1975 as compared to 10 percent in 1987. The Caucasian population *shrank* slightly, from 53 percent in 1975 to 49.5 percent in 1987.

These changes mean that, more than ever, business people need not go abroad to encounter the problems of cross-cultural communication. They must develop flexible and excellent communication skills for various cultures even if they confine themselves to working with employees, customers, vendors, or others in Los Angeles, Chicago, or New York. By some time in the twenty-first century, perhaps the year 2075, the population in the United States will be much more homogeneous, requiring business people to have a relatively small range of communication skills for various cultures. But those of us involved in management situations in the last portion of the twentieth century must be as conscious of the cultural differences within the cities of the United States as we are of those in Seoul, South Korea; Osaka, Japan; Riyadh, Saudi Arabia; Frankfurt, West Germany; Helsinki, Finland; or Mexico City.[4]

[4]Source for these background demographics data: Professor D. Nakashini, Graduate School of Education, University of California at Los Angeles.

CONTRASTS IN CULTURES

Managers who travel to foreign countries to do business are aware that they will encounter many more variations in communication than they do in their plants and offices in the United States. Being aware of those variations and adapting to them can often make a most significant contribution to the success of a business transaction. Although there are so many differences (and even conflicts) among cultures that it would be impossible to list and discuss all of them in these few pages—or even in a whole book—we can note a few to arouse your awareness.

The Perception of Space

We all know that animals, both wild and domestic, guard their territory. Some species of turtles, salmon, and pigeons use specific rivers, bays, or other territories for mating and laying eggs, returning year after year until they die.

We are also aware of questions of territoriality and space in our nation, our culture, and even our own homes. To protect and define our territory we put up flags, fences, rows of bushes, "no trespassing" signs, and so on. How many times have you seen students walk into a classroom for the first time, carefully select a seat, and occupy it every class period for the rest of the term? Interestingly enough, no other class member will take that seat from the second class session to the last.

Societal norms often govern "territory." The instructor occupies the space in front of the class; the students sit out there. However, if the instructor wishes to communicate (nonverbally) that "the rules have changed for today," he or she will arrive early and rearrange the students' chairs into groups of six and move the instructor's chair to the side. The "rearranged" space communicates a message.

Primary territories are items such as your bed, toothbrush, or comb; *secondary* territories include the chair you usually sit on at dinner or the desk in the chemistry class you usually occupy each day at 2:00 P.M. *Public* territories are places such as the library, parking lot, beach, or picnic area. But even here you can communicate a claimed space within the public territory by placing your books and jacket on the table in the library, unrolling your blanket on a spot of beach, painting your name or title on a parking space, or placing your food basket on a picnic table. *Personal* space is an area around an individual that expands or contracts because of the situation and/or cultural background.

It is usually felt that if you do business with someone from Mexico or Italy, you should expect them to occupy much more of your personal space than someone from Germany. Perhaps you have personally been involved, either here or abroad, with an Italian speaking with great excitement to an American. He may well be advancing, you may be retreating, and each is puzzled. "Why is he moving into my space?" you wonder; "Why is she backing away from me as I address her? Does she disagree?" the puzzled Italian ponders.

On the other hand, one source points out that the belief that Italians and Latin Americans are comfortable with little personal space and Americans not may be nothing more than a generalization. Personal status or rank may play a more dominant role in space relationships.[5] Nevertheless, it is true that space is used differently between a father and son or two males who are good friends in many Hispanic and Near Eastern cultures as compared with males in the United States.

Look at the designation of space in an American corporation. The president, in splendid isolation, occupies a large office on the top floor with corner windows. The French or Near Eastern managing director sits among his subordinates so he can "see" all activities. Or consider the Japanese home owner, who often values a small home that is well proportioned and includes only the items needed for daily use; the American measures his or her home in thousands of square feet and often fills it with furnishings that may never be used but are meant to communicate status.

The utilization of space among individuals in a culture or between cultures is not only a fascinating aspect of nonverbal communication study, it is also a revealing one for the cross-cultural communicator. One need only think of how individuals react in a crowded elevator as compared with an elevator containing only four people; how the people density in a rock concert, or prison yard may contribute to violence; and how space is viewed in the small but heavily populated nation of Japan as compared to the United States.

The Perception of Time

Different cultures certainly observe time differently. Time is of major importance to the United States businessperson. His or her background is thoroughly time oriented: we "save time," "buy time," "make time," "spend time," "waste time," and "invest time." We are so time oriented that we are often irritated when others don't observe time commitments the way we do.

The American businessperson dealing with someone whose cultural orientation is different—whether here or abroad—must be aware of the possibility that that person may view time differently. The American kept waiting

[5]L. A. Malandro and L. Barker, *Nonverbal Communication*, Addison-Wesley, 1983, pp. 228–29. This paperback is an outstanding source for a thorough discussion of the differences in nonverbal communication among different cultures. We highly recommended it as a source to the interested reader.

for a half hour past his 2:00 P.M. appointment should not interpret the wait as an affront; it is "merely time." The businessperson in Latin America, the Near East, and some nations of Western Europe may have attitudes toward time very different from those of the typical American.

It is interesting to note the change that takes place in the perception of time by cultures as they move towards industrialization and become more Westernized. The Japanese, for example, have become more and more time conscious as they have become more industrialized.

Material Items

In our consuming culture, many individuals prize highly such material items as impressive cars, jewelry, furnishings, clothes, and so on. Large diamonds, full-length mink coats, and a new Mercedes may be important items to communicate status in our society but they may be looked upon as ostentatious and even in poor taste in other cultures.

Although jewelry has frequently been a factor of status in most societies, the particular item varies. Diamonds and emeralds may only be colored stones of little value to some. On the other hand, a shell or animal tooth may be something to be highly prized by others.

We usually perceive "big as better": a giant redwood, a large car and home, or a large precious stone. The Japanese, who find space limited in their nation, admire beautifully proportioned items that are small: a bonzai tree, a home, a garden, a carved netsuke, or an intricately worked piece of jade or ivory. It's all in the perception!

Friendships

Friendships and how they are viewed differ from culture to culture. Most people in the U.S. have moved from one city or state to another. Wherever we go, we usually "make friends" quickly and easily. New neighbors, church members, and work associates almost immediately become "Joe" or "Jenny" or "Bud." When we attempt the same approach in England, Germany, Japan, or Finland, communication may frequently encounter barriers. They're not immediately "Nigel" or "Karin" or "Togo" and we aren't immediately "Jim" or "Jane" to them. They expect to be addressed as "Mr. Salisbury" or "Fräulein Baumann" or "Mr. Tamasaki," and they will call you "Mr. Stevenson" or "Ms. Wright."

Friendships develop slowly and carefully in many cultures. Neighbors in England or Germany may address one another quite formally for years if that is the preference of one or both parties. In many nations friendships are not infrequently based on loyalties, feuds, or physical encounters sometimes going back generations. Americans make friends quickly and easily; many other cultures do not.

Agreements

To us an agreement completed with a signed contract is almost sacred. To many businesspersons in the Near East, however, a contract is just "a piece of paper" that is dissolved when the paper is destroyed. But a handshake, made after deliberate and thorough discussion over many small cups of coffee, that is an agreement! Unfortunately many U.S. construction firms who have embarked on major projects in the Near East have found their carefully worded contracts to be looked upon as the *beginning* of negotiations, not the end. In recent years, however, the perceptions of the two cultures of what constitutes an agreement have come much closer together.

Eating Customs

Customs in eating vary tremendously around the world. Who is served first? The men or women at the table? Or are women even present at an "important" meal? What about utensils—which ones should be used when, or are there none at all? What about liquor (never served in the Middle East)? Should you match your host toast for toast? Can you decline to drink? And be careful how you pass or reach for food at the meal. The left hand is never used in serving food in many of the Middle Eastern nations for that is the hand usually reserved for "unclean" (toilet, for example) functions. Must you partake of the raw fish? braised brains? sauteed kidneys? stuffed intestines? boiled stomach? It's best to learn of the customs before you go "there" so you may be prepared.

Male-Female Relationships

What of male-female relationships abroad? Be careful when you are in the company of businessmen in the Near East not to discuss or even inquire about the health of Abdul's wife or 19-year-old daughter. Much too personal and forward! And where are the wives of Togo, Taki, and Mako as these three men prepare to serve as your hosts for an evening out in Tokyo? Don't ask. Wives rarely accompany their husbands at an evening "business" dinner.

What some cultures perceive as the "natural" subordination of women to men strikes many Americans as unfortunate and unjust. The political and moral issues involved come to a head when an American businesswoman faces hard choices: can she do business in cultures that suppress women and, if so, how can she cope?

The answers to those difficult questions, of course, differ according to the culture and situation at hand. But three trends can be observed in recent years:

- businesswomen are visiting sexually hostile cultures in increasing numbers.

- when these women anticipate problems due to sexual assumptions, they take time in advance to establish their professional status with their foreign clients by correspondence, telephone conversation, and the agency of mutual acquaintances.
- women sometimes make initial business contacts in the company of male colleagues, who then withdraw as the business relationship develops.

A favorite tenet of cultural relativism is that mores and customs are neither right or wrong, just different. But in the case of sexual discrimination, cultures like individuals can simply be wrong-headed. Attitudes change, however, as women assert themselves as professionals equally capable with men to do business. Attitudes also change as economically disadvantaged cultures face the fact that wealthy trading cultures respect women. In short, if they want our dollars, they can learn to accept the equality of American women, if not their own.

Miscellaneous

There are many other areas where perceptions differ from one culture to another. An American who brings his Berlin dinner hostess red roses (signifying romantic love) would probably arouse the hostility of his host. And white flowers (signifying mourning) might bring displeasure to a girlfriend in Belgium.

Different cultures view odors differently. In the United States, millions of dollars are spent annually on deodorants designed to eliminate body odors. However, Arabs may often breathe in each other's faces while speaking. Not to do so is to "deny one's breath" and is considered a grave insult.[6] Eskimo, Maori, Samoans, and Philippine Islanders rub noses or inhale as they place their noses against the cheeks of another.

Scents or odors are often associated with cultures, and these frequently come from diets. The scents are neither good nor bad, merely different. The American manager traveling abroad must recognize that accepting or rejecting an individual based on odor may be very unwise.

Paralanguage is behavior that interrupts, accompanies or takes the place of speech. It may be a gesture or movement of a hand, eyebrow, face, or posture. Or it may be sound such as a grunt, whistle, or sigh. And it can even be a short or extended silence. All these may vary from culture to culture.

The physician's "ummm" while staring intently at the X ray or lab report; the inward rush of breath as one reads the bad or good news in a letter, are both examples of paralanguage that communicate a message. But we must be careful not to misinterpret. The long silence on the part of the Jap-

---

[6]Malandro and Barker, *Nonverbal Communication*, pp. 228–29.

anese seller is not a sign of rudeness or a ploy; he is attempting to examine the offer carefully from all points of view. The frequent nod of the head of this man as you speak to him probably means he understands you, but it may not mean he *agrees* with you.

COMMUNICATION IN DIFFERENT CULTURES

Nonverbal Communication

A great deal of communication in all cultures occurs nonverbally. Nonverbal cues can range from touching and smells to gestures and body movement. Our culture's attitude toward the nonverbal area of touching is vastly different from that of many others in the world. It is not unusual in Europe or the Middle East to see two men walking together with hands clasped or even encircling a shoulder. Such a sight would be as unusual here as seeing two men greet each other with a light kiss on each cheek—a relatively common sight in many nations.

Discussion between a manager and a subordinate in the United States may have them both in a very relaxed posture in the former's office. They might both be sipping coffee. If the manager is a man, he may have a foot hooked over an empty chair or planted on a nearby table top as he sprawls in his chair. Not so in the Middle East where crossed legs or facing the soles of your shoes toward another individual is a sign of rudeness. In so many nations and certainly in much of Western Europe, the subordinate is almost "at attention" when briefly addressing a superior. And keeping your hands in your pockets as you speak to your German or Austrian boss is just "not done."

We in the United States are sometimes concerned when the other person does not look us in the eye or seems visually evasive. Is there a lack of honesty or integrity here? Yet in Japan, it may be interpreted as a lack of respect if the individual *does* look directly at you. We also have no hesitancy, when asked, to list our accomplishments. In the Orient such a presentation by the individual would seem out of place and in bad taste. Someone else may do it, but even then it would be accomplished with discretion. And it would not be wise for the American manager to praise one Japanese worker for an outstanding performance in the presence of his or her co-workers. It would be embarrassing because the Japanese feel it necessary to be simply one of the group. "The nail that protrudes must be knocked down" say the Japanese.

Language Communication

Fortunately for Americans, communities of the world are moving toward making English an international language. But "American English" is often not the same as "British English." And what happens to American English when it is translated into foreign tongues can be even more disastrous.

As an example of the above, many of us still have difficulty remembering that in England "bonnet" and "boot" are not items of clothes but refer to the hood and trunk, respectively, of an auto. "Dust bins" are refuse containers and a "scheme" may be a plan and not a conspiracy. "Satisfactory" to us is acceptable but to the British it may be interpreted from acceptable to excellent. An apartment is a "flat;" a band-aid an "elastoplast;" a diaper a "nappy;" a druggist a "chemist;" liquor is "spirits;" and what comes at the end of this sentence—what we call a period—is called a "full-stop" by the British.[7]

When phrases in American reports and letters are translated to other languages, they are sometimes incorrect and often even humorous. The important point, however, is that delays, confusion, and misinterpretations often result. What are the answers? Certainly we must do a better job of learning the language of the nations with whom we carry on business. They in turn are certainly learning more English. In many of the countries of Western Europe and in the Orient, several years of English are "required" in the educational programs of school children.

However, the problems of semantics will continue to occur in English or in translations from the English to another tongue. Some of those we hear about come from our advertised products. A group of Hispanic ad agencies in Los Angeles have begun a new organization called "Merito," which they have subtitled "The Society for Excellence in Hispanic Advertising." The organization expects to go national to further their aim of eliminating "misunderstandings, bad translations and bad advertising by non-Hispanics to the Hispanic market." One example cited by the group is the Braniff slogan of "travel on leather." The Spanish word for leather ("cuero") also means "naked." Thus, some Latin Americans interpreted the Braniff ad as "travel naked."[8]

Other mistranslations (which often happen with colloquialisms) are "Come alive with Pepsi" which turned into "Come out of the grave" in Germany and "Pepsi brings your ancestors back from the grave" in Asia, where "Body by Fisher" became "Corpse by Fisher." And the phrase "The spirit is willing but the flesh is weak" became in Russian "The ghost is ready but the meat is rotten."

Of course these are extreme examples. The point, however, is that the American manager must be especially careful of language choice. He or she should also try to secure feedback or some type of response in an effort to monitor the accuracy of the translation.

[7]A. Bickerton, *American English, English American*, Abson Books, Bristol, England, 1974.

[8]*The Los Angeles Business Journal*, September 7, 1987, p. 7.

SHOULD YOU DO UNTO OTHERS AS THEY . . . ?

According to the Golden Rule, we should treat others as we would like to be treated. That assumes that we would all like to be treated similarly because we *are* similar. However, from a cultural point of view, we *are not* similar, and that often makes a profound difference in the verbal and nonverbal communication we send and receive in our interaction with individuals in foreign nations.

Let's look at the Golden Rule as it applies to just a few aspects of nonverbal communication. As stated earlier, men in some parts of Europe or the Middle East walk together with hands clasped and greet each other with a kiss on the cheek. Their wives may follow several steps behind as they walk. All of these communicate a message. Would they communicate the same message if they occurred in the United States? You might argue that these are really rather superficial factors in a culture, that "deep down" people are the same all over the world. But even at a less superficial level we find basic differences between cultures. We know, for instance, that different cultures have different ways of looking at the meaning of a contract, polygamy, or drinking alcohol.

Of course, many cultures have customs that are decoded the same way. But they also all have a multitude of differences, both superficial and at the core, that may be interpreted differently and which may create misunderstanding in attempts at cross-cultural communication. In other words, be wary of following the Golden Rule across cultures.

AMERICAN VALUES[9]

It is important for Americans to understand how their values contrast with those in other cultures. An appreciation by Americans of these differences in values among cultures will permit us to better see how individuals from other cultures look at us.[10]

Personal Control Over Environment

In the United States, people consider it normal and proper that Man should control Nature. That may mean changing the size of a mountain, the type of weather, the direction in which a river flows, and perhaps even the genetic structure of living organisms. Most of the world's population feel that such

[9]This discussion is based on an intriguing and important paper titled "The Values Americans Live By," by L. Robert Kohls, Executive Director, the Washington International Center, Washington, D.C., 1984.

[10]The term "Americans" in this discussion refers to the population of the United States.

changes should not be made. Fate has made certain decisions which must be obeyed.

Change

Americans usually feel change is good. It is often associated with progress, development, growth, and advancement. However, older cultures often feel change is disruptive and destructive. Stability, tradition, and an ancient heritage are valued.

Control of Time

As noted earlier in this chapter, Americans are often controlled by time; it is valuable and highly prized. Not to observe time commitments in the United States is a sign of discourtesy. But people in many other cultures do not permit the clock to control their activities as do Americans.

Equality

Still another American value which differs significantly in many other cultures is the concept of equality. We say "People have been created equal" and we view equality as an important civic and social goal. But in most of the world, rank, status, and authority are viewed as part and parcel of everyday life. To many individuals in other cultures, knowing who they are and where they fit in the various strata of their society is reassuring and offers a sense of security.

Individualism/Privacy

People in the United States feel very strongly that they are individualists; that they each march to a different drummer. "I'm a little special, a little different from others."

Other cultures, where space is at a premium in homes, offices, and work places, and where large numbers of people are treated similarly, often do not appreciate the American's concept of individualism and need for privacy.

Self-Help

Americans take great pride in "making it" on their own. Inherited wealth is accepted but the individual is given little personal credit for wealth secured from a parent. The same view is not often the case in foreign cultures. The "self-made man" or woman is looked up to much more in the United States than he or she would be in many other nations.

Competition and Free Enterprise

We value competition and stress it as a desirable quality from the classroom to the sports field and the boardroom. But in societies which value cooperation, our intense competitiveness is not easy to comprehend. Almost every one of our fields fosters competitive values. Even our economic system is based on free enterprise. For millions of people in the world, however, that value is not easy to accept and may be viewed as a "lack of cooperation."

Future Orientation

Americans constantly work, plan, and strive for an "improved" future. We set long- and short-term goals; we devise strategies to improve the future whether it is economic, social, athletic, or medical. But in much of the world, an attempt to alter the future may be perceived as futile and perhaps even sinful. "What will be, will be." That is what must be accepted.

Action/Work Values

Americans usually work hard—the day is planned; activities are scheduled weeks or even months in advance. We are often so involved in our work that we become "workaholics." This constant attention to accomplishing productive labor is not shared by many cultures, where spending a day strolling, meditating, or even "doing nothing" is an important activity.

Informality

Most people in the United States prefer informality in discussions, relationships, and dress. First names are frequently used not only by boss and worker but even by those who have just been introduced. But the use of titles (Mr., Mrs., Dr., etc.) is expected and followed in much of the world. Addressing the division manager as "Karl" by a line worker would be unthinkable in Germany.

Directness, Openness, and Honesty

Americans are looked upon by many foreign people as being blunt, perhaps even unfeeling. But the American very often prides himself on "telling it like it is." That is very difficult to understand for an individual who comes from a society where saving face is important or one in which an indirect method is used for conveying bad news or an uncomplimentary evaluation.

We seem to lose interest in the individual who hints at what is intended rather than stating the situation directly. Yet members of other cultures often lose trust in us *because* of our directness.

The Value of Practicality and Efficiency

Most Americans look at situations and ask "Will it pay off?" "Can it be done in the time provided?" "Have we found the most efficient solution?" But in some cultures decisions are made in answer to such questions as "Is it aesthetically pleasing?" "Does it advance the arts?" "Will it increase knowledge?" "Will it prove enjoyable?"

Materialism/Acquisitiveness

Most people in other cultures perceive Americans as being much more materialistic than Americans perceive themselves. We usually feel that our appliances, cars, TV sets, and computers are our just rewards for hard work. However, many others see Americans as being almost obsessed with acquiring and maintaining "things."

CULTURES IN PERSPECTIVE

We wish to emphasize that the term "foreign trade" may be a relic. There is international trade, and it is difficult to even determine what is foreign. Autos with Japanese made bodies, German made motors, and components from a dozen foreign countries as well as our own, are assembled by Americans in the United States. Shall we call this a "foreign car"?

What are foreign products? When components are manufactured abroad on an American license, and then returned to this country to be integrated or assembled into an "American made" product, how should it be designated? American made or foreign made? And the same is true when we send components of a doll, toy, or electronic item to a foreign nation for assembly which are then returned here for final packaging. How shall it be designated?

These are problems better left to the U.S. Department of Commerce. What is important for American managers to keep in mind when dealing with foreign cultures—either in this country or abroad—is that the foreign individual's receptions of verbal and nonverbal factors in the environment may be different from ours. While we can't expect "them" to always see our perceptions, we *must* always see theirs.

Toward that end, more and more American companies are carefully training employees in the ways of "other" cultures before they are sent abroad. However, the training that is provided and required by foreign companies is considerably greater for their employees who are sent to the United States. In fact, many American firms stated they had no "cross-cultural" training for employees sent abroad and indicated, "They either sink or

CULTURAL VALUES

In the United States	In Some Other Cultures
Personal control over the environment	Fate
Change	Tradition
Time and its control	Human interactions
Equality	Hierarchy/Rank/Status
Individualism/privacy	Welfare of the group
Self-help	Birthright inheritance
Competition	Cooperation
Future orientation	Past orientation/tradition
Action-work orientation	"Being" orientation
Informality	Formality
Directness/openness/honesty	Indirectness/ritual/"face"
Practicality/efficiency	Idealism
Materialism/acquisitiveness	Spiritualism/detachment

swim."[11] Such a short-sighted view is sure to prove negative in the long run.

We must become more aware of how other cultures view the United States. And, most important, we must be much more sensitive to the needs and perceptions of individuals whose cultural background differs from ours whether we travel abroad or interact with them in our daily activities in the United States. Education, foreign affairs, the print and electronic media, trade and a dozen other factors have contributed to making the world "smaller" and all of us closer members of the "family of man."

QUESTIONS FOR STUDY

1. Do you feel that the current opportunities for instantaneous communication among various world-wide cultures has improved or worsened international communication effectiveness? Explain.
2. Why have changes in culture not kept pace with changes in technology?
3. Why has the population of blacks, Asians, and Hispanics changed much more dramatically in large urban centers in the United States than in small rural towns and cities?
4. Why do you feel "securing of consensus" before a decision is made is much more important in Japan than in the United States?

[11]John W. Gould, "Intercultural Communication," in N. Sigband and A. Bell, *Communication for Management and Business*, Glenview, Illinois. Scott, Foresman and Co., 1986, p. 81.

5. In what way doesn't the Golden Rule hold true for U.S. citizens when they travel in foreign countries?

6. How do your perceptions of space differ when you are walking on your campus as compared to when you are in a crowded elevator? Why?

7. Is there any reason why a group of workers should be consulted before assigning them to new large clothes lockers (for changing from "street" to work clothes) from their present very small accommodations? Why? Are there cultural factors involved in this?

8. Is there a relationship between the size of the United States and "beautiful redwood trees" and the size of Japan and "beautiful bonsai trees"? Explain.

9. What cultural habits in the United States led to the incidence of stress as compared to the cultural factors and stress in Tibet?

10. Do you ever resent being addressed by your first name on an initial contact with a stranger? Why? Are reactions, on the whole, to this situation different for teenagers as compared to seniors? Why? Can you make a strong argument for or against training U.S. managers in intercultural communications whether they work in the United States or are sent by their organizations to a foreign nation? Explain.

11. List five stereotypes Americans entertain for Japanese? For Middle Easterners?

12. What are five common stereotypes people in other nations have of Americans?

13. Explain how time and space communicate differently in American culture under different circumstances.

14. Carry through a research project on the "Changing Role of the Japanese Wife in the 1990s." Make a presentation to your class of your findings.

15. Choose among your friends an American, an Asian, and a Latin from Western Europe. Carefully record the type and quantity of their nonverbal communication for one day. Report on your findings to the class.

16. Carry through a research project titled "Jewelry and Its Make-up in Various World Cultures." Report your findings to the class.

17. Select three different cultures and determine how 1) decision making and 2) participative management are viewed in each.

18. Interview a foreign businessperson who is in the United States on a temporary basis. Determine his or her office size and location, the nature and time of "business" lunches, management style, the input of subordinates to decision making and other factors which interest you. Compare your findings with the information gained from a U.S. businessperson.

19. Indicate how the use of time differs in the United States for most individuals depending on the day of the week. A log, maintained for one week, on "time utilization" by members of your own family should prove valuable.

20. Interview two individuals, one from an Asian and the other from a Hispanic background and record three cultural customs of Caucasians in the United States which they find perplexing, unusual, or illogical.

21. Spend time with an Asian family that has come to the United States within the last ten years. Indicate the differences in cultural patterns between the parents and the children of that specific family.

22. Working with three or four other students, prepare a research report on how three major U.S. corporations prepare employees who are sent overseas to work in the company's operations or that of a company subsidiary. Evaluate the training and preparation received.

23. Recent press reports indicate that most students in China are required to take classes in basic English. As we know, relatively few students in the United States study Chinese, or for that matter, any other language. Present a report (oral or written) on what implications this has—from an economic, social, and cultural point of view—on both nations over the next 25 years.

4

The Electronic Communication Revolution

By the year 2000, getting information will be easy. But managing and interpreting information will remain a challenge.

The electronic communication revolution continues to sweep through business and academic life. Business communicators during the 1980s, for example, saw the symptoms of change transform the office. Typewriters were pushed aside for word processors. Bulky file cabinets gave way to data storage devices no bigger than a breadbox. Coast-to-coast business meetings began to take place by teleconference, not transcontinental flights. In colleges, registration was given over to the computer. For many students, access to a personal computer became a virtual necessity for some accounting, finance, and communication courses.

Consider the importance of the electronic communication revolution in relation to other revolutions. The tool revolution—hammers, saws, combs, brushes, pens, scissors—extended the power of our *hands*. The transportation revolution—trains, planes, cars, bicycles—extended the power of our *feet*. The optical revolution—telescopes, microscropes, televisions—extended the power of our *eyes*. The auditory revolution—stereo speakers, compact disks, hearing aids—extended the power of our *ears*. The aesthetic revolution—trumpets, pianos, sculpture, painting, choreography—extended the power of our *emotions*. But one centrally human power remained body-bound until the mid-twentieth century: the power to *think*. The electronic communication revolution extends the power of *mind*.

The electronic communication revolution is a crucially new way to solve an old human problem. Our physical means of communicating—our voices, gestures, and expressions—have severe limitations. Adam no doubt noticed those limits the first time he tried to call Eve home from the back forty.[1] She didn't hear him. He had to get up, put on his leaf, and trudge all the way to the apple orchard (thereby creating the first path) to communicate with his rib.

Left to their natural physical equipment, human beings had to stand within range of hearing and seeing to communicate. But the inconveniences Adam had to tolerate didn't end there. Eve had a short memory. "You did *not* tell me to avoid the snake—and if you did, you can't prove it." She also had a point.

Human communication—a matter of waves (both sound and light) dashing through the air—had an aggravating way of disappearing just when you needed it most. What did she say? How did she say it? What did her hand, face, and body movements tell you? Those questions could be resolved only by memory. The physical evidence—the words that passed between Adam and Eve, their looks and gestures—could not be recalled for examination. The sound and light waves that made up those communications were literally on their way out of the galaxy. Out of sight and, probably, out of mind.

If memory were more accurate, of course, Adam's problem with disappearing words would have been less severe. He and Eve would have remembered their conversations word for word, pause for pause, raised eyebrow for raised eyebrow. Unfortunately, Adam thought Eve had a perversely selective memory, and Eve thought Adam had little or no memory at all.

The twin problems—our limited range of communication and our inability to preserve communication—proved good for the travel business for thousands of years. Need to talk to Huzah in Persia? It's a six-week journey by foot. Invention soon came to the rescue, of course, reducing the time to three weeks: you could run (or send a runner).

THE FIRST REVOLUTION: PEN ON PAPER

Problems have a wonderful way of eliciting solutions for improvement. Without a doubt the inventors of paper, pens, and ink had the problem of tired legs and aching feet. The paper/pen revolution must have seemed a bit awkward at first: beat reeds or rice husks until you have a paperlike slab. Then make inked marks on the slab and hand it to someone else, with an oral explanation of what the marks mean. ("An ×, Huzah, means to milk the cow. A + means to kill the cow.") The weak link, of course, was (and continues to be) our overtaxed and undertrained memories. Huzah no doubt confused his marks from time to time, leading to the first milk shortage.

---

[1] By borrowing the Adam and Eve story for illustrative purposes, we intend no inappropriate comment on material which, for some, bears religious importance. Nor do we wish to offend those for whom the story has marked sexual biases.

FIGURE 4–1
Ancient hieroglyphics

But consider the essence of this communication revolution: for the first time, the message sender could stay home. A set of marks on paper could be carried across scorching deserts and frigid mountain passes not by the message sender, but by his brother-in-law (the first "gofer"). Progress came quickly thereafter, led, no doubt, by the brothers-in-law of the world. Paper messages could be tied to pigeons or inserted into bottles and cast into the sea.

Our physical limitations as communicators had been extended in two ways. First, our range of communication was no longer limited to the distance we could be seen and heard. Messages on paper could extend as far as birds could fly or bottles could bob. Second, we no longer had to rely on memory alone to recall communication events. The paper bore the marks, indisputably, long after the last echo of our voice pierced the ionosphere on its way to outer space.

The cultural changes precipitated by the paper/pen revolution seem inevitable by hindsight. Laws and agreements could be set down in writing and preserved. Harvests could be recorded and compared with harvests of other years. Religious and secular tales could be artfully preserved, their expressive power now fixed and independent of the teller.

THE SECOND REVOLUTION: TYPE

Repeated copying of long documents like the Bible gave the original meaning to the term writer's cramp. Clearly, communicators needed a way to distribute written words broadly. As the need to know became more and more critical to social mobility and power, the demand for documents like books, pamphlets, sermons, letters, and journals increased exponentially. Just as Adam had noticed with regret his limits in calling to Eve, so communicators felt the strain of a new limit: the ability of scribes to produce and reproduce culturally important documents. Handpenned documents, where they did exist, often had to be chained for safekeeping, as in the case of the Vulgate during much of the Middle Ages. The problem of access had changed little from Adam's dilemma: legs still had to carry you to the physical spot (whether in the church or apple orchard) where a message could be received.

Enter movable type, typesetting, typewriters, carbon paper, and photocopying machines. Spanning the last 500 years, these inventions made up the print world as it was known to us at mid-twentieth century. With superior technological cleverness, typing machines in various forms sped up the scribe's hand, allowing readable (if not artistic) letters to appear on paper almost as fast as a person could speak.

Through reproduction techniques, many copies of such typed information now can be distributed to message receivers. The problem of access to written documents has been resolved. The public library movement led by Benjamin Franklin symbolized the availability of written words for everyone. Bibles no longer must be chained in churches, but instead can be stolen from hotel drawers.

The pain of hand-copying original sources has been allayed. But a secondary and more influential pain, the pain of waiting, lurked in the days when scribes penned documents letter-by-letter. That pain has been the driving force in the history of modern communications.

The hand, as scribes knew well, can draw letters on paper up to a certain speed, beyond which the letters cease to be readable. Early business men and women probably nagged their scribes interminably: "It's not done *yet*? Well, when *will* it be done?" The pain of waiting was exacerbated by the problem of multiple copies: "Fine. Now I need thirty more copies without a mistake. And could you *hurry*?"

Consider this interesting dilemma. The human range of communication had been pushed forward dramatically by the paper/pen revolution, but with a sacrifice about which even Adam would have complained. The time between the wish to communicate and the act of communicating had been lengthened. In other words, the paper/pen revolution ignored our need for speed in communication. When Adam needed to speak to Eve, he hated that long walk out to the apple orchard. The will to speak has little patience with delays of any kind, whether it is walking to reach Eve or penning letters one by one. The wait becomes all the more painful if circumstances shift between the moment of will-to-speak and the actual communication. In the most important matters of business and law, time is of the essence. In ancient times, the scribe's painfully slow drawing, re-drawing, and copying of documents no doubt caused the loss of many opportunities. We can be thankful that the Magna Carta was not a 600-page document.

FIGURE 4–2
Printing press

The lack of speed also became an increasing problem in terms of the physical delivery of messages. Though the message sender no longer had to personally travel to the intended message receiver, the penned message still took an irritatingly long time to deliver. Settlers in the New World often had to wait the better part of a year to receive news of births, deaths, and the latest gossip from their homeland. In short, the transmission of human communication by paper could proceed no faster than legs could run, ships could sail, or horses could gallop.

THE THIRD REVOLUTION: ELECTRONICS

In the history of electrical research, monumental minds like those of Michael Faraday and James Clark Maxwell noticed what Adam noticed: that electrical impulses move faster than human legs or pigeon wings. For communicators, the goal seemed quite straightforward. A way had to be found to load words and images onto electrons instead of runners, bottles, pigeons, or ships. How efficient it would be to let electrons carry messages to others at the speed of light, so that once again, a raised eyebrow or harrumph—like Adam's—would bring an immediate effect undisturbed and undelayed by scribes and delivery boys. And, better than Adam could have dreamed, that message could be broadcast instantaneously to millions of message receivers.

That work was undertaken by epic names in the history of communication—Thomas Edison, Alexander Graham Bell, Samuel Morse, Marchese Guglielmo Marconi—and less well known but important contributors like Philo T. Farnsworth (television), Lee De Forest (vacuum tube), and Heinrich Hertz (radio theory). They are the architects of a communication network without which the modern world would be inconceivable. These inventors literally helped create who we are and what we do.

Important communication theories flowed from the work of such early pioneers. Shortly after World War II, Claude E. Shannon and Warren Weaver published *A Mathematical Theory of Communication* (Urbana: University of Illinois Press, 1949). This significant contribution to communication theory, largely developed by Dr. Shannon at the Bell Telephone Laboratories, examined the technical problems of transmitting a message from sender to receiver.

In Shannon's and Weaver's model, the message begins with an *information source,* which is the mind of the speaker or writer. The speaker or writer chooses words and organizes them into sentences to encode a *message.* This message is transmitted as a *signal* (sound or light waves, or marks on paper). The signal is sent through a *channel,* but it can be garbled by *noise* (distractions, poor handwriting, static, and so forth). Finally, the *receiver* (person or machine) receives the message and decodes it into meaningful symbols. As a case in point, communication by computer follows the essential patterns described in the mathematical theory of communications.[2]

Some aspects of the electronics revolution have already stopped seeming new—much less revolutionary—to us. Radios, telephones, stereos, tape recorders, and even VCRs seem like standard furniture. They "belong," somehow, and we can't imagine life without them. These familiar appliances of the electronic communication revolution are largely one-directional, however; they bring the world to our living rooms, but they do little to bring our living rooms to the world. In other words, even by the mid-twentieth century, average citizens found their communication range to be severely restricted. True, the telephone could be picked up anytime and another person called almost anywhere. But what of printed messages?

It seemed that you had to own a publishing house or a newspaper to enjoy the full benefits of the electronic revolution. Placing printed messages in others' hands, especially across great distances, was prohibitively expensive for the lay person. Telegrams were reserved for life's most important occasions, like deaths or marriages. Our access to visual communication devices was equally restricted. Johnny Carson could be a guest in our bedrooms, but we could reach his only by breaking an extended list of laws. The major networks became the message senders, and the viewing audience settled for the role of message receiver.

The first to feel the discomfort of this relationship were American businesses. Most companies felt they definitely had something they wanted to say to their market. The biggest and wealthiest of these businesses wedged their way into a position of communication power by means of commercials. On radio and television and in magazines and newspapers, these corporate giants demonstrated their desire to play a shaping role in mass communication.

ELECTRONIC MEDIA AND YOU

For the first time, during the last two decades of the twentieth century, smaller businesses and individuals are feeling the impact of what it means to be a message sender as well as a message receiver in the electronic revolution. For costs that are already moderate and quickly becoming even lower, individuals and business entities can send oral and printed messages virtually anywhere on the planet and beyond.

---

[2]The mathematical theory of communication has been taken up, altered, and extended in the work of general system theorists like Anatol Rapoport and William J. Horvath (see "Thoughts on Organization Theory," *General Systems*, Vol 4, 1959, pp. 87–91). Recent contributions are treated well in Walter J. Severin and James W. Tankard, Jr., *Communication Theory: Origins, Methods, Uses* (New York: Hastings House, 1979), Nancy Harper, *Human Communication Theory: The History of the Paradigm* (Rochelle Park, NJ: Hayden, 1979), and Frank E. X. Dance, *Human Communication Theory: Comparative Essays* (New York: Harper and Row, 1982).

FIGURE 4–3
Modern business telephone

The Telephone

None of us needs instruction on how to use the familiar household telephone. But telephone companies warn that we will all have to pay attention to use the "new" phones effectively. These instruments have many new features to offer to business, with more features waiting in the development stage.

First, the modern business telephone answers calls rather than postponing them. Your caller either reaches you directly or is transferred to a line where you can be reached. If you cannot be reached at all, you can prerecord a message for callers (even individual messages can be left for callers with prearranged access codes).

Second, a "new" phone helps you screen calls by displaying the caller's number before you answer. The caller's number can be automatically sorted by the telephone for later callback.

Third, business telephones can open both ends of the conversation to several speakers. With conference microphones, one group of business people can talk freely with another individual or group. At the press of a button, the proceedings can be recorded for later analysis.

Fourth, modern phones help you reach your party. Using "camp'on" capability, the phone virtually stands in line when it receives a busy signal. You don't have to call back. Your intended party, meanwhile, receives a flashing "call waiting" signal. He or she knows you're waiting because your telephone number has already appeared on his or her telephone's display.

Finally, and most important, "new" telephones need not be plugged into the wall. Through the use of radio frequencies, cordless telephones can accompany you into meetings, on sales calls, and even (alas) on vacation. With the advent in the mid-1980s of cellular automobile telephones, business men and women can be in touch with the office or clients while on the road.

The conference call, of course, has been common in business communication for more than a decade. Speaking from separate locations, business men and women can hold joint discussions by interlinked telephone connections. Certain rules of the road have to be established in such calls to prevent confusion (Who is speaking now? What did she ask? Is it my turn to speak?) Business leaders quickly learn, however, to adapt personal communication styles to conference calling. They do not interpret silence as suspicion or reticence on the part of their listeners, as they certainly might in face-to-face conversation. Instead, moments of silence in conference calling may simply indicate courtesy. All speakers are waiting a moment to avoid inadvertent interruptions. As will be discussed later in this chapter, communication habits appropriate in conference calling go far in preparing managers for the world of teleconferencing (visual conference calling) which is sweeping business in the 1980s and 1990s.

The Microcomputer

Though not yet as common as the telephone, the **microcomputer** has passed the "fad" stage in large and small American businesses. By the mid-1980s, most earned their keep. The following discussion will not be concerned with such uses of microcomputers as processing data, handling payroll functions, running milling machines, and scheduling trains. Instead, we will focus on the five aspects of the microcomputer that are critical to the business communicator.

The Microcomputer as Word Processor   Using **software** (magnetically coded computer programs) such as WordStar, Multimate, WordPerfect, and others, the microcomputer permits relatively easy entry into and manipulation of text. A business letter, for example, can be typed into the microcomputer. Letter by letter, the words appear on the screen as you type, as much as they would appear on a piece of typing paper in a conventional typewriter. Unlike a typewriter, however, the microcomputer lets you perform a variety of corrections at the press of a key. A misspelled word, for example, can easily be deleted or replaced. If the correct spelling contains more or fewer let-

FIGURE 4–4
Personal microcomputer

ters than the incorrect spelling, the lines of the letter—all of them, in the case of a longer document—automatically and instantly adjust to accommodate the new spacing.

Writers find such flexibility conducive to free, relaxed writing. With a conventional typewriter, making such mistakes as a misspelled word or a forgotten line has always entailed a slow, irritating correction process: retyping the page, erasing or covering up the mistake, waiting for the whitening material to dry, and then retyping. Even correcting typewriters pose correction problems if the paper has been removed from the typewriter before the error is noticed. The sheet must be reinserted and readjusted with great care before the correcting tape can be applied to lift off the incorrect letters. In the case of an omitted line, of course, the correcting typewriter is of no more help than the conventional typewriter.

The word processor, by contrast, permits effortless insertion of lines, paragraphs, and whole pages. In addition, a "search and replace" function allows the person using the machine (the **user**) to select a particular word (let's say, "Brown") that has been misspelled throughout a manuscript and a replacement word ("Braun"). At the press of a key, all occurrences of "Brown" in the manuscript will be replaced by "Braun." In addition, sophisticated spelling software enables the user to check all words used in a document against a dictionary of words stored in computer memory, all in a matter of seconds. Progress is being made in the area of grammar as well, though the definitive grammar checker is still years away.

Once a document has reached final form on the computer screen, it can be stored on a **disk** (either floppy or hard) for later retrieval. A disk costing no more than a few dollars can store 300–400 pages, with advances in technology increasing that amount each year. From the disk, the document can be printed out by a **dot-matrix printer** (with high speed but low-quality print) or a **letter-quality printer** (a slower method with carbon-ribbon quality print). **Laser printers** can produce text and graphics virtually identical in quality to this page.

Recent advances in *facsimile transmission* promise to enhance the visual quality of materials we receive from computer printers. Using laser technology, sophisticated processing units can now print the image of whole pages without going through the difficult and limiting task of printing the page character by character, as done by a traditional typewriter. In this way, complex graphic images can be stored, retrieved, and transmitted using computers.

Such materials become all the more useful when they can be broadcast onto a large screen for business meetings and conferences. Programs like Storyboard convert the microcomputer to a well-equipped graphics laboratory, complete with colors, shapes, type fonts, and motion routines. With a little practice, even a beginner can create illustrative materials to accompany a business presentation or to be printed in a business document.

With a microcomputer, appropriate software, and a laser printer, individuals can produce documents—brochures, newsletters, even whole books—previously possible only through traditional publishing techniques. Such *desktop publishing* has dramatically expanded the number and types of printed communications available within businesses and to the public. Of the estimated 26,000 different types of newsletters now published in the United States, more than half are produced on desktop publishing equipment.

What do you need for such an operation? First, locate a reasonably powerful microcomputer, usually with at least 640 K of memory. Next, choose desktop publishing software that can be run on your system. Two popular systems are Xerox's Ventura Publisher and Harvard Professional Publisher. Finally, obtain a laser printer, such as Apple's LaserWriter or Hewlett Packard's LaserJet II. With practice, you can produce documents that, in format, typefont, layout, and print quality, have a truly professional appearance.

MAKING COMPUTERS INTO SPEEDY READERS

Teaching office computers to read used to be daunting: Operators of the scanning machines that translate printed data into computer language had to cut pages into single columns, paste them onto paper, and feed them in by hand. Even the scanners introduced in recent years require tutoring to recognize more than a few type fonts, and none can handle both text and pictures efficiently. Now Palantir Corp., a private, four-year-old Silicon Valley company, is offering a device that can identify any typewritten character or image and store it in a computer virtually at the touch of a button. "It's the next step in scanners." says Richard A. Shaffer, editor of the *Technologic Computer Letter* in New York.

Sales of scanning machines totaled $56 million last year, according to Dataquest, a market research firm. Law and accounting firms use them to store the reams of documents they encounter; other businesses use them to spruce up manuals and in-house documents by adding graphics from other sources.

Scanners typically send images and words to a computer's memory by using different techniques. In image scanning, sometimes called bit-mapping, a scanner breaks a picture into a pattern of thousands of light and dark dots. A light-sensitive semiconductor converts the pattern into a digital code that can be stored in a personal computer. An image scanner can process a full-page picture in about 30 seconds.

Excerpt from "Making Computers Into Speedy Readers," *Fortune*, July 7, 1986, p. 66. Reprinted by permission.

The Microcomputer as Trainer   Because it stores and presents information reliably and inexpensively, the microcomputer is attracting growing attention as a trainer. The need for training, of course, can hardly be overstated in an era when outmoded technologies and product lines are giving way to modern ones. Workers across the whole business spectrum must learn new concepts, skills, and applications—and they must learn them from someone or something.

The old training model is centered on a human teacher with a limited number of students. Although public education continues to fund that model, American business is looking for a less labor-intensive and expensive way to communicate ideas, concepts, and skills. Videotape has some usefulness for this purpose: a skilled teacher can record his or her training lesson, to be replayed numerous times in different company training locations around the country.

Unfortunately, people do not learn effectively merely by watching. They must participate by making choices and learning both from their successes and failures. Videotape has no place for such participation. It simply plays on, without regard to student responses.

The microcomputer, however, can be programmed to respond to student input. Especially when coupled with videotape, the computer can offer a high-quality, repeatable training experience. If a mid-level manager, for example, is learning negotiation skills, the computer can switch on a few minutes of videotaped negotiation. The tape can then pause for the computer to pose questions to the student. If the student's responses are correct, the computer can proceed with the lesson. If the responses show that the student misunderstood or misinterpreted the material presented, the computer can branch to a series of remedial lessons.

Although the creation of such programs takes time, money, and intelligence, they are cost-effective training tools once they are in place. Microcomputers can play and replay training lessons without absenteeism, job burnout, midlife crisis, union strikes, or any of the other overhead associated with human teaching.

The Microcomputer as a File Cabinet   The storage and retrieval of business documents has long been a human and financial burden. Staff members must complete the dreary task of hand-filing originals and copies of business documents. Expensive floor space—even entire rooms—must be devoted to bulky file cabinets.

The microcomputer offers an appealing solution. Business documents that arrive by means of computer can be transferred immediately to a storage disk. Filed there under descriptive headings, the documents can be recalled at any time to the screen for review or to a printer for hard copy production. The space required for storage is minimal. Literally hundreds of thousands of business pages can be stored on disks occupying no more space that a shoe box.

The risks inherent in such a storage system must be mentioned. Paper documents can be destroyed by fire or flood, but otherwise last rather well decade after decade. Documents stored on disk, by contrast, can be erased or ruined by serendipitous events: a magnet passed too close to the disk, a slight crease in the disk itself, or hot temperatures that distort the disk surface. For this reason, most businesses make a practice of backing up all data stored on disks. When information is irreplaceable, as in the case of bank records, the duplicate computer storage tapes or disks are kept in separate locations at all times, sometimes miles apart.

However, these risks seem minor when the storage capacity of a computer is compared with that of file cabinets, In addition, the sums of money that can be saved by *not* using space for filing cabinets can be substantial.

The Microcomputer and Security   As the computer becomes the main channel through which business sends, retrieves, and stores information, business leaders have every reason to question the machine's security mechanisms. How can we be sure that sensitive financial data entered into the office computer cannot be accessed by a fourteen-year-old "hacker" with a home computer and **modem** (an electronic link joining one computer to another)? Or, worse, by a competitor?

Another concern for those who use and rely upon data in large computer systems are "computer viruses." These unauthorized programs, often introduced by saboteurs and vandals, destroy or alter data and computer functions. Like a virus, they spread from level to level within the computer impervious to an easy cure. In 1987 such destructive programs were responsible for millions of dollars in lost data.

Any computer attached to other computers for communication purposes is subject to user commands. When such a command says, in effect, "reveal business data," the computer obeys. Business computer specialists have therefore developed mathematical ways to make authorized user commands *special* to the computer in a way that nonauthorized user commands are not. By analogy, they give the authorized user a mathematical key to the locked portion of data within the computer.

Few keys, unfortunately, have proved as foolproof as they were intended to be. Unlike physical keys, with notches carved into brass, the key to a computer is just a series of numbers—let's say, 39204939592. Intuitively, it would seem difficult, if not impossible for anyone to guess that number and gain access to the protected data within the computer. But intuition fails us. A competitor or vandal bent on breaking into the protected data files can use the computer's vast speed to a criminal end; the "enemy" computer tries number combination after number combination, thousands every minute, until it happens up the right number to break the electronic lock.

As newspapers and magazines feature stories of illegal entry into computer credit files, legal records, and so forth, business people may be wary of revealing any sensitive business secrets to computers. While such reticence is understandable, it can be overcome by knowledge. Businesses must take the lead in proving and publicizing the worth of reliable-looking mechanisms. Only by such effort can business communicators share the kind of confidence a bank manager feels after slamming shut the door on a two-ton vault.

The Microcomputer and Data Bases   Business decisions are based on knowledge—and knowledge can be expensive and time-consuming to accumulate if it is gathered first-hand. An alternative is to access a business-related data base by means of microcomputer. Such a **data base**—in effect, a huge library of cross-referenced information—allows the user to enter "search" words relating to the business need at hand. For example, an executive might need information on an issue in business law from the ABI/Inform data base located in Louisville, Kentucky (see Chapter 7 for data base lists and addresses). When a search word such as "libel," is entered, all articles pertaining to that term from more than 500 journals are available for review on the screen or for printout. Brief synopses of articles help the executive pick the ones he or she needs to read in full. A hard copy of these articles can be printed out on a long-distance basis from one computer to another. Without leaving his or her desk, the executive has visited one of the best business law libraries in the country.

This is just one data base; there are literally hundreds of others. Most of these will access materials only in specific areas such as business, medicine, or finance.

Several communication companies now offer videotext service, a means of accessing printed information from data base sources. These services allow the user to order individual pages, whole reports, or longer documents for review, research, or inclusion in published company materials. Videotext materials can be previewed on the computer screen before the decision is made to have hard copy printed. An increasing amount of videotext source material is uncopyrighted, providing the user with a virtual encyclopedia from which to draw in preparing company proposals, reports, and publications.

A GLIMPSE AHEAD

The microcomputer is changing quickly in terms of memory capacity and computing power. With the advent of laser-disk storage of computer codes and images, new horizons will open for computer training systems, self-contained data bases (in effect, a library on your desk), and vastly expanded document storage systems. Two developments in particular already seem destined to impact the future of computing in an especially powerful way. First, led by Japanese fifth-generation computers, the **voice-driven computer** is no longer a dream or curiosity. At its heart is a voice chip that digitizes sound waves, making it possible to convert them to letters of the alphabet. Given the varieties of pitch, inflection, and accent in our speech, the task of speech-print conversion involves powerful discriminatory powers on the part of the computer. Just imagine the possibilities: to be able to sit before your computer and leisurely command business documents onto the screen. When you want to change a word or line, or when the computer has misprinted or misunderstood what you've said, you simply instruct the computer—orally—to make a few changes. When the document is done, you probably will find yourself saying, "Thank you." And no doubt the computers of the future will answer, "You're welcome."

The second and more compelling advance that lies in the near future is **artificial intelligence.** The term means no more or less than it suggests: a machine will have the necessary capability to carry on intelligent processes. In short, it will *think.*

What will a thinking machine do for us? This scenario may hit close to the mark: we tell our computer that we need a shipment of parts that was ordered three weeks ago and is now late. The computer asks a few questions: Who is the supplier? Do you know why the shipment is late? Do you want to maintain a friendly tone? We answer the questions in words, talking as if to a business associate. The computer proceeds to generate a letter for our inspection. If the letter says what we like, we instruct the computer to forward the message electronically to our supplier. If it needs correction, we mention particular lines and suggest improvement. Better yet, we "teach" the computer how to improve the poor lines so that next time a similar letter will be perfect the first time.

In an extension of this scene, an answer arrives from the supplier. The computer reads and understands the message. All we have to do is pose the question, "Computer, have we heard from the supplier yet?" We can then ask what the message was. Or we may choose to leave it up to the computer: "Did we get things straightened out?" The computer, after all, knows our production schedule, our inventory, and our shipping requirements. It is in a key position to assess whether or not the message from the supplier solves the problem.

More imaginative minds may want to drive the case a bit farther. Why ask a highly skilled computer anything? Why not let it generate a "hurry-up" letter every time parts are late (parts the computer ordered in the first place). Why not let it develop weekly or monthly reports that *it* can then analyze to see how business is going? And who should it tell if things are going poorly? Certainly not the human manager. He or she has long since opted out of the complexity of computer-managed business. The report properly goes to a human specialist—a systems expert—who tweaks the program to bring different and— with luck—better results.

Research into artificial intelligence is in progress at major academic centers around the world. Computers have already demonstrated their ability to master limited areas of understanding in English. Each month, that area of understanding grows, almost the way a child learns to speak. In time, machines will talk and write in an understandable way. They will master language word by word, with ever-growing flexibility and naturalness. Then Milton's prophecy will be true: "We have lent out our minds."

Teleconferencing

In 1987, American business spent $20 billion in expenses related to flying business bodies around the world. In most cases, only business *minds* needed to travel.

A **teleconference** is a visual telephone call in which cameras and microphones in one meeting room transmit visual and auditory signals by satellite or ground line to another similarly equipped meeting room. With the assistance of trained camera technicians, geographically separated business men and women can talk almost as naturally to one another as if they were in the same room.

Teleconferences have many communication advantages over business travel. They avoid the stress of travel, including the time away from family and friends. They let participants speak from their own turf, secure and confident. All the charts, models, and other visual supports that couldn't fit on the plane are available for display. Other personnel can attend the teleconference to lend support or participate.

For such reasons, major corporations like ARCO and Hughes Aircraft, as well as hotel chains like Hilton and Holiday Inn, have invested heavily in teleconferencing equipment. While none of these companies has expressed outright regret at the investment, some have made reference to "learning the hard way." They have discovered that teleconferencing, unlike radio and television, is not a phenomenon that has gained quick or common acceptance.

The reasons for the slow growth of what seems like such a good idea are instructive. First, business conferences depend as much on social chemistry as on information sharing—and chemistry is created from posture, manners, asides, glances, chuckles, and all the other subtle signals of communication by which we learn to trust or distrust, like or dislike one another. Even business leaders skilled in personal contact are not automatic media presences like Dan Rather or Barbara Walters. Such business people have difficulty trusting big deals and important negotiations to teleconferences because of unknowns: What do they look like on camera? On what will the

FIGURE 4–5
Teleconferencing

camera focus? How will they know when to speak, or when someone on the other end wants to speak? How will they look eye-to-eye with decision makers in the group?

These issues cannot be resolved by improvements in teleconferencing hardware. Instead, people must be trained to use teleconferencing effectively. Major business schools are now undertaking this task. In the last decade of this century we can look forward to the widespread use of a technology that comes close to total communication, relaying not only voices but also gestures, expressions, postures, and all other nonverbal signals.[3]

Electronic Mail

As American business turns increasingly to interstate and international markets, the lag factor in mail delivery becomes more expensive. Major financial decisions, such as dividend changes, bond prices, or new borrowing, often are deferred pending written confirmation of new contracts and successful negotiations. Having such messages held up for even a few days in the channels of traditional mail can cost thousands of dollars in lost time and, too often, lost opportunities.

Electronic mail proposes nothing less than almost instant written communication between computer terminals. A message sender in New York, for example, can type a message onto a computer screen, check it over for accuracy, and press a key for the "send" command. The message is sped by local telephone line to a main-frame computer in New York, which in turn races the message by satellite or ground lines to the message receiver in Los Angeles. There, the message can be read on the terminal screen and printed out, if a hard copy is desired.

Mailgrams, Telex, TWX, and other electronic transmission systems from the 1960s and 1970s have already made a solid case for the advantages of fast, accurate delivery of messages. Such systems were relatively expensive to the user, however, and hence were often reserved for urgent and often emergency messages. The impact of a telegram or mailgram, therefore, depended in large part upon its rarity: a mailgram each day would quickly cease to arouse special interest or curiosity. Electronic mail, similarly, quickly seems old hat to businesses already using services like Telenet and Western Union's EasyLink. The impact of such messages relies, as always, on fundamentals: the writer's ability to motivate readers through persuasive use of language.

Saving and filing electronic messages is easy. Each user has a file directory where hundreds of electronic messages can be filed under user-chosen guide words. A message from Ms. Smith of IBM, for example, might be

---

[3]See Arthur Bell and Thomas Housel, "Teleconferencing Comes of Age—Again," *T.H.E. Journal* (Nov., 1986), p. 24.

TELE-NOIA: THE PRIVACY ISSUE IN TELECONFERENCING

The telephone has had almost a century to build its reputation as a relatively confidential medium for communication. The same mistrust that Granddad felt for "who might be listening in on the party line" is echoed by modern managers leery of teleconferencing. They point to newspaper stories of signal-stealing, ingenious hackers and backyard satellite dishes. When it comes to discussing personnel matters, tax planning, financial disclosures, product information and personal career plans, many business leaders simply don't trust the teleconference.

Vendors in the last two years have spent millions developing and publicizing encryption codes that supposedly make teleconference transmissions inviolable. But whether or not a particular code is breakable, *belief* is the issue. If managers believe that somewhere a hacker with a satellite dish is taking notes—perhaps for a competitor or a government regulator—teleconferencing will be reserved for only the most innocuous business transactions. Such tele-noia is reflected even in the architecture of teleconferencing centers. At ARCO, for example, the teleconferencing room was purposely designed to exclude even the equipment operators from any knowledge of what transpired within.

Add to such general mistrust the uneasiness many speakers feel when they talk room-to-room instead of person-to-person. No matter how broad the visual scan, speakers complain that they don't know the size or nature of their audience at the other end. Am I speaking to the face I see on the screen or a roomful of listeners? Will others enter the room while I'm speaking? Can others not on camera hear what I have to say? How can I adjust my words if I can't see their faces?

These questions cause many teleconference speakers to think and speak without taking any risks. The wooden, empty statements that result please no one. The speaker feels awkward, the listener feels disappointed and the business purpose is too often aborted.

Excerpt from "Teleconferencing Comes of Age—Again" by Arthur H. Bell and Tom Housel from *T.H.E. Journal,* May 1986. Copyright © 1986 by Information Synergy, Inc. Reprinted by permission.

stored under the guide word "Smith/IBM." The correspondence can be stored at a press of a key, and recalled to the monitor or printer just as quickly. In most cases, the physical tapes or disks holding the user's files do not reside in the user's building at all. Instead, they are given maximum security and hazard protection at a specially designed computer center, often at a distant location. Physical distance, of course, makes little difference when transmissions take place at speeds approaching that of light.

By the mid-1980s, several companies and government agencies provided electronic mail service on a fee basis. The most popular of these among the private sector's electronic mail services is GTE's Telenet. The service features not only a flexible and extensive set of commands for sending and receiving mail, but also bulletin boards where companies or individual can post information to be read by all (or selected) users of the systems. Company announcements or training materials, for example, can be "published" and distributed electronically at far less cost and effort than traditional typesetting, printing, and physical distribution. Employees are simply told by memo, "Please read Bulletin #16 on Telenet before next Thursday's meeting." Employees can choose to read the material on the computer screen, or print out a copy to take home.

In January 1982, the United States Postal Service inaugurated E-COM (Electronic Computer-Originated Mail). Major post offices around the country can receive messages entered from the computer terminals in their locale. The messages are then electronically transmitted to the post office of their destination. There, the message is printed out and placed in an envelope for delivery by traditional carrier.

In November 1984, Western Union placed its hat in the ring of electronic mail providers with EasyLink. For a fraction of the cost of a traditional telegram, computer users can send electronic messages to be delivered by Western Union either in electronic form—that is, directly to the receiving computer terminal—or as printed message packaged in a Western Union envelope. Businesses are finding this an attractive service for two reasons. First, Western Union provides handshake compatibility between a great variety of different computers. An Apple in Pennsylvania can talk to an IBM personal computer in Michigan. Second, the Western Union name provides an identity and suggestion of urgency for messages delivered in envelopes.

What do actual users have to say about their experiences with electronic mail? Ellen Siler, Director of Sales, Marketing and Training for TRW, comments:

> *The work of my particular unit depends upon electronic mail. I travel extensively, but my people have no trouble sending me documents for review and approval by electronic mail. I can keep in touch anywhere there's a terminal served by Telenet.*[4]

Other users, while acknowledging the many conveniences of electronic mail, are quick to point out its problems. Some find that messages sent by electronic mail are taken less seriously than traditional business letters. Senders tend to dash off their thoughts in rough draft form, bypassing the review and correction often provided by associates or secretaries. Other users say they miss the pizzazz of traditional mail communication—classy black type on crisp, expensive stationery, with paragraphs and signature all calculated to amplify the persuasive effect of the message. "I miss signatures especially," says one executive. "I formed impressions of the individual I was dealing with by the way the name was signed."

The future of electronic mail seems assured, if only because it provides two important factors to message transfer: speed and accuracy. Improvements are being made each month. Competition will encourage companies to provide more formatting capabilities for electronic messages, returning

[4]Personal communication, March 1, 1985.

margins, paragraphing, and other graphic aspects of business messages to the control of the user. Company letterheads, too, may soon accompany printed messages. All of these refinements suggest that business messages are not and never have been mere words; instead, they are a combination of words and impressions gathered from the total effect of the written communication at hand.

An interesting footnote to the use of electronic mail involves business schools. In the last decades of the twentieth century, successful business schools find themselves blessed with many more students than they anticipated. The problems arising from such programs are largely physical in nature; for example, not enough parking, classrooms, and eating facilities. Electronic mail offers an attractive, if partial, solution: students can often send their minds to campus without sending their bodies. In other words many assignments, questions for the professor, and contacts with fellow students can be sent by electronic message from the student's home rather than

FIGURE 4–6
Integrated office system

in person. Lecture notes and, in some cases, student assignments can be posted on electronic bulletin boards, all accessible by the college community. These practical applications of electronic mail will surely increase in frequency and creativity as more and more colleges require students to own a microcomputer as an entrance requirement.

Integrated Office Systems

Despite the claims made in computer advertisements of the 1970s and 1980s, the computer and its peripheral devices were not immediate stars in many offices. The problem was compatibility. In many cases, the desktop computer could not access records already held in main-frame computer storage. The two computers simply spoke a different language. Additionally, companies had trouble achieving tight working relations among electronic storage of documents, computer telephone information (who called? when? message?) photocopying equipment, and—most of all—graphic facilities.

Major computer companies like IBM, Xerox, and Wang took the lead in producing not just stand-alone equipment but whole office systems integrated to work harmoniously together. Achieving this sort of coordination among machines meant determining common specifications for hardware and software. The result is an office system that takes over many of the tedious chores of the business day. In a lawyer's office in Chicago, for example, the computer telephone rings. At the push of a button by the lawyer who answers the phone, the central computer receives a message from the phone that the call is to be billed at the rate of $2.00 per minute, with an invoice automatically sent to the client within ten days. The computer, in turn, sends invoice information, complete with letterhead, to the laser printer. It prepares the invoice with lightning speed, along with an envelope complete with metered postage. The communication only awaits the lawyer's signature to go out of the door. If the client is served by electronic mail, of course, the process is even simpler: the computer sends an electronic billing directly—and is paid, perhaps by electronic transfer of funds.

By 1988 well over half of America's work force was white-collar. The integrated office offers time-saving advantages for such highly skilled and well-paid workers, thereby increasing the efficiency and profitability of the company. Time-motion studies of American executives consistently show significant "down" time per day for trivial tasks: standing at a photocopy machine waiting for 20 copies of a document, adding up figures by hand for purposes of billing or inventory, searching through bulky, ill-organized files to find a necessary document, and so forth. These frustrations of the business day not only interfere with creative, insightful management; they also rob workers of energy. The integrated office system, as it continues to evolve, strives to put information and electronic helpmates at the fingertips of each office worker and manager.

THE BUSINESS RESPONSE TO THE COMMUNICATION REVOLUTION

As we look forward to communication techniques and technologies in the last decade of the twentieth century, what important changes can we foresee? While the future always has a way of surprising us, the truth of the following three basic propositions seems assured:

Proposition 1: We Will Read More in the 1990s

There will be more words to read. Writing will be a national and perhaps international obsession, due in large part to word processing. Word processing, as discussed earlier, simplifies the act of typing. Words, phrases, sentences, and whole paragraphs or pages can be transposed at the press of a key. But word processing also makes the compositional process much less tedious.

When word processing takes threat away, the fingers fly freely across the keys with the knowledge that they can't do irreparable harm. Typing speed increases dramatically (on the order of 20 to 30 percent, some studies show). Not only do experienced typists increase their typing speed, but new office workers take up typing who previously found it too difficult or painstaking. Even hunt-and-peck typists find the word processor a forgiving and flexible production instrument.

The net effect of all this new capability is words, words, words. Whenever a bottleneck of difficulty is removed, the floodgates open to a new surge of productivity. We can expect our business lives to be awash in documents of all kinds, each competing for our attention. Many executives, as they compare their work in the 1980s with that in the 1970s, claim to have twice as much to read now.

Add to the effects of keyboard word processing the inevitable tidal wave of words that will sweep over us as voice-driven word processors come on line in the early years of the 1990s. At first, the mere novelty of the machine will cause a surge of print from office experimenters. After that, the ease we all feel in talking as compared with writing will ensure more documents, probably of greater length.

Proposition 2: We Will Reproduce Our Words More Often

Not only will we produce more words; the documents we create will be distributed much more globally than they are at present. Let's say, for example, that we have produced a three-page memo reporting production delays. If the memo report must be duplicated by carbon copy, there is a good chance that we will send it to no more than four or five people (the maximum number of clear carbon copies on most typewriters). If, however, we have access

FIGURE 4–7
Text capabilities of word processing

1   **TEXT CAPABILITIES OF WORD PROCESSING**

November 19, 19__   6

2   Mr. Jack Bevins
1928 Western Ave.
Los Angeles, CA 90083

3   Dear Mr. Bevins:

4   How pleased we at Victory Transport were to receive your note of thanks.   7
It was our pleasure to provide assistance to the Children's Charity.

5   Count on us for one truck and two men for next year's fund-raiser.   8
We're eager to do our part.
9

Sincerely,

Frank Baxter

Frank Baxter
Manager, Victory Transport

FT302:vw   10

1 Can set all capital letters and headline fonts	6 Can place individual lines at left or right margin, or center them
2 Can move entire text or individual lines anywhere on page	7 Can reformat a paragraph or page
3 Can insert extra lines or spaces	8 Can insert extra words
4 Can correct misspelling	9 Can search for/change given words through the entire text
5 Can set spacing between lines	10 Can store text on disk for later editing, reprinting

to a photocopying machine, we may send the document to many more people, even though the job entails collating, stapling, and addressing the various copies.

Now imagine the same three-page document composed for electronic mail. A menu appears asking us where we want the memo distributed. One of our choices is "All authorized recipients," in this case all supervisors, managers, and directors. The temptation is overwhelming: at the press of a button, the document is on its way to over a hundred people. Some of these need to read your memo report, and others don't. You tell yourself that it's better to include too many readers than to leave out someone. The effect? Words, words, words pouring in upon each manager at an unprecedented rate. Everyone, it seems, has something to say through electronic mail, and copying the entire company is almost easier than picking out selected readers.

For documents that are not distributed by electronic mail, we will have high-speed, multi-task copiers at our disposal. Laser printers and copiers reproduce the "image" of each page, rather than breaking it down letter-by-letter, like a traditional typewriter. As a consequence, hundreds of original copies can pour from the machine each minute. On many standard office copiers, these can be automatically collated and stapled. What's more, the process is fun to watch. Office workers who operate the new generation of printer/copiers report fascination with the way pages pour through the machine at a dizzying rate. Again, the effect? More documents for every manager to read, digest, and file.

Proposition 3: We Will Have Access to More Information

More than 2400 data bases now serve the needs of business, medicine, law, engineering, and a dozen other fields.[5] Taken together, these information services make available billions of printed pages from journals, reports, studies, books, and dissertations. In past years our office desks were not heaped with such materials because we had a good excuse: the business library was across town, and research there was too costly in time and personal energy. A bottleneck of inconvenience prevented us from getting information we may have needed.

That bottleneck has been shattered by computer access to data bases. From our offices, we can enter search words that within minutes can bring up pertinent information on virtually any topic relevant to business.

The effect of this new availability? More words.

---

[5]"Let the Data Base Get You the Facts," *Changing Times*, Oct. 1984.

HOW WILL WE HANDLE MORE WORDS?

These three propositions build a clear case for the future: we will face vastly more printed words in our business lives. But this phenomenon would matter less if the big chip—the one between our ears—kept pace with changes in all the microchips around us. That is, more words don't matter if reading speeds and comprehension rates keep up.

Unfortunately, there is no evidence to suggest that we read any faster or comprehend any more completely than business people in previous decades. Nor are there significant plans on the books at major business schools to change this situation. The implications are clear, if somewhat frightening. Something has to give, as words pouring through microchips back up against a bottleneck impervious to technology: the human brain.

What will give, most likely, is the way we communicate. In the way we write, speak, and even think, we will make crucial adjustments necessitated by the new world of words. At the present time, the form of these adjustments can be observed only in part; therefore, the following descriptions of possible changes in communication are hypothetical and should be construed as suggestions, not facts. Measure their accuracy against your own communication experience as you contemplate or confront a business career overflowing with words.

More Verbal or Oral Contact

Printed communication will lose effectiveness to the extent that it gets lost among piles of letters, memos, reports, and advertisements. On many important business matters, we will find ourselves making contact in person, by telephone, or by teleconference rather than by printed media. After initial business understandings have been reached, we may agree to confirm points in a backup letter or memo of some type.

This will have implications for business schools, where the major emphasis still falls upon writing. Business majors will want to be prepared to do business by means of interpersonal conversations, group discussions, interviews, telephone/teleconferencing meetings, and other forums requiring practical oral skills.

Early Messaging

In his well-known video presentation, "Effective Writing," Joseph Florin demonstrates what a busy executive does with a pile of printed matter. There is the initial shuffle to see what looks interesting or important. Then there is the tentative selection of a few likely candidates for reading. After a glance here and there at how they begin, the "winners" are selected for serious attention. The rest remain unread, often for days or weeks, until they are filed or discarded.

What determines which document is chosen? Clear, early messages let the reader know what you plan to discuss and why. Too often that "headline" gets buried deep in memos, letters, and reports. Consider, for example, two opening paragraphs from a report. The first hides the central intent of the report; the second displays it early and openly.

Delayed messaging:

The mission statement of the Office of Employee Safety within Entron Corporation requires that we review potential hazards within the company, and report on a quarterly basis to management. This report, though not our usual quarterly report, is felt to be justified by circumstances uncovered last week during routine maintenance of company air conditioning ducts. That maintenance was performed by Caudwell Associates and has now been completed.

Early Messaging

Carcinogenic asbestos fibers in Entron's air conditioning ducts pose a health threat to every employee. The Office of Employee Safety reached this conclusion after examining ducts exposed during recent servicing. This report describes our findings and makes recommendations.

Notice that a reader is "caught" by the first line in the second example. He or she does not have to wade through boring preliminaries. **Early messaging** recognizes that each piece of writing has a short "window of opportunity" to catch the eye of the reader. If that moment—really a matter of only a few seconds—is lost due to irrelevant language, the document may go entirely unread.

You can enhance your ability to produce early messages by emphasizing "Subject:" lines in memos and letters. Make these phrases attention-getters as well as describers. Observe how a flat "Subject:" line with a minor revision, can breathe new life into the statement without verging over into type.

Subject: *Upcoming Sales Convention* (descriptive but not urgent)

Subject: *Your Role in the Upcoming Sales Convention* (personalized to gain attention)

In longer works such as reports and proposals, the subject line is expanded into a succinct paragraph or two called the Executive Summary. This extended early message may be your only chance to attract the interest and the reading time of a busy executive. Use words early in your paragraphs that get to the heart of what he or she may care about in your longer document. For example, notice how this short executive summary places emphasis on what matters most to the executive reader:

Executive Summary

Employees at VRC Corporation use virtually all of the sick time allotted to them each month. This practice costs the company more than half of its current profit margin. None of our competitors experiences a comparable rate of absenteeism.

Are VRC employees truly ill? The evidence suggests they are not (Section II). Only in four cases have employees been disciplined for taking unnecessary sick leave (Section IV). Three company policies should be changed to bring down the number of absentee hours due to the abuse of sick leave (Recommendations, Section VI).

The test for early messaging in any business document is simple: hand it to a business associate to peruse for five seconds. Then take it back and ask for impressions. If, in those five seconds, your associate has not at least glimpsed the central message and purpose of the document, your early message needs improvement.

Increased Emphasis on Format

We form important judgments about business documents long before we read a single word. In the era of the electronic communication revolution, these first impressions will be crucial in determining whether or not a document gets our attention.

One way to attract the eye and mind is to format the document in a **user-friendly** way. This term comes from the language of computer manuals, in which computers are described—often inaccurately—as machines that are patient and forgiving to user errors and misunderstandings. In the case of documents, however, *user-friendly* has a more specific meaning: user-friendly formats don't scare the eye away.

Notice, for example, in this dense jungle of prose how the eye immediately decides, "Thanks, I'd rather not."

Heavy blocks of print unrelieved by white space prove uninviting to the eye. Even before the mind has a chance to consider what the words themselves have to communicate, the eye has already decided "too dense, too dark, too difficult." That predisposition influences how we read the words on the page. The task of reading such a dense block of print is comparable in many ways to remembering a long number: 41112345678910198577510020. Notice how a bit of white space makes the number visually more approachable, and hence memorable: 411 12345678910 1985 775-1020. Use white space in the form of indentation, margination, and spacing to create visually interesting and attractive paragraphs and pages.

By contrast, the following paragraphs invite the eye's attention by their generous use of white space, indentation, and short paragraphs.

Heavy blocks of print are difficult to read. Even before the mind has a chance to consider what the words themselves have to communicate, the eye has already decided "too dense, too dark, too difficult."

That predisposition influences how we read the words on the page. For example:

- *Try to remember this long number: 411123456789101985775 1020*
- *Now notice how a bit of white space makes the number visually more approachable and memorable:*

411 12345678910 1985 775–1020

Use white space in the form of indentation, margination, and spacing to create visually interesting and attractive paragraphs and pages.

Again, the test for adequate user-friendliness in documents is a human one. Hand the document to a business associate and ask, "How does it look?" Watch the person's eyes and expression for your answer. if the reader squints and frowns while looking over your document, you've missed your mark. Revise your format (easily done through word processing) so that there is more "breathing space" for the reader's eye and mind.

Increased Use of Graphic Enhancements

In every era of business communication, there have been "prestige cues" that indicate, at a glance, the relative importance of the document. In the 1970s, for example, letters typed on fabric ribbon seemed somehow more amateurish than letters typed with carbon ribbon (producing a booklike clarity in type). The letter style became standard practice for attorneys, accountants, and other professionals whose credibility depended in part on a "class" impression.

With advances in word processing in the 1980s, prestige cues changed. Now everyone seemed to have access to a letter-quality printer with carbon ribbon type. The new cues had to do with the type itself: could the writer justify (make even) both right and left margins? Could the writer emphasize some words through the use of boldface? Could the writer create large-letter headings? These changes raised the stakes in the game of looking professional. Popular word processing software like WordStar went through several revisions in an effort to provide more and more flexibility with type.

The game, with its new set of cues, continues as we approach the twenty-first century. Now all business communicators seem to have access to WordStar-like systems for turning out eye-catching type in letters, reports, and proposals. The new prestige cues—the keys to who's ahead in the communication game—are pictures within business documents.

Several software packages now available for computers like the Apple Macintosh and the IBM personal computer enable the user to create charts, graphs, maps, schemata, and photographlike pictures for inclusion in business documents. Once created on the screen of the microcomputer, these graphics can be placed anywhere in a business document and printed out by a printer with graphics capability (typically, a variety of a dot-matrix printer). The graphics can be reduced or enlarged, rotated to any position, and, in many systems, printed out in a variety of selected colors. Once these graphics have been placed within the business document, they can be stored onto disk for recall at a later time. Thus, companies with a given product line can create a number of visuals depicting their products. This collection forms a visual library to be called up by any writer within the company who needs a handy illustration.

Far more than cosmetic decoration, such graphic enhancements confirm the wisdom of the ancient saying, "a picture is worth a thousand words." Visual diagrams and representations catch the reader's eye more powerfully than mere print and can be used to reinforce central points in a lasting way.

To use these new prestige cues, familiarize yourself with a prominent graphics package as recommended by your college learning resource specialist or professor. You might also check with computer stores to find graphics software compatible with the microcomputer and printer at your disposal.

FIGURE 4–8
Graphics system

Test your own response to a business page containing graphic enhancements (see Figure 4–9).

FIGURE 4–9

Graphically enhanced page

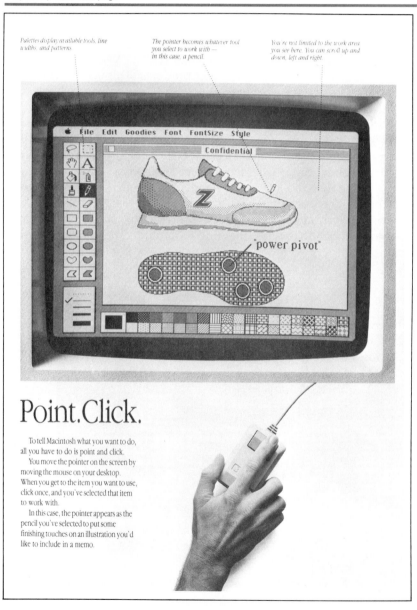

The Return of Friendliness

One might think that communication, as it grows faster and more mechanical due to new technologies, would lose its human warmth. "It was great to see you, Frank" might inevitably degenerate into "Per our recent meeting . . ."

Just the opposite seems to be occurring. Perhaps because we fear a sterile, brave new world, we already seem to be pouring our personalities into communication carried electronically. Notice, for example, how this actual sample from electronic mail manages to say, "Hey, there's a person behind this message—one you might like to know."

Formal it's not. But is it effective communication? Mary tells Bob exactly what she needs and when. In frank, friendly terms she explains the reason for the rush and seeks Bob's cooperation. In tone and substance, the message could be considered a written telephone call.

Shrewd communicators can use this general relaxation in formality to business advantage. Business relationships are still based to a remarkable degree on interpersonal chemistry and warmth: the key ingredients of trust. By striking a friendly but not presumptuous or brash tone, communicators

FIGURE 4–10
Electronic mail sample

```
EMS 3987 January 4, 19__     Storage Disk:2238


We need the results of your marketing studies no later
than January 20, 19__, to complete redesign of label and
packaging for BerryTarts.  Contact us ASAP by EMS when
you receive computer runs, particularly for urban areas.
By January 30, 19__, we will send preliminary redesigns
to you by FAX for your signoff.  Thanks, Bob--and sorry
for the rush.  We're all under the gun to beat the market-
ing effort of General Foods.  Happy New Year!
Mary Gilford
```

can put their reader at ease—the best posture for persuasion. The act of communicating itself becomes easier as we let ourselves write in a friendly, open mode. Few of us find it easy to generate paragraph after paragraph of the business clichés we never use in ordinary speech: "Regarding your . . . , thereby eliminating . . . , in full expectation of . . . , with all due respect." Those may (or may not) have been the words of our grandfathers; they certainly are not our sincere words. By letting ourselves write as though to a friend, we find words flowing more naturally and more persuasively. Often, we make a friend of our reader in business simply by treating him or her that way in words.

The Advent of Shared Writing

Historically, American business people have considered writing a private act, a form of self-expression. As such, criticism of one's style was tantamount to criticism of one's personality. "What Do You Mean, I Can't Write?" asks the title of one of the *Harvard Business Review*'s most often reprinted articles.[6]

That attitude—that a person's writing is private and personal—has roots that every business writer must understand, especially at a time when the attitude is changing dramatically. With the Romantic era of the nineteenth century came the idea that writing was based primarily on inspiration. Waiting for such inspiration came to be known as "writer's block"—that painful staring at a blank sheet of paper. Poets like Byron talked of the "lava of the imagination" pouring forth into words.

Through our schooling, we are all heirs to such Romantic assumptions about where words come from. Once we have cast language onto paper, we adopt an almost parental attitude toward our choice of diction, phrasing, and even punctuation.

Such protective attitudes may be appropriate for poets, but are not well-suited to today's business communicators. Words in business are like nails in carpentry: items with which to get the job done. Business writers, especially in the fast-paced days of a communication revolution, put words on paper with much the same attitude as a builder frames a house. He or she welcomes constructive comment by others, because the goal is to build a good document or house, rather than to immortalize personal expression or inspiration. In short, the era of electronic communication will emphasize the *craft* of business communication—skills that workers are eager to share in the same way that craftsmen compare techniques.

This attitude is already giving birth to communication **quality circles** (Q-circles) in American corporations. Writers within a work group circulate a

---

[6]John Fielden, "What Do You Mean I Can't Write?" *Harvard Business Review,* May-June 1964, pp. 46–54.

document to test its effect on other readers before releasing it for public scrutiny or company use. From their fellow workers, business communicators get straightforward advice on what works and what doesn't work in the piece of writing at hand. In this way, personnel learn writing skills in a way they were never taught in school.

A final word must be said in this period of communication revolution. Anxieties tend to run high as the skills ensuring yesterday's job security are rendered nearly obsolete for tomorrow's technologies. Frustration also increases for some adults who are learning something completely new, often the first really new learning they've undertaken in years. Disappointment is rampant as new technologies hit expensive, time-wasting glitches—with the proverbial egg on the faces of those who recommended the new computer, new mail system, or new teleconference room. Finally, jealousies run high as comparative youngsters are promoted into responsible positions (with big salaries) based on technological insight and skills.

These are the growing pains and signs of ferment in the communication revolution. Business communicators will do well to get used to them. Unlike past revolutions, the third revolution in communication promises almost perpetual change and a dizzying onslaught of new possibilities. We now type our words into the computer; soon we will probably talk them in. By the year 2000 will we simply *think* our words into the computer? Will we establish our credibility as communicators with a card or code so we can concentrate on essential messaging? Will we develop special shorthand languages for rapid reading and writing?

The answers to these and other questions we cannot imagine are our not-so-distant inheritance. What an exciting time this is, to have something to say and to care about how it is said.

QUESTIONS FOR STUDY

1. Discuss the advantages of the word processor over the traditional typewriter, including the correcting typewriter. Do you see any disadvantages?
2. Describe the technological communication links that make it possible for more and more business people to do part of their work from their homes.
3. What is teleconferencing? Placing yourself in the role of an executive, what would attract you to this communication technology? What might cause problems for you?
4. How will computerized telephones help to prevent "telephone tag," lost phone numbers, and other inconveniences? (Telephone tag occurs when

business people leave messages for each other in a frustrating effort to make contact.)

5. Make and discuss a list of terms associated with the microcomputer. Include such common terms as *floppy disk* and *monitor.*

6. What is a data base? How can it prove useful to businesses with microcomputer access?

7. What forces will contribute to a glut of words across business desks in the coming years?

8. "Memos have nine lives," one executive complained. What technological developments make it easier and easier to locate, reproduce, and distribute portions of previously distributed documents?

9. In an age when print can be generated and distributed quickly, what place remains for verbal contacts?

10. What is early messaging? Why it is important?

11. Discuss how impressions are formed about the importance and credibility of business documents. Include a consideration of format in your discussion.

12. What kinds of graphic enhancements can be included in business documents today? Speculate about enhancements that will be possible in the future.

13. What place can personal warmth play in the fast-paced future world of business communication?

14. Writing has long been considered a personal and private act. What advantages do you see in learning to share your business writing with colleagues?

EXERCISES

15. Work with a knowledgeable individual on the subject of desk-top publishing. Secure several examples of materials produced in that manner. Present a report (oral or written) on the subject to your class or instructor indicating the value of this method of communication to small firms.

16. Investigate the topic of "computer graphics." Make an oral presentation to your class members on the value of using computer graphics in their future reports.

17. Survey ten executives on the value and/or dangers to today's students who become accustomed to using a "spelling correction" or "reference segment" in their computer use. Report on your findings.

18. Survey ten executives and ten middle managers in a large corporation. Determine what percentage of their time is spent on the computer installed in their office. Report on your findings. (You may have some difficulty securing frank replies; a carefully worded questionnaire may be needed.)

19. Let each member of a group of four or five students develop a short business document such as a memo or letter. Pass the rough drafts around the group for comment and suggestions. After you have seen one another's writing, discuss the usefulness of second and third opinions. What did you feel as others were criticizing what you had written?

20. Using a word processor, make the changes in your document suggested by the group. Report to the group on your ease or difficulty in using the word processor. Compare the techniques you used on the word processor with the steps you would have taken on a traditional typewriter to make the same corrections.

21. Identify five business occasions when instant written messages via electronic mail would be vastly preferable to delivery by ordinary mail.

22. Take time to try out a word processor on campus or at a computer store. Report your impressions to your classmates.

23. Interview three business people who work with computers. Ask them to comment on the advantages and frustrations of such experiences.

24. Develop an oral or written presentation (as your instructor suggests) about the value of microcomputers for a business of your choice. Aim your presentation at a traditional business that has not yet brought computers on-line.

25. Browse through at least two recent issues of a computing magazine such as *Byte* or *Personal Computing*. In the advertisements or articles, choose at least three technological devices not discussed in this chapter. Suggest for each a possible business application.

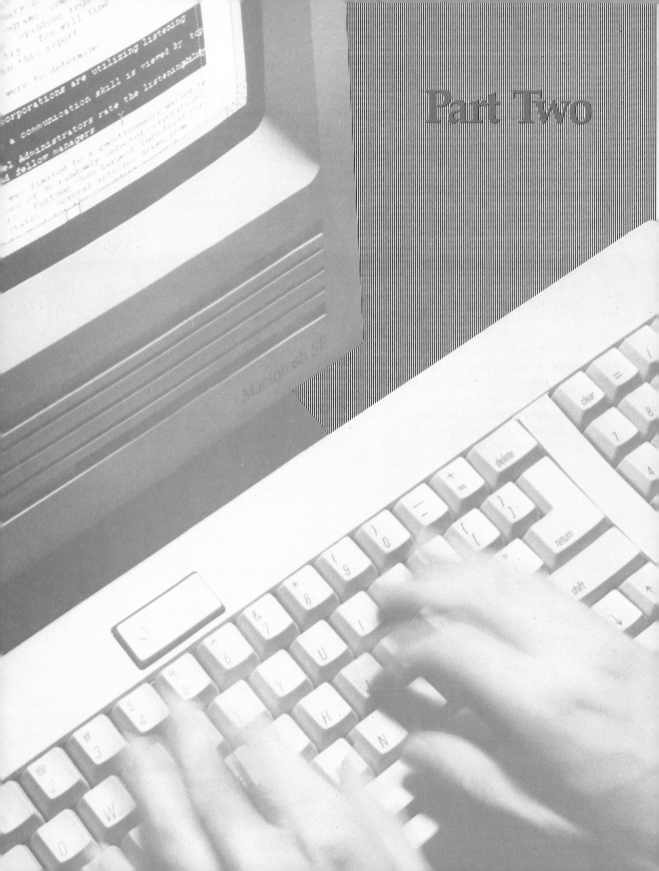

Part Two

Writing that Works

5 The Writing Process

Plan to communicate, plan your communication, and then plan what to say and how to say it.

Planning, organizing, writing, and editing are intimately associated. We will focus on the first two in this chapter and the last two in the following chapter.

Whenever we face the task of writing a report, preparing a proposal, completing a staff study, or composing a business letter, we go through the same series of logical steps. First we recognize the problem and/or the purpose with which the message must deal. We then plan the content of the communication to achieve our goal. Next we organize our ideas so that they will be presented in an order that is logical and psychologically effective. Then comes the task of writing the first draft, which must be followed by careful editing. It is imperative to make sure that what we have written is stated clearly, completely, correctly, and concisely. Writing the final draft from that edited version then becomes almost a simple formality.

INITIAL STEPS IN THE PLANNING PROCESS

Good planning and organizing are the keys to the success of a great many activities in our society. Without them it would be impossible for a rocket to function properly, a building to be erected solidly, a surgical procedure to be carried through successfully, or a piece of oral or written communication to be presented effectively. Few activities, from baking a cake to going on a journey, take place without a plan or blueprint. But often we write or speak without following a plan, though of course we should not.

How often have you thrown down a magazine, slammed shut a book, snapped off a television set, or tapped someone on the shoulder with a "well, what's the point?" How often have you lost interest in an article, a report, or a speech because its theme or argument seemed to be going in circles? Perhaps this was because it was not properly planned.

PLANNING

Business writers take time to plan their writing efforts for several reasons. First, planning helps the writer determine what details, evidence, and argument to include. Second, a good working plan provides a writing agenda of sorts, giving the writer a step-by-step pattern to follow in writing the document. Last and of utmost importance, a clear, logical plan makes the document easy to read and understand.

Some business communicators make the mistake of skipping the preparation of planning, reasoning that "well, it will change anyway." While it is true that good plans do evolve as the document develops, writers should begin with at least a tentative outline.

But where do planning efforts start? Begin by answering five key questions:

- What is the precise problem addressed in the report, proposal, memo, or letter?
- What is the primary purpose of the communication?
- Who is the reader?
- In what ways should the topic be limited?
- In what depth should the topic be treated?

The answers to these questions put the writer well on the way to developing a tentative plan for writing.

Identifying the Problem

Not every piece of communication deals with a problem, but a great many do. Whether the problem involves declining sales, an unusual increase in accounts receivable, or the rise in employee pilferage, it is imperative that the precise problem be identified before you move to the next step.

Too often an executive notes that something is wrong in a particular area. In an effort to get to the bottom of the case and solve the problem, he may request of the subordinate, "Let me have a report on the situation." If the specific problem is not recognized, the report may not solve the problem.

Let us look at two examples. Records indicate that employee pilferage is up 10 percent. If a report is requested on that problem, the writer may try to explain the situation in an eight-page report by concentrating on inadequate security measures. However, that report will serve no purpose because the *real* problem is not inadequate security. It may be that pilferage is up because of what employees perceive as an inadequate pay raise, poor management, or unfair promotion practices.

The point is simply this: if the problem is not recognized and all efforts are focused on a side issue, the resulting report will make no contribution to the solution of the problem. As a result, time and effort will have been wasted.

Let's consider another situation. Mr. George of Foremost Pharmaceuticals has just received a letter from one of the firm's retail accounts, Drayer's Drugs. Mr. Drayer requests that one of the free attractive signs, "Prescription Drugs," offered to Foremost accounts with $2500 per month in sales, be sent to him.

Mr. George checks and finds that Drayer's sales have never exceeded $1500 per month in the three years in which Drayer's Drugs has been making purchases from Foremost. Now, what is the problem? Is it the sign or is it retaining Mr. Drayer's sales?

If Mr. George decides the problem is simply the sign, he may refuse to give Mr. Drayer one and, as a result, lose him as a customer. If, on the other hand, Mr. George feels the problem is how to retain Mr. Drayer's good will and sales, he will write a different type of letter.

Thus the first step in the planning process is recognition of the problem. Now we must determine the purpose of the written communication.

Deciding on the Purpose

If we decide, in the preceding case of employee pilferage, that our purpose is to inform the reader, that would be one purpose of the report. On the other hand, our purpose could be to persuade the reader to purchase a new security system. It is possible that our purpose might be to compare method A of cutting employee pilferage with method B.

When we establish the primary purpose of a communication, its organizational pattern begins to fall into place. For example, a letter arrives from a customer asking for our firm's credit terms. Our purpose is simply to inform him of our credit terms, and we will organize our reply this way:

1. Acknowledge letter requesting credit terms.
2. Spell out our credit terms in detail.
3. Add a friendly closing.

However, if the customer is asking for credit and we discover that his or her asset-liability ratio is unsatisfactory, our purpose will be to persuade the customer to accept an alternative (e.g., COD instead of credit), and therefore we will organize our reply differently:

1. Acknowledge letter requesting credit.
2. Explain why it would be of benefit to the customer to improve his asset-liability ratio.
3. Offer the option of COD, explaining its advantages. (The refusal to extend credit is implicit in the positive statements made here.)
4. Add a friendly closing.

By following this plan, the correspondent need not say, "Therefore we cannot . . ." "We find it impossible . . ." or "We must refuse . . ." Under ordinary circumstances, if the writer first explains the reason for the refusal, a negative statement may be implied rather than stated.

Identifying the Reader

Our next basic question is, who is the prospective reader? The answer tells us at what *level* we should write. Should the discussion, charts, graphs, and related materials be presented in a simple or a complex fashion?

Is the reader one of the persons involved in financing this building project, a relatively uninterested shareholder who owns three shares of stock, or the consulting architect? Are we writing a release to the newspapers for publicity purposes or a detailed report to the board of directors? The style, level, and amount of detail will surely differ for each.

The *organizational plan* may also change according to who the reader is. In one case, a chronological approach, which is relatively easy to follow, may be better; in another case, a cause-and-effect order may be appropriate. More technical detail will be included in one organizational plan, and less in another; complicated financial facts will be integral to one outline but not to another. Other variations may be reflected in the outline concerning visual aids, financial data, and the length and detail level of the narrative. In this way, the outline (and, therefore, the final paper) is designed with the reader in mind.

The *tone* of the communication may also vary according to who the reader is. Is he or she someone with whom you have been doing business for 15 years or a new account who has just entered a second order with you? Is the reader one of your vendors with a total work force of ten, or an impartial reader of proposals involving hundreds of millions of dollars that have been submitted to the U.S. Department of Defense?

Once you have defined your problem, purpose, and audience, it is imperative to record them on paper or your computer screen. At times, a purpose that seems logical as we drive down the highway loses its validity on paper or a flat computer screen.

Let's say, for example, that we have been told by the company vice president that, "We have spent several hundred thousand dollars on scanning equipment for the checkout counters of our sixteen stores. However, there is a problem: the equipment isn't being fully utilized. Look into this."

THE READER'S INTEREST[1]

No matter what your letter is about, the reader will want to know: "How does this affect me?"

It is a literary vice not to seek out the reader's interest. You may tell him what you want in impeccable language and forceful manner, but you fall short of success unless you pay attention to what he wants or can be made to desire. Your ideas must enter, influence and stick in the mind of the recipient.

As a writer, you may protest that some of the failure in communication may be blamed on the receiver, but it is your responsibility as sender to determine in advance, to the best of your ability, all potential causes of failure and to tune your transmission for the best reception.

Granted, something must be expected of the reader. Every writer is entitled to demand a certain amount of knowledge in those for whom he writes, and a certain degree of dexterity in using the implements of thought. Readers who demand immediate intelligibility in all they read cannot hope to go far beyond the limitations of comic strip language.

However, the writer is bound to eliminate every possible obstacle. He must not grow away from people. He must anticipate their questions. Let the salesman stand at a bargain counter and listen to what goes on in the minds of prospective customers. He will see women who spend ten minutes examining socks advertised at 35 cents a pair—do they stretch? are they washable? will they stay soft? are they tough enough to wear long? Those women are not up on the plateau of bulk sales, but down where a nickel counts.

That is the imagination of preparation. Then comes the imagination of expression. The most important demand of customers is for friendliness in those who seek to do business with them. A man may pride himself upon being an efficient, logical person, unswayed by sentiment in business matters, but at some stage in his every business deal there is a spark of emotional appeal and response.

You need to study your audience and then write what you want them to understand in the form that is most likely to appeal to them. Any other course is like the childish custom of writing a letter to Santa Claus and burning it up the chimney.

[1]Royal Bank of Canada. Monthly Letter, "Imagination Helps Communication," Sept., 1960.

||||||||||||||||||||||||||||||||||||||||||||||||||||||||||||||||||||||||||||||||||||||||||||||||||||||||||||||||||||||||||||||||||||||||||||||||||||||||

On the surface, the problem seems clear. But further thought, as we begin to formulate and write down the purpose, reveals flaws in our assumption. What exactly is meant by the problem, "scanning equipment . . . not fully utilized"? Is the problem that checkout clerks are simply ringing the items' costs on the register and *not using* the scanning equipment to read the universal price code? Is the problem that the scanning equipment is often "down" and *can't be used?* Is the scanning equipment not being fully utilized because some checkout clerks are *not familiar with* the capacity and potential of the equipment? Or is it possible that store managers are *not using the data* gathered by the scanners in relation to inventory control, pricing, and purchasing?

What if we accept the problem as: scanning equipment . . . not fully utilized? If we should now move to our **purpose** "To determine why the checkout clerks are not fully utilizing the scanners," we may be 180° off base. It is quite possible that the checkout clerks are fully utilizing the scanning equipment but the store managers are not! Although store managers can secure product turnover and inventory status from the scanners, it's possible that they are neglecting to do so. Or, further, perhaps it's headquarters personnel who are not fully utilizing the equipment.

The point is that until the precise problem, purpose, and reader are identified, it is quite possible for a writer to move in the wrong direction and work for days or weeks on a topic that does little to solve the problem.

How can this type of well-intentioned but wasteful effort be avoided? One answer is by clearly defining these variables and *discussing* them with the person for whom the work is being completed. When an understanding has been reached between the two, the writer may move into the next phase: the organizing stage.

ORGANIZING THE MATERIAL

The next step is to make a tentative outline and choose the major topics to be covered. This builds a foundation upon which the entire paper will be constructed.

Let us say, for example, that our topic will be "The Marketing of Our Product in Western Europe." We may choose six major areas for examination:

1. Market acceptance
2. Competition
3. Advertising and sales promotion
4. Method of distribution
5. Legal restrictions
6. Cost of distribution

These may be arranged in a different order when the final paper is written, but we do know that they will be the major areas for analysis and investigation. They also become the major headings in our tentative working outline. Now we can begin to divide each one into fairly obvious subcategories:

1. Market acceptance
       Households
       The teenage market
       Institutional purchasers
       Governmental agencies
2. Competition
     From similar local products
       Brand A
       Brand B
       Brand C

From North American products
  Brand AA
  Brand BB
  Brand CC
  Brand DD
From similar products manufactured abroad
3. Advertising and sales promotion
  To the consumer
    Newspaper
    Radio
    Television
    Direct mail
    Point of sales
    Miscellaneous
  To the distributor
    Trade publications
    Direct mail
    Sales force
    Miscellaneous

Each of the major points has been subdivided, as indicated above, into sub-points that can be divided further.

The method of developing an organizational plan is very important. Always begin by listing your major topics for discussion and examination. After these areas have been identified, develop each into subdivisions.

It is fairly simple to list the major points in an analysis. They are usually the specific questions that need to be answered. For example, let us say we are faced with a problem of whether we should undertake to manufacture new product X. The obvious questions are:

- Do we have the facilities to manufacture it?
- Is there a market for it?
- What competition exists?
- What costs will be incurred?
- What advantages do we stand to gain?

Each of these questions can be easily reworded into a more succinct major topic heading, and then the subpoints under each developed. Let's try another topic for presentation. This time let us assume that we are faced with "The Advisability of Publishing and Distributing a Monthly Employee Magazine." Some of the primary questions to be answered here are, will such a publication make a significant contribution to employee morale? What will the annual cost of such a venture be? What personnel must we secure to handle the project? What alternatives may accomplish similar ends? What are the experiences of similar industries in this area? Here again, subtopics may now be developed under each major topic. The writer should always select or identify the major topics *before* subdividing.

LIMITING THE TOPIC AREAS

Before the investigator proceeds too far in analyzing and developing the organizational plan, boundaries and limits should be checked. In the report on marketing in Western Europe, for instance, certainly there is no point in carrying out research in the area of legal restrictions if the legal restrictions have already been determined and are part of company records. Or perhaps the legal restrictions are known to be minor and are not worth the time and effort to investigate. If an area need not be pursued, why expend time and energy on it?

The number and content of subtopics also must be limited. There is no need for in-depth coverage if it serves no purpose, as it may even prove detrimental by giving readers much more information than they want. If our concern is competition from similar products manufactured only in France, then let's not get involved with those manufactured in North America or other countries in Western Europe.

Limitation of the subject area is vital if the communicator (or encoder) is to get to the heart of the precise area being investigated. It will also help prevent creative efforts from being dissipated. Let us say we are writing a report titled "The Advisability of Constructing a New Plant in Bennington, Ohio." Our major foundation blocks for investigation are:

Labor supply available	Community attitude
Physical plant	Availability of utilities
Market	Tax structure
Source of raw materials	Transportation facilities
Financing	

Now let's examine these major points to see if we can limit the study. If company records contain adequate material on the source of raw materials and community attitude, let's not waste time on research; let's use what is already available to us.

Our next step is to break down each of the remaining points above into a logical series of subpoints. The number of subpoints will determine the depth of the analysis and usually the length of the presentation. If the prospective reader only wants to know if there are rail, air, water, and truck lines going into Bennington, that information can be covered in one paragraph:

Transportation Lines into Bennington
   Rail
   Air
   Water
   Trucking

If, however, the reader wants to know which transportation companies are involved, along with specific rates, schedules, guarantees, and history of performance, the result may be twenty pages of narrative, charts, and tables based on the following outline:

Transportation Facilities
   Shipment of finished products
      Rail
         Santa Fe Railroad
         Mid-Continent Railroad
      Truck
         Commercial trucking firms
         Company trucks
         Leased trucks
      Air
         Commercial air freight
         Chartered air freight
   Comparative analysis
      Cost
         Rail
         Truck
         Air
      Shipment time
         Rail
         Truck
         Air
   Analyses of roads, air terminals, water, and rail facilities
      Roads
         Freeways, highways, major roads
         Secondary roads
         Access roads (to plant)
      Air terminals (75-mile radius)
         Passenger
         Freight
      Water facilities
         Ports (import-export)
         Rivers (raw material; bulk products)

Rail facilities
    Track spurs (on company property)
    Condition
    Ownership
Terminals
    Railroad companies involved
    Accessibility
Receiving and shipping points
Employee transportation
Public
    Commercial bus routes
    Rapid transit
Private
    Individual automobiles
    Car pools
    Routes to and from residential areas
Cost analysis

Obviously, if a reader wants one level of depth and receives another, the writer is to blame for poor organization of the basic outline. The solution is simple: plan and organize according to specific needs and expectations of the prospective reader.

REVIEWING THE FIRST STEPS IN PLANNING AND ORGANIZING

Let us review quickly the initial steps of planning and organizing:

Problem Our sales have declined. Is the problem due to the fact that we have a smaller segment of the market than our competitors? Is it the result of price increases? Is it a direct result of the change in the demographics of the area? Certainly, once we see the problem, we will plan accordingly. But we must first decide what the problem really is. If we don't, we may, as the old saying goes, "jump on our horse and ride off in all directions."

Purpose Just what is the purpose? Is it to compare two systems? Is it to analyze a situation? Is it to cite information for record-keeping purposes? Is it to sell a course of action to a prospect? To explain a technical procedure to a reader? To defend and argue for the acceptance of a procedure?

Reader Is the reader of the message a technically oriented engineer or a business-minded member of the board of directors? Is he/she a potential customer or a steady account?

Limitation and Scope   Has the topic been accurately limited on the basis of the reader's needs, desires, and level? Has the depth of the research and of the report, letter, or speech been properly determined?

The tentative outline is developed, of course, as the writer carries through the steps above. At no time should he or she hesitate to add to or delete from the outline or change its order to a more logical form. The outline is completely flexible and should be treated as a guide to be shaped, changed, and molded as the need arises.

DRAWING UP A TENTATIVE OUTLINE

As the writer begins research using primary and secondary sources, he or she may find that completion of some of the points in the tentative outline is neither logical nor possible. Conversely, he or she may discover in the source material that certain areas were inadvertently omitted from the outline. And so the tentative outline is revised and polished. The writer cuts two points here and one there, and inserts a new item here and one there. The new, revised outline quite frequently will be extremely different from the original outline.

Value of an Outline

Too often we may feel that drawing up an outline or guide prior to the presentation of the report or speech is an extra and unnecessary step. Why, we may ask, go through the work? Why not just write the report or prepare the talk? On the following pages there are several good reasons why all reports should begin with an outline.

1. The length or depth of treatment of one part of the outline in comparison to the other sections can be **easily evaluated.** If a section is out of proportion—with either too much or too little data—it is easier to make the correction in the outline than in the finished presentation. The example below illustrates such an imbalance.

Employee Training at Allied Telephone
  I. Employee Training in the Fairview Plant
     A. Executive training
     B. Engineering training
     C. Shop supervisory training
        1. Leadership classes for superintendents
        2. Foreman training

D. Office personnel training
  1. Written communications
  2. Office equipment training
II. Employee Training at the Leance Plant
  A. Executive training
  B. Engineering training
    1. Electronic-control systems
    2. Engineering cost control
  C. Shop supervisory training
    1. Leadership classes for superintendents
    2. Foreman training
    3. Interpersonal relations
III. Employee Training at the Stone Plant
  A. Executive training
  B. Engineering training
    1. Engineering cost analysis
    2. Operations research
    3. Manufacturing processes
      a. Heat treatment of alloys
      b. Casting and molding
      c. Material joining
      d. Metal-surface treatment
      e. Material cleaning
    4. Computer use
      a. Analog and digital
      b. Computer codes
      c. Programming principles
  C. Shop supervisory training

It would appear, in the numbered outline above, that point B under section III has been developed to an extent that is out of proportion to the other topics. If all of the material is needed, then perhaps a new major heading should be included; if all details are not necessary, they should be excised mercilessly. Section III will then be in better proportion to the other major headings.

2. If the outline is logical, the writer is assured of the **logical development** of the report. It is simple, for example, to move point B under section IV to another section of the outline if an analysis of the organization so indicates. Think how difficult it is to move that section after the report has been completed. And it is much easier to expand or reduce a section in the outline than in the finished report. The following example illustrate how easy it is to make changes in the outline to secure a more logical plan.

Employee Fringe Benefits
  I. Insurance Programs
     A. Hospitalization
     B. Major medical
     C. Life
 II. Pension Plan
     A. Company retirement program
     B. Social Security
III. Miscellaneous
     A. Sick leave
     B. Annuity program (employee-sponsored)
     C. Discount purchase of merchandise
     D. Surgical coverage (employee-sponsored)

3. The communicator can use the outline to check on the **completeness** of the presentation. It is certainly simple to evaluate an outline to determine if all necessary points have been covered; if they have not, additional items may be inserted easily.

4. The communicator can evaluate the **order of development** used. This is closely related to logic, as discussed previously. There must be some method of logical development to any presentation: chronological, geographical, cause and effect, for example. Here again, it is easier to check the outline and correct inconsistencies than it is to rework the finished version, even with recent advances in word-processing technology.

5. An outline **saves time.** This fact is obvious. As the communicator evaluates the outline, he or she can quickly make additions, deletions, corrections, and revisions. How much more effort is required—and how much more inconvenient it is—to take the same action on a finished paper!

In business, time is money. But some managers use that truism as an excuse for skipping the outlining step for documents. Consider the case of Raymond Simmons, new products manager for a computer company. Simmons hears a number of distressing messages from his subordinates:

- key employees are thinking of quitting
- a rumor is circulating that massive layoffs are coming
- someone has sabotaged one of the VAX mainframe computers
- employees misunderstand the new "flex-time" rules in the company
- news is circulating that managers will soon receive substantial raises at a time when other employees will receive none

Clearly, Simmons must communicate with his workforce. But an "off the top of the head" memo may do more harm than good. He takes time, therefore, to work out a tentative outline:

1. The truth about layoffs
2. Facts about flex-time—for all employees
3. Encouraging news about new company contracts (to counter in an indirect way the rumor that key employees are going to quit)
4. Facts about managerial raises

Simmons chooses not to deal with the sabotage issue in this company memo, lest workers come to look upon vandalism as a way of expressing displeasure. By following his outline, he is able to write a cogent, cohesive memo that goes far to allay anxieties and misunderstanding.

Outline Mechanics

How you design your outline is often a matter of personal preference. Some people prefer an elaborate numbering system of Roman numerals and letters all carefully arranged on clean, white stationery; others simply indent subordinate ideas under major headings on the back of an envelope. The mechanics of organizing are personal, and most of us eventually develop our own system.

Designate Major and Minor Points   It is always wise to arrange the items in your outline so that a glance will reveal major areas, as opposed to minor ones. It is helpful to think of the most important points as the key ideas and the subordinating ones as items of substantiating evidence.

The most frequently used numbering system is the *numeral-letter combination*. Roman numerals are used for major points, capital letters for subtopics, and Arabic numerals and lowercase letters for topics of lesser importance. If a further breakdown is necessary, parenthetical Arabic numerals and letters are used.

    I. First Main Heading
        A. First subtopic under main heading
        B. Second subtopic under main heading
            1. First subtopic under B
            2. Second subtopic under B
                a. First subtopic under 2
                b. Second subtopic under 2
                    (1) First subtopic under b
                    (2) Second subtopic under b
                        (a) First subtopic under (2)
                        (b) Second subtopic under (2)
    II. Second Main Heading

The *decimal style* is favored by engineers, as well as others in science and technology. This system is logical, easy to use, and affords a quick method for referring to specific points:

1. First Main Heading
    1.1 First subtopic under first main heading
    1.2 Second subtopic under first main heading
        1.21 First subtopic under 1.2
        1.22 Second subtopic under 1.2
            1.221 First subtopic under 1.22
            1.222 Second subtopic under 1.22
2. Second Main Heading
    2.1 First subtopic under second main heading
    2.2 Second subtopic under second main heading
        2.21 First subtopic under 2.2
        2.22 Second subtopic under 2.2

There are other methods of outlining, such as simple indentation and the use of specialized symbols. Any system that is accurate, permits easy analysis, and works for you is the one you should use.

Ensure Parallel Development   In designing the outline, give items of equal importance similar levels of designation under major headings. Thus if *cost of materials* is an immediate subhead to Roman numeral I, it would hardly seem possible that under Roman numeral II *cost of materials* should slip to the level of a subtopic. Points of parallel interest should be listed at similar levels in the outline.

Avoid Overlapping Ideas   If headings and subheadings are chosen properly, there should be little overlapping of ideas. The most common error of this sort lies in making a subordinate topic equal in placement to major topics. In a report on passenger safety in automobiles, for example, the major topics might be seat belts, air bags, and padded dash/steering wheel. The subordinate topic of quick-release seatbelt buckles should not be given equal placement with such major topics but should be discussed instead under seatbelts.

Use a Consistent and Logical Order of Development   Whether your communication is long or short, written or oral, simple or complex, you want it to be understood and accepted. This requires that you analyze the content of the message, the nature of the audience, and the purpose you hope to achieve. You go through these steps to secure the most logical order of development for your message. This attribute of logic is vital, for regardless of the excellence of your word choice, the clarity of your sentences, and the appearance of the report, all will fail if the message lacks logic.

The critical business person may well overlook a misplaced comma or a faulty phrase. But if the presentation lacks logic, the ideas then become suspect, and the reader may simply tune out. You have certainly read such a presentation and noted at some point that, "this doesn't follow; it's not logical; I can't accept it."

Obviously we cannot expect that everything we say or write will be accepted, but when it is rejected because we did not present it logically, then the fault is ours. Listed below are several methods to ensure the logical development of your communications.

Analysis and Synthesis   Before we design a plan for presentation, we must be sure we have recognized all or most of the important factors in the situation.

Sales of our products on the West Coast have declined very dramatically. Let's **analyze** (identify the elements) to find out why the decline has taken place. We do not have a West Coast distribution plant; a large market for patio furniture exists on the West Coast; shipping our outdoor furniture from the Midwest is costly; freight rates for shipping have risen steadily; our West Coast customers have complained about high shipping costs; surveys show we are not competitive on the price with West Coast manufacturers of similar lines . . . . Thus we began with a condition: decreased sales. We then analyzed the situation and attempted to identify the contributing factors.

Or we may be confronted by a number of diverse elements that require **synthesis** (putting together) to form a logical whole or pattern. Production has declined very rapidly since the early part of June. Employees have complained about the level of illumination in the production area; a new supervisor of the section took over in May; the safety equipment for the presses is slow and outdated; compensation is on a piece-rate basis; the lead worker was discharged after she and the new boss had a severe argument on June 1 . . . . Can these various facts be related or synthesized with one another into some pattern that would result in an overall theme?

Inductive Development   **Inductive development** proceeds from the particular or specific to the general. Here the writer cites details, specific events, and examples and finally arrives at a general conclusion. We might, for example, explain that the quality of the product was high, the price very competitive, the service excellent, and delivery fast, all of which resulted in a year of high sales.

Deductive Development   **Deductive development** proceeds from a general statement to particulars, details, and facts. We might begin by stating that a firm's primary activities depend on communication. From here we could point out how most external transactions are based on business letters; advertising in newspapers, radio, and TV; reports to government agencies; and proposals to potential customers. Internally, communication takes place through such media as news bulletins, company magazines, management memos, interdepartmental correspondence and reports, conferences, and meetings.

Chronological Development In **chronological development,** a specific period of time is selected from which our discussion moves forward. Guiding phrases such as "In the past . . ." or "In the 1970s . . ." signal the first stage of such development. The middle stage comes next: "At present . . ." or "This year . . ." and so forth. Finally, chronological development usually looks forward with sections beginning "Looking ahead . . ." or "In the future . . ." or "As we plan for the 1990s . . . ."

In chronological development, avoid the "post hoc ergo propter hoc" logical error (literally, "after this therefore because of this"). Just because one event happened in 1986 and another in 1987 does not mean that the first event caused the second event. A new manager, for example, may have been hired in 1986. Employee turnover in her division may have been exceptionally high in 1987. That fact does not automatically mean that the new manager caused the turnover. In using chronological development, do not be content merely to imply causality between events. Instead, use evidence and argument to show causal links.

Geographical Development In **geographical development,** we begin at one location and then move to the next. If we are analyzing sales for a corporation that has four district sales offices, plus sales headquarters in New York, it would seem logical to begin with a discussion of the activities of the New York office, then go on to an examination of the Chicago office; to Waterloo, Iowa; to Denver; and finally to Los Angeles. Or we might look at warehousing facilities in Camden, N.J., Fort Wayne, and Dallas before analyzing that they should be in the new warehouse going up in San Francisco.

Spatial Development When the order of development moves from one logical space designation to another, it is called **spatial development.** In a plant, areas might be designated as administrative, manufacturing, packaging, storage, and shipping. If we were to examine the illumination levels (or safety hazards, or decorating schemes, or noise levels) in the entire plant, we would first discuss the aspect in one space (administrative, for example) and then discuss each of the others.

Directional Development A simple description of a process or product as it moves in a predetermined direction is called **directional development.** For example, the piece part must first be cleaned and sprayed. From there it goes to cutting and polishing. It is then sent to inspection, after which it is sent to production, where diodes are attached. Again it is returned to inspection, after which it is sold and taken from stock. Those are the steps followed and the directions in which the item moves.

If we were to follow a state legislative bill from the time it was introduced in the House by a legislator, moving from Committee A to Committee B to the Senate to the executive branch to the governor, we would be describing the direction of movement of the bill.

Simple-to-Complex Development **Simple-to-complex development** is appropriate when we are faced with explaining a relatively involved situation to a reader who may not have a clear understanding of the fundamentals of the subject. If we begin with simple, easy-to-understand situations and gradually move to more complex areas of the same topic, the reader will be able to follow the explanation presented. If we wish to discuss a new automated production process, we might begin by explaining the fundamentals of a standard production process, then go on to the principles of a semiautomated situation, and finally to the complexity of a completely automated arrangement.

TYPES OF OUTLINES

The two most frequently used outline forms are the topic type and the sentence type. In infrequent cases, a paragraph outline may be used. In addition to a list of items in topic, sentence, or paragraph form, the outline also has a title and often a thesis sentence. This thesis sentence should state clearly and concisely the purpose or objective of the message.

Topic Outline

Each entry in a topic outline consists of a few words or a short phrase. This type of outline has several advantages: the writer can jot down ideas quickly and need not bother with structuring each thought into a sentence. With a list of brief topics, the writer has little hesitation about adding several, dropping a few, or moving one from one section to another of the outline, and making other revisions as the need arises.

A disadvantage of this type of outline is that it requires a good memory. When the two- and three-word headings are examined three weeks after they were written, the writer may have quite forgotten what the cryptic phrase "Losses—unexpected circumstances" refers to. Yet when that entry was made, he or she knew perfectly well what to discuss under that point.

A Survey of Fringe Benefits in Industry
  I. Insurance Programs
      A. Life insurance programs
          1. Executive level
          2. Other employee level
      B. Hospitalization insurance
          1. Individual
          2. Family plans

     C. Major medical plans
        1. Company sponsored
        2. Insurance-company sponsored
     D. Surgical plans
     1. Individual
     2. Family plans
  II. Vacation and Holiday Plans
     A. Vacation plans
        1. Standard vacation (specific period each year for all employees)
        2. Nonstandard vacation
        3. Time
            a. Weeks associated with years of company service
            b. Specific periods of time for different levels with no reference to length of service
     B. Paid holidays
        1. In conformity with union contracts
        2. As announced by the specific organization
     C. Extended leave periods (for research, travel, illness, etc.)
        1. With compensation
        2. Without compensation
 III. Annuity and Pension Plans
     A. Government sponsored (Social Security)
     B. Annuity programs
        1. For executives
            a. Company-employee contributions
            b. Company contributions only
        2. For other employees
     C. Pension plans
        1. Company sponsored
        2. Company-employee sponsored
 IV. Profit-Sharing Plans
     A. Broad coverage based on net earnings
     B. Limited employee participation

Sentence Outline

In a sentence outline, each entry is a complete sentence. This requires that writers structure their thoughts a little more carefully than with the topic outline. Ideas are stated completely, and the danger of forgetting what an entry refers to is considerably lessened. A major disadvantage of this style, however, is that it tempts writers to convert their sentence outlines into reports. That is sometimes done through the simple expedient of connecting the sentences with a few transitional words or phrases. Of course, the results are poor. The writer of a sentence outline should remember that the outline must serve only as a guide to the writing assignment, not as an initial effort to be converted into the final paper.

Paragraph Outline

In planning an extensive report, a proposal, or a fairly detailed paper, it is sometimes wise to use a paragraph outline. In this instance a paragraph is used to summarize a major idea, another paragraph for the next major idea, and so on. Once the broad portions of the entire report are broken down into individual paragraphs, these can then be subdivided (or outlined) into their component parts.

CONCLUSION

In sum, the planning step pays dividends to both the writer and the reader. A working outline gives the writer an agenda to follow in creating a clear, organized document. That outline, as translated into headings and paragraph beginnings, serves the reader as a road-map for following the writer's thoughts. The end result of such orderly sending and receiving is successful communication.

QUESTIONS FOR STUDY

1. Discuss the improvisational approach to writing, in which the writer begins the document without a guiding plan.
2. Outlines take time to create. In your opinion, is that time well spent?
3. Crisp, clear writing seems to flow from point to point in a logical, easy-to-follow way. How can outlining prove valuable in achieving this logic?
4. Why is it important to decide in advance upon the depth with which the topic at hand will be treated?
5. What is chronological development in a business document? Suggest an example (not found in the text) for which chronological development would be appropriate.
6. Discuss the common organizational error of making a subordinate topic heading equal in importance to main headings. How can the error be avoided?
7. Explain why the detail included in the outline will change with the reader of the eventual communication.
8. In the planning process, what is the general foundation?
9. What is parallel development? Cite an example not found in the text. Why is it important?

10. Readers like headings. Why?
11. Explain why limiting the topic is so crucial to the success of a business document.
12. What is the difference between stating a topic and stating a problem statement?
13. Why does a topic outline call for a good memory?
14. Why will the final outline often be substantially different from the original tentative outline?
15. What comes first, the purpose or the outline? Explain.
16. What is the relationship between the number of subpoints in an outline and the eventual length of that portion of the writing?
17. What is the basic difference between the inductive and deductive development methods?

EXERCISES

18. Find a current business article. Create an outline of its major and subordinate points. Write a paragraph in which you evaluate the organization and development of the article.
19. Time is probably the executive's most precious commodity. Preparing outlines takes time. As a cost-conscious manager, support or refute the development of outlines for communications in the organization.
20. Create an outline for a business document dealing with employee theft. Make sure the topic headings are parallel in form, as discussed in the chapter.
21. As a city planner, you are preparing a report on the growth of suburbs around your city. Outline your report, using directional development.
22. Writing, it has been said, involves selecting a target and the right arrow to hit the target. Explain the sense of this analogy with regard to business documents.
23. You are a member of a student group in your academic department. To assist the department, your group wants to prepare a brochure that can be distributed to high school seniors. The purpose of the brochure will be to attract majors into the department. Outline the contents of the brochure.
24. A group of junior high school students is intrigued with college students and wants to know about the typical day in the life of a collegian. Outline two presentations—one using the chronological scheme and the other using the geographical scheme.
25. You think your company should co-sponsor a rock music festival. Create two outlines of how you would present your idea. One outline should be created for fellow employees, most of them under 35. The other should address senior managers, most of them over 55. Be prepared to discuss differences in the outlines based on readership.

26. Your institution is considering building an addition to the student center. You have viewed and studied the situation and feel that the addition (which would primarily add recreational facilities like bowling, pool, and electronic games) is needed. Prepare an outline of a report that could be presented at a meeting of the Student Senate.
    a. Prepare the first outline in an inductive manner.
    b. Prepare the second outline in a deductive manner.

27. Find a display advertisement (a long ad, often boxed) in a newspaper or magazine. Read the ad with care. Then develop an outline of the basic ideas, in their order of appearance, in the ad. Write a brief critique of the success or failure of the advertisement in following a consistent topic design. Can you find a persuasive thread of argument through the entire ad? Where does it stray from that path? Submit the ad and completed assignment to your instructor.

28. Here are bits and pieces of an outline. Place them in a logical, persuasive order that you are willing to explain and defend. Rephrase any headings that seem clumsy or unclear.
    What Has Been Done to Date
    Recommendations
    Budgetary Considerations
    Definition of the Problem
    Conclusion
    We Should Analyze the Causes of the Problem
    Alternatives Need to be Examined

29. Identify a problem or situation that you understand very well. However, other members of your class will generally be much less knowledgeable.
    a. Identify the problem.
    b. Develop an outline that proceeds from the simple to the complex.

30. The following is an outline concerning the development of an employee communication program at a large corporation. However, the outline is not in parallel form; shape it up!
    I. The Need for Improved Employee Communications
        a. Our employees do not know their employer
        b. Progressive companies keep employees informed
    II. Information = Productivity
        a. Knowledgeable employees work harder
        b. Pride and productivity
    III. A Plan to Upgrade Our Employee Communication Efforts
        a. Bulletin boards will help
        b. Newspaper
        c. Meetings

31. Your instructor will assign one of the articles in the Readings section of this book. Draw up an outline of the article and submit it along with your brief evaluation of the organization of the article.

6 Drafting and Editing

Material that is easy to read is the result of good writing—which is difficult to complete.

In the last decade of the twentieth century, managers at all levels will need to know how to write fast and well. Many people will depend on their clear, complete messaging. Subordinates need to know the whats, whens, hows, and whys of tasks assigned to them. Superiors need to know about progress, projections, and problems. Clients rely on unambiguous assurances, warranties, and guarantees. The public needs to know what the company does and what impact company actions will have on social and environmental areas.

The messages that answer these needs must often be written, in the form of memos, letters, reports, and proposals. No manager, therefore, can ignore his or her writing abilities with the excuse that "I'm great in person and on the phone." Nor can a manager throw together a few thoughts for later "wordsmithing" by a secretary. The reality in modern business is that no company can buy writing skills at the secretarial level that it cannot buy at the managerial level. Managers set the level for clarity, organization, completeness, and accuracy in company writing.

WRITING AND EDITING

Because written messages at all levels are crucial to company operations and image, managers today often find themselves in the role of editor for company communications. They are responsible for a final "approval point" before a given document goes on to its intended audience. If an assistant underwriter in commercial insurance drafts a letter to a client, for example, the unit manager will read and approve the letter before it goes out. In doing so, she examines the communication in several areas:

1. Mission   Has the written communication responded successfully to its task? Have the client's questions been answered, complaints addressed, orders filled, and so forth?

2. Company interest   Does the communication reflect well upon the company in both form and content? Do all claims and assurances fall within company policy? Is any portion of the communication questionable from a legal or moral point of view?

3. Style   Does the written communication "flow" in a professional way? Has the writer used vocabulary, format, sentence and paragraph length in effective and appropriate ways?

4. Tone   Does the communication, read from the recipient's point of view, strike an appropriate and helpful tone? Has the writer communicated feelings that fit the occasion and business purpose of the communication?

5. Accuracy   Down to the last apostrophe and comma, has the writer taken care to create a literate, careful document that reflects well upon the company and prevents misunderstanding?

Busy managers form judgments (often problematic) about written communications evaluated by these standards. On one hand, managers can be glad they stopped ineffective and sloppy communications from going forward. But on the other hand, who has the time to rewrite poor communications? Usually not the manager. Yet to hand the document back to an unskilled writer may only recycle the problem.

Faced with the "editing crunch," managers must be able to perform three editing functions quickly and accurately:

- spot writing problems
- make some corrections on the spot
- briefly describe errors for correction so that subordinates don't make the same errors over and over

Creating and maintaining high standards for written communication in the workplace is hard work on the part of the manager. But the effort is well repaid as subordinates begin to practice the same standards set by the manager. The alternative—simply letting poor writing go forward—backfires eventually on the bottom line, as clients, stockholders, and the public lose faith in a company that can't communicate accurately and clearly.

THE PROCESS OF WRITING: WE COMMUNICATE MORE THAN FACTS

Effective written communications succeed in both rational and emotional ways. Skilled business writers convey and arouse feelings as well as communicate facts and ideas. In the following sentences from a poorly written memo, you can feel the sarcasm "between the lines"—sarcasm that will undercut the message of the memo and the relationship between the sender and receiver.

An Unnecessarily Sarcastic Tone:

I received your request for a personal leave day—your second in the last 60 days. It's always surprising to me how requests for personal days coincide with the opening of fishing season. But I'll take you at your word that you need this day "for pressing personal matters." Your request is granted.

Far from feeling any gratitude for the day off, the reader of this message has every reason to feel personally insulted. How much better if the writer had been more in control of feelings conveyed and aroused.

A Revision:

I'm granting your request for a day of personal leave. While the company doesn't want to pry into personal affairs, we will appreciate as specific a reason as possible in requests for such leaves. Your cooperation helps us plan work loads and schedules for the good of all.

In both cases, the employee has been "put on notice" that a vague request for personal leave won't do in the future. But what a difference! The first communication left the reader angry, insulted, and demotivated for company tasks. The second memo has a much better chance of winning the employee's cooperation and loyalty.

THE WRITER'S JOB

One of the greatest "hidden costs" of business is Writer's Block—those agonizing periods when words just won't come. Based on an approximate hourly rate of $30 per hour for managerial time, writer's block costs American businesses literally millions of dollars in lost productivity each year.

Why is writing so difficult at times? Motivated by friendship, most of us can generate personal letters very quickly. Motivated by anger, we can dash off complaints with equal speed. But faced with an extended letter, memo, report, or proposal to write, we may dawdle for minutes, hours, and even days. In doing so, we consciously or unconsciously accept three mistaken myths about business writing:

> The Just-Begin Myth   Business documents don't unfold "top-down" like steps on a ladder. Don't begin by trying to write the first sentence, then the next, and so forth. Instead, plan your entire communication (see Chapter 5) before beginning the first draft.

The Easier-Tomorrow Myth   If writing is viewed as inspiration (which it's not), tomorrow always seems preferable to today for making a start. Recognize that whatever holds you back today will probably hold you back tomorrow. Make a start even if you don't "feel like it."

The More-Research Myth   Reading what others have written is always a convenient retreat from the hard work of writing. Research, of course, can be crucial to the success of your argument. But don't allow the research activity to be an escape from your own production efforts.

Chapter 5 described a step-by-step method for determining your purpose, limiting your topic, analyzing your audience, and outlining your material. Those steps should be seen not simply as preparation for writing but as part of the writing process itself. Viewed in this way, we will be less tempted to skip over the planning work for the "real" writing that takes place in drafting. We will also avoid the pain of writer's block—by planning, we've chosen a target and know which arrows to use to hit it.

The First Draft

In a first draft, most of us do not say precisely and clearly what we mean. However, there is a simple system you can use to achieve that final well-written communication. First, develop a satisfactory outline. Refer to it as you write a first draft; then edit, revise and rewrite until you are satisfied that your paper says just what you mean it to say in the manner in which you mean to say it.

After you have gathered all the material, tabulated and interpreted the data, carefully checked the outline, and are confident that the paper will achieve the stated purpose, you are ready to begin to write.

Write as rapidly as possible. The purpose at this stage is to get the thrust of your ideas on paper. Never mind the somewhat awkward sentence, the word that doesn't quite fit the situation, the obvious repetition, and the wordy paragraph. Those will be taken care of in the editing process. The most important effort now is to make thoughts concrete by documenting them.

This stage should proceed rapidly, since you have finished the research, done your outline, and are familiar with the material. The detailed and logical outline serves as a guide, and cards are filled with vital information waiting to be turned into sentences. All that needs to be done now is to write the first draft from the materials at hand.

Editing and Revising

A primary purpose of an expository piece is to present data, discussions, descriptions, conclusions, and recommendations as clearly and as accurately as possible. Faulty sentence structure, confusion in ideas, negligence in word choice, or any other carelessness in presentation that impedes the free flow of ideas should be corrected during the editing process.

People who have not done a great deal of writing may be somewhat surprised at how much work there is yet to do after the first draft has been completed. That first draft, as a matter of fact, is just the beginning. The serious job of rewriting must now be undertaken.

Sometimes sentences must be completely reworked, paragraphs thoroughly revised, and entire sections reorganized. Many successful contemporary authors attest to the fact that the major portion of their time is spent not on the original composition, but in revising and rewriting—again and again—the initial draft (see "Editing Suggestions," pp. 145–150).

One traditional roadblock to effective revision is the sensitive matter of disturbing a clean-typed page. Many of us have the understandable, if unfortunate, tendency to allow slipshod writing to remain uncorrected once it is typed. But word processing has removed that roadblock to revision. Using software such as WordStar, MultiMate, or Word, a business writer can easily change words, sentences, and even whole paragraphs and pages without having to retype every word. In essence, word processing permits the user to place words onto a computer screen where they can be electronically rearranged by simple keystrokes called **commands.** In one popular system, for example, pressing two keys reformats a document from single-spaced to double- or triple-spaced—certainly an improvement over complete retyping. When the document appears on the screen as the writer wishes it to look, it can be "saved" (*i.e.,* stored) on a computer disk and printed out.

At the drafting stage, writers must not cling too tenaciously to each and every word, as if dealing with sacred script. Many of those words—whole paragraphs and pages at times—will have to be cut in the revision process. It is perhaps best to look at the rough draft as a jeweler looks at a diamond in the rough. Much will be cut away and polished before the intended gem is realized.

THE PARTS OF THE WHOLE

When we communicate, we attempt to transmit ideas. We select words, order them into sentences, and connect the sentences to build paragraphs. The way we handle those three elements—words, sentences, and paragraphs—largely determines how effective we are in making ourselves understandable to others.

Words

It is estimated that in the English language there are well over half a million words. Many are compound words or words borrowed from other languages. Other entirely new words come from advances in the sciences, changes in the world of recreation, and the effects of unusual events, such as war.

In using words we find that some are suited for communicating ideas on a golf course, while others are preferable at a technical conference devoted to the use of transistors in new electronic components. Different levels of words, like different styles of dress, are designed for use in specific situations. You would not wear formal dress to a baseball game or a T-shirt and slacks to a wedding. Similarly, you would not ordinarily use slang and jargon in an article for the *Harvard Business Review* or highly complex technical terms in explaining the use of lasers to a Cub Scout group.

Correct Usage   If they are to communicate ideas effectively, words must be used carefully and correctly. There are two categories of commonly misused words: those that sound alike but have different meanings and those that are somewhat similar in sound or have the same root (see Appendix B).

Words that sound alike but are spelled differently and have different meanings (homonyms) are very common in English: where, wear, ware; bear, bare; would, wood; principle, principal; and many others. Most people know what these words mean; the difficulty comes in spelling them. If in a business letter you write *principle* when you mean *principal,* the recipient will figure out what you mean, but he or she may feel that you are careless in communication and perhaps equally careless in how you handle an order or request.

Examples of the second group of misused words also abound: uninterested, disinterested; imply, infer; credible, creditable; incredible, incredulous. A judge on the bench should be disinterested in the case being tried before him but surely not uninterested. When I am speaking, I imply something; when you are listening, you infer something.

The writer or speaker who uses *disorganized* when *unorganized* is meant or *healthy* when *healthful* is meant not only lessens the exactness of the statement but also confuses the reader or listener and, in the long run, helps corrupt and weaken our language.

The carpenter who uses a screwdriver when a chisel is required will probably produce a less-than-perfect cabinet; when we use second-rate words (our tools), the ideas that we advance have less impact because they are not expressed as they should be.

Accuracy and Precision   Words have two distinct traits: they denote and connote. The **denotation** of a word is its factual meaning or definition. Its **connotation,** on the other hand, is the sum of thoughts and emotions it arouses or contains.

A word may have several denotations. The word *vessel,* for example, may refer to a component of the body's circulatory system, a container for liquids, or a waterborne vehicle. As a noun, *rest* may mean repose, something used for support, a pause in music, or the remainder. Yet there is little chance of confusion among these meanings; the context will make obvious which denotation is intended.

It is the connotations of words that create difficulties in communication. The word *capitalism* denotes the same thing to Americans and Soviets, but the connotations are opposite. Everybody knows what *soldier* means; but consider the different emotions the word arouses in a man who has been recognized as a war hero and in an individual who now lives in Canada because he left the U.S. to avoid the draft. What different feelings do you have about the words *fat, obese, roly-poly,* and *plump*? All have the same denotation. Makers of a diet food would never say it makes you *skinny*; they say it makes you *slim* or *slender.* Do you want an after-shave lotion that has a *smell,* a *scent,* a *perfume,* an *aroma,* or an *odor*? They all have the same denotation, but different connotations. The picture we wish to paint can be conveyed very accurately with the words we choose for our colors.

Attention to connotation is of primary importance in business communication. We have already seen its significance in advertising; and business letters and reports are a form of advertising—for yourself and your firm. A letter over your name is your image to the recipient; if it creates unpleasant feelings, it may be worse than no letter at all.

Remember *who* your readers or listeners are, and choose your words in light of their feelings, their educational level, their social status, and their needs.

Sentences

Writing that is clear and concise motivates and persuades others. Such writing is based on sentences that are well structured and cogent. In some material we read, sentences seem to flow into one another smoothly and effortlessly. Other material must be read and reread, for the prose seems choppy, difficult, and awkward.

Even the Rand Corporation, one of America's most prestigious "think tanks," recommends to its researchers-authors that their reports be as clear, concise, and as simple as possible. As an example of how *not* to write, the Rand writer's guide quotes the following and then comments on it.

> *A processing skill of symbolic reasoning, sustained by the interfacilitation of an intricate hierarchy of substrata factors that have been mobilized as a psychological working system and pressed into service in accordance with the purpose of the reader.*
>
> *That is a definition of "reading" presented by a professor of educational psychology. It is doubtful that even specialists in reading understand it, and it is almost certain to baffle, let us say, a physician or metallurgist. Writers who "implement," "facilitate," and "utilize" too much, and whose busy needles*

string "which" and "as well as" clauses into festoons like cranberries and pop-corn at Christmas, run the risk of becoming unable to talk any other way even when they long to stop.[1]

Take a moment to consider that curious ability you have to feel the ebb and flow of pleasing writing. Where did you get it? Certainly not in formal classes on prose rhythm. Like a surfer on a wave, you have the ability to feel and flow along with the rise and fall of words, phrases, and sentences. You know when writing sounds abrupt and juvenile, or long-winded and pedantic.

But how do you know? You've trained your ear to the rhythms of English since you first learned to speak. That training became refined through your reading over the years and now is one of your best allies when it comes to writing. Even before you find the exact words, you have a feel for approximately how the next few words, phrases, or even sentences should go.

What factors contribute to a writer's style? How does one write sentences that flow rather than stumble? There are, of course, no simple answers, but there are some directions you can follow. To begin, you should be familiar with sentence structure and classification.

Types of Sentences   There are four primary kinds of sentences. The most common is the *declarative*, which is a positive or negative assertion. Other kinds are the *interrogative*, which asks a question; the *imperative*, which expresses a command or a wish; and the *exclamatory*, which ends with an exclamation point. All begin with a capital letter, end with the appropriate punctuation, and usually contain a subject and a verb.

Sentences may be formed in several ways. A simple sentence consists of one independent clause; a compound sentence consists of two or more independent clauses. A complex sentence is composed of one independent and one or more subordinate clauses; and a compound-complex sentence is made up of two or more independent clauses and at least one subordinate clause.

Variety of Sentence Structure   It is important to make writing clear and interesting. One way to do so effectively is to vary sentence structure. Paragraphs composed entirely of compound sentences are monotonous and boring; paragraphs constructed only of simple sentences are choppy, childish, and lacking in grace. However, the judicious use of a simple sentence can give writing force and impact. Complex sentences, because they are made up of independent and dependent clauses, clarify meaning and make for easier reading. Compound-complex sentences, in that they have inherent variety, also give vitality and interest to writing.

---

[1]*Author's Guide to the Rand Publications Department.* Copyright © 1976 by The Rand Corporation. Reprinted by permission.

For variety within a sentence, use an occasional command, exhortation, exclamation, or question to replace the usual declarative sentence. Or why not modify the usual subject-verb sequence, beginning a sentence with a phrase or subordinate clause to give details as a lead-in to the main idea of the independent clause?

Notice the differences in the examples that follow. Compare the abruptness and unnecessary overlapping of the simple sentences, and the monotony of the compound sentences, with the smoothness and variety of the sentences in the third example.

Simple Sentences   Management in any large corporation is dependent on information. This information is secured from many departments within a company. Sales, credit, production, research, advertising, and other departments forward information. This information is sent up to management. Often this information is in the form of reports. The information in these reports is usually gathered by each department. It is necessary that the content of these reports be accurate and complete. This is necessary because decisions are made on the basis of the content. Obviously decisions cannot be made if the reports do not contain adequate substantiating data. These data are usually statistical.

Compound Sentences   Management in any large corporation is dependent on information, and this information is received from many departments within the company. Sales, credit, production, research, advertising, and other departments forward information, and this information is then sent up to management. Often this information is in the form of reports, and this information is usually gathered by each department. It is necessary that the content of these reports be accurate and complete and this is necessary because decisions are made on the basis of the content. Obviously decisions cannot be made if the reports do not contain adequate substantiating data, and these data are usually statistical.

Variety of Sentence Types   Management in any large corporation is dependent on the information it receives from the sales, credit, production, research, advertising, and other departments. This information, which is sent up to management, is usually in the form of reports. The substantiating data (usually statistical) in these reports must be accurate and complete, for decisions are made on the basis of the facts provided.

Revising Sentences   The best way to write, as the old saw goes, is to write. Get your ideas down in black and white; let the sentences flow from your mind to the paper. After you have written down a complete block of ideas, go back and revise the awkward and wordy sentences. As you become more critical of your own writing and more adept at revising sentences, you will find that your ability will steadily improve.

The following examples demonstrate what can be done when a serious attempt is made to edit and revise.

Faulty Sentence Structure	*Improved*
Burns worked in his dad's store while attending school, and although he majored in management, I don't think he liked it.	Burns worked in his dad's store while attending school. He majored in management, but I don't think he liked the field.
To fly efficiently, a good pilot should check his plane after every flight.	If a plane is to fly efficiently, it should be checked after every flight.
Arriving home late, dinner was started immediately.	Because we arrived home later than usual, we prepared dinner immediately.
Running down the sidewalk near the hospital which was a new modern building built to handle children's cases.	John ran down the sidewalk adjacent to the new children's hospital.
When I first started to play tennis with John, I found that my serve was quite good. Although I had not played for six years.	When I first started to play tennis with John, I found that my serve was quite good, even though I had not played for six years.
When I write a report, I find that it requires a good deal of concentrated effort and work, this is, as I think of it, necessary when I do any type of writing.	When I write a report, I find it requires a good deal of concentrated effort and work. The same thing is true, now that I think of it, of any type of writing I do.
The annual report serves, by and large, two very important purposes today and the first of which is the presentation of financial information to stockholders and the second is to build company public relations in the business community at large.	The annual report serves two primary functions: the presentation of financial data to stockholders and the building of company public relations in the business community.
You will find enclosed, as per your basic request, the report which we have taken the liberty of forwarding to you.	The report that you requested is enclosed.

Improvement is not difficult; all that is necessary is a merciless blue pencil and an acceptance of nothing less than excellence in sentence structure. Perhaps the first step in editing is to be sure the thought and ideas you have in mind are clear. Peter Drucker, in an article titled "What Communication Means," wrote:

> *There is a very old saying among writers: "Difficulties with a sentence always mean confused thinking. It is not the sentence that needs straightening out, it is the thought behind it." In writing, people attempt, of course, to communicate with themselves. An "unclear sentence" is one that exceeds the writer's own capacity for perception. Working on the sentence—that is, working on what is normally called communications—cannot solve the problem. The writer has to work on his own concepts first to be able to understand what he is trying to say—and only then can he write the sentence.*[2]

The experienced editor often evaluates a sentence by reading it aloud and listening. If it sounds awkward to the ear, it should probably be revised. Many people, when revising an awkward sentence, will scratch out a word here and move a phrase there. The usual result of this minor surgery is that although some improvement takes place in the sick sentence, it cannot be placed on the healthy list. More often drastic surgery is called for. Delete the sentence and begin again. The new version will usually say just what you mean.

Another valuable editing technique involves the first few words in each of your sentences. Are they important words that catch the reader's eye and mind, or are they mere fillers like "There is . . ." and "In the opinion of . . ." Just as advertisers always put product names first in slogans such as "Coke is it!," so business writers should put the words they care most about in the most prominent sentence position.

Yet another technique is to use your dictionary and thesaurus constantly; don't be satisfied with the almost-right word. Search until you find the word that conveys precisely your intended thought and also gives your sentence the rhythm and tone you desire.

Paragraphs

A paragraph is a group of related sentences that help advance the development of a paper. Each paragraph, though joined to the one before and the one following, develops an individual idea, whether or not that idea is explicitly stated. Thus, carefully constructed paragraphs serve the double purpose of joining and separating.

The *expository* paragraph tells about the topic. It is linked at top and bottom with other paragraphs, but it develops, explains, illustrates, or supports a particular point. It can do so by particularization, by example, by definition

[2]P. Drucker, "What Communication Means," *Management Today,* March 1970.

of terms, by contrast and comparison, by analysis, by classification, or by narration.

The *transitional* or emphatic paragraph, on the other hand, assists the reader. A paragraph of transition says, this is where we have been; that is where we're going—so get ready. The paragraph of emphasis says, that was an important point we just passed; did you get it?

When you rewrite your paper, be sure not only that you have chosen the right words and put those words together into clear sentences, but that those sentences are combined into logical, useful paragraphs.

Be aware that readers judge your paragraphs at a glance before they begin to read your actual words. Paragraphs that look huge and heavy on the page proclaim to the reader, "Hard work ahead! You're really going to have to plow through all these words to find meaning." Therefore, build in "at-a-glance appeal" when constructing your paragraphs.

Can paragraphs be too short?

Yes, as these paragraphs are intended to show.

Do you notice that the eye and mind weary of putting together such disconnected pieces into one pattern of meaning?

Too many short consecutive paragraphs can strike the reader as jumbled pieces of a jigsaw puzzle. The reader may resent the fact that the writer never took time to put the pieces together.

QUALITIES OF WRITING STYLE

In a discussion of writing style, most authorities list the three standard qualities of rhetoric: **unity, coherence,** and **emphasis.** There are others, however, that certainly deserve more than a passing glance: consideration for the reader, clarity, liveliness, and grace.

It is a writer's style that makes the work unique. One author's work may be lively, while others' may be dull, persuasive, or consistently entertaining. These qualities come from the heart of the composition and make up the rather indefinable quality that we label *style.*

Every communication written by a businessman or businesswoman should have an effective style. Of course, few executives will approach the excitement of Hemingway, the humor of Thurber, the insight of Shakespeare, or the precision of Churchill. On the other hand, the writing need not be as dull as an inventory form or as uninspired as a page of stock quotations.

Unity and Coherence

Every paragraph should develop an idea; a group of paragraphs should move a single topic forward; and the sections of the paper should all contribute to the development of the specific topic with which the message is concerned.

Irrelevant details and materials not directly related to the core idea must be eliminated. Then the paper must be checked to determine if it possesses this quality of "oneness" or unity. Each sentence, each paragraph, each section must march forward toward the objective the writer hopes to achieve. If it does not, strike it out.

Coherence is attained when ideas are logically interconnected, follow one another smoothly, and are clear and easily comprehended. When sentences and paragraphs are connected with transitional words, phrases, and sentences, the whole body of material seems to move interestingly and coherently from one idea to another. Thoughts are not isolated but related to one another, and together they proceed logically toward a specific conclusion.

Courtesy and Consideration

In any kind of communication, oral or written business or personal, one of the prime requisites is consideration for the recipient. Courtesy and consideration are easy to achieve, requiring from you only sensitivity and a little care.

In business communication, much more than common courtesy is involved. Discourtesy or thoughtlessness might cause the loss of a good customer or of a large sale. It might contribute to loss of prestige and status. It would almost surely mean a lessening of respect for and approval of you and your company.

 Basic to consideration is a knowledge of your readers. If you know who they are, what they want, and why they want it, you can even refuse them without offending. Remember to write in terms of "you" rather than "I." Customers are interested in *their* requests or complaints, and you must be too.

The second ingredient for a courteous business letter or memo is "Please," "thank you," "I'm sorry," "I'm delighted." Liberal—but not excessive use of these words will give your readers the feeling not only that you are polite but that you care about them.

Interestingly, every significant study of electronic mail concludes that writers pour more personality, not less, into this new communication convenience. Perhaps because electronic mail robs us of the pleasantries of attractive letterhead, sharp type fonts, and flashy signatures, we attempt to compensate by including more personal warmth through our choice of words.

Skilled business writers know the value of person-to-person emotional contact. Communication may happen faster in the years ahead, but there is no sign that sincere human warmth has ceased to be important in the electronic revolution.

The third ingredient in consideration goes back to knowing your readers.

Use words and phrases and ideas that are on their level. If you talk over their heads, they will feel unhappy, insecure, and inferior. This is not way to gain confidence. If you talk beneath them, they will be insulted. This, too, will defeat your aims.

Emphasis

At times we wish to persuade our reader to take specific action as recommended in certain segments of our writing; or perhaps we wish to bring a particular section of the paper into sharper focus. This requires that significant sections be emphasized.

A variety of methods can be used by the business writer to achieve emphasis. There is the simple method of *proportion,* which involves giving more space to a key point than to items of less importance. If a writer spends four pages discussing sales and only half a page on credit, production, and research, it is obvious that he or she wishes to focus the reader's attention on sales.

Emphasis helps satisfy the reader's hunger for your point. Particularly in the middle of a hectic business day, your reader has no desire to wander through paragraphs in search of a key idea. Use every technique at your disposal, including choice of words, placement on the page, headings, and type face to make your point in an obvious way.

Repetition of facts, ideas, or words also helps. An idea may be discussed in the paper, presented factually in a table, and commented on again in a further analysis.

The thoughtful *placement* of ideas within the body of the writing may also be a device to secure emphasis. Statements made in the early portion of the presentation, or at the beginning of a section, will often receive special attention.

Attention-catching words or phrases may be used to emphasize ideas. The use of dramatic words or alliterative phrases need not be limited to advertising writing: they can be used effectively in expository writing as well.

The use of *mechanical methods* has some value when the writer wishes to emphasize a particular point: capitalizing words, underscoring phrases, using colored inks, or inserting cartoons, sketches, and photographs. In addition, an idea or thought can be set off by itself with a dramatic amount of white space around it.

But perhaps the most effective way to emphasize a point is through *excellent writing.* One's writing should be so effective, so clear, so persuasive that the reader will remember the ideas because of the quality of the writing and not because of capitalized phrases or underscored ideas.

One of the best examples of securing emphasis and impact through excellence in composition was achieved by John F. Kennedy in his inaugural address of January 20, 1961. In the first portion Kennedy stated:

The world is very different now. For man holds in his mortal hands the power to abolish all forms of human poverty and all forms of human life. And yet these same revolutionary beliefs for which our forebears fought are still at issue around the globe—the belief that the rights of man come not from the generosity of the state, but from the hand of God.

He then went on to say:

We dare not forget today that we are the heirs of that first revolution. Let the word go forth from this time and place to friend and foe alike, that the torch has been passed to a new generation of Americans—born in this century, tempered by war, disciplined by a hard and bitter peace, proud of our ancient heritage— and unwilling to witness or permit the slow undoing of those human rights to which this nation has always been committed, and to which we are committed today at home and around the world. . . .

Let every nation know, whether it wishes us well or ill, that we shall pay any price, bear any burden, meet any hardship, support any friend, oppose any foe to assure the survival and the success of liberty.

And then after stating the philosopy for his term in office, Kennedy concluded with his memorable quotation:

And so, my fellow Americans, ask not what your country can do for you. Ask what you can do for your country.

Securing emphasis through this method—good writing—is not easy. It requires analysis, time, and constant reference to the dictionary and thesaurus. But it is worth it, for effective writing makes an indelible impression in the reader's mind. A well-written statement may be recalled for years, while an underlined sentence may be forgotten in a few minutes.

Imagination

Imagination is important in business writing. Achieving it requires a sensitivity to words and a desire to find the exact words and combinations of words to impart not only facts but feelings. Prose that is a pleasure to read— emphatic phrases, clear and concise statements, ideas imaginatively presented—is more likely to achieve its purpose than writing that is dull, awkward, heavy-handed, or pompous.

Writers with *imagination* not only will put themselves in the place of the reader, but will also look for the word, the analogy, the figure that best expresses what they want to say. They will avoid clichés and ambiguities, worn-out similes, and irritating redundancies.

Here is a sample of energetic, imaginative prose from a great intellect and leader Adlai Stevenson:

Today we are no longer poor and defenseless. We are by far the richest nation on earth and, until recently, the most impregnable. Yet, ironically, our actions have been timid and irresolute. Our leaders talk of freedom—and embrace dictators. We do not act as frightened as we did during the shameful McCarthy era. But to millions of people just emerging from feudalism or colonialism we still look like a nation that has forgotten its revolutionary heritage and moral purpose, and that prefers its political status quo, business profits, and personal comforts to the traditions on which our republic was founded.

Rich and endowed as we are, the dominant concerns of our leadership have been almost wholly defensive. Our foreign policy has been dominated by sterile anticommunism and stupid wishful thinking, our domestic policy by fear of inflation and mistrust of government. . . .

Our strength does not lie in the iron discipline of the state. Nor does it lie in the balance of a budget. It does not even lie in the productive capacity of our farms and factories. These are instruments of power, and we must wield them to accelerate our growth. In the final analysis, as Jefferson said, our national strength lies "in the spirit and manners of the people."[3]

EDITING SUGGESTIONS

You should review your first draft several times; in each review, give special attention to a specific aspect of the writing. Step back, so to speak, from the paper and determine if every sentence, every paragraph, every section contributes to the theme and purpose. If any portion, whether a word or a paragraph, can be construed as being irrelevant or unnecessary, it should be cut without compunction.

Writers, of course, are not always objective judges of which words should live and which should die in their work. By all means, reach out to colleagues for their **feedback** to your drafted document. The technique can be simple: give your work to a friend you trust, asking him or her to jot a question mark in the margin beside any sentence or paragraph that seems foggy, unnecessary, or misplaced. Then go back to revise and clarify those passages. Your helper may even have some good ideas for your editing.

Then check for **coherence**. Is there good transition between ideas? Do the sentences and paragraphs seem to be logically associated and connected? Do the sections flow into one another easily and smoothly.

What about **clarity**? Does every sentence say precisely what you mean it to? Do the words have the exact connotations intended? Does this phrase or that clause result in the proper picture in the reader's or listener's mind? No second-choice word or group of words is acceptable here; use your dictionary or thesaurus to find the exact words, the words that will convey the precise idea, tone, and mood. Take every opportunity to use lively words, similes,

---

[3]Michael H. Prosser, ed., *An Ethic for Survival: Adlai Stevenson Speaks on International Affairs 1936–1965*. New York: William Morrow & Company, Inc. 1969.

metaphors, and other figures of speech that will give your writing vitality and color.

Emphasis can be achieved by proper placement of key ideas, by inserting topic and subtopic headings, and by the judicious use of detail.

Examine carefully all **statistical data** in your paper. Would the use of charts or graphs make your presentation clearer and easier to read? Tables, charts, diagrams, and other visuals must be used with restraint, but they are an important tool in communication. (See Chapter 12 for a detailed discussion of visuals and how they can be used most effectively.)

What does a piece of writing look like before and after editing? Figures 6–1 through 6–6 show examples of part of a report, a memo, and a letter in their first drafts and then after editing.

FIGURE 6–1

Page from a short report (rough draft)

WESTERN MANAGEMENT SERVICES, INC.

In addition, I think it would be appropriate here to include some mention of how often employees have been absent during the first half of this year as compared to the first half of last year. (I am assuming the beginning of fiscal year as January 1.)

Overall, absenteeism was lower is some job categories and higher in others, with some categories about the same. For example, managers tended to come to work more often while programmers slipped a bit (though only by a day or two). In my opinion, the improvements we have seen in absenteeism, in those categories where improvement exists, is due to the company's new incentive programs, such as "Pay per Day," which, as you know, provides an extra 15 percent hourly pay for each sick/personal/legal day not taken during the year. Employees generally have responded favorably to this incentive. At least so I've heard in the lunchroom from time to time.

The only problem I can see with the incentive plan is that, at lower levels, that 15 percent really doesn't add up to much for low hourly wage employees, while upper level employees have much more to gain by coming to work as often as possible. We should discuss this and make changes.

FIGURE 6–2

Page from a short report (final)

WESTERN MANAGEMENT SERVICES, INC.

III. Absenteeism January 1 through June 30, 19___

　　At all employment levels, absenteeism dropped significantly (an average of 24 percent) when compared to the same
period in 19___. Two employee surveys (summarized in Appendix
A) attribute the drop to the company's new "Pay per Day"
incentive plan.

　　By employment category, absenteeism occurred as follows:

	Ave. Days Absent	Ill	Personal	Legal	Misc.
Management I	4	2	1	1	
Management II	7	2	3	2	
Supervisor I	8	4	3	1	
Supervisor II	8	3	4		1
Foreman	11	5	3	2	1
Group Leader	14	8	4	1	1
Technician	14	6	4	2	2
Programmer	17	11	6	1	

IV. Interpretation of Absenteeism Records

　　The company's "Pay per Day" incentive program offers
proportionately higher incentives for upper management to
avoid absenteeism than for rank-and-file employees. As a
consequence, the categories of Foreman through Programmer have
shown less improvement (an average increase of only 7 percent)
over comparable absenteeism records from 19___. At the
Programmer level, in fact, absenteeism has actually been worse
in 19___ than in 19___, by an average of 4 percent.

FIGURE 6–3

Memo (rough draft)

Apex Reproductions, Inc.

To: Richard Hall
From: Sylvia Leaven
Subject: What have you been telling your clients???
Date: October 9, 19__

Apparently you have been telling your clients that we will give them a loaner copier
if theirs breaks down during the warrantee period. This is not true, as you are well
aware from your training classes in this company and my memos dated February 2
and March 16, 19__. The policy of this company is not to exceed or in any way
elaborate upon the specific contractual provisos drawn up by our legal department
and intended to accompany each respective product. This applies to all company
personnel, from the president on down. Obviously we have to solve the problem
you have created, and I need your input on how to best go about it. It is very
important that we meet tomorrow morning.

FIGURE 6–4

Memo (final)

Apex Reproductions, Inc.

To: Richard Hall
From: Sylvia Leaven
Subject: Policy regarding verbal assurances
Date: October 9, 19__

This morning I spoke with three of your clients. All had purchased the #702 copier
through you during the last year (see invoices attached) and all have a common
complaint: they say you gave them verbal assurance that the company would provide
loaner copiers if their copiers had to undergo warranteed repairs.

I will not prejudge the case by accepting the clients' version of this matter at face value.
Let's meet at 9:30 a.m., October 10, in my office to discuss what was and wasn't said.
Company policy, as you are aware, strictly prohibits employees at all levels from giving
verbal assurances, warranties, or guarantees beyond the specific written language
accompanying our products.

Please bring your notes and records of these transactions to our meeting. I'm anxious to
resolve these misunderstandings quickly.

FIGURE 6–5
Letter (rough draft)

Victor Financial Partners, Inc.
392 Liverpool Avenue
Miami, FL 30233
(203) 398-2839

January 7, 19__

Mr. Thomas Evans
3028 Henderson Drive
Fort Lauderdale, FL 30203

Dear Mr. Evans:

You called last week to discuss possible investments that stand a good chance of providing significant return on investment, and I recommended a new offering we will have going beginning February 1, 19__, the Medinvest II limited partnership.

It involves buying a magnetic resonance unit and leasing it back to doctors. We think the lease arrangement when added to the tax benefits (see the new tax laws regarding depreciation of medical equipment) can provide a healthy return. We are putting some of our best clients into this investment because we view it as a "sure thing."

There is some literature enclosed about the investment. I can help you interpret it if you wish. Give me a call and we'll find a time to get together.

Don't delay, though. This investment is "hot."

Sincerely,

Robin J. Matthews

Robin J. Matthews

FIGURE 6–6
Letter (final)

Victor Financial Partners, Inc.
392 Liverpool Avenue
Miami, FL 30233
(203) 398-2839

January 7, 19__

Mr. Thomas Evans
3028 Henderson Dr.
Fort Lauderdale, FL 30203

Dear Mr. Evans:

Thank you for your inquiry about the Medinvest II limited partnership we will offer beginning February 1, 19__.

As we discussed briefly by telephone, the Medinvest II program will create an investment team of fifty individuals for the acquisition of a General Electric Magnetic Resonance Unit, model #297. The purchase price to the partnership, less cash discount, will be $1.7 million. Medinvest partners will then lease the unit to physician groups in the greater Miami area.

Because of favorable tax treatment given to depreciable medical instruments, the general partner projects an annual return on investment of 24 percent, beginning with Year 2 and continuing through Year 7, at which time a lump sum distribution of additional accumulated capital will be made.

I have enclosed a Medinvest II Prospectus for your review. I would be pleased to discuss its major points with you at your convenience. May I ask you to give me a call when you're ready to meet?

Again, thank you for your interest in what we feel is an excellent investment.

Sincerely,

Robin J Matthews

Robin J. Matthews
Vice President

IMPROVING READABILITY

Over the years, various theories have been advanced on how to improve the readability of material. These theories have usually been accompanied by formulas for measuring the readability—how much difficulty will the average reader have with any given material?

One of the best-known of the readability experts is Robert Gunning. Some years ago he offered a series of suggestions to keep in mind when writing.[4] His points sound deceptively simple and, like most recommendations, are much easier to make than to achieve. Of course, there is much more to effective composition than the points Gunning makes. Yet his list is a convenient guide against which to check your own writing.

1. Keep sentences short, on the average. Gunning points out that there is nothing wrong with a clear forty- or fifty-word sentence, as long as it is balanced with a few that are six, eight, or ten words long. Of course, a short sentence that lacks other qualities of effective communication will have no value.

2. Prefer the simple to the complex. If we can say, "It was difficult to free the youngster's leg from the drainpipe." why should we say, "Major difficulties of a complex nature were encountered in the process of extricating the lower left limb of the adolescent from. . . ." Write directly, simply, and to the point.

3. Prefer the familiar words. Use a vocabulary that is familiar to your reading audience. In one case the best term may be *concomitant strabismus;* in another, it may be *cross-eyed.*

4. Avoid unnecessary words. Much contemporary business writing is padded, wordy, and pompous. It is simple to eliminate unnecessary words and thereby improve the writing. Rather than saying, "May we take the liberty of saying that in accordance with your request, you will find enclosed Baxter drawing #305," it is better to state, "Enclosed is Baxter drawing #305."

5. Put action in your verbs.
Passive: A sharp drop in production was noted.
Active: Production dropped sharply.
Writing in the active rather than the passive voice results in more lively, vivid, and interesting prose.

6. Write as you talk. Gunning does not expect a *literal* interpretation of this recommendation. If so, your writing would contain a good deal of rep-

---

[4]See Robert Gunning, *The Technique of Clear Writing* (New York: McGraw-Hill, 1952). See also Gunning, *New Guide to More Effective Writing in Business and Industry* (Boston: Industrial Education Institute, 1962). Gunning is also responsible for an excellent readability index commonly called The Gunning Fog Index.

etition, awkward phrases, and most certainly an inexcusable quantity of unnecessary words. What he is suggesting is that your writing reflect the friendly, natural tone you usually use when you talk. Perhaps it would be more accurate to say that when you write, you should sound as though you are talking.

7. Use terms your reader can picture. We noted earlier in our discussion that words make pictures in people's minds. When the words are concrete (chair, pen, lamp), the picture in the communicator's mind will probably be similar to that in the receiver's mind. The task of securing the same picture in the minds of the sender and the receiver is more difficult, however, when abstract terms are used. Therefore it is better to say, "Please pay within three days" than to say, "It is highly desirable that payment be forthcoming at your earliest convenience." Why talk about "unavoidable exigencies which may result from the complexities of morality which infringe on the juvenile's activities" when it is easier to say, "Problems of morality frequently confront today's teenagers"?

8. Tie in with your reader's experience. Your writing should present material from the reader's point of view. It isn't enough to explain the company profit-sharing program; you must explain it in relation to the employee and his or her family, job, and experiences.

9. Make full use of variety. go from simple to complex sentences, from long to short statements. From time to time, choose words that will make your reader sit up and take notice: "If you do not wish your letter to be read yawningly, write it wide awake."

10. Write to *express* and not to *impress*. Many of us feel that it is necessary, in our everyday activities, to impress someone with the importance of our job, the outstanding facts in our education, or the world-shaking impact of what we way. Skip such artificiality in writing or speaking. It fools no one. Pomposity is always recognized for what it is. Throw out the long words, the unusual words, the pompous phrases, and the cumbersome sentences. They will impress no one, and they do not help express ideas.

Those, briefly, are Gunning's suggestions for achieving clarity in writing. Several of them are very closely related and appear to overlap. Furthermore, the reader may feel that Gunning reduces effective writing to a too-simple formula. But his suggestions have much to recommend them, and they can be adapted to individual needs.

His formula for measuring the readability of a piece of writing follows.

1. Find the average number of words per sentence. Use a sample of at least 100 words. Divide the total number of words by number of sentences. This gives you average sentence length.

2. Count the number of words of three syllables or more per 100 words. Don't count: (a) words that are capitalized; (b) combinations of short easy words like *bookkeeper*; (c) verbs that are made three syllables by adding *ed* or *es*—like *created* or *trespasses*.

3. Add the two factors above and multiply by 0.4. This will give you the Fog Index. It corresponds roughly with the number of years of schooling a person would require to read a passage with ease and understanding.

If the material has an index of 8, it is at the eighth-grade level in the American school system and is easy to comprehend. If the index is 12, that is equal to senior high school. When the index reaches 16, it is at a level where reading and comprehension are not easy. Over 20, and few readers will bother to plow through the material.

It is usually recommended that a Gunning Fog Index of between 10 and 12 is quite safe for most readers of business materials.

THE FINAL PRODUCT

Now that the writing and editing of the final draft have been completed, you should check one more aspect of your paper: the overall appearance.

Topic Headings

Is each new section properly headed? Will readers be required to read through the 15 pages on employee fringe benefits to find the section on sick-leave pay, or will they be able to find that section quickly because it is preceded by a heading? You can assist your readers by using topic and subtopic headings. Choose your words for these headings carefully. Be sure these headings are concise and to the point.

Busy executives are delighted when they can skim through a paper and see at a glance the major and minor areas that are discussed. They can quickly note the organizational pattern (or outline) the writer had in mind and thus appreciate the method of development and emphasis. With such knowledge, they can then select the specific section or sections that require detailed study.

The use of headings also assists the writer in that headings are a constant reminder to deal only with the topic noted. It is difficult to digress when a guide of three or four words heads the section. Thus, topic headings serve as road markers for both reader and writer.

White Space

It is foolish to spend a good deal of time and money on a report or letter and then economize on paper. The generous use of white space in the margins, between sections, above and below tables and charts, and on a title page adds immeasurably to the appeal of your presentation.

The well-balanced page looks inviting; the material is easy to read and easy to assimilate. This is in contrast to the appearance of a "heavy" page that has typing from the very top to the very bottom and only a half-inch margin on either side.

Appendixes, Charts, Supplements

The technical paper may require various supporting documents. To include this material in the text may upset the continuity of the discussion. That is especially true if such material is relevant but not vital to the topic. In such cases the information should be placed in a footnote, if it is brief, or in an appendix. Sometimes a complete set of supporting documents must accompany a study; these can be placed in an appendix.

At times, extensive tables or charts may serve their purpose better when placed at the end of a paper. Here clever foldouts, gate folds, and layovers[5] can be used.

Various supplements may also be made part of the whole presentation to aid in understanding. These include sales promotion materials, statistics, and company records. Of course the table, graph, or supporting material should be placed in the text when it is vital to the ideas being presented.

These items are all valuable to include, but if they are not *vital* to the message being presented, they should be attached as additions to the report proper. Nothing should be permitted to interfere with the reader's understanding and assimilation of the core idea of the presentation.

Bindings, Introductory Pages, and Reproduction

Some type of binder is vital for a study, research document, or report. It is usually an important document, and a good binder helps the reader examine it, file it, or forward it to others.

The firm that issues many reports may use a standard binder; other companies may use anything from an inexpensive folder to an attractive plastic spiral affair. Here again, one should not be penny-wise and pound-foolish.

Introductory pages, such as the title page, table of contents, and list of illustrations, should be tastefully designed.

How the paper is reproduced depends on the number of copies desired and the size of the budget available. The report writer may profit from the advice of a printing consultant. Of course, if only a limited number of copies is needed, the report should be typed. The results achieved by a competent secretary, using an electric typewriter with a contemporary type style, are invariably excellent.

---

[5]A graph reflecting trend lines may be drawn on transparent paper and so inserted that it may be laid over a related graph or chart, making contrasts more obvious.

Well-written and well-formatted documents make a positive and lasting impressing on readers. But just as important is the impression the finished product makes on you, the writer. As you hold the completed work in your hands, you have every reason to feel proud of a creation—something valuable that did not exist before your hard work. Your confidence in your ability to produce such work makes the next writing task a more pleasant challenge. You know that you can do it; set about your work without crippling doubts and perpetual writer's block.

In short, good writing pays double dividends: once to the business community that reads your work, and again to you, the writer.

|||||||||||||||||||||||||||||||||||||||||||||||||||||||||||||||||||||||||||||||||||||||||||||||||||||||||||||||||||||||||||||||||||||||||||||||||||||

QUESTIONS FOR STUDY

1. The first draft has also been called the "rough" draft. What aspects of writing remain to be polished in the typical rough draft?
2. What is the danger when a writer "falls in love" with particular sentences and paragraphs in the rough draft?
3. Differentiate between denotation and connotation of language.
4. How does a writer decide whether to use a simple, compound, or complex sentence at a given time in a business document?
5. Writing is both a mental activity and a physical one. Draw an analogy with some form of sports to explain the statement, "The best way to write is to write."
6. Headings obviously help the reader keep track of the flow of ideas in a business document. But how can headings also be helpful to a writer in the act of composing the document?
7. Skilled business writers make their business documents sound as natural and straightforward as if they were speaking to us. But how does writing differ from speaking? Should you try to write as you actually speak? Explain your responses.
8. Some writers have learned to rely on the adrenalin surge of panic to make words flow just before an important deadline. The resulting document is seldom satisfactory. Why?
9. Why can connotations get the manager-communicator in more trouble than denotations?
10. What is the difference in the transitions used in connecting sentences and the transitions used in connecting paragraphs?
11. Imaginative business writing often makes use of analogies. In a well-developed paragraph, use an analogy to describe what it's like to be a new employee in an organization.

12. The text suggests that "you should review your first draft several times; in each review, give special attention to a specific quality of writing." Prepare a list of items you will specifically accomplish on each individual reading of a first draft.

13. Why should a manager attempting to do a good job in his or her specialty have to be concerned with white space?

14. We hear much about protecting the environment in our society and nation; what is meant by the manager's protecting his or her writing environment?

15. Briefly discuss and illustrate the uses of a thesaurus.

16. List three "do's" and three "don'ts" to guide a writer using appendixes, charts, and supplements.

EXERCISES

17. In a recent business article, identify transitional paragraphs. Explain in writing how key words and synonyms for key words are used to make smooth transitions.

18. Rewrite the following paragraph, adding or subtracting words as necessary, to restore sentence variety (in grammar, structure, rhythm, and length). Strive to make verbs active where appropriate.

Baudford Corporation is the object of a hostile bid by Wilson Enterprises. Baudford is a company that makes electrical connectors and cables. Wilson Enterprises is a firm that manufactures electrical switches and breakers. The takeover bid is being resisted by Baudford because Wilson Enterprises plans to replace top Baudford management. Baudford's past success is due to the skill and foresight of these men and women.

19. Rewrite each of the following flawed sentences, adding or subtracting words as necessary:
    (a) The multimillion-dollar transaction due in large part to Frank Williams' creative ideas for attracting investors.
    (b) Closing the Portland factory meant layoffs, most of the workers simply could not afford a month without pay.
    (c) The manager asking her to handle the Fitzpatrick account.
    (d) The employees left the building bundled in heavy overcoats.
    (e) Reputed to be a tough manager, the delivery boy said Mr. Foster actually told a joke from time to time.

20. The practice of reading documents aloud can help you discover stylistic problems. Choose one paragraph from your own writing. Read it aloud, then explain in writing the possible areas for revision you discovered by

your reading. Go on to discuss why reading aloud uncovers problems that are difficult to spot by silent reading.

21. Using one of your own pieces of writing, look at it in terms of unity, coherence, emphasis, reader consideration, clarity, liveliness, and grace. Then on a separate sheet of paper, describe your writing style. Submit both the original writing and your analysis.

22. Rewrite and combine the following sentences as one longer paragraph. Do not merely recopy the sentences. Instead, rearrange them as necessary for an organized, coherent paragraph. Add words where necessary.
    We all remember the spirit of cooperation while Sandra Ortiz was Chief Executive Officer.
    The best leaders have come from among the company's own ranks.
    She rose from quality control inspector to unit supervisor to vice president and finally CEO.
    The company has never experienced a significant downturn in profits while led by a leader from among its own.
    Because employees knew that Sandra looked out for them, they worked hard for her.

23. Name and exemplify each of the three ingredients for achieving courtesy and consideration in business writing.

24. Throughout our education we are explicitly and implicitly encouraged to write in an impressive manner. "Simple" seems to be the antithesis of modern education. But profit-making organizations don't have time for "impressive" missives; they need simple, straightforward communication. List and explain at least three recommendatiions you would make to students graduating from college as to how they should switch gears. That is, explain what they should do as they move to the workaday world, which will require letters, reports, memos, and other writing done simply rather than in a complex manner. Be very specific in listing and explaining your recommendations.

25. Revise the following statements as necessary to improve clarity, conciseness, and style.
    (a) Betty promised Mark in June she would marry him.
    (b) One Zenith employee, Mark Webster, constructed a sail plane, "The Butterfly," with both sling and sail near his home in San Jose.
    (c) In order to lose weight, the doctor suggested to Marie that lunch not be skipped.
    (d) Recently I found that no food seems satisfactory to my dog which comes in a can.
    (e) Our basketball coach spoke about how to win the tournament on television.
    (f) Her future, full of questions, but also of hope and desire, and perhaps pain and disappointment, was never realized.

(g) Peter exercised, such as jogging for 40 minutes, swimming forty laps, doing pushups for ten minutes, and jumping rope forever, on a daily basis.

(h) Frank, noting the approach of the fire, the high winds, the lack of water, and his own physical incapacity, was frightened.

(i) The winning of the games plus the increased salary which the players received brought the team full circle. This was, however, not what management desired.

(j) The owner insisted that the color of the car be green. This irritated the dealer.

26. Read the following sentences carefully. If you find an error in punctuation, rewrite the sentence, inserting the correct punctuation.

(a) The competition among automobile manufacturers has become intense, the solution, if there is a solution, is to offer higher quality and lower prices.

(b) If you believe it will solve the problem and I have my serious doubts, why not attempt to pay the account, that should satisfy Martin even though it may not please his partner.

(c) I released the emergency brake and then I put the car in gear.

(d) You will find that a turbo charged system will consistently save fuel, however that is not always the most important objective for the motorist.

(e) I called Herb and learned he was not available today but I did determine that he would be at the party on Friday under any circumstances.

(f) Betty could not find her husband in the crowd, nevertheless she went directly to their seats and greeted her guests.

(g) This situation, however, is different from the one which follows.

(h) I don't believe he will ever become a reliable and efficient parts manager, however, he does have the ability to become a competent personnel director.

(i) You may be correct about the mechanical features of foreign cars, however I do feel GM may match Nissan when styling is compared.

(j) I went to the class, which I always found interesting but Frank stayed home to watch the final game in the series.

27. Each occupation has its own set of "jargon" words. List several items of jargon you had to learn in a past or present job. For each, write an equivalent expression you would use in communicating that item to an uninitiated reader.

28. The following text of a letter was intercepted from word processing before it left Hudson Restaurant Supply on its way to a prospective customer. Put yourself in the shoes of Hudson's general manager, who now reviews the letter. What changes would you recommend? More impor-

tant, how would you go about educating the writer of the letter about better writing habits? (Only the body of the letter appears here.)

You're giving your customers less than they deserve if you're not buying from Hudson Restaurant Supply. And you're probably wasting money as well.

We can show you economical ways to begin serving a quality product at your eating spot, not second-rate fare. Our representative will be driving through your part of town next Thursday or so. If his schedule permits, he'll stop by to let you look over our product line. You'll be impressed.!

We look forward to supplying all your restaurant needs.

29. As a new employee at Midwest Agricultural Products, you've already gained a reputation as a good writer—the "office wordsmith." Your supervisor asks you to lead a two-hour meeting on effective writing. What will you cover? Draw up a working agenda for your session, indicating the approximate amount of time you will devote to each topic.

30. The connotation of the word or words you choose can either work for you or against you. Select three advertisements and show how the connotation of the language is used to build a positive image of a product.

31. The Maynard corporate president happened to see some correspondence various executives were sending to customers and vendors. The president labeled the materials rude, crude, and lacking completely in consideration. As Assistant to the VP for Administration, you have been charged with developing a brochure that will be presented to all letter writers in the company. The brochure is tentatively titled, "Don't Be a Grouch—Be Courteous in Your Writing." You are to meet with the VP and the president next week and show them an outline of what will go in the brochure. Prepare the outline—and remember, the managers will probably need many examples.

Part Three

Research and Reports

7 The Research Process

Investigate what was done yesterday if you wish to contribute to advances tomorrow.

In previous eras, wealth and power stemmed directly from control of resources: oil, gas, uranium, and so forth. But the last decades of the twentieth century have seen a new form of wealth and influence by means of access to information. Especially in business, finding answers to pressing problems by access to appropriate data can spell the difference between success and failure.

As we shall see in this chapter, our ways of storing, accessing, controlling, and distributing information are changing in revolutionary ways. The essential process for gathering and using information, however, is as old as Aristotle. We have all used that pattern, in one form or another, since we were children.

Consider, for example, how we negotiated our first allowance from our parents. First, we considered the problem: no money for the convenience store. Then we defined our purpose and objective: to get money legally. We went on to analyze our audience, those loving but penurious parents. In the light of that analysis, we narrowed and limited our central purpose and specific topic to a workable range: $5 per week. Finally, we put our developing idea (our hypothesis) to the test, paying particular attention to feedback ("We'll think about it . . . ") and revising our hypothesis accordingly.

That basic process of topic formation and information gathering underlies even the most complete research projects in business life. Luckily, we do not have to reinvent the wheel in our search for available information on our topic. Once we know where we are going and why, we can try to find out what others have discovered about our subject or about related areas. There is really no point in our duplicating work that others have already completed. When we have reviewed the work of others—referred to as secondary research—we can break new ground through primary research.

SECONDARY SOURCES

Let's say we have a problem to solve. The company president wonders how consumers will react if all our stores switch from paper bags to plastic bags. Significant sums can be saved if we use the latter. Find the answer!

In this case there are dozens of *similar* problems that have been described in various books, magazine articles, reports, and research studies. Of course, they won't necessarily be concerned with our precise topic, but they will cover impinging aspects. The material they present can guide and shape our thinking.

For example, in researching the paper bag vs. plastic bag question, there are a half-dozen reports on how consumers reacted to change when food stores put in scanners and discarded registers; how consumers reacted when full-service gasoline stations changed to self-service; and how consumers reacted when plastic versions of many previously metal parts began appearing in automobiles. Surely these reports could contribute to a foundation for further research. Don't ignore existing knowledge. Search secondary sources and build on the information others can give you.

Secondary sources may be divided into several general categories: (1) books; (2) periodicals, newspapers, and other serials; (3) government documents; (4) business or trade directories; and (5) miscellaneous sources. In this chapter are general comments on all of these categories. At the end of this chapter you will find a listing of useful reference guides, plus suggestions on using the computer to assist you in your research efforts.

BOOKS

Because the time required to turn manuscripts into books is now often a matter of weeks instead of months, researchers have no reason to look upon recently published books as "out-of-date" for research purposes. In many cases the lag time between completion of manuscript for a book and for a journal or magazine article is comparable. Therefore, don't discount the value of recently published books. Even older books can often contain classic studies or background material vital to your research efforts.

Using the Card Catalog

Most library researchers begin by looking through the card catalog for books on their topic. Title, subject, and cross-reference entries should be checked. The advent of electronic card catalogs has greatly reduced researchers' time in locating desired sources. As discussed later in this chapter, the computer makes it possible not only to locate sources of information quickly, but also to find related sources and abstracted summaries of books and articles.

Using the Library Stacks

Using the library stacks, a researcher can browse through actual studies instead of making research judgments based only on catalog card information. Such browsing often pays the additional dividend of turning up new avenues for investigation and new sources for evidence. While in the stacks, look for back issues of magazines and journals in addition to books.

PERIODICALS, NEWSPAPERS, AND OTHER SERIALS

Using Periodicals

Sometimes you will be given a hint by a helpful friend who says, "I read a great article on your topic a couple of months ago. I think it was in *Business Week*, but maybe it was in *Forbes*—or *Fortune*. I don't remember the exact title, but it was really good, and you should use it. I think you'll be able to find it; I'm sure it wasn't more than six months ago that I saw it."

Where do you begin? Preferably not by thumbing through stacks of *Business Week*, *Fortune*, and *Forbes*. Use one of several excellent periodical indexes that cover the business and social sciences fields. (See end-of-chapter listing.) To discover which of these indexes will best suit your particular needs, it may be helpful to check the list of periodicals indexed in each. Those indexes containing abstracts may be of special interest because of their descriptive notes, but they usually do not cover all articles in a journal.

Using Newspapers

Newspapers carry tremendous quantities of valuable information of all types: statistical, political, financial, and so forth. But how do you get at it? Again the answer is to use an index. Some newspapers, such as the *Wall Street Journal*, the *Christian Science Monitor*, and the *New York Times*, have their own indexes. These papers are also indexed collectively in the *National Newspaper Index*. The dates of relevant issues of these newspapers will guide you to promising issues of others.

Using Other Serials

Each year thousands of excellent reports, bulletins, brochures, and studies are issued by universities, foundations, corporations, cultural and social institutions, and professional societies and organizations. Unfortunately, there is no one guide to this valuable information. However, some useful reference guides are included in the end-of-chapter listing.

Government Documents

More than two hundred government departments, bureaus, ministries, agencies, and committees issue a wide variety of technical reports, pamphlets, bibliographies, periodicals, translations of foreign documents, and other publications each year. Thus, the U.S. government is probably the world's largest publisher. Many of these publications are extremely sophisticated and of very high quality. Since much of this literature is vital to business people and researchers, the appropriate reference guides can be of great assistance.

Statistics

Statistics are so vital to business that a separate section in our end-of-chapter listing is necessary to describe the most important sources. In addition to the U.S. government, there are many other compilers and publishers of statistical information. If you are not familiar with the more specialized sources, it is often useful to turn to the comprehensive statistical compilations. These will usually refer the user to appropriate specialized sources. Fortunately, there are also some excellent statistical reference guides and indexes available to help point the way through the maze of available data.

Business or Trade Directories

In addition to names and addresses of individual companies and product listings, business or trade directories carry a wide variety of information on organizations and individuals. These directories may be used for many purposes: to identify company officers or directors, to identify competitors in a particular area, to verify company names, and so forth. Many are published annually, with supplements appearing throughout the year. Job seekers will also find background information in company directories that may be useful during employment interviews. Major directories and reference guides to directories are described in our end-of-chapter listing. Almost every field, from automotive products to wholesale jewelry, has its own directory of national and international listings.

International Information

Because of the rapid development of international business, you may soon deal with many political, economic, and social differences among nations. The reference guides and indexes described in the end-of-chapter listing can be invaluable in developing a global perspective.

Miscellaneous Sources of Information

Many additional sources of information, including atlases, annuals, and yearbooks, provide a wealth of reference materials. See the reference guides to such compilations at the end of this chapter.

THE COMPUTER AS A RESEARCH AID

Computers now store literally billions of pages of business information in memory structures called "data bases." By telling a computer which data bases to search for information on a given topic, you can save yourself many hours of manual research. In addition, you stand a good chance of coming up with articles and studies that you may not have found in your company or university libraries. Several business-related data bases are listed at the end of this chapter.

To begin a computer search, you must first specify "descriptor terms" that the computer can use as guides. If, for example, we were investigating new plant construction, we would ask the computer to search for articles classified under "plant construction," "relocation," "labor availability," "city tax structure," etc. The computer searches its data bank and provides a listing of articles on these subjects. Usually included in the reference are the author's name, title of the article, journal name, date of publication, and a brief abstract of the paper itself (see Figure 7–1).

There are a variety of data bases (banks of research information) that may be rapidly searched by the computer.[1] And there are tremendous advantages to the researcher who uses computerized literature searches. Among these are the following:

> Speed. A computerized literature search can save enormous amounts of time. Contrast a ten-minute computer search with the dozens and dozens of hours spent in the library searching through card catalogs, indexes, and old magazine and journal files.

---

[1]Cuadra Associates publishes a directory of data bases. The same company was quoted in December 1984 *Wall Street Journal* news item: ". . . 2453 information banks are commercially available, about sixfold the total five years ago."

FIGURE 7–1

Printout page from a computerized data base search

```
85024498
The PC Explosion
 Ross, Melvin M.
 Best's Review (Prop/Casualty) v86n3  PP: 64,67 Jul 1985  CODEN:
BRPLB3
ISSN: 0161-7745  JRNL CODE: BIP
 DOC TYPE: Journal Paper  LANGUAGE: English  LENGTH: 2 Pages
  AVAILABILITY: ABI/INFORM
 When personal computers (PC) entered the market in 1982, Travelers
Corp. (Hartford, Connecticut) recognized their potential for use as
professional tools.  PCs were first placed in the offices of 15 top
executives at the firm to encourage companywide use; presently,
Travelers has 3,000 PCs in its home and field offices and 3,500 in the
hands of independent agents.  Travelers has also established a support
system for PC users, including a computer store, an information center,
personal computing coordinators, and a PC service center.  PC applica-
tions at the company include: 1. the Interactive Agency Company
Computer System that provides a communications link between
independent agents and the Travelers' data banks, 2. teleconferencing,
which allows a meeting among people at several sites who share their
material electronically, 3. development of customer information files
and telemarketing packages, and 4. the tracking of storms to help
estimate and prevent losses.  Popular software packages at Travelers
are Lotus 1-2-3, Multimate, and Decision Images.
  DESCRIPTORS: Microcomputers; Travelers Corp-Hartford; Insurance
companies; Case studies; Office automation; Applications; Software
packages
  CLASSIFICATION CODES: 8200 (CN=Insurance industry); 9110
(CN=Company specific); 5210 (CN=Office automation)
```

Thoroughness. The computerized search ensures that *all* issues of relevant journals, periodicals, or other sources are reviewed. Your library search, by contrast, is often frustrating because of missing volumes, issues, and information.

Timeliness. The printed index is made from the data base tapes. Thus citations are available from the computer at least a month before the published index is on the market.

Convenience. There is no need to take dozens of notes on available sources. The printout lists the author, title, name of journal, date of publication, and an abstract of the article as well as other information.

Document Delivery Service. If the researcher desires, he or she can obtain copies of most articles cited (for an additional fee). This rapid service is especially valuable if a file of a particular journal is not easily available in your library.

Using COM (Computer-Output Microfilm)

Computer-output microfilm, in which pages are reduced to less than postage-stamp size images, is generated by a microfilm printer that now can substitute for line-printer or tape output. This technology has facilitated development of microfilm indexes, which are totally self-contained on one reel and which are completely cumulated with each new monthly issue of the index. Since a researcher need only look in one place for all entries on each subject or author, using such an index is more convenient than using multiple issues of paper indexes.

PRIMARY SOURCES

In the modern busy world most of us depend on newspapers, radio, and television to tell us what's going on. They, in turn, get much of their information by asking questions.

"Interviews with key government officials in Washington," begins one story. "A survey of workers at the Danbury plant," runs another. A politician is disposed of with the words, "A nationwide poll showed that Throttlebottom ranked far down in the public's preference."

Information obtained by asking questions is called **primary information.** Other kinds of primary data include company records, diaries, original reports, letters and notes, and personal observation.

The data secured from primary sources are considered "raw" because they have not been subjected to interpretation and analysis by others. The researcher may very well be the first person to analyze, evaluate, and interpret the information. We may be interested in finding out whether the company's new product should be packaged in the red and blue carton or in the brown and green one; whether the new plant should be built in Topeka or in Kansas City; or whether we should advertise on TV instead of on radio. Companies devote substantial resources to find answers to such questions.

Selecting the Sample

When we make a survey to find out what large numbers of people are thinking or feeling, we don't try to approach everybody. To survey everybody would be too expensive and perhaps impossible. Instead, we take a sample of the people whose opinions we're interested in. If the sample is carefully selected so that it is representative of the group (or "universe") as a whole, surprisingly accurate results can be obtained from a very small sample.

The important point to remember is that the sample should be a reliable cross-section of the group you're studying. If it isn't, you'll get results that are not valid. A statistician or market analyst can tell you best how to go about it. For some purposes a random sample may be the answer. In other cases it may be wiser to use a stratified, cluster, double, selective, or area sample.

Perhaps the most popular samples are *random* and *stratified*. In a truly **random sample,** every item in the universe has an equal chance of being selected. One way to accomplish this is to put everyone's name or every item's number into a hat and then draw out a predetermined number. Thus each person or item has an equal chance of being selected. In actual practice, researchers use a table of random numbers, thus saving the chore of drawing designations from a hat.

A **stratified sample** is one in which the universe has been segmented into homogeneous groups first: lawyers, physicians, nurses, professors, engineers, and chemists. If each of these segments or groups is made up of different numbers and we draw ten from each group, our stratified sample is *nonproportional*. However, if we draw a number from each group that represents 15 percent of the total of each group, our sample is a **proportional stratified sample.**

Other types of samples are explained in more detail in almost any basic statistics book.

In almost every instance the validity of a survey increases with the sample size. However, a plateau of validity will be attained with a specific sample size beyond which confidence in results does not increase significantly. And although the cost of continued sampling increases, the level of validity rises very slowly after the plateau level has been established. Thus a return of 5000 will give us, let us say, a validity level of 90 percent. If we secure 5000 *additional* returns, our validity level may only rise to 92 percent. The researcher must now determine whether the added expenditure from further surveying is worth the increase in validity from 90 to 92 percent. Of course, if one is assessing consumer response to a blue versus white packaging, a 90 percent validity level is fine. On the other hand, if a researcher is checking an anti-virus serum to be injected into millions of children, he or she probably wants to feel 99.999 percent confident that results are correct. In such a case, the added cost is worthwhile.

Conducting the Survey

Even with a good sample and a well-planned questionnaire, a survey may fail if it is not conducted properly. Respondents to a survey are doing us a favor, and they should be treated accordingly. The investigator should be courteous at all times. He or she must also be perceptive, in order to locate and record the "real" responses.

Types of Surveys

Questions are not difficult to ask; the problem is getting reliable and truthful answers. Several different methods are used to secure information from people. Basically they all involve asking questions or presenting situations, securing reactions, and then determining how the respondents will behave in a practical situation based on their responses to the survey. Sometimes the conclusions run like this: "Of those interviewed, 53 percent preferred the smaller package, 26 percent preferred the larger, and 21 percent had no preference." Among the methods used are mail questionnaires, personal interviews, telephone interviews, unstructured or depth interviews, and observation. The first three use series of questions to secure information. However, each is very different from the others and has its own advantages and disadvantages.

Mail Questionnaires   The advantages of the **mail questionnaire** are several. Chief among them are its low cost per response and the ease of securing responses from a wide geographical area. Respondents can also be assured of anonymity, which helps increase the proportion of questionnaires returned. Securing answers from hard-to-see people (such as company presidents) is easier with a mail questionnaire. Also, there is no possibility of interviewer bias, which can influence the responses.

But there are disadvantages to the mail survey. It must be relatively brief, or people won't bother with it. Persons who feel strongly—pro or con—are the most likely to respond; thus it may not accurately reflect the attitudes of those lacking strong opinions. It is also difficult to know whether the intended respondent personally completed the questionnaire or gave it to some member of the office staff or family to do so. Many respondents fail to answer a mail questionnaire because of the effort involved. For these reasons we are never quite certain whether those who reply are really representative of our sample, and of the population at large.

Personal Interviews   Perhaps the biggest disadvantage of the **personal interview** technique is its cost. Competent interviewers are expensive. And even when professional interviewers are used, there is the risk that the interviewer's bias may influence the answers obtained. Securing data through interviews is time-consuming as compared with mail surveys. And often respondents don't have the time or inclination to stand and chat with an interviewer.

On the other hand, interviewers can go into more specifics than is usually possible by mail. They can also obtain answers to questions in sensitive areas (income tax, sex, politics, religion) and bring in a reply where a mail survey may fail. Because they can choose their respondents to a certain extent, their surveys usually include more representative samples.

Telephone Interviews   The **telephone interview** has several major limitations. Questions must be brief and generally limited to not more than three or four. Questions requiring discussion or even careful thought cannot usually be included, nor can any that are concerned with personal relationships. Not every telephone call will lead to an interview. On the other hand, telephone interviews are inexpensive, almost anyone can be called regardless of his or her position or office, and simple information can be secured quickly and easily.

The Depth or Unstructured Interview   Respondents don't always answer questions truthfully. Because of societal conventions and individual inhibitions, we often answer questions as we think they should be answered. We don't want to admit that we hate our boss, dislike bridge, or find certain television programs entertaining. We may not lie, but we evade. Naturally, if the replies are not honest, the survey results cannot be valid.

Some experts believe that if you let people talk to a skilled interviewer about a topic freely and easily, their true feelings will become apparent regardless of the conventions of the society in which they live. This is the theory of **depth interviewing:** to set up a climate for the respondent so that he or she will talk freely and frankly about the topic under discussion. For example, "Tell me how you select the candidate for whom you vote" may produce some key information, even though the answer lasts five minutes and contains a great deal of irrelevant material.

Personal Observation   A great deal of information can often be obtained simply by **personal observation.** Researchers watch how a shopper makes a choice of one breakfast food from among thirty, how he or she selects a cut of meat, or whether a conference with a friend is necessary before choosing a cake. Observers also collect data by watching traffic patterns, counting shoppers, noting people's restaurant habits, and so on.

Designing the Questionnaire

Whatever type of survey is used, the most important point is to ask the right questions. Nothing is easier to design than a poor questionnaire, and nothing is more difficult than a good one. But there are a few rules which, if carefully followed, will greatly increase your chances of success.

Almost every detail of a questionnaire is important, even the title and introductory comments. To call it "Executive Survey" may appeal to the respondent's ego. The title "Confidential Analysis Among Our Retailers" encourages a sense of close relations between researcher and respondent. At times a carefully worded introductory sentence or two, appealing to the respondents' professional knowledge or responsibility, their loyalty, or even their sense of humor, may motivate them to complete the survey.

The precise wording of the questions can be a significant factor in the percentage of returns. Here are a few suggestions:

1. **List questions in logical order.** There is no point in asking a respondent in question 3 what flavor icing he or she prefers on cakes, and then asking in question 6 if he or she ever eats cake. If the questionnaire does not seem logical and sensible to the respondent, it may be discarded.

2. **Provide easy-to-answer questions early in the questionnaire.** The respondent who has gone quickly and easily through the first eight questions may be reluctant to discard the questionnaire when he or she encounters difficulty on question 9. This suggestion may conflict with the preceding one about following a logical order, but the researcher can only do what is most advantageous under the circumstances.

3. **Create smooth transitions between questions.** That and parallel wording help the respondent to move easily from one question to the next.

4. **Word each question so that it is concerned with one topic only.** If respondents are faced with giving two answers to one question—and only one space is provided—they may discard the form. Or, if they do answer, their responses may not give a clear indication of their preferences. Consider, for example, the question: "Would you like movies on commercial air flights at a slight extra charge?" If respondents answer "no," does it mean they wouldn't like them even if they were free? And if they would like movies on long flights but not on short ones, how do they answer? And if they don't want movies at all, whether there is an extra charge or not, how do they so indicate?

5. **Design the questionnaire so that it looks (and is) easy to answer.** Arrange questions so that respondents see clearly where to indicate their

replies. There should be plenty of white space, and the numbering should be easy to follow. Choose words carefully so that everyone will understand. And provide addressed, stamped envelopes in which to return the questionnaires.

6. Avoid words that may provide a biased or emotional response or carry an undesirable connotation. These are usually abstract words, (happiness, morality, democracy, communism) or words relating to politics, sex, religion, and race.

7. Eliminate ambiguity; clarity is of the utmost importance. A question like "What type of soup do you prefer?" can cause difficulty. One respondent will answer "hot," another "Campbell's," a third "beef noodle," a fourth "frozen," and a fifth "inexpensive." One way of handling this problem is to provide the respondent with a list of alternative answers from which to choose.

8. Avoid questions that "lead" the respondent to specific answers. Certainly a bias will enter into most respondents' answers if we ask, "Do you prefer General Motors cars?" "Do you usually purchase the best seats when attending a play?" "Do you always drink moderately?" "Do you prefer imported wines?" Here again, it helps if you give the respondent a list of choices.

9. Do you expect respondents to search their memories or carry through computations. We can't expect an accurate answer to "In what year did you take your first jet trip?" Not many people will bother to compute the answer to "How much does your family spend each year on movies?" Questions such as these can cause the questionnaire to be tossed into the wastebasket.

10. Avoid personal questions if possible. People dislike being asked questions about their political or religious affiliation, sex habits, income, or age. A promise of anonymity may help, but it is better to avoid the whole issue if possible.

11. Don't ask skip-and-jump questions. People are likely to give up in despair when confronted with "If you answered yes to question 4, skip questions 7 and 8 and go directly to question 9, unless you live in New York, in which case do not answer question 9."

12. Avoid questions with blanket meanings. Some words are open to a variety of interpretations. For example, the word *often* in the question, "Do you often take your wife out to dinner?" may mean once a month to some husbands and once a week to others.

Figure 7–2 shows an example of a mail questionnaire. You may wish to evaluate the quality of the questions, their wording, and the order in which they are presented. Note the different kinds of questions that appear. A *check* question requires only that the respondent make a mark to choose from among predefined alternatives. A *scale* question asks the respondent to locate his or her opinion or feeling on a continuum of possible responses. *Open-end*

FIGURE 7–2

Mail questionnaire using check, scale, and open-end questions

23. Please add any relevant comments you may have concerning the executive's role to-day in communicating with the media and/or special interest groups as well as the attention paid to the skill of communication in today's schools of business.

17. How frequently have you appeared before special interest groups in the . . .

past two months? _____   past two years? _____

18. Do you anticipate such appearances with . . . (Check once.)

Enthusiasm

Excellently

corporate officers . . .

11. In the last 10 years have you received any special training to assist you in becoming more competent in speaking . . . (Check all those applicable.)

☐ before large groups such as stockholders?
☐ before the print media?
☐ before the TV media?
☐ before sp
☐ before ot

12. Was the training you

☐ an emplo
☐ an "outsi
☐ a firm wh

13. If you received suc company facilities to you, etc.).

_____
_____
_____

14. What effect do you

_____
_____

15. Does your firm sp competent in comm

If "yes" please desc of time, who provid

_____
_____

16. How frequently hav

past two mo

University of Southern California
School of Business Administration

SURVEY OF CHIEF EXECUTIVE OFFICERS

Please complete the following questionnaire and return it no later than November 14, 1983. Your response is vital to our results. Thank you.

1. What is your present title? _____

2. How long have you occupied this position? _____ years _____ months

3. What was your position prior to this one? _____

4. Your age?   ☐ 30-40   ☐ 40-50   ☐ 50-60   ☐ over 60

5. Your academic degrees? _____

6. Number of employees in your company? _____

7. In what area(s) have you spent most of your industrial time (production, engineer-ing, marketing, finance, administration, other)?

_____

8. In our firm policies concerning communication with the media and/or special inter-ests are . . .

☐ printed and distributed to managers.
☐ in the process of being printed.
☐ discussed but no formal action taken.
☐ not discussed.

9. Time spent communicating (to employees, community members, reporters of all media, government agencies, etc.) on *public affairs* by you (or your predecessor) has gone from what percentage of your work time 10 years ago as compared to today?

10 years ago   _____ percent of work time
Today   _____ percent of work time

10. Of the total amount of time you spend in communicating with the various groups listed below, indicate the percentage breakdown in a typical month.

To the media   _____ percent
To special interest groups   _____ percent
To community groups   _____ percent
To other public groups   _____ percent
To employees   _____ percent

questions allow the respondent to generate answers without predefined limitations.

Figures 7–3 through 7–8 are examples of several other questionnaire formats. They show alternative ways of arranging the questions. Where an attempt is being made to measure levels of attitude and feelings, a *semantic differential* is often used, as in the horizontal format of the first two examples. This permits the respondent to choose among answers ranging from one extreme to another. Placing numerical designations on the **scale** makes it possible to measure just how strongly the respondent feels about his or her answer. The answers from all respondents can then be charted and correlated to show how groups differ in the strength of their feelings.[2]

Direct-Mail Surveys

We have already mentioned some of the advantages and disadvantages of mail questionnaires. Such questionnaires are probably used by more researchers, and certainly are better known to the public, than any of the other survey methods. In order to obtain the best results possible, it is important not only that the questionnaire be well done but also that the accompanying letter be well written and courteous.

The Cover Letter   In a direct-mail survey, the quality of the cover letter will strongly influence whether or not the respondents return completed questionnaires. A well-written cover letter may well motivate them to check the answers carefully and return the questionnaires promptly.

There are many reasons a questionnaire may not be completed and returned, and there is no way to design a survey instrument that will ensure a 100 percent response. The person who receives a questionnaire may have no interest in the topic under discussion; he or she may be busy; or perhaps his or her employer does not permit completion of such surveys. These are all understandable reasons for not completing a questionnaire. But why are so many simply discarded? The answer may lie in a poor cover letter: one that is writer-centered, pompous, too demanding, or lacking an explanation of the survey's purpose. If the recommendations below are followed, the percentage of responses will usually be good.

1. Keep the cover letter brief. Go over the draft with a blue pencil, striking out every extra word and phrase. The reader is busy and in a hurry. State what you want, why you want it, how he or she will benefit from giving it to you, and then stop. With rare exceptions, the cover letter should never be longer than one page.

[2]Basic texts on research carry detailed discussions of the semantic differential.

FIGURE 7–3

Scaled questionnaire (one page of several)

20. Do managers and executives above you communicate frankly and honestly to you and others at your level?

(24)

Never Communicate				Seldom Communicate			Often Communicate			Always Communicate	
1	2	3	4	5	6	7	8	9	10	11	12

21. Is your immediate superior interested in knowing about your problems at work and at home?

(25)

Never Interested				Seldom Interested			Often Interested			Always Interested	
1	2	3	4	5	6	7	8	9	10	11	12

22. Is your immediate superior interested in your suggestions concerning necessary changes within your company?

(26)

Never Interested				Seldom Interested			Often Interested			Always Interested	
1	2	3	4	5	6	7	8	9	10	11	12

23. Are you helped, rather than blamed, by your immediate superior when you encounter a problem in your work?

(27)

Never Helped				Seldom Helped			Often Helped			Always Helped	
1	2	3	4	5	6	7	8	9	10	11	12

24. When you do a job well, how often does your immediate superior commend you for it?

(28)

Never Commends Me				Seldom Commends Me			Often Commends Me			Always Commends Me	
1	2	3	4	5	6	7	8	9	10	11	12

25. Once you have completed a job, does your immediate superior personally evaluate your work and give you feedback.

(29)

Never Does				Seldom Does			Often Does			Always Does	
1	2	3	4	5	6	7	8	9	10	11	12

FIGURE 7–4
Scaled questionnaire (one page of several)

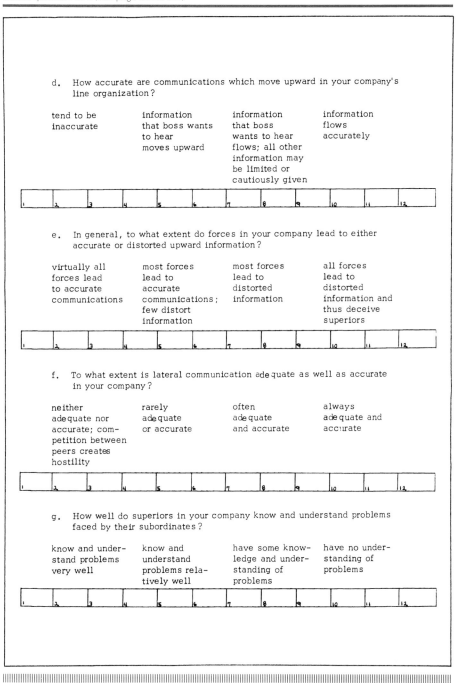

FIGURE 7–5

Checklist and scaled questionnaire

September 23, 1983   HUGHESNEWS   Page Three

Hughesnews readership survey
We have questions. You have the answers.

For more than 40 years, the Hughesnews has been publishing articles and news items for and about employees, the products they produce, and the services they perform. This survey will help us find out how well we have been doing our job and whether there are things we could be doing better.

Please check the boxes or fill in your answers in the spaces provided. The small numbers alongside and above the possible answers are for computer tabulation only, so ignore them.

We do not want to know your name but we do ask that you fill in the few "personal" questions at the end of the survey, which will enable us to learn how particular segments of our readership

(age groups, company organization, etc.) feel about the Hughesnews.

To return the questionnaire, tear out this page, fold it in half and then in thirds along the dotted lines. (Instructions on back of page.)

Send the questionnaire to us by company mail. If you do not have access to the company mail distribution system, you may send it through the U.S. Postal Service.

Remember, the more people we hear from, the more we will know about how to make the Hughesnews as useful and informative as possible. Help us reach those who may not be reading the paper regularly—encourage them to participate, too.

1. The Hughesnews is published every other Friday. Do you feel this is too often, not often enough or about right?
   - Too often ....( )1
   - Not often enough ...( )2
   - About right ....( )3

2. Is the Hughesnews readily available to you every two weeks?
   - Yes ....( )1
   - No (please explain and include your closest Hughesnews pick-up point) .( )2

3. How often do you pick up a Hughesnews?
   - Most issues ....( )1
   - Occasionally ....( )2
   - Rarely ....( )3

4. How much of the paper do you *usually* read?
   - All of it ....( )1
   - Most of it ....( )2
   - About half of it ....( )3
   - Selected articles ....( )4
   - Very little, just glance at it ..( )5

5. Who, besides yourself, usually reads your copy of Hughesnews? Please check all that apply.
   - Family ....( )1
   - Friends ....( )2
   - Other employees ....( )3
   - No one ....( )4

6. Is your overall opinion of Hughesnews favorable, unfavorable or neutral?
   - Favorable ....( )1
   - Unfavorable ....( )2
   - Neutral ....( )3

7. Listed below are groups of words and phrases. In each group, please check the one response that comes closest to expressing your opinion of the Hughesnews in general or that applies to its stories.

   11-1 ( ) Informative
   2 ( ) Not informative

   12-1 ( ) Educational
   2 ( ) Not educational

   13-1 ( ) Employee-centered
   2 ( ) Mouthpiece for management
   3 ( ) Balanced

   14-1 ( ) Believable
   2 ( ) Not believable

   15-1 ( ) Objective
   2 ( ) Slanted

   16-1 ( ) Complete
   2 ( ) Missing information

   17-1 ( ) Useful
   2 ( ) Useless

   18-1 ( ) Candid
   2 ( ) Doesn't tell me everything I'd like to know

   19-1 ( ) Thorough
   2 ( ) Superficial

   20-1 ( ) Willing to speak on any issue
   2 ( ) Unwilling to speak on some issues

   21-1 ( ) Accurate
   2 ( ) Not accurate

   22-1 ( ) Interesting
   2 ( ) Dull

   23-1 ( ) Story length too long
   2 ( ) Story length too short
   3 ( ) Stories are the right length

   24-1 ( ) Well written
   2 ( ) Poorly written

   25-1 ( ) Too technical
   2 ( ) Over-simplified
   3 ( ) Right amount of detail

   26-1 ( ) Clear
   2 ( ) Confusing

8. Hughesnews covers a number of different subjects. Please indicate your interest in the subjects listed below.

	Very	Somewhat	Not usually	Not at all
	-1	-2	-3	-4
Program or product-related stories .	( )	( )	( )	( )27
Heir Fare	( )	( )	( )	( )28
Anniversaries	( )	( )	( )	( )29
Announcements (such as HEA events)	( )	( )	( )	( )30
Classified ads	( )	( )	( )	( )31
Leisure Life	( )	( )	( )	( )32
Stories about employees' activities on the job	( )	( )	( )	( )33
Stories about employees' activities off the job	( )	( )	( )	( )34
Who's News at Hughes	( )	( )	( )	( )35
Patents awarded	( )	( )	( )	( )36
Management's industry-related activities (speeches, appearances before Congress, etc.)	( )	( )	( )	( )37
Information about Employee Benefits	( )	( )	( )	( )38
Graduations from company-sponsored classes	( )	( )	( )	( )39
Award presentations	( )	( )	( )	( )40
Savings Plan Unit Values	( )	( )	( )	( )41
Credit Union stories	( )	( )	( )	( )42
Employee sports activities	( )	( )	( )	( )43
In Memoriam	( )	( )	( )	( )44

9. Are you interested primarily in reading about the activities of your Group (GSG, RSG, etc.) or organization (Support Systems, Research Labs, subsidiary), your Division, or the entire company? Check only one of these.
   - Group or organization ....( )1
   - Division ....( )2
   - Entire company ....( )3

10. How well does the Hughesnews usually satisfy this interest?
   - Very well ....( )1
   - Fairly well ....( )2
   - Not very well ......( )3
   - Poorly ....( )4

11. What types of articles or stories would you like to see *added to* the Hughesnews? Check as many as you like and feel free to write in other suggestions.
   - Editorials from management ....( )1
   - Question and answer column ....( )2
   - Industry news ....( )3
   - Interviews with management about industry or company problems ....( )4
   - Letters from employees ....( )5
   - Stories about our competitors ....( )6
   - Other suggestions _____( )7

12. We want your comments. Please see reverse side of this page.

(More on back of page)

(Separate along dotted line)

FIGURE 7–6

Unusual checklist and scale or semantic differential questionnaire

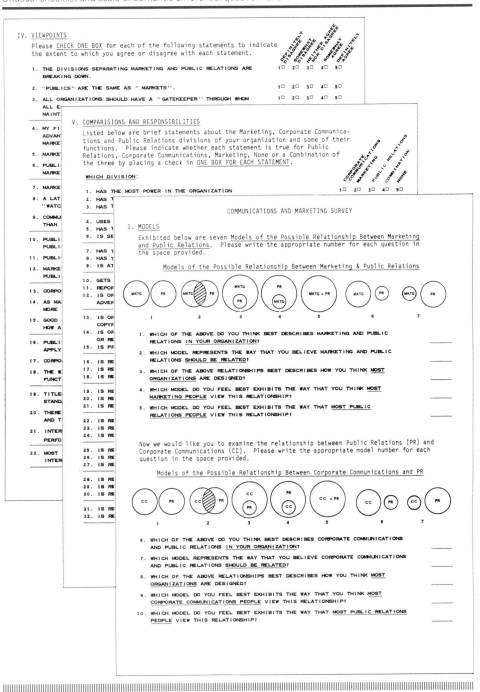

FIGURE 7–7

Typical questionnaire

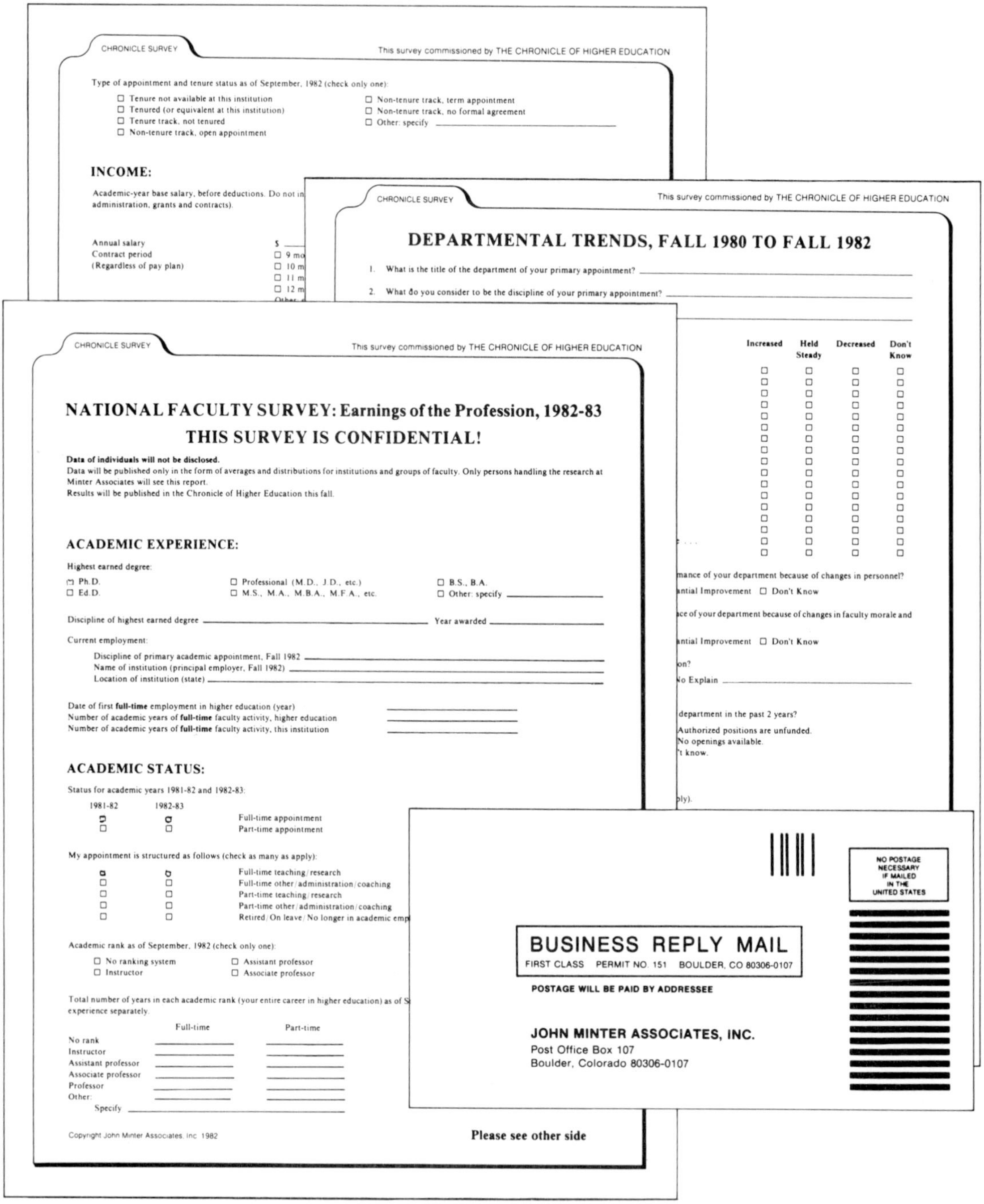

FIGURE 7-8

Check and fill-in questionnaire

8. Please answer the following questions for the purpose of classifying your responses:

a. Are you: □ Male □ Female

b. Your age: □ Under 25 □ 25-34 □ 35-49 □ 50-65 □ over 65

c. Your Marital Status: □ Married □ Single

d. How many dependents under

e. Which of the following classi

□ Manager
□ Proprieto
□ Office w
□ Police, p
□ Sales wo

f. Which of the

□ Reading
□ Cooking
□ Boating,
□ Hunting,
□ Jogging,
   Aerobics
□ Photogra

9. Please give us
   like us to hear.

_____
_____
_____
_____
_____

Once again, we

5. When you buy a car to replace the one you drive most often, what year, make, and model cars would you seriously consider and shop for? Will it be new or used?

New Used
□   □

First Choice: ____ ____ ____
              Year Make Model

2a. In each of the following areas, how much progress do you feel Ford Motor Company has made compared to other manufacturers?

	Compared To Domestic Manufacturers			Compared To Import Manufacturers		
	A Lot	Some	A Little	A Lot	Some	A Little
Overall Quality						
Body Engineering						
Styling/Design						
Engine Technology						
Fuel Economy						
Ergonomics						
Aerodynamics						
Employee Involvement						
Management Philosophy						
Response to Consumers' Needs and Wants						

b. Would you be interested in dealership?

□ Yes □ No

c. If yes, please specify model

3. To help us understand your h (Example: 1981 Chevrolet Cit **PLEASE LIST THE VEHICLE**

a. ____ ____
    Year Make
b. ____ ____
    Year Make
c. ____ ____
    Year Make
d. ____ ____
    Year Make

4. Please circle the letter to th following questions about th

Ford

M066000078

Please correct any mistakes in your name and address as shown.

Mr. Norman B. Sigband
Univ Pk. Sch Bus Adm
Los Angeles, CA   90007

_____
_____
_____

At Ford Motor Company, we value your opinion and would appreciate your candid reaction to the material you have received. Thank you for taking the time to answer these questions. Your opinions will be treated confidentially and will allow us to better serve you in the future. When you've completed the evaluation, simply fold it in half, enclose it in the postage-free envelope, seal, and mail.

1. Based on the material you have received from Ford Motor Company, please answer the following questions:

	Agree Completely	Agree Very Much	Agree Somewhat	Disagree Somewhat	Disagree Very Much
a. The information gave me a more positive feeling about Ford Motor Company	□	□	□	□	□
b. I think Ford Motor Company is making better products than it did five years ago	□	□	□	□	□
c. Ford Motor Company does seem committed to making the best cars and trucks in the world	□	□	□	□	□
d. I believe that Ford Motor Company vehicle design and engineering are at least as good as any manufacturer's in the world	□	□	□	□	□
e. I think Ford Motor Company is far ahead of other manufacturers in the involvement of workers and management in the product development decision process	□	□	□	□	□

279356

2. Show the respondent the importance of participating in the survey. We all want to be needed, and we like to know that we are making a contribution. Tell the respondent what the survey aims to accomplish and why it is important. Couple this with the role of the respondent in the survey, and you will usually involve him or her to the extent that he or she will want to help you.

3. Show the respondent how he or she will benefit from completing the questionnaire—the *you* attitude. Although at first this may seem almost impossible, it usually can be done after some thought. Explain the situation honestly. Perhaps you are trying to develop an improved delivery or packaging program, which will eventually produce a better and more salable product. Or perhaps you want to improve your use of computers, so as to lower your costs and pass the savings on to consumers.

4. Inject a personal tone. Research substantiates the value of making the cover letter seem personal. This can be done with a handwritten signature, a handwritten postscript (it may be necessary to simulate this if a large mailing is planned), use of the respondent's name in the salutation and/or body of the letter, and the overall tone of the letter itself. Abandon all hackneyed and obsolete phrases. Give the letter a conversation-across-the-desk tone.

5. Mention a due date for returning the questionnaire. Most of us tend to put things off. If we are asked to do something by a certain date, however, most of us will do it. The due date should always be given in both the cover letter and the questionnaire:

> *So that we can begin our new, faster delivery service to you as quickly as possible, please return the completed questionnaire no later than August 3.*

6. Where possible, assure the respondent of confidence or anonymity. If you feel that some questionnaires will be discarded because potential respondents do not wish to divulge confidential information, or because they fear the embarrassment of being identified, take precautions. Sometimes a simple statement will increase returns by 20 percent:

> *You may be sure that all the information you include will be kept completely confidential.*
>
> *Of course we don't want you to sign the questionnaire; we are interested only in your answers.*

7. Offer to send the respondent the results of the survey—if it won't be too expensive or won't divulge findings you want to keep confidential. Most respondents are interested in or working in the field with which the study is concerned. If you tell them you will send them a copy of your findings, this may spur them to complete the questionnaire. You can maintain their anonymity by including a post card, addressed to you, which the respondents may return separately from the questionnaire. Or you can suggest that they "write to the address above anytime after December 3 for a copy of the survey."

These are the major factors that govern the percentage of responses to questionnaire surveys. There are others, but in the sample letters shown here (Figures 7–9 through 7–12), you will notice that most of the principles listed have been included.

Motivating the Prospective Respondent   Research directors have found that giving the prospective respondent a "reward" usually will significantly increase the percentage of completed questionnaires returned. A freshly minted quarter, a coupon that may be traded for a package of the company's product, a ballpoint pen, or a crisp dollar bill ("to be passed on to your favorite charity") are some of the devices used. (See Figure 7–10.) When using a coin, avoid saying anything like "Here is a quarter for your effort." Other researchers have reported the following:

> *Promised incentives of two dollars and entry into a lottery with awards of fifty dollars, thirty dollars, and twenty dollars in return for a completed questionnaire did not significantly change the response rate to the mail questionnaire relative to the no incentive (control) group response rate. . . . These same researchers, however, found that the response rate was significantly improved with an enclosed one dollar bill.*[3]

Interestingly enough, a promised contribution of one dollar to "your favorite charity" drew a higher response than a promise of the same amount to the respondent.[4]

Sometimes attachments to the cover letters can save the researcher a significant amount of money. Let's say that 5000 questionnaires are sent out, each of which costs 60¢ (printing, folding, postage, and such). If 400 completed questionnaires are received, the cost per completed questionnaire will be $7.50. If, on the other hand, 2000 are mailed, each of which has a 25¢ enclosure (cost per questionnaire: 60¢ plus 25¢) and 550 are received, the unit cost will drop to about $3 including the expense of the coin. Thus these premiums should be considered, but they should always be used with caution. Some prospective respondents may feel that they are unethical. And there is also the danger that the respondent who has accepted the coin or coupon may answer the questionnaire as he or she thinks the researcher desires, rather than as he or she honestly feels.

[3]J. Paolillo and P. Lorenzi, "Monetary Incentives and Mail Questionnaire Response Rate," *Journal of Advertising*, Vol. 13, No. 1, pg. 46.

[4]D. Furse and D.W. Steward, "Monetary Incentives Versus Promised Contribution to Charity: New Evidence on Mail Survey Response," *Journal of Marketing Research*, Aug. 1982, p. 375

FIGURE 7–9

Cover letter to questionnaire

October 23, 19__

Mr. Harry L. Blomquist, Jr.
President
Coastal States Gas Corp.
5 Greenway Plaza E.
Houston, TX 77046

Dear Mr. Blomquist:

Is is true that the CEO's role in the corporation is changing and that he or she is spending less time in decision making-planning-finance, and more time in communication with employees? With special interest groups? With the media?

Today's newspaper, radio, and TV reporters want to question the CEO, not his or her subordinate. Special interest and employee groups want answers from the CEO and not his or her representative. And the CEO has not only become the organization's spokesperson on sensitive and controversial issues, but even its marketing representative as he or she sells the company's products on TV!

In an effort to determine how much time and activity the CEO spends communicating on public issues today as compared to ten years ago, I have undertaken this research project. Will you take a few minutes of your valuable time to complete the attached questionnaire and return it to me no later than November 14, 19__, in the enclosed, stamped envelope? Of course all replies will be respected as anonymous.

Obviously, the input received from you will have an impact on curriculum content at the MBA and Executive Program levels. Surely if the CEO and upper-level managers are spending more time in oral and written communications before the media and special interest groups, we must do something in our Schools of Business to make them as competent as possible in these activities.

Such curriculum changes should supply you and your firm with more articulate and decisive managers and CEOs in the years ahead.

If you would like a copy of the results of this survey, please let me know after December 15, 19__; I shall be happy to send one to you.

Thanks again for your cooperation.

Cordially yours,

Norman B. Sigband

Norman B. Sigband
Professor

Enclosure
F89T4:Y

FIGURE 7–10

Combination cover letter and questionnaire

Important LOWE'S Corporate Relations Survey

Dear Reader:

We want to make our investor relations program as inclusive and as effective as possible. Consequently, we rely on the views and opinions expressed by all recipients of our Annual Reports. You can help by taking a moment or two to complete the following questionaire. No postage is required to return it to us. As a token of our

appreciation for your time, we would like to send you our unique Lowe's Stock Market Calculator, a special slide rule for fast computation of yields, growth rates, p-e ratios, etc. Thank you for your interest and participation.

Robert L. Strickland
Senior Vice President

1. From which of the following groups does your interest in Lowe's stem? (Check more than one if applicable.)
   ☐ Shareholder ☐ Financial Press
   ☐ Security Analyst ☐ Mutual Fund
   ☐ Financial Advisor ☐ Lowe's Employee
   ☐ Stockbroker ☐ Other (specify)

2. Are you ☐ male or ☐ female?

3. In which age group would you be listed?
   ☐ Under 25 years ☐ 45 to 54 years
   ☐ 25 to 34 years ☐ 55 to 64 years
   ☐ 35 to 44 years ☐ 65 years and over

4. When did you first become interested in Lowe's from an investment standpoint?
   Within the past: ☐ Two to five years
   ☐ Year ☐ Over five years
   ☐ One to two years

5. How did you first become aware of Lowe's? (Check one)
   ☐ Through my stockbroker ☐ Newspaper or Magazine Article
   ☐ Through a Lowe's employee ☐ Other (please specify)
   ☐ Receiving your Annual Report _____

6. Which section of our 1972 Annual Report did you like best? (Check one)
   ☐ Chairman's Letter ☐ Lowe's Sources and Resources
   ☐ President's Report
   ☐ Audited Financial Statements ☐ Lowe's How We Grow
   ☐ Graphs and Charts ☐ 16 year Review
   ☐ Market Dimensions ☐ Other (please specify)

7. If not already included on one of our Financial Mailing Lists, please check here if you desire to receive future mailings.
   ☐ Yes ☐ No

8. How much of this Annual Report did you read?
   ☐ Cover to cover ☐ Only the Highlights
   ☐ Almost every page ☐ Gave it a quick glance
   ☐ About half ☐ Didn't read any

9. My overall judgment of the report was:
   ☐ Excellent ☐ Marginal
   ☐ Good ☐ Poor
   ☐ Average ☐ Unsatisfactory

10. If you are presently a Lowe's shareholder, are you satisfied with your investment?
    ☐ Satisfied ☐ Moderately dissatisfied
    ☐ Moderately satisfied ☐ Dissatisfied
    ☐ No opinion

11. Based on your knowledge of Lowe's, whether shareholder or not, how would you rate the Company?
    ☐ Up with the times ☐ About average
    ☐ Behind the times ☐ No opinion

12. As a Lowe's shareholder, do you feel your comments, suggestions and inquiries receive appropriate attention?
    ☐ Yes ☐ No ☐ No opinion

13. As a Lowe's shareholder, do you feel you receive sufficient information from the Company on a regular basis to keep you adequately informed of the Company's progress and future plans?
    ☐ Yes ☐ No ☐ Not entirely

14. As a Lowe's shareholder, what is your primary investment objective by investing in Lowe's?
    ☐ Capital appreciation ☐ A little of both
    ☐ Dividend income ☐ No opinion

15. Any other comments?
    _____
    _____
    _____
    _____
    _____

Again, we thank you for your assistance. Please complete the following so we may send you the Lowe's Stock Market Calculator.

Name_____

Address_____

City   State   Zip Code

Lowe's Corporate Relations Survey. Reprinted by permission.

Note the offer of a gift to improve response rate

FIGURE 7–11

Cover letter with incentive

Simmons Market Research Bureau, Inc.

April 25, 19__

Dear Survey Member:

Please help make our 21st annual TV and radio study a success. Your experience will help us to better understand viewing and listening habits in all parts of the United States.

Whether you watch TV or listen to radio a little or a lot, we need to hear from you. You have been selected to represent people like yourself. This was done according to scientific research procedures and we are not permitted to make substitutions. Your cooperation is, therefore, most important to the success of the study and will be most appreciated. Please be assured that all the information you provide is used only in a statistical form.

The TV diary and the radio diary we mentioned in the letter we sent you about ten days ago are enclosed.

We have only a limited time to complete our 19__ study and so we are asking participants to keep their TV diary for specific two-week periods. Kindly start your diary on Monday, May 2 and go through Sunday, May 15.

Please note that we are interested only in the programs you yourself watch in your own home. If on a particular day you did not watch TV, there's a place to tell us. Please answer the questions on the cover page. As an aid, some instructions are printed in the TV diary.

On each of the two days printed in your radio diary please fill in all the listening you do. We would like to know about your listening to, or hearing a radio played, in your own home, in a car or anywhere else.

On Monday, May 16 please mail us your completed TV diary and your completed radio diary in the enclosed pre-addressed return envelope. No stamp is necessary.

Thank you for your help,

Frank Stanton
President

FS:npd
Enclosures

P.S. Within 4 weeks after receiving your completed TV and radio diaries, we will mail your $5 check for your thoughtfulness. Meanwhile, please accept this $1 bill as a token of our appreciation.

SMRB 219 East 42 Street, New York, NY 10017 (212) 867-1414

FIGURE 7–12

Cover letter to questionnaire appealing to respondents' sense of altruism

NEWSTIME

Newstime Incorporated
1020 Addison Avenue
New York, NY 10020
EXECUTIVE OFFICES
(212) 555-3106

Dear Reader:

May we ask for your help?

Every so often, we at NEWSTIME survey our readers to ensure that the magazine remains relevant to their needs. You have been selected as part of a small, scientific sample of readers; thus, your response is very important to the accuracy of the survey. Your answers will, of course, be held in the strictest confidence.

This questionnaire will take only a few minutes of your time. We'll be very grateful for your help and so will these important charitable organizations:

The American Cancer Society
The United Way
The American Red Cross

Why will your participation benefit these charities? Because for every 20,000 responses we receive, we will contribute $5,000 to charity. With your help, our contributions could reach $50,000.

Won't you please complete the questionnaire now and return it to me in the postpaid return envelope.

Sincerely,

Nancy J. Hany

Nancy J. Hany
Publisher

NJH:dd

QUESTIONS FOR STUDY

1. What is a data base? How can it be accessed by computer?
2. What is the primary disadvantage to the personal interview technique?
3. In the telephone interview, what seems to be the approximate limit to the number of questions that can be asked?
4. What (or who) is the world's largest publisher?
5. Define *primary source* and *secondary source.*
6. Define and provide an example of a question that "leads" the respondent. Why are such questions unsatisfactory in questionnaires?
7. What source may be helpful in attempting to secure reports, bulletins, and brochures?
8. Books used to be considered a good source but a stale one. Has the situation changed? Explain.
9. "Tell me how you select a can of coffee when you shop," would be a question from which type of survey: mail questionnaire, telephone interview, depth interview? Explain.
10. Consider this question: "Do you approve of the terror tactics employed by leftist revolutionaries in South America?" What terms are biased in the question? Rephrase the question so that it produces a more accurate response on a questionnaire.
11. What should a cover letter accompanying a questionnaire do? List at least three objectives for the letter.
12. Why is it important that a questionnaire look easy to answer?
13. What are skip-and-jump questions? Should you use them in your research? Why?
14. What advantages does a computer search offer over manual research methods?

EXERCISES

15. Write survey questions that will produce the type of response specified:
    Structured responses

    - a question on soft drink preferences
    - a question on sleeping garments
    - a question on automobile colors

    Unstructured responses

    - a question on clerk friendliness
    - a question on company image
    - a question on customer loyalty

16. For each of the following topics, suggest three sources you would use in beginning your search for useful information. Make use of the list of sources that appears in the supplement to this chapter.
    a. financial information about a major corporation
    b. recent books on economic theory
    c. U.S. government publications on agriculture

17. Define and give examples of a "descriptor term" used in computer searches.

18. Certain words should be avoided in questionnaires. In addition to the examples cited in the text, list six words you would recommend banning from questionnaires.

19. On your campus it seems that most students are apathetic about student government and its role. Develop a cover letter that will accompany a mail questionnaire, the purpose of which is to determine why the students are uninterested in their government.

20. Secure a questionnaire, preferably one that is not more than two pages long. Evaluate it thoroughly, basing your judgments in part on the standards for questionnaires described in this chapter. You may wish to organize your comments along the lines of (1) design and content of questions, (2) logic of organization, and (3) the format of the questionnaire.

For exercises 21–29, evaluate each question posed and state whether or not it should appear in a questionnaire. Defend your choice of keeping or discarding the question.

21. Do you often purchase items other than gas and oil at service stations?
22. How much money did you make last year?
23. Consider the following attitudes toward movie theatres:

    A. too expensive   B. too crowded
    C. too dirty   D. too little parking

    Which of the following attitudes reflects your own?

A and B are true	B and C are true	A, B, C are true
B only is true	C and D are true	A, B, D are true
C only is true	A and C are true	A, C, D are true
D only is true	A and D are true	B, C, D are true
A and B are true	B and D are true	A, B, C, D are true

24. Express in writing your viewpoint on the harassment and domination of women in modern business.

25. Would you favor a greater choice in yogurt flavors even if it meant a slightly higher price?

26. Do you usually select fruit that has not been artificially ripened?

27. To begin this questionnaire, we want to know if you consider the automobile you now own, or one you have owned in the recent past (within

the last five years), to be something more than mere transportation for you or members of your family who must commute to work or school.

28. If you responded with numbers 1 or 4 to question 3, proceed to Section II. If you responded with either numbers 2 or 3, do not go on to Section II, but instead turn the page to Section III and continue with question 4 on that page.

29. How many times have you attended a movie in the past three years? How many times have you listened to a record album in the past six months? How many times have you listened to a radio broadcast of music for more than thirty minutes in the past two years?

30. Asking a question like, "What type of soup do you prefer?" can result in a wide variety of answers. That can be a problem. Take the intent of the inquiry and develop a question that will secure uniform and useful data.

31. A former professor has hired you to aid in some research. For the course the professor teaches, students are required to do a considerable amount of studying in the college library. However, the professor is not pleased with student performance. Your job is to use observation research and determine how students are studying. Then you are to make recommendations on what can be done to improve student performance. In some detail explain how you will implement the research.

32. Develop a short questionnaire to assess preferences in ice cream. Do respondents favor cones or dishes? What flavors? What brands? With what frequency do they buy? Administer the questionnaire to a specific demographic sample of at least twenty-five people. Tabulate your results.

33. Visit your university or public library to discover what facilities are available for computer searches of research topics. Develop a brief guide for others seeking to use the service.

34. Collect as much information as possible on computer-assisted data base searches available through your college. What must the researcher provide? How much does it cost? How long will it take? What does the researcher eventually receive? Draw up a short guide to computer-aided research for use by your classmates.

A RESEARCH SUPPLEMENT

The pages that follow include general comments on each secondary source category and a basic listing of useful reference guides. Since the scope of business research is often global, a section on guides to international information has also been included. Starred items in this listing (*) are available on-line.

GUIDES TO BOOKS AND BOOK REVIEWS

Guides to Books

Books in Print: An Author-Title-Series Index to the *Publishers' Trade List Annual*, New York, R. R. Bowker Co. 1948 to present.

> Issued annually, this guide lists books currently in print (with a few exceptions such as Bibles) in the United States. Entries include author, title, price, and publisher. Author and title indexes appear in separate volumes. The title volume includes a list of publishers and addresses. *Books in Print Supplement* (beginning in 1973) appears midyear between annual issues.

*Business and Economics Books and Serials in Print. New York, R. R. Bowker Co. 1981.

> This comprehensive bibliography of books and serials provides access to more than 50,000 books and 7500 periodicals in all areas of business and economics. Full bibliographic data and thorough author and/or title and subject indexing are provided for each entry. *Books in Print* and *Subject Guide to Books in Print* also list these same books along with other volumes on nonbusiness topics.

Cumulative Book Index: A World List of Books in the English Language. Bronx, NY, H. W. Wilson Co. 1928 to present.

> Issued monthly (except August) and cumulated at intervals with eventual permanent cumulations, this index lists books published in the English language throughout the world. Entries are arranged by author, title, and subject. Each cumulation includes a list of publishers.

*National Union Catalog. Washington, DC, Library of Congress, Card Division. 1942 to present.

> Printed monthly with quarterly, annual, quinquennial cumulations, this catalog includes works cataloged by the Library of Congress and by other major North American Libraries. Entries are indexed by author. Coverage has varied through the years.

Subject Guide to Books in Print: An Index to the *Publisher's Trade List Annual*. New York, R. R. Bowker Co. 1957 to present.

> Books currently in print in the U.S., as listed in *Books in Print,* are presented annually under Library of Congress subject headings.

Guides to Book Reviews

Book Review Digest. Bronx, NY, H. W. Wilson Co. 1905 to present.

> Issued monthly (except February and July) and cumulated annually, this publication lists books reviewed in more than 80 periodicals. Arranged by author, entries include quotations from a few reviews and citations to others. Subject and title indexes are included.

Book Review Index. Detroit, MI, Gale Research Co. 1965 to present.

> Issued bimonthly and cumulated annually, this index covers more than 380 periodicals in a wide range of disciplines. Citations are listed under the author reviewed with full title index in each issue. *Book Review Index 1969–1979: A Master Cumulation* provides access in a single alphabetical sequence to eleven years of material.

Current Book Review Citations. Bronx, NY, H. W. Wilson Co. 1976 to present.

> Published monthly and cumulated annually, this comprehensive index includes more than 1200 book-reviewing periodicals and subject periodicals in all major fields including business, the humanities, and the sciences. Entries are arranged by author and indexed by title.

GUIDES TO PERIODICALS, NEWSPAPERS, AND OTHER SERIALS

General Guides

Ayer Directory of Publications. Bala Cynwyd, PA, Ayer Press. 1880 to present.

> Issued annually, this directory covers some 22,800 newspapers and periodicals published in the United States. Entries include circulation statistics, rates, name of publisher, size of page, etc. The directory also includes 69 custom-made maps on which all publication cities and towns are indicated.

National Directory of Newsletters. Robert C. Thomas, ed. Detroit, MI, Gale Research Co. 1978–81.

> Issued in four parts, each part contains about 750 entries with vital information about newsletters issued on a regular basis by businesses, associations, societies, clubs, government agencies, and other groups.

Standard Periodical Directory. New York, Oxbridge Communications, Inc.
1964 to present.

> Issued annually, this classified directory provides subject access to more than
> 66,680 U.S. and Canadian periodicals. Entries, which include subscription
> rate, circulation, and basic advertising rate, are indexed alphabetically.

Periodical Indexes

Business Periodicals Index. Bronx, NY, H. W. Wilson Co.
1958 to present.

> Issued monthly (except August) and cumulated annually, this basic subject
> index for the business field covers about 275 periodicals in all business-related
> fields such as finance, labor relations, insurance, management, and advertis-
> ing. For materials prior to 1958, use the *Industrial Arts Index.*

*Engineering Index Monthly and Author Index. New York, Engineering
Index, Inc. 1896 to present.

> This monthly index (formerly *Engineering Index*) provides abstracting and index-
> ing services for the world's engineering literature. Data from technical maga-
> zines, government bureaus, and research laboratories are recorded as well as
> abstracts of reports, book reviews, and articles. This index is available on-line
> as *Compendex.*

*F&S Index United States. Cleveland, OH, Predicasts, Inc.
1960 to present.

> Issued weekly and cumulated monthly, quarterly, and annually, this index pro-
> vides a brief summary of articles from about 1200 published sources reporting
> U.S. business and technical events. It is a companion index to *F & S Index Inter-
> national* and *F & S Index Europe.* Entries are arranged in two parts: part one, by
> SIC number or product; and part two, by company. Major articles are desig-
> nated by a black spot preceding the journal title. This index is available on-line
> on the *Predicasts Terminal System.*

Index of Economic Articles. Homewood, IL, Richard D. Irwin, Inc.
1965 to present.

> This index (formerly *Index of Economic Journals*) lists articles in English for more
> than 140 principal economic journals of various countries. Coverage varies: vol.
> 1, 1886–1924; vol. 2, 1925–1939; vol. 3, 1940–1949; vol. 4, 1950–1954; vol. 5, 1955–
> 1959; vol. 6, 1960–1963; vol. 6A, 1960–1963 Collective Volumes; vol. 7, 1964–1965;
> vol. 7A, 1964–1965 Collective Volumes; and vol. 8, 1966. Frequency is annual
> after 1966. Arranged by a detailed classification scheme, citations are full and
> precise with an author index in each volume. Beginning with vol. 6A, coverage
> includes collective volumes such as Festschriften, conference reports and
> papers, and collected essays.

Readers' Guide to Periodical Literature. Bronx, NY, H. W. Wilson Co. 1900 to present.

> Issued semimonthly (except monthly in February, July, and August), this index provides author and subject access to about 190 popular periodicals. This valuable guide contains references to articles in a broad range of fields.

Social Science Index. Bronx, NY, H. W. Wilson Co. 1974 to present.

> Issued quarterly and cumulated annually, this index (which supersedes, in part, the *Social Science and Humanities Index*) provides author and subject access to articles in more than 275 journals. Subject areas covered include anthropology, area studies, economics, environmental science, geography, law and criminology, planning and public administration, political science, psychology, sociology, and related topics. An author listing of citations to book reviews follows the main body of the index.

More Specialized Indexes

*Accountants' Index. New York, American Institute of Certified Public Accountants. 1920 to present.

> Issued quarterly and cumulated annually, this index provides author, title, and subject access to English-language journals, books, and government documents in accounting and related fields. Frequency of earlier volumes varies.

Index to Legal Periodicals. Bronx, NY, H. W. Wilson Co. 1908 to present.

> Published monthly and cumulated annually, this index covers 417 major legal periodicals in all areas of jurisprudence. This three-part index includes a subject and author index, a table of cases, and a book-review index.

*Management Contents. Northbrook, IL, Management Contents, Inc. 1975 to present.

> Issued biweekly, this guide reproduces the tables of contents from about 285 of the best U.S. and foreign business journals, proceedings, and transactions.

*Social Sciences Citation Index. Philadelphia, PA, Institute for Scientific Information. 1972 to present.

> Issued three times a year with the third issue cumulating the year, this international, multidisciplinary index covers more than 1500 journals and 200 books in the social, behavioral, and related sciences. It enables the user to identify related writings by indication of sources in which a known work by a given author has been cited. The "Permuterm Subject Index" provides subject access. Available on-line as *Social Sci-search*.

Newspaper Indexes

Bell & Howell Newspaper Index. Wooster, OH, Bell & Howell.

> Issued monthly and cumulated annually, newspaper indexes are issued for the following papers: *Chicago Sun Times,* 1979 to present; *Chicago Tribune,* 1972 to present; *Christian Science Monitor,* 1949 to present; *Denver Post,* 1979 to present; *Detroit News,* 1976 to present; *Houston Post,* 1976 to present; *Los Angeles Times,* 1972 to present; *New Orleans Times Picayune,* 1972 to present; *St. Louis Post Dispatch,* 1970 to present; *San Francisco Chronicle,* 1976 to present; and *Washington Post,* 1971 to present. Entries in each index are arranged by subjects and by personal names.

*New York Times Index. New York, New York Times Co. 1913 to present.

> Issued twice a month and cumulated annually, this index summarizes and classifies news alphabetically and chronologically by subject, by person, and by organization name. This index is available on-line on the *New York Times Information Bank.* (The *Wall Street Journal,* the *Washington Post,* and the *Financial Times* are also included in this data bank.)

The Wall Street Journal Index. New York, Dow Jones and Co. 1958 to present.

> Issued monthly and cumulated annually, this index covers the New York edition of the *Journal.* Entries are arranged in two parts, corporate news and general news.

GUIDES TO GOVERNMENT DOCUMENTS

General Guides

Andriot, John L., ed. Guide to U.S. Government Publications, McLean, VA, Documents Index. 1981 (available only in microfiche).

> This annotated guide (formerly *Guide to U.S. Government Serials and Periodicals*) lists publications of the various U.S. government agencies. Volume 1 lists those publications in existence as of January 1, 1975; volume 2 covers publications of abolished agencies and discontinued publications; volume 3 contains a detailed description of the SuDoc classification scheme and agency chronology.

Directory of Government Document Collections and Librarians. 3rd ed. Government Documents Round Table, American Library Association, comp. Washington, DC, Congressional Information Service. 1981.

> Arranged alphabetically by state and city, this directory covers the government document holdings of more than 2700 U.S. libraries. Entries include detailed descriptions of libraries and their collections and names of staff members working with documents as well as information on library policies concerning public access, circulation, and interlibrary loans. Entries are indexed by library name, library staff name, and subject.

U.S. Catalogs, Indexes, and Bibliographies

*CIS/Index. Washington, DC, Congressional Information Service, Inc. 1970 to present.

> Published monthly and cumulated quarterly and annually, this source provides access to U.S. congressional publications and legislation. Coverage includes both depository and nondepository committee hearings and prints; House and Senate reports, documents, and special publications; and Senate executive reports and documents. Issued in two parts: part one is an index of briefly annotated entries corresponding to full document descriptions in part two.

*Federal Index. Cleveland, OH, Predicasts, Inc. 1977 to present.

> Issued annually, this index is divided into three sections allowing subject access by government agency, by government function, or by affected industries, persons, institutions, or countries. Coverage includes more than 60,000 key articles appearing in the Congressional Record, the Federal Register, and the Weekly Compilation of Presidential Documents. Entries include government agency involved, action taken or proposed, citation to U.S. Code, code of Federal Register, etc., and journal abbreviation, date, and page reference. Available on-line on the *Predicasts Terminal System*.

*Selected United States Government Publications. U.S. Superintendent of Documents. Washington, DC, Government Printing Office.

> Issued monthly, this annotated guide lists new publications for sale by the Government Printing Office as well as important older publications still in stock.

GUIDES TO U.S. STATISTICAL SOURCES

General Guides and Indexes

*American Statistics Index. Washington, DC, Congressional Information Service, Inc. 1974 to present.

> Published monthly and cumulated quarterly and annually, this comprehensive guide provides access to data in more than 7000 statistical publications of the U.S. government. Coverage includes every type of U.S. government document, regardless of depository status, whether issued by the Government Printing Office or an individual agency. The index is published in two parts: part one is an index of briefly annotated entries corresponding to full document descriptions in part two. This is a companion service to *Statistical Reference Index*.

Statistical Reference Index. Washington, DC, Congressional Information Service, Inc. 1980 to present.

> Published monthly and cumulated quarterly and annually, this companion service to *American Statistics Index* includes significant statistical publications from more than 1000 non-U.S. government associations and institutes. Topics covered include business, industry, finance, and economic and social conditions. The index is published in two parts: part one is an index of briefly annotated entries corresponding to full document descriptions in part two.

Comprehensive Statistical Compilations

Standard & Poor's Statistical Service. New York, Standard & Poor's Corp. 1941 to present.

> Issued monthly and cumulated annually, this service provides statistical time series in the following areas: banking and finance, production and labor prices indexes; income and trade; building and building materials; transportation and communications; electric power and fuels; metals; autos, rubber, and tires; textiles; chemicals; paper; agricultural products; and securities prices.

*Statistical Abstract of the United States. U.S. Bureau of the Census. Washington, DC, Government Printing Office. 1978 to present.

> Issued annually, this guide serves both as the prime source for U.S. industrial, social, political, and economic statistics and as a bibliographic guide. The majority of tables are national in scope, providing one or two years of consecutive annual data. Source notes are given at the foot of each table. The "Guide to Sources and Statistics" section lists important statistical publications by subject including a descriptive list of recent Census publications. The *Statistical History of the United States from Times to the Present* (New York: Basic Books, 1976) serves as a historical supplement to *Statistical Abstract.*

BASIC SPECIALIZED COMPILATIONS

*Business Statistics. U.S. Bureau of Economic Analysis. Washington, DC, Government Printing Office. 1951 to present.

> Issued as a supplement to *Survey of Current Business*, this publication provides a historical record of the more than 2500 statistical series appearing in the *Survey.* Tables give annual averages, beginning with 1947, and monthly figures for the most recent five years. Sources, references, and explanatory notes are included.

*Handbook of Labor Statistics. U.S. Bureau of Labor Statistics. Washington, DC, Government Printing Office. 1924–26 to present.

> This compendium of major BLS statistics provides figures for as many years as they have been compiled. Statistics given include those for the labor force, employment, unemployment, productivity, prices and living conditions, and foreign labor statistics.

GUIDES TO DIRECTORIES

General Guides

Guide to American Directories. 10th ed. New York, B. Klein Publications. 1978.

> Arranged by subject, this directory includes more than 6000 major industrial and professional directories. Entries include description and price and are indexed alphabetically. Industrial directories are listed under the "Manufacturers" heading.

Basic U.S. Company Directories

Dun & Bradstreet, Inc. Million Dollar Directory. New York, Dun & Bradstreet, Inc. 1959 to present.

> Issued annually, this three-volume directory lists over 120,000 U.S. companies with an indicated worth of $500,000 to $1 million or more. Volume 1 covers 49,000 of the top companies ranked by net worth; volumes 2 and 3 cover the remaining companies (many of them privately held). Entries include names of officers and directors, products or services, SIC number, approximate sales, and number of employees. Each volume contains a complete alphabetical index to all companies in the set. Entries within each volume are also indexed by geographical location and by industry.

Standard & Poor's Register of Corporations, Directors and Executives. New York, Standard & Poor's Corp. 1928 to present.

> This three-volume directory lists more than 37,000 U.S., Canadian, and major international corporations. Volume 1 is an alphabetical listing with information on officers, products or line of business, stock exchange listing, SIC number, sales range, and number of employees. Volume 2 lists executives and directors with a brief profile on each. Volume 3 contains an index of companies by SIC and by location, a list of companies and a list of executives added for the first time, and an obituary section.

COMPUTERIZED INFORMATION SYSTEMS/DATA BASES

Computerized information systems place mountains of information at your fingertips.[5] You or your library can subscribe to various on-line data base sources. In so doing you can secure continuously updated news reports, stock quotations, bond listings, and other data. You can also get a list of all, or almost all, of the articles available on a topic you are researching. In other words, you can eliminate most of the tedious hours spent in library research by using computerized data bases. Think of the data base as a computerized library organized in such a way that many users may secure what they wish quickly and easily.

Some data base services such as DIALOG and Bibliograph Research Services (BRS) were designed to be used primarily by research specialists working in business, professional, and educational institutions. On-line data bases can be classified into three types:

1. Reference data bases direct the user to articles, books, and other reference sources on a specific topic. You may search for items by using key words, dates, and authors' names. Summaries or abstracts (see Figure 7–1) of the sources cited are often available on-line. Some services will also provide a copy of the full printed text for a fee of $5 to $12. DIALOG provides such a service.

2. Full-text data bases will place on your computer screen a full text copy of an article or news story. Several data bases having this capability are available from LEXIS, NEXIS, Dow Jones News Retrieval (DJNR), and NewsNet.

3. Source data bases provide information on stock market quotations, airline schedules, physical and chemical properties of various items, and miscellaneous topics.

Various data bases have been designed for professional use. Among these are LEXIS for lawyers; MEDLARS for medical specialists; Data Resources, Inc. DIALOG Information Retrieval Service, DJNR, for business people; and Bibliographic Retrieval Services, Inc. (BRS), for specialists in a variety of areas.

There are now some 350 on-line services that offer at least 2400 data bases. This number is growing rapidly. You can keep track of them with Cuadra Associates' *Directory of On-Line Data Bases*. It lists data bases by producer and subject, describes each one, and indicates which on-line service offers it.

[5]See "Let a Data Base Get You the Facts," *Changing Times,* Oct. 1984.

Data Base Services

The following are just a few of the more frequently used services:

Bibliographic Retrieval
Services (BRS)
1200 Route 7
Latham, NY 12110

Over 80 data bases covering physical
and social sciences, business,
education, medicine

Data Resources, Inc. (DRI)
29 Hartwell Avenue
Lexington, MA 02173

Over 100 economic and financial data
bases, including demographic and
stock market data

DIALOG Information
Retrieval Service
3460 Hillview Avenue
Palo Alto, CA 94304

Over 200 scientific, technological,
general news and business data
bases. Abstracts and some full texts
available

Dow Jones News Retrieval
P.O. Box 300
Princeton, NJ 08540

Full text news from Wall Street
Journal and other Dow Jones sources.
Emphasis on business and finance

LEXIS
Mead Data Control
9393 Springboro Pike
P.O. Box 933
Dayton, OH 45401

Federal and state laws, tax codes,
specialty law

NEXIS
Mead Data Control
9393 Springboro Pike
P.O. Box 933
Dayton, OH 45401

Full text articles from over 120
newspapers, magazines, and
periodicals; NAARS is a data base of
annual reports and proxy statements

MEDLARS
National Library of Medicine
8600 Rockville Pike
Bethesda, MD 20209

Biomedical data bases referencing
international medical literature

Data Bases

ABI/Inform. Louisville, KY, Data Courier, Inc. 1971 to present.

> This management data base provides on-line access to citations and abstracts from 475 English language journals covering such subject areas as finance, management, economics, business law, and marketing. Offers information similar to what can be found in the *Business Periodicals Index*.

Management Contents. Skokie, IL, Management Contents, Inc. 1975 to present.

> This management data base provides on-line access to citations and abstracts from about 325 U.S. and foreign management journals, proceedings, and transactions (the printed index is also listed later).

Predicasts Terminal System. Cleveland, OH, Predicasts, Inc.

> This comprehensive on-line system combines bibliographic and statistical data elements. Individual files on the system include *F & S Indexes,* from 1972 to present, and *Federal Index,* from 1976 to present (both printed indexes are listed here), *PTS International Time Series* and *PTS International Forecasts* (both described here as *World Product Casts* and *World Regional Casts*); *PTS U.S. Time Series* (described here as *Predicasts Basebook*); *PTS U.S. Forecasts* (described here as *Predicasts*); and *PTS Promt,* which includes selected materials from *F & S Indexes,* which have been abstracted in detail.

Accountants' Index. American Institute of Accountants, New York. 1974 to present.

> The hardcopy equivalent is the *Accountants' Index.*

Dissertation Abstracts On-line. Ann Arbor, MI, University Microfilms International, 1861 to present.

> The hardcopy equivalent is *Dissertation Abstracts International.*

Guides to Information Systems and Services

*Directory of On-line Databases. Santa Monica, CA, Cuadra Associates, Inc. 1979 to present.

> Issued quarterly, this directory includes more than 400 on-line bibliographic and nonbibliographic data bases. Entries for data bases include producer name, organization through which it is available, type and amount of information, geographical and chronological coverage, and frequency of updating. Entries are indexed by subject, data base name, producer name, and on-line organization name.

*Encyclopedia of Information Systems and Services. Anthony T. Kruzas, ed. Detroit, MI, Gale Research Co. 1971 to present.

> Issued biennially, this international guide includes about 2000 organizations, including many in countries other than the U.S. Types of organizations include computerized data bases, SDI services, data base publishers, clearing houses and information centers, library information networks, data collection and analysis centers, micrographic systems and services, and consulting research and coordinating agencies. Arranged alphabetically by organization or service and indexed in multiple ways, entries include description of system or service, input or data sources, microform or computer applications and services, and computer and information-processing equipment. The supplements are called *New Information Systems and Services.*

RESOURCES IN BUSINESS COMMUNICATION

Bibliographies

Alred, G. J.; Reep, D. C., and Limaye, M. R., *Business and Technical Writing: An Annotated Bibliography of Books, 1880–1980* (Scarecrow Press, 1981)

Renwick, George W., *The Management of Intercultural Relations in International Business: A Directory of Resources* (Intercultural Press, 1982).

Walsh, R.M., and Birkin, S.J., *Business Communications* (Greenwood Press, 1980).

Journals

ABCA Bulletin (Quarterly)

Communications News (Monthly)

Journal of Business Communication (Quarterly)

Journal of Communication (Quarterly)

Journal of Communication Management (Quarterly)

Journal of Management Communication (Quarterly)

Telecommunications (Monthly)

Helpful Subject Headings in Card Catalogs

Americans in Foreign Countries

Business Report Writing

Commercial Correspondence

Communication

Communication in Management

Corporation Reports

Information Theory

Intercultural Communication

International Business Enterprises—
   Personnel Management

Interpersonal Communication

Interviewing

Listening

Meetings

Negotiation

Nonverbal Communication

Office Management

Oral Communication

Persuasion

Proposal Writing in Business

Public Relations—Authorship

Public Speaking

Report Writing

Technical Writing

Telecommunication

Word Processing

Legal Considerations

BUSINESS RESEARCH AND THE LAW

To what information do you have a legal right? The answer to that question differs dramatically, depending on whether you seek data from private or public sources.

PRIVATELY HELD INFORMATION

The Fair Credit Reporting Act of 1970 (Title VI of the Consumer Credit Protection Act) restricts access to information about your financial and employment history. Credit reporting agencies are required by this legislation to tell you the names and addresses of those to whom information is reported. Any organization reporting second-hand information or making subjective statements about your credit has the legal responsibility under Title VI to

- provide protection from false information
- inform you of communication regarding your credit
- allow access to you to your own credit information

Libel and slander laws further constrain the release of subjective judgments about people's actions and characters, even in such areas as recommendation letters. If an employee asks for a letter of recommendation from you, remember that you may be subject to suit if, in the employee's view, your letter misrepresents his or her abilities or character. Specific damages to be awarded to the employee could be substantial wages supposedly lost as a result of your letter.

Due to such cases, fewer negative recommendation letters are written today than in previous decades. Instead, managers choose a "code language" of less-than-enthusiastic but nonactionable euphemisms. Words like "capable," "diligent," and "steady" can be used to describe an unmotivated low performer. Managers sometimes decline the request for a recommendation letter altogether, or ask that a waiver be signed by the employee, foregoing his or her right to see your letter.

Your ability to seek information from private sources, therefore, is often a matter of law, not simply what the private source will permit.

PUBLICLY HELD INFORMATION

Much more legislation guides the handling of information by public institutions. The Freedom of Information Act of 1966 permits individuals greater access to records maintained by the federal government. As amended in 1974, the legislation defines what kind of information the government must release and in what time frame the delivery of information must occur.

One result of "sunshine" legislation such as the Privacy Act of 1974 and the Family Education Rights and Privacy Act of 1974 has been the discovery of many sensitive business secrets. The many forms and registrations that must be filed by companies large and small are now, in large part, available for public scrutiny—including the eyes of competitors. One difficult task for security-conscious managers is how to meet governmental filing requirements without giving away valuable or sensitive company secrets.

As a case in point, until 1980 the reprimands, orders, and instructions of bank regulators to banks under their scrutiny were hidden from the public. But late in that year the Consumers Union, acting under the Freedom of Information Act, successfully sued three bank regulators for release of consent agreements and cease-and-desist orders to banks. For the first time, consumers were able to read and evaluate those agencies' orders and to make their banking decisions accordingly.

The cumulative result of such legislation and court action has been the elimination of most "secret files" from government agencies. Managers of those agencies are now forced to make a regular review of what kinds of information they hold on file. Private sector managers, at the same time, have become more cautious about information they release to such "transparent" government files. An ongoing struggle continues between the need for "sunshine" freedom of information versus the understandable desire of companies to protect their product and marketing secrets.

8 Reports for Decision Making

Effective decision-making is completely dependent on effective reporting.

Managers at all levels are required to make decisions. Sometimes these decisions are simple, such as a decision to hire a part-time clerk to assist in the office, or to ship merchandise via rail instead of truck. At other times a decision may involve closing down one of the company's plants and throwing 1400 people out of work, or acquiring a firm with annual sales of $42 million. These decisions, major or minor, simple or complex, near-term or long-range, are arrived at after all the necessary information has been reviewed and evaluated.

The information is given to the decision maker through some form of report. The report may be written or oral, long or short, a hefty computer printout or a combination of several formats. Whatever its length, the report must be complete, specific, and accurate. All necessary facets of the problem or situation must be presented; all conclusions must be carefully drawn; and all recommendations must be thoroughly substantiated.

A report should be factual, objective presentation of information. Some reports also interpret and evaluate the information given. Others not only present and interpret information, but are also persuasive in tone. When the purpose is other than the objective presentation of data, that fact should be stated clearly.

Most reports are part of the decision-making process. Even the short personnel status information report issued each Monday will eventually play a role in the quarterly action (decision) of the vice-president of personnel. His or her future, that of associates, and not infrequently that of the company, are dependent on the decisions he or she makes. And these decisions are dependent on the reports received.

DIRECTIONS OF FLOW

A variety of reports move up to the manager. Some deal with special problems. Others are turned in by each department head at periodic intervals. The periodic reports are frequently written, but they may also be oral, as in an interview or a conference. The manager also receives data through informal communication: while waiting in the lunch line, in a casual chat while walking down the corridor, from the attitudes reflected by various persons in conversations and at meetings. In addition, the modern manager receives data reports from the computer: sales volume, personnel turnover, inventory levels, production quantities, and a dozen other facts concerning an organization's activities. These data, when properly interpreted and evaluated, are of enormous help to a decision maker.

Reports also travel down, bringing information to every member of an organization. The data contained in these reports help guide employees and give further direction to continuing activities.[1]

And for each department or division to function most efficiently, reports should travel laterally. Certainly it helps the sales manager to be aware of the status of production, the problems of personnel, and the plans of marketing. However, such lateral communication operates rather haphazardly in most companies. Many department heads *must* send information up because their superiors require it. The manager *must* send information down if his or her department is to function effectively. But managers are often too busy (or think they are too busy) to communicate laterally. Furthermore, managers' interest in other departments is usually minimal, unless something arises unexpectedly that forces them to consult with other department heads. For these reasons, lateral communication does not always take place effectively.

CAN REPORTS BE CLASSIFIED?

As you have seen, a **report** is a message (usually objective) that conveys information from one organization (or organizational level) to another to assist in decision-making and problem-solving. This definition characterizes all reports. But there are many ways of classifying reports:

Formal or Informal The *formal* report often is very elaborate and well organized, with carefully drawn conclusions and thoroughly substantiated recommendations. In most cases, this report is detailed and objective. Such

---

[1]See P. Drucker, "What Communication Means," in the Readings section, for comments on downward communication.

reports may be the result of scientific and technical research or investigative business research. An example of an *informal* report is an interoffice memo used to transfer relatively routine information from one department to another.

Long or Short This classification is not very useful. Certainly the routine half-page memo is a short report, while the 35-page "Analysis of Consumer Preferences for . . ." is a long report. But how does one classify a five-page progress report? A four-page letter report? A three-page periodic report? Because the long report is usually formal and the short report is informal, formal-informal designations are used most often.

Informational vs. Other Purposes Many reports are strictly *informational;* their primary purpose is to convey information for problem solving or decision making. Other reports may be analytical, persuasive, comparative, or argumentative. These are usually rather detailed (see Chapter 11 for an expanded discussion).

Internal or External When we look in the organization, we find reports called *progress* reports. These usually permit a superior to know the progress an individual or team is making (sometimes out in the field) on a particular assignment or problem. There are also *periodic reports,* which may be distributed either internally or externally at designated times: daily, weekly, monthly, quarterly, semiannually, and annually. These are often quantitative in nature and used for comparison with a previous period or periods.

Computer-Generated or Written by Humans With the increased processing power of new silicon chips and programming advances spawned by artificial intelligence ("AI") research, many reports can now be generated by computer. It is important that they be clearly labelled as such. Readers must understand that selection and interpretation of data within computer reports are only as good as the program that generates them. More than one executive has picked up the phone to ask about a particular point in a report, only to hear the response, "We don't know. The computer generates those."

Functional Reports These are often issued by a functional department such as accounting, marketing, or finance. Obviously, the same "marketing report" may also be called an analytical, formal, or even progress report, depending on its content.

Here's the point: report classifications are quite arbitrary and any one report may quite often be placed—quite legitimately—in any one or more different classifications. However, you should be familiar with the terms, as you will undoubtedly hear them during your business career.

REPORT CONTROL

The management of every company must place report control high on its list of cost-saving exercises. Report requirements, including those from the computer, should be reviewed periodically. In this way some reports can be eliminated, others combined, and, where necessary, news ones initiated.

Many firms find that it is efficient to conduct a **report inventory** each year. Necessary reports are continued; others are dropped. Eliminating an ongoing report is obviously difficult without the support of top management; therefore, the person responsible for report control must possess adequate authority. Some people in the organization will be unhappy when their reports are eliminated or incorporated into existing ones. Part of their work responsibility has been dropped, and they are likely to feel that their importance has been lessened. However, once an inventory policy is announced, supported, and carried through for two or three years, the task becomes routine and—more important—valuable to the firm.

Carrying through a report inventory is not easy. Whoever is responsible for this task must first list all reports issued in a department or the organization. He or she must then visit each of those designated as a receiver on the report distribution list. Each designated recipient must then indicate whether he or she found a given report to be "of no value," "of some value," or "very valuable." Once the recipients' responses are on record, a decision by a senior person is made to retain, eliminate, or combine reports.

Keep in mind, however, the task is not easy. Eliminating a report is sometimes viewed as eliminating "good old Marty's job." Of almost equal importance is the report author's identification with the report and his or her ego involvement. Nevertheless, report control (or elimination) is a critical function in today's business world.

REPORT SECURITY

A ten-page report can cost the company thousands of dollars in labor and overhead to produce. But that report in the wrong hands can cost the company millions. Because reports contain new-product information, market projections, personnel assessments, strategy formulations, and other matters of proprietary interest, they are a popular target for industrial theft and espionage.

Increasingly, therefore, companies are limiting the "hard copy" distribution of sensitive reports to only the most trusted readers. Channels of distribution, similarly, are guarded: hand-picked couriers within the company may be the only ones besides readers to have physical possession of the document. "For Eyes Only" is often marked at the beginning of the report, indicating that any photocopying of its pages is strictly against company policy.

Shredding also plays a part in report security. When reports have served their communication purpose, all copies—usually numbered for inventory—are routinely gathered and shredded. Reference copies are retained in company vaults and in protected computer files.

WHAT TO REPORT

A question that frequently arises is: what does management want in reports? A number of years ago a study was made at Westinghouse in an effort to find some answers to this question. Here is an excerpt from the article describing the study.

> *When a manager reads a report, he looks for pertinent facts and competent opinions that will aid him in problem solving and/or decision making. He wants to know right away whether he should read the report, route it, or skip it. To determine this, he wants answers fast to some or all of the following questions:*
> *What's the report about and who wrote it?*
> *What does it contribute?*
> *What are its conclusions and recommendations?*
> *What are their importance and significance?*
> *What's the implication to the Company?*
> *What actions are suggested? Short range? Long range? By whom? When? How?*
>
> *The manager wants this information in brief, concise, and meaningful statements. He wants it at the beginning of the report and all in one piece.*
>
> *For example, if a summary is to convey information efficiently, it should contain three kinds of facts:*
> *1. What the report is about;*
> *2. The significance and implications of the work; and*
> *3. The action called for . . .*
>
> *Such summaries are informative and useful, and should be placed at the beginning of the report . . .*[2]

This study also indicates that several conferences should be held while the report is being written. The first conference should define the problem and the project. At this point, the report writer learns just what he or she is to do, what kind of report is desired, and how his or her work relates to the decisions to be made.

A second conference should be held after research and investigation have been completed. At this time the report writer can discuss with the manager the findings, their implications, and the evidence discovered. The manager, on the basis of greater experience and overall view of company

---

[2]From "What to Report" by Richard W. Dodge, in *Westinghouse Engineer,* Westinghouse Electric Corporation. Used by permission.

activities, can suggest further investigation or additional areas to be surveyed. He or she may also suggest areas of emphasis, along with the order and methods of presentation.

In the third conference, the final outline should be reviewed. If changes in organizational structure are needed, this is the time to make them—*before* the report is written.

A fourth meeting should take place after the report is written. At this time the manager may suggest a distribution list, the strategy of presentation, and minor changes.

WRITING A REPORT

Long or short, simple or complex, most reports follow a basic pattern. Some of the steps may be touched lightly in very short reports or even skipped, but the order is common to all. Almost anyone can write an excellent report if he or she will (1) observe the communication rules of clarity, conciseness, completeness, and accuracy, and (2) follow the logical series of steps given below:

Define the problem clearly and accurately

Understand the purpose

Identify the reader

Limit the topic

Draw up a tentative outline

Define the depth or scope of the report segments

Formulate a research plan

Carry through research
   From secondary sources
   From primary sources

Tabulate the quantitative data gathered

Evaluate all material

Edit the data

Interpret the data

Complete a detailed outline

Write a rough draft

Insert tables, graphs, and other visuals

Draw up supplements

Edit the rough draft

Write the final copy

Plan the presentation strategy

TEN FATAL ILLS IN BUSINESS WRITING[1]
... and what to do about them

1. **Anemic Verbs** (is, are, was, were, seems to be)
   Not: It is the policy of this company to promote creative thinkers.
   Instead: This company promotes creative thinkers.
2. **Impotent Verbs** (passive constructions)
   Not: The account was handled carelessly.
   (The perpetrator can escape visibility if passive constructions are used.)
   Instead: Jack Bevins handled the account carelessly.
3. **Atrophy of the Position of Emphasis**
   Not: There are two financial packages suited to our needs.
   (Initial strong position wasted on meaningless words)
   Instead: Two financial packages suit our needs.
4. **Distended Sentence Length**
   Not: While seven of our managers at the midlevel range object to the idea of moving our corporate offices, the majority of our senior staff is agreeable to the move and sees it as an opportunity to live in the sun belt.
   Instead: Seven midlevel managers object to moving our corporate offices. Most of the senior staff, however, welcome the move as a chance to live in the sun belt.
5. **Hypertrophy of the Noun**
   Not: The unification of companies will prove beneficial to the establishment of financial arrangements more conducive to solvency and profitability. (Avoid swollen Latinate nouns.)
   Instead: Merging our companies will help solve our money problems.

[1]Arthur H. Bell from *Nation's Business*, Nov. 1984 Copyright © 1984 by Nation's Business. Reprinted by permission.

This plan should be carried out for every report; actually, many of these steps become almost mechanical for the efficient writer. And a few may even be skipped if the nature of the report or the situation permits.

Because many of these steps were discussed earlier, we won't review them here. However, it is important to keep in mind that an excellent report can usually be produced when a series of logical steps is followed.

Once the initial steps (the identification and/or design of the problem, purpose, reader, specific topic area, tentative outline, and establishment of the depth of each subtopic area) have been carried through, the report writer may proceed to information and data collection.

Research Design and Hypothesis

Here again care must be taken. It would be easy to collect a truckload of material. But it is pointless to send out thousands of questionnaires, hold dozens of interviews, examine hundreds of company documents, and evaluate the

6. **Slow Sentence Pulse**

Try mixing Subject-Verb-Object sentences with other types:

Frustrated, Jerry wrote a scorching memo.

(-ed beginning before the subject)

The storeroom, long an eyesore on the fourth floor, is scheduled for remodeling.

(Subject, break, verb)

His taxes were due, but his wallet was empty. (Subject/verb, then subject/verb)

7. **Obese Paragraphs**

Try "easy in and easy out," using very short paragraphs at the beginning and end of business letters, memos and short reports.

8. **Noun Clots**

Not: Please write a minorities opportunity evaluation report.

Instead: Please write a report evaluating opportunities for minorities.

9. **Spastic Repetitions**

Not: We reviewed the benefits package. The benefits package provided for . . .

Instead: We reviewed the benefits package, which provided for . . .

10. **Contagious Prepositions**

Not: We ran an advertisement in a trade journal in May for a manager of the sales division at our subsidiary in Wisconsin.

Instead: "Sales manager," "Wisconsin subsidiary" (Combine prepositional phrases into adjective/noun combinations.)

contents of scores of articles, bulletins, reports, and pamphlets, if such effort is not required. The questions to ask are: what research design will best serve our needs and at the same time conserve our time and funds? How can we obtain the data we need with the least amount of time, money, and effort?

We may decide, in a particular case, that our research design should include:

A search of company records

An evaluation of secondary sources
Magazines
Journals
Newspapers

A check of government publications
Technical reports
Translations

A series of 20 interviews with company production managers

After we get into the research, we may have to modify our design. Perhaps the material in the journals doesn't fill our needs, and more emphasis must be placed on interviews; or perhaps the findings presented in the government reports are so definitive, complete, and up-to-date that there is no need for the questionnaire or interview survey. But we can't be sure until we begin to use the research materials and evaluate their adequacy.

To help give direction to the research, the investigator will usually formulate a hypothesis. A **hypothesis** is a statement that may be proved or disproved as a result of research findings. For example, we may wonder if premiums will increase the sales of our Sunshine Cake Mix by 10 percent per month, as measured against monthly sales last year. Our hypothesis might then be: *Sales of Sunshine Cake Mix will rise 10 percent during 19___ as compared to 19___ when Kitchen Brite premiums are given with the product.* This is a positive hypothesis whose validity can be tested through research.

Because of the importance of research to the business manager, Chapter 7 is devoted to that topic. A research supplement at the end of that chapter lists guides and indexes to information sources as well as techniques for research in primary and secondary sources.

Documenting the Report

Readers rely on footnotes and bibliographic references as substantiation for points within the report and as resources for further investigation. Not every assertion in a report can or should be documented, of course. Let's say, for example, that you refer in your report to America's 255 million citizens. It would not be necessary to cite the latest census or the World Almanac—your assertion can be accepted on its merits as commonly known information. If, however, you assert information that is not generally known or relies heavily on the work of others, that information should be referenced by a footnote and bibliographic entry.

A footnote can be used for purposes other than to provide citation references. It can be used effectively to

- cite information relevant to the report but not important enough to appear in the body of the report itself
- cite data in support of statements made in the body of the report
- cite other points of view
- note differences among authorities in the field
- offer critical evaluations of major sources—for example, a comment on the large sample in a survey or inaccuracies in a book

Footnotes can appear at the bottom ("foot") of the page or, as endnotes, at the end of the chapter, section, or report. Many readers prefer the latter system since all notes are gathered there in one location for ease of reference.

There are several accepted forms of footnotes. The system exemplified below, that of the Modern Language Association, remains the most common for nontechnical/nonscientific reports. For documenting the latter reports, see the American Psychological Association (APA) stylesheet.

A number of abbreviations are used in source documentation, though the use of Latinate terms is fading. Two terms still common (but becoming less so) in report documentation are *ibid.* and *op. cit. Ibid.*, from the latin *ibidem*, means "in the same place," indicating that the source is identical to the one preceding. *"Ibid., p. 45"* means that the source is the same except that the page to which reference is made is now 45. *Op. Cit.*, from the latin *opere citato* ("in the work cited"), refers the reader to a source previously cited but not immediately preceding. As noted in the examples below, the author's last name is now usually used in place of *ibid.* or *op. cit.*

SUGGESTED FOOTNOTE FORMS

Single Book Author

F.W. Morgan, <u>Electronic Communication for the 1980s,</u> 2nd ed. (New York: Brendon Press, 1986), p. 230.

Two or More Book Authors

Victor Velasquez and Ramon Ortega, <u>Management Techniques in South America</u> (Houston, Texas: International Press, 1987), p. 392.

Edited Books

Martin C. Benson, ed., <u>Speakers on Speaking,</u> 3rd ed. (Boston: National Publishers, Inc., 1988), p. 334.

Journal or Magazine Article

Henry Gwent, "Communicating Bad News," <u>Personnel Development,</u> 60, no. 3 (March, 1988), p. 78.

Later References

`Morgan, p. 235.` (If more than one book by Morgan has been cited, refer also to the intended title.)

`Velasquez, p. 399.` (Note that for multi-author books and articles, only the first author need be cited.)

Articles Without Named Authors

`The Wall St. Journal,` Feb. 6, 1988, p. 34. (Titles of articles may be cited, if relevant, and are included before the name of the journal or newspaper.)

Placed at the end of a report after endnotes, a bibliography differs from footnotes primarily in that it gathers together not only works referenced in the report but also works that the reader may wish to consult for further reading. Bibliographic items appear in alphabetical order, not order of appearance in the text. When books, articles, and other sources are grouped separately, items within each group are alphabetized.

Note that the author's last name appears first.

SUGGESTED BIBLIOGRAPHY FORMS

`Gwent, Henry. "Communicating Bad News," Personnel Development,` 60, no. 3 (March, 1988), 70–84.

`Morgan, F.W. Electronic Communication for the 1980s,` 2nd ed. New York: Brendon Press, 1986.

`Velasquez, Victor and Ramon Ortega, Management Techniques in South America.` Houston, Texas: International Press, 1987.

`The Wall St. Journal,` Feb. 6, 1988, p. 34.

For other reference situations, consult the MLA Stylesheet, the Chicago Manual of Style, or another standard reference.

ALTERNATIVE DOCUMENTATION STYLES

Most technical documents and some business documents use the APA (American Psychological Association) style for documentation. Note the differences particularly in placement of date and use of abbreviated author citation. These examples follow the style of the APA Publication Manual.

Book—One Author

> Johnson, B. (1987). Social Welfare for the 1990s. New York: Brandson Press.

Book—Two Authors

> Kevinson, J. & Lester, P. J. (1986). Business Approaches to Social Problems. San Francisco: Western Publishers.

Journal—One Author

> Victors, L. (1988). What does "agent relationship" really mean? Journal of Law in Business, 48, 110, 98.

Citations Within a Report or Paper

Short Quotation

> One expert asserts that "financial inducements may attract employees to new positions, but certainly cannot hold them there" (Crashaw, 1986, p. 182).

Long Quotation (Several Lines)

> Crashaw (1986) asserts the following:
> Financial inducements may attract employees to new positions, but certainly cannot hold them there. While 61 percent of new employees attributed their job change to better salary offers, fewer than 8 percent of exiting employees pointed to salary as the primary reason for quitting.

The APA style does not use the title of the work within the citation, but includes it for reference in the endnotes.

THE FINAL PAPER

At this point, let's skip a few stages. We'll assume that the report writer has carried through the research, evaluated the data, interpreted the findings, drawn up a final outline, selected the visuals, and written and edited the draft of the report.[3] With the final draft in mind, he or she recognizes that

---

[3]Suggestions for effective writing may be found in Chapters 5 and 6, the use of visuals in Chapter 12.

other writers will be competing for the attention of the reader. Every busy person has too much material to read and digest effectively. Every report writer must try to make his or her material so attractive, complete, and interesting that the reader will turn to it in preference to competing material.

The best way to achieve this goal, of course, is to have something important to say and to say it effectively. There are some rather mechanical procedures that will do a great deal to increase the attractiveness of a report: the use of topic heads; the use of white space; the use of supplements; good binding, format, and reproduction; and a strategy of presentation.

Topic Heads

Mountains of words can be frightening. It is certainly disheartening to open a report and find fourteen pages of type staring us in the face—paragraph after paragraph after paragraph. We need help penetrating it. Assimilation is so much easier when the writer puts a few signposts along the way. "Here," he or she might say, "is a section on supervisory training, and here is another dealing with management training, and over here is a third section covering cost of training."

When these signposts or topic heads are placed throughout the report, they give the reader a sense of direction. They also save time. Perhaps the executive vice-president wishes to review only the segment on participants' evaluation of training. With topic heads throughout the report, he can find that section easily. And if the report is pulled from the file two years from today, and the reader wants data only on the cost of sales training, he can find it quickly.

Figures 8–1 through 8–4 give examples of original and revised reports, respectively. Notice how much easier it is to read the second version of each pair than the first.

White Space

We all know that the appearance of a page is enhanced by generous use of white space and careful arrangement of the material. Yet it is amazing how many times the pages of a report are solidly typed from top to bottom and side to side, with narrow margins and heavy, block paragraphs. That probably results from lack of awareness on the secretary's or manager's part. It is well worth fussing a bit. Keep your paragraphs short and your margins wide (See Figure 8–5).

FIGURE 8–1

Original memo report. The reader has difficulty picking out key ideas and statistics because they are not well formated or clearly expressed.

To: Wilson Reilly, Director, Company Operations

From: Wanda Reynolds, Real Estate Specialist

Date: February 6, 19__

Subject: On-site Inspection of City Ice House

You were essentially right in your intuition, expressed to me on January 10 in our meeting in your office, that the company might find advantageous use for the old "Ice House" building now subject to demolition by the City. We discussed other matters that day, but you may recall that you wanted me to look into the structural and locational factors pertaining to the building and get back to you as soon as possible. I hope this memo is soon enough to serve your decision-making processes, and I will certainly be happy to answer any questions you may have as a result of reading my evaluation of the subject property. You can contact me most mornings at my office extension (3923); in the afternoons I'm usually in the field, but of course can be reached by beeper. I try to respond to all beeper calls within ten minutes, so feel free to reach me this way (and try, if possible, to be near a phone yourself for ten minutes following your call so I can call you back).

Well, getting back to the Ice House, here's the situation. The timbers inside are essentially sound, without dry rot or termite damage. This fact amazed me, since some of the structural beams are probably 60 years old. One of the caretakers at the building told me the beams had been prepared in a special way to withstand the moisture of the ice-making process. The electrical system is another story entirely. It is the old "fuse" system, not breakers, and will need to be replaced almost entirely. Heating in the building is by oil furnace. The unit was inspected by Central Heating, Inc., and is said to be in good shape. The roof needs immediate repair. It is rolled composite asphalt that has not been maintained since the 1950s. Estimates run between $16,000-$20,000 to strip off the old roofing material and replace it with new material. The estimate for the new electrical system, by the way, was $26,000 for a 400 amp, 60 breaker panel and new copper wiring throughout the building.

As for location, I don't see a problem. The area around the ice house is undergoing a "yuppie revolution," with older buildings being renovated for up-scale apartments and restaurants. The police told me the area was considered very safe at all hours. We should have no particular problems with vandalism during construction or later during leasing and maintenance. Insurance is relatively cheap in the area.

I hope these observations have answered your questions about the building. Feel free to contact me if I can be of further help.

FIGURE 8–2

Revised memo. White space, indentation, numbering, and clear, specific points make the memo easier to read and understand.

To: Wilson Reilly, Director, Company Operations

From: Wanda Reynolds, Real Estate Specialist

Date: February 6, 19__

Subject: On-site inspection of City Ice House, with recommendations

Background

On January 10, 19__, you instructed me to inspect the old City Ice House and to prepare an evaluation of its suitability for conversion into ten "boutique" shops. I visited the building three times (January 12, January 28, and February 1). The findings summarized below are supported by a photo record, which I will be happy to provide if you request.

Observations

On January 12 I inspected the Ice House for structural soundness with the assistance of Martha Victors, city Building Inspector, with the following result:

    1. Main rafters and joists are in good condition and can be retained in renovation.

    2. Approximately 30 percent of bracing and spanning lumber has been attacked by termites and/or dry rot and will need to be replaced. Estimate: $6,000.

    3. Roofing is composite asphalt and in need of immediate replacement. Estimate: $16,000.

On January 28 I returned to the site with Milton Grift, electrical engineer. We inspected all electrical circuits, with these findings:

    1. The present system is outdated and cannot be retained within current building codes. Grift recommends conversion to a 400 amp, 60 breaker system with new copper wiring (Romex, #12) throughout the building. Estimate: $26,000.

2. Fixtures cannot be reused without extensive repair. Since many are desirable as antiques, you may want to sell them. Estimated income from sale: $10,000. Estimated expense for new fixtures: $14,000.

On February 1 I visited the site to inspect the area for eight blocks in all directions:

1. Within the boundaries of this area, 80 percent of available commercial space is currently rented (primarily as professional offices, shops, and art studios).

2. Approximately 6200 people live within the area (walking distance to the Ice House), with a median income of $42,000.

3. Six building renovations are now underway within the area, with two more in the permit stage. These are condominium projects intended to sell to young professionals in the $90,000-$160,000 range.

4. Police records show a dropping crime rate, comparable to that measured in outlying suburban areas.

Recommendations

Based on these finding, I recommend proceeding with the Ice House project in three steps:

1. Enter into an escrow on the building with contingencies for undiscovered damage.

2. Put major repair items to bid with both union and non-union contractors.

3. Work with Marketing to develop an initial "early lease" program to attract pre-completion tenants.

Contact me at 3923 if you have immediate questions. I look forward to working with you on this project.

FIGURE 8–3

Original report

TO: J. L. Wyatt, Exec. Vice Pres., Southern California Power Co.

FROM: Martin Weston, Bellville Manager

DATE: June 15, 19___

SUBJECT: Trouble in Bellville

As you're aware there was community trouble in the Bellville substation area during the last portion of March, and here is the report you requested on the situation as I see it. As you're aware, the Bellville Substation is located in Los Angeles County, five miles east of the city of Halliday on the north side of Halliday Road. The substation is a new 220-66 kV substation consisting of 2-220 kV line positions and 2-220 kV Transformer banks, 75 MVA each. The purpose of this substation is to provide adequate service for the Carlson area including various pumping facilities associated with the State Water Plan. The project costs (approved June 4, 19___) include $1,840,000 for engineering and $18,575,000 for construction. Actually, the situation revolves around major issues which have arisen: the student protest concerning ecological issues and the neighborhood reactions concerning property values. The student issue began on January 5, 19___, when a group of approximately 150 young men and women from Bellville Community College marched on the construction site. Unfortunately, there were only two representatives present from Southern California Power Company at the time. The remainder of the men on the site were workers and supervisors of the subcontractors. Both R. T. Franks and M. T. Martin, Southern California Power employees, did the best they could but were unprepared and could give the students no satisfactory answers to their demands to halt the use of soft coal to generate power, abandon the Keystone Nuclear Power Station and all future plans for atomic energy plants, and immediately channel major funds into research which would result in a drastic reduction of pollutants discharged into the air. Attempts were made within three days of this confrontation to meet with the students, and on January 12, Frank Brackling, Director of Environmental Planning, addressed the Bellville Students for Ecological Planning.

Mr. Brackling did an outstanding job and then met on three subsequent occasions with student groups. Attendance at these four sessions was approximately 80, 40, 35, and 25 students. Unfortunately, a good deal of vandalism has occurred on the construction site since February 10, 19___. On March 2, the employee toilet, washup, and locker area was broken into, with some $10,000 worth of fixtures of all types broken. The mirrors were spray painted with, "Don't Pollute Bellville-BSC (Bellville Student Club)." In addition, plate glass windows have been broken, stacked lumber pilfered, and equipment damaged. Of course, this is not to say that students have been responsible, but it would seem to be a good bet. More recently we have had problems with the citizens who live in the neighborhood of the substation. Initially it began in April when a delegation visited Councilman George Myers and attempted to get him to have all construction on the substation halted. The group felt the substation would be

Heavy block paragraphs containing a great amount of data tend to repel the busy reader unsightly and lower property values. Of course, there was nothing the councilman could do. On April 25, a group called the Bellville Neighbors visted our headquarters building and met with Vice President Bell. He assured them of the care we took with landscaping and actually showed the representatives the renderings of the substation. Certainly anyone can see that the station will add materially to the appearance and beauty of the area. However a few troublemakers insist the substation will have a "factory like" appearance that will destroy neighborhood property values. Of course, this situation is somewhat similar to the student group that called on Mr. R. Stiner and insisted that Southern California Power was determined to pollute the environment. At the same time they would not permit any reasonable dialog with Mr. Stiner to take place. But what I do feel is important is that we take several steps to cut down on damage and property loss. One of these suggestions is to bring in Bill Green's Special Agents--quietly and discreetly to cut losses at the Bellville Substation. And those losses are outlined below. And I might also add that the neighbors were not happier meeting with Vice President Bell than they had been before. Another recommendation is to have Mr. Brackling, or a member of his staff, meet with the Ecology Club on a monthly basis at Bellville Community College. Representatives of Southern California Power should also meet with the Bellville Neighborhood Group, and lastly a committee should be established.

In the period of April 1 to June 30, 19___, vandalism included broken windows valued at $34,300, compared with a similar type of vandalism for the January 1 to March 31 period, at $22,500. In addition, spray paint removal from the walls of the structure cost $6,600 for the second quarter as opposed to $3,500 for the first quarter. Broken locks, fences, and signs accounted for $5,550 in the January-March period, but rose to $9,500 in the second quarter. Pilferage and theft were harder to measure because there is no doubt that some items stolen may have been taken by company personnel. However, that figure is surely a fraction compared with losses due to thefts by individuals outside the Southern California Power Company. It is estimated that $33,500 worth of lumber and lumber products were lost in April-June, while $17,500 disappeared in the previous period. Building materials such as cement and plaster accounted for $1,500 in the first quarter as opposed to $2,800 in the second. Electrical products, such as wire, switches, and related materials, accounted for $24,500 in April-June, while $12,500 was lost in the previous period. These figures and those responsible must be viewed with caution. There is no evidence that this vandalism and theft are caused by students and/or neighborhood residents. It is possible, of course, but it is also possible that outsiders have done this. And we have evidence that individuals do come to a construction site from some distance at night and carry out acts of vandalism and theft. But back to the citizen-neighborhood groups. It is my recommendation that we immediately assign a senior engineer to the site on a full-time basis whose primary and only purpose is to act as liaison and work with the community, the school, the contractor, and other groups whose efforts impinge on this structure. He, of course, should have excellent abilities for communication, for essentially this whole affair is a communications problem. He might even consider holding weekly meetings of himself and representatives from the school and neighborhood. In any event, the recommendations I have made should be followed.

FIGURE 8–4

Revised report

TO: J. L. Wyatt, Executive Vice President, Southern
           California Power Co.

FROM: Martin Weston, Bellville Manager

DATE: June 15, 19__

SUBJECT: Bellville Substation, Community Trouble

Student Protest

On January 5, 19__, 150 students from Bellville Community College marched on the Bellville substation construction site. They made four demands of the Southern California Power Company:

    1. That SCPC halt soft-coal power generation.

    2. That SCPC stop construction on the Keystone Nuclear Power Station.

    3. That we immediately fund research to reduce air pollution.

    4. That we abandon all future plans for atomic energy plants.

In response to these demands, Frank Brackling, Director of Environmental Planning, addressed four student group sessions. Attendance declined with each successive meeting, indicating a decrease in student hostility. In addition, Mr. Brackling satisfied the students' questions.

Neighborhood Protests

In April, a citizens' delegation requested Councilman George Myers' support in its efforts to halt construction on the Bellville substation. The group felt that the substation would lower neighboring property values and also prove unsightly. On April 25, the Bellville Neighbors met with Vice President Bell, who assured them of the care taken with landscaping. A few members of the group still insisted that the substation would have a "factory-like" appearance that would drive down property values.

Property Losses and Vandalism

Vandalism and pilferage have increased tremendously in the recent past. Although graffiti noting "Bellville Students Association" has been found, there is no solid evidence of student involvement in this problem. At the present time we have no solid proof that either neighbors or students are responsible for the vandalism and theft. However, it is quite possible that some theft can be blamed on "outsiders" coming to the Bellville project.

Topic headings, numbering, indentation, and the use of a visual aid all assist the busy manager in assimilating information

Theft and Vandalism

Nature of Loss	Quarter 2 April-June 19__	Quarter 1 Jan-Mar 19__	% Change
Vandalism			
Broken windows	$14,300	$ 8,500	+ 68%
Spray paint removal	3,600	1,550	+132%
Broken locks, fences, signs	4,500	2,550	+76%
Subtotal	$22,400	$12,600	+ 77%
Pilferage			
Lumber products	$ 3,500	$ 1,500	+133%
Building materials	800	500	+ 60%
Electrical products	4,500	2,500	+ 80%
Subtotal	$ 8,800	$ 4,500	+ 95%
Total	$31,200	$17,100	+ 82%

Recommendations

1. Hire Bill Greene's Special Agents to come in and work in the Bellville substation area on a discreet basis.

2. Have Frank Brackling meet monthly with the Bellville Community College Ecology Club.

3. Have our representative meet with the Bellville Neighborhood Group. This should also be done on a monthly basis.

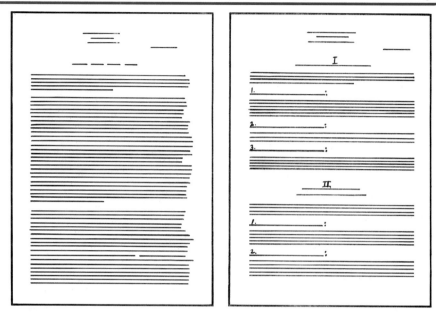

Appendixes and Supplements

Some report writers will examine a segment of their material and conclude that, though it isn't relevant to the subject at hand, it's really too good to discard. So it goes into an appendix. Sometimes, conversely, the report writer has important information that ends up in an appendix instead of the body of the report.

Of course, both approaches are unwise. If the material isn't useful, discard it. If it supplements the text data and may be of value to the reader, place it in an appendix. If it is vital to the understanding of the report, then put it in the body.

When appendixes and supplements are used, they should be made as easy as possible to refer to. Use color dividers or separators so the reader may turn to the correct supplement easily. A color- or number-coding system may help.

Bindings, Format, Reproduction

Firms that require periodic reports have usually found it convenient to use standard title pages and binders. It is often helpful to use one color binder for engineering, another for finance, a third for production, and so on.

Most companies have excellent equipment for reproducing reports as well as mechanical devices for heavy-duty stapling or for placing reports in spiral binders. Once a system is established for reproduction and binding, distribution of reports is made easier, as is their handling, storage, and retrieval.

Strategy of Presentation

All too often the report writer spends six weeks gathering information, a week evaluating it, three days writing, and—alas—only five minutes making the presentation. He or she carries the report to the executive vice-president's office and quietly leaves it on the desk or with the secretary. Or if he or she does talk about it to a few people, the stage isn't set properly.

Here's how it ought to be done.

When the report—oral or written—is ready to be presented, the writer should secure a block of time for the purpose. Not just any time, either, but the right time. And it's wise to make sure that the climate is such that the report will receive the attention it deserves. There is a right time and a right climate for explaining the purpose of the report, what it accomplishes, and what it does not accomplish. The writer should plan the presentation with the following considerations in mind.

Who should be present when I submit the report?

What needs to be said or explained when I submit the report?

What visual aids should I utilize at the time the report is submitted?

What advance work is needed, and with whom, before I submit the report?

The one basic principle to remember is that the end of the project is as important as the beginning. Never submit a report that has been requested for a special purpose without planning the strategy behind the presentation.

QUESTIONS FOR STUDY

1. "Research without an hypothesis is just guesswork." Explain this assertion as it applies to research for business documents.
2. In what direction does the weakest communication flow go?
3. What can an organization do in an attempt to conserve dollars spent on reports?

4. If knowing what the audience wants or needs is indeed important to report writing, how can a writer get to know his or her audience? Suggest several ways.
5. When you send a report to upper management, are you entering a competition of sorts? Explain the nature of that competition.
6. What can you do to end up a "winner"?
7. Are readers becoming more or less patient with lengthy documents? Explain your answer and offer advice for writers who want to determine a readable length for documents.
8. What main purposes do reports serve in businesses?
9. Concerning white space, complete the following advice in the text: "Keep your _____ short and your _____ wide."
10. How can color help an appendix or supplement?
11. How does "climate" relate to report presentation?
12. Is it ever recommended to alter the research design after the information gathering process has begun? Why?

EXERCISES

13. You notice with some surprise that your boss has instructed you to issue your routine monthly report only on a quarterly basis from now on. Discuss possible reasons for this change.
14. What to report? Obviously, the answer is dependent upon the particular situation. However, after reading this chapter, summarize in a paragraph what you feel is important to include in a report.
15. "Writing good business documents just involves following common sense." Test this assertion by making a list, in order, of the steps you would follow in preparing a report for an executive audience. Then compare your list with the steps suggested in this chapter. Discuss in writing any steps you overlooked or combined.
16. Write down the presentation strategy you would use in delivering the report prepared in the exercise above. Assume that you are delivering the report to Millicent Brady, a busy 55-year-old vice president in charge of human resources. She knows that you are preparing the report, but did not order its preparation.
17. Explain the rationale for the report writer's holding conferences during the entire process of the report writing; explain why only one meeting generally will not be satisfactory.
18. The report-writing process is intellectual. That being the case, why should the report writer be concerned with such mundane items as report bindings and reproduction?
19. Report discipline: is the discipline in the report or in the report writer? Explain.

20. The Cortex Corporation is a typical organization. That is, it has good upward communication, adequate downward flows, and horrid lateral transfer of information. As an example, in a personnel area there are six departments, and although they are literally within a few feet of one another, they might as well be located on different planets. As head of the personnel area, what would you do to improve the information flow, especially of reports, among these units?

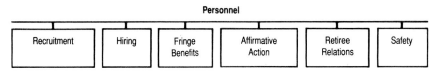

21. As assistant to the personnel director in the organization cited in Problem 20, you are to make a presentation two weeks from today. The presentation, to be made to the director and the heads of Recruiting, Fringe Benefits, and Affirmative Action, concerns how clearly written brochures may assist the activities of the department. Your report is completed. What can you do to set the stage properly so that you will receive a fair hearing—perhaps even an enthusiastic response—to the ideas you will want to share?

22. Using a ruler, calculate the approximate proportion of white space to printed matter on a page that, in your opinion, uses white space well. Apply the standard you develop to a page that uses white space poorly. In general, what percent of a page should be devoted to white space?

23. One step in the process of developing a report is limiting the topic. Limit each of the following broad topics to one on which you could carry through research and present a valuable report: taxes, employee benefits, company goals, and qualities of company leaders.

9 Short Reports

Data and information are not communication.

Most business decisions are based on reports. A well-conceived and clearly written report frequently brings favorable action—and focuses attention on the writer.

The power of a carefully organized report with a logical conclusion and thoroughly substantiated recommendations is demonstrated in the following incident. A young manager working for a Southern California aerospace firm tells of his frustration in his effort to sell what he considered to be an excellent idea:

> *I discussed it with my boss and his boss at lunch; I talked about it to them at coffee breaks; I mentioned it on the golf course, in the parking lot, and at meetings. Nothing seemed to work. They listened politely (and not so politely if they were in a hurry), asked questions, requested that I repeat data, and almost always ended up saying, "Well, let's see something tangible when you get the bugs worked out."*
>
> *And then I woke up. When they said, "Let's see something," that "something" was a written report or proposal. I sat down and worked on that document, off and on for a week. I carefully developed my ideas, included a cost analysis, listed carefully thought-through recommendations, added the necessary tables and charts, had it carefully typed and then put it all together. Copies went forward to the four decision makers involved. The letters of transmittal asked for a response in ten days. I received them, and in every case the reply was affirmative. The product that I recommended went into production. It's done extremely well, and so have I. It's all the result of my report-proposal which was read, analyzed, evaluated, and approved!*

That is what a good report always does: it turns the spotlight on the topic and the writer, and frequently gets action. It may start production lines rolling, halt expenditures on TV advertising, or even bring about a merger.

Let's examine, in the chapters following, the types of reports used most frequently in American companies. Although their purposes may differ, many of the principles of effective reports are found in all.

THE MEMORANDUM REPORT OR SHORT REPORT

Companies often urge their employees to use written memos. One obvious reason for this is to avoid the distortions and misunderstandings that occur when oral statements are transferred from one person to another. But there are several other reasons also. **Memo reports** (also called **short reports**) serve to:

- Make specific information a matter of record. Such reports can be pulled from the file, referred to, and used as the basis for review and action or as a source material.
- Inform individuals of policies, procedures, and/or action. Each of the recipients of the message has the identical information presented in precisely the same way.
- Fix responsibility by naming specific individual(s) to take clearly defined action(s).
- Record policies, decisions, and/or action items agreed to at a meeting, conference, or interview.
- Provide summaries of meetings for participants as well as for those who were absent from the session.
- Confirm a decision, an agreement, or a policy previously agreed to by concerned individuals.

The format of the memorandum report has been consistently established regardless of the form in which it is written. It may be on a half- or full-size ($8\frac{1}{2}$-by-11-inch) sheet of paper. It almost always carries a four-part heading: the recipient, the sender, the date, and the subject.

```
TO:     Robert Andrews,          DATE:  June 27, 19__
        Vice President
        Marketing

FROM:   John Kane, Supervisor    SUBJ:  Budget allocation,
        Consumer Research               Project 248
```

Note that the individuals' full names and titles are given, rather than just a first name, initials, or even the complete name with no title. As more and more pieces of business communication become a part of court cases, the need for completeness—even in a memo—becomes important. A company's liability may depend on what corporate position the memo writer held when the memo was written.

As for the subject line, it should be as specific as possible. A concise but complete subject line not only sets the stage for the reader, but may even eliminate all or part of the introductory paragraph.

Memos may transmit more than information, policies, and summaries of meetings. They can also transmit attitudes that build barriers. Some managers send out an inordinate number of interoffice memos. They fly from their desks like snowflakes in a storm, often hastily written and not even proofread. When a manager's attitude is, "Well, it's only a memo—nothing official; I'll put my ideas down and straighten this guy out," trouble is likely to result.

A memo will be read not only by the designated receiver but by all others who receive copies of it. And if it is tactless, much needless antagonism can result from the fact that several people have read it besides the person it was addressed to. One of the comments heard most frequently in company offices is, "Well, I don't know why he was so sore; I only sent him the memo to keep the record straight." We can understand why "he" was so upset if we keep in mind that copies of that memo also went to his superiors and fellow supervisors.

FIGURE 9–1

Typical short memo

 Dennison Furniture, Inc.

To: Warehouse Personnel

From: Madeline Johnson, Manager

Date: April 6, 19__

Subject: Water Damage to Furniture

During this period of heavy rains, report directly to my office even the slightest roof leakage.

Showroom staff reports twelve furniture items sent from the warehouse with water damage in the last 30 days.

If you will let me know right away about roof damage or other water problems, we can avoid costly damage to our merchandise.

Memo to File

Very often information will be received or transmitted by telephone, in an interview, at a meeting, or during a business lunch. Because that information may make an important contribution to a transaction, procedure, project, or ongoing negotiations, it should be recorded. Once it is documented, the information not only is in less danger of being distorted, but it is also available—in five days or in five years—in exactly the same words, to the various individuals who are involved.

Such information is noted in memo form and filed with the appropriate and related papers; thus the name, **memo to file** (see Figures 9–2 and 9–3). It is also not unusual, although not necessary, to send a copy of such a memo to the other party or parties involved.

Informational Memos

In an effort to transmit information precisely and swiftly to sales personnel, department managers, section supervisors and others, the **informational memo** (see Figure 9–4) is often used. It can help reduce or avoid distortion,

FIGURE 9–2
Blank form for memo to file

MEMO TO FILE

☐ Phone call to _____   File No. _____
☐ Phone call from _____   Date: _____
☐ Interview _____   Time: _____
☐ Meeting/Conference _____
   Place _____

FIGURE 9–3

Memo to file

MEMO TO FILE

☐ Phone call to Antonio Vasquez, Conway Industries

☐ Phone call from Rita Givings, Vice President

I assured Mr. Vasquez that this company would extend warranty
on the #392 unit to June, 19__. Legal staff has been instructed to prepare an addendum to the present warranty
agreement.

FIGURE 9–4

Informational memo

To: Marketing Department

From: Ronald Lions, Director of Advertising

Date: March 12, 19__

Subject: Theme for wallpaper media ads

After more than three weeks of meetings, the theme "Color My World" has been selected
for the upcoming series of radio and television wallpaper advertisements.

A "walk-through" of the theme, as it applies to individual ads and products, has been set up
in the executive lounge. Please take an hour during the next five days to get to know the
exhibit.

Reserve March 26, 19__,10:00 a.m. to noon, for a meeting with advertising and production
staff members. The purpose of the meeting will be to firm up our approach to the selected
theme and to make specific plans for a multi-level marketing approach.

misunderstandings, and rumors. Often a simple visual aid such as a chart, table, or graph will help readers assimilate the information (see Figure 9–5).

When information is to be disseminated to all employees, an employee bulletin is often used. However, if the information has time-important data in it (Figure 9–4), a memo may be used that would be read to all department members or affixed to employee bulletin boards, or both.

Policy Memos

Because a memo is a more official and formal piece of communication than a bulletin, it is used quite often to change, eliminate, or establish policies or procedures (see Figure 9–6). The details of a policy change—or a completely new policy—usually follow in a printed, three-hole-punched format that can be added to the policy or procedure manual concerned.

Memos Fixing Responsibility

As most of us know from sad experience, two or more individuals can carry on what seems to be a clear, intelligent conversation for fifteen minutes, but they will each come away with a very different perception of what was said. Problems that arise from such situations are costly in loss of time, goodwill, understanding, and trust. A brief memo (see Figure 9–7) will often eliminate such problems.

THE LONGER MEMO REPORT

Although memos and memo reports are usually quite brief, ranging from half a page to a full page, some may be as long as two or three pages. Reports not classified as progress, periodic, formal, or analytical are simply called **memoranda reports.** These should, of course, follow all the suggestions that apply to more extensive reports. They should be clear, complete, concise, correct, and courteous. In addition, the memo or memo report should be as readable as possible, with excellent format, short paragraphs, plenty of white space, carefully selected topic headings, and signature or initials. (See Figure 9–8.)

THE LETTER REPORT

For those accustomed to writing or dictating business letters, completing a brief report in letter form is convenient and easy. However, there are differences between the business letter and the letter report that should be kept in mind.

FIGURE 9–5

Informational memo with visual aid

TO: All District Sales Managers

FROM: Ron Toshiba
              Vice President, Sales

DATE: November 15, 19__

SUBJECT: Sales, Mercury Program
              January-November, 19__

This is to give each of you some indication of the success of our Mercury Sales Force Incentive Program. You will receive specific data and figures for all items (by district) on December 20.

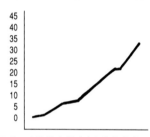

Congratulations, and keep up the great work!

FIGURE 9–6

Policy memo

Memo

TO: All Department Members

FROM: Tom Martin, Executive Vice President

DATE: September 5, 19__

SUBJECT: Change in Employee Appraisal Policy

Beginning on January 1, 19__, we will complete appraisals (or reviews) on all Class I, II, and III employees twice each year.

Appraisal (or review) forms will be submitted to the Head of Personnel between May 1 and May 15, and again between November 15 and November 30.

Employees with three months or fewer of service will be reviewed during the period following.

Forms 24 and 26 will continue to be used.

FIGURE 9–7

Memo fixing responsibility or confirming an agreement

To: Shane Travella, Manager, Accounting Division

From: Ellis Worth, Vice President

Date: May 7, 19__

Subject: New Assignment to <u>Forecast</u> Newsletter

I'm glad we had a chance, on May 5, to discuss at length your role as supervising editor for our new executive newsletter, <u>Forecast</u>. You know how much a steady stream of reliable financial information can mean to our executive leadership in the company.

As agreed in our meeting, effective June 1 you will be released from 1/3 of your present duties to assume direct responsibility for production of this bi-weekly in-house communication. We agreed, further, that the first issue will appear no later than July 1.

Thank you, Shane, for your enthusiasm in leading this important new effort. I look forward to its success.

FIGURE 9–8

Memorandum report

MEMORANDUM REPORT

To: C.E. Johnsen   Date: April 30, 19__
        Executive Vice President
From: T.E. Kerwin, Manager   Subject: Review of Employee Communication Activities
        Employee Communications

This is in response to your memo of April 25, 19__, in which you requested a review of our current employee communication activities at our headquarters facility.

Print
At the present time we issue three publications:
      1) The Farmington News (Begun in 1948)
      2) The Management Review (Begun in 1970)
      3) The Supervisor's Bulletin (Begun in 1975)

Publications and Costs (as of January, 19__)

	No. Pub. Jan. 19__	No. Pub. Jan. 19__	Cost perCopy Jan. 19__	Jan. 19__
Farmington News	18,500	17,100	41¢	37¢
Management Review	600	570	12¢	11¢
Supervisor's Bulletin	1,500	1,400	9¢	8¢

in addition, from time to time we issue the following:
1) Employee Orientation Manual
2) Brochures describing new and/or ongoing benefits such as hospitalization and insurance

Oral and Interpersonal
1) Monthly Farmington Quality Circle (6 representatives from the work force and 6 from management)
2) Annual president's report (to all employees)
3) Quarterly division manager's reports (to respective divisions only)

Personnel Involved
The number of personnel assigned to the Employee Communications Department has remained static over the last 24 months. This is significant inasmuch as we have assumed three new major responsibilities in that period:
1) Inception of monthly Quality Circle meetings.
2) Inception of the Supervisor's Bulletin.
3) Assignment of one individual, on a full-time basis, to speech writing for Farmington officer personnel.
The department staff consists of
1 Director
4 Assistants to the Director
2 Clerical Personnel
1 Photographer/Graphics

The tone of the **letter report** is formal and objective. The writing style is factual, and the letter report often contains substantiating data in the form of tables and charts. The inside address, salutation, and complimentary close may be dispensed with, although letterhead stationery is used. Topic headings and subheadings are used liberally.

The letter report illustrated in Figure 9–9 is quite formal and uses the typical "To, From, Subject, Date" format. In some cases, however, the originator of a letter that contains a significant amount of data may prefer the traditional "Inside Address, Salutation, Signature" format. This is when it would be most practical to arrange the communication in report form and simply call it a letter report (see Figure 9–10).

COMPUTER REPORTS

Certainly two of the most significant electronic contributions being made are (1) the generation of data for purely informational purposes, and (2) the generation of data that are vital in the decision-making process.

Reports can be produced almost automatically through the modern miracle of computer programming by simply requesting data stored in the computer's bank. No longer is it necessary for the manager to review, analyze, tabulate, and record dozens of pieces of information concerning product sales, personnel changes, advertising expenses, shipping completions, and a dozen other items to secure a report. The manager can program the computer to do all the work, and the printer provides the manager with a well-organized report. That report can appear either on the computer screen or in a hard copy on sheets of paper.

Take, for example, your last visit to the grocery store. Most major stores now use scanners. The check-out clerk passes each item over a glass screen, exposing a series of vertical lines printed on each item. The number and width of these lines varies according to a predetermined standard called the Universal Product Code. The code is "read" and immediately decoded on the screen as well as the sales slip: 6 cans of Coke, $2.59; 1.5 pounds of bananas, 30¢ lb., 45¢; 1 Kellogg 6-ounce package of cornflakes, $1.39; etc.

That is a familiar way that the consumer receives information electronically. Let's see how the supermarket's District Manager can use the same data for decision making. Because all scanners record information at a central terminal, he or she can determine sales of not only each store but of individual check-out lines; the speed with which each checker works; the average number of items purchased per consumer; the rate of returns; and the use of coupons per store or check-out line. In addition, determining which items are selling and which aren't is simplified. Because of the computer's capacity to keep a running score, the manager can monitor each product's inventory level and easily decide when to reorder. Alternatively, the computer can be

FIGURE 9–9

Letter report

 Electronics, Inc.

751 MacLean Avenue
Dallas, Texas 75223

October 21, 19__

TO: Mr. Albert Hill, Manager
            Hill, Adams and Hill, Management Consultants
FROM: Roberta T. Black, Personnel Director
            ZRM Electronics
SUBJECT: Summary of Training Activities, 1987-89

You indicated that it would be helpful to your firm to learn of the training activities for employees which we carried through from 1987 to 1989. The data which follow are a summary of those activities.

Management Training, 1987-89
Personnel at the management level have been offered three specific courses. These have been well attended.

Course	Approximate No. Eligible	No. Enrolled	No. of Classes Held
Supervision and Human Relations	260	65	3
Decision Making	260	50	3
Effective Written and Oral Communication	260	85	5

Engineering Training, 1987-89
Although a number of courses have been offered to the engineering personnel, the response has been very weak. Perhaps the reason for this lies in the engineering work load, which is very heavy due to military and space orders.

Course	Approximate No. Eligible	No. Enrolled	No. of Classes Held
Cost Control for Engineers	350	45	3
Advance in Electronics	250	25	1
Engineering Reports	350	80	4

Clerical and Office Training, 1987-89
Response by these personnel to the training has been consistently
high. However, the company has not offered as many courses as
could be filled because of the high turnover of employees in
these categories.

Courses	Approximate No. Eligible	No. Enrolled	No. of Classes Held
Office Techniques and Management	425	150	6
Business Letters	300	110	6
Telephone and Filing Techniques	250	50	3

On the basis of your request, shop training has not been included
in this report. However, information is available.

Instruction
Instructors for all management-level training plus the engineer-
ing-reports classes have been secured from outside the company.
Most of the teachers used were university professors or professional consultants.

All other courses were taught by company personnel.

Administration
All training was carried out under the direct supervision of the
Personnel Department. Mr. Asquith was specifically charged with
coordination and supervision of recruitment, assignment, and
class direction.

Concluding Comments
This will give you some idea of the training that has been
carried through. If there are any questions I can answer, I
shall be happy to do so. I am eager to work with you on long-
range training plans for our company.

R.T.B.

FIGURE 9–10

Letter report with inside address, salutation, and signature

Central Computing Supply
3928 Frederick Highway
Waslount, Virginia 89283

May 1, 19__

Mr. George Loesing
Loesing Business Consultants
98 Sixth Street
Macon, Georgia 98283

Dear Mr. Loesing:

Thank you for requesting our evaluation of your inventory levels and pricing structure
for computer supplies. Based on the information you provided us (by letter, April 8,
19__), we offer the following observations and recommendations:

Inadequate Inventory of Essential Software
Your current inventory levels of such basic software programs as WordStar, WordPerfect,
Lotus 1,2,3, Symphony, Fastback, Xtree, and other standard products should be raised by
40 percent. At your present pace of retail sales, you will find yourself out of stock on
many of these items during the expected summer peak in computer sales. Reorder time
is now 10 to 15 days—too long to suit your potential customers, who may choose to shop
elsewhere.

Inadequate Inventory of Laptop Computers
In your region, laptop computers for both personal and business use are increasing in
sales more than 30 percent each month. At the same time, laptop manufacturers are
experiencing difficulty filling mounting backorders. We recommend that you increase
inventory of laptop computers by 60 units to last through the summer.

Adequate Inventory of Printers
You now have on hand a good retail stock level of both dot matrix and letter quality
printers. You may, however, wish to stock 10 more units of the Okidata laser printer.

I have enclosed a partially completed order form for your review and signature. Again,
thank you for the confidence you've shown in Central Computing Supply. We look
forward to providing you with the best advice, the best products, and the best prices.

Sincerely,

Nancy Springfield

Nancy Springfield
Sales Manager

FIGURE 9–11

Computer-generated inventory report

```
MIDWEST MUSIC SUPPLY, INC.

Wednesday, January 16, 19__              Inventory Report     No. 6

Note:  covers all transactions through January 14, 19__

STOCK ON HAND

Item         Quantity      Serial No.     Wholesale      Retail

Bundy          4            29384          $178          $275
Trumpet                     29385           178           285
                            39284           195           320
                            39824           295           455

Selmer         2            48A670          302           486
Flute                       46B392          340           505

King           1            J2943           485           675
Trombone

Victor         3            39243           138           245
Clarinet                    38592           184           299
                            39853           295           405

Armstrong      1            AC392           507           785
Tuba

Brandford      2            ZZex44          605           940
Cello                       ZXff98          640           975

Rickami        4            29853           495           786
Violin                      29834           495           786
                            29385           520           820
                            48923           730           990

ON ORDER

Item         Quantity     Order Date  Purchase Order   Unit Cost

Czylo          6            10/5/89       #39205        $98.00
Cymbals

Basco          24           11/8/89       #39235        $ 5.50
Reeds

Comston        24           11/12/89      #39240        $ 2.12
Valve Oil
```

programmed to generate a reorder form when certain products reach a designated reorder level. If the computer inventory level doesn't match the actual level, the manager has some indication of the level of pilfered products ("shrinkage") or those misplaced or shipped in error. Figure 9–11 shows a computer-generated inventory report.

Obviously, what we have described is only a bird's-eye view. The point is that dozens of routine reports, highly dependent on quantitative data, no longer require laborious hand recording, tabulation, evaluation, and presentation. Many of these functions are now computer-generated—daily, monthly, or at the flick of a switch. The danger is obvious: the temptation to generate unnecessary or lengthy printouts so that we are inundated with an overwhelming amount of data. Not only are such quantities of information not used, but they actually lead to user frustration. Too often the same person who submits printout after printout assumes that he or she is communicating, when all that is occurring is the production of data.

In his excellent article "What Communication Means," Peter Drucker emphasizes that there is much difference between data and communication. And, further, he says that too much data, or unused data, will almost invariably make communication between encoder and decoder *worse*.[1]

Nevertheless, computer reports, when properly generated and used, can supply us with enormous amounts of vital information.

QUESTIONS FOR STUDY

1. Why are most important business decisions based on written reports, as opposed to conversation?
2. Memos often accompany or confirm verbal discussions and agreements. Discuss three examples of this use of the memo.
3. How does the fact that others besides the addressee will read a particular memo influence the writer's choice of words and topics? Discuss examples from your experience.
4. The text asserts that a good report always "turns on a spotlight." On what and whom does the spotlight shine? Explain your answer.
5. Why are titles commonly placed beneath names in the "To:" and "From:" headings of a memo, even though the two parties know one another well?
6. Is a subject heading necessary in a memo of only a page or two? Explain your response.

[1] See P. Drucker, "What Communication Means," in the Readings section of this book.

7. In what ways do memos fix responsibility?
8. What reader aids should be used in longer memo reports?
9. Consider a manager's demand for a thorough activity report every three days from each of her twelve unit heads. Describe the probable results of such a policy.
10. What sets the stage in the memo report?

EXERCISES

11. A manager has verbally instructed you to take home an expensive piece of company word processing equipment so that a report can be completed. Write a memo to file in which you cover yourself against charges of taking company equipment without authorization and against liability for the equipment.
12. Write a policy memo to workers. In the memo, explain why the company is not taking a day off for a nationally recognized holiday.
13. Call to mind three businesses or industries that make regular use of computer reports. After describing what computer reports are typically issued and why, describe how such information had to be produced prior to the advent of computers in business.
14. Below are three introductory paragraphs to memo reports. If there were a good subject line in the heading of the memo report, the paragraphs would not be needed. For each of the following, write an appropriate subject line that would eliminate the need for the paragraph.
    a. Following up on your request for a status report on the Baxter project, the following data and recommendations have been assembled.
    b. The need for providing additional work space for our support staff is obvious. Following an extensive three-month study, we have determined an efficient and cost-effective means of gaining the needed space.
    c. Beverly Beven has done an extraordinarily good job on projects that are actually beyond the scope of her job description. The purpose of this memo is to put her effort on record and inform you of her fine, cooperative spirit.
15. From time to time, we all want to establish policies for those around us. Take, for example, those influencing your living space: roommates, spouse, parents, landlord, or neighbors. Address a memo to one or more of these groups. In it, establish policies that, in your judgment, will lead to more harmonious relations.
16. Identify a problem on your campus that students have been discussing with the administration for years—but nothing ever seems to happen. Perhaps the problem is that oral messages can be forgotten or ignored rather easily. Write a short memo report on the problem.

17. Choose one of your courses, perhaps the one you are taking in connection with this text. Write a memo from the professor to the students fixing responsibility for major class activities (grading, homework, reports, attendance, and so forth).

18. One kind of memo report covers updates on important topics for superiors. Your boss has asked that any time you see an article that is germane to the operations of the firm, the Balsley Biscuit and Tea Company, you are to summarize the item and send it forward in memo form. Premised upon your area of expertise (be it accounting, marketing, finance, etc.) find a recent article that would have application to the firm. Place your ideas in memo form and keep your memo report to one page. On the back of the memo report indicate your major or area of interest.

19. "I wish I could remember . . ." "There was an important point in that meeting I should have written down." How many ideas get lost because we forget them? One way to attempt to keep a record of good ideas is to write memos to file. Drawing on either a good idea you recently learned in class or an important point that should be retained from a student group meeting, write a memo to file.

20. Imagine that you own and manage Bristol Auto Supply. Each item in your large inventory is computer-coded. When an item sells, the computer takes note of what it was, how long it sat on the shelf, and how many other like items remain in stock. What kind of computer report would you, as manager, like to receive? How often? What information should the report contain? How will you use the information?

21. As Vice President of Marketing for a large corporation, you've been receiving paper by the bale from your employees—much of it in the form of unintelligible computer printouts. Write a memo addressed to all of your employees. Delineate the difference between data and communication. Emphasize that you want the latter in all future memos and reports.

22. Keeping items brief and to one page is often necessary. Your boss, C. E. Johnson, has decided that only short memo reports will be acceptable unless the issue is most unusual. You have prepared one of the long reports printed in this chapter. Without losing the intent of the message, revise the report downward so that it will fit on one sheet (one side) of letterhead stationery.

23. Read the material below and edit it for content, clarity, conciseness, and organization. Submit your ideas in a memo to John Farnsworth, Vice President, Marketing.

Your firm, Zenith, manufactures auto parts and equipment. Approximately three weeks ago, the head of your department—Marketing—called a meeting. The primary topic was "How Can We Motivate Our Dealers Into A More Aggressive Sales Posture." You've come up with some ideas. You discussed them briefly with your boss and halfway through your comments he said,

"Let's see a memo; then we can approve or disapprove your suggestions."

What you had in mind was a program of *cooperative advertising*. Actually the theory behind C. A. is that both manufacturers and dealers will make a cost contribution to the premium item. Thus, each (the manufacturer and the dealer) has a stake in the program and usually greater commitment. The trick in C. A. is, of course, to require the dealer or distributor to make a financial contribution that is significant as well as attractive to him or her. However, the financial contribution should never be so large that it would cause the dealer or distributor to decline to participate in the program. Finding the fine line between dealer participation and rejection is the most delicate task the manufacturer has in such a program.

Among your ideas is to offer all dealers custom-made all-wool navy blue blazers for salespersons. They would carry the individual company logo or crest and could be purchased by dealers for $40.00 each. A minimum purchase by a dealer would be 12 jackets. You've checked this out with Martin as well as Fairview Garment Manufacturers. The former would charge Zenith $58 per jacket and the latter, $60. Both require a minimum purchase of 400 jackets. You would also like to offer Zenith dealers a neon "Zenith Super Ride" sign that is extremely attractive and could be mounted in a dealer's window or in the dealership itself. Your thought is to provide the sign free to any dealer whose purchases of parts in the last quarter of this year is 120 percent or more of parts purchased in the last quarter of the previous year.

In addition, you wish to encourage dealers to purchase individual dealership radio time in their local towns and cities. You know that radio time is quite expensive, but you feel that it will pay. Your plan is to pay 100 percent of radio time cost over $500 per week which any dealer purchases. Thus, if a dealer purchases $600.00 one week, $750 the second week, $500 the third week, and $850 the fourth week of the month, Zenith will reimburse the dealer $700 for that month. The maximum monthly reimbursement would be limited to $1,000.

Incidentally, the crest on the jackets noted above is removable in the event the salesperson wished to use the garment as a sports jacket for leisure wear. As for the neon signs, they are extremely attractive and would cost $350 each if purchased from the sign division of General Electric. Of course, this price is for an order of 200 signs minimum. If the request fell below that number, the price would go to $475 each.

Also, your rough figures indicate that a dealer's parts purchases for the quarter would have to increase about $20,000 over the previous quarter to pay for each sign, breakage, descriptive flyers to describe the program, transportation, etc. But the signs are very attractive advertising items.

As for the radio time, you would limit that offer to the first quarter of 19__ only. And the monthly expenditure would be for station payments only. It would not include payments to script writers, singers, etc.

The benefits of your three suggestions are quite obvious. It has been proved that automobile dealers, television manufacturers, and heavy home appliance distributors (washers, dryers, etc.) increase sales about 15 percent with sustained, minimum radio advertising offered to local communities.

Research by General Electric has proved that neon signs are 20 percent more effective than regular nonelectric signs and 30 percent more effective than direct mail in securing prospective customer interest and attention in a product or service. As for jackets for sales personnel, the benefits are obvious. Sales personnel receive a $150 jacket for no cost or nominal cost. It is an attractive garment to add to their wardrobe. When the crest is worn, it increases esprit de corps, morale, and productivity.

Furthermore radio time increases listener awareness and identification of the dealership even if a sale does not result.

Routine Reports, Proposals, Policies, Procedures, and Business Plans

10

It is as important in an organization to eliminate unnecessary reports as it is to retain vital ones.

W hen companies consider how to save money and work more efficiently, they often redesign office space, computerize utility usage, and reorganize administrative hierarchies. But smart companies also make changes in one of the greatest hidden costs to corporations large and small: the writing of reports, proposals, policies and procedures.

Take a typical case from an Ohio insurance company. The manager of the commercial underwriting unit assigns three of her employees the task of drawing up a report on excessive and suspicious claims under the company's WR307 policy, an inexpensive small claims program for renters. At worst, those claims may be costing the company $4,000 to $5,000 annually in unnecessary expenses.

Much to the manager's displeasure, the three employees take a total of ten working days to research and write the report (a total of fourteen pages). Consider the expense to the company—the average salary of these employees is $30,000, or about $15 an hour. ($30,000 divided by 2000 hours in a work year is $15 per hour.) They each spend a total of 80 hours on the report, for a total of 240 hours. The expense of their labor to the company is astronomical: $3600 (240 hours × $15), not counting the additional expenses for typing, duplication, filing, and so forth. The cure for a business problem has, in this case, cost almost as much as the disease.

Companies are learning from such horror stories to eliminate unnecessary reports, to standardize the writing and distribution of necessary reports, and, above all, to train business writers in fast, effective research and composition strategies.

ROUTINE REPORTS

Among the most routine reports submitted in organizations are periodic reports and progress reports. Both are primarily designed to transmit information for its own sake or to be used as the basis for decision making. In many firms, other routine reports may carry other designations: justification report, monthly accounting (or marketing or personnel report), recommendation report, and sales report are just a few. For all of these the basic principles of good business communication should be kept in mind:

- the prose should be clear and concise
- adequate quantitative data should be included
- dramatic changes (within a period, or comparatively between periods) should always be explained
- quantitative differences between periods should be noted numerically and as a percent
- questions about data should be anticipated and answered
- data should be complete
- recommendations should be substantiated
- the design and format should be attractive and readable

THE PERIODIC REPORT

One of the most widely written reports in industry is the **periodic report of activities.** Bank cashiers prepare daily reports. Factory foremen write weekly reports. Department managers write weekly or monthly reports to their supervisors. Corporations send out annual reports to their stockholders. Not all periodic reports are written by people, however. As noted in the previous chapter, the computer printout now may be used as a report. If evaluations, interpretations, or recommendations must accompany the data, a series of covering comments may be attached to the printout.

Reports are generally composed of certain standard elements: the opening; the various sections, each with an appropriate topic heading; and the signature or initials of the writer at the end. The periodic report almost invariably begins with a summary of activities for the period covered. This is followed by a fairly detailed discussion of the primary topic (sales and sales volume, for example, if sent out by the sales manager; production accomplishments and problems if done by the production manager; numbers of employees, separations, and employee additions if written by the personnel manager).

The primary discussion is supported by facts and figures. These almost always include data for a previous period or periods so that current performance can be compared with past performance. The amount and depth of this information depends on what the company wants. For the monthly sales analysis, some companies will want only data on sales; others will require data on sales personnel, sales advertising, competition, sales problems encountered, and perhaps still other data. In the monthly personnel report, one firm may be satisfied with data covering the present employee level, the number added, the number dismissed, and the number separated. Another firm will want more—perhaps a careful presentation of compensation levels, training, safety, union-management relations, and so on.

Figure 10–1 gives an example of a typical periodic report. Note in the Hawthorne report that any situation that is somewhat unusual, as compared to the previous month, is explained. This is evident in the section devoted to Group V sales. Also note that the recommendations appear at the end.

Figure 10–2 presents a different format. Here, the various recommendations are noted from time to time throughout the body of the report. The method used, whether as in 10–1 or 10–2, depends on the complexity of the material, the reader's identity, and the company's preferred format.

Firms that rely heavily on periodic reports (usually monthly) would be wise to study the value and feasibility of (1) using a standard format to be completed by all personnel who are similarly titled and (2) developing a program that permits the computer to generate a report at specific time periods.

Use of Forms for Periodic Reports

Some companies develop a standard form for the periodic report, and all that is necessary is to fill in the blank spaces. This has obvious advantages: it is concise, it elicits the exact data desired, and it lessens the work of the department head. It also ensures that the various managers reporting, who may be stationed in different cities throughout the country, will all send about the same quantity and level of information. Of course, this form may also inhibit discussion and expression of ideas on the part of the writer.

Each firm can develop its own. The form illustrated in Figure 10–3 is used by a relatively small organization in all its divisions (sales, production, personnel, finance, advertising, and administrative).

THE PROGRESS REPORT

Some managers have to supervise half a dozen activities simultaneously. A single department may have four people carrying on research within the plan, five others engaged in a government project 800 miles away, and four attempting to install a new operation in a customer's plastic division. The manager must know what progress is being made on each assignment, what

FIGURE 10–1

Periodic report

Hawthorne Toy Corporation
Newton, New YOrk 10800

Monthly Sales Report
May, 19__

TO: Robert T. Montgomery, Executive Vice President
FROM: Frank Levin, Sales Manager
DATE: July 1, 19__

Summary
Sales for the month of May have proved to be somewhat heavier than
anticipated, and almost 10 percent above those of May last year.

All items in Group II (metal-mechanical) and Group III (packaged
games) have sold as expected. Group IV (plastic items) has moved
up to a very satisfactory level. Group V (bicycles) has declined.

Sales of all groups for November delivery are up 15 percent as
compared to the same period last year.

Sales expenses have risen again this month. This has taken place
in spite of new efforts to achieve economies.

Sales personnel and advertising expenditures have remained static.

Sales
Although The Toy Manufacturers Monthly for April indicated that
overall toy sales should be expected to rise approximately 7
percent in May over last year's figures, our sales reflect about a
10 percent increase. This may be accounted for by our sales
incentive program as well as our introduction of five new items in
May.

Group V figures are a cause for concern. Certainly sales in this
category should reflect, as they traditionally have, increases in
May over April. The reasons for our decline are not clear.
However, there may be two important contributing factors:
1. Our higher price to the dealer for our entire bicycle line
    (as compared to our competitors).
2. Increase in advertising on the part of competitors. Hi-Flyer,
    for example, has purchased large blocks of TV time.

SALES VOLUME MAY, 19__ (IN DOZENS)

ITEM	MAY 19__	APRIL 19__	MAY (previous year)
GROUP I (misc.)			
A 100	5750	5700	5200
A 101	6500	6400	5800
B 300	9750	9500	8800
B 303	6700	6500	5900
GROUP II			
M 101	3150	3100	2800
M 102	2500	2500	2200
M 103	2300	2100	2000
M 104	2400	2300	2100
M 105	3500	3400	3250
M 106	3000	2850	2750
GROUP III			
G 405	8500	8450	7800
G 407	7500	7300	6500
G 408	7000	7100	8200
G 409	9500	9350	8200
G 410	3500	3400	3100
Group IV			
P 600-5	21,000	20,000	23,000
P 610-5	23,500	24,000	26,000
P 620-5	22,500	22,100	25,000
GROUP V (in single units)			
Whippet			
Girls'	8500	9300	9000
Boys'	12,500	14,000	14,500
Hi-Ride			
Girls'	16,000	16,000	16,500
Boys'	19,000	21,000	20,500
Speedsters			
Girls'	12,500	14,000	13,900
Boys'	16,500	17,500	18,500

Advertising Expenditures

According to Bob Carlton, Advertising Manager, expenditures for
magazine and newspaper ads were 5 percent above May of last year.
However, he indicated that we will, for the first time, use TV spot
commercials during the summer months. An initial expenditure of
$45,000 for TV will be made in two carefully selected areas on the
east and west coasts. Sales will be observed carefully and corre-
lations, if any, drawn.

Sales Personnel

The number of personnel, with the exception of trainees, has
remained stable.

SALES PERSONNEL

	MAY 19__	APRIL 19__	MAY (previous year)
Sales Personnel			
Area I	40	38	39
Area II	20	20	22
Area III	25	23	23
Trainees			
Area I	6	3	0
Area II	3	0	0
Area III	3	1	0

Recommendations

1. Carry through an immediate cost analysis to determine if
    wholesale prices on the Group V line can be cut 10 percent to
    meet competition.
2. Gain additional savings by using plastic instead of rubber
    handle grips, drop battery-powered road light (as standard
    equipment), and apply two (instead of three) coats of enamel
    to the bike frame.
3. Cut all prices in Group III 15 percent when purchases are made
    in gross lots.

FIGURE 10–2

Periodic report with recommendations appearing throughout

MONTHLY SALES REPORT
MARCH, 19__

To: Douglas Shoemaker, General Manager
From: Harold Palmer, Sales Manager
Date: April 5, 19__

SUMMARY

Sales are up 1.2 percent from last month and 10.7 percent from the same period of a year ago. Net profits are up a corresponding amount in spite of added advertising expenditures and increased personnel costs. High unit contribution margins have enabled us to maintain our net return on sales.

While the overall sales picture looks good, the outlook for individual product lines varies from "terrible" to "tremendous." We are passing up opportunities with great growth potential: yet at the same time, we are continuing to carry some product lines which should have been dropped long ago. Inventories have taken a significant jump (4.6 percent) from last month, but this is largely attributable to the change in accounting procedure. Our monthly inventory turnover ratio has improved from .70 for March 1988, to .74 for March 1989.

SALES VOLUME

Sales volume data are presented below. Items with an asterisk are discussed in the following section.

	Sales Volume			
Product Line	March 1989	February 1989	March 1988	% Change 3/88-3/89
Group One				
*Air Conditioners	102,000	100,000	85,000	20.0
*Heaters	23,000	24,000	37,000	(38.0)
	$125,000	$124,000	$122,000	
Group Two				
Chrome Tailpipe Extensions	22,000	22,000	25,000	(12.0)
Headlamp & Door Trim	20,000	20,000	25,000	(20.0)
Mirrors	21,000	20,000	15,000	40.0
*Ski Racks	4,000	4,000	28,000	(50.0)
Miscellaneous	13,000	14,000	10,000	(30.0)
	$ 80,000	$ 80,000	$103,000	
Group Three				
*Stereo Tape Players	104,000	100,000	50,500	105.9
Radios	83,000	82,000	80,000	3.8
Clocks	15,000	14,000	10,000	50.0
	$202,000	$196,000	$140,500	
Total Dollar Sales	$407,000	$400,000	$365,500	

<u>PRODUCT LINES</u>
I. <u>Air Conditioners</u>. Sales forecasts continued to be very bright.

<u>Recommendations:</u>
1. We should continue our heavy emphasis on this line.
2. Truck "camper" market for air conditioners should be investigated.

II. <u>Heaters</u>. Sales of auto and truck heaters are showing a downward trend. Analysis of past sales records indicates that this decline has continued for the past five years. Automotive industry statistics on cars sold without heaters as original equipment point out a far greater decline than our own sales drop. As automotive "no heater" sales and our heater sales have always shown a direct positive correlation—<u>but</u> with a three-year lag—we appear to be headed for real trouble in this area.

Our sales personnel report repeated inquiry about heaters for truck "campers." This appears to be an excellent market.

<u>Recommendation:</u>
We should drop standard auto heaters from our sales line. To replace this item, we should consider developing a heater, or heater conversion unit, for truck "campers." Growth potential appears great in this field.

III. <u>Ski Racks.</u> Sales have dropped 50 percent this year. This decline is due to the heavy competition from the new rubber-plastic Hi Snow model. For the foreseeable future, we will not be able to manufacture a similar item because of our production limitations.

<u>Recommendation:</u>
We should drop this product line as soon as possible.

IV. <u>Stereo tape players</u>. Sales increases in this area have been fantastic. But, we are merely holding our share of the market! This is our big opportunity to push American Automotive Accessories into a period of rapid and profitable expansion. Let's not pass it up.

Evidence continues to support the popularity of the cassette player, particularly in the secondary equipment market. We should continue our policy of specialization on the cassette models.

<u>Recommendations:</u>
1. In spite of sales gains, we should <u>increase</u> our efforts on this product line. Increased market penetration is important. Innovation, quality, and availability of product should be of prime concern. Continued heavy advertising to let people know what we have to offer is a must.
2. Strong consideration should be given to stocking a tape library as an addition to our product line.
3. Further consideration should be given to <u>producing</u> our own cassettes from marketed stereo "33-1/3's." (Many "garage shop" operators have been finding this a profitable venture.)

ADVERTISING

Our first-quarter increases in advertising expenditures appear to have paid off well in added sales and profits. However, our Accounting Department feels we should cut back advertising "now that we're rolling." I'm strongly opposed to this. Coca-Cola tried cuttting back advertising a few years ago—with highly negative results. And what product is better established than Coke?

Recommendation:

We should not only maintain but expand our advertising program.

PERSONNEL

While our sales have increased 10.7 percent from one year ago, our sales personnel staff has increased 25.0 percent for this same period. This situation continues to have me perplexed, but I'm holding off on any staff reduction pending (1) developments in our stereo and air conditioning product line, and (2) the results of our just-completed sales training program.

Recommendation:

Sales personnel strength should be maintained another 90 days. The personnel situation will be re-evaluated at that time.

FIGURE 10–3

Periodic report form used by a small company

To:
From:
Date:

Number of Employees Entered on Payroll
      Unit A _____
      Unit B _____
      Unit C _____

Total Regular Rate Hours Paid
      Unit A _____
      Unit B _____
      Unit C _____

Total Overtime Rate Hours Paid
      Unit A _____
      Unit B _____
      Unit C _____

Sick Leave Hours Taken (if any employee exceeds 16 hours, attach employee name, work I.D. number, and brief statement of circumstances to this report)
      Unit A._____
      Unit B _____
      Unit C _____

Personal Leave Hours Taken (if any employee exceeds 8 hours, attach employee name, work I.D. number, and brief statement of circumstances to this report)
      Unit A _____
      Unit B _____
      Unit C _____

Unaccounted Absence Hours (attach employee name, work I.D. number, and brief statement of circumstances and action taken by manager)
      Unit A _____
      Unit B _____
      Unit C _____

Additional Information or Recommendations:

_____
  (signature)

_____
  (date)

problems have been encountered, and when the jobs will be completed. **Progress reports** help the manager to maintain control by keeping him or her informed as a project progresses.

Progress reports have a further value. A review of progress reports filed on projects in the past assists the manager in planning and working up cost and time estimates for similar operations contemplated for the future. The reports may tell where problem areas existed, what to avoid, and where to focus attention. Thus they serve as a reference guide.

Every project has a beginning, a work period, and an end. Progress reports conform to this arrangement. They consist of an initial report, continuing reports, and a terminal statement.

The initial report should cite the background of the project, along with its purpose, specific goals, and sponsor. In addition, it should review the progress made on the assignment in the period covered by the report. Continuing reports merely recount the activities of the period, and the terminal report presents a final summary and analysis.

Most managers prefer progress reports that provide a brief background to the situation, a detailed summary of the period covered, and a statement of the work to be carried through during the next time block. Problems and obstacles encountered are usually noted in some detail with recommendations for solutions. (See Figure 10–4.)

Like the periodic report, the progress report may also be prepared by filling out a standard form. When a firm has several teams in the field, each working on a somewhat different project, this method can be valuable and assures a certain uniformity.

OTHER WRITTEN COMMUNICATION

In addition to reports, there are many other rather formal items of communication completed in most companies. Among them are policy statements and manuals, procedure manuals, job descriptions, and proposals. For each of these, every firm usually establishes its own format and formula. However, there are basic similarities among each type from one company to another.

PROPOSALS

The primary document by which most companies acquire work is the **proposal**. As discussed later in detail, this important business form can be as short as a few pages or as long as several bound volumes.

Probably the two principal preparers of proposals are companies competing for federal, state, county, and municipal contracts and individuals or

FIGURE 10–4

Progress report

Progress Report #4

Period: January 1 - - April 30, 19___
Date: May 5, 19___
From: Rachel Thomas, Sales Supervisor
Subject: HumidAir Direct Mail Promotion

Overview:
As created by Jenkins, Williams, and Todd Agency, Inc., the HumidAir Direct Mail campaign seeks to develop customer leads for the sale of HumidAir 607 units (humidifiers which attach to both gas and oil furnaces).

Activities This Period:
6700 homes in Sector C received the "Dry Air and Your Health" mailing by January 30. A total of 92 information request cards were returned (a response rate of 1.5 percent) by March 1, and an additional 21 cards from the original mailing by April 30.

These lead cards were distributed as they arrived to sales representatives according to area.

Results of Sales Calls from Lead Cards

	Total Leads	Calls Made	Contracts Signed	Follow-Ups
Area 7	12	12	4	2
Area 8	10	10	3	3
Area 9	31	26	10	9
Area 10	34	29	11	8
Area 11	27	27	9	8
Totals	114	104	37	30

Comments on Activities:
Sales representatives for Areas 7 and 8 completed their training on December 15, and, therefore, have been assigned lighter client loads for their first quarter. We were pleased to see that both of these new salespeople achieved a 33 percent contract-to-call ratio. Based on those results, we will balance the distribution of leads as evenly as possible in future quarters.

Planning for Next Period:
We anticipate the new HumidAir incentive mailing in late April to produce comparable results to the January mailing, assuming that temperatures remain cold through the early spring. Our "May in Milan" drawing should yield an increase in information cards received. Jenkins, Williams and Todd Agency will monitor contract-to-card ratios to evaluate the cost effectiveness of the vacation trip incentive approach.

groups in colleges, universities, and research agencies seeking funding for projects. Proposals are also prepared within organizations and submitted to management or to committees.

But whether intended for an in-house audience or an external review panel, all proposals have one common element: they seek an affirmative response.

What Is a Proposal?

In essence, a proposal is a reasoned request for action. By logic and persuasion, it tries to convince its audience that (1) there exists a significant need, and (2) that need is best met by the proposed action contained in the document. Effective execution of both halves is crucial for proposal success. Many proposals have fallen flat because they have not directly addressed the need perceived by the funder: "You may have a good idea, but it certainly doesn't meet our needs." Or a proposal writer can err by supplying too few specific details about the action it recommends: "You understand our needs, but we can't figure out what you plan to do about it." These elementary considerations can spell success or failure. Winning a major aerospace contract can send a company's stock zooming, and with it an increase in thousands of jobs. On the other hand, losing an important proposal can result in massive layoffs. Successful proposal writers must squarely confront two business realities:

Competition is stiff. When submitting a proposal to government agencies and funding groups, it isn't enough to possess the organization, the personnel, the facilities, the experience, and the creativity to secure the contract. The proposal defining and describing all of this must *communicate* with such excellence that readers sitting hundreds or thousands of miles away will examine it and conclude, "The proposal award goes here."

Funding agencies do not always know exactly what they want. In large part, proposals must often educate when analyzing the audience's need. A mid-sized city, for example, may seek proposals to alleviate a summer swarm of mosquitoes, but where and why mosquitoes are breeding may not be common knowledge or immediately apparent. The proposal writer who manages to clarify and define the reader's need has a huge advantage when it comes time to develop plans to meet that need.

Types of Proposals[1]

Although proposals may run from thousands of pages (an aircraft carrier-based plane) to a few pages (drinking fountains for the three new buildings

---

[1]For a detailed discussion of proposals see H. Holtz and T. Schmidt, *The Winning Proposal . . . How to Write It*, New York, McGraw-Hill, 1982.

in Chicago's Franklin Children's Park), they are essentially the same in *makeup*.

Governmental agencies usually issue a Request for Proposal (RFP). There are usually very precise, formal documents that list specifications for the product or service, due date, delivery schedule, testing procedure, guarantees required, performance minimums, and so on. Some elements may be included in a separate document called a Statement of Work (SOW). This item specifies the product, a list of regulations or references to them, forms to certify compliance, a contract for the supplier to sign, and other details.

These documents, whether from a Federal or city agency or from a company, must be studied with extreme care. Every item must be answered clearly and honestly. To bypass one of the requirements, regardless of how minor, or to indicate the firm's inability to handle even one item, makes your proposal *nonresponsive*. A nonresponsive proposal is a sure loser.

Planning the Proposal

The first step, then, is to be sure you have a clear idea of the customer's *needs*. If the manufacture and installation of 40 drinking fountains are required, exactly what is needed? Stainless steel or white vitreous china? Are they to stand alone or to be recessed in a simple wall dispenser? Should some be designed for children or handicapped persons? Must the water be iced or just cold from the line's tap? And these are just a few questions to ask!

The next step is to clearly analyze how your organization's *capabilities* fill those needs: your equipment, experience, facilities, personnel, finances, etc. Once you have matched your abilities with the customer's needs, look at the competition. Of course, the purpose is not to mention the competition in your proposal but to recognize your comparative strengths and weaknesses so you may deal with those intelligently.

In most cases, the RFP will request a detailed response in the areas of facilities, equipment, and personnel. In addition, information will be requested concerning schedule dates (start-up, production, and delivery), funding, training, subcontracting (if necessary), guarantees, replacement parts, technical manuals to accompany the product, and other related items. In the area of facilities, it is important to note whether they are already available or must be constructed or extended. The same is true of equipment. However, a firm that lacks adequate facilities or immediately available equipment should not drop out of the competition. At times the contract generator may pay for such expenditures. And it is quite possible that competitors may be in the same position as you are.

One of the most important sections of any proposal is the list of personnel who will be involved in the assignment. The proposal should contain resumes of key personnel to include clear descriptions of their experience, education, and awards. If the RFP is for a new type of armored helicopter or assault landing craft, or computer-based inertial aircraft guidance system, the proposal submitted in response may run a half dozen volumes with dozens of appendixes covering a variety of areas. In such cases, the best results are secured through a team effort. No one person can be expert enough to submit detailed plans, drawings, and schedules for not only what goes into that armored helicopter but also the many peripheral areas involved. Thus individuals are needed with expertise in such areas as engineering, manufacturing, production, computer information systems, design, avionics, finance, and testing. Of course, there is a team leader, and perhaps a proposal writing expert, who are responsible for consolidating the entire work. However, in the final analysis, a major proposal must be a team effort.

Although the outline of every major proposal will differ, on the whole the organizational pattern will probably be close to the following:

Introduction

Definition of the problem

Proposed solution

Description of facilities available

Description of equipment available

Description of key personnel

Overall work design to include manufacturing and production plan

Manufacturing, production, and delivery dates

Financial data to include pricing

Concluding statements

Miscellaneous (evaluation, testing, replacement parts, guarantees, etc.)

As is true of the long report (see Chapter 11), the proposal contains an introductory section (letter of transmittal, title page, table of contents, table of illustrations, abstract, summary, and preface), a discussion section, a conclusion, and appendixes.

The Short Proposal

The short proposal, running from five to twenty pages, is essentially quite similar to the long proposal. Again, the customer's needs must be carefully recognized and responded to. As shown in Figure 10–5, the short report condenses the various steps listed above in the organizational pattern for proposals. The description of available facilities, for example, may take only a paragraph in a short report, while the same topic may occupy most of a volume in an extended aerospace proposal.

FIGURE 10-5

Short proposal

Proposal to Retrain Economart Gardening Personnel

submitted to

Ms. Morgan Henderson Baillison
Vice President, Retail Sales
Economart Corporation

by

Patricia C. McKay, Ph.D.
Director, Training Specialist, Inc.

May 16, 19__

I. Proposal Overview

At your request, this proposal examines the problems Economart Corporation faces in its retail gardening sector and suggests
how Training Specialists, Inc., can help to solve those problems
efficiently.

Background

In 1982, Economart opened the doors of its seventeen departments for the first time. Success came at different rates for
different departments, but within a year all sectors of the store
showed healthy profits. Based on that success, the company
decided in February 1986 to add a large outdoor addition to the
store: the gardening department.

In the past two years, the gardening sector has shown
substantial losses for each quarter, with no significant potential
for a turnaround. This proposal will argue that the company risks
further, more serious, losses by continuing the operation. The
key, however, to a smooth phaseout of the gardening sector lies in
a retraining plan for gardening employees.

II. Problem Analysis

The financial problems of the gardening operation have been
apparent to management since late spring 1986.

The Record

Except for a brief sales peak during the initial Grand
Opening month (February 1986), the record of gross receipts vs.
expenses clearly demonstrates the worsening financial situation of
the operation (see Graph I).

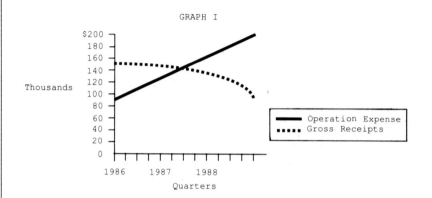

GRAPH I

Observe that expenses (including facility overhead, salaries, merchandise, supplies, and losses) have risen almost 100% during the past two years. During that same period, gross receipts from the gardening sector have fallen 24%.

Reasons for Unprofitability

     The gardening operation has proven unsuccessful for internal and external reasons:

     1. Product waste. Because Economart has no facility for restoring or treating damaged plants, an average of 18% of all plants displayed for sale each month end up in the trash. These rejects include plants damaged by customers or insects, by improper feeding or watering, and by moving and storage.

     2. Rising labor expenses. Because each plant must be cared for while on display, the gardening operation requires a full-time staff of sixteen gardeners and salespeople to maintain the department. As Graph II indicates, both the number of employees and the total cost of salaries/benefits have risen dramatically in the last eight quarters:

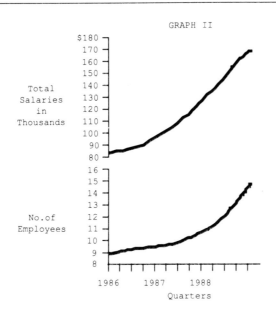

GRAPH II

Observe that the total salary/benefits cost has risen more rapidly than the expansion of the gardening staff because of the unionization of the workers beginning January 1987. Given present union demands for salary/benefit increases, we can expect the trends illustrated in Graph II to continue into the foreseeable future.

3. Competition. The market area served by Economart now has three retail nurseries, all larger than Economart's gardening department. One of these nurseries, Kwai Gardens, is able to charge significantly less for plants than Economart because of the family nature of the Kwai organization.

Prices charged by the other two nurseries are roughly equal to those of Economart, and these competitors also offer attractive delivery and consultation services.

III. Evaluation

Because of waste, labor expense, and competition, the Economart gardening department stands little chance of reversing

its record of unprofitability. Although one of these factors--
waste--could be lessened by the purchase of a company plant farm,
the expense involved outweighs benefits to be achieved.

The problem can also be evaluated by considering the profits
in relation to each square foot of floor space in the Economart
store. Excluding the 6800 square feet of interior floor space now
used by the gardening department, the store's remaining 24,000
square feet produce an average of $3.20 profit per square foot
each month. By contrast, the gardening operation produces a loss
per square foot of $.43.

We can conclude, therefore, that the interior space now used
by the gardening department might be more profitably occupied by
another product line. Several departments have long-standing
requests to management for expansion. The great majority of these
requests present statistically persuasive arguments that additional floor space will produce additional profits at or above the
rate already established in the department at hand.

IV. Proposal Specifics

Economart management should phase out the gardening operation
by dealing effectively with three factors:

1. Labor retraining and relocation. Present labor relations
make it unwise for management to simply dismiss the workers now
employed in the gardening department. While legally such a
dismissal might be upheld, Economart would no doubt be the target
of boycotts, picket lines, and unfavorable advertising in the
coming months. Management may therefore decide to retrain the
present nursery workers for jobs as stock persons, shipping
clerks, and floor staff.

2. Stock reduction. Current inventory in the nursery now
totals $204,000 retail value. Assuming that the loss factor of
18% will remain accurate during the coming months, the company
should reduce inventory as quickly as possible. With spring and
summer gardening seasons upon us, management may authorize a 15%-
off sale on all gardening merchandise. In the highly competitive

gardening field, this price break will significantly undercut the prices of other nurseries. If the sale prices bring quick reduction of stock, the store may actually make a greater profit per month because less merchandise is lost to the 18% waste factor.

   3. Store image. Management will not want the closing of the gardening operation to be perceived by customers as a failure on the part of Economart. Hence, the 15% sale referred to above may be cast as a "Remodeling Sale," an event marking the transition from a gardening operation to a Patio and Outdoor Furniture operation, or whatever retail line is chosen for the gardening floorspace.

   In summary, management should act quickly to relocate staff, reduce inventory, and redirect advertising to put the best face possible on the closing of the nursery.

Proposed Retraining

   Training Specialists, Inc., will retrain the 16 workers now employed in the gardening department. For each employee, Economart management can select a retraining route:

   1. Sales person
   2. Shipping clerk
   3. Floor staff

Training Location

   All training will be conducted on Economart premises during regular business hours. Our trainers will use your Conference Room A or a similar room of your choice.

Training Time

   Each employee will receive ten hours of training, divided into four 2.5 hour sessions spread over four consecutive days. Thus, all employees will finish training within four work days. Scheduling will be arranged so that ordinary work patterns within the gardening department are not significantly compromised during the training period.

<u>Training Personnel</u>

Sessions will be conducted by personnel with extensive experience in training and a successful history of training with Economart personnel:

Patricia C. McKay, Ph.D. (specialist in training program development)

Andrew Ortega, M.A. (specialist in sales/marketing training)

<u>Training Costs</u>

Total expense to Economart for employee retraining is $4480, including all materials and personnel supplied by Training Specialists, Inc. Here is a breakdown of specific expenses: 16 workers x 10 hrs. training (Economart premises) x $28/hr. training cost = $4480.

V.   Conclusion

Training Specialists, Inc., trusts that you will find this problem analysis and proposal helpful in your planning for continued corporate success. We look forward to working with you on the project described in this document. Certainly we will welcome your questions or comments on the action we propose. Thank you for the confidence you have shown in Training Specialists, Inc., in the past, and for inviting our proposal in this case.

Short proposals do not, however, leave out any major portions of the proposal argument. A carefully worded description of the problem, the plan, equipment, facilities, and personnel still is vital and must be handled with thoroughness and integrity.

In the following example of a short proposal, the writer (an independent analyst/trainer) tries to "sell" Economart Corporation on a retraining program for gardening department employees. Note that the writer does not make the case solely on the grounds that "training is good," or "I'm quite capable," though both assertions may well be true. Instead, the proposal is grounded solidly in the *specific needs* of the company: the gardening personnel must be retrained and relocated to save the company money.

Persuasion in Proposals

Just how do proposals go about persuading their readers to say "yes"? Consider the influence of logical order, psychological order, and solid evidence.

Logical Order   Business writers arrange the parts of a proposal to appeal to an audience's sense of reason. When one point logically follows from a previous point, we feel reassured that the writer has thought through the proposal with care. When at last the writer calls upon us to make a decision on the proposal, we feel it is only natural to continue the chain of logic that has been established. We forge the final link by saying "yes."

Notice in the following illustration how logic snares us. The proposal writer creates a series of links similar to this circular chain. The proposal needs only one more link to be complete. Because the pattern has been worked out with such care, we feel an almost irresistible urge to complete it, to finish the circle by saying "yes."

For example, observe the development of a logical train of thought in the following propositions (briefly summarized) from a consultant's proposal.

Ensign Engineering has determined that it can save $2800 per day by leasing a mainframe computer costing $800 per day. The company leased the computer.

Unfortunately, Ensign Engineering is presently able to use the computer to only 20% of its capacity due to a lack of programming and hardware knowledge. Hence, the company is saving only $560 per day (20% of $2800) though the computer still costs $800 per day.

By consulting for Ensign Engineering for one month, I can ensure 100% use of computer capacity through my knowledge.

The company now loses $2240 per day. My consulting fee is $300 per day for one month.

To save money, hire me. I'm worth it.

Without Consultant

A	B	C
Computer Cost/day	Theoretical Savings	Actual Net Savings
$800	$2800	20% of $2800
		minus $800 = − $240

With Consultant

A	B	C
Computer Cost/Day	Theoretical Savings	Actual Net Savings
$800	$2800	$1700
+ 300 (consultant)		(B − A = C)
$1100		

Before considering the logic of the argument, the proposal's readers may have cringed at the thought of spending $9000 (30 days times $300) for a consultant. But although the fee is substantial, company officials may conclude that hiring the consultant is reasonable in the light of logic.

Too often, however, logic goes astray and the proposal fails. Faulty logic may be compared to scattered links of a chain. We feel no attraction to fulfill an inevitable pattern of any kind when faced by the chaos of an illogical argument.

Be on guard for these logical disasters in business proposals you write and read.

Hasty generalization—a conclusion based on too little evidence.

Buy my product because it worked last year for your sister's roommate.

Circular reasoning—a purported explanation turns out to be a mere restatement.

> *We require employee contributions to the retirement fund because it is the policy of this company to fund retirement benefits by means of deductions from employee wages.*

Personal bias—using personal judgments as the standard for evaluating ideas.

> *Morgan's a good chap. Why would you want to oppose his plan for a stock split?*

Non sequitur—a conclusion that does not follow from the evidence.

> *Frank's clients love his jokes. Make him sales manager.*

Either/or thinking—two alternatives posed as the only alternatives.

> *Either we raise prices or go bankrupt.*

Straw man—setting up a fake target as if it were a true target for your argument.

> *The whole question comes down to personalities. Fire Jenkins and the entire company will turn around.*

False cause—incorrectly taking an earlier event as the cause of a later event.

> *Jenkins came aboard at the beginning of 1982. Nine employees quit that year. That must show you what kind of president Jenkins has been.*

Stacking the argument—piling up biased evidence while ignoring other valid evidence.

> *The Rolls Royce Silver Shadow has only fair acceleration, gets poor gas mileage, and costs too much to repair. I think I've made my case: the Silver Shadow is an overrated automobile.*

Faulty syllogism (a syllogism is pattern of thought)—drawing incorrect conclusions from correct assumptions.

> *All managers arrive at 8 A.M. I arrive at 8 A.M. Therefore, I must be a manager. (The correct version: All managers arrive at 8 A.M. I am a manager. Therefore, I arrive at 8 A.M.)*

Although these faulty arguments may stand out clearly here, they hide themselves cleverly in many business proposals and other documents. Can you spot the logical errors in these assertions?

Example 1   *Benson Lamination's profits soared 42 percent higher within nine months of their purchase of the new Quadrex computer-driven plywood press. We here at Star Lumber can expect similar results by purchasing a Quadrex press.*

Example 2   *For years, all of the best life insurance companies in America have offered double indemnity policies in case of accidental death. Miller Farm Insurance has just announced its policy of double indemnity for accidental death. In so doing, Miller Farm proves itself to be one of the best life insurance companies in America.*

In the first example, the error is "false cause." Benson Lamination's profits soared *after,* not necessarily *because of,* the purchase of a Quadrex press. In the second example, the error is "faulty syllogism." The argument asserts that all A have B characteristics; C has B characteristics; therefore, C must equal A. If this were true, then we could argue that, "All toads have warts; Fred has warts; therefore, Fred is a toad."

Though such logical slips may make us smile, they tend to emerge in less humorous ways in multimillion dollar proposals. Too often faulty arguments go unnoticed until, in the final stages of proposal review, a sharp executive adjusts his or her glasses and says, "Wait just a minute. Am I to understand that . . . ?" Like a card castle built on shifting ground, the whole proposal can collapse due to flawed logic.

Psychological Order   The best business proposals move both our minds and our wills. We develop not only thoughts about the merits of the plan, but strong feelings as well. Proposal writers manage our feelings by carefully timing the length and placement of bad news and good news.

The Placement of Bad News   Any message that threatens our welfare and survival is *bad news.* A company seeking to minimize training expenses may hear the bad news that employee turnover is rising by 24% per year. A traditional stock brokerage may hear the bad news that discount brokers are doubling their business each year.

Why would a proposal writer ever want to mention such bad news? For the same reason, perhaps, that fire-and-brimstone preachers begin each sermon with vivid descriptions of hell's hot agonies: to get the audience ready for later rescue.

The skillful use of bad news topics creates a need for an answer or solution—a need emotionally felt by the reader. When later in the proposal the writer presents *good news*—the solution, the proposed idea—the reader welcomes it with satisfaction and some relief.

There's a joke about a leftover 1960s activist who was chided for giving in to the Establishment. "Man, I've still got the answer," he complained, "but no one remembers the question anymore."

The writer of a good proposal makes sure that readers will appreciate the good news by setting the stage, as it were, with well-chosen items of bad news. Placing negative aspects effectively has the additional advantage of anticipating any questions and objections that may occur to the reader. Such anticipation reduces the negative effects of these questions and objections.

Whatever negative influence remains can be overcome by the good news suggested in the proposal.

The Placement of Good News   When turning to the good news of a proposal, a business writer must show that the benefits of the proposed idea are not only *possible* but *probable*. The readers of most business proposals, after all, said goodbye to wishful thinking long ago; they know the ways of the business world, with its hard-earned rewards and its ready disappointments. Therefore, readers are suspicious of proposals that naïvely broadcast the good news of a proposal without also examining accompanying risks, resistances, and liabilities.

Consider, for example, the good news promised in a "Proposal to Substitute Look-Alike Plastic for Genuine Leather in Lejax Wallets." The proposal writer sets forth three items of good news for the Lejax Company:

1. Plastic costs 75 percent less than leather.
2. By using plastic, Lejax can rid itself of bothersome regulation and inspection entailed in the use of leather.
3. Unlike irregular pieces of leather, premeasured sheets of plastic can be machine-fed into pattern-cutting machines. Waste is cut by 40 percent.

The proposal writer feels that his good news is unassailable, and that the company's approval of his proposal is certain. He simply can't believe his ears when a high-level management committee returns the proposal for more extensive analysis.

"Haven't I spelled out the advantages to the company?" he asks.

"Yes," a vice president tells him. "Now make them real."

In order to demonstrate what she meant, the vice president plays devil's advocate to each item of good news offered by the proposal writer:

Good News	**Devil's Advocate**
Plastic is cheaper than leather.	Of course. But we built our reputation on the feel and smell of real leather. Convince me that plastic won't destroy our image.
Goodbye to government inspection.	Government inspection keeps foreign wallets off the market here. Will inspectors still be around to shield us from competition after we've gone to plastic?
We can mechanize production.	We're a union shop through and through. Prove to me that plastic won't invite massive labor problems.

The art of delivering good news, then, is not simply a matter of listing bright, desirable ideas. In fact, the challenge of writing good proposals lies in another direction entirely: showing how a bright idea can surmount obstacles. The bright idea earns its right to persuade us by conquering real-world objections.

The Influence of Solid Evidence   Persuasion depends upon the use of examples (termed **evidence** when used to prove a point). Proposal writers often steer a middle course between general and specific evidence.

General Evidence   ("The world's oceans are warmer this year") is composed of a great number of examples gathered together (generalized) in the form of a statement, mathematical measurement, or illustrative chart.

Specific Evidence   ("The water off Pierce Pier in San Diego on May 9, 1985, was 73 degrees") focuses on the precise details that make up generalized evidence. Both general and specific evidence can strengthen or weaken a proposal.

Notice in the following example that general evidence can support a point well, but in a clinical, aloof way. While we may agree with a point supported by general evidence, we are seldom moved:

> *Grocery store managers are prone to health problems. In a recent survey of 900 grocers, 37 percent of store managers had chronic symptoms of stress-related illness.*

What is the strength of this bit of general evidence? We grant the weight of the fact that 900 men and women were polled. But this statistic, like the many numbers that clutter our lives, suffers from rigor mortis. Hundreds of grocers may be suffering, but not a single one suffers before our mind's eye.

By contrast, consider a brief sample of specific evidence:

> *Grocery store managers are prone to health problems. Blaston, Pennsylvania, has three large supermarkets. The managers of each, all in their 30s, began work in the mid-1970s. Today, one suffers from ulcers, one works half-time owing to acute hypertension, and the third doesn't work at all: he suffered a fatal heart attack at age 36.*

In this case, we feel the impact of the words "on our pulses," as the poet Keats said. The suffering grocers appear to us visually in imagination. Words like "ulcer" and "heart attack" strike us more powerfully than percentages.

The weakness of specific evidence, of course, is its severe limitation of sampling. Do the illnesses of three sick store managers really prove whether grocery store managers are more or less prone to stress-related illness? No. Only broad, quantified studies can prove broad assertions.

Skilled proposal writers steer a middle course between the strengths and weaknesses of general and specific evidence. They try to bring out the general truth of statistical evidence without sacrificing the emotional appeal of specific evidence.

Notice how the following statement combines the best of general and specific evidence:

> *Grocery managers are prone to health problems. In a nationwide survey of 900 of them, 37 percent were found to suffer from such stress-related illnesses as ulcers, hypertension, skin rashes, and heart irregularities. In some communities like Blaston, Pennsylvania, virtually all supermarket managers in town are chronically sick.*

To sum up, persuasion in a proposal has little to do with slick fast talking or tricks. Proposal witers *earn* influence over their readers by constructing tight, logical arguments, psychologically effective patterns of good news and bad news, and convincing demonstrations of general and specific evidence.

Appearance Counts   Because proposals are often judged competitively, they must win attention and respect by how they *look* as well as what they have to *say*. Wandering margins, long, heavy block paragraphs, bleary type and smudged graphics all say "unprofessional" and "unreliable" to an evaluator trying to get value for money invested. Here are five ways to give your proposals a crisp, professional appearance:

1. Use carbon typewriter ribbon rather than fabric ribbon. Your stationer can demonstrate the dramatic difference in effect.
2. Use heavy bond white paper. Beware of pastel shades, especially if you plan to photocopy the work.
3. Abide by strict margins on all sides of the page. Word processing systems now make right-justified margins possible without typesetting.
4. Decide if the effect of your proposal will be more powerful if it is bound with a vinyl or heavy paper cover rather than unbound. Proposals of just a page or two, of course, are not bound. Most photocopy and fast-print businesses now can bind your work for a few dollars per copy.
5. Make sure that photocopied versions of your proposal are, in clarity and crispness, comparable to your original. Some writers feel that grey and blurred photocopies are acceptable, as long as they are readable. The excuse? "They wanted a copy—and you know how bad those copy machines can be." Actually, most photocopy businesses have modern, well-maintained machines that produce quite clean copies that often are almost indistinguishable from the original. Don't compromise for grey, "wet" copies from an old corner drugstore copy machine.

Proposals and Desktop Publishing

Companies are aware that the form of the proposal adds or detracts substantially from its persuasiveness. More and more proposal writers, therefore, are turning to desktop publishing to produce proposals that appear to be typeset. The proposal in Figure 10–6, for example, was prepared entirely on an IBM PC, the software program Ventura Publisher, and a laser printer.

Final Tricks of the Trade   We have discussed how to make proposals logical, orderly, persuasive, accurate, and attractive. Finally, consider a few hints, the final touches, to help you create winning proposals.

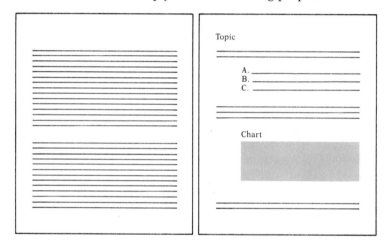

1. Use topic headings and inset material freely. Judge for yourself the difference in effect.
2. Never bury crucial information in appendixes or footnotes. If the reader needs to know a fact to make sense of your proposal, include that fact in the text itself. If necessary, you can state the fact briefly in the text, elaborating elsewhere in a footnote or appendix. Never, however, should the reader simply be told "See footnote 34" for important information.
3. Be direct and specific, rather than vague and general.

   Vague, General   (a proposal to remodel the floor plan of a factory):
      Production has been hampered by the physical separation of related work units.

   Direct, Specific:
      The company loses $400 per day in lost time as employees from the graphic and the word processing units walk the 700-yard path between their two related work areas.

FIGURE 10–6
Proposal prepared with personal computer and desktop publishing software

A Marketing Plan for Regent Street Hotels
proposed by
Victor A. Ramirez
Ramirez Marketing Associates, Inc.
Seattle, Washington

Proposal Overview

The seven hotels located between the 300 and 900 blocks of Regent Street, Bellevue, Washington, enjoyed brisk year-round business throughout the 1970s, when State Highway 17 brought thousands of tourists past their doors each day. With the opening of Interstate 9 in 1981, however, the traffic flow on Regent Street decreased dramatically, and with it the profitability of the seven hotels in question. This proposal describes an affordable way to recapture, in 1989, up to 45 percent of the tourist traffic lost to Interstate 9, and up to 80 percent in later years.

Key Marketing Factors

All seven hotels share basic marketing advantages that should be developed:

- *clean, attractive, and reasonable lodging*

- *price and location advantages over urban Seattle hotels or rural motels*

- *a cooperative spirit among hotel owners, allowing joint effort to solve joint problems*

The missing factor, of course, is **exposure**--all due to the rerouting of traffic flow. Tourists who might spend one or more days in Bellevue speed on through to Seattle hotels simply because they don't see available lodging along the Interstate. To date, state laws have prevented individual businesses from displaying billboard advertising along Interstate routes.

The Proposed Solution--A Shared Plan with Shared Advantages

Ramirez Associates proposes to significantly increase the exposure of Regent Street hotels in three ways:

- *to negotiate on behalf of the hotels with Miller Grain Storage, Inc., to place an eye-catching advertisement for the hotels on Miller's 22-story grain silo beside Interstate 17. (Such advertising has not been prohibited by state billboard laws.)*

- *to design brochures for distribution at all three Interstate Information rest stops. From these brochures, tourists will learn how to find Regent Street and what kind of accommodations are available there.*

- *to work with city and state departments to install prominent "Lodging" markers at the Regent Street off-ramp of Interstate 17.*

Terms

Corporate representatives of Ramirez Associates will be pleased to meet with hotel owners at their convenience to discuss methods, personnel, milestones, and costs for this marketing plan. We will be pleased to present the concept in more detail at a future meeting of the Regent Street Hotel Association. To arrange for this presentation, please contact Judith Foster at 983-2832.

Ramirez Associates is grateful for this opportunity to help you achieve your business goals.

Vague, General   (a proposal to market a new perfume):
> In the past, our company has had success marketing floral fragrances.

Direct, Specific:
> Since 1980, our company has marketed "Orchid Memories," "Gardenias in May," and "Roses are Red." Each of these flower fragrances produced a quick profit margin of well over 50 percent in the first nine months of sales.

Proposals are the primary means by which business asks for work to do, for money to earn. Long or short, the proposal requires a writer's sharpest writing skills. Business writers who demonstrate the ability to write winning proposals reap substantial professional and financial rewards. These writers quickly make themselves indispensable in businesses small and large.

THE COMBINED PROPOSAL/CONTRACT

Especially when independent contractors and small businesses are involved, proposals may be combined with contracts, as in the popular format shown in Figure 10–7. Using this simple and straightforward model, a proposal writer can treat key proposal items in a brief way: a description of the proposed work, specification of payment, including terms and time, and necessary qualifications protecting both the proposer and reader.

Note that the reader of this proposal need only say "yes" by a signature to finalize the contract. In this way, small firms avoid the lost business that often comes with lengthy periods of contract preparation, legal consultation, and second thoughts.

Can a company or researcher very well qualified to do a job not receive the assignment? The answer is an unqualified and resounding "Yes!" Such instances are not uncommon, and the reason for the rejection is simply that the proposal submitted was either (1) nonresponsive to the request, and/or (2) it did not communicate clearly, concisely, completely, and correctly.

It is wise to check the format and layout of the proposal for visual attractiveness. Is there plenty of white space? Effective use of topic headings? Easy-to-understand charts, tables, and graphs? Is it clearly and logically organized? Are references, supplements, and appendixes easy to find? Companies have lost multimillion dollar contracts because the proposal submitted was poor. But the story doesn't stop there. When a contract is not received, it may well mean not only the loss of major funding but the loss of jobs for hundreds of employees.

FIGURE 10–7

Combined proposal/contract

PROPOSAL and CONTRACT

Date_____, 19_____

TO_____

_____Telephone_____

Dear Sir:

_____propose to furnish all materials and perform all labor necessary to complete the following (if proposal is for a swimming pool, see important provisions on reverse):

_____
_____
_____
_____
_____
_____
_____
_____
_____
_____
_____

All of the above work to be completed in a substantial and workmanlike manner according to standard practices for the sum of_____ Dollars ($_____)

Progress payments to be made_____

_____as the work progresses

to the value of_____per cent (_____%) of all work completed. The entire

amount of contract to be paid within_____days after completion.

This proposal is valid until_____and if accepted by that time work will commence _____days after acceptance and will be substantially completed approximately_____working days thereafter subject to delays caused by acts of God, stormy weather, uncontrollable labor trouble, or other unforeseen contingencies.

Any alteration or deviation from the above specifications involving extra cost of material or labor will only be executed upon written orders for same, and will become an extra charge over the sum mentioned in this contract. All agreements must be made in writing.

"NOTICE TO OWNER"
(Section 7018, 7019—Contractors License Law)

Under the Mechanics' Lien Law, any contractor, subcontractor, laborer, materialman or other person who helps to improve your property and is not paid for his labor, services or material, has a right to enforce his claim against your property. This means that, after a court hearing, your property could be sold by a court officer and the proceeds of the sale used to satisfy the indebtedness. This can happen even if you have paid your own contractor in full, if the subcontractor, laborer, or supplier remains unpaid.
Under the law you may protect yourself against such claims by filing, before commencing such work of improvement, an original contract for the work of improvement or a modification thereof, in the office of the county recorder of the county where the property is situated and requiring that a contractor's payment bond be recorded in such office. Said bond shall be in an amount not less than fifty percent (50%) of the contract price and shall, in addition to any conditions for the performance of the contract, be conditioned for the payment in full of the claims of all persons furnishing labor, services, equipment or materials for the work described in said contract.

Respectfully submitted,

By_____

_____
Address

_____
Telephone

Contractor's State License No._____

Name and Registration Number of any salesperson who solicited or negotiated this contract:

Name_____   No._____

If this Proposal and Contract is for a Home Improvement and the Proposal and/or the Acceptance is made at other than the premises at which the contractor or the owner normally carries on a business, then the additional terms and conditions on the reverse side of this form are applicable and so incorporated into this contract, and you, the buyer, may cancel this transaction at any time prior to midnight of the third business day after the date of this transaction. See the attached notice of cancellation form (Wolcotts Form 560) for an explanation of this right.

ACCEPTANCE

You are hereby authorized to furnish all materials and labor required to complete the work mentioned in the above proposal, for which_____agree to pay the amount mentioned in said proposal, and according to the terms thereof. I have read and agree to the provisions on the reverse side of this Proposal and Contract, and any attachments hereto.

_____
Owner's Name

_____
Street Address

_____
City   State   Zip

_____
Place of Business

Date_____, 19_____

ACCEPTED:_____
(Owner's Signature)

Contractors are required by law to be licensed and regulated by the Contractors' State License Board. Any questions concerning a contractor may be referred to the registrar of the board whose address is:

Contractors' State License Board
1020 N Street
Sacramento, California 95814

IMPORTANT: SEE REVERSE SIDE FOR IMPORTANT INFORMATION

WOLCOTTS FORM 564—REVISED 6-77—PROPOSAL AND CONTRACT

POLICY MANUALS

Almost every organization has a series of policy statements, bulletins, and even manuals. When firms become large, with locations in various cities or even countries, it is necessary to record policies in a dozen different areas of company activities to secure uniformity of internal action.

Certainly there are policies needed on recruitment, retention, and termination of personnel; quality of product levels; manufacture and distribution of goods; consumer, community, and government relations; financing; handling of receivables, payables, and advertising; press standards and relationships; and a dozen other areas.

A detailed discussion of this subject is obviously beyond the scope of this book. However, it should be noted that policies must be decided on very carefully, be approved by top management, distributed carefully, and discussed thoroughly with those personnel charged with policy implementation. In addition, the writing style used in policies must be clear, objective, and concise.

PROCEDURE MANUALS

The documentation of procedures can vary depending on the audience for whom the procedures are intended. For example, Procedure X, for shipping a new line of TV sets nationally and internationally, has been changed. A new procedure must be written for the shipping departments for six warehouse locations. Note, however, that one set of procedures must be written for the line employees involved, one for managers (to include all new documentation instructions concerning bills of lading, government forms, tariff regulations, computer entry, etc.), and one for company management to appreciate the various steps and implications involved. Most procedures will reflect the following steps to a greater or lesser degree, according to who the reader is:

- Introduction: why the procedure has been instituted together with background needed to understand the rationale for carrying through the procedure.
- Description of major steps and functions.
- Specific step-by-step instructions using short, clear sentences together with explanatory visuals.
- Conclusion recapitulating major procedural steps, with an added statement of why the work is vital and how it fits into the company's overall goal or design.

As in the case of policies, many organizations, because of size and complexity, have drawn up carefully tailored procedures manuals for dozens of activities.

JOB DESCRIPTIONS

Job descriptions naturally derive from procedure statements. However, many organizations either have manuals of job descriptions, and no procedure manuals, or procedure manuals and no job descriptions. In any event, job descriptions are usually designed for situations where a number of employees carry out the same or very similar jobs.

Job descriptions usually give the employee a detailed step-by-step description of what should be done to accomplish a specific assignment. Very often the steps are numbered; the language is concise and clear; and almost invariably the words are supplemented by visual aids. One successful method is to divide the steps of the job description into two columns. The left-hand column describes what must be done. An adjacent right-hand column describes the result of the action.

5. Tighten wing bolt B to maximum	5. Yellow heat bar should now protrude from side approximately 2 inches
6. Attach identification number to *smooth* surface of yellow heat bar	6. Identification number should be directly above imprinting "Garrison Corporation" in metal frame

Obviously the language of job descriptions must be in accordance with the technical and educational level of the reader. With the influx of foreign workers into the U.S.A. in recent years, many job descriptions are now written in other languages, among them Spanish, Korean, Vietnamese, and Chinese.

WRITING A BUSINESS PLAN

Background

Today there are many individuals who have excellent ideas for various entrepreneurial ventures but are short of cash to fund such efforts. On the other hand, venture capital organizations exist which possess financial resources for just such investments. How to bring them together—for the benefit of both parties—is basically a matter of communication. And the communication vehicle usually used is designated a Business Plan.

Obviously, there are many more plans written than there are plans accepted and funded. The fault at times is not in the entrepreneurial idea itself, but in the written document which does an inadequate job in its attempt to secure the funding to implement the plan. One Boston venture capital firm received 1200 plans during the period of several months. Of these, 600 were read, 45 were researched, and only 14 funded.[2]

Venture capital experts indicate that many business plans are too long: they include data and information which are not vital, gloss over areas that are critical, and sometimes completely ignore central issues such as "the competition," marketing steps, and the experience (or lack of it) of the key personnel involved.

The View of the Venture Capital Organization

Funding organizations may be classified as "high risk" businesses. However, in an effort to lessen the risk, every precaution is usually taken to insure that investments made will almost certainly provide a viable return. For that reason, the investor wants to know as much as possible about the product or service being offered, who will manage the organization (background, expertise, experience, knowledge, commitment), the market and the marketing plan, the competition, the manufacturing plan and process, the distribution network, long range goals, and a dozen other vital factors. All of this should (and must) be set down clearly, concisely, and completely in a business plan.

Writing the Business Plan

Perhaps the first step in writing the business plan is to determine what topics and in what depth the venture capital organization perceives as vital. This can usually be determined through a conference or from a guide booklet or form that has already been prepared by the funding group. Certainly this will vary based on whether capital is desired for a product or for a service; whether the funding amount requested is $5 thousand or $5 million; whether the business will be cyclical or on-going; and whether the market is local, national, or international.

Following is a checklist which briefly outlines the format of most business plans. Please consult more detailed guides for further development of the subject. Other guides, however, only elaborate on this basic checklist.

[2]*The Wall Street Journal*, May 15, 1987, p. 36D.

Section One: An Executive Summary This section should contain a brief description of the product and service, why it is marketable, possible future demands for the product or services, and an overall view of the present position of the company and personnel involved.

Section Two: Products and Services This should cover a rather full description of the product or service, where it stands in its life cycle (is it a new product or a mature one that has been in the market for some time), the present status of patents or copyrights, and future plans for product research.

Section Three: Manufacturing and Distribution A treatment of the manufacturing process should be noted in this section: how complex the operations are and what logistics are required, what the production capacity of the present organization is, and at what percentage (of 100 percent production) is the present level. In addition, the distribution system necessary should be presented along with how complete (or incomplete) it is at the present time.

Section Four: Marketing Plans This is certainly a critical segment of the business plan. It should cite facts on the industry in which the product is competing and what the present sales trends are. What are the short- and long-term profit potentials?

In addition, a specific marketing plan should identify the market segment(s) targeted. A customer profile should also be included as well as an analysis of market needs, market segments, sales by geographic areas and how these areas will change with the passage of time, increased competition, and environmental, social, and economic changes. Also included in the marketing section should be a brief analysis on how and why "this" marketing plan is not only different but also superior to that of competitors.

Section Five: Financial Information The business plan should contain a financial statement for the current year and (if possible) for the previous three years. Financial projections should also be presented for the next three to five years. These should include projections for sales, cost of sales, cash flow, pro forma balance sheets, and key statistics (current ratio, debt-equity ratio, and inventory turnovers).

Included in this section, or perhaps a separate one, should be a comment on pending lawsuits by or against the organization, the potential for liability, insurance coverage in force or needed, and related areas.

Section Six: Management Personnel This critical area should list the key management individuals with a summary of their personal background, work experiences, education, community activities, and memberships.

Overall Comment on the Business Plan

In essence, the business plan is a type of proposal. It is directed to an organization for the primary purpose of selling the company presenting the plan. If the effort is successful, funds are advanced so the original concept or idea for a new product or service may enter the market. However, those who assume the risk of advancing their funds and those of *their* investors, are critical individuals. They must not only be convinced of the potential market for the product or service, but every detail of the enterprise must be substantiated and explained to their satisfaction. That is the task the successful business plan must complete.

QUESTIONS FOR STUDY

1. How would you describe unnecessary reports in business? Why are they written? How can they be prevented?
2. A progress report has three basic parts. What are they?
3. Reports are expensive to produce. Using the figures suggested in the chapter, calculate the cost to a company of producing 75 reports per year, each averaging 18 hours of preparation time. Discuss how substantial cost savings can be achieved by better report management.
4. What two kinds of reports can sometimes be written with the aid of a form?
5. Many companies attempt to streamline the report process by providing standardized report forms for use by report writers. What advantages or disadvantages do you see in this practice?
6. Give an example of a form report beyond one that is mentioned in the text.
7. What value do progress reports have?
8. What is an RFP? How does it relate to the writing of a proposal?
9. What categories are common to both long and short proposals?
10. Do proposal awards always go to the most capable bidder? Explain your response.
11. Name six areas in which policies are commonly established and published within business.
12. What is the difference between a procedural guide and a proposal?
13. What is a procedure manual? Give an example describing the use of such a manual.
14. What is the two-column approach to job description? Create a brief example not found in the text.
15. Both employers and employees may take written job descriptions very seriously. Why?

EXERCISES

16. Assume that your CEO has given you the task of shortening company reports. Develop a list of guidelines for use by company writers seeking to have their say in fewer words. Make your suggestions as specific as possible.
17. You're in charge of developing a new product line for the company. You want to receive progress reports from your development team. Make up a product line, then describe in detail each of the progress reports you would want to receive from start to finish with regard to the project.
18. As a manager of a small glass company (manufacturing mirrors, windows, and windshields), you are concerned about the frequent bickering among your six employees over who does what. List at least four duties for each of the six employees.
19. You've invented "Lopside," a board game for children and adults. A wealthy friend shows interest in backing your developmental efforts, but first requires a proposal from you. In no more than three pages, propose your plans to the prospective investor.
20. Create an RFP for some improvement that needs to be made at your campus or workplace.
21. Western Ways Mail Order Company is interested in including your handmade Christmas decorations in an upcoming catalog. The company requests that you sum up in a brief proposal what you will do for them and what you expect in return. Do so in not more than three pages.
22. Imagine that you are chief developer of a new office tower. Your funding agencies have requested regular progress reports from you. List six stages at which you plan to send progress reports. (For example, you might send one report after land acquisition.)
23. As office supervisor, you're tired of repeated questions about common office procedures. Choose an office activity or procedure, and then write a clear description of the process, as if for a procedures manual.
24. Consider the following facts. Use them as the basis for a short progress report directed to Ms. Harriet Conway, Executive Director, Publications Division, Western Enterprises, Inc.

Facts: You recently conducted a survey to determine who reads what in the monthly company magazine, *Western Worlds*. On February 6, the current issue was mailed to the home addresses of 2804 company employees. A February 25 telephone interview of 200 employees chosen at random showed that:

- 24 percent did not know if the February issue had arrived at their homes
- 55 percent had not looked at the issue

- among those who had at least looked through the magazine, 26 percent could recall no single detail, article title, picture, or advertisement from the issue

The magazine costs the company $1.86 per issue delivered to an employee's home. Total publication costs are escalating at 17 percent per year.

As Director of Communications for the company, you have assumed responsibility for publishing and distributing the magazine.

During the past three months, you have spent $16,500 making the magazine look more professional. You have three unsolicited letters from employees praising the "new look" of the February issue. In addition, you have received one scorching letter condemning the February issue as "more company money spent on frills when it could be spent on salaries."

The company is trying to decide whether the magazine should be expanded, cut back, or dissolved. No statistics exist for determining how readers responded to the magazine at an earlier period. Ms. Conway has asked you to sum up in a progress report how your efforts to improve the magazine are being received by employees.

25. Four months have passed since you submitted your progress report to Ms. Conway in Problem 24. She has asked you for monthly periodic reports detailing the essential facts about that month's issue of *Western World:*

- number of pages
- cost per issue delivered
- number delivered to employees
- standard features
- new features
- use of company contributors
- use of freelance writers
- number of photographs
- number of full-time employee hours spent in editing, production, and distribution
- percentage of your work time spent on *Western Worlds*
- number of unsolicited letters received within 14 days of delivery
- number of complaints, written or oral, received within 14 days of delivery

She has told you that your periodic reports will help establish a suitable budget for the magazine at the end of the current fiscal year. Prepare a periodic report satisfying the director's criteria. Design and submit a report form that can be "filled in" each month and submitted to Ms. Conway.

Long Reports

The reader of the corporate annual report must be aware of what has not been said as well as what has.

The long report is written after careful investigation and research. Its style is formal, and its statements are carefully substantiated with facts and fig-ures. The subject may be a possible corporate merger, a proposed marketing plan, a corporate five-year program, the development of a shopping center, or any other matter calling for thorough and careful study. Such a study may include trends in population growth, economic analysis, sales potential, cul-tural contributions, ethnic considerations, national and international affairs, industrial change in a particular area, and other contributing factors.

OBJECTIVES

The objectives of the long report may be one or more of the following: to per-suade, to inform, to compare, to analyze, or to argue.

The Persuasive Report

Suppose we want to convince our readers that a new forty-eight story apart-ment building to be constructed next year should be heated and air-condi-tioned with natural gas. We will aim our arguments at several groups: the architects, the financiers, the contractor, and probably the firm that will operate or sponsor the building. Because these are all intelligent, analytical readers, the report must be buttressed with statistical data and information at every point. A good deal of logical reasoning is required. The purpose is to demonstrate why the building's heating and cooling systems, as well as its kitchen equipment, should be gas rather than electric. The report must persuade through the logic of its arguments and the strength of its substantiating data and should avoid an overly emphatic or hard-sell approach.

The Informational Report

As the name suggests, the **informational report** serves only to present data that may be used as a record or as the basis for decision making. Perhaps the most frequent fault of such reports is overkill: they smother the reader with too much information. The scope and limitations of the topic should be carefully defined. The informational report is sometimes referred to as an *investigative* or *research* report.

The Comparative Report

When management wants to make a decision, it may call for a report comparing alternatives. Should we purchase this plant or that one? Should we introduce a new line of brushes or not? Should we open another outlet? Should we stock Product A or competitive Product B? The **comparative report** is primarily concerned with an evaluation and comparison of two or more products or services.

The Analytical Report

It is the purpose of the **analytical report** to appraise a situation and sort out the factors affecting it. For example, we may want to examine the future of our industry in relation to "Our Growth and Expansion in the Next Five Years." We state our firm's goals and objectives and suggest strategies for reaching them. The report should examine all supportive activities within the firm such as personnel, finance, manufacturing, marketing, production, distribution, and research and development. It should also analyze the external environment: the market, consumerism, raw material supply, lifestyles and values, legal and legislative forces, energy, and so on. Typically an analytical report concludes with recommendations for a specific course of action.

The Argumentative Report

The **argumentative report** strongly urges a specific course of action and substantiates its recommendations with data and documentation. There is nothing subtle about this "selling job," as contrasted with the persuasive report. The writer wants the reader to follow a specific course of action, and argues for it.

COMPONENTS

When a report runs to six pages or longer, it covers a fairly wide area and includes a good deal of information. It is at this point that we begin to think of helping the reader assimilate the material by including a title page, a table of contents, a summary, and perhaps an appendix for statistical and/or reference data.

Some of the specific sections of the long report, in the order in which they would appear, are discussed in the pages that follow. Few reports contain all the divisions listed, although most long reports carry a letter of transmittal, title page, table of contents, and summary, in addition to the basic body.

Preliminaries

Letter of Transmittal   A letter of transmittal almost invariably accompanies the formal report and attempts to set the stage for the reader so that he or she will understand why and for whom the report was prepared. Placed at the top of the report or clipped to the title page, it usually covers the following items (see Figure 11–1, p. 294):

1. Authorization for research.
2. The purpose of the project.
3. The limitations of the report, noting legal restrictions and the boundaries of time and funds. This can be of great help to the writer because it tells the reader what to expect and what not to expect.
4. A listing of certain key sources.
5. Reference to any finding in the report that is of particular importance or interest to the reader. Recommendations and/or acknowledgments of assistance may be included in the letter of transmittal.

Title Page   The title page should carry the report title; the name of the person, group, or organization for whom the report is written; the author's name; the name of the group or company issuing the report; and the date (see Figure 11–1, p. 295).

"Cute" titles should not be used (such as "Pressing Problems: Parker Garment Co."), although there is no reason why a title cannot be informative and interesting. For example, a General Electric report was titled "What They Think of Their Higher Education." And an aircraft company issued one titled "Flying High: A Survey of Supersonic Aircraft."

Letters of Authorization and Acceptance   The first page in government reports often cites the meeting, conference, or legislative action that authorized the appropriation of funds for the survey reported on. By clearly setting down the problem, scope, and limitations for research, the letter of authorization can prevent later misunderstanding. This letter is not usually found in business reports.

Some reports also include a letter of acceptance. Although such a letter is not common, it can be used to accept, revise, or change the terms or conditions established in the letter of authorization. If it serves as an agreement between two companies, it may also be used to cite times, fees, and other contractual obligations. The letter of acceptance is part of the mechanics leading to the report's assignment and acceptance. It is usually not part of the report, although some government reports display it in an appendix.

Table of Contents   The table of contents (see Figure 11–1, p. 296) is prepared after the report has been typed. It lists chapter or section titles and subdivisions, with page numbers indicated for each. The headings should agree with those in the final outline. Lists of illustrations and tables may also be included (see Figure 11–1, p. 297).

Foreword or Preface   Because the letter of transmittal normally sets the stage for the reader, a foreword or preface is not usually found in a report. When it is, it goes into some detail about the general scope and purpose of the report.

Summary   The summary, sometimes included and often referred to as a review, brief, abstract, synopsis, digest, or executive summary, is designed to give the busy reader a concise overview of the entire report. It should state the problem, the scope of the investigation, the research methods used, the key ideas in the report proper, the conclusions reached, and the course of action recommended. The writing style should be crisp, penetrating, and objective. Topic headings may be used in the summary to assist the reader further.

Body

The body of most reports can be divided into three major sections: introduction, discussion, and conclusions and recommendations.

Introduction   If the report has a letter of transmittal, a summary section, or other prefatory sections, probably a good part of the introduction has already been presented. In any event, the introduction should give the reader sufficient background to fully understand the report (see Figure 11–1, p. 300).

The introduction may include a history of the situation and a clear statement of the problem to be solved or examined. Limitations of the investigation should be noted and the purpose of the report stated. The research methods used should be explained as well as how validity or reliability of the survey was secured. If specific definitions are important to the clear understanding of the report, they may be presented at this time. The introduction may also explain the plan of presentation of the report. If the reader is told that all statistical data may be found in the appendix, that sample questionnaires are in the body, and that this report is based on the initial study dated March 15, 19___ , then he or she will be better oriented to the report.

Discussion   The discussion is the vital part of the report and makes up 75 to 85 percent of the total length. It is in the discussion that the investigator presents, analyzes, and interprets the information and points out significant facts and relationships among the data.

Throughout the discussion, the write should assist the reader by conciseness and clarity of presentation. To this end, it is helpful to use topic and subtopic headings and to present some of the data in easy-to-analyze tables, charts, and graphs.

Conclusions and Recommendations   Conclusions and recommendations are given in most types of reports. The writer must be sure that each conclusion or recommendation is thoroughly substantiated in the body of the report. At no time should the executive reading the report ask, "Well, where is the evidence for this?" The evidence should be in the discussion section of the report.

Lately there has been a trend toward placing the conclusions and recommendations immediately after the summary or introduction rather than at the end of the report. This makes sense. The top executive receives reports from every division and department of his organization. These are vital if he is to know about all the firm's activities and to appreciate the big picture. He doesn't need to know all the details but should be familiar with each division's broad plans. If he can get that information from the summary, conclusions, and recommendations sections of a report, then he need not plow through the entire text.

Addenda   Following the body of the report are the appendixes and various supplements, such as copies of questionnaires, interview schedules, diagrams, statistics, maps, and any other information related to the subject of the report that may be of interest to the reader.

THE CORPORATE ANNUAL REPORT

Perhaps the best-known example of a long report is the once-a-year summary of company activities that is issued by thousands of corporations.

Modern shareholders want to know how "their" company is being managed. Their desire for a clear, concise, and complete picture, coupled with

FIGURE 11–1

A long report

April 15, 19__

Mr. John M. Wanamaker
Personnel Director
Webster Manufacturing Corporation
15335 Morrison Street
San Francisco, CA 94111

Dear Mr. Wanamaker:

The attached report is the result of the research project that you
requested in your letter of January 20, 19__. It is a study of corporate
listening training programs, combined with an analysis of top Personnel
Administrators' opinions regarding the importance of listening training
in industry. You will find our conclusions and recommendations included
in this report.

    The purposes of the study were to determine:

      1. How extensively corporations are utilizing listening
         training programs
      2. How listening as a communication skill is viewed by
         top Personnel Administrators
      3. How top Personnel Administrators rate the listening
         ability of both their employees and fellow managers

The primary research used was limited to a questionnaire mailed to top
Personnel Administrators of 98 randomly selected corporations that were
members of the 19__ Fortune "500 Largest Industrial Corporations" in the
United States. Several articles drawn from journals and magazines were
used for the secondary research.

This project was both a challenging and rewarding undertaking. We
believe that our findings will aid you and other top Personnel Administrators in acquiring further understanding of corporate listening
training programs in the event you wish to implement your own program at
Webster. If you have any questions, please call on us; we will be happy
to answer them.

Cordially yours,

John Newton   *Michael C. Horasanian*

John J. Newton   Michael C. Horasanian
Research Associate   Research Associate

THE VALUE TO INDUSTRY

OF

LISTENING TRAINING PROGRAMS

Presented to

John M. Wanamaker
Personnel Director

Webster Manufacturing Corporation

Submitted by

John J. Newton and Michael C. Horasanian
Research Associates

Church and Keeling Corporation

April 15, 19___

TABLE OF CONTENTS

i

LIST OF TABLES

EXECUTIVE SUMMARY

Most persons have had courses in reading, writing, and speaking. However, listening, the communication skill used most often, is not usually part of the American educational system. In this report, we have attempted to determine the importance industry places on listening as a communication skill and the extent to which it has implemented listening training programs.

The report is based on a nationwide mail questionnaire sent to randomly chosen members of the <u>Fortune</u> "500 Largest Industrial Corporations" in the United States; it is also based on secondary research from magazine and journal articles.

The results of the survey indicated that top Personnel Administrators consider listening to be the most important communication skill. A slight majority of corporations are utilizing listening training programs, and these programs seem to be effective over time.

Since listening is frequently looked upon as an important communication skill, we recommend that industry implement listening training programs for their employees in order to increase productivity and efficiency of operations in general.

1

CONCLUSIONS

1. Top Personnel Administrators consider listening the most important communication skill for industry.

2. Currently a significant number of major corporations utilize listening training programs.

3. Top Personnel Administrators feel that both their employees and fellow managers are not listening at optimum levels.

4. Corporations that encourage their employees to give feedback to their superiors report higher levels of listening efficiency among both employees and managers.

5. The longer listening training programs have been in effect, the more they have increased levels of listening efficiency among both managers and employees.

RECOMMENDATIONS

1. Corporations should implement listening training programs if they feel that their managers and employees are not listening at desired levels of efficiency.

2. Corporations should encourage their employees to give feedback to their superiors in order to increase levels of listening efficiency among both employees and managers.

2

INTRODUCTION

Background Information

Miscommunication due to poor listening costs industry billions of dollars every year, according to Dr. Lyman K. Steil, a consultant to Sperry Rand Corporation.[1] The importance of good listening skills in business today cannot be emphasized enough. Persons in business today spend more than 50% of their work time in listening-based activities.[2] Even though listening is so vital in business, it is the least taught communication skill in the American educational system. This is a major problem facing American industry today. The way many companies are battling it is by using special listening training programs and techniques of their own.

Purpose of the Report

The purpose of this report is (1) to discover how listening as a communication skill is viewed by top Personnel Administrators, (2) to determine the extent to which corporations are utilizing listening training programs and techniques, and (3) to discover how top Personnel Administrators rate the listening ability of both their employees and fellow managers.

Hypothesis

Listening is a vital communication skill in industry that can be significantly improved by utilizing training programs.

Scope and Depth of the Project

The object of this report is to give Personnel Administrators a general idea of the importance of listening as a communication skill in industry, and to urge them to study further the benefi-

3

cial impact that implementing a listening training program and
listening techniques might have on the corporation.

The primary source of this information was a mail questionnaire (see Appendix II).

The secondary sources, such as journal and magazine ar-
ticles, were found in the University of Southern California Roy
P. Crocker Business Administration Library, the University of
California at Los Angeles, and other libraries.

SPERRY'S LISTENING TRAINING PROGRAM

One of the leading companies implementing a listening training
program is the Sperry Corporation. Sperry began its program in
mid-1979. This company has not only increased the efficiency of
its corporate operations, but it also has created a highly successful advertising campaign that promotes the importance of
good listening.

Sperry started by using seminars to train its 700 most
senior U.S. and European managers. After its advertising campaign began to take effect, demand for the seminar from employees at all levels virtually exploded.

Because of the enormous number of requests for the listening seminars, more practical methods of presenting listening material had to be implemented. Sperry's next step was to produce
a videotape that explained why listening was important, followed
by a record covering the basics of good vs. bad listening, and a
booklet on good listening techniques sent to all of its 55,000
U.S. employees' homes.[3] By the fall of 1982, a staggering 10,000
employees attended just the formal listening seminars alone.

4

Sperry's most recent program consists of a self-test to reveal retention of material, films illustrating poor and effective listening habits, and role playing models for employees to practice what they have learned (see Schedule A). According to Jim Van Horn, Sperry's Internal Management Consultant, 75% of participants from the engineering division have experienced a change in attitude toward listening, and 45% have experienced a change in behavior as a result of participating in the program.

When asked if he could specifically point out any costs from poor listening in his company, Sperry's CEO, J. Paul Lyet, replied, "How about $1,000,322?" Apparently a customer asked for a quote on a large order, and no one heard him. Here is what happened:

> Of the two employees who were present when the customer asked for the quotation, one said he didn't hear it. The other said he had not heard that it was wanted within two weeks. They lost the business because they didn't react in time. They didn't react in time because they didn't listen.[4]

This example clearly demonstrates that good listening skills are invaluable in order to conduct business successfully in today's world.

SCHEDULE A

Following are ten bad listening habits that the Sperry training program tries to eradicate.[5]

1. Calling the subject uninteresting

2. Criticizing the speaker's delivery or mannerisms

3. Getting stimulated by something the speaker says

5

4. Listening primarily for facts
5. Trying to outline everything
6. Faking attention to the speaker
7. Allowing interfering distractions
8. Avoiding difficult material
9. Letting emotion-laden words arouse personal antagonism
10. Wasting the advantage of thought speed (daydreaming)

CORPORATE LISTENING TECHNIQUES

The implications of good listening skills are not only external, but also internal. Poor management-employee relations can lead to high employee turnover. This is expensive. Employees must feel that they can approach management to discuss not only on-the-job problems, but also personal problems. According to Dr. Earl Planty, executive counselor for the pharmaceutical firm of Johnson & Johnson:

> By far the most effective method by which executives can tap ideas of subordinates is sympathetic listening in the many day-to-day informal contacts within and outside the work place. There is no system that will do the job in an easier manner. . . . Nothing can equal an executive's willingness to hear.[6]

Maintaining good management-employee relations and keeping employees happy add to the unity of the corporation, and, as a result, employee turnover is reduced.

Techniques used to listen to employees vary from company to company. A good example of how a large corporation undertakes this task is the Bank of America. Even though Bank of America is the world's largest bank, with 77,000 employees, it has outstanding management-employee relations.

6

One of the bank's techniques is the use of employee surveys. These are used to reveal the moods and attitudes of its
employees toward management, benefits, their salaries, their
jobs, their image of the bank, and other job-related concerns.[7]
The bank surveys a cross-section of its employees every six
months, keeping the questions basically the same in order to
spot changes in employee opinion and see trends. With this constant influx of information, management is able to recognize
potential problems and react accordingly.

Surveys are but one of Bank America's methods of listening
to their employees. Others include an employee assistance department, where employees can contact officers confidentially
for assistance with a problem; Let's Talk It Over, a formal,
six-step employee problem-solving procedure; and Open Line, a
system that provides employees a channel to make anonymous inquiries of bank officials and receive answers within ten days.

General American Life Insurance Company's method of listening to its employees is called "listening posts." Listening
posts are various methods by which management receives feedback
from employees. These include surveys, exit interviews, an employees' advisory panel, and a grievance procedure. All of these
programs ". . . are vital in any effort to remain alert to potential problems and keep management from isolating itself in an
ivory tower."[8]

HOW GOOD LISTENING PRODUCES RESULTS

Management's listening to employees has not only increased the
efficiency of operations, but also has helped restructure operations for the better. Employees on the line are the first to
discover if there is a better way of getting work done. Histori-

7

cally, this precious information has been suppressed because of the dictatorial structure or yesteryear's management. Every modern manager must listen well to his or her employees.

One such manager is Knut Rygh, production manager for Norwegian bicycle manufacturer Jonas Oglaend. What Rygh and his associates did was to listen to line workers' ideas regarding the layout of the plant. Originally, the plant made use of an assembly-line system, but now, after allowing line workers to develop their own production structure, the plant has sixteen highly autonomous work groups. The employees now view their work groups as if they were managing their own company. They are responsible for their own production levels and quality control, and must solve their own problems. During the four years that the new plan has been in effect, workers' attitudes toward management have changed for the better, and employee turnover rates have dropped from 11.5% to 9.6%. Management's main aim was to improve quality, but productivity rose too, about 20%.[9] Jonas Oglaend discovered that listening to employees was a profitable investment.

SURVEY METHOD

Our specific survey of Personnel Administrators was conducted over a fourteen-day period from March 4 to April 6, 19__.

Sample Size

A random sample of 100 corporations was selected from the 1982 _Fortune_ "500 Largest Industrial Corporations" in the United States.[10]

Questionnaires were mailed to the top Personnel Administrators of 98 of the corporations we selected, making an effective sample size of 98.

Analysis of Questionnaire

The questionnaire was formulated to assess three general issues:

1. How top Personnel Administrators valued the importance of listening as a communication skill for their industry.
2. What percentage of major industrial corporations were using listening training programs.
3. How top Personnel Administrators rated the ability of their employees and fellow managers to listen to them.

SURVEY RESULTS

The results on the following pages are separated into five sections. The first section deals with questionnaire returns. The other four sections cover each of the three general issues just described, along with several results extrapolated from the comparative results of different combinations of questions.

Response to Questionnaire

The response rate by the cutoff date was 28 returns out of the effective sample 98, or 28.69%.

Six members of our sample population returned unusable answers. Four corporations sent letters of refusal, while two returned questionnaires containing incomprehensible data.

9

The Importance of Listening

When asked to rate the two most important communications skills out of a list of five, the greatest number of respondents, 42.8%, selected listening as the most important. The skill chosen by most respondents as the second most important, by a slight margin, was speaking (see Table A). According to the responses, the respondents view listening as a critical skill for both managers and employees. On a 10-point scale, listening as an employee skill received a mean score of 8.11, while listening as a management skill received a mean of 8.50. The rating most frequently given for both managers and employees was 10 (out of 10). These results tend to indicate that while listening is regarded as very important for both managers and employees, it is crucial for managers to listen well. Interestingly, not a single respondent selected a value of less than 5, or "important," for this question.

TABLE A
The Importance of Listening

Rate these communication skills in order of importance for your industry.

Choice	Reading	Writing	Listening	Speaking	Nonverbal	Total
First	6	2	12	8	0	28
Second	5	6	7	8	2	28

These results indicate that top Personnel Administrators viewed listening as the most important communication skill, with speaking the second most important.

The Utilization of Listening Training Programs

A majority, 57.14% of the respondents, indicated that they do, in fact, use listening training programs. When asked why they

10

implemented the programs, the overwhelming majority, 75%, selected the answer "other." No respondents selected "low employee
morale," and only 12.5% each selected "labor inefficiency" and
"misunderstood orders" (see Table B).

Respondents were also asked, "If your company has been
using a listening training program, how long has it been in
effect?" To this question, 26.27% answered "one year or less,"
and 33.33% answered "more than five years."

Of the 42.68% of the respondents who do not have a listening training program, only one out of eleven had plans to implement a new program.

When asked, "How valuable would a listening training program be to your company?" the respondents averaged a score of
6.92 on a 10-point scale. This number is somewhat lower than the
mean for question 2, regarding the importance of listening.
Presumably, a number of firms see listening as an important
skill, but feel that implementing a listening program would not
be worthwhile.

TABLE B

Reasons for Implementing Listening Training

If your company uses a listening training program, what prompted
this action?

Low employee morale	Labor inefficiency	Misunderstood orders	Other	Total
0	2	2	12	16

This indicates that our assumptions as to why listening training
programs were introduced were not accurate.

11

The Ability of Management and Employees to Listen

When asked, "How well do your employees listen to you?" respondents indicated a mean score of 6.74 out of 10. However, when asked the same question of managers, the mean score was 7.11. Again, these results are somewhat lower than the mean scores indicated for question 2, regarding the importance of listening. Apparently, both management and employees are listening at a somewhat lower level than desired (see Table C). Not a single respondent said that employees listen "very well," or a score of 10.

In response to question 8, "Are your employees encouraged to give feedback to their superiors?" the greatest number of respondents selected "always," or 10 out of 10. The mean score was 7.25.

Extrapolated Results

Eight respondents answered "always" to question 8, regarding employee feedback. Those firms, when asked questions 9 and 10, regarding employee and manager listening ability, responded with a mean score of 7.00 for employees and 8.125 for managers. These 6.74 and 7.11, respectively (see Table D).

A significantly lower result was obtained for questions 9 and 10 from respondents who answered 4.00 or 5.00 to question 8. For this group, the mean for question 9 was 5.25, and the mean for question 10 was 5.875. Also, none of the respondents in this group answered any higher than 7.00 on question 10, while in the other group, none answered <u>lower</u> than 7.00 on question 10.

12

TABLE C

Actual Listening vs. Importance of Listening

Responses for question 2:	Responses for questions 9 and 10:
A. Management Average = 8.50	A. Question 10 Average = 7.11
B. Employees' Average = 8.11	B. Question 9 Average = 6.74

This indicates that the attained levels on the right do not meet
the levels of importance given for listening on the left.

TABLE D

How Employee Feedback Affects Listening

Group	Feedback always encouraged	Feedback often encouraged
Managers	Mean listening score = 8.125	Mean listening score = 5.875
Employees	Mean listening score = 7.00	Mean listening score = 5.25

This indicates that when feedback from employees to their superiors is encouraged, the listening efficiency of both managers
and employees increases correspondingly.

The general trend shown here is that corporations that encourage
employees to give feedback to their superiors also employ persons who are better listeners than those employed by firms that
do not encourage feedback.

An interesting pattern was discovered when the data for
question 6, "If your company has been using a listening program,
how long has it been in effect?" were correlated with those of
questions 9 and 10. For the 26.67% of respondents who answered
"one year or less" to question 6, the mean responses for questions 9 and 10 were 6.00 and 6.25, respectively. As the duration
of the training program increased, the level of listening ability moved correspondingly. For those firms with programs in
effect more than five years, the mean scores for the listening

13

ability of employees and managers were 8.25 and 8.00 out of 10 (see Table E).

These results demonstrate that as listening training programs were implemented and utilized, they did, in fact, aid personnel at both the management and employee levels in improving their listening ability. Presumably, the longer the program had been in effect, the more it had contributed to improving listening within the company.

TABLE E

Length of Program and Listening Level

Age of Program

Group years	One year or less	Two to five years	More than five
Managers	Mean = 6.25	Mean = 6.83	Mean = 8.00
Employees	Mean = 6.00	Mean = 7.67	Mean = 8.20

Mean = mean of scores attained when rated for ability to listen

This indicates that as listening training programs have more time to take effect, they do improve the listening ability of both management and employees.

14

APPENDIX I

March 24, 19__

Personnel Administrator's Name
Company Name
Address
Location

Dear Personnel Administrator:

We would appreciate your help in determining to what extent
major corporations are utilizing listening training programs,
and what effect these programs have on business. We are surveying 100 top Personnel Administrators from around the nation
regarding the state of corporate listening techniques and training programs today.

Because you are a highly respected leader in the industry, your
opinions will be invaluable to the success of this survey. The
results of this survey will assist growing organizations such
as yours in deciding if listening techniques and training programs are profitable investments.

Please take a few minutes from your busy schedule to complete
the enclosed questionnaire. Because of our carefully selected
and limited sample size, every response is vital. So that we may
have the results available as soon as possible, please return
the completed questionnaire on or before April 5, 19__. For your
convenience, a stamped, self-addressed envelope is provided.
Please respond today.

Thank you for your cooperation. If you would like a summary of
our survey, contact us at the above address after May 10, 19__.

Very sincerely yours,

John Newton

John J. Newton
Research Associate

Michael C. Horasanian

Michael C. Horasanian
Research Associate

15

APPENDIX II

28 responses from a sample of 98 (28.69% return)

Listening Programs Questionnaire

1. Rate these communication skills in order of importance for your industry. Please indicate #1 (most important) and #2 (second most important) in the spaces provided.

<u>3</u> Reading *21.43%*
<u>4</u> Writing *7.14%*
<u>1</u> Listening *42.86%*
<u>2</u> Speaking *28.57%*
<u>5</u> Nonverbal *0*

2. Rate listening as a management and employee skill. Check appropriate box for each.

Management

Not important   Very important

1	2	3	4	5	6	7	8	9	10
0	0	0	0	2	2	4	3	6	11

Employees

Not important   Very important

1	2	3	4	5	6	7	8	9	10
0	0	0	0	1	5	4	6	4	8

3. Does your company utilize an established listening training program?

Yes *16*   No *12*
   57.14%   *42.86%*

4. If so, what prompted this action? Check appropriate box or explain other.

Low employee morale *0*
Labor inefficiency *2* *12.5%*
Misunderstood orders *2* *12.5%*
Other: _____ *12 75%* _____

16

5. If your company does not utilize a listening training program, does it plan to in the future?

Yes *1*   No *10*
    9.09%   *90.9%*

6. If your company has been using a listening training program,
how long has it been in effect?

1 year or less *4* *26.27%*
2-3 years *3* *20.00%*
4-5 years *3* *20.00%*
More than 5 *5* *33.33%*

7. How valuable would a listening training program be to your
company? Check appropriate box.

Not
valuable   Valuable   Very
                                                         valuable

1 *0*	2 *0*	3 *1*	4 *1*	5 *6*	6 *3*	7 *5*	8 *4*	9 *2*	10 *4*

  3.85% *3.85%* *23.08%* *11.54%* *19.25%* *15.39%* *7.69%* *15.39%*

8. Are your employees encouraged to give feedback to their
superiors? Check appropriate box.

Never   Often   Always

1 *0*	2 *1*	3 *0*	4 *4*	5 *4*	6 *2*	7 *1*	8 *6*	9 *2*	10 *8*

  3.57% *14.29%* *14.29%* *7.14%* *3.57%* *21.43%* *7.14%* *28.57%*

9. How well do your employees listen to you? Check appropriate
box.

Not   Fairly   Very
well   well   well

1 *0*	2 *0*	3 *1*	4 *2*	5 *5*	6 *3*	7 *4*	8 *8*	9 *4*	10 *0*

  3.7% *7.41%* *18.52%* *11.11%* *14.81%* *29.63%* *14.8%*

10. How well do your fellow managers listen to you? Check
appropriate box.

Not   Fairly   Very
well   well   well

1 *0*	2 *0*	3 *0*	4 *0*	5 *6*	6 *3*	7 *6*	8 *7*	9 *4*	10 *1*

  22.22% *11.11%* *22.22%* *25.93%* *14.82%* *3.7%*

PLEASE RETURN THIS QUESTIONNAIRE NO LATER THAN APRIL 5, 19___

THANK YOU

17

SCHEDULE B

Explanations for the selection of "other" in response to question 4: "If your company does utilize an established listening training program, what prompted this action?"

"An effort to improve skills."

"Job content structuring."

"Recognition as integral training skill."

"General need to be an effective listener."

"Belief in importance of improving total communication."

"We realized the importance of listening in the communication process."

"Needs analysis."

"Listening is a basic communication skill necessary for conducting business."

"Realization of the need to maintain skills at high level."

"Recognition of employee development needs."

"Communication enhanced."

"Company survey of employees."

18

NOTES

[1]Susan Mundale, "Why More CEO's Are Mandating Listening and Writing Training," <u>Training</u>, Vol. 17, October 1980, p.39.

[2]David Cushing, "Reading, Writing, and Listening Courses," <u>Training</u>, Vol. 18, February 1981, p. 54.

[3]David Clutterbuck, "How Sperry Made People Listen," <u>International Management</u> (UK), Vol. 36, February 1981, p. 21.

[4]Clutterbuck, p.23.

[5]Clutterbuck, p. 24.

[6]Ralph G. Nichols, "Listening Is a 10-Part Skill," in <u>Communication for Management and Business</u>, 3rd ed., by Norman B. Sigband, p. 618.

[7]David W. Ewing, et al., "Listening and Responding to Employees' Concerns," <u>Harvard Business Review</u>, Vol. 58, January-February 1980, p. 102.

[8]John R. Hundley, "Listening Posts," <u>Personnel</u>, Vol. 53, July-August 1976, p. 39.

[9]Jules Arbose, "Listening to the Workers Produces Results," <u>International Management</u> (UK), Vol. 35, February 1980, p. 40. See also Norman B. Sigband, "Proaction, Not Reaction for Effective Employee Communications," <u>Personnel Journal</u>, March 1982, and Norman B. Sigband, "Face to Face," <u>Communicator's Journal</u>, May-June 1983.

[10]"The 500 Largest Industrial Corporations," <u>Fortune</u>, May 3, 1982, pp. 269-78.

19

BIBLIOGRAPHY

Arbose, Jules. "Listening to the Workers Produces Results." International Management (UK) 35 (February 1980): 40-41.

Clutterbuck, David. "How Sperry Made People Listen." International Management (UK) 36 (February 1981): 21-23.

Cushing, David. "Reading, Writing, and Listening Courses." Training 18 (February 1981): 52 & 54.

Ewing, David W., et al. "Listening and Responding to Employees' Concerns." Harvard Business Review 58 (January-February 1980): 101-14.

Hundley, John R. "Listening Posts." Personnel 53 (July-August 1976): 39-43.

Mundale, Susan. "Why More CEO's Are Mandating Listening and Writing Training." Training 17 (October 1980): 37-41.

Nichols, Ralph G. "Listening Is a 10-Part Skill." In Communication for Management and Business, 3rd ed., by Norman B. Sigband: 617-21. Glenview, IL: Scott, Foresman, 1982.

Sigband, Norman B. "Listen to What You Can't Hear." Nation's Business (June 1969).

_____. Communication for Management and Business. Glenview, IL: Scott, Foresman, 1982a.

_____."Proaction, Not Reaction, for Effective Employee Communications." Personnel Journal (March 1982b).

_____."Face to Face." Communicator's Journal (May/June 1983).

"The 500 Largest Industrial Corporations." Fortune (May 3, 1982): 269-78.

management's awareness of its public responsibility, have contributed to better and more complete reports.

The corporate annual report is no longer a drab summary statement of company activities. Today it is usually a well-written document, divided into narrative and financial sections, and enhanced by attractive colors, excellent visual aids, and appealing format.

Although most financial analysts would agree that the annual report is a good way for companies (both public and private) to communicate with their diverse publics or readers, they would not usually recommend that a heavy financial investment be based on the report's content alone. More and more critical readers are requesting the firm's 10-K, which is the report that must be filed with the Securities and Exchange Commission. This report is far more detailed and complete than the annual report insofar as significant financial data are concerned. And there now are a few firms that issue to their stockholders the 10-K rather than the usual annual report. Most companies feel the stockholder enjoys the color and photos of the annual report. If those can be retained while improving clarity, adding vital details, and increasing candor, the best of the annual report and the 10-K will be achieved.

Purposes of the Annual Report

The primary purpose of the annual report is to present an informative summary of company activities to stockholders, each of whom owns a share of the company and is interested in learning about the progress the firm has made during the previous year, its financial structure, its profits, its union-management relations, its expansion of facilities, its new-product development, its relationship with government agencies, its long-range objectives, and so on.

But the modern annual report has still another purpose. It attempts to build good will among its shareholders and sell its products, stock, and company image to others. This is one reason why corporations distribute many more reports than they have stockholders. The additional copies go to employees, educators, suppliers, government agencies, libraries, securities analysts, brokerage firms, banks, foundations, financial institutions, insurance firms, university endowment officers, financial editors of newspapers and magazines, legislators, and many others.

With this wide readership, the annual report writer is confronted with a major problem in composition. How should style, word choice, financial data, complexity of charts, and overall content be adjusted to the variety of reader levels and interests?

To do a good job, the writer must weigh every word, examine every sentence, check every graph, and evaluate every page to make sure that all readers will find the report interesting and valuable. It is possible to write an

FIGURE 11–2

Annual report covers

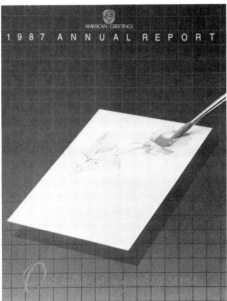

annual report with these qualities for two different readerships: the company shareholder and the security analyst. Of course, this requires consummate skill—but a good writer can discuss the necessary activities and select and explain financial data that will prove acceptable to both technical and non-technical readers.

Content and Makeup of the Annual Report

The content of the annual report can usually be divided into three major sections: the introductory section (letter of transmittal and table of contents), narrative portion, and financial information.

The president's or chairman's letter to the stockholder, or letter of transmittal, is usually a crisply worded summary of the highlights of the year's activities (see Figure 11–3). It gives the reader a bird's-eye view of the entire report and serves a purpose similar to that of the letter of transmittal in the typical formal report. This letter should be friendly and written from the stockholder's point of view. A stiff, formal, "boardroom" tone will make few friends among stockholders. This letter *is* the corporation to many; it is vital that it build good will.

The narrative portion of the report may discuss the company in relation to the following:

1. Products and services. The stockholder is interested in learning about the specific products the company handles and what services it makes available to its customers. A word should be offered on new items contemplated, future markets, advertising and marketing programs, the reactions of customers, and other areas related to the firm's products.

2. Plants and equipment. Present operations should be reviewed. Future acquisition of plants and equipment should be noted together with projected capital costs and return on investments. Investments in foreign plants and equipment should also be discussed together with possible implications.

3. Employees. The report should discuss how many employees the firm has, the benefits extended to them, payroll information, educational activities, affirmative action programs, employees in community affairs, employee health and safety records, and so on.

4. Labor relations. A clear and frank discussion of company relations with unions should be presented. If the firm has had labor problems, strikes, or disagreements during the year, they should be discussed objectively. The stockholder will have learned of the firm's problems from newspaper articles; he or she deserves a clear and honest explanation of them in the report.

5. Stockholders. How many stockholders does the company have? How and where are they distributed? What are their interests?

6. Government. What percentage of the firm's production goes to the government? What are the future trends likely to be? What interest do federal agencies have in the company? Have investigations been completed? Are they contemplated?

7. Community. Some comment should be made on the firm's relations with, and contributions to, the community. Have employees held public office? What recognition or complaints have been directed to the company?

8. Research and development. Where is the firm going? Does it contemplate expanding its product line? Is it going to diversity? Will it merge with other firms?

9. Social issues. More and more firms are giving some indication of their views on various social issues such as toxic waste disposal, involvement or noninvolvement in political activities, medical costs, and even housing, immigration, and import quotas.

10. Legal issues. Because of the enormous growth in government regulations, plus a strong trend to a more litigious society, most firms are deeply involved in court suits. Many firms comment on pending suits and their probable financial impact on the firm, along with the firm's perception of its liability.

These are only some of the areas that can be dealt with in the annual report. There are many others.

The financial information in the annual report is vital to most readers. It should be complete, objective, and presented in a style that is easily understood by the average stockholder.

The report should include a comprehensive balance sheet that permits comparison with previous years' records. As for the narrative text, the American Management Association feels that it is almost as important as the figures themselves. It can serve to amplify the statistics, to explain certain conditions, to qualify various items, and, in general, to throw additional light on the firm's financial picture.[1]

Howard Sherman, director of *Financial World's* annual report survey, has drawn up this list of ingredients for the well-designed report:

A minimum of twelve pages, including the cover.

Highlights, for a quick summarization of the year's results in comparison with the prior year's performance. Inclusion of percentage change figures enhances the value of this section.

An informative, easy-to-read message from the chairman and/or president.

---

[1] "Preparation of Company Annual Reports," American Management Association, Inc., Research Report Number 10, New York.

FIGURE 11–3

Letter to the shareholders

Report to Stockholders

We are very pleased to report that fiscal 1987 was one of the most successful and productive years in the history of Delta Air Lines. The financial results were excellent as the Company established records for net income and income from operations. Throughout the year, the Company made good progress in achieving its plan to expand its operations and to strengthen its route system, competitive position, and financial foundation. These accomplishments are particularly significant because they were achieved while maintaining Delta's tradition of outstanding customer service.

The financial results for fiscal 1987 showed a substantial improvement over the prior year. Net income was $263,729,000 ($5.90 per share) compared with $47,286,000 ($1.18 per share) in fiscal 1986. Income from operations totaled $404,525,000 compared with $34,488,000 last year. The previous record amounts for net income and operating income were $259,453,000 ($6.50 per share) and $366,010,000, set in fiscal 1985.

A central element of the Company's strategic plan to achieve its goals and objectives as a major international airline is the expansion of its route system. During its successful history, Delta has developed a strong, balanced route system covering most of the major domestic air travel markets. The acquisition and merger of Western Airlines into Delta during the year gave the Company immediate strength in virtually all sections of the United States in which it had lacked a substantial presence. The acquisition of Western, the country's ninth largest airline measured by revenue passenger miles, increased Delta's revenue base by more than one-quarter; added 44 cities to the Delta system, including important markets in Alaska, Hawaii, western Canada, and Mexico; gave Delta both size and strength in the very dense airline markets along the Pacific coast as well as in the western and northwestern United States; provided Delta with new hubs at Salt Lake City and Los Angeles; and afforded Delta the opportunity to use its market strength and customer appeal to gain a substantially greater share of the air travel market than the two carriers could have achieved individually. Another important aspect of the acquisition was that more than 11,000 Western personnel joined the Delta family. Like Delta personnel, they have consistently demonstrated dedication to their company and to providing the best possible service to its customers.

In addition to the external growth provided by the acquisition of Western, the Company implemented an internal growth plan designed to expand Delta's hub operations. The hub and spoke system, which Delta pioneered, has become the keystone of route development in the increasingly competitive airline industry. Delta has major hubs in Atlanta, Dallas/Ft. Worth, Salt Lake City, Cincinnati, and Los Angeles. The operation at each is designed to gather traffic from the geographical region surrounding the hub and connect it with principal travel destinations throughout the world. A major hub development project under the internal growth plan was implemented in December 1986 when the Company more than doubled its daily flights at Cincinnati. By the end of the fiscal year, Cincinnati's operation had almost tripled since the end of fiscal 1986. Traffic growth in the last quarter of the year indicated that Cincinnati had become an effective competitor to the midwest hubs of other carriers. The Company's growth plan calls for significant new service additions at all its hub operations over the next several years.

A major part of the Company's route development strategy is growth in international markets. In addition to the new international markets Delta received in the merger, new service was added from Atlanta through the Portland, Oregon, gateway to Tokyo. Later in fiscal 1988, the Company expects to extend this route beyond Tokyo to Seoul, South Korea. Delta also inaugurated new service between Cincinnati and London, and initial results have been excellent.

To support its growing flight schedule, the Company took delivery of 35 new aircraft during the year, in addition to the 92 aircraft gained in the acquisition of Western. These new aircraft, with a market value of approximately $1.1 billion, were financed primarily through operating lease arrangements. While the Company used lease financing extensively in fiscal 1987 because it was advantageous under the new tax law, this does not represent a permanent shift from the Company's strategy to own its aircraft.

On December 18, 1986, the Company paid $384 million in cash and issued 8.3 million shares of Delta stock valued at $403 million to acquire Western. In addition, Delta assumed $456 million in long-term debt, capital leases and other non-current obligations. Capital expenditures during fiscal 1987 totaled $1.2 billion, including $1.1 billion for flight equipment and $114 million for ground property. Despite these expenditures, Delta was financially stronger at the end of fiscal 1987 than at the end of fiscal 1986. The Company ended the year with its strongest working capital position in many years. Bank debt was eliminated, and the Company has a one billion dollar bank line of credit available. The debt-to-equity position was 35% debt and 65% equity at the end of fiscal 1987, compared with 40% debt and 60% equity at the end of fiscal 1986.

Delta's operating financial strength was reflected in the significant reduction in its unit cost during fiscal 1987. The average cost per available seat mile was 7.12¢, down 14% from the 8.30¢ average in fiscal 1986. In the June 1987 quarter, the cost per seat mile was 6.94¢. This decline in seat mile cost from one of the highest among the major carriers to one of the lowest, resulted from the reduction in the price of fuel, changes in accounting policies related to depreciation and pension expenses, and increased productivity by Delta personnel. The decline in seat mile cost is especially important in the competitive struggle among the airlines because low fares are a primary competitive tool in the industry and will continue to be a major marketing thrust for the foreseeable future. Accordingly, Delta will continue to work to lower its unit costs. We still have substantial improvements to make to meet our unit cost goal, but we made an excellent start in fiscal 1987.

The Company's commitment to provide excellent customer service continued to be recognized around the world. Delta was again voted the best airline by the readers of Travel Holiday Magazine. For the 13th consecutive year, Delta had the best customer service record among major U.S. airlines, according to U.S. government records. Unfortunately, Delta's commitment to customer service is not shared by all other airlines; and, as a result, Congress is considering consumer service regulation of the airlines. Whether or not this legislation is adopted, Delta will continue to seek new and better ways to serve its customers.

Subsequent to the end of the year, Dave Garrett reached his mandatory retirement age. Effective August 1, 1987, the Board of Directors elected Ron Allen Chairman of the Board and Chief Executive Officer and Hollis Harris President and Chief Operating Officer. Also subsequent to the end of the year, the Board chose to increase the Company's dividend 20% to an annual rate of $1.20 per share.

While the results of fiscal 1987 were excellent and the people of Delta have a right to be proud of their achievements, we must look to the future. We are optimistic that the Company is moving strongly ahead to achieve its goals. In the coming year, we will continue to take full advantage of the opportunities gained in the past and to seek new avenues for development. The plan to grow and build a stronger Delta Air Lines will continue to be pursued with great energy and commitment. The family of more than 51,000 Delta professionals is dedicated to keeping our Company the nation's premier airline.

R. W. ALLEN
*President and
Chief Operating Officer*

DAVID C. GARRETT, JR.
*Chairman of the Board and
Chief Executive Officer*

July 30, 1987

FIGURE 11–4
Certification by independent public auditors

REPORT OF
ERNST AND WHINNEY,
INDEPENDENT AUDITORS

Board of Directors
American Greetings Corporation
Cleveland, Ohio

We have examined the consolidated statements of financial position of American Greetings Corporation and subsidiaries as of February 28, 1987 and 1986, and the related consolidated statements of income, changes in financial position and shareholders' equity for each of the three years in the period ended February 28, 1987. Our examinations were made in accordance with generally accepted auditing standards and, accordingly, included such tests of the accounting records and such other auditing procedures as we considered necessary in the circumstances.

In our opinion, the financial statements referred to above present fairly the consolidated financial position of American Greetings Corporation and subsidiaries at February 28, 1987 and 1986, and the consolidated results of their operations and changes in their financial position for each of the three years in the period ended February 28, 1987, in conformity with generally accepted accounting principles applied on a consistent basis.

Ernst & Whinney

Cleveland, Ohio
April 6, 1987

A comprehensive narrative review of the twelve-month period just concluded. Operating and financial matters to be covered include, for example, prospects for each of the company's divisions, research and development, nature and cost of acquisitions, marketing and advertising details, sales breakdowns, and future financing plans.

A comprehensive balance sheet and profit-and-loss statement, with comparative figures for two years and adequate footnotes.

Statement of earnings and dividends on a per share basis, for both the current and the previous year, at a minimum.

Statistical data for a sufficient number of items, preferably for ten years.

Source and disposition of funds statements.

Certification by independent public auditors (see Figure 11–4).

A high degree of technical excellence in design and typographic art so as to help the reader absorb the hard information in the quickest possible time.[2]

---

[2]Howard L. Sherman, "Twenty-five Years of Annual Report Progress," *Financial World Magazine*, June 30, 1965, p. 69.

Presenting figures for the previous five or ten years is now common-place; longer periods are not unusual. This is vital for the serious reader who wishes to follow financial trends in the firm.

The guidelines set down by the American Management Association for good reporting are excellent: the report must be complete; it must be interesting; and it must possess clarity of expression.

DEALING WITH COMPANY PROBLEMS

More and more, the annual report is a way for management to speak directly to investor worries. Such concerns are often dealt with in the introductory letter from the president and/or chairman of the board. In the following excerpt, the senior corporate officers of American Greetings assure stock-holders that better times lie ahead:

As COMPETITION SUBSIDES AND INVESTMENTS IN OUR BUSINESS TAKE HOLD, MARGINS WILL IMPROVE AND WE WILL ONCE AGAIN SEE ANNUAL GROWTH

Our desire is not to mislead you with exaggerated statements. Your confidence in us has reflected our policy of eschewing hype, relying instead on solid financial performance to speak for our future prospects.

Candidly, our optimism for the future is based upon confidence. The long term outlook is very positive. There is every reason to be optimistic.

We thank you once again for your loyalty and support. Hopefully, this pause in earnings, albeit unpleasant, will be the springboard for mutual prosperity in the future.

Sincerely,

Irving I. Stone
Chairman of the Board
Chief Executive Officer

Morry Weiss
President
Chief Operating Officer

H. W. Bloch, in his letter to stockholders, informs them of new challenges the corporation will face. In this way, he prevents later charges that Bloch management didn't foresee adverse legislation and business conditions.

We do not believe that the new tax law will appear to the public as "simplified." However, many returns will be shortened because certain forms and entries will be entirely eliminated. On the other hand, new forms will be required by the new law. With its effect on the makeup of the average return, the simplification aspect of tax reform will directly affect our average fee. We see this as an opportunity to hold down and even decrease the average charge. This means that the profitability of our tax preparation business will be more directly dependent upon increasing the number of clients and keeping a tight control over expenses. It should also be noted that an estimated six million low income people will be taken off the tax rolls in 1988, another result of tax reform. Nevertheless, we believe that many of those having no income tax obligations will continue to file to get a refund on any withholding or to take advantage of the earned income credit, a negative income tax entitling nontaxpayers to refunds. These are but some of the many factors which will influence next year's business.

Respectfully submitted,

Henry W. Bloch

Henry W. Bloch
President and Chief Executive Officer
July 20, 1987

Finally, investor concerns can be dealt with in question-and-answer form within the annual report, as in this "Q and A" excerpt from the H & R Block 1987 annual report:

Q How will the national shortage of nurses, which is expected to continue into the 1990s, affect the business of Medical Personnel Pool (MPP)?

A The present nursing shortage is not significantly different than the one a little more than a decade ago, although it may be more acute now due to low enrollment in nursing schools, new career options for nurses, and increased demand for home care services. Medical Personnel Pool, by offering alternative professional career path opportunities, with flexibility consistent with an individual nurse's needs, actually helps expand the availability of licensed personnel. MPP believes that its attractiveness to these nurses will provide not just a buffer from the shortage but allow MPP the opportunity to increase its business.

Production and Distribution

Collecting information from various divisions or subsidiaries of a large corporation, securing excellent photographs, and amassing accurate statistical data are major tasks in themselves. Wrapping everything up clearly and concisely in a limited number of pages—to the satisfaction of the company's officers and stockholders—requires creative planning.

That is why most firms make one competent person responsible for the production of the annual report. A wise employee prepares a timetable and holds to it: narrative explanation of the following areas is due on this date; financial data on that date; selection of photographs and drawings of graphs must be completed by this time; and presses are to roll on this date. The lack of a timetable often means that information will trickle in, changes will be made constantly, and confusion will result.

A careful plan for the distribution of the annual reports should also be followed. Of course every stockholder receives a copy, but many other persons and groups should be considered, for, as noted earlier, the annual report can be a potent goodwill builder. Among those to whom copies might be sent are:

Company employees	Investment club officers
Company suppliers	Community leaders
Financial analysts	Newspaper and magazine editors
Educators	Brokerage firms
Government agencies	Legislators
Bank officers	Radio and TV commentators
University and foundation investment officers	Libraries
	Members of the clergy
Customers	Officers of service groups

With stock ownership so widespread in America, a company that does not produce an excellent report does itself a disservice. Many firms have found that an outstanding report helps their stock sales and improves their public image.

For those interested in the writing and distribution of the annual report, the following references may prove valuable:

"Annual Report Madness," *Public Relations Quarterly*, Spring 1980.

H. Bruce, "Perfectly Unclear," *Canadian Business*, March 1987, pp. 84–85.

J. A. Byrne, "This Year's Annual Reports: Show Business as Usual," *Business Week*, April 13, 1987, p. 42.

B. G. Grabow, "The 10 Laws of Annual Report Production," *Public Relations Journal*, August 1981.

A. E. Jensen and I. Mulligan, "Writing a Better Annual Report," *Canadian Business Review*, Winter 1983.

L. Jereski, "Beware of What You Don't See," *Forbes*, March 23, 1987, p. 102.

W. D. Lutz, "Corporate Doublespeak: Making Bad News Look Good," *Business and Society Review*, Winter 1983.

J. Sebestyn, "The Annual Report Hassle and Ways to Avoid It," *Bank Marketing*, September 1981.

QUESTIONS FOR STUDY

1. "Information is limited only by the needs of the audience." Discuss the truth and limitations of this assertion.
2. What does the comparative report compare?
3. What kind of long report is least subtle? Why?
4. Of the various items that can be included in the preliminaries, which one is least commonly included? Why?
5. Why are succinct, thorough introductions crucial to the success of long reports?
6. Where might conclusions and recommendations be found in the long report, and what is the current trend in placing these items in long reports?
7. What misunderstandings could arise if the letter of authorization is not attached to the long report?
8. In what ways can a company's annual report be viewed as a sales document?
9. What issues must be considered in the distribution of annual reports?
10. Should companies mention legal entanglements in their annual reports? Explain your opinion.
11. Long reports are made up of thousands of words. Discuss at least three ways in which the writer can help the reader avoid boredom, confusion, and tedium while reading so many words.
12. What are the differences between a corporation's annual report and its 10-K report?
13. Besides financial data, what other kinds of information are often included in a corporation's annual report?
14. Why would a corporation send its annual report to people and institu-

tions other than shareholders? Who might be included in the "noninvestor" category to receive the report?

15. With what do the titles in the long report's table of contents agree?

EXERCISES

16. A student group of which you are a member has completed a long report on the advantages of placing modern electronic games in a special room in the Student Center. Prepare three different title pages for the report. Give considerable attention to the report title. The report is to be presented to the director of the center.

17. For the report in exercise 16, write a letter of transmittal. As chairperson of the group, you will want to recognize the contributions of the group members and also of Mary Lee Sunquist, assistant to the student center director, and Bob Lee, manager of Video and Electronic Games (VEG), a company that distributes games like the ones you are proposing be placed in the center.

18. For the situation in exercise 16, explain some potential addenda that could be added to your long report.

19. Make a list of visual elements, including a balanced title page, that can add to the positive effect of a long report.

20. Find a long written report that lacks a summary or synopsis. Prepare this part of the long report and keep it to one page. Submit the long report with the summary you write. The long report may be one that a fellow student has written, a document you discover in the records of an organization, or a government report on file in the library.

21. Obtain an annual report from a business that interests you. Prepare an evaluation of the content of the document, noting both strengths and weaknesses. Pay particular attention to ways in which the document slants its material toward special readers. What is intended to appeal to stockholders? What will catch the eye of company employees? What seems designed to attract potential investors? Do not attempt to evaluate the format, typography, and printing details. Concentrate specifically on the writing.

22. How would you communicate in a long report to alumni of your college or university? Describe the sections you would include in the report and any recommendations.

23. Organizations besides profit-making companies often produce annual reports. Select a nonprofit organization with which you are familiar and:
    a. Name and explain the group, summarizing its purpose.
    b. In some detail outline what could be included in the annual report.
    c. Indicate the categories of people and organizations that might receive this annual report.

24. Select a real company and assume you are to make recommendations to this firm about the content and presentation of its annual report. Prepare a memo in which you make your recommendations. Also, to illustrate your ideas, select two annual reports—one good and one bad. Append these reports to your memo so that the reader can actually see favorable and unfavorable attributes of annual reports.

25. The 10-K report is an important document to business people. Obtain a 10-K report on a company. Then prepare a memo in which you explain the purpose and data of the 10-K report to a person who is unfamiliar with 10-Ks.

26. Many television commercials now emphasize the advantages of desktop publishing for report writing. List those advantages and, if possible, provide an example of a desktop published document.

27. As CEO of Alpha Industries, Inc., you're aware of the large investment it took to produce 10,000 copies of your annual report. You have only 3,000 stockholders and 400 employees. Develop a distribution plan for the remaining reports.

28. Consider the following facts about Beta Engineering, Inc.

   - For the first time since 1977, annual earnings per share have sunk below the $1.00 mark ($.97 per share in 1988 vs. $1.34 in 1987).
   - The company faces an infringement of patent lawsuit ($38 million) that probably will not reach court until 1990.
   - The Research and Development funds invested in teleconferencing devices show no sign of recovery within the current fiscal year.
   - Company real estate holdings have increased in value by 12 percent since 1984.
   - Long-term company debt ($178 million), while not being reduced, has not been increased during the year.
   - The Machinists' Union has formally threatened a strike against the company if current wage demands are not met.
   - The company has won a major proposal competition for a $22-million Navy contract, due to begin in mid-year.
   - The number of employees has declined by nine percent. Most of these were technically trained personnel.
   - Two former employees have filed "unlawful work termination" suits against the company.
   - Two small companies were purchased in the last 8 months: Eaton Electronics ($2,750,000) and Charter Chips ($3,150,000). It was felt that the addition of these two firms would give Alpha a strong professional edge over the competition.

   Use these facts and others of your own creation to write the President's Letter of Transmittal for inclusion in the company's annual report.

LEGAL
CONSIDERATIONS

REPORTS AND THE LAW

Of the many common business reports one type is especially significant from a legal perspective. Companies devote considerable effort and expense to producing "stakeholder reports" for both internal and external audiences. Management must provide shareholders and owners with sufficient information to permit them to make intelligent decisions on company issues and to evaluate the stock. The Securities and Exchange Commission (SEC) administers the relationship between management and the owners. The Commission directs how and when management is to communicate with its stakeholders. It also regulates what may not be communicated. For example, "inside" information (information that may influence the price of the stock) may give some the opportunity to profit unfairly. During the 1980s, some notable Wall Street and corporate figures have been fined or jailed for either releasing or acting upon such privileged information.

Consider a case in point. As a director of a company, you participate first-hand at the board meeting in a decision to split company stock 3 for 1. The decision will almost certainly cause the stock to rise substantially. But how and when must that information be released? To your best friends in the company first? To your brother-in-law, to whom you owe a "tip"? All such handling of the stock information would be deemed illegal by the SEC, which specifically defines the time table and channels for the release of potentially influential information.

Even the language of such reports is being monitored closely by regulatory agencies and the courts. No longer can companies hope to hide deleterious information from the public by ambiguous "bureaucratese" or obscure jargon. In reports as in warranties and contracts, the language used must be clear to bear legal tests.

Visual Aids

Be alert to words that confuse and figures that lie.

Ever since ancient artists first drew pictures on the walls of their caves, people have understood the value of symbols that speak directly to the eye. Drawings, sketches, pictograms, charts, graphs, and tables are certainly not new devices for communicating ideas. Most of those ancient devices continue to communicate their ideas clearly and interestingly even today. But we are still struggling to make sense of the peculiar lettering some civilizations have left us. That is because graphic representation tells a story directly, while written words do so only when we understand their key.

Beyond this, a well-designed graph, chart, or table will sometimes convey a complex relationship much more quickly and easily than can words. Have you ever tried to read a memo citing many different sums of money, tons of production, yearly changes in costs, or percentage differentials? You plow through such a discussion several times without understanding it. Finally you resort to making a table that will present the numbers in a more meaningful way. How much better it would have been if the *writer* had supplied the table!

COMPUTER GRAPHICS

Some ten to fifteen years ago, the computer was almost a status symbol for the large corporation. Now it is an absolute necessity for virtually every organization, large and small. The computer stores, retrieves, and outputs information not only on inventory, sales, payroll, and financial transactions, but on dozens of other activities as well. Reports and more reports are generated daily by the computer. The number continues to increase almost overwhelmingly. One reason for this is the refinement of laser technology, which has greatly increased the speed of the computer printer.

What all this means is a tremendous increase in data. In many organizations the flow of information has become a flood. Reports are longer, and the numbers produced increase daily. They are filled with statistical data and information, but they are rarely read completely.

One event has taken place in computer technology to improve the communication of computer-generated data. That step forward is computer graphics. Modern computer software now has the capability of automatically converting volumes of data into easy-to-assimilate visual aids. These graphic representations are made by six-color pen plotters, electrostatic plotters, graphic-colored cathode-ray tube terminals (CRT), and digitizing boards. Gantt charts, pie charts, organizational charts, bar charts, musical scores, three-dimensional representations of almost anything, in virtually any color, can be produced through the use of computer graphics. Figure 12–1 shows examples of computer-generated graphics.

FIGURE 12–1
Examples of computer-generated graphics

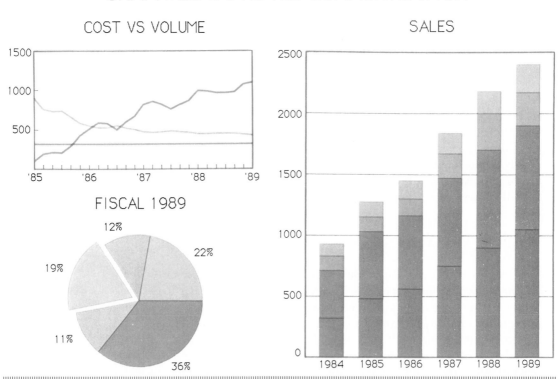

VALUE OF COMPUTER GRAPHICS

The value of computer graphics cannot be overstated. Enormous quantities of data can be converted into a graphic representation that.is not only easy to comprehend but saves a great deal of time in a decision-making process. Pages of data can be represented in an easy-to-comprehend visual aid (see Figure 12–2).

In addition, computer-assisted design and computer-assisted manufacturing (CAD/CAM) help engineers and product designers manufacture new items. Advertising artwork, architectural units, newspaper layouts, clothing patterns, auto designs—almost anything—can be drawn graphically. These designs can be revised until the desired results are achieved. They can then be fed back into the computer system for implementation of the final product. Figure 12–3 shows a pen plotter that is compatible with many personal computers. Note the variety of graphic images it can generate.

FIGURE 12–2

Computer-generated graphic representation of statistical information (originals in four colors)

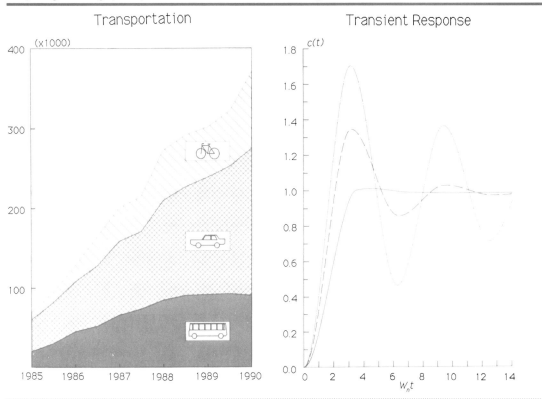

FIGURE 12–3

Graphic aids produced by modern pen plotter

HOW COMPUTER GRAPHICS WORK

The operation of the *pen plotter* is really the key to computer graphics. Computer programs (or software) can reduce data to a series of X and Y coordinates. The first XY coordinate is the starting point, and the second coordinate becomes the ending point. The pen starts at the first point and draws a straight line until it reaches the second coordinate. This process continues until all data are plotted. Some lines are so short that when they are put together, they can result in a circle. Different sets of XY coordinates may be selected for different colors.

Six-pen as well as two-pen graphic plotters are available together with a wide range of graphics software. These plotters draw on paper (as large as 11 x 17 inches) or transparent film. They can draw up to fifteen inches per second, and a top-quality chart can be produced in three to four minutes. Compare that with the time needed for freehand drawing! And with the advent of *flat-screen monitors* (those with displays less than one inch thick), it will be possible to create computer graphics on the screen and then actually place the screen on a photocopy machine to transfer the image from the screen to the paper.

Animation also is becoming a part of computer graphics. Once a shape has been defined mathematically within the computer so that it can be rendered in three dimensions, that shape can be made to "move" through space on the screen as directed by the computer operator. In this way, a manufacturer, designer, or an engineer may see an animated portrayal of the product before it actually exists in a prototype model.

SELECTING GRAPHIC AIDS

One word of warning: graphic aids should not be used only for cosmetic reasons. Their purpose is to clarify the data being presented. If they have no instructional function, they will only confuse the reader.

Defining the Reader

As in all phases of report writing, writers must ask themselves, "Who is the reader?" before choosing graphic aids. If the report is directed to a group of aerospace engineers, the charts, graphs, and tables used can be complex. But a logarithmic chart, for example, would not be appropriate in an annual report to stockholders. An illustration fulfills its purpose only if the reader finds it clear, informative, and easy to understand. This may seem obvious, but if you look through an annual report or a scientific journal, you will often find charts that are not in keeping with the level of the audience.

Choosing the Best Graphic Aid

A second question report writers must ask themselves is, "What type of chart or table will best tell my story?" At times writers get in the habit of using a table for one type of representation and a bar chart for another, adapting them to almost every situation. They know them well and can use them effectively, but they run the risk of not stretching their imaginations enough to determine if there might be a better way to present the data. If the reader is interested in *trends,* a series of bars or a line graph may be useful. If, however, he or she is concerned with specifics and precise data, a table may be most appropriate.

Designing the Content

Report writers must not only determine which type of graphic aid best presents their data, they must also decide how complex or simple it should be in reference to the data and the reader. One reader will be comfortable with five different information designations on one chart; for example, solid, broken, dotted, dashed, and dot-dash lines. Another reader requires five separate charts. This type of reader doesn't have the interest, motivation, or ability to analyze a single complex visual aid.

An Example of Choice and Design

Which is the best visual aid to represent the data contained in the following excerpt from a periodic report?

> *Twelve of our Star-Economy gasoline stations in the Chicago area were selected to check the effectiveness of the two display stands in generating sales. For purposes of the survey, the stations were designated with numbers from 1 to 12 (see Appendix A for number and address of each station).*
>
> *The test was conducted from June 5 to June 10, and the total sales for three items were recorded: "Road Safety Flares, package of 4," Unit 201; "All-Purpose Med Kit," Unit 404; and "All-Purpose Wrench Kit," Unit 605.*
>
> *Two different cases were used to display these three items for sale. Six of the cases were our regular five-foot walnut with chrome-trim affairs, while the other six were newly manufactured by the Greeley Company. These were only two feet wide, constructed of heavy cardboard, and equipped with a continuously flashing red and yellow electric blinker. Stations, 1, 4, 5, 7, 9, and 10 received the five-foot case, and stations 2, 3, 6, 8, 11, and 12 the two-foot case with blinkers.*
>
> *Total sale of the three items during the six-day test period (Monday through Saturday) were as follows: Stores 1, 2, 3, and 4 sold 350, 820, 870, and 440 respectively. In stores 5, 6, 7, and 8 sales were recorded at 375, 950, 475, and 675 units. Sales of the same units in Store 9 were 550; Store 10, 525; Store 11, 1150; Store 12, 1050. It would certainly appear that there is a correlation between sales and type of display case. This correlation was also apparent in a similar survey conducted in Detroit early this year.*

On the basis of the data given, you must decide whether to present *trends* in sales, *specific sales figures,* a combination of both, or a "picture" of the information (pictogram).

A quick review of the data tells you that the key is to be found in the question, "Which display case resulted in more sales?" Not, "Which stations(s) had the greatest sales?" If you were to present the data as in examples 1, 5, 6, and 10 (see Figures 12–4 and 12–5), you would not communicate very effectively. When the data are grouped by type of display case, as in examples 2, 3, 4, 7, 8, and 9, the reader will see immediately what is important.

FIGURE 12–4

Various presentations of identical data in tabular form

SALES OF UNITS 201, 404, AND 605, JUNE 5–10

Example 1

Station No.	Total Sales
1	350
2	820
3	870
4	440
5	375
6	950
7	475
8	675
9	550
10	525
11	1150
12	1050

(Reflects specific data, though not effectively presented)

Example 2

Station No.	5 ft. Display Case	2 ft. Display Case (Blinker)
1	350	
2		820
3		870
4	440	
5	375	
6		950
7	475	
8		675
9	550	
10	525	
11		1150
12		1050

(Reflects specific data)

Example 3

Station No.	5 ft. Display Case	2 ft. Display Case (Blinker)
1	350	
4	440	
5	375	
7	475	
9	550	
10	525	
2		820
3		870
6		950
8		675
11		1150
12		1050

(Reflects specific data; distinguishes types)

Example 4

Station No.	5 ft. Display Case	Station No.	2 ft. Display Case (Blinker)
1	350	2	820
4	440	3	870
5	375	6	950
7	475	8	675
9	550	11	1150
10	525	12	1050

(Reflects specific data; well organized)

FIGURE 12–5

Various presentations of identical data in graph form (bar charts and line graphs)

Example 5

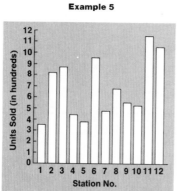

(Reflects trend but difficult to assimilate)

Example 6

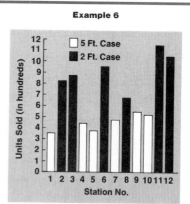

(Reflects trend but is confusing)

Example 7

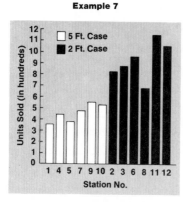

(Reflects trend; well organized)

Example 8

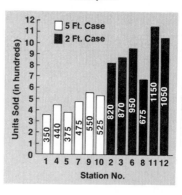

(Reflects trend and cites specific data)

Example 9

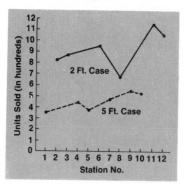

(Reflects trend; subject to misinterpretation)

Example 10

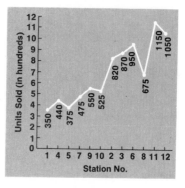

(Reflects data)

MISREPRESENTATION

Everyone has heard the saying, "Statistics don't lie, but statisticians do." It's true: some writers who use statistics sometimes fail to present them so as to show the whole picture. Sometimes a writer will present some facts in a table, chart, or graph but omit others. The data presented may be accurate, but the *impression* they create is basically misleading. The bar chart in Figure 12–6 is an example of **selective omission.** The casual reader might simply assume that sales have been climbing steadily from 1980 to 1982. However, an examination of the section that has been omitted (ostensibly to save space) reveals quite a different story. Sales have *not* gone up consistently. The chart is therefore accurate but misleading.[1]

Visual distortion is another way to subtly misrepresent statistics. Perhaps the ordinary bar graph in Figure 12–7 is not sufficiently impressive. Why not convey the information as illustrated in the center image—or even the right-hand one? Note that the tops of the money bags are precisely at 30 and 60 on the vertical axis in each image, but the horizontal dimension has been stretched in two of them.

FIGURE 12–6
Selective omission illustrated by bar chart

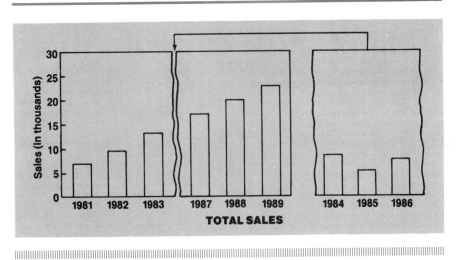

[1]See Darrel Huff's and Irving Geis's instructive and entertaining book, *How to Lie with Statistics* (New York: W. W. Norton). Each of us can find in it examples of misleading statistics which we have accepted—or perhaps transmitted.

FIGURE 12–7

Identical information conveyed three ways, with a touch of visual distortion in the center and right-hand images

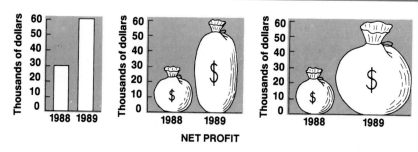

NET PROFIT

Then there are statements that seem to convey facts, but, like double talk, really say nothing. The ad that shouts "50% bigger" but neglects to indicate what its product is bigger than is an example. Or the "giant 256-square-inch TV screen"; why "giant"? Certainly 256 square inches is 256 square inches, and adjectives do not increase the size—except to the suggestible mind.

When we read charts, graphs, and illustrations, or interpret statements citing statistics, we should do so critically. Are the ideas conveyed to us accurate and complete? And when we *transmit* ideas through graphic aids or statistics, we should continually ask ourselves whether we are being complete and thorough.

There is probably no statistical reference more commonly used (and misused) than the term *on the average* is to designate the common characteristics or central tendency of a group. Because this term is often loosely used to mean several different things, it may be used in one context but interpreted in another. For example, in the Dependable Car Sales Company, automobiles were sold in the quantities listed on the dates designated below:

Date	No. Sold	Date	No. Sold
July 1	16	July 11	6
July 2	16	July 12	5
July 5	0	July 13	7
July 6	2	July 14	8
July 7	1	July 15	4
July 8	3		

The *mean* (or arithmetical average) number of cars sold per day is 6.88. This figure is obtained by totaling the number of cars sold and dividing by the number of days. The *median* number of cars sold, 5, is the middle number in the array of daily sales arranged from high to low: 1, 2, 3, 4, 5, 6, 7, 8, 16. This too is an average, although quite different from the mean.

Thus "on the average" can be easily misconstrued or misused. The report writer should use it with caution, and the report reader should always question an "on the average" figure. You should determine whether the writer is referring to the mean or the median—or perhaps to some other measure of central tendency such as the *mode*. (The most frequently occurring number in a distribution. In the example above, the modal average is 16!) Beyond that, you should ask how many cases were included in the sample to secure the figure. A small sample size (or too selective a sample) should signal extreme caution in interpreting and applying statistical results.

TABLES

What would your reaction be to the following paragraph encountered in a sales report for a large auto dealership?

January, 1988, proved to be one of the best months ever. We sold 275 Ranger pickups as compared to 250 in January, 1987, amounting to a 10 percent increase. The popular Mustang series saw a 5 percent jump in sales, with 220 in 1988 and 210 in 1987. Due to rising gasoline costs, the larger Thunderbird line decreased slightly in sales (a 5 percent decrease), with 380 sold in 1988 and 400 in 1987.

Now compare that with the table in Figure 12–8. Can there be any question that a table is far superior to a series of sentences in communicating quantitative ideas? In addition, tables have many other advantages:

- Materials can be listed concisely.
- Reference to specific facts can be made quickly.
- Comparisons between and among statistics can be made easily.
- The reader can comprehend and assimilate quantitative data in tables much more quickly than if the same information were presented in paragraph form.

Authorities in the field of visual aids classify tables in different ways. One group speaks of a **dependent** table, which does not carry a title or subtitle and is explained in the text. The **independent** table, with its title, headnote, and explanatory comments found in the caption and/or footnote, stands by itself. Even when examined apart from the text on the page, it conveys a clear and complete idea to the reader.

Automobile Sales			
	January 1988	January 1987	Percentage Change
Ranger	275	250	+10%
Mustang	220	210	+5
Thunderbird	380	400	−5

Tables are also designated as *spot, special purpose,* and *reference.* The **spot** table may be made up of a few figures, set apart from the text in an organized way, to make understanding easier. The **special purpose** table is somewhat more complex, usually contains column headings and rulings, and often carries a title. (See Figure 12–9).

The **reference** table usually contains a fairly large quantity of data. The table is ruled, titled, and arranged to facilitate comparisons and evaluations by the reader. It is not unusual to find government reports containing a great deal of information that has been distilled and refined into one or two excellent tables.

Faculty Size at Midwest University			
	1987	1986	1985
Professors	110	90	62
Associate Professors	240	230	205
Assistant Professors	320	402	390
Instructors	340	320	290

Production of Printed Circuit Boards (in thousands), Circuit Switch Corp., Mansfield Plant						
	Radio			Television		
Year	#101	#102	#103	#301	#302	#303
1986	150	250	90	580	300	250
1985	120	220	115	510	310	220
1984	110	220	120	420	290	205

A checklist for constructing tables follows:

- Head each vertical column clearly and concisely.
- Assign a number and a title to each reference table. Use subtitles, if necessary, to further clarify or explain the caption.
- Place comparative data on a horizontal plane from left to right (the usual direction of the eyes in reading).
- Note fractions in decimals.
- Use standard terms throughout the table (yards, meters, and fathoms should all be converted to a standard unit of measure and explained in a footnote).
- Always design tables so that reading and understanding are easy. This requires careful use of rules, generous use of white space, and clear titles.

CHARTS AND GRAPHS

Charts, graphs, pictograms, and sketches can present information dramatically and skillfully. With a glance at a bar or line chart, the reader can determine the *trend* of an activity. For example, have sales increased? Declined? Remained stationary? Has the gross national product gone up? If readers see a tiny money bag next to a bigger one, they will have their answer right away.

Of course, charts and pictograms do not contain the quantity of specific data found in a table, but their purpose is different. They indicate trends, rather than precise data.

Pie or Circle Charts

The **pie chart** (also called **circle chart**) is one of the most commonly used visual aids. It is easy to interpret, does not require extensive artwork, and communicates its basic ideas with clarity and simplicity. Although each segment represents a different percentage, the total comes to 100 percent. The pie chart can be presented in a variety of different ways. Some firms use a picture of their product to represent their "pie," and divide it into appropriate segments to represent cost of materials, salaries, depreciation, and so on. One electric company used a pie chart reflecting percentage and amount to depict its distribution of revenue (see Figure 12–11).

A pie may contain all sorts of things, including falsehoods. Report readers should beware of the pie whose segments are labeled only in words, with no percentage figures. And they should also be skeptical of the pie that has segments numbered consecutively and explained at the bottom of the page. One of the most common ploys in the game of "lying with statistics" is the pie (or product) chart with out-of-proportion segments. Each segment in the pie chart should be identified and should show the percentage it represents.

FIGURE 12–10
Well-constructed reference tables

Sales and Operating Income by Industry Segment
(in millions of dollars)

	1989		1988		1987	
	Operating Income	Sales	Operating Income	Sales	Operating Income	Sales
Industrial and Power Equipment	$ 88.6	$ 626	$ 77.3	$ 600	$ 55.2	$ 516
Fluid Control Systems	35.2	391	50.0	367	48.4	320
Materials	9.6	734	59.4	808	44.3	664
Industrial Seals and Components	44.0	307	40.0	303	31.9	250
Shock Mitigation Systems	19.1	145	6.7	106	14.2	92
Intersegment elimination	—	(37)	—	(43)	—	(34)
Total segments	196.5	2,166	233.4	2,141	194.0	1,808
Interest expense	(24.4)	—	(29.6)	—	(29.8)	—
Interest income	16.4	—	14.3	—	13.1	—
Corporate unallocated	(20.0)	—	(15.6)	—	(14.7)	—
Consolidated	$168.5	$2,166	$202.5	$2,141	$162.6	$1,808

Sales of Hi Deb Sportswear
(listed in dozens)

	June 1989	June 1988	Percentage Change (approx.) June 1989 with June 1988 (Basal Year)
Bel Air Line			+10%
Swimsuits	220	200	+10%
Sailing Jackets	400	300	—
Summer Blouses	2360	2350	
Summer Skirts	310	300	+5%
Blazers	1000	900	+10%
Brentwood Line			
Swimsuits	3400	3000	+10%
Sailing Jackets	3600	4000	−10%
Summer Blouses	4200	3500	+20%
Summer Skirts	5500	5000	+10%
Blazers	6300	6000	+5%

Use of Color and Dimension in Visual Aids

EXHIBIT 1

Pie Charts: increasingly complex rendition of data in a pie chart format

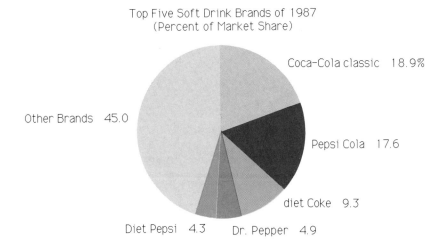

Top Five Soft Drink Brands of 1987
(Percent of Market Share)

Coca-Cola classic   18.9%

Pepsi Cola   17.6

diet Coke   9.3

Dr. Pepper   4.9

Diet Pepsi   4.3

Other Brands   45.0

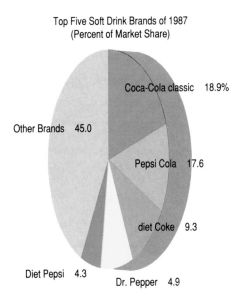

Top Five Soft Drink Brands of 1987
(Percent of Market Share)

Coca-Cola classic   18.9%

Pepsi Cola   17.6

diet Coke   9.3

Dr. Pepper   4.9

Diet Pepsi   4.3

Other Brands   45.0

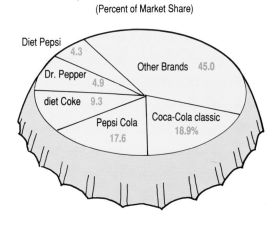

Top Five Soft Drink Brands of 1987
(Percent of Market Share)

Diet Pepsi   4.3

Dr. Pepper   4.9

diet Coke   9.3

Pepsi Cola   17.6

Coca-Cola classic   18.9%

Other Brands   45.0

EXHIBIT 2

Bar and Line Graphs: different renditions of the same data

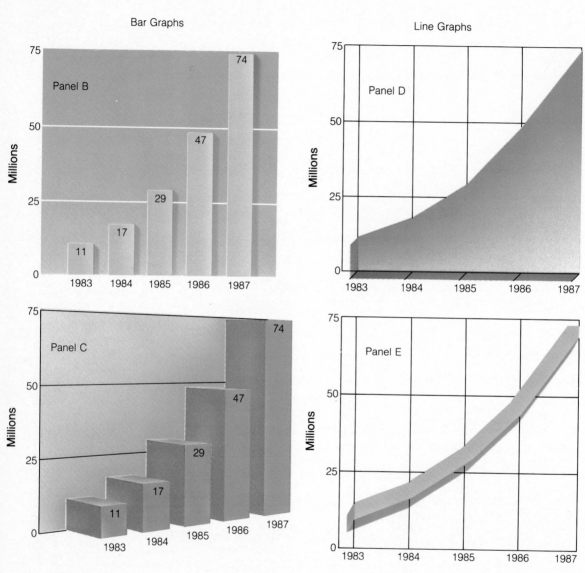

Bar Graphs

Line Graphs

EXHIBIT 3

Time Line Graph: inflation since 1860

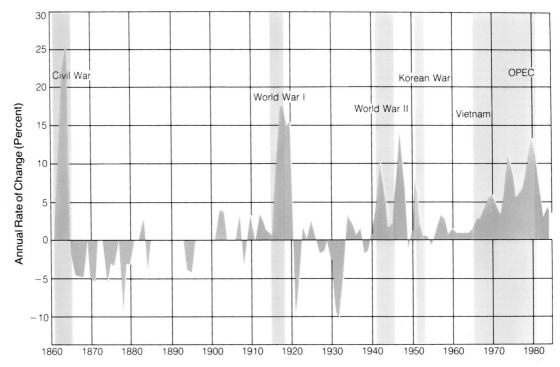

This figure highlights the various inflationary periods experienced by the United States since 1860. The majority of these periods have occurred during extended military hostilities; however, although the 1970s and early 1980s were relatively peaceful, the price level crept up briskly.

Source: U.S. Department of Labor, Bureau of Labor Statistics.

EXHIBIT 4

Process Diagram: satellite telecommunication

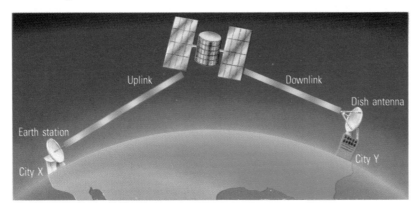

EXHIBIT 5
Process Diagram:
the oceanic food chain

EXHIBIT 6

Exploded Diagram: the color monitor process

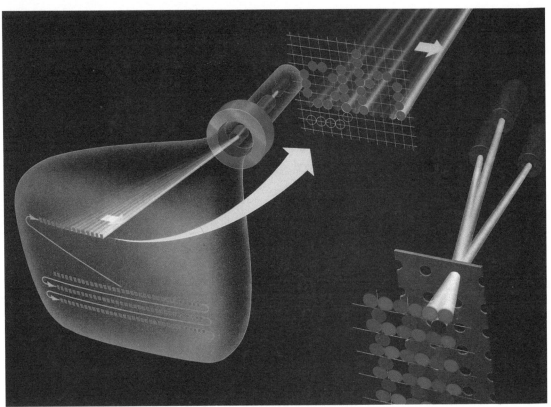

Red, green, and blue are the three primary colors that are "electronically" mixed to produce other colors. A spectrum of color is generated by turning on different combinations of the RGB electron guns on a triad of phosphor dots. This process is called raster scan.

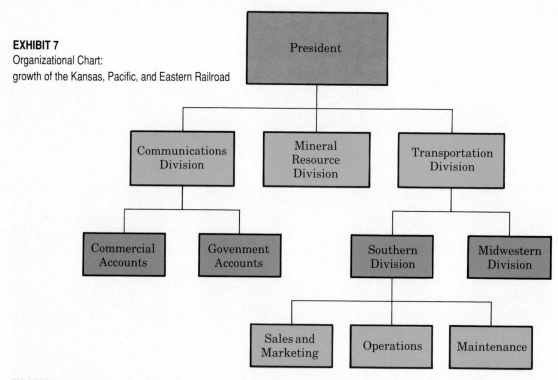

EXHIBIT 8
Map: the Western Trails

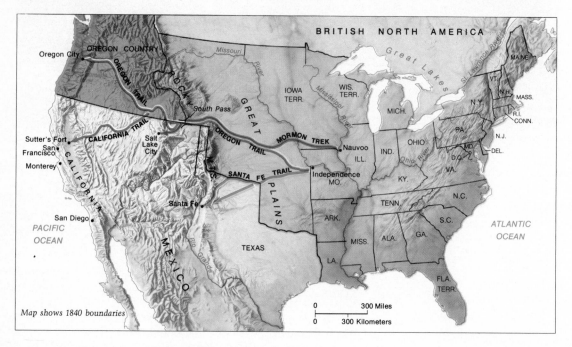

Visual Aids Generated by Computer

EXHIBIT 9
Line Drawing: CAD CAM

EXHIBIT 10
Line Drawing: increasingly complex stages generated by computer

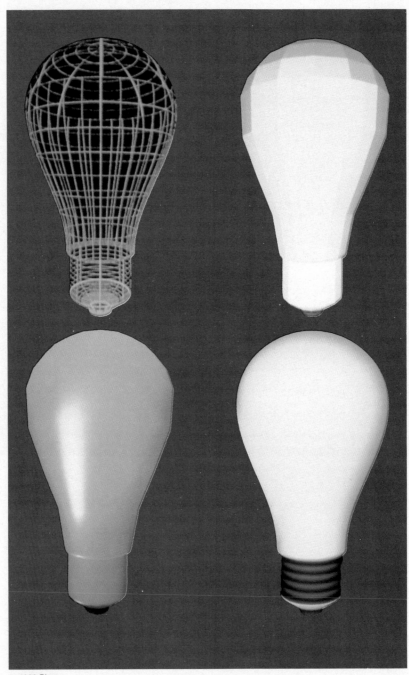

FIGURE 12–11
Pie (circle) chart

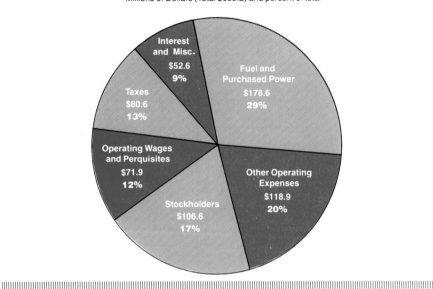

Distribution of Revenue

Millions of Dollars (Total $609.2) and percent of total

Bar Charts

The **bar chart** is constructed so that each point is located in reference to two variables: one a quantity—like money, temperature, or volume—usually indicated along the vertical axis; and the other a time, distance, load (etc.) factor, most frequently indicated along the horizontal axis (see Figure 12–12). Bar charts may be presented either vertically (often called **column charts**) or horizontally; the length of the bar normally indicates quantity. Ordinarily the variation in bars should be only in length. If a bar is changed in length *and* width, to designate *two* variables, confusion in interpretation is likely to result.

Various techniques can be used to make the bar chart more interesting: bars in a second color, hatching effects, projective drawing, or sketches of the company's products in a stylized column form.

One valid criticism of the bar chart is that it does not reflect quantities with precision and accuracy. When the reader's eye moves from the top or end of the bar to the scale axis, it is impossible to determine the *exact* quantity designation. However, this weakness can be overcome by placing the figures within the bars or at the top of each bar.

The **segmented bar chart** is a simple variation on the pie chart. A single bar represents the total data. However, it is split into segments that are in

FIGURE 12–12

Bar charts—vertical format

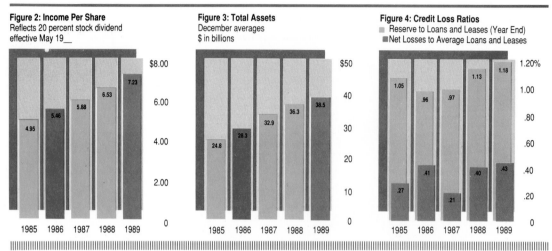

Figure 2: Income Per Share
Reflects 20 percent stock dividend
effective May 19__

Figure 3: Total Assets
December averages
$ in billions

Figure 4: Credit Loss Ratios
■ Reserve to Loans and Leases (Year End)
■ Net Losses to Average Loans and Leases

proportion to the quantities designated (see Figure 12–13). Here also the bar may be horizontal, vertical, or designed to duplicate the company's product.

Curve Charts

The **curve chart** is sometimes referred to as a **line chart** or **line graph.** The reader can quickly and easily see trends over periods of time. It is easy to make; once the various items have been plotted on the chart, it is a simple matter to connect the points with a curved line.

FIGURE 12–13

Segmented bar chart—vertical format

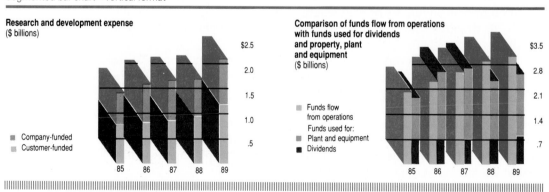

Research and development expense
($ billions)

■ Company-funded
■ Customer-funded

**Comparison of funds flow from operations
with funds used for dividends
and property, plant
and equipment**
($ billions)

■ Funds flow
  from operations
  Funds used for:
■ Plant and equipment
■ Dividends

A further advantage of the curve chart is the large quantity of information that may be depicted on one chart. It is relatively simple to use multiple curves on one drawing to depict related data. Of course, each curve is slightly different (through the use of dashes, dots, and other graphic elements), enabling the reader to easily tell them apart (see Figure 12–14).

Band Charts and Component Bar Charts

The **band chart** is similar to the multiple-curve chart except that it has shadings (see Figure 12–15). Each shaded section (usually beginning at the bottom with a dark color and moving up to lighter colors) represents a quantity. The same pattern is followed with the **component bar chart** (see Figure 12–16).

FIGURE 12–14
Multiple-curve chart

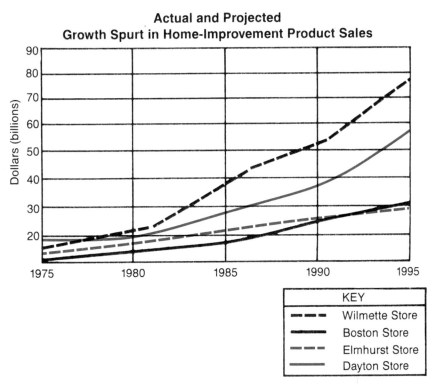

**Actual and Projected
Growth Spurt in Home-Improvement Product Sales**

KEY

▬ ▬ ▬	Wilmette Store
▬▬▬	Boston Store
─ ─ ─	Elmhurst Store
─────	Dayton Store

FIGURE 12–15
Band chart

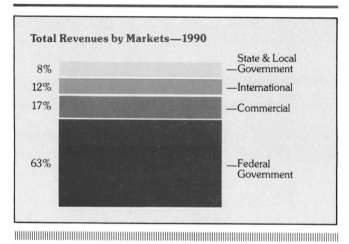

These charts should be used only to give an impression of general relationships. If the report writer wishes to give exact relationships or precise data, some other visual aid is preferable.

Ratio Charts

For comparisons of growth, **ratio charts** are often used. These are drawn on semilogarithmic paper. For example, on an ordinary chart a change in Army reserve strength from 3000 to 30,000 and Navy reserve strength from 10,000 to 100,000 would be difficult to represent. The major change in the large Navy figure might well force the line or bar designations off the chart completely. The same figures can be represented more compactly on a ratio chart, which telescopes quantity. Since the scale is based on percentages instead of on absolute units, it permits comparisons of growth rates or percentage increases. The chart in Figure 12–17 shows that the Army and Navy forces grew at exactly the same rate, each increasing by ten times.

MISCELLANEOUS GRAPHIC AIDS

Organizational Charts

Modern organizations are so complex that it is sometimes difficult for the manager to have a clear understanding of who reports to whom. And employees usually feel more comfortable when they know precisely what is

FIGURE 12–16
Component bar chart

LINES OF BUSINESS
(in millions)

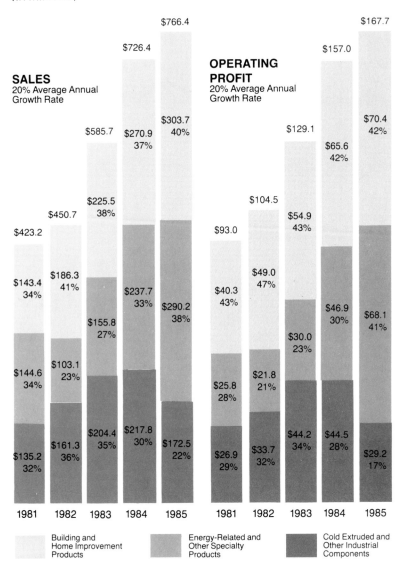

SALES
20% Average Annual
Growth Rate

$423.2
$450.7
$585.7
$726.4
$766.4

OPERATING PROFIT
20% Average Annual
Growth Rate

$93.0
$104.5
$129.1
$157.0
$167.7

	Building and Home Improvement Products	Energy-Related and Other Specialty Products	Cold Extruded and Other Industrial Components

The Oil-Field and Related Products, Personal Communications, and a portion of the Other industry segments, as presented in the Segment Information Note to the financial statements, are included in the Energy-Related and Other Specialty Products line of business. The Transportation-Related and the remaining portion of Other industry segments are included in the Cold Extruded and Other Industrial Components line of business.

FIGURE 12–17
Ratio chart

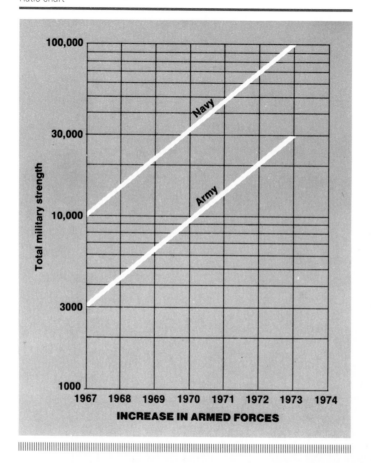

their position within the company, exactly who is their supervisor, and who is their supervisor's supervisor.

There are several kinds of organizational charts. Most common is the vertical chart shown in Figure 12–18, which reads from top to bottom. There are also horizontal charts, which read from left to right, and circle charts that show authority emanating from the center. A variation of the circle chart is the beehive chart. In most organizational charts, solid lines indicate direct relationships; broken lines indicate indirect relationships.

Although authority and the *real* chain of command are not always accurately depicted on paper, the organizational chart does serve an important purpose. Something is needed to give an appreciation of the structure of the company, and nothing does it quite so quickly and easily as an organizational chart. At the same time, it is well to remember that the actual centers of authority in an organization usually differ from what is shown on the chart.

FIGURE 12–18
Organizational chart

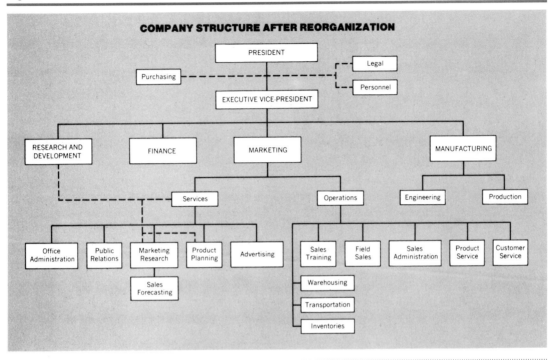

Flow Charts

Flow charts indicate the direction of movement of a product or a process from the initial stages to completion. Sometimes simplified drawings or symbols are used to represent stages, with arrows to indicate direction. The flow chart, flow sheet, or routing diagram can be invaluable to the new employee or anyone who wishes to gain rapid familiarity with the sequence of activity in a process (see Figure 12–19).

Pictograms or Pictorial Charts

The **pictogram** (see Figure 12–20) is ideal for readers who are in a hurry or who are disinclined to interpret a six-line curve chart. They can quickly see, for example, that the cost of living has gone up if little market baskets are shown marching up a chart, or that more office buildings were constructed this year than last year if five additional skyscrapers are shown on a pictogram.

FIGURE 12–19
Flow chart

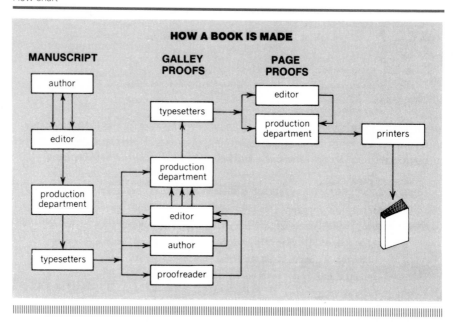

The symbols, such as dollar signs, autos, homes, planes, tires, should all be of uniform appearance and size. (Sometimes, as in Figure 12–20, the size of symbols suggests relative importance or quantity.) Each should represent the same quantity or dimension. The symbols should be simple and so representative that it would be almost impossible for two readers to interpret them differently.

Only a limited amount of uncomplicated information can be presented in a pictogram. For data having several facets and requiring thoughtful interpretation, other visual aids are preferable.

Map Charts

For representation that is dependent on geographical or spatial relationships, **map charts** are excellent (see Figure 12–21). Symbols (trees, oil wells, people, livestock, and so on) can designate quantities, and their position on the map can indicate location.

A map drawn out of proportion to its true land areas can be used to indicate the disparate characteristics of various areas of the nation. For example, a map of the United States depicting manufacturing output will have the eastern and midwestern states drawn out of proportion so that they appear much larger than the other states.

FIGURE 12–20
Pictogram

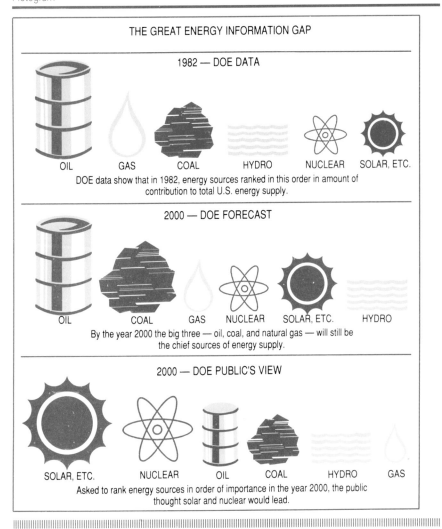

THE GREAT ENERGY INFORMATION GAP

1982 — DOE DATA

OIL   GAS   COAL   HYDRO   NUCLEAR   SOLAR, ETC.

DOE data show that in 1982, energy sources ranked in this order in amount of contribution to total U.S. energy supply.

2000 — DOE FORECAST

OIL   COAL   GAS   NUCLEAR   SOLAR, ETC.   HYDRO

By the year 2000 the big three — oil, coal, and natural gas — will still be the chief sources of energy supply.

2000 — DOE PUBLIC'S VIEW

SOLAR, ETC.   NUCLEAR   OIL   COAL   HYDRO   GAS

Asked to rank energy sources in order of importance in the year 2000, the public thought solar and nuclear would lead.

Cutaway and Exploded Drawings

Cutaway and exploded sketches or photographs are excellent for showing the reader the component parts of a piece of equipment, as well as subsurface areas. They are usually arranged to give a perspective view. A **cutaway** drawing can often convey a much clearer picture of the interior working parts of a complex mechanical device than could a 5000–word description.

FIGURE 12–21
Map chart

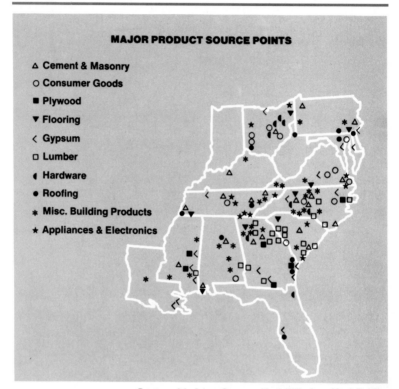

MAJOR PRODUCT SOURCE POINTS

△ Cement & Masonry
○ Consumer Goods
■ Plywood
▼ Flooring
< Gypsum
□ Lumber
◀ Hardware
● Roofing
✳ Misc. Building Products
★ Appliances & Electronics

Courtesy of the Lowes Company, North Wilkesboro, North Carolina

An **exploded diagram** presents the component parts of a device. Each piece is drawn to show how it fits into, or next to, a contiguous piece. If it is a piece part, for example, each of its segments is exploded. Dotted lines are sometimes used to illustrate how the entire unit is attached to the larger mechanism.

The cutaway and exploded diagrams are most often used in technical reports. They require the services of an artist who can draw with care, precision, and imagination (see Figures 12–22 and 12–23).

Photographs

The use of photographs in reports has increased in recent years, and with good reason. They are most persuasive as visual evidence in support of the text. If a report writer wants to indicate that a shield does not bend on impact, a picture can be taken at the precise instant of impact. If the writer

FIGURE 12–22
Cutaway diagram

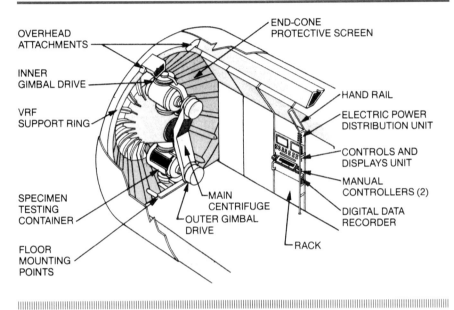

OVERHEAD ATTACHMENTS

INNER GIMBAL DRIVE

VRF SUPPORT RING

SPECIMEN TESTING CONTAINER

FLOOR MOUNTING POINTS

END-CONE PROTECTIVE SCREEN

HAND RAIL

ELECTRIC POWER DISTRIBUTION UNIT

CONTROLS AND DISPLAYS UNIT

MANUAL CONTROLLERS (2)

DIGITAL DATA RECORDER

MAIN CENTRIFUGE

OUTER GIMBAL DRIVE

RACK

wants to prove that a cement support cracked, a photo can be used. If someone wants a view of a piece of property, one need only snap the picture and then pencil on it the width, depth, frontage, or other pertinent data. The contractor need not draw a diagram of a kitchen to be remodeled; the room can be photographed from several angles and the dimensions needed can be written in, saving hours of drafting time.

Another advantage of photographs is the speed with which they can be made. A Polaroid instant photo can be snapped and printed in minutes, in black and white or color. Photographs are also easier, less time consuming, and less expensive to prepare than charts and graphs, although they are more expensive to reproduce in printed form. If only ten or twenty copies of four or five pictures are needed, an industrial photo lab can supply them at a very nominal charge.

PLACEMENT OF ILLUSTRATIONS

A table or chart should appear in the text if the material it presents is directly related to the topic under discussion. Any explanation, interpretation, or analysis of it should appear in the body of the report immediately before or

FIGURE 12–23
Exploded diagram

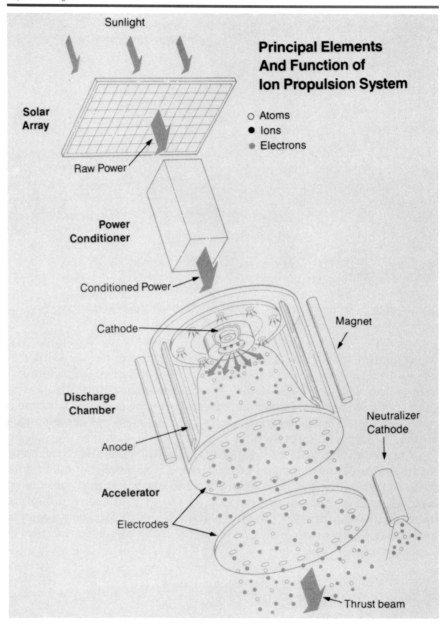

Sunlight

**Principal Elements
And Function of
Ion Propulsion System**

**Solar
Array**

○ Atoms
● Ions
● Electrons

Raw Power

**Power
Conditioner**

Conditioned Power

Cathode

Magnet

**Discharge
Chamber**

Anode

Neutralizer
Cathode

Accelerator

Electrodes

Thrust beam

after. On the other hand, when tables and charts are meant only to present material that is related to text information or that amplifies—but is not vital to—it, they can be placed in an appendix or supplement.

The report writer should keep in mind the obvious danger of placing anything important in an appendix. If readers can refer to a chart easily and quickly, they will use it. If they are required to flip back and forth between the body of the report and charts in the appendix, they may stop referring to the illustrations altogether.

At times a table or chart may be found in a footnote, but it usually seems out of place. The footnote area at the bottom of a page is not recommended for illustrations.

This chapter has presented only a few of the visual aids that can be used to convey ideas in report writing. There are many others, such as PERT charts, schematics, and block diagrams. The writer who is convinced that there is some truth to the old cliché about one picture being worth a thousand words will search out the best visual aid for a particular message and a particular reader.

QUESTIONS FOR STUDY

1. What graphic aid would be most useful in comparing two exact figures? Justify your choice.
2. Explain the different meanings of the phrase *on the average.*
3. Differentiate between a dependent table and an independent table.
4. Do you agree or disagree with this statement? "Include as much data as possible whenever you have the chance. It demonstrates your expertise." Explain your answer.
5. Identify and explain two common problems with bar charts.
6. Illustrate a flow chart for a simple procedure in either a student organization or a job you have held.
7. Do you agree or disagree with this statement? "Never place graphics or tables at the end of your text. They will be lost there." Explain your answer.
8. In what specific ways can graphics be used to distort statistical information? Illustrate your answer with a drawing of your own creation.
9. What is a multiple-curve chart? Suggest one example in which it might be used appropriately.
10. How is a segmented bar chart like a pie chart? In what way can both prove deceptive?
11. For what reasons can we expect more, not less, graphics in business documents in the years ahead?

12. In your view, how does color influence our perception of graphics in business documents?

13. What are the possibilities of distorting data (and thus interpretations) when pictograms are used? (A pictogram is a graphic representation of a quantity: bags of money; rows of "stick" people; airplanes; buildings; etc.)

14. Research and determine the Dow-Jones stock average for January of 1984, 1986, and 1988. Present the average for each month graphically in three different charts. Indicate the audience for each chart.

EXERCISES

15. Words must explain their message in linear fashion, one at a time, while graphic images communicate more immediately. What advantages and/ or disadvantages do you see in the speed with which graphic aids create impressions?

16. You are to prepare a report that explains the nature of your academic department's curriculum. The report will be presented to high school juniors (who are unfamiliar with the college), to alumni of your program (who will be familiar with some of the operations of your college), and to parents of current students in the program. Although the substance of the report will be basically the same, how will the visuals change?

17. Write our clear definitions for mean, median, and mode. Invent an advertising scenario in which inaccurate impressions could be conveyed by mixing up or ignoring these definitions.

18. Collect at least five graphic aids from recent business magazines. For each, discuss what was done well or poorly in the communication of ideas and statistics.

19. Develop a bar chart representing student enrollment in, for instance, your college, department, or student organization. However, besides just focusing on the data over a specified period (such as the past eight to ten years), also indicate the changes in the male/female makeup of the total numbers. After you have completed the bar chart, prepare a one-paragraph critique of your work.

20. Find a table in a business document (perhaps from a report in your business library). Write an evaluation of the table based on the "Checklist for Constructing Tables" in this chapter. Then redesign the table, using a photocopy of the data to avoid recopying.

√ 21. As manager of Home Medical Devices, Inc., you've seen profits explode in the past ten years. For your annual report, you must decide on a graphic way of representing the increase. Make up net sales figures for each of the past ten years, and then draw up three different graphic representations of the figures. Choose one for your annual report. Explain why you chose it over the others you prepared.

22. Discover what graphics capabilities students can gain access to on your campus. Make use of the facilities to generate one or more of the visual aids described in this chapter. Then write a short summary of what is available for student use. If no facilities exist on your campus, suggest how students can generate graphs and charts on their own, without a significant financial expenditure.

23. Concerning computer graphics the text states: "These graphic representations use six-color pen plotters, electrostatic plotters, graphic-colored cathode-ray tube terminals (CRT), and digitizing boards. Gantt charts, pie charts, organizational charts, bar charts, musical scores, three-dimensional representations of almost anything, in virtually any color, can be produced through the use of computer graphics."

If one has seen computer graphics in use, the above statement is clear. However, if a person has not seen a computer terminal, display screen, and other elements, it may be a bit confusing. Assume you need to make a written presentation concerning the potential use of computer graphics in the Murphy CPA firm. The report will be reviewed by office staff, some old-time personnel (pencil and eyeshade accountants), and recently educated accountants who are up to date on the latest technologies. Develop a single graphic or a series of graphics that will make the statement more understandable.

24. Find three examples of visual aids in a current business magazine. For each, evaluate the effectiveness and integrity of the visual in representing data and communicating impressions to readers. Make suggestions for improvements where possible. Remember to cite the source for each visual used.

25. Chart your own academic progress (approximate grade average, perhaps?) beginning with elementary school. Estimate where necessary. Without resorting to trickery, choose a visual mode of representation that puts your academic path in as complimentary a light as possible.

26. Identify the vocation you plan to enter and specify a particular industry you hope to join—perhaps even a particular organization. For your future job, industry, and perhaps company indicate: (a) the current status of computer graphics and (b) the potential for using computer graphics in your vocation, industry, and/or organization.

27. Misrepresentation via visuals can be a serious problem. Advertisers are expected to represent their product in the best possible light. Find an advertisement (in either the print or video media) that you feel may misrepresent the actual situation. Identify the advertisement, describe it, and explain how it tends to distort reality.

LEGAL CONSIDERATIONS

MANAGEMENT COMMUNICATION AND THE LAW

In choosing the method and medium for their communications, managers consider a variety of approaches: what will the audience find interesting? What will best convey the idea? What will prove persuasive? What can the company afford? Every manager must add another crucial question to that list of considerations: what is legal?

Virtually all managerial communications must be evaluated with an eye toward legal responsibilities and liabilities. The manager, after all, stands in an "agency relationship" with the company—he or she is empowered to act for the company and to stand under the supervision of the company. For these reasons, the company must accept responsibility for the work-related actions and communications of its employees.

The agency relationship, in fact, is difficult to put aside, even when both the manager and company involved wish to do so. Simply labelling an interview "off the record" or writing "Confidential" on a memo does not put the communication beyond the reach of the courts. All managerial communications, including memos, phone records, files, and minutes of meetings can be ordered into court as evidence under the power of subpoena (the court's legal demand for the submission of evidence).

Are such circumstances rare? Not at all. Hundreds of cases are brought each day against managers in communication-related charges, especially in these areas:

- violation of equal opportunity legislation
- failure to provide proper credit information or notification
- violation of right-to-privacy laws

- improper or discriminatory practices in hiring, supervising, and firing
- inaccurate or misleading consumer information, including advertising, labelling, and warranties
- suppression or destruction of information available under "sunshine" legislation

In these and other areas, modern managers must exercise the utmost care in what they communicate. When charges are brought against a company and its agents, what counts in court is not what a manager meant to say or write, but what in fact he or she *did* commit to paper or "publish" (make known) to third parties through conversation or oral presentation.

Consider, for example, the manager of a large mall in New York who communicated, by posted notice, that leaflets could not be distributed by non-merchants on the mall premises. In this instance, an anti-nuclear group had tried to distribute protest and information leaflets in the mall corridors. Before the New York Court of Appeals in 1985, the manager lost his case. His letters, memos, and notices were brought forward by the plaintiff as evidence of an attempt to suppress freedom of speech. The court agreed, defining the modern mall as a "town center" where citizens have a right to speak out in oral and written forms.

Do such cases imply that managers should avoid communication altogether? No. To manage *means* to communicate, and contemporary managers spend as much as 90 percent of their business day in communication activities. But court precedents and common sense do suggest that managers educate themselves about the legal dimensions of every document or presentation in which they are involved. Throughout the text, therefore, we have provided information on the legal aspects of managerial communication in the following areas:

Business Research and the Law   p. 204

Reports and the Law   p. 330

Employee Communication
and the Law   p. 456

Credit, Collection, and the Law   p. 602

Products, Promotion, and the Law   p. 630

In each of these cases, our intent is not to provide legal advice for direct application in your business life; only an attorney can provide specific guidance in such areas. Instead, we intend to alert you to legal "hot spots" where common sense and legal precedents urge managers to exercise judgment and caution. The cost of being a careful communicator is low, especially when measured against the devastating financial, corporate, and personal consequences of legal action based on your communications.

Part Four

Professional Speaking and Listening

13 Principles of Oral Communication

What and how you communicate often determine what you are to the world.

Business people are called upon to speak frequently in a variety of formal and semiformal situations. There are occasions that involve a twenty-minute presentation to a group of prospective customers, visitors to the plant, or security analysts. At other times we may be called upon to express ideas and opinions at meetings and conferences. Then there are panel presentations frequently used at Chamber of Commerce sessions; recruiting, appraisal, and counseling interviews; and a dozen other occasions when we are called upon to express ourselves. Each of these is an opportunity—an opportunity to express yourself and impress others not only with your knowledge of the topic, but also with your ability to convey that knowledge.

An interesting aspect of speaking is the correlation listeners frequently draw between the effectiveness of the presentation and the ability of the speaker in his or her field. Even if the speaker is an outstanding accountant, engineer, or financial analyst, speaking inarticulately or fumbling and bumbling may cause the listener's perception of his or her ability to suffer severely. We may say that such an evaluation is unfair, but that negative evaluation—fair or not—remains.

Because people in a variety of areas and professions have occasion to speak—and therefore present themselves—in a dozen different situations, they must do so effectively. Speakers actually have an obligation to do as good a job in their oral presentations as they do in their professional areas. And doing so is really quite simple when specific steps are carried through in the preparation, content, and delivery of the message.

Although we all recognize the importance of making effective oral presentations, many of us still face the task with some fear and trepidation. As a matter of fact, when large numbers of Americans have been asked about their greatest fears, they frequently list "speaking before a group" as a situation they fear over and beyond heights, accidents, insects, financial problems, and even death itself.[1]

However, there are a variety of steps each of us can take to lessen that fear and eventually overcome it. Those factors, such as preparation, knowledge of the topic and the audience, plus others, are discussed thoroughly in the following pages.

TYPES OF PRESENTATIONS

We usually think of oral communications as being persuasive, informative, or entertaining. Whether the presentation is long or short, taking place in an interview, a panel, or at a meeting, it usually falls into one of these three categories.

The Persuasive Talk

Gaining the listener's acceptance or approval is the objective in the persuasive presentation. One method of doing that is to use a logical order of development that includes the following:

Arousing Interest   Capture the audience's interest by making a startling statement, telling a story with which the members of the audience can identify, demonstrating an activity, holding up a sample, or carrying through any action that will cause the audience to become alert and receptive to your message.

Describing and Explaining   Your description should be clear enough so that listeners can easily understand and appreciate your ideas and concepts. And the explanation should revolve around the benefits the listeners will accrue: the fulfillment of their needs, their hopes, their desires.

Proving and Visualizing   Substantiate your claims by citing past experiences, testimonials from others, or some guarantees that the members of the audience will find acceptable and believable. Statements that help visualize results are also important in persuading others:

> *You will therefore be able to dispose of eight out of ten filing cabinets now in use. Picture the added work space secured!*
>
> *With this equipment, your production line speed can be increased by almost 40 percent. That should almost double your output, thus making a sizable contribution to your profit margin.*

---

[1]See the movie, "Speaking Effectively to One or One Thousand," CRM/McGraw-Hill Films, 1979, and D. Wallenchinsky and Irving Wallace, *The Book of Lists*, New York: William Morrow, 1979.

Moving to Action or Approval   Now that the interest of the audience has been secured, the idea, concept, product, or service described, the need for it noted, and its value proven, you should ask for approval. This step should be carried through specifically and positively.

> *Now that you have the facts, an accurate evaluation of the return on investment we will receive, and the overall benefits to our company, I request your written approval for the project by May 15.*

The Informative Talk

In this presentation, it is vital that the audience clearly understand the concept presented. For that reason, pay special attention to clarity, organization, and coherence in the presentation. An essential factor is, therefore, an outline, which will assist both the speaker and listener.

Good visual aids can make an important contribution in the informative speech by helping the audience see as well as hear how the important points in the concept are related.

The Entertaining Speech

This speech may have as its basis such things as humor, description, picturesque language, drama, mystery, or a combination of these. Certainly the interest level must be kept high and the organization clear.

It is well to remember that although humor may be an attribute of the entertaining speech, it is not the only one.

ORGANIZING THE SPEECH

Very often speakers feel that once they have their key concepts selected, their research completed, and their visual aids arranged, they are ready to give their speech. However, there are other steps to complete: the design of the introduction, the body, and the conclusion, and the selection of the central theme.

The Introduction

The introduction is vital, for it will often determine the overall reaction of the audience to the entire speech. Getting off on the right foot is important. The old saw, "We never have a second chance to make a good first impression," has much merit.

Good introductions result from careful planning, which may involve beginning with an unusual statement or story; referring to the audience or a problem or situation with which they can identify; posing a rhetorical question; or even injecting humor that is associated with the topic. Beginnings such as the following are sure to lose or alienate the audience:

> *Well, I'm not sure why Mr. Baxter selected me to address you, but here goes anyway . . .*
>
> *I really have little or nothing to add to what has already been said on the topic, but . . .*

The Body

The body of the speech usually will account for 70 to 80 percent of the speech time. It is the heart of the presentation. In organizing it, the speaker should select and write out the central theme, main ideas, and supporting ideas.

The central theme is what the speaker wants the audience to remember even if all or most of the other ideas are forgotten. It is best if the central theme can be stated in one sentence. And if that sentence can be alliterative or somehow distinctive, so much the better. Once that theme has been selected, a series of main ideas should be chosen to buttress that concept. Normally, listeners will be able to retain four or five such main ideas, but not more.

The supporting ideas to the main ideas are then brought in. Their primary function is to substantiate, prove, and reinforce the main ideas. Statistics, analogies, examples, and quotations are often used to serve as support.

After the speaker has selected the central theme and main and supporting ideas, he or she should take the time to arrange them in a consistent and logical order of development. Some methods of developing a presentation are chronological sequence, spatial sequence, causal sequence, deductive sequence, inductive sequence, and problem-solution sequence.

The Conclusion

The conclusion should "fix" the central theme in the minds of the audience and serve as a closure. The speaker may wish to summarize the main points, suggest a specific course of action to the audience, propose a solution, or request approval. At times even a quotation from an authority will tie in perfectly with the speaker's theme idea and serve as an effective conclusion.

QUALITIES OF THE EFFECTIVE SPEAKER

The members of the audience to which the manager speaks—in business, industry, and government—do not expect or demand a spellbinding, polished presentation. However, they do expect the speaker to be *knowledgeable*, *prepared, well-organized,* and *honest.* If, in addition, speakers deliver their comments with impressive gestures, careful enunciation, and excellent inflection and remember to maintain good eye contact, so much the better. But at the least, the speaker must do an effective job with the "formidable four":

Be Knowledgeable   Speakers should possess excellent background knowledge of both the audience and the topic. Their research should be complete and the information they possess should be sufficiently thorough so that they can anticipate questions, comments, and objections.

Speakers should know something of the areas related to the topic as well as ideas which oppose their own. With knowledge on this level, rebuttals as well as answers to questions can be handled with some degree of confidence.

Be Prepared   Speakers should be prepared in several different ways. The presentation should include selecting a thorough outline of the presentation, along with a theme idea, a main idea, and supporting points. Preparation should also include useful and readable visual aids, handout materials, samples, recordings, photos, and any other materials that will add to the substance of the presentation.

It goes without saying that notes should be part of the presentation. But the notes should never be so detailed as to require word-by-word reading. (For a sensitive or extremely important topic, it may be necessary and even wise to read a very carefully prepared talk.)

Be Well-Organized   Perhaps this is part of being prepared. If speakers prepare properly, they usually organize at the same time.

One of the best ways to retain the attention of the audience is to make the presentation well organized, concise, and clear. Conversely, there is no quicker way to lose an audience than with a rambling, illogical, poorly organized talk.

Be Honest   Probably no activity reveals a person more completely than speaking. An ancient philosopher said, "Speak that I may know you."

Somehow, some way, one's personality, knowledge, truthfulness, emotions, and self are revealed when one speaks. And because speech is so revealing of ourselves, we are ill-advised to pretend to be something we aren't. Such attempts will almost always be recognized by the audience, and the speaker will suffer in the balance.

That is why speakers should be honest in the presentation—in action and in statements—if they wish to maintain the goodwill of the audience. And they should also respect the audience. Finally, they should recognize the value of a straightforward, "I'm sorry, I really don't know the answer to that question."

DELIVERING THE SPEECH

If all steps leading up to a speech (preparation, research, organization, gaining knowledge) are well taken care of, the speech will probably be effective. Nevertheless, we cannot discount the importance of the delivery. It isn't quite enough to "just give it," even if you do have the "formidable four" well in hand.

The delivery will surely be affected by your emotional state. And if you are like most of us, your emotional state will contribute to your presentation. Your pulse rate will probably be higher than usual; your breathing may be shallow and rapid; and your stomach and mouth will not feel the way they usually do. But this condition, you may be sure, will be much more apparent to you than the audience. And, as a matter of fact, it may give you a slight edge because you are so alert and sensitive to the climate in which you are involved.

Fortunately, this nervousness decreases in direct proportion to the work you do on the "formidable four." When you are prepared, organized, knowledgeable, and honest, you can't help but be confident and thus much less nervous.

FACTORS IN THE DELIVERY OF THE SPEECH

Although your audience may not demand that the delivery of your speech be accomplished with the perfection of a first-rate orator, they will appreciate some degree of care on your part concerning the basic principles of volume, enunciation, eye contact, and the like.

Choice of Words and Word Usage

A primary purpose of communication is to transfer ideas. Ideas are made up of words; therefore, the more extensive our vocabulary is, the easier is the task of selecting the exact word for every meaning. Then ideas can be expressed with precision, force, and clarity.

Our choice of words must be based on the audience. Often we become so deeply involved in our own areas of specialization that we forget that our technical terms are not known to everyone. Remember, too, that certain words arouse emotional reactions which increase prejudice, build support, or evoke opposition. Words such as *strike, scab, delinquent, hippie,* or *warmonger* may cause a strong reaction among our listeners. It is one thing to choose emotionally charged words intentionally so as to better convey ideas. However, you should be aware that a careless choice of such words may cause listeners to tune you out.

It is not sufficient to know what one ought to say; one must also know how to say it.

Aristotle

Pronunciation of Words

You should take care to enunciate clearly the words you choose. Careless or sloppy enunciation is usually the result of sheer laziness in the use of mouth, tongue, and lips. A "yeah" for a "yes," "dontchathink" for "don't you think," and "we're gonna" for "we are going to," neither help present ideas nor enhance your image to the audience.

Inflection

At times it is vital to give specific inflection to ideas as we speak. That change in tone, emphasis, and volume will often reflect, better than the words, feelings of emotion, anger, enthusiasm, humor, or support. The speaker who will not permit his or her voice to reflect feelings usually misses an important factor in oral communication.

Volume

It is obvious that the audience must be able to hear the speaker easily before it can accept his or her ideas. If members of the group strain to hear the speaker, they will eventually find the effort too taxing and give up. On the other hand, if the speaker's voice is too loud or scratchy, or pitched too high, the audience may find that an irritation, and again the speaker will lose. It takes very little effort on the speaker's part to determine and maintain the proper volume and pitch.

One of the most important factors in volume is variation. A one-level presentation becomes monotonous, and it is helpful to vary the volume, not, however, in a way that sounds mechanical or affected. Changes in volume should be related to the idea being presented.

Rate of Delivery

Changes in the rate of delivery, like changes in volume, help arouse audience interest and dispel monotony. The speech that is delivered too rapidly is sometimes difficult for an audience to follow. And even if an audience does comprehend easily, it is taxing for most people to stay with someone who speaks extremely rapidly for more than thirty minutes or so. On the other hand, the speaker whose words come out at a snail's pace finds that the audience becomes bored, inattentive, and even irritated. Rate of delivery should always be adjusted to the subject matter, the audience, and the speaker's personality.

Gestures and Posture

Freely motivated and natural gestures can add immeasurably to the communication of ideas. Effective nonverbal communication by means of the torso, hands, head, face, and eyes all help convey your message, mood, and attitude. But your gestures must be spontaneous and natural. It is important that they not look artificial.

You must also watch your posture. If you slouch or drape yourself on the lectern, the audience may feel that your ideas are as slovenly as your posture. A speaker who stands erect and is vigorous commands the attention of the audience.

Eye Contact

Eye contact, carefully and naturally maintained, helps keep the audience involved. One way is to pick several individuals in the audience and speak directly to them. Then pick others and focus on them. Soon most of the audience begin to feel an involvement with you and with what you are saying.

Most of us can recall speakers or teachers who stared out the window or at the floor, or glued their eyes to their notes. The speaker lost directness, and the audience, interest. But the speaker who looks at the listeners arouses their interest and captures their attention.

Evaluating the Audience During a Speech

It is important to be alert to the feedback you receive from the audience while you speak. The content, depth of analysis, organization, use of humor, and a dozen other factors must often be varied according to the response.

The effective speaker is not tied to notes and outlines. On the contrary, alert speakers quickly become aware of the questions on the faces of many in the audience and add another example. They immediately sense that this point has been covered very adequately. To continue would be to belabor it and lose many of the group. They therefore move on quickly.

On a total basis, they "feel" the audience and respond accordingly.

USING VISUAL AIDS

The adept use of visual aids can add an important dimension to the effect-iveness of your oral communication. The very fact that your comments are not only *heard* but elaborated on or further explained as they are *seen* increases the impact of your message.

Like the report itself, the visual aids must be prepared with careful attention to the audience. Should a table or pictogram be used in this instance? A chart or a graph? In every case, the item (table, chart, graph) should have a minimum number of factors on it. In an oral presentation, two or, at most, three lines are recommended for a graph or chart. Tables should not be made up of more than two or three columns of figures. All in all, you should keep in mind that it is not as easy to assimilate data from a visual aid that is on a chart or screen some fifty feet in front of the viewer as it is from an item in your hand and only twelve inches from your eyes.

Flip Charts

Flip charts are easy to use and certainly inexpensive. Felt-tip markers are excellent for designing easy-to-read charts. Here again it is wise to keep the information on each sheet to a minimum and to be positive every word and number is visible from every chair in the room.

Most speakers find it wise to prepare their charts *before* they speak. Few of us are so expert that we can talk, maintain eye contact, and record legible data on a flip chart simultaneously.

The flip chart has other advantages: The room lights do not have to be lowered, and there are no mechanical items to burn out or otherwise go wrong. And of course the speaker can place tiny penciled notes between the heavy colored lettering on the chart and thus be liberated from dependence on note cards.

Slide Projectors

Using slides is very effective. The color, spontaneity, and visual impact of professionally made slides can prove very effective. With modern projectors few problems arise, and the speaker can project slides forward easily or even go in reverse at the press of a button. Of course the room lights must usually be dimmed, but if the speaker keeps the lights lowered for only a short period of time, the full attention of the audience will usually be retained.

Overhead Projectors

This is one of the most versatile pieces of audiovisual equipment. Transpar-encies can be prepared beforehand, or you may make them up as you speak.

You can easily add or delete key points to a prepared transparency while the audience watches. Perhaps the chief advantage is that the projector may be used without lowering any of the lights.

Blackboard or Whiteboard

Information can be added or erased easily, and almost every room that can accommodate a speaker and an audience is equipped with the old standard blackboard or the newer, easy-to-erase whiteboard.

Whatever visual aids you use, make sure they are not too "busy." They must be attractive, easy to comprehend, and visible from every seat in the room.

Visual Aids Must Be Informative

Too often individuals will prepare a slide or a chart that adds nothing to the presentation. To have a table that adds little information or a chart with such broad terms as "Advantages," "Conclusion," or "Liabilities" will not normally contribute to the speech. On the other hand, recapitulating the key closing points and *listing* those points under "Conclusion" are good ideas. Or it may be that the speaker decides to discuss the four "advantages." In such a case, listing them on the chart reinforces those four supporting ideas.

The final test should always be: Will the visual aid (a table, chart, heading, or listing) clarify, reinforce, supplement, or explain an idea or concept? If the answer is yes, it should be used. If it serves only as window dressing, it should be discarded.

QUESTIONS FOR STUDY

1. What are three specific methods which can be used to "arouse interest" in a persuasive talk?
2. What "proof" methods could you use to persuade an audience of college students to purchase a new personal computer?
3. Can your "move to action" or "approval" in a persuasive talk ever be too strong? Explain by selecting a product, an audience, and a "move to action" statement.
4. Is it possible for an "entertaining presentation" to be so entertaining that the message is lost? Explain and give an example.
5. A good conclusion can sometimes "make or break" a presentation. List several methods of concluding a speech that can prove effective.

6. What are the "Formidable Four" attributes for a speaker who wishes his presentation to be successful? List and explain why each of the four is important.

7. If one of the four attributes which you listed in your answer to question 7 above is not present or is poorly handled, can the speech still be successful? Explain.

8. What is meant by "enunciation" in speaking? List ten words or phrases with which you are familiar that are frequently not properly enunciated by many Americans today. Can you explain why this happens?

9. What are two valuable effects on the audience that result from an effective "rate of delivery"?

10. For the speaker who does use gestures, why is it vital that such nonverbal communication be "natural"?

11. When the President of the United States addresses a national audience of millions, he seems to maintain excellent eye contact by looking directly at the camera. Yet, he is obviously *reading* a prepared speech from a *teleprompter.* Present a brief report (orally or in writing) explaining how a teleprompter works.

12. How can a speaker "evaluate the audience" at the same time that he or she is giving a speech? And, why should the speaker evaluate the audience?

13. What visual aid do you find most effective and convenient to use? Explain why.

14. Why is "preparation" so important in using a visual aid? And further, what items need to be prepared? Be specific.

EXERCISES

15. You are to give an oral presentation to a group of high school seniors. The topic is "Your College Campus." Select three different organizational sequences and outline each.

16. Research the "sales letter" and then report (orally or in writing) on the similarities between that type of message and the persuasive presentation.

17. Some gestures command attention and others detract from the presentation. Select a recognized television personality and list the gestures he or she uses that command attention. Then list the gestures that are distracting. Be very specific in identifying and explaining the items you list.

18. Listen to an extended address by a politician, religious figure, or other personality (perhaps on television or radio). For that speaker, discover where pauses are characteristically placed, then develop a short speech of your own, placing pauses in those locations. Assess the influence of such pauses on your own effectiveness as a speaker.

19. It sometimes appears that we are becoming slovenly in the way we pronounce our language or substitute inappropriate words for correct English. Besides the examples cited in the chapter, list at least ten words you frequently hear that are either mispronounced or misused, or are slang terms.

20. Study the speaking habits and techniques of two TV newscasters. Then, using at least six categories of comparison, write down their similarities and differences as speakers. Decide which, in your view, is the most effective speaker.

21. Using a tape recorder, conduct the following experiment. Choose a longer paragraph in this text (or another) and read it slowly and distinctly into the tape recorder. Then read the same passage again into the recorder, this time very quickly. Listen to the two versions. For each, write down the impression you gain about the speaker based on the pace of speech. (Does a fast pace, for example, make the speaker sound ill-at-ease and impatient? Or does the speaker sound more compelling to listen to?)

22. There are at least three types of presentations: informative, entertaining, and persuasive. However, besides being types of speeches, the elements of information, entertainment, and persuasion can be parts of a total speech. You are a concerned student who feels that the academic standards of your institution have declined. You have met with the dean to explain your feelings and after several discussions the dean said, "I want you to make a seven-to-ten-minute presentation to a faculty group." The purpose of your speech will be to convince the audience to increase the institution's academic standards. However, to achieve your purpose you want to inform them and include some appropriate humor along the way. Outline your presentation and specifically identify the elements of information, entertainment, and persuasion in the outline.

23. As one of the better speakers in your company, you've been assigned as a personal speech coach to help a company vice president overcome "speaker's nerves." You have two weeks to help this executive before an important presentation must be given. Describe the steps you would take to lead this person to confident speaking.

24. Thirty minutes before a business meeting your boss tells you to say a few words about the history of the company for the benefit of guests at the meeting. In that amount of time, what information must you gather? What personal preparation and planning must you make?

25. Often student presentations in classes can be represented in one word: dull. You are to make an oral presentation in a class; other students in the class will be making speeches on the same topic. You want to differentiate yourself from the others by gaining the attention of the audience immediately. Write the introduction on a sheet of paper and explain

what you will be doing to gain the audience's attention. Select one of the classes and topics:

Course	Topic
Basic Accounting	Why Accountants Must Be Precise
Secretarial Studies	Men Enter the Secretarial Profession
Personnel	Fringe Benefits of the Future
Finance	Changes in Banking Regulations
Marketing Sales	Salesmen Aren't Necessarily Men Anymore

26. Locate a public figure reputed to be honest and sincere in his or her speaking manner. List specific verbal and nonverbal techniques (whether conscious or unconscious) used by the speaker in creating this impression.

Short Presentations

Memorable words can produce memorable results.

There are obviously many situations in business where short oral presentations must be delivered. It is important for a brief talk to be as effective as a long, formal one. Short presentations may be given by you before employees, community members, business and professional organizations, and government representatives. You may be the only speaker or you may be participating as a panel representative or a committee member at a meeting.

Among the many occasions that arise in which short, oral presentations are needed are:

- The informational talk to a small group or an individual
- An explanation of a new project, procedure, or concept to colleagues, company personnel, or conference attendees
- Introductions of individuals, projects, or concepts to an audience
- Recognition of individuals or groups for their contributions
- Welcoming visitors or others on behalf of your organization or company
- Luncheon or dinner presentations
- Briefings on technical or semitechnical projects to those who need to know about the project.

THE INFORMATIONAL TALK

There are a great many situations in which an informational talk is used. You may be called upon to inform employees about new rules, regulations, or procedures. Or you may wish to inform students, community members, or stockholders about your firm, its activities, products, or organization. You may wish to give customers information about a new sales allowance or a new product.

The primary purpose of the informative talk is to provide listeners with information they did not previously possess. Members of the group usually have very little knowledge of the topic. Of course you must still determine the level of knowledge they possess so that you do not speak above or below their heads.

Visual aids will often serve a useful purpose in this type of talk. A chart, cutaway drawing, model of a piece of equipment, or diagram can assist in the transfer of information.

THE EXPLANATORY TALK

This presentation is similar to the informational talk. Certainly in any explanation, information must be transmitted. However, the explanatory talk usually requires that sufficient details be presented to ensure that listeners will *understand* how a piece of equipment or machinery works, how a procedure is carried through, how a routine is followed, or how an item is constructed.

This type of talk goes beyond informing to explaining. Certainly any visual aid that assists in the explanatory process should be used.

THE INTRODUCTORY TALK

The purpose of this talk is to motivate the audience to want to hear the speaker—not the introducer.

For that reason, introductions should be short, attention-catching, and pithy. They should make the speaker feel welcome; certainly they should not embarrass him or her by being too effusive, humorous, or long. Introductions that state, "This individual needs no introduction," "I really don't know what I can tell you about our speaker that you don't already know," or "Last, but not least . . ." are all trite and only make the speaker's job more difficult.

The introduction can (1) emphasize the accomplishments of the speaker, (2) concentrate on the topic, (3) examine both, or (4) discuss the speaker and the topic and their relationship to the audience. In most cases, this last suggestion will arouse the greatest audience interest.

The introducer should learn as much as possible about the speaker as well as the interests of the audience, attempting to find a common ground that can be used to heighten audience interest. If the speaker is a corporate officer of a food manufacturer and is scheduled to address two thousand chain-store managers, the introducer may point out that the speaker himself was a store manager some eighteen years ago: "His knowledge and appreciation of the daily problems you face are derived from hard work and experience, not reports read in a walnut-panelled office."

Another technique is to cite names of several members of the audience and their relationship to the speaker. At times a relevant quotation can arouse interest, for instance, a statement made about the speaker by a national authority. Or perhaps the speaker or the topic can be linked to a quotation from a major source such as the Congressional Record, Shakespeare, or the *New York Times*. Quoting the section of the Bible concerned with the Tower of Babel was an interesting and effective method one introducer used in presenting a speaker in the field of communications.

The key is to learn about the speaker and the audience. Then draw interesting elements from the backgrounds of each to serve the mutual interests of all concerned.

In introducing concepts or projects, the same thing holds true. What in the concept or project will be of significance to *this* particular audience? Once the introducer knows what to select concerning the project or concept, it should be quite simple to bring those factors into focus for a specific audience.

Perhaps the firm is introducing a new product to its sales force. Some members of the sales force may call on distributors, others on chain-store buyers, still others on independent retail outlets, and others on government agencies. One device is to have several short presentations, each made by someone who is familiar with one of those groups. Credibility rises, for we all realize no one can be an expert in *every* area. However, we will accept the fact that certain individuals have a better feel for the needs and desires of a particular group than others have.

THE RECOGNITION SPEECH

Sometime in your career you will be asked to present an award or special item of recognition to an individual or a group. The audience has gathered, of course, to honor the recipient—not the presenter. Therefore the speaker is wise to comment on the award, the achievement of the recipient or recipients that prompted the award, and the honor or significance of the recognition.

Most of us who work hard or perform beyond the call of duty appreciate recognition as much as financial payment. For that reason the recognition is important, but care must be taken to avoid embarrassing the person honored. The words chosen and the method of presentation or recognition are most important, and the place and manner in which the ceremony is held should be planned with care.

In the speech of recognition or presentation, keep the following in mind:

MOBILIZING THE ENGLISH LANGUAGE[1]

If anyone should ever doubt the power of speech, just bear in mind that one leader, by speeches, kept his country free. In England's dark year of 1940, the resolute defiance of Churchill convinced Franklin Roosevelt to lend aid and deterred Adolph Hitler from launching a sea invasion. In the words of John Kennedy, "Churchill mobilized the English language and sent it into battle."

Churchill, no doubt, is "the speaker of the century," but it is a forgotton fact that he was a self-made speaker. The stuttering, lisping Churchill was an unlikely oratorical prospect. At five-foot-five, he hardly had an imposing presence and his gutteral snarl lacked the resonant timbre of a MacArthur or Martin Luther King. Churchill did not even have the advantage of a university education. He had not only to surmount these handicaps, but also the fear of speaking. In one of his first speeches in the House of Commons, he collapsed in the middle of his remarks.

Yet Churchill in early manhood determined that eloquence would be his ladder to power and greatness. While a lieutenant stationed in a far-flung empire garrison in India, Churchill studied the parliamentary addresses of the great British statesmen such as Disraeli and Gladstone to find the winning recipe for oratory. His conclusions were jotted down in 1897 in an unpublished article, "The Scaffolding of Rhetoric."

To Churchill, the elements of an effective speech were rhythm, diction, analogy, and a central argument. By "rhythm" Churchill meant an oral style drafted not to be read but to be listened to. Cumbersome sentences with more than one subordinate clause are too complex for the ear to digest. Speech writers should break up unwieldy "Germanic" structure into simple declarative sentences. And they shouldn't sacrifice the force of an active verb to a lifeless passive voice. Such construction may read well in an article or editorial, but sounds dead to the ear in a speech, Churchill believed.

Diction, or the right word, was the next important factor in Churchill's view of effective expression. He was aware that the right word or phrase which caught the essence of the speech could be the headline in the next day's paper. One such phrase was "summit confer-

1. Be brief. Honest and sincere recognition should be given. However, the statement should not be a eulogy or so long as to be boring or make the recipient or the audience uncomfortable.
2. Identify the award or gift or read the certificate. Many in the audience may have contributed money for the purchase of the award or they may simply want to hear the words describing the recipient's accomplishments.
3. Conclude the comments with the presentation of the gift or certificate.

In a busy, hurried society of giant organizations, accomplishments of individuals are often overlooked or not handled well. When there is recognition, therefore, it should be accomplished with care, good taste, discretion, and professionalism. After an individual is recognized, both the person honored and the audience should feel a real glow of inner satisfaction.

ence," which he proposed in 1951. It is now forgotten that the slogan "business as usual" was coined by Churchill when he was War Minister in World War I. And in 1946 when Churchill said, "An iron curtain has descended across the continent of Europe," the whole world could almost hear the clanging down of a steel wall between East and West.

The most useful tool in communication, wrote Churchill, is "the analogy." In his unpublished article, Churchill cites as an example the Bishop of Derry's remark, "A strong nation may be no more confiding of its liberties than a pure woman of her honor." Churchill would liken the appeaser to "one who feeds the crocodile hoping it will eat him last" and "dictators who ride to and fro upon tigers from which they dare not dismount." He described Ramsey MacDonald as "a sheep in sheep's clothing" and John Foster Dulles as "a bull who carries his china closet with him."

Churchill knew that in an oral presentation, the message must be simple and direct. In his words, there has to be a "central argument." Complex reasoning may serve the purposes of an essay but a good talk, wrote Churchill, should be "a series of facts all pointing in a common direction." To put it another way, Churchill said the writer should not begin his draft of a speech unless he has the closing message fully in mind: "The end appears in view before it is reached. The words anticipate the conclusion and the last words fall amid a thunder of assent."

The ending should have the impact of a symphony finale. If the first four-fifths of a speech should be a highly focused succession of facts designed to win the mind, the last fifth should be aimed at the heart. Churchill had studied the climactic closings orators such as Gladstone had delivered to their audiences and became convinced that an emotional call to arms should cap the logical argument.

Some four decades later, the emotional closing in Churchill's Dunkirk speech ("We shall fight them on the beaches . . .") not only steeled the will of the English people but persuaded a neutral America to give timely and decisive aid.

[1]Adapted from James C. Humes, "Mobilizing the English Language," The Toastmaster, February 1981. Used by permission.

THE WELCOME SPEECH

Plants, offices, schools, or other facilities are often visited by individuals or groups. In almost all instances, the visitor or visitors should be welcomed. The statements should be brief and sincere.

It is always wise to note in a speech of welcome the accomplishments of the visiting group and add the hope that they will gain from their visit. Perhaps the key in this brief presentation is to keep in mind that although the welcome to your facilities should be noted, it is even more important to mention what the visiting group or individual has accomplished or achieved. This would not be at all difficult with the astronaut who visits an aerospace firm. But it can even be accomplished with a high school computer club that is touring the data-processing division of a large corporation. In that instance,

the group might be commended for its conscientious efforts and the students' desire to learn more by making the visit.

In some situations the welcome must include some specific information regarding safety or security. This can be a reference to the wearing of a hard hat or safety goggles in certain areas, the prohibition against taking pictures or interrupting a worker's assignment, or returning to a designated point at a specific time. Such information can be handled in a positive, courteous way and from the point of view that such suggestions are made for the visitors' benefit and safety.

In almost all instances, the welcoming speech (1) should be brief; (2) should recognize the accomplishments or position of the visitor or group; (3) should contain a little humor or "light" reference; (4) should offer the good will and assistance of the host organization; and (5) should list any rules or regulations that should be observed.

THE AFTER-DINNER OR AFTER-LUNCHEON SPEECH

Because the groups to which an after-dinner speech is delivered can vary so much, it is difficult to suggest any one pattern to follow. Some groups appreciate a brief, humorous presentation. Others want to learn and come prepared to ask penetrating questions. Because these two kinds of groups have such a tremendously different set of objectives, it is vital for the speaker—to be successful—to determine in advance what type of presentation is expected.

The "light" after-dinner speech has a theme running through it, but also has a fair amount of humor. The stories should be in good taste and associated with the theme. It is also sometimes wise to introduce a quotation or short poem that applies to the occasion and that can be remembered.

The serious after-dinner speech (to a professional accounting, dental, or financial organization, for example) should not be overly long. Here, however, the speaker wants to leave a message, introduce a new concept, or have some learning take place. For this reason it is vital not only to present the necessary ideas in a speech of this type but also to reinforce them. That can be accomplished with a story, a little humor, a demonstration, and/or the use of visual aids. A flip board with large-sized lettering might prove appropriate, but to turn down the lights and use slides is to take a calculated risk. A group of individuals who have worked hard all day, enjoyed predinner cocktails, and then consumed a prime-rib dinner might find the arms of Morpheus more attractive than your presentation.

Whether the after-meal speech is light or serious, it should be comparatively brief, carefully worded, and, to a greater or lesser degree, humorous. The speaker who includes a quotable phrase or two is wise, for in so doing he or she makes it somewhat easy for the audience to retain a key idea.

In almost all instances, the toastmaster plays a vital role in helping make the after-meal speech successful. The introduction of the speaker should be light and humorous, and give an indication of the topic to be discussed; the comments afterwards should not only reflect appreciation but also reinforce (very briefly) the key ideas.

THE BRIEFING

The oral briefing is precisely what the name implies. It is a *brief* presentation of a complex topic designed to inform the listeners of a planned or ongoing project or activity.

A nuclear engineer may present a briefing to a group of physicians on a new medical-nuclear piece of equipment; a shop manager may explain the functions of a new machine to the maintenance crew; or the office manager may inform the company board of directors on the functions, objectives, and work of a new word-processing center. In every case the presentation must be brief and not too detailed, and both words and ideas must be easily understandable to those who listen.

The **informational briefing** presents ideas in easy-to-understand terms and attempts to list concepts for easy retention. Charts or handout materials are often used to make sure the key ideas are not only *heard* but *seen*. This reinforcement can be very helpful in conveying basic information of what might be a complex operation or procedure.

The **instructional briefing** is designed to *teach* the listener or listeners how to operate or carry through a practice or a procedure. Here again, the basic ideas are presented, not the detailed or complex concepts.

In the instructional briefing the listeners should be given, if at all possible, an opportunity for a hands-on application. If they can actually handle, closely observe, or even participate in working with the item with which the instruction is concerned, the briefing will be aided tremendously.

Briefings are usually given by individuals. A team briefing is not at all unusual, however. It might be that a team will present a briefing to the new members of a board of directors. One person will brief the group on the organization's financing, the next on production, the next on marketing, and the last one on personnel activities. Each is limited to his or her topic and by time. The briefing team leader usually serves to coordinate the presentation with opening and closing comments.

The briefing is an important oral activity in today's business world. The person who can give a good briefing is recognized as articulate and competent—as someone who knows how to strip away details and present key concepts so they may be easily comprehended and assimilated. Such an individual stands out in any organization as one well qualified to move to the top.

OPPORTUNITIES TO PRACTICE THE SHORT PRESENTATION

Because practice is vital to becoming a good speaker, you should seize every opportunity to make an oral presentation. The next time your conference leader asks for a volunteer to present "a brief report on the new benefit program," raise your hand. When your association, fraternity, sorority, or club director is looking for someone to preside at the annual convention, push your arm up. When your boss requests an employee to visit the "upcoming conference and represent us," be the first to say, "I'll do it." The more times you practice, the more confident you'll become. And if you have an ability for self-evaluation, you will be able to spot weak points and eliminate them.

Better than self-evaluation, at times, is to seek the constructive criticism of colleagues and peers. One effective method for doing this is to involve yourself in regular on-going speaking activities. Some organizations exist primarily to promote such activity. One effective organization that is easily available to most individuals in the United States is Toastmasters International. It has representative chapters in thousands of companies, corporations, hospitals, government agencies, and other organizations—both in the public and private sectors. Each chapter holds weekly, semi-monthly, or monthly meetings. All members have frequent opportunities to speak and receive the constructive comments of friends. The atmosphere is pleasant, non-threatening, and, overall, very enjoyable.[1]

Organizations that provide speaking opportunities for their members have grown rapidly during the last twenty years. Toastmasters, for example, has grown from approximately 50,000 members in 3,000 chapters worldwide in 1975 to 135,000 members in 6,000 chapters in 47 countries today.

||||||||||||||||||||||||||||||||||||||||||||||||||||||||||||||||||||||||||||||||||||||||||||||||||||||||||||||||||||||||||||||||||||||||||||||||||

QUESTIONS FOR STUDY

1. For your future profession, name at least three situations in which you will probably be called upon to give a short speech.
2. Is there any basic difference between introducing a person and a concept/project?
3. In what specific ways can the presenter/introducer draw attention to the introduced person or concept rather than to himself or herself?
4. In seeking interesting things to say about a guest you are introducing, what areas might be investigated?
5. What are the differences in the information bases of the audience listening to an informational talk and the audience listening to a briefing?
6. What is a briefing? What is its importance and use in business?
7. Once ideas are presented in a speech, how can they be reinforced?
8. Why would you use an oral presentation for an "informational talk" instead of simply distributing the information in a written format of some type to those in your audience? Explain.
9. Is a visual aid usually needed more in making an explanatory rather than an introductory talk? Explain.
10. Making a good introductory talk preceding a speaker is said to be a most difficult and "delicate" task. Why is this so?
11. Can an introduction be so laudatory as to do a disservice to the speaker? Explain.
12. Why is it difficult to make an *effective* after-dinner speech which is technical in nature?
13. What steps can a speaker take in an effort to be successful in the case of question 12?
14. Visual aids may be most important and useful for what kinds of short speeches? Explain.
15. Differentiate between the explanatory talk and the informational talk.

[1]For membership and chapter information, write to Mr. Terrence McCann, Executive Director, Toastmasters International, 2200 No. Grand Avenue, Santa Ana, CA 92711.

EXERCISES

16. Assume that you supervise six managers. Write them a memo in which you emphasize the importance of "social" speaking situations to the company's image in the community.

17. Organizations such as colleges and universities are often known for their particular policies, procedures, and rules. People know the material but often do not know why these restrictions exist. Identify such an item that students would know on your campus. Outline the explanatory short talk you could give that would present the "why."

18. Present a briefing of your last class to a group of fellow students. You are to assume none were present for the session.

19. Write three humorous stories that would be appropriate in introductions and welcome speeches for a general business audience.

20. You are to give a welcoming talk to a group of college students from another state who are visiting your campus for the weekend. What would be some items of specific information that they would need to know and must be included in the welcome in addition to a sincere greeting?

21. We live in an era of technological explosions. Each day we learn of new technology applicable to our profession. Identify your profession and then outline a short informative speech that would report on a new technology (or new application of an existing technology) for your profession. The speech would be given to a group of people who have the same professional interests as you have.

22. You are to introduce the head of your academic department to a group of visiting high school students. Find a fitting quotation from the literature that would aid your introduction. Name the speaker and cite the quotation and its source.

23. Break into groups of three. Person A interviews person B in the area of "What I Want from a Career." Person C records the results, then organizes them into a short speech of introduction. As time allows, persons may switch roles so that all have a chance to interview, be interviewed, and speak.

24. Identify a subject with which members of your class would be familiar. Then obtain additional information so that a briefing can be prepared for them.
    a. Name the subject.
    b. Identify the new information.
    c. Prepare the visuals that would help the audience understand the information.
    d. Be prepared to present the briefing if called upon.

25. Imagine that you are being introduced to a business audience. Write a short introduction you would like to hear about yourself. Study it as a potential model for the kind of introductions others probably want to hear about themselves.

26. You are to make a short recognition speech at the college's coming Honors Day Program. Select one of the following situations and prepare your recognition speech. Work with a fellow student in developing the data; that is, use information about the fellow student in preparing your presentation. Also give the speech and have the person being recognized (who will receive a plaque) standing near you. Be sure you establish appropriate eye contact with the recipient and the audience. Potential recognitions, to which you may add, are as follows:
    Student with Highest GPA in the Department
    The Most Likely to Succeed Award
    Leadership Award to Student Making Contributions to the College
    Kindness Award to Student Considerate of Others
    Award to Student Getting the Highest Test Scores on Statistics Examinations in the College

27. Develop a visual aid to be used with a hypothetical informative talk. Create a checklist of at least six points you will want to consider in using the aid. (For example, when should it be shown to the audience?)

15 Longer Presentations

Preparation: the key to effective presentation.

Because organizations are becoming more complex, there is a greater need than ever for the exchange of information. The research and development department must present its ideas to the engineering and manufacturing department if a concept or sample is to be turned into a product. Marketing must explain to production what the buyer will accept or reject. Finance must discuss budgetary constraints with marketing and manufacturing. Top management is required to review plans, policies, and objectives with directors and stockholders.

And the list goes on.

The need for the exchange of technical information among knowledgeable people is an absolute necessity. Few people possess *all* the information required to carry through an activity or a project. Sharing is required as ideas, concepts, and data are discussed, evaluated, and integrated. This sharing often takes place during or after a long presentation.

What we have said previously concerning the planning, organizing, and delivery of the short presentation applies, in large measure, to the long speech. However, there are factors concerning strategies and content in the long presentation that require special attention.

HOW LONG AND SHORT PRESENTATIONS DIFFER

There are several ways in which long and short presentations differ.

Ideas. The concepts and ideas presented in the long speech are almost always more complex and involved than those in the short talk. The long presentation may analyze the financial, marketing, and manufacturing aspects of a product. Or it may carefully build a series of ideas designed to persuade the audience to take specific action. Or it may involve a team approach, with one individual presenting the design concepts and another the manufacturing process involved.

Length.   The time required to make a long presentation may vary from ten minutes to an hour. This is in contrast to the three to five minutes usually required for the short talk.

Use of Visuals.   Whereas the short talk rarely includes the use of visual aids, the long presentation almost requires them. Charts, graphs, samples, cutaways, handouts, and similar items that help communicate an idea are frequently used in the long presentation.

Exchange-Involvement.   The long presentation permits the interaction of ideas between members of the audience and the speaker. Exchange and involvement provide opportunities for ideas to be explored, questions to be raised, clarification to be offered, and concepts to be reviewed. All of this assists in attaining objectives.

The following are examples of the different types of long presentations:

Persuasive.   A presentation to the firm's executive council by the plant manager in which the latter attempts to have the council approve the purchase of a new piece of automated manufacturing equipment. Not only must the equipment be described, but the effect it will have on productivity must be analyzed and its financial implications reviewed as well.

Informative.   A presentation by the executive vice president to all department heads. The purpose is to inform the department leaders of changes in government regulations concerning the hiring of minority personnel, the completion of documents, and guidelines for job interview procedures.

Technical Exchange.   A presentation by a marketing representative to production and manufacturing personnel. In this case an "exchange" is required so that the marketing representative may explain what the potential buyer will or will not purchase. The technical representatives can then present the manufacturing constraints under which they must operate. Through this exchange or sharing, problems can be explored and solutions found.

Comparative.   A presentation involving the explanation and discussion of two or more products, concepts, policies, or activities. The primary purpose is to present all the facts to the audience so that a decision concerning a specific course of action may be made. Careful substantiation and objective analysis of data are vital in this situation.

Analytical. A presentation by the controller to the firm's financial committee regarding the possible acquisition of a small company. In this case the controller would analyze the present financial position of the firm being considered, its potential for increased sales, its debt structure, and a dozen other facets that will influence the committee's decision. In every area careful analysis is vital if the decision is to be accurate. This type of analytical presentation may be used by personnel from various company areas in many different situations, but it is found most frequently in a persuasive presentation.

SIX STEPS FOR A SUCCESSFUL SPEECH

Almost any activity requires that we follow a specific plan, system, or series of steps. Certainly that is true when we wish to deliver an effective long report or speech. These steps are as follows: (1) select the purpose and objectives; (2) plan the presentation; (3) analyze the audience; (4) select a presentation method; (5) use visual aids effectively, and (6) select a strategy to secure desired results.

Step 1: Select the Purpose and Objectives

We have all had the rather disturbing experience of listening to someone for fifteen or twenty minutes and not knowing what we should do when the speaker has finished. Did the speaker intend merely to inform us? Did he or she want us to vote? Or was the intention to motivate us to ask questions? Or was it his or her hope that we now go out and buy the product or service? Or perhaps the speaker wanted us to go back to our departments and discuss (or not discuss) his or her ideas with our associates. The error of leaving an audience frustrated or confused about the purpose of a speech is probably more serious than the error of delivering it poorly. People are busy; they need specific direction and guidelines. Of course they will make their own decisions, but the material upon which their decisions are made must be clear, concise, and well organized.

Specify your purpose: whether it is to inform, to persuade, or to compare. Indicate clearly that you are going to "list the four alternate fuel systems available to our firm and show why solar power will prove to be the most advantageous.

Obviously, the purpose of the presentation and the objectives you hope to achieve are selected as your first step. These (the purpose and your objectives) should be written out so you may examine them critically and evaluate every word to be sure you have selected those words which will convey exactly what you mean in your statement of purpose. Once the purpose or purposes have been selected to your satisfaction, you may wish to transfer them to flip charts (or other visuals) to be used at the most appropriate time in the course of your presentation.

Knowing precisely what your purpose and objectives are will assist your audience in evaluating and acting in response to your speech. And it will certainly help you plan every segment of your presentation.

Step 2: Plan the Presentation

Planning the presentation is simply organizing the talk for the most effective results.

The first activity to carry through is to write a tentative outline and then evaluate it to determine if it covers your purpose and objectives. When that has been completed, research is needed to gather facts, figures, and details. Company records, questionnaires, interviews, journal articles, reports, and the many other sources available are all possibilities. During the course of research, the tentative outline will probably be edited, revised, and restructured so the speech can have its greatest impact. Out of this comes a final outline that is used for the actual presentation.

Planning also includes anticipating logical questions that may be raised, objections that could be voiced, and requests for information in related areas. The speaker should have the answers or information ready, even if they may not be called for or used during or after the speech.

Designing the proper visuals and selecting the meeting site also are part of planning. Obviously the type and complexity of the visuals are dependent on such factors as the makeup of the audience, the nature of the topic, and the room size.

The meeting place plays an important role in the success of a presentation. Attempting to speak before forty people jammed into a tiny room or before nine people seated in an auditorium can prove disastrous.

In preparing or planning, the visual aid equipment, microphone, light switches, and other mechanical items should all be checked. All too often, if something can go wrong, it will! But if you plan well, the odds are usually in your favor.

Step 3: Analyze the Audience

If your presentation is to be delivered within your firm, you will have a better opportunity to know the makeup of the group. How many in the audience are from engineering? From finance? From marketing? If you are speaking to an external group, you may know only that in the audience are community residents, members of a particular association, or elementary school teachers. But even knowing just that, and exploiting that knowledge, can help you.

Not only should you know the makeup of the audience by background or vocation, but you also should know something about their attitudes, biases, sympathies, or opinions. In addition, are there specific cliques or factions in the audience that agree or disagree with each other?

A second major factor in audience analysis involves knowing what knowledge they already possess and what knowledge they *should* possess. If you cover material with which the audience is familiar, you may bore them and, in effect, lose some of their support. If, on the other hand, you assume they possess knowledge which in fact they do not, the results can be equally harmful.

Your analysis should also determine what the audience wishes to know. If you are aware that most members would react favorably to a 6 percent increase in prices and you intend to request 9 percent, that knowledge may assist you in your planning. If you are aware the audience wants thorough substantiating data plus proof before they will accept a recommendation to purchase an $80,000 piece of equipment, again you can plan accordingly. Without that knowledge, you might not have possessed adequate data to win your point.

It is also prudent, if possible, to determine who the "influentials" are in the audience and their points of view. With this knowledge, it may be to your advantage to elicit a comment from such an individual early in your presentation, late in your presentation, or not at all.

Step 4: Select a Presentation Method

For the long presentation, it is almost imperative that you use some materials, such as notes, for reference. Not only will such data keep you on the topic and prevent digressions, but they will also remind you to "make points 3 and 4." And very often we may wish to read an important statement or quote an authority. Having the precise words in front of us on the podium is very important.

What format should the notes for a long presentation take? Certainly the choice has much to do with what you find comfortable and the type of speech you are making.

Manuscript.   Because of the importance of a talk and the need to use specific wording, it may be wise to read your speech.

In that case, the type used should be large and clear, and the body of the text should be arranged with plenty of white space. Double or triple spacing with very wide margins can be helpful. Add side notes in color such as: "pause," "emphasize this point," "repeat name," "look up and smile," "gesture toward head table," "wait for slide," and "indicate cost date on flip chart." The manuscript should always be prepared with enough white space to permit notes, changes in content, and additions.

Note Cards.   The use of 5-by-8 inch note cards (3-by-5 inch cards are too small) can be very helpful. Usually an outline of your presentation plus a quote or two are about all that is needed on cards. Such an arrangement keeps you on track and permits you to read a key statement or quotation. Remember to number your cards consecutively in the event that the packet is inadvertently dropped.

Notebook.   Using an $8\frac{1}{2}$-by-11 inch three-ring binder can prove valuable if you must maintain items in precise order. You can even insert transparencies in the notebook so they will be available at the precise moment you need them.

Of course a notebook is very obvious; turning pages may distract the audience, and the notebook does tie you to the podium. Nevertheless, it is a method many people, especially chief executive officers, find very satisfactory.

Hidden Notes.   If you wish to have your long presentation appear extemporaneous, or if it actually is, you can assist yourself by placing key ideas in hidden notes.

It is possible, for example, to list in large, heavy print your three key methods for cost reduction on the flip chart. Under each you can pencil in, in small print, your substantiating ideas. These are effectively hidden from the audience but not from you. Or you may simply present, on a transparency, your five key points, each listed as one word. That "outline" and those five words clearly remind you of everything you intend to discuss concerning the five areas. Or you may wish to add more detailed notes on the cardboard frame that holds your transparency.

The important point is to select and use some type of presentation method. Too often when we attempt to wing it, we fall instead of fly.

Step 5: Use Visual Aids Effectively

The long oral presentation usually contains some financial, production, manufacturing, or development data that are not simple to assimilate. The listener will often find the task of assimilation easier if the oral message is supplemented and complemented by a visual aid.

It is usually difficult to follow a presentation of thirty to forty-five minutes. However, a good visual aid often retains the attention of the audience, brings variety to the message, and helps clarify it.

In Chapter 12 we discussed the various visual aids usually used to accompany a speech: handouts, reports, chalkboards, slides, flip charts, transparencies, table flip charts, and overhead projectors. It is impossible to designate the best type of aid for every situation. Obviously the complexity of the topic, nature of the audience, type and size of room, purpose of the visual aid (to introduce, to clarify, to reinforce) all play important roles in the choice. However, basic principles apply to all visuals. They should complement, clarify, or reinforce the idea presented orally; be easy to see; and be easy to assimilate.

The effective speaker always spends a little time not only preparing a visual aid but also preparing for its use. Do you know where the light switches are? How to change a projector bulb quickly? Are the markers at the podium dry, or will they write? Will the cord on the projector extend far enough to reach the electrical outlet? Can the flip chart be seen from all parts of the room? Are the pages of the handout in correct order? This preparation requires only a few minutes, but they are minutes well spent.

Step 6: Select a Strategy to Secure Desired Results

The usual purpose of the long presentation is to secure some desired action or result. It may be the sale of a product, approval of a proposal, or understanding of a concept. Getting that precise response is often based on the strategy of the presentation. That strategy may involve a number of factors.

Time and Timing.   Always be sure you have been provided with adequate time to cover your material as you wish. If the chairperson says, "Well, we seem to have about seven minutes left; why don't we hear from you?" and you have prepared a twenty-minute presentation, politely decline his or her invitation. Furthermore, your strategy calls for you to be the only presenter on a specific date. Don't let that well-intentioned chairperson upset your plan.

Timing, as the actor knows well, can be vital in a performance, and that is often true in speaking. When is the right time for you to make your presentation? Yesterday we learned the firm will show a $600,000 loss this year. Will that fact prove to be an asset or a liability to you if you make your presentation today? Should you follow or precede the sales manager in the list of presenters? Mr. Johnson, who has consistently opposed your ideas, is in the audience today. Would you be wise to postpone your presentation?

Order of Development.   Which order of development will prove strategically sound considering the topic and the audience? Should you go from general to particular or vice versa? Perhaps using a geographical order might be better than a chronological one. Should you start by telling the audience what action you want them to take and then list the reasons why? Or would it be strategically wiser to reverse that order? Should you close with specific recommendations or permit the audience to draw their own from the material presented?

Involvement and Participation.   Very often an excellent strategy is to first present the basic fundamentals and then invite audience participation for the purpose of decision making. From the point of view of strategy, we know people are much more likely to accept and support a decision which they have had a hand in shaping than a decision proposed by someone else.

Participation is usually a plus. A confident speaker who can remain in control can usually use audience participation to his or her own advantage.

Recognition of Audience Makeup.   How far the speaker can or should go in pushing for a desired response often depends on who is in the audience. If it is made up of many obvious supporters of your idea, you will follow one plan; if there are opposing or unsympathetic cliques, you may follow another.

No speaker should approach an audience without knowing its makeup. Just as the politician first determines if the audience favors or disapproves of price supports, or whether they are conservative or liberal Republicans or Democrats, so should you first determine the attitudes and perceptions of your audience.

Calling for Action.   The experienced salesperson knows there are times when he or she should press for the sale, ask for the sale, or let the prospect do it. This also applies in a good presentation.

At times it is strategically wise to tell the audience specifically and precisely what action to follow; at other times it is best to suggest. And in still other instances, it is preferable to let the audience come to its own conclusion.

There are many factors involved in the strategy of presentation, and each of these has its own subpoints to consider. But just as the successful general determines the strategy of the attack, so too a successful speech maker considers the strategy of the presentation.

PARTS OF THE LONG PRESENTATION

Like every speech, the long one is made up of an introduction, body, and conclusion. Each segment has a purpose, and it is sensible for the speaker to determine what these are in the planning phase of the presentation.

The Introduction

The introduction should accomplish the following objectives:

Indicate the Topic.   It is quite possible that some members of the audience don't know what you are going to talk about. Make sure that everyone in the room knows precisely what you are covering and why. It may be that two of the managers who were invited could not attend today's session and sent substitutes. These alternates may not be aware of the agenda; thus you are wise to take a minute or two to set the stage.

Define Your Terms.   Because the long presentation is often complex, it is wise to begin with a definition of technical terms as you will use them. Or it may be helpful to indicate certain parameters or constraints that you will observe.

Establish Rapport.   Often the audience will not be familiar with you or your ideas, and it is important for you to establish a good relationship immediately. There are many factors that will help you achieve this, but the most important are sincerity and honesty.

If you sincerely feel that what you are saying is important and in the best interests of the listeners, that feeling will somehow be transmitted to them. Conversely, if your intent is to manipulate or hoodwink, that too will be conveyed.

In addition, it may also be helpful to voice some of the concerns you know members of the audience have. Or, why not refer by name to some of those in the audience?

A smile is certainly an asset, as is an approach that makes people feel you are talking *with* (instead of *at*) them. And a bit of humor, always in good taste, tends to relax a group.

The speaker should be confident, convinced he or she has an important message to deliver, and in control. To begin with a statement such as the following is to invite disaster:

> *If you will go along with me for a moment, I'll get on the track and probably convince you . . .*
>
> *Many of you, I'm sure, know more about this than I, but it was my misfortune to be sitting in front of Mr. Bendix when he was looking for a speaker . . .*

The introduction is a vital part of the long presentation; it should be planned carefully so that it may be executed excellently. The introduction to the speech is an important part of the listener's first impression of the speaker.

The Body

The body is the heart of the presentation. Of course one cannot estimate precisely what portion of the speech should be given over to this segment. But again, clarity and conciseness are vital. In planning the body of the presentation, the speaker should give special attention to the following:

Organization.   Considering the audience, what is the best organizational plan to use? Should you present the financial aspects first and then the marketing plan or vice versa? It is questions such as these, as well as those concerned with the method of development, which must be answered.

Visuals.   What kind and when should they be used? Are you better off with charts? Handouts? Slides? Cutaways or samples of the actual items?

Audience Involvement.   Should you encourage participation or involvement during the presentation?

The body of the presentation may well utilize 80 percent of the time of your speech. How you handle that time depends on the many factors we have already discussed: content, knowledge, organization, delivery, visual aids, strategy, and a dozen others.

The Conclusion

The conclusion, an integral part of any speech, is a critical factor in the strategic planning of your presentation. To end by saying, "Well, I guess that does it," or, "That brings me to my last note, but if anyone has any questions . . ." or, "I'm sorry I took longer than anticipated, but I didn't think you folks would mind sitting a few extra minutes," is to invite a negative response.

In your conclusion, you may wish to recapitulate key points. Or as teachers often were told in the early 1900s: "First you tell them what you're going to tell them [Introduction], then you tell them [Body], then you tell them what you told them [Conclusion]."

If the long business presentation is other than informative in nature, it usually contains conclusions and recommendations. Conclusions should be thoroughly substantiated by material presented in the body and the recommendations completely justified by the facts.

Because recommendations (to buy, to sell, to construct, to change, or to take some other course) are the key to action, it is often practical to list them on a visual aid and review them. This may very well fix the recommendations in the minds of the audience and motivate them to take the action you desire.

Concluding Comments—The Long Speech.   Long presentations may be vital factors in the advancement of your career. Seize opportunities to give them, and when you do so, be sure they are so well organized, so clear, so concise, so impressive that every person in the audience will remember you gave them and want you to receive the credit the presentations merit.

QUESTIONS FOR STUDY

1. Name four aspects which frequently differ between long and short presentations.
2. Would you assume that the "Technical Exchange" presentation is made more frequently among a group of engineers or sales personnel? Explain.
3. What is one of the most important objectives of a comparative presentation?
4. Why is it wise for a speaker to state in writing, as the first step in preparation, the purpose and objectives for his/her speech?
5. There are usually several steps to be carried through in *planning* a presentation. List at least four of those steps and discuss each briefly.
6. When a speaker analyzes an audience, what are several of the specific attributes of the listeners with which he or she should be concerned?
7. What advantages do 5-by-8 inch note cards have over 3-by-5 cards as reference sources in making a presentation? Explain.
8. What specific contributions do visual aids bring to an oral presentation? List and briefly discuss at least three types of visual aids.
9. Why should you check specific mechanical devices of the room prior to giving a speech in it? List several of those devices.
10. What are "hidden notes" and how can they be used by a speaker?
11. Why is it important for listeners to know in advance what the speaker intends for them to do with the information being communicated in a presentation?
12. It is often necessary in a long presentation to "define technical terms." Should that be done orally or in a written (printed) handout? Defend your choice.
13. Observe a well-prepared instructor use: 1) slides, and 2) an overhead projector in his/her presentation. Which device do you prefer and why? Explain why each is valuable in specific situations.
14. If a speaker intends to use visual aids employing electronic devices, what preparation is necessary?

EXERCISES

15. For your profession and for the specific job you hope to assume, identify a common kind of "technical exchange" that would take place.
    a. Specifically indicate the parties involved in the exchange.
    b. Indicate the elementary gaps in their knowledge or information bases.

    c.   Create concrete suggestions on how you could attempt to bridge the gaps in your long oral presentation.

16. Assume that you will be speaking to the local Rotary Club, a group made up of business men and women. Choose your own topic, then describe in specific ways what you would like to know about your audience prior to speaking, and how you could find that information.

17. You are to make a long presentation to the faculty of your academic department on "Student Suggestions for Revisions in the Curriculum." A student group has spent months developing the materials and there are a number of issues to present in some detail. You have decided to speak from a prepared manuscript.
    a.   Write the first page of the introduction to the speech that you plan to give.
    b.   In the margins, insert appropriate and helpful side notes.
    c.   Explain how you plan to secure the pages of the manuscript. Are you going to place them loose in a folder, staple them together, place them in a bound notebook, or use some other method?

18. Interview a manager who holds the kind of job you hope to attain eventually. You want to find out from the manager (a) how long presentations are used in the modern organization and (b) what the executive thinks are the major pitfalls in the long presentations he or she must sit through. Prepare a three-minute speech in which you report your findings.

19. Timing is important—the long presentation given at the inappropriate time may mean months of hard work are wasted. In the situation identified in exercise 17, you are called upon to make the presentation today. However, much to your surprise, the chairman of the department and the department's chairman of the curriculum committee are not present. Will you give your presentation? Explain and justify your answer.

20. What is rapport? Make a list of specific ways in which you would attempt to establish rapport with an audience unsympathetic to your point of view. (You may invent details to make this situation as realistic as possible.)

21. Watch an extended television interview of a business or political figure. Make two lists of observed techniques: one applying to the interviewer and one for the interviewee. Based on the lists, decide which was more skillful in the encounter.

22. Lectures can be considered a form of public speech. Based on your experiences as a student, draw up a list of do's and don'ts for lecturers.

23. Observe your own attention span while listening to a presentation (perhaps a lecture) more than ten minutes long. Report to the class on how often your mind wandered and what the speaker did (or could have done) to regain your attention.

24. Watch a business or political interview on television. Evaluate the interviewee's use of facial expressions. What do they communicate? Whom do they influence? For your own use, make up a guide sheet regarding the use of facial expressions during interviews.

25. Establishing rapport with the audience in the beginning of a speech can be crucial in getting them to listen to and perhaps accept the ideas you are going to present. As chairman of the student group that has studied your academic department's curriculum (See exercise 17), you are to make a long oral presentation to the faculty on how the curriculum can be improved from the students' viewpoint. The presentation will be in a manuscript speech. Write your introduction and leave plenty of space in the margins. Then, in the margins, identify how you are attempting to establish rapport with the audience.

    Remember, you must walk on eggs. Why? (a) The faculty may think the curriculum is theirs, not the students'; (b) many of the faculty might initially be insulted by thinking "these young kids think they know everything—we've been teaching twenty years," and (c) many faculty members will have definite vested interests in the curriculum and specific courses—they won't want their sacred cows addressed in a speech. Good luck in establishing rapport—a vital concern in this kind of speech.

26. Humor can establish rapport, but sometimes a speaker's use of it can backfire. For the situation in problem 17, would there be any spot in the speech—in the introduction, in the body, or in the conclusion—where humor could be inserted in an appropriate way to ease tensions and to aid in getting the audience to listen to your ideas? Or, is humor too dangerous in this situation? Indicate a way in which humor might be used in the presentation and then decide and justify your decision on whether you would keep it or drop it from the final draft of the speech.

27. Give an eight- to ten-minute presentation to the managers, owners of a company, college administrators, board of directors, or any group that has authority to accept or reject the proposal you will make to them. Your persuasive presentation may involve a change in policy, purchase of a piece of equipment, acceptance of a new regulation, or any item of your choice. You are required to use visual aids to accompany your presentation.

28. Give an eight- to ten-minute presentation that is explanatory/informative to a group. Identify the makeup of the group. You may explain how to carry through a procedure, process, or activity. You are required to use visual aids to accompany your presentation.

Crisis Communication and Coping with the Media

As more and more attention is given to conservation, food and drug purity, toxic wastes, and consumer and worker health and safety, we can only look at crisis management as a "growth" industry.

People and products do not always perform at a maximum level of efficiency. Equipment malfunctions, accidents happen, mislabeling occurs, packaging errors take place, and people do not act rationally. Such problems are usually minor and easily corrected. Sometimes, however, serious problems cause illness or even death. When that happens, the situation becomes a crisis in the life of the organization. And crises are almost always newsworthy and extremely costly to turn around.

CRISIS AND THE MEDIA

An organization that has spent dozens of years and millions of dollars building an image of its product or service that reflects quality, dependability, integrity, and excellence can have all that shattered overnight. In the few hours between a consumer's complaint and the media's headline on page one, picture story on the evening TV news, and comments on a radio broadcast, the firm's image begins to crumble.

Recall the wide media coverage given the following highly volatile situations:

- In 1983 seven people died as the result of alleged product tampering with Extra Strength Tylenol.
- In July 1984, twenty-one men, women, and children were killed by random gunfire from one man in a McDonald's restaurant.
- In 1980 Proctor & Gamble's Rely tampons were linked to deaths from toxic shock syndrome.

"Testing cars is a good idea. Disconnecting odometers is a lousy idea. That's a mistake we won't make again at Chrysler. Period."

Lee Iacocca

LET ME SET THE RECORD STRAIGHT.

1. For years, spot checking and road testing new cars and trucks that come off the assembly line with the odometers disengaged was standard industry practice. In our case, the average test mileage was 40 miles.

2. Even though the practice wasn't illegal, some companies began connecting their odometers. We didn't. In retrospect, that was dumb. Since October 1986, however, the odometer of every car and truck we've built has been connected, including those in the test program.

3. A few cars–and I mean a few–were damaged in testing badly enough that they should not have been fixed and sold as new. That was a mistake in an otherwise valid quality assurance program. And now we have to make it right.

WHAT WE'RE DOING TO MAKE THINGS RIGHT.

1. In all instances where our records show a vehicle was damaged in the test program and repaired and sold, *we will offer to replace that vehicle* with a brand new 1987 Chrysler Corporation model of comparable value. No ifs ands or buts.

2. We are sending letters to everyone our records show bought a vehicle that was in the test program and offering a free inspection. If anything is wrong because of a product deficiency, we will make it right.

3. Along with the free inspection, we are extending their present 5-year or 50,000-mile protection plan on engine and powertrain to 7 years or 70,000 miles.

4. And to put their minds completely at ease, we are extending the 7-year or 70,000-mile protection to *all major systems:* brakes, suspension, air conditioning, electrical and steering.

The quality testing program is a good program. But there were mistakes and we were too slow in stopping them. Now they're stopped. Done. Finished. Over.

Personally, I'm proud of our products. Proud of the quality improvements we've made. So we're going to keep right on testing. Because without it we couldn't have given America 5-year 50,000-mile protection five years ahead of everyone else. Or maintained our warranty leadership with 7-year 70,000-mile protection. I'm proud, too, of our leadership in safety-related recalls.

But I'm not proud of this episode. Not at all.

As Harry Truman once said, "The buck stops here." It just stopped. Period.

 **CHRYSLER MOTORS**
CHRYSLER · PLYMOUTH · DODGE CARS · DODGE TRUCKS

We just want to be the best.

- In October 1987, Northrop was alleged to have falsified test results for a missile guidance system it manufactures.
- In 1978 steel-belted Firestone tires were blamed for numerous highway deaths.
- In 1985 Union Carbide's gas leak in Bhopol, India, caused thousands of deaths and injuries.
- In June 1987, Chrysler Corporation was accused of selling as "new" (with odometers turned back to zero) cars that had been driven by employees, and had even been in accidents.

That is the way our instant-communication news media work. They serve an interested society in a climate that labels almost every crisis newsworthy. There is nothing wrong with that: crises *are* newsworthy.

Cases like these all create crises for the organizations involved. The direct losses in millions of dollars are not as serious as the loss in customer confidence and goodwill. The organizations' responses to crises are of critical importance.

RESPONDING TO CRISIS

Obviously, every crisis is different and must be handled differently. An examination of various responses to crises shows that some organizations bury their heads in the sand while others seize the initiative, purchasing media space or time and announcing corrective action.[1] What is the most effective way to attack the problem?

Again and again, we see that the best defense is a good offense. The organization that immediately takes action and announces its responsibility in the situation and the action it will take is usually highly respected by the buying public.[2] Its sales losses are usually recovered fairly quickly. On the other hand, the organization that does nothing or says "we are not responsible" finds its credibility damaged and the purchase of its products or services declining significantly.

The key players in most of these crisis situations are the media, the corporate policy, and the corporate spokesperson(s). What an organization does or does not do in relation to the media will often determine success or failure for the firm in handling its crisis.

Every firm seems to go through similar steps in managing a crisis:

- Identify the cause of the crisis. Is it internal (product? employees? equipment?) or external (a supplier? community? environment?)?
- Develop specific plans and policies for coping with and solving the crisis.
- Name a senior executive as the organization's primary spokesperson. He or she should have authority for decision making and for speaking for the company.
- Determine specific roles for key executives and other personnel for responding to the media as well as to employees.[3]

All of these steps can be taken more easily if the firm already has a broad crisis-management plan in place. The plan itself should be based on input from senior staff members and should be familiar to all management personnel. Quite obviously, plans will differ widely in depth and length according to the size of the company (50 employees *vs.* 50,000), level of risk to the industry (commercial aviation *vs.* trouser manufacturing), and location (major urban center *vs.* rural area).

[1]"How Companies Cope with Disaster," *Toronto Star,* March 9, 1986; *The Wall Street Journal,* Chrysler advertisement, July 2, 1987; E. Reidenback and D. Sherrell, "Negative Press: Is Your Company Prepared?" *Business,* January–March, 1986.

[2]"Crisis Control Becomes a Growth Industry," *The Los Angeles Business Journal,* Nov. 9, 1987, pp. 9, 40.

[3]"Crisis Control Becomes a Growth Industry," pp. 9, 40.

Perhaps the best reason for crisis planning is to minimize the risk of a change in the organization's image. However, a second reason is simply "the times." With today's instant communication worldwide, any incident—major or minor—can become a crisis, instantly known from coast to coast. In contrast, 75 years ago the same incident would have been classified as a local tragedy or accident.

COPING WITH THE MEDIA

A recent survey of *Fortune 500* companies found that corporate chief executive officers spent four times as much time communicating to various public and private groups as they did ten years previously. In most cases these same executives indicated they faced the media with more than a little trepidation.[4]

However, whether the modern manager likes it or not, he or she has become the corporate spokesperson. A carelessly conducted press conference can result in "bad press" and cost the company millions in loss of goodwill and reputation. An angry retort to a reporter, a careless statement that implies possible company negligence, or a comment that can be used as backup for "unlawful termination" may all be read back to the CEO months later in a court of law. In modern times, with regulations by the dozen, court awards running into astronomical dollar amounts, and a society involved in thousands of lawsuits, caution and care in communication are vital.

What can upper management do to achieve the best possible return when appearing before representatives of the media and special-interest groups, in sensitive and controversial situations? The first step is to recognize the obligation *they* have to make the results of the interview as unbiased and as factual as possible. Appearing before an investigative group should be viewed by the manager as an opportunity to build the reputation of the organization, rather than an adversarial situation to be feared.

Establish Policies of Communication

Before we even discuss what to say and how to say it, we must recognize the need for a company policy on communication to various publics concerning sensitive issues.[5] Such a policy must be drawn up, published, and distributed to company managers. It should list company rules on precisely who in

---

[4]Norman B. Sigband, "The Changing Role of the CEO," *Bulletin of the Association for Business Communication*, Summer, 1985.

[5]Norman B. Sigband, "Needed: Corporate Policies on Communication," *Advanced Management Journal*, April, 1969. Used by permission.

MAKING THE CHORE LESS OF A BORE

"Most press releases are an abysmal waste of time," says Donald A. Davis, editor of *Drug & Cosmetic Industry,* Cleveland. He has a great deal of experience to back up his opinion: A trade magazine editor for more than 32 years, Mr. Davis gets 40 to 50 press releases per day.

But like other editors I talked to, Mr. Davis considers press releases a necessary evil. Because he has a small staff, he relies on releases for industry news he couldn't get any other way.

Still, Mr. Davis thinks that most press releases could be much improved. Here are some suggestions from Mr. Davis and other trade editors on how to make press releases more effective:

● **Know the publications on your media list.**

"Most press releases we receive are not appropriate for our magazine," says Janet Dona-hue, editor of *Soap, Cosmetics & Chemical Specialties,* New York. "Public relations people put us on a media list because they think our editorial content applies to their product. But if they read our magazine, many would realize that we don't cover their market. In that case, sending us a release is just a waste of paper and postage."

● **If possible, craft the release to fit the publication's editorial needs.**

"Many releases seem as if they're written to please the company president, not provide information for publication," says Mr. Davis. He recommends making releases as straightfor-ward and "non-fluffy" as possible, and editing out information that does not directly apply to the subject matter.

● **Don't sacrifice substance for style.**

Too many companies spend big budgets on press kits with fancy graphics, printing, and packaging. "That may be effective for consumer magazines, but it doesn't influence trade edi-tors," advises Ms. Donahue. "I'd rather see a well-written release any day than all the fancy packaging on Madison Avenue."

● **Use the press release only when appropriate.**

Other public relations methods often work better. "We appreciate getting releases, but often a well-timed phone call is more effective," says Michael L. Sangiovanni, editor-publisher of *Aerosol Age,* Fairfield, N.J. "For instance, if a company is doing something really newsworthy, I'd like to hear from them right away. That way, we can get it in our magazine immediately—and not have to wait for the whole press release process."

||||||||||||||||||||||||||||||||||||||||||||||||||||||||||||||||||||||||||||||||||||||||||||||||||||||||||||||||||||||||||||||||||

the company is permitted to talk to outside organizations or individuals regarding catastrophic, sensitive, and unusual or highly negative situations.

Guidelines should also be noted as to what may be said and to whom, and the legal implications involved in explaining the accidental death or injury of an employee or visitor. Other items should also be noted and policy statements indicated: terminations, layoffs, plant closures, labor problems, product quality, consumer complaints, environmental issues, and so forth. Of course, every contingency cannot be noted. But everyone in the organization should clearly understand that only designated people may respond in critical situations. When this is noted companywide, the danger of an unauthorized field manager or other employee responding to an inquiring reporter—and saying the wrong thing—is clearly diminished.

Hewlett-Packard's booklet, "How to Deal With the Press," lists a series of guidelines for the manager. The introduction from the Director of Public Relations, Dave Kirby, states in part,

> We hope the booklet will serve as a useful guide to you and other people in your organization who may be exposed to the press. For easy reading, we've put the information in an informal, question-and-answer format. Despite this informality, please consider the information as corporate policy.[6]

As for the interview itself, whether it is with print media, radio, television, special interest groups, or employee groups, preparation is the key.

Preparation: The Key to Winning

Certainly the manager or CEO must prepare answers to almost every possible question that may arise. A wise plan here is to prepare specific answers to be sure that the words come out correctly. Rather than stating, "We haven't had any serious accidents in five years . . . ," it is better to say, "Our safety record in the industry is outstanding; as a matter of fact, last year we received an award . . ."

Preparation should include recognition of terms and phrases to be avoided:

Negligence	Fired
Death	Catastrophe
Accidents	Layoffs
Discrimination	Probably could happen . . .

Similarly, it's prudent to recognize those that should be stressed:

Safety	Long record of excellent relations
Care	Equal opportunities
Concern	Satisfactory
Employment opportunities	

The wise manager can also prepare by requesting that the media representative give him or her a list of questions before their meeting. Although

---

[6]Hewlett-Packard Corporation, "How to Deal With the Press," as quoted in Norman B. Sigband, "Coping Successfully With the Media," *Advanced Management Journal*, Winter, 1985.

some journalists may not desire to do so, there are situations in which this may work out.

In preparing answers to possible questions, make every effort to secure strong substantiating information, dates, facts, and statistics. These all give authority and credence to your answers. These data should be readily at hand. As a matter of fact, don't hesitate to refer to a few note cards that contain facts, figures, and numbers.

Your Relationship with the Interviewer

If at all possible, learn the name and identity of the interviewer (e.g., whether he or she is a media person or a special-interest group representative). Use the individual's last name with respect and sincerity. If he or she addresses you as "Mr., Ms.," or "Miss," follow suit and use the interviewer's last name.

The interviewer has a job to do. And, with rare exceptions, he or she is trying to do it honestly. If you remember this, you will welcome the media and set the tone for an honest and open exchange. Media representatives are professionals who want to do a professional job.

These people represent the public and feel the public has a right to know. Certainly no one can argue with that. For that reason, your replies should reflect your *appreciation* of the public's point of view. You may disagree with that point of view or feel it is unacceptable under the circumstances, but you must begin by appreciating it.

Handling Questions and Making Statements

How the manager handles the questions posed will usually determine how effectively he or she has come through the interview. A few critical concepts to keep in mind are these:

1. Answer the question concisely and directly. Don't get involved in a discussion that may take you far afield or even into quicksand. Simply reply and stop.
2. Never repeat an incorrect statement made by the reporter. You may be quoted and if your statement is taken out of context, it will appear that you accept or agree with the misstatement. A wiser policy is simply to say:

    That is incorrect. The precise situation is this: . . .

3. Have facts, data, and figures readily at hand, if possible, to lend weight to your answers. A reply that is based on proof will be appreciated by your interviewer. It makes strong copy and places you in a position of authority.
4. Learn how to *bridge*. This is a technique of taking a question, answering

it, and then moving to a comment, usually related to the topic, which reflects credit on your firm.

Yes, I imagine that is a possibility in handling toxic wastes. However, in the 10 years our firm has been involved with the XYZ product, I am happy to state that we have been successful in . . .

It is also important to note that at our St. Louis facility, 98 percent of our workforce rated company safety programs as either "excellent" or "superior." As a matter of fact, our firm received the Railroad Association's award for "Outstanding Safety Measures" last year and for the three previous years.

5. Turn a negative into a positive. If an interviewer phrases a question or a statement negatively, don't pick up on it or repeat it. Answer it, but rephrase it or state your reference to it positively.

Question
Isn't it possible that some employees could be killed or seriously injured in a situation like that?

Answer
I really can't speak to that. Our safety experience is outstanding. Not one of our employees at this facility has ever been involved in a reportable accident. This is surely due to the attention given to safety procedures and employee welfare in our organization.

Question
Although your bank has some 35 vice presidents, how do you explain the fact that only five are women?

Answer
All appointments to vice president are made on the basis of Board selection and an examination. Every opening is posted and any employee of the appropriate grade is eligible to apply.

In the past three years, we have had nine openings for vice president. Ten women took the examination and two were appointed. In the same period, thirty men took the examination and seven were appointed. Thus 20 percent of the women and 23 percent of the men taking the exam were appointed. I would say that we had a similar level of treatment and equality in both cases, wouldn't you?

Also, in handling questions, never accept facts or figures the interviewer cites as being reliable if you haven't checked them or are unaware of the information. A simple statement such as the following will handle the situation: "I'm sorry but I haven't personally checked those figures and therefore can't accept them as accurate at this time. I will, however, follow up on it."

Above all, if you don't know the answer to a question or prefer not to respond, don't hem or haw. Don't let words be put in your mouth. A straightforward statement is best: "I'm sorry I don't have an answer to that question." Or, "I don't have the information at this time; I'll try to get it for you as soon as possible." And for a question you don't want to (or can't) answer, a brief, "No comment at this time," is perfectly within your rights.

Using Time to Your Advantage

In addressing representatives of the media or special-interest groups, use time to help you. There are several ways to do this. Perhaps one of the best is to use the "ten-second rule." Ten seconds is not a long period, but if you use that time correctly, it can prove very helpful.

Before responding to any question, take ten seconds to formulate your answer. This will help eliminate negative words and terms that can be mis-construed. It will also reduce the likelihood that a "possibly could happen" statement will creep into your reply when it should not.

You should also not hesitate to indicate to an interviewer that, "I'm sorry I can't work with you just now. If you will return at 10:00 A.M. (or "in 45 minutes" or "early this afternoon"), I'll be happy to meet you and other representatives of the media in our sixth-floor conference room."

There is no reason why you should be expected to give an answer at the convenience of the interviewer. Granted that time is vital to the media, be wary of answering too quickly in a highly sensitive or catastrophic situation in which all facts are not necessarily at your disposal. Express concern and compassion if necessary, but make no statements that can prove damaging later.

Nonverbal Aspects of the Interview

Nonverbal communication is a highly important area, especially if you are being taped for a television broadcast or you are appearing on live television. It isn't so much the way you dress that counts; you will use common sense on that. For men, a dark suit, knee-length socks, light blue or white shirt, and a conservative tie should be worn. For women, a conservative suit with a plain white blouse—or a tailored dark-hued dress—is appropriate.

It is the *gestures* that are vital. Preparation should be made to secure and carry through those that reflect credit on you. If you appear before a group, either stand behind a rostrum or be seated behind a table. Choose whatever feels most comfortable to you. Some speakers feel that a standing position, offering a downward view of a seated audience, gives them a certain psychological advantage. Others prefer to sit with notes carefully arranged in front of them on a table top or on a "table" podium. Regardless of the method used, *you* should make the selection. It is your show and *you* have the right to call the shots. If you are appearing on live television, the choice should still be yours as to how, where, and in which surroundings or situation you wish to be photographed or taped.

Whether you appear "live" on camera or in front of a group, be careful of your eye contact, hand and body gestures, and facial expressions. Maintain direct eye contact with the individual who asked the question. Look for response in his or her eyes or face and react. When presenting a prepared statement to a group, avoid reading it. Use notes and look directly at people in the group who are to your left, right, and straight ahead. Don't look at areas; select people and look directly at them. If you know who the "influentials" are in the group, address your remarks directly to them.

Pay attention to your hand and body gestures to avoid conveying nervousness or defensiveness. Don't drum on the table or podium, inch nervously back and forth in your seat, or slouch defensively or discourteously in your chair.

Finally—and perhaps most importantly—be conscious of your facial expressions. The value of a smile or a pleasant expression can't be overestimated. A smile, sincerely made at an appropriate moment, can be invaluable in conveying honesty and believability.

Make the audience feel you're speaking *with* them, not *at* them. Use your head and face to show agreement with a statement made. Let your features reflect "that's a good question; I'm glad you asked it." Try not to exhibit anger, irritation, fear, or shock. The best way to avoid that is to prepare and maintain a mental frame of mind of desiring to work with those who are interviewing you.

Maintaining Control

Maintaining control is vital to keep in mind because it can sometimes "make or break" you in an interview. Remember, in the interview situation, *you* are in charge; *you* can accept a question or pass on it; *you* can answer or not answer; *you* can make the point or points *you* wish to make. Do all this with firmness, courtesy, tact, and, when possible, a smile. Never, never get angry, nasty, or sarcastic or "lose your cool." You are in control; maintain that control in a firm, participative, cooperative, democratic manner.

Specific Factors in Maintaining Control There are several specific ground rules that will assist you in maintaining control.

Using the Best Space and Position Do not permit yourself to be interviewed or videotaped in the middle of a noisy crowd, on a busy factory floor, or surrounded by a crowd of reporters, bystanders, or employees—unless you feel that is to your advantage.

You select the interview site. If you feel more comfortable standing behind a rostrum with the interviewers seated in front of you, request that arrangement. If you feel more comfortable sitting behind a table or desk, with or without a small podium, see that that is arranged.

If you prefer to have the interview take place in your office or in the company conference room, schedule the discussion for that site.

Making Vital Statements   Because you are in charge, don't hesitate to state what you feel must be said. This can be an opening statement or an add-on to one of your answers.

Don't feel constrained to simply answer questions. Certainly you have a vital point to make or an issue to address. Make that statement and if an interviewer breaks in on you, override the interruption and complete your comment.

Choosing Questions and Questioners   In many cases you will be aware who the professional journalists in the group are or the reasonable individuals among the special interest representatives. Call on those people for questions. You are probably also aware of who the rabble-rousers are. Ignore them if at all possible.

Keep in mind that it is not necessary to recognize the individual who shouts the loudest or jumps up most vigorously. Of course, such a person may attract the most attention, but you can always say, "Thank you. I know you have an important question, but there were two hands on this side of the room that I have yet to call on. I'll try to get to you in a minute."

Using Time Advantageously   You may wish to announce at the beginning of the interview that, "Because of meetings (other obligations, the need to work on this problem, etc.), we will take just 15 minutes at this time to answer your questions."

Keep in mind that if it is not convenient for you to be interviewed "now" (because you are not prepared, aren't completely familiar with all necessary details, lack vital statistics or data, etc.), there is absolutely no reason for you not to say, "I will be happy to meet with you at exactly 3:00 P.M. today."

In addition, you should control the length of an interview. If you feel you have done your part and nothing further may be gained (or an advantage may be lost) by fielding more questions, call a halt to the session. Remember to add a courteous, "Thank you for attending," or "I'll be happy to meet with you again if you feel that would be valuable."

Adopting a Positive Attitude   Your mental approach to the interview can also prove to be a vital factor in handling the session successfully. Remember, you are in charge; you are in control; and you are honest. If you are in a position to accept these three statements in what you say (or what you don't say), you will have the advantage.

Go into the interview with a cooperative attitude and the knowledge that you have the option of answering those questions you wish to answer, and the authority to make the statements you wish to make. When you walk in and face your questioners, simply say to yourself, "I am in charge; I am in control."

Making a Strong Closing   Your opening and closing statements can often be the most critical ones. Naturally, you will prepare the opening to set the stage to your best advantage. But remember that the closing can be equally important.

Distill vital points in a strong closing statement. And make it clear that what you said was indeed a closing statement. Don't let your ideas be diluted by further questions or digressions. After you finish your statement, the interview should end.

Overall Suggestions

In addition to the suggestions made above, there are a few others to keep in mind. First, your responses should address the situation from the public's point of view, rather than that of your company. If you must state your organization's differing point of view, do so. But do so only after appreciating "their" perception. In this way you can avoid the adversarial us-against-them syndrome.

Next, never allow yourself to participate in a shouting match with a questioner. He or she may purposely be attempting to goad you in that direction.

Statements from questioners such as "just between you and me," "not for publication but to give me background only," and "this is off the record," are unreliable. You may receive all kinds of assurances that "your statements of this will never see the light of day." Don't buy them. Anything you say is fair game primarily because so much confusion exists between the interviewer's and the interviewee's perception of the meaning of "off the record," "background only," and similar phrases. Don't risk making a statement that is "off the record" today. It may well appear on the front page of the newspaper tomorrow.

Finally, never lie in an interview. If you can't make a statement, simply say, "no comment." Otherwise you will live to regret your lie.

Being interviewed on a sensitive or controversial issue may not be the most enjoyable way to spend a morning. On the other hand, you may well turn the session into an advantage for you and your organization. As is true of any venture, being prepared and playing the game professionally are vital factors in achieving your goals.

QUESTIONS FOR STUDY

1. How can a crisis situation, which is ignored, materially damage the image of a well established 50-year-old firm in a matter of two weeks? Explain.
2. Can a crisis situation ever be turned to an advantage by the organization involved? Explain.
3. Research Union Carbide's Bhopal, India, tragedy and the Johnson & Johnson Tylenol crisis. Determine how each company handled its situation, the time involved in the firm's response to the media, and other vital factors. Report (either in writing or orally) the key facts in both cases and your analysis of whether one firm did a better job than the other and why.
4. Do you feel there is ever a situation when a firm should not communicate about a crisis situation even after it has been presented by the media? Explain your stand.
5. Determine through your research whether or not an organization has ever been ill-served by careless and inaccurate reporting of a crisis. Report (in writing or orally) the facts in the case.
6. In the case of question #5, above, what possible steps should have been taken (or what steps would you have recommended) to alleviate or correct the problem after the careless and/or inaccurate reporting?
7. Why are crisis situations different today from what they were 75 years ago? Explain.
8. Do you agree with the frequently heard comment that the only incidents that are aired by the media are those that are "bad news." Explain your stand.
9. Do corporate CEOs spend more or less time communicating with the media now than ten years ago? Why?
10. What risks does a CEO face in media appearances?
11. What is a company policy on communication? How can it help executives prepare for media appearances?
12. Why might media interviewers resist providing a list of questions in advance to the executive they plan to interview?
13. What is "bridging"? How can it be used effectively in media appearances?
14. How can executives use time to their advantage in a crisis interview situation?
15. Watch a television panel discussion on a national issue. Select one participant and comment on his or her nonverbal communication during the interview and what it tells you. Note also how the nonverbal agrees or disagrees with the verbal. Document your report as to date, place, and participants in the panel, plus the topic discussed.
16. Why is "control" so important in the crisis interview situation? Explain.
17. List and discuss briefly four methods for maintaining control.

18. How can the "you attitude" (reader or listener orientation) be used effectively by the firm's representative in addressing the media in a crisis interview situation?

19. Why is it unwise to repeat an incorrect statement of the interviewer in replying to questions or comments?

20. If you do not wish your comment to be used or quoted, will the statement to the interviewer of "this is off the record" be adequate? Explain your answer.

EXERCISES

21. Visit five corporations in your area and interview top management members in each. Determine, through a carefully formulated questionnaire, what steps or policies they have for "handling the media in a crisis situation" should such action be necessary. Report on your findings.

22. Determine in your above interviews if any of the firms have been involved in a "crisis situation." If so, what action was taken, and what were the results?

23. Watch a television interview of a prominent individual being questioned by a skilled interviewer. What did the "prominent individual" do right and/or wrong? How could he or she have improved his or her position?

24. Design a policy statement which you feel leading newspapers and TV networks should issue to personnel for "equitable and responsible interviewing of news subjects."

25. Collect five manuals on "Handling Crisis Situations" issued by five different corporations. Report to your class, and explain the manuals' distribution (who in the organization receives them) and their individual strong and weak points.

26. Break into groups of ten. Each person should assume he or she is a CEO, president, or director of an organization. Select one topic from among the six listed below, prepare and make a four- to five-minute statement, and then accept questions from the other nine individuals. These nine will play the role of media representatives (such as reporters and newscasters) or members of a special-interest group concerned with such issues as the environment, the rights of minority groups, religious groups, and toxic wastes. The "CEO" and the "reporters" should do their best to play their roles as authentically as possible according to real-life situations. At the conclusion of each exercise, hold a five-minute debriefing to explain to the "CEO" what he or she did correctly and what could be improved and how.

    (a) One of your firm's trucks badly injured a six-year-old youngster in a school zone just two hours ago. The driver involved today has an excellent record and maintains that the youngster unexpectedly dashed into the street after a ball. There apparently are witnesses who have stated that the truck was exceeding the speed limit (15 mph) by at least 20 mph. Unfortunately, one of your trucks was involved in a similar situation (in the same school zone) five years ago. At that time, damages of $100,000 were levied against your firm.

(b) The League of Black Citizens has voiced its concern over the fact that among fifteen company officers and fifty-five managers there are only two blacks. Why? Is this blatant discrimination?

(c) Fred Kochinsky, one of your vice presidents, just resigned. Apparently there was some question concerning the way he handled company funds and the possible misappropriation of significant amounts. However, the company has not brought legal charges against Mr. Kochinsky. Interestingly enough, Mr. Kochinsky is also a member of the City Council. This group must act frequently on your company's requests for zoning variations, changes in ordinances, etc. Is there a connection?

(d) The special-interest group "Equity for Women" is concerned. Your firm professes to be an equal opportunity employer with a policy of promotion from within among present employees, but EFW doesn't agree. Although your firm has 145 individuals in Grade 4 and up (department head and higher) only two women have been promoted to that grade as contrasted to sixteen men in the last twelve months. Why?

(e) Your firm has manufactured dry cereals for almost 90 years. Yesterday a child choked to death on a foreign object, which the family claims was ingested as she ate her Wheat Pops. "The object was definitely in the box of cereal and that is what caused her death," the mother told the press. All of your products go through two careful checks before packaging in a primary effort to eliminate all foreign objects. At this time, you have no other information. Answer the reporters who want to know precisely what happened and "why is your firm permitting dangerous items to get into your products?"

(f) Determine your own topic. Explain it briefly to your group and then make a four- to five-minute presentation.

17 Listening

*If **you** don't listen to **them**, they will always find someone who **will**.*

For years, people in business and education have been aware of the importance of speaking, writing, and reading as facets of the communication process. Employees have been encouraged to improve their abilities to speak effectively, write clearly, and read rapidly. They have been encouraged to attend courses offered at schools in the community or within the company.[1]

The fourth area of communication—listening—has been almost totally ignored until recently. Now, however, more and more attention is being given by educational as well as business institutions to listening as an important aspect of learning as well as of effective management.

In addition, a variety of programs are available from commercial organizations. These are tapes, records, books, pamphlets, exercises, tests, and other instructional media designed to improve the individual's ability to listen.[2]

HEARING IS NOT LISTENING

We are often told that managers spend approximately 60 to 70 percent of their working hours in some area of communication. And of that percentage, some 65 percent is spent not in talking, writing, or reading, but in listening.

[1]An excellent paperback is available for the interested reader: James J. Floyd, *Listening, A Practical Approach*, Glenview, Il: Scott, Foresman, 1985.

[2]It may prove helpful to use the Paramount Communications film "Listening: A Key to Problem Solving," Norman B. Sigband, consultant, available from AIMS Media, 6901 Woodley, Van Nuys, CA, 91406.

And yet only an average of six to eight managers out of a hundred have had any formal instruction on how to listen effectively. Fortunately, that number is steadily increasing.

One reason for that increase is the fact that more and more individuals are becoming aware that hearing is not listening. Hearing is an almost automatic, physiological function that occurs with little or no conscious reaction. When you drive your car you hear a horn blaring, a child shouting, a truck roaring, a jet flying, a winch whining. But you don't *listen* to them. Hearing requires almost no effort. Listening does.

Listening requires both physical and mental effort to overcome the barriers in our environment as well as those in ourselves. Philosopher Mortimer Adler said, "The most prevalent mistake that people make about listening is to regard it as passively receiving rather than as actively participating."[3] People can't really listen with full effectiveness if they completely relax, slouch in their chairs, and stare in the general direction of the speaker. They may be "hearing" but it is not "listening." The latter requires as much effort on the part of the receiver as does effective effort on the part of the sender. Dr. Adler states, "Catching is as much an activity as throwing and requires as much skill, though it is a skill of a different kind. Without the complementary efforts of both players . . . the play cannot be completed."[4]

BARRIERS TO EFFECTIVE LISTENING

Perhaps the most important barrier to effective listening results from the fact that most of us talk at about 125 to 150 words per minute, while we can listen to and comprehend some 600 to 800 words per minute. Quite obviously if the sender talks at 125 words and the receiver listens at 600, the latter is left with a good deal of time to think about matters other than the message; and he or she does: illness, bills, cars, the baseball game score, what's for dinner tonight, and so on. This is the **internal competition** for attention.

However, there is also the **external competition** to effective listening. These are the distractions caused by clattering typewriters, ringing telephones, noisy production lines, heated arguments, intriguing smells, captivating sights, and dozens of other factors we all encounter in a busy, complex society.

Time, or more accurately, the lack of it, also contributes to inefficient listening. Effective listening requires that we give others a block of time so they may express their ideas as well as their feelings. Some individuals require more time than others to do this. If we are—or appear to be—impatient, they

---

[3]T. Montalbo, "Listening: Not a Spectator Sport!" *The Toastmaster,* July 1987, p. 8.

[4]Montalbo, 1987, p. 9

> The most prevalent mistake that people make about listening is to regard it as passively receiving rather than as actively participating.
>
> *Mortimer Adler*

||||||||||||||||||||||||||||||||||||||||||||||||||||||||||||||||||||||||||||||||||||||||||||||||||||||||||||||||||||||||||||||||||||||||||||||||||||||||||||||||||||||||||||||||

will either not express themselves fully or will require more time than usual. And yet the listener possesses a limited amount of time also. In addition, there are some individuals who will monopolize *all* of your listening time. If you begin to listen to such a person at noon, you could still be listening at 3:00 P.M.

You must turn off a person like this as tactfully as possible. However, there are others with whom you work or live that you should give time to so that you may listen with undivided attention. Remember, if *you* don't listen to *them*, they will always find someone who *will*.

If employees feel their supervisor won't listen to them, they will find other employees or the union representative who will; if young people feel their parents won't or don't listen to them, they may find friends, gang members, or people whose influence might be detrimental. And if customers feel a supplier really isn't listening, they will find a competitor to the supplier who will. There is no such thing as a vacuum in communication.

Conditioning is still another factor that contributes to poor listening. Many of us have conditioned ourselves not to listen to messages that do not agree with our philosophy or that irritate, upset, or anger us. TV and radio play a role in this conditioning. If the program we see or hear doesn't entertain or intrigue us, we have been conditioned to reach over and simply change channels or stations. And we carry this habit of changing the channel to tune a message out into our daily listening activities.

Evaluating what we hear may constitute still another barrier. So often we listen and almost immediately evaluate and reject the idea before it is completely voiced. Or we listen and then detour mentally while the individual is still talking. Of course, it is not possible not to evaluate, but one should continue to listen after evaluating. The problem is that most of us tune out as soon as we hear an idea or point of view that does not agree with ours.

Emotions, if colored or at a high level, may also get in the way of effective listening. Surely if you hear ideas that are counter to yours, or if you are involved in a confrontation or are emotionally upset because of fear, anger, or happiness, effective listening becomes very difficult.

Lack of training on how to listen is still another barrier. Most of us have received much instruction on how to write more concisely and clearly, read more efficiently and rapidly, and speak more forcefully and effectively. But few of us have every received any instruction on how to listen. Perhaps this flaw in our educational system stems from the belief on the part of many educators that if one hears, one is listening. The fact remains that more effective listening can be taught. Fortunately, increasing numbers of schools today are teaching pupils how to listen more effectively, and there are even programs available in many universities.

Our **failure to concentrate** is another barrier to effective listening. That may be due to the fact that many of us have not been taught how to listen, or to the fact that we don't work at listening.

All you need do is look around the room at the next meeting you attend. Note how many people are sitting in a completely sprawled posture; some even have their feet stretched out on the chair next to them or on top of the meeting table or desk. How can anyone really work at listening while in a completely relaxed posture? And even if the individual does listen well in that position, think of what that posture conveys nonverbally to the speaker!

It does little good, except as items of information, to name (as we have) eight reasons why many of us don't listen well. What is really of concern to us is how we can become better listeners . . . and most of us *can* become better.

TYPES OF LISTENING

We usually think of three types or levels of listening:

1. *Casual listening* is the way most of us listen to music or news reports while driving or reading.
2. *Attentive listening* is done when important information is directed at us. This is information we may analyze, remember, and question. Attentive listening is assisted when we can question, get feedback, and see and hear simultaneously.
3. *Empathetic listening* requires that we listen with the other person; that we attempt to understand his or her emotions, feelings, and attitudes about the item under discussion. It is the listening that is often referred to as between the lines, active listening, or listening from the other's point of view.

MESSAGE CONTENT

If we analyze the content of most of the messages directed at us, we will conclude that they contain facts or facts and feelings. A simple statement such as, "I would like two packages of spearmint gum," contains several facts. Frequently an entire class lecture, if delivered with no enthusiasm, contains only facts.

On the other hand, a statement such as the following contains both facts and feelings: "Well, I really worked on that assignment—night and day for three weeks—but the results are terrific and I'm sure you'll agree. The payoff will place our firm in the lead position among all solar-panel manufacturers!"

In both quotations, attentive listening is required, but only in the second is attentive and empathetic listening necessary.

LISTENING FOR FACTS

If you are a student, you have probably experienced missing an important class. If you are a manager, you have occasionally missed a meeting. The problem is playing "catch up." As a result, you approach Mitchell and ask about Monday's class and what you've missed.

If Mitchell can tell you little more than it was "an interesting class and I really thought the financial analysis of the case was OK," he probably is not very efficient in his attentive listening for facts. If you continue to press him, he may go on to say, "It was a great case," or, "It emphasized financial aspects of a major corporation." Then you surely know that he doesn't listen very well (or attentively) for facts.

On the other hand, you may find Jan's response to the same question on the same class quite different. "Yes," says Jan, "it was a very interesting class. First, Professor Maxwell set the stage by indicating we would look at three aspects of high interest rates and the problem of getting residential mortgages: the trend in home sales, the cost of mortgage money, and the tax benefits secured by the residential purchaser."

Jan may then go on to list the specific subpoints under the three items noted and even give you Professor Maxwell's summary statement.

What is the difference between Mitchell's ability to listen for facts and Jan's ability? To some extent, Mitchell has not used his class time very well and will surely spend much more time reviewing for his final exam than Jan will. And the real pity is that his store of knowledge doesn't grow as quickly or as efficiently as Jan's.

Jan listens and retains facts; Mitchell does not. How do you listen? Like Jan or like Mitchell?

How to Improve Your Ability to Listen for Facts[5]

Catalog Key Words. In almost every discussion or presentation, several key ideas are presented. Each of these ideas can be retained if a key word is remembered that can be associated with each of the key ideas. In the discussion above, Jan probably remembered "home sales," "cost of money,"

---

[5]See also R.G. Nichols, "Listening Is a 10-Part Skill," *Nation's Business*, July 1957, and Norman B. Sigband, "Listen to What You Can't Hear," *Nation's Business*, June 1969.

and "tax benefits." Because she remembered these key words, she was able to discuss intelligently the concepts presented during the class.

Resist Distractions.   A dozen distractions take place while you listen. Whether you are in a group listening to a speaker or having a conversation with one other person, distractions are present. There are the external ones such as heat and humidity, noise and smell, bickering, illumination, and competing activities. Internally there is our own tendency to daydream, evaluate, and think of other important matters as well as our emotions, values, and the speaker's personality.

But we must resist these distractions and focus on the key concepts and words. No one maintains that such concentration is easy. It requires effort, but the task is made easier if we assume a posture of attentiveness and mentally force ourselves to pay attention to the task at hand. Many people find that taking notes during the presentation assists them in resisting distractions. If our friend Jan took notes during the class in question, she possibly wrote and underlined the key words, "home sales," "cost of money," and "tax benefits."

Review Key Ideas.   In the course of Professor Maxwell's lecture, both Mitchell and Jan had a good deal of free time. Professor Maxwell spoke at an average pace of about 140 words per minute. Both Mitchell and Jan comprehend approximately 650–700 words per minute. Mitchell used the "extra time" to think about last night's dinner with Betty and the fact that Chablis might have been a better wine to order than Blanc de Blanc. Jan, on the other hand, used her "extra time" to review the evidence Professor Maxwell cited in relation to home sales, cost of money, and tax benefits. Learning is a constant search for key ideas. As Keith Davis stated in his book, *Human Behavior at Work*, "Hearing is with the ears, but listening is with the mind."[6]

Be Open and Flexible.   The old saw, "Don't bother me with the facts, my mind is made up," may be humorous, but it is also true for many people. Their biases are so strong that they may prefer not to listen. Or perhaps their instant assessment of the speaker's clothes, ethnic background, hair style, accent, or beard is enough for them to fix their opinions.

Obviously this attitude is an injustice not only to the speaker but most certainly to the listener as well. It is true that Mitchell had a very unhappy experience in a real estate transaction last year. But is that any reason for him not to listen to Professor Maxwell today?

Listen to whatever is being directed to you. Be flexible and receptive. No one suggests that you must *accept* the idea and concepts presented by others. However, you should listen to them.

[6]K. Davis, *Human Behavior at Work*, Prentice-Hall, 1977, p. 9.

Evaluate but Don't Tune Out.   Closely associated with being open and flexible is this suggestion: evaluate but don't tune out. If your evaluation results in your rejection of a concept or idea, that is perfectly acceptable. However, don't immediately tune out. The information that follows may place a new light on the matter, but if you don't even listen to those subsequent ideas, you may be the loser. Or it is possible that the subsequent material may introduce a completely new topic. If you are still tuned out from the previous one, you may miss important data. The point is, disagree with what you hear if you feel disagreement is correct. But continue to listen.

Work at Listening.   Effective listening—like effective speaking, writing, and reading—requires the expenditure of energy. That energy is used for planning, organizing, and assimilating. Listening is no different. It requires effort to concentrate, to sit up attentively, to review ideas, to remain open, to resist distractions, and to remain alert mentally and physically while someone else is talking. And that person may well be talking and presenting ideas with which you disagree.

But the fact remains that you have an obligation to listen. As a matter of fact, when you elected to sit in that classroom, in that office, or in that easy chair, you made—in effect—a contract that the other person would talk and you would listen.

None of us can evade the issue and say that "I couldn't listen to him. His accent (mannerisms, pacing, emotions, scratchy voice, hot room, noisy audience) made it impossible for me to listen intelligently." That is a cop-out.

If we begin a one-to-one relationship in an office, in a class, at home, the contract is in effect and we must work at listening effectively.

This ability to listen attentively for facts is not difficult to develop. Following the six points listed above may not be easy but it may not be terribly difficult either. If you are a student and you have the ability to listen effectively for facts, you will not only assimilate more knowledge but will find great satisfaction as you watch your grade level rise. If you are a manger, you will find your decision-making ability increased as your body of facts expands.

The greatest satisfaction will come, however, in the knowledge that you are using your time more efficiently.

LISTENING FOR FEELINGS, OR LISTENING EMPATHETICALLY

Earlier in this chapter we noted three types of listening, one of which was empathetic listening. Certainly one must also listen attentively while listening empathetically. But with **empathetic listening,** we are very concerned that an individual's feelings are heard and, in most cases, responded to.

Let's say, for example, that Chief Nurse Higgins just walked on the floor at 7:00 A.M. The first person she encounters is Registered Nurse Murphy, who looks frazzled, exhausted, upset, and concerned. Before Ms. Higgins can even offer a "Good morning," Ms. Murphy blurts out:

What a night! Two of our staff didn't show up for work, we had three emergencies, and both Jane Baxter and Mrs. Cox had terrible problems. In fact I thought we would lose Cox when she began hemorrhaging again, but we saved her.

And then you wanted me to complete the monthly status report in my free time, which I did, but even though I began my shift two hours early, it was a job that proved almost impossible. And if I never have another night like this last one, it will be too soon.

If Chief Nurse Higgins now says, "Well, take off now, get a good rest; I'll see you tomorrow," then it is obvious that she hasn't listened to what Nurse Murphy did not say!

What was Nurse Murphy *really* saying? If Ms. Higgins was listening empathetically for feelings, she might have heard one or more of these messages:

I deserve some praise.

I worked over and beyond the call of duty.

You were unreasonable to ask me to complete the status report.

I'm an exceptional nurse.

I should really be paid at least two hours' overtime.

Which of the above *possible* messages should Ms. Higgins respond to? Obviously she can't ask Nurse Murphy what she was really saying. If Nurse Murphy could have really said what she meant, she would have said it. However, Ms. Higgins could make a rather neutral statement such as, "You really must have had a difficult night," or "You must certainly be exhausted." Or Ms. Higgins may restate or make a "mirror" statement of what Nurse Murphy said. And in response, Nurse Murphy may say what is in her heart. Or it is even possible that Ms. Higgins knows Nurse Murphy so well she can select the correct response to make from the five alternatives listed. Certainly couples who live together or work together for many years know precisely what the other individual is really saying in what they are not saying. That ability results when individuals listen empathetically; when they listen for feelings; when they listen sensitively.

How effectively do you listen to the feelings of others? Following are several suggestions that may prove valuable.

Listen Empathetically.   Listen with the speaker: with his or her emotions, hopes, desires, perceptions, point of view, values, age level, and so on. It is not necessary that you agree or even accept that perception, point of view, or value structure, but make an effort to *understand* it. And it is helpful to articulate to the speaker your understanding.

Appreciate the Speaker's Meaning for the Words Used.   As we know well, words have different meanings for different people. Try to appreciate the speaker's connotation for the words he or she used. What does the speaker mean by *immediately, costly, responsible, early*? In our fast-changing world there are often differences in meaning for the same word between a forty-eight-year-old parent and a sixteen-year-old son; a fifty-year-old teacher and twenty-one-year-old coed. As a matter of fact, words even take on new meanings that may not be understood the same way by the communicating parties.

Listen for Nonverbal Communication.   Hand gestures, drumming fingers, tapping heels, voice inflections, worried glances, facial expressions, perspiration, cracking knuckles, voice level and intensity, and body tension are just a few nonverbal messages that may constitute an important part of the message conveyed. Watch, listen, and evaluate carefully every part of the message directed to you. Listening with your eyes (that is, observing the nonverbal messages) can sometimes be as important as listening with your ears. Although there has been much written on interpreting body language, you must also be cautious. A specific mannerism doesn't always mean XYZ, although some authors would have you believe it does. You must always interpret body language as well as other nonverbal communication within the context and cultural norms of the situation and according to the personal style of the individual.

Be extremely aware of *paralanguage* as you listen. This includes the tone and quality of the voice, the rate of delivery, sounds such as a sigh or a grunt, pauses, and the length of silences. Any one of these may reinforce or contradict the verbal message; if you are alert to them they will assist you to listen effectively.

Listen and Respond to What is Said Within What Isn't.   In many instances, when we listen empathetically, it is relatively simple to respond to what isn't said within what is. Such a response will assist the communication to continue or it will close the loop. What is he or she really saying with the comment, "Since I took over the department, production is up over 60 percent," or "It's almost too hot to fix dinner tonight," or "I guess I was lucky winning three sets in a row," or "What do you think of this necktie?"

If it is appropriate and we are empathetic to the feelings expressed, we can respond to what wasn't said in each message. Doing so assists the communication process. However, we must also recognize that a response should not always be made, even when the speaker hopes it will be voiced. For example, Bob says, "Boy, I really worked twenty-eight hours yesterday to have that report ready for you today at noon." Because you know Bob, you also know that this is his oblique way of saying, "Give me a pat on the back; tell me what a great job I did." But Bob doesn't deserve a pat on the back; he has had a month to finish the report. Had he planned carefully, he would not have had to work "twenty-eight hours yesterday."

Certainly in such cases, it may be perfectly acceptable not to reply to what wasn't said. However, the "loop" should be closed in the most appropriate and tactful way under the circumstances.

Listen With an Open Mind. In an effort to listen empathetically to another person, it is tremendously helpful if you can recognize your own biases on the topic under discussion. This is not to say that you should drop or change your point of view, but you should be able to weigh and recognize it in relationship to the views of the other person. Poor listeners often hear the first few sentences and reach a decision of agreement, friendliness, hostility, or indifference. They should not. Listen to the message; appreciate the speaker's perceptions and viewpoints; and then weigh the facts and analyze carefully before making a judgment. In a word: don't jump to conclusions or give up your ideas. Just listen with an open mind.

Select, if Possible, the Right Time and/or Place. At times we really want to listen to the other person but if adequate time is not available or the place is too noisy, how can we? There is nothing wrong, however, in saying, "This is really important to both of us, but I have a class in five minutes, and it just isn't fair to you if we begin to discuss this and I'm required to rush off. When would be a convenient time for us to get together?"

Listening for feelings or listening empathetically is not easy in a highly competitive, busy society. Our usual tendency is to first think of our needs, our desires, our "winning." How do we condition ourselves to do a better job of listening to the other person's needs, desires, or "winning"? It can be done, and when we recognize the rewards of such listening, we will make the effort and take the time to do it.

ACTIVE LISTENING

Dr. Carl R. Rogers probably was the originator of the term "active listening." He states, "It is called 'active' because the listener has a very definite responsibility. He does not passively absorb the words which are spoken to him. He actively tries to grasp the facts and the feelings which he hears. . . ."

Rogers makes the point that when we listen, we should attempt not to evaluate or judge what is said. Once a positive or negative response is made by the listener, the speaker will have a tendency to halt the discussion. After all, he has received the listener's judgment. However, active listening encourages the speaker to continue to speak. That may be done with non-judgmental responses such as "You sound upset; tell me more," "Can you expand on that so I may see more of the picture?" "Perhaps you could tell me in a little more detail why you feel that way; I think I'm beginning to see your point."

Rogers goes on to say:

> *Active listening is an important way to bring about changes in people. Despite the popular notion that listening is a passive approach, clinical and research evidence clearly shows that sensitive listening is a most effective agent for individual personality change and group development.*
>
> *When people are listened to sensitively, they tend to listen to themselves with more care and make clear exactly what they are feeling and thinking. Group members tend to listen more to each other, become less argumentative, more ready to incorporate other points of view. Because listening reduces the threat of having one's ideas criticized, the person is better able to see them for what they are, and more likely to feel that his contributions are worthwhile.*
>
> *Not the least important result of listening is the change that takes place within the listener himself. Besides the fact that listening provides more information than any other activity, it builds deep, positive relationships and tends to alter constructively the attitudes of the listener. Listening is a growth experience. . . .[7]*

We can see the value this type of listening has for not only professionals (such as counselors, interviewers, therapists, etc.) but also for business managers. The latter group will obviously conduct more effective interviews with subordinates, customers, and vendors and better group staff sessions and business meetings by being aware of Carl Rogers' suggestions.

THE VALUE OF EFFECTIVE LISTENING

Up to this point we have reviewed the factors that cause us to listen inefficiently, differentiated the types of listening, and considered how to improve our listening ability. The obvious questions are, "Why make the effort? What do we gain?"

The gains are significant and can easily have a strong influence on our work relationships, personal life, and almost every other facet of our daily activities.

Information.   Careful and attentive listening gives us information that helps us in our classes, work situations, and personal activities. The added information assists us in decision making, in learning, and in dealing with problems.

[7]Carl R. Rogers and R.E. Farson, "Active Listening," Industrial Relations Center, University of Chicago, 1975.

Ideas.   Effective listening will often give us new ideas that will help us advance on the job, deal with others, or earn a better grade in a class. It is amazing how many new ideas are available for our use if we only listen for them.

Understanding.   Empathetic listening will often provide us with insight and understanding about those around us. We come to understand that Betty has difficulty saying what she really means, that Phyllis requires a great deal of praise, that Mike is an extrovert and Perry an introvert. The fact remains that when you understand what motivates, drives, inhibits, or turns others off or on, you can usually communicate more effectively with them.

Cooperation and Improved Listening on Their Part.   When individuals feel that you are listening attentively and empathetically to them, they may very often listen more effectively to you! People do not necessarily want you to agree with them. They do, however, want you to listen. Your full, open effort to listen and understand them may very well motivate *them* to cooperate and listen to you.

CONCLUSION

In a world of communication overload—where too many people, media, institutions, and organizations are shouting louder and louder to be heard— effective, attentive, and empathetic listening is not practiced very often.

But it should be.

There is little you can do to make others better listeners. Certainly telling them to "listen better" will result in antagonism rather than in improvement. However, there is much you can do to make yourself a better listener. And when you listen better to them, they may then listen better to you.

But good listening is not easy. It takes time; it often takes emotional control; and it often requires courage to listen and find that someone else's way is better or more correct than yours. Listening may not be difficult in a passive situation. But it is difficult in a situation of confrontation. And it is precisely when it is most difficult—in a conflict situation—that effective listening is most needed.

||||||||||||||||||||||||||||||||||||||||||||||||||||||||||||||||||||||||||||||||||||||||||||||||||||||||||||||||||||||||||||||||||||||||||||||||||||||

QUESTIONS FOR STUDY

1. Explain the difference between hearing and listening.
2. Often we end up listening poorly without really deciding to do so. What obstacles to listening can influence our attention without our conscious knowledge?

3. In terms of your professional work and your personal life, explain the statement, "Always remember that if *you* don't listen to *them*, they will will always find someone who *will*."

4. What are the pros and cons of evaluating a message as it is transmitted to you orally?

5. Though your judgments will necessarily be broad, appraise the listening habits of today's 13 or 14 year olds. Are their schooling, music, television habits, and other life experiences teaching them to be good listeners? Explain your response.

6. Paraphrase and provide an example to illustrate the concept of *listening for feelings*.

7. Explain the possible dangers of "not listening to what isn't said."

8. In an era of communication overload, why is it important for people to listen? Instead, shouldn't they be listening less? Explain.

9. Define and give examples of *paralanguage*.

10. Identify (in your classroom) distractions and potential distractions to effective listening.

11. What implications do you see in the fact that we talk much more slowly than the pace at which we can comprehend?

12. What is the difference between attentive listening and empathetic listening? Provide an example of each type.

13. List at least six nonverbal cues that must be listened for by an effective communicator.

14. What is the payoff for managers who learn to listen well? Explain your response.

EXERCISES

15. Identify and explain a situation where you have conditioned yourself *not* to listen.

16. Ask five of your classmates if you may see their lecture notes after they have all attended the same class. Analyze their notes and present your findings and the relationship of those findings to the topic of "Listening for Facts."

17. Examine your relationship with your girlfriend, boyfriend, mother, boss (select one from this group—or any other person). Determine a specific major listening barrier that you encounter in this relationship and attempt to explain why it exists.

18. Conduct a listening experiment: turn the "contrast" or "brightness" control on your television so that no picture shows. Listen to a news or informational program for fifteen minutes. Make a check mark on a score sheet each time you catch your attention wandering from the program. Then repeat the activity, this time with full picture and sound. Again, make a check mark on your score sheet when your attention wan-

ders. Based on your results, write an evaluation of the importance of sight and sound to listening effectiveness.

19. Work at listening! It is easy to say and difficult to do. Take a few moments and evaluate your listening skills and habits. Then in a concise list, indicate what you need to do in order to improve your ability to "work at listening."

20. "Appreciate the speaker's meaning for the words used." Discuss this quotation in relation to semantics broadly and word connotation and denotation specifically.

21. How can an "Effective Listening Program" for all the employees of Webster Electronic Corporation have an effect on the company's "bottom line"?

22. Ask a classmate to speak to you about some topic for three to five minutes. Next, try to sum up and repeat back the major points to the satisfaction of the speaker. Then switch roles and repeat the experiment. Finally, write a final evaluation of this activity as an aid to training in listening.

23. Managers spend a considerable amount of their time involved in some aspect of communication—talking, reading, writing, and listening. There are a variety of estimates on how the manager's total time is spent communicating and how time breaks down among the four activities.

Find a cooperating executive in the profession you plan to pursue and ask to observe his or her normal work route for a specified period of time (e.g., two hours or a half day).

During that time be a silent observer and carefully audit how the manager's communication time is allocated; specifically identify:

a. the situation

b. how your figures (percentages) compare to those given in the chapter

c. the listening environment

d. what could be changed in the physical placement of people and things and in individual habits to improve the quality of listening

24. As an employee known for good listening skills, you've been assigned confidentially to help Hugh Melton, a company vice president and notoriously poor listener, to improve his listening skills. You'll have four two-hour sessions with Melton. Sketch our how you'll use the time.

25. What are the signs to use to tell if someone has truly listened to what you have said? Make a list of the specific symptoms that tell you whether or not a person is really listening.

26. Draw up a list of five irritating listening habits you have observed in:

a. your present or past boss

b. an instructor you now have or have had

c. your girlfriend (boyfriend, wife, husband, friend, mother, etc.)

In each case, identify the individual as specifically as possible.

18 Interviews and Meetings

To change others, try listening instead of talking.

Many of the activities of an organization are transacted through people, and those transactions often take place during interviews or meetings. Both take place frequently. There are interviews between purchasing agent and vendor, salesperson and customer, personnel director and job candidate, plant superintendent and manufacturing manager, chief engineer and director of research. In addition, there are the meetings held among a group of individuals to solve organizational problems. Like the interview, this one-to-group communication situation is the medium for the exchange of important information in most organizations.[1]

Despite the frequency with which these meetings and interviews are held, probably no two other communications activities are carried on so inefficiently. Surprisingly enough, few managers have been trained to conduct interviews effectively; yet almost every manager must do so frequently. The same is true of meetings. Although managers often call them, not many lead them effectively.

And yet both interviews and meetings are vital activities for the exchange of information and for reaching the solutions to problems. Interestingly enough, they are both as important in the small retail store as they are in the corporate walnut-panelled office.

---

[1]An excellent book on meetings is R. K. Mosvick and R. Nelson, *We've Got to Start Meeting Like This!* Glenview, IL: Scott, Foresman, 1987.

THE INTERVIEW

The purposes of the interview are many. In general, the interview should be recognized as an effective communication method for

- sending and receiving information;
- gaining understanding and the acceptance of ideas;
- developing and changing attitudes and behavior; and
- motivating others to work for a common goal.

These are the broad, general purposes. Some of the more specific types of interviews are:

Selection Interview—for choosing new employees

Orientation Interview—for orienting employees, new and old, to organizational policies and practices

Transition Interview—for guiding employees through periods of change, especially during transitions in leadership or company directions

Training Interview—for instructing employees in new skills and attitudes

Information Interview—for securing the knowledge and experience of others so organizational objectives may be more easily attained

Appraisal Interview—for evaluating employees, reviewing job performance, establishing objectives, and analyzing future directions

Problem-Solving Interview—for discussing company, departmental, or individual problems

Disciplinary Interview—for dealing with disciplinary or behavioral situations on the job

Counseling Interview—for advising employees on family, health, financial, or other personal matters

Exit Interview—for recording valuable input given by employees who are leaving the company

Persuasive Interview—for assessing needs, then applying suggested solutions to those needs. This form of interview is commonly used in sales.

Of course every interview will be different, depending on the purpose, the personalities involved, the emotions of the participants, and the complexity of the topic. The successful interview is a two-way process. Each of the parties must be an adept listener (receiver) as well as sender; each person must be sensitive to the other's needs and be able to listen intelligently, skillfully, and understandingly. In all cases the successful interview is planned, with objectives carefully defined.

Although many think the interview is simply a situation involving two people—one asking questions and the other answering—it is much more. The interview is an *exchange* of thoughts, feelings, and attitudes in which ideas, goodwill, and understanding can grow as a result of the efforts of the individuals involved.

Major Categories of Interviews

There are many different types of interviews. Of course, it is not unusual for them to overlap. Obviously the information interview is used in the appraisal interview, the selection interview, and all other types of interviews. And the disciplinary interview certainly has aspects of the persuasive interview in it.

1. The Selection Interview   In many respects, this is also a modified information interview. The interviewee attempts to get as much information as possible about the organization, the benefit package, the job responsibilities, etc. The interviewer attempts to get as much data as possible about the qualifications, personality, potential, and background of the applicant. This means that both must plan carefully and design a series of cogent questions prior to the interview if their objectives are to be achieved.

Because word choice is so vital, it is wise to write out each question to make sure the wrong word is not used. For example, it is perfectly acceptable for the prospective employee to ask about promotion, but to use that precise word even before he or she has been hired may seem to be presumptuous. However, the applicant may wish to phrase the question in writing this way and test it out: "Assuming hard work and excellent performance, what is your firm's policy on moving employees up?" That sounds better than, "When can I expect a promotion?"

Today it is probably more true than ever that the prospective employer should first prepare a list of questions. With the many government regulations such as the rules of fair employment practices legislation and equal employment opportunity guidelines, it is imperative that the interviewer only ask questions that are acceptable. As is well known, there is a long list of questions concerning age, marital status, race, religion, and so on, which if asked can be the basis for legal action.

Insofar as the interviewee is concerned, he or she must do an outstanding job in this interview assignment. Otherwise it is very unlikely that there will be another opportunity.

2. The Orientation Interview   New employees or visitors to corporate facilities can, of course, be given an orientation by means of a presentation or a meeting. But these tend to be one-way forms of communication that focus on what the company has to offer, not what the employee or visitor seeks. The orientation interview, by contrast, involves the newcomer in the process of "finding a fit" in the communication of company information. A typical orientation interview begins with inquiries into the newcomer's interests and experiences. Company information is doled out in direct response to those interests and experiences. The result is mutual orientation; the newcomer knows what the company is all about, as viewed from his or her point of view, and the company knows a great deal about the newcomer's attitudes and background.

3. The Transition Interview   The "personal touch" afforded by the interview is never as important as during stressful times of transition. When employees change jobs within the company or take on additional responsibilities, the give-and-take of the transition interview gives management the chance to hear and feel how the employee reacts to the transition. The interviewer not only presents the facts about the transition but also feels out the interviewee on personal reactions, possible problems, and suggestions.

4. The Training Interview   The attention span of even the most intelligent trainee is remarkably short when information is presented by the lecture method. But that same trainee can be attentive and tuned in for hours at a time when training occurs by more interactive means, such as in the training interview. Let's say, for example, that we want to upgrade a report writer in the company from word-processing skills to desktop publishing skills. Instead of simply presenting desktop publishing techniques, we could instead use the interview format, in which we inquire about what worked and what didn't for the person in the word-processing position. As the shortcomings of word processing were uncovered, information about the advantages of desktop publishing could be given. In this way, trainees feel they are part of the training process. They feel motivated to learn because they recognize how new skills and abilities can help them.

5. Information Interview   The primary purpose of this interview is to obtain or provide information in which prices, weights, delivery schedules, and other data are of vital importance. But of course the information interview takes place in a hundred situations beyond a buyer-seller relationship. There are the patient-physician, the teacher-student, the parent-child, and the lawyer-client interviews, to list a few. As in all interviews, each party must listen carefully for facts and feelings to determine what information has been omitted, avoided, distorted, or expanded.

One common form of the information interview focuses on technical exchange and often involves several individuals. It takes place when a problem has been isolated and its solution requires the input of several technically oriented people. Not only is their input necessary but their cooperation and support as well. A good technical exchange interview will accomplish that.

Take, for example, the problem of designing a more efficient missile to be mounted on a new, smaller fighter aircraft. This missile must be able to reach its target regardless of interceptor devices. Certainly the design engineer requires the knowledge of the research-department manager as well as the directors of manufacturing, finance, production, aeronautical design, and ballistics. All these people must meet, exchange ideas, and slowly build the blocks of knowledge that will result in goal achievement. This technical exchange, if handled well, can begin with any number of reasonable concepts and develop them into finished projects. The organization that emphasizes effective technical exchange and does a good job at it can usually become a leader in its field.

More good ideas in more organizations have been lost or destroyed because the technical-exchange sessions have not been handled well or are simply not productive.

6. Appraisal Interview   Employees seem to complain more about company appraisals than almost anything else. Many managers will let the interviews for which they are responsible "accumulate." One day they look at their calendar and say, "Darn it, all appraisal interviews are due tomorrow and I haven't even begun mine yet! If I space 'em ten minutes apart beginning at 8:00 A.M. tomorrow, I should be done by noon."

That is certainly no way to hold effective appraisal interviews. How can objectives be established thoughtfully; how can the work load be reviewed; how can plans be made for further professional training; how can mutual goals be developed and agreed to? All of this requires open discussion and time.

The primary purpose of this interview is to mutually evaluate the employee's performance in such areas as production, efficiency, responsibility, creativity, initiative, judgment, delegation, and professional growth. In addition, it is an opportunity to determine how well previously stated goals have been achieved and also to design new ones for the future. In some organizations that operate on a management-by-objectives basis, these goals are noted and then accepted by both parties by initialing or signing the interview form (or contract).

7. The Problem-Solving Interview   Businesses can save much time by putting face-to-face those people who are likely to have the answers to given problems. When they function as they are supposed to, these meetings can produce results (though too often meetings devolve into lecture sessions). In a problem-solving interview, both parties usually come to the occasion aware that there is a problem. The business of the interview is to define the nature of the problem, review attempts to solve the problem, discuss barriers in the path of that solution, and develop new approaches that will prove more successful. As a case in point, the communications director of a corporation may interview a senior manager with the goal of removing blocks in the company's communication channels.

8. Disciplinary Interview In this interview, the manager, parent, or teacher hopes to correct the situation while retaining the goodwill of the interviewee. Because there is so much potential for a confrontation, this interview is not easy to conduct.

An important point to keep in mind in the disciplinary interview is that one should criticize the *action* and not the individual. The interviewer, for example, should criticize the action of smoking while handling highly sensitive gauges, rather than the person. In another instance, the manager may evaluate the action of missing section meetings but not the person who has missed them.

In a disciplinary interview it is also vital to be very careful of words selected. When negative, tactless expressions are used, the potential for arousing antagonism is great. Rather than saying, "You neglected to complete . . ." it might be more appropriate to say, "When you complete . . ." Instead of saying, "I was dismayed to find that your work was unsatisfactory," it is better to say, "I will be extremely pleased when your satisfactory efforts . . ."

There are also certain disciplinary interviews where it may be very appropriate to "come on strong." If you have stated your point of view carefully, tactfully, and diplomatically on more than one occasion and the results have proved fruitless, then it may be time to prove forceful and very direct. Some individuals respond to that style only.

However, the successful disciplinary interview is one that brings problems into focus, suggests solutions, and maintains goodwill and an open line of communication.

9. Counseling Interview One of the tasks of the manager is to assist subordinates by offering suggestions and advice. The manager may wish to counsel the worker on how to improve productivity, mediate a problem, deal with suppliers or vendors, establish goals, solve a specific problem, cut costs, reschedule an operation, or develop a new process. At other times, a supervisor may wish to counsel a subordinate, if appropriate, on personal problems such as finances, health care, interpersonal relations, and other sensitive areas.

Counseling, both job and personal, lies within the province of the manager. However, in the case of personal-area counseling, managers should recognize that they have limitations. How deeply should they get involved, or should they get involved at all, in the areas of marital affairs, alcoholism, drug abuse, and financial problems? If the manager is not qualified and does offer advice, he or she may do more harm than good. It is for that reason that many firms now retain professional staff to work with employees in sensitive, personal areas.

10. Exit Interview   The exit interview can supply an organization with valuable information if it is conducted properly. However, such sessions all too often become highly vocal complaint, or gripe, sessions with unhappy employees disparaging (whether true or not) former supervisors and fellow employees but never themselves. They are trying simply to relieve their own guilt. When employees who leave the firm voluntarily or involuntarily are questioned carefully, the information they supply can prove valuable for future operations.

The exit interview should be conducted by an objective individual in an impersonal and professional manner. In almost no instance should the employee's former supervisor conduct the interview. A well thought out series of questions should be covered; personalities should not. The focus should be on the manufacturing process, the production procedure, the office routine, or whatever primary activity the employee was involved in.

What actually took place? What flaws did you observe? What interrelations existed? What specific barriers arose? What changes in procedures do you suggest? How should they be implemented?

11. Persuasive Interview   We often think of the salesperson as one who is involved in a persuasive interview. And that is true. However, almost every interview has an element of persuasiveness in it. The manager is attempting to persuade a subordinate in the counseling interview; the supervisor is attempting to persuade the worker in the disciplinary interview; the job seeker is attempting to persuade the personnel director in the selection interview. And so persuasion enters into many one-to-one relationships.

On the other hand, we also recognize that we can rarely persuade others. We can only listen understandingly and supply the information that will permit the other person to persuade himself or herself. As a matter of fact, when we do attempt to persuade others and use an aggressive approach, we meet resentment and are accused of using a hard-sell method.

About all we can do is supply information, listen attentively and empathetically, appreciate the situation from the other person's point of view, and hope that he or she will then be self-persuaded.

Those are the most common types of interviews encountered in industry. There are others; however, the basic principles noted above can be modified to serve almost any interviewing situation which may arise.

PLANNING THE INTERVIEW PROCESS

There are three basic steps in planning an interview: the preparation for the interview, the interview itself, and the follow-up to the interview.

Preparing for the Interview

Although there are many different types of interviews, they all require the same preparation:

1. **Establish goals and objectives for the meeting.** Because this step is so important, it is advisable to write these out. It is only when objectives are set down in black and white that they can be properly evaluated to determine if that is precisely what was meant.

2. **Obtain necessary background data.** It may be background on the problem to be discussed, on the individual with whom the discussion will take place, on factors that might impinge on the solution, or on other related areas.

3. **Formulate critical questions.** Here again, setting these down in black and white prior to the meeting is wise. Because one carelessly chosen word can result in problems in an interview, the writing-it-out procedure pays major dividends.

4. **Determine the interviewee's needs, personality, and attitudes, and attempt to adapt to them.**

5. **Determine possible solutions, courses of action, or even appropriate reactions to items that may arise during the interview.**

6. **Secure data or other items that will be needed during the interview.** These may include reports, samples, or company records.

7. **Select an appropriate interview site.** This point, though it appears to be minor, is really quite important. Nothing will destroy the climate of an interview more quickly than a noisy interview site. You should check to see that the site is quiet, comfortable, private, well-equipped with chairs, and adequately illuminated.

Although these seven points seem simple and obvious, they each require time. Nevertheless, if they are completed, you will find that the interview will start on the right foot.

Conducting the Interview

You hope to secure specific information from the interviewee during the course of the interview and also attain the objectives you established. Here again, guidelines are helpful.

THE INTERVIEW: WHO SHOULD BE TALKING TO WHOM?[1]

A senior partner in a mid-size Manhattan law firm recently described his approach to interviewing prospective associates as follows: "I like those candidates who turn the interview around and end up interviewing me." This might work well for the applicant—people in positions of power like to talk about themselves—but it never works for the interviewer. By the end of the interview the latter may indeed feel that he likes the candidate, but in truth it is only his own image, skillfully mirrored by the interviewee, that he likes. Needless to say, he has learned little about the candidate.

This is one of the most common mistakes interviewers make—talking too much. As an interviewer, you must learn the art of engaging another person silently. Remaining silent without assuming a withholding, harsh interpersonal stance is difficult for most interviewers, but the general rule is that the interviewee should do about 80% of the talking.

[1]Excerpt from "The Interview: Who Should Be Talking to Whom?" by Alon Gratch, *The Wall Street Journal*, February 29, 1988. Reprinted by permission of the author.

1. **Establish a comfortable climate.** This can be accomplished with a cordial and sincere greeting and by beginning the interview at the time scheduled and having adequate reference sources and information available.

2. **Prepare and ask key questions of the interviewee.** These should be noted beforehand so that none is forgotten. At the same time, the interviewer should anticipate the questions and topics about which the interviewee will very probably inquire.

3. **Observe, evaluate, and note the interviewee's verbal and nonverbal communications and reactions.** At times nonverbal behaviors may prove more valuable to the alert interviewer than the verbal ones.

4. **Be alert to crucial junctures (or crucial periods) in the conversation.** These key moments may be vital signals for closure, new directions, counternegotiations, agreements, or compromise.

5. **Establish key items for action (or action items) and a schedule for follow-up.** These should be noted in writing and a copy given to the interviewee immediately or within twenty-four hours. Such action items fix responsibility on specific individuals (most usually, the interviewer and interviewee) for completing specific tasks by specific dates.

6. **Terminate the interview in a thoughtful, appreciative manner.** The interviewee who finds the conversation brought to an abrupt halt as a result of the interviewer's jangling telephone has every right to be resentful. The same is true when a secretary interrupts or the interviewer jumps up after a hurried glance at his watch and a muttered, "I had no idea it was getting so late . . ."

And with all the guidelines listed above, the most important for both parties is to listen attentively and empathetically. Effective listening insures effective participation.

Again let us emphasize that good interviews don't just happen. They require careful preparation and follow-through. Both parties must take into consideration not only the guidelines noted above but also the personalities involved, the type of problem or situation under discussion, the objectives of both the individuals, and the environment in which the interview is taking place.

After the Interview

The interview has been prepared for and has been held. But that isn't the final step. If the "transaction" is to be successful, the parties have further obligations. It is imperative that the agreements made and the decisions reached be completed. Too often the parties concerned complete an interview, shake hands, and go on to their respective tasks. But somehow one or more of the items each person was to follow up on fall between the cracks. Here are several guidelines the interviewer should follow subsequent to the interview:

1. The interviewer should follow through on all action items that have been designated as the interviewer's responsibility.
2. The interviewer, if possible and applicable, should assist the interviewee in those action items designated as the interviewee's responsibility.
3. The interviewer should supply the interviewee with all items promised: brochures, application blanks, reports, and so on.
4. The interviewer should maintain contact with the interviewee if such an action was agreed to.
5. The interviewer should sincerely and honestly be available to the interviewee for follow-up to the interview or to supply data not available at the time of the discussion.

The interview is a vital communication activity in which we all engage frequently. In our activities at work, at home, or at play, we are involved in a one-to-one (interview) situation. These are held for the purpose of solving problems, reaching decisions, setting goals, exchanging information, and for simple day-to-day relationships. Each of these has the potential for building goodwill and assisting both parties in achieving their objectives.

Of course, every interview will be different. Sometimes the guidelines listed here will fit perfectly. At other times you will be required to design your own. And that is because you are dealing with people in an interview— and people are different.

You will frequently play the role of interviewer or interviewee. To be proficient, practice the suggestions made here. And above all, remember to listen. The interview is a communication situation where receiving ideas, feelings, and attitudes may be more important than sending them.

PSYCHOLOGISTS' ADVICE ON THE HIRING INTERVIEW[1]

Ten Warning Signals an Interviewer Should Be Alert For:

1. Inconsistent answers by a candidate, such as saying at one time that he loves his job and at another that his boss is impossible.
2. Inconsistencies between what he says and what he does or has done. He may say that he is ambitious and career-oriented, but his job history may show that he is content to muddle along.
3. Abrasiveness or any other personality quirk that makes the interviewer uncomfortable.
4. Evasiveness.
5. A pattern of unhappiness in former jobs.
6. Psychopathic personality, which might show up in a pattern of taking advantage of other people, to get revenge on the world.
7. Split personality, which might show up as a dullness in responding to questions.
8. A candidate who blames others for all his troubles.
9. One who tries to take charge of the interview by attempting to dominate the interviewer or by turning the questioning in a different direction.
10. One who admits to patterns of deceit—habitually fooling people at work and elsewhere.

Ten Tips for an Interviewer:

1. Take a course on interviewing.
2. Do no more than 15% of the talking; concentrate on listening.
3. Ask open-ended questions, such as "Tell me about your upbringing," rather than specific ones, like "Did you have a happy childhood?" Always ask, "What did you do in your last job?" The answer will tell you how the candidate perceived the scope of that job.
4. Ask about personal goals and plans.
5. Ask what the candidate thinks other people—family, friends, bosses and subordinates—think of him.
6. Ask what was easy and what was hard in school, in his jobs and in other relationships.
7. Don't ask questions that can be answered "yes" or "no."
8. Keep in mind the psychological demands of the job he is seeking.
9. In judging a candidate, keep your own biases in mind.

CONFERENCES AND MEETINGS[2]

How many times have you heard the following conversation at the lunch table . . . or perhaps even participated in it yourself?

Are you supposed to go to that meeting this afternoon on new products, Alice?

Yup, and I can't figure out any way to get out of it. What time is it supposed to start, Ed?

The notice I received said it's scheduled to begin at 1 P.M. sharp.

Yeah, and end at 3:30—dull.

Perhaps there is no corporate activity that is blamed for wasting more time and creating more antagonism than the meeting or conference. And yet it need not be so.

An unorganized, unplanned, bickering conference results in frustration, antagonism, and confusion. And one doesn't need a complex mathematical formula to determine how costly it is to confine sixteen people in a room every Tuesday afternoon from 1:00 to 3:30. At a rate of approximately $30 per hour per person (salary plus overhead), it is easy to see how one two-and-a-half-hour meeting can "cost" an organization over $1200.

But conferences should not waste money. They should not create hard feelings. They should not result in confusion.

On the contrary, they can and should produce acceptable plans, worthwhile goals, profit-making decisions, and a climate that establishes the will to work together. All that is required is the formulation of a philosophy for conferences and then attention to a three-step system for organizing them. If you are ever a conference leader or a conference participant (and almost everyone in business is at one time or another), you have a responsibility to help make every meeting you attend a success.

Management's Conference Policy

If the top personnel in the firm really believe in participative management, then they must give the conference the dignity and the recognition it deserves. Furthermore, a basic fact must be accepted and must become a part of management philosophy: that the group meeting or conference, where plans are made, objectives established, and decisions reached, is an integral and vital part of the company's management procedures and deci-

---

[2]This section was summarized in Norman B. Sigband, "Meetings with Success," *Personnel Journal*, May, 1985. See also Norman B. Sigband, "How to Meet with Success," *Nation's Business*, March, 1971.

sion-making process. Once that concept is accepted, the firm's meetings and conferences are on their way to success.

Meetings will have an excellent opportunity for being successful if management establishes, announces, and supports a list of meeting policies. These should include the following:

1. Hold only those meetings for which there is a demonstrated need. Of course, in many organizations there is so much activity that a weekly or biweekly meeting is justified. The same may be said for staff meetings that bring department members up-to-date. But under no conditions should a meeting be held every Monday or the third Wednesday of every month on the expectation that "we will surely have some items to review."

2. State a purpose and objectives for every meeting. These should be written out. In most cases the purpose is rather broad: "to discuss," "to evaluate," or "to compare." The objectives are more narrow: "to purchase Brand A or Brand B," "to construct a $40,000 addition to the plating room or not."

When meetings are called to exchange ideas, they are on their way to being bull sessions. On the other hand, a meeting purely for brainstorming is acceptable provided the brainstorming has a specific purpose with stated objectives.

3. Invite only those individuals who can make a positive contribution. People should not be invited because of protocol, politics, or fear of offending "good old Harry."

4. Prepare and distribute an agenda prior to every meeting. In the case of emergency meetings called on very short notice, the meeting leader may post or list the agenda in the meeting room prior to the start of discussion.

5. Begin and end meetings precisely at the times scheduled on the agenda sheet.

6. Distribute a set of minutes or a recapitulation of the meeting within twenty-four hours of the close of the session. This should list decisions reached and action items with completion dates and the name of the individual responsible for each action.

What Makes a Successful Business Meeting?

An effective meeting is a forum where knowledgeable individuals come together to solve organizational problems through open and participative communication. It is a place where the will to work together is developed. It is also a group session that participants find exciting and provocative; it's one where every member who has something to say is heard; it's one where everyone is on an equal level; it's one where decisions are reached. After such a conference, participants may be overheard saying, as they leave the meeting room, such things as: "Well, I personally don't agree with the way the vote went, but we *did* reach a decision on the Sunnyvale Plan, and it's on its way."

The background to a successful meeting is management's acceptance of the fact that a conference is an important, worthwhile activity, and that the ideas, suggestions, and decisions reached at such meetings *will* be put into practice as soon as is reasonably possible.

Once this philosophy is established, following the three-step plan becomes almost a matter of mechanics.

Step 1: The Preconference Period

Establish the Need   The preconference period requires a brief discussion among key personnel in which the need for the conference is clearly established. Too many meetings are called simply because "we always meet on Tuesdays at 1 P.M." If no useful purpose can be accomplished, a conference should not be called.[3]

Define the Problem or Topic for Discussion   A clear statement of the problem or discussion topic must be agreed to and set down on paper. All too often the conference leader and participants have only vague ideas of what they are to talk about. Discussion then goes in circles, and solutions or decisions are difficult to reach.

Let's not look into "Fringe Benefits with Special Attention to a Profit-Sharing Program." Instead, let's be specific: "An Analysis of Profit-Sharing Programs in Companies Similar to Ours," or "Cost of a Profit-Sharing Program to the Jono Company," or "Should the Jono Company Adopt a Profit-Sharing Program?"

Defining a problem or selecting a topic usually requires careful analysis. Certainly a *symptom* of a problem should not be designated as the problem. It is true that production has slowed down, but installing faster punch presses will not solve the problem. The slowdown is only a symptom of the real problem, which may be low morale among people in the production department. That is the issue with which the conference should deal—not the possible acquisition of newer and faster punch presses.

Determine the Type of Conference   Once the need for the meeting has been agreed to, the next step is to decide what type of conference will best serve the immediate situation. The types of conferences include:

Informational, where information is provided in the same way at the same time to everyone concerned. Questions may be answered and facts explored.

---

[3]Paul R. Timm, "Let's Not Have a Meeting," *Supervisory Management*, August, 1982.

Problem Solving, where questions or problems are dealt with and people concerned with them are expected to help work out solutions. This is the type of conference with which the major portion of the following discussion deals.

Training, where specific skills, concepts, or ideas are explained. There may be demonstrations and question-answer periods.

Brainstorming, where almost anything goes as long as it has to do with solving or exploring the topic or problem under discussion.

The difficulty that frequently arises involves a conference leader who tries to accomplish the activities of at least all four of the preceding conference types in one meeting. It is almost impossible to disseminate information, solve problems, train, and brainstorm all in one session!

Selection of Participants   Only those individuals who are clearly and specifically concerned with the topic should be invited. Persons who occupy management positions should not be asked "just to keep them informed." There are easier and less time-consuming methods of informing such persons. And under no conditions should individuals be invited whose feelings might be hurt if they are not asked.

It is important that the company policy on conferences clearly state that only those directly concerned, or who have knowledge or experience to contribute, will be asked to conferences.

Designation of the Conference Leader   A conference often flies or falls depending on the conference leader. Actually the term *leader* is a misnomer, for the best leader is one who doesn't formally lead but who acts as a catalyst, a stimulator, a moderator, or an arbitrator. The leader who talks least and stimulates most usually does the best job.

There is also good reason to advise that the highest ranking member of the group *not* be designated as the leader. When that person is in the position of conference leader, too often he or she can't forget who's boss, nor can the participants. Why not ask one of the knowledgeable people in the group to serve as the leader? Or—an idea that is gaining some popularity—have the assistant to the president serve as leader. One might consider rotating leaders so that a different individual in a common group would serve at each meeting.

But whoever is designated as the leader, an effort should be made to see that it is someone who:

Has an ability to think quickly and clearly	Is tactful
Is analytical	Is poised
Is impersonal	Is self-restrained
Is unbiased	Expresses himself or herself easily
Is patient	Possesses a good sense of humor

And where is that saint with all these qualities to be found? Perhaps nowhere, but there is no reason why the leader can't attempt to strive for most or all of these qualities.

Designation of Topic Areas   Now that we have the specific topic, the leader, and the participants, we can move ahead and select subareas for discussion. Obviously these should be chosen with care, keeping in mind the complexity or simplicity of each point, how much discussion may be needed, and the overall time allowed for the meeting.

To list more topics than can reasonably be discussed in the time scheduled is frustrating since it means that discussion of some of them will have to be cut short.

Distribution of the Conference Announcement/Agenda   The announcement/agenda should be sent out to everyone concerned approximately three to seven days prior to the meeting. It is important to provide the following information:

- Date, time, and place of meeting
- Topic(s) for discussion
- Subareas for discussion
- List of participants
- If applicable, materials to be reviewed prior to the meeting

Figure 18–1 shows an example of a satisfactory announcement/agenda form. It is obvious that there are many advantages in distributing such an announcement. First, participants who wish to prepare for the meeting may do so. No one can say later, "Holy smoke, if I had known we were going to discuss this, I could have brought tons of statistics!"

Second, digressions can be easily and tactfully curbed by the conference leader: "That's a good point, Jeff, but I think we will defer it until later. At the moment we are trying to tie up point number 2 on the agenda sheet, so let us turn to Suzanne who has a comment on that area."

Third, all participants know who has been invited, and thus they can plan their strategies, if necessary.

Finally, the conference leader (who makes up the agenda sheet) is forced to *plan* and prepare for the session.

Preparation of Physical Facilities   The mechanical aspects of the meeting seem so obvious as to require no mention, yet breakdowns in this area have ruined countless meetings. What's the good of having twelve people congregate in front of the meeting room at the appointed time only to find it occupied, or locked and the key in the possession of somebody's secretary who is on a coffee break? Irritation and confusion are certain to follow as some make their way to the substitute meeting room while others drift back to their

FIGURE 18–1

Announcement/agenda form

JONO COMPANY

DATE: February 2, 19__

TO: Mr. R. T. Carter, Production Manager

FROM: Mr. J. M. Kean, Vice President

SUBJ: Conference, February 15, 19__
          1:00 p.m., Lounge #2

Topic for Discussion:

    Shall the Jono Company Establish a Training Division?

Specific Items for Discussion:

    1. Advantages of a training unit for salary and hourly
       personnel.
    2. Disadvantages of a training unit for salaried and
       hourly personnel.

    3. Training staff required.

    4. Cost (first 3 years).

    5. Other business.

Distribution:

Ms. G. G. Berg	Ms. I. M. Hernandez
Mr. L. A. Strong	Mr. R. T. Carter
Mr. J. R. Garro	Mr. A. B. Burton
Mr. R. B. White	Mr. M. X. Green
Mr. K. L. Mace	Mr. L. O. Cox
Ms. R. J. Foreman	Mr. L. M. Gates

desks. For this reason, it is probably wise to prepare a checklist on the physical arrangements.

1. **Room setup**   Reservations for room made? Enough chairs? Podium needed?
2. **Audiovisual materials**   Projectors? Flip charts? Mikes? Display materials? Tape recorders?
3. **Handout materials**   Adequate number of copies for distribution?
4. **Refreshments**   Coffee? Sandwiches?
5. **Miscellaneous materials**   Pads? Paper? Pencils? Ashtrays? Marking pens? Name cards?

These are some of the areas that should be checked out prior to the meeting. Now we're ready for the meeting itself.

Step 2: The Conference Period

A basic concept that companies must accept is that various aspects of the management of the firm, and of management development, can and should be built into the conference. Let's make this point by looking at a typical situation.

Of the six reports presented at today's meeting, three hit strongly at customer dissatisfaction with the carrier we are now using. One of the young men present, with a degree in marketing, made some thoughtful remarks on the advantages of using commercial carriers. Several of the old-timers wondered if we shouldn't transfer our entire delivery operations to a third party. The conference leader turned back to the young man, who volunteered to complete a study on this vital issue for the next meeting. A final decision on the problem is expected to be made at that time.

This certainly is more than discussion; it is management of the firm and, in the case of the young man, personnel development.[4]

If the conference is to go well, the leader must set the right climate. He or she must know the participants and watch the time. Care must be taken not to march down the list from first point to last, pushing discussion here, cutting off comments there. Rather, discussion must be stimulated so that the topics are covered while at the same time the participants feel they have made significant contributions.

Developing the technique for doing this is not really too difficult. It requires a sincere feeling on the part of the leader that the participants, taken

---

[4]An excellent article that touches on management development during the course of the meeting is "The Meeting-Goer's Lament," by Herbert E. Meyer, *Fortune*, October 22, 1979.

together, are smarter than he or she, possess a wealth of experience, and are equally as eager to solve the problem before the group as he or she is.

Thus the meeting begins on a positive note in which the leader communicates, verbally and nonverbally, his or her respect for each person in the room. The climate that is set in the first few minutes will either motivate the participants to contribute actively and effectively or cause them to retreat into their shells.

Note-Taking   Someone should take notes. It may be a participant who is respected by the group (not someone who will say, "I'm invited only because I write fast") and is quite impartial. Or a secretary can be brought in. However, it may inhibit discussion if some of the participants feel that the secretary is not discreet.

In the past the general procedure was for a secretary to take notes on a note pad. These were later transcribed and a set of minutes issued. The problem with this is that the secretary will record what she or he heard. If incorrect, many days pass before the record is set straight.

A trend today is to have the secretary (who may very well be a participating group member) record brief notes on a flip chart. In that way, if the secretary records his or her perception of what was discussed, said, or voted on, and if the recorder's perception is incorrect, everyone in the room will make that fact known immediately.

Time Management   The meeting leader should begin and end at the times scheduled. No one has "enough" time these days, and if the leader doesn't begin the meeting until twenty minutes after the time scheduled or holds the group an extra twenty minutes at the close, he or she will surely encounter antagonism.

Leading the Meeting   The conference leader should be careful not to dominate the meeting physically. A leader standing at a podium that is separated from the conference tables conveys the feeling, "I'm in charge." If the conference leader sits in front of the group with space to the left and right (as in a **U** arrangement), this again suggests that the leader is in charge by the way the space in the room has been used. In most situations an unbroken rectangular or oval arrangement is preferable. The conference leader need not sit at the head; discussion may flow more easily if he or she takes a seat as part of the team. Perhaps the most important point for the meeting leader to keep in mind is not to dominate the meeting. The less you talk and the more the participants contribute, the more successful you will be in attaining your objectives.

Encouraging Participation   It is wise for the leader to prepare a few pertinent questions for each topic on the agenda. Then if discussion slackens, a question can be tossed to the group. Sometimes a leading question can be fed to someone who has much to contribute but for some reason prefers to play the role of Silent Sam at meetings.

The leader should also step in at an appropriate moment to summarize discussion on a topic and move the group on to the next point. Otherwise a topic may be talked to death and nothing more accomplished.

The Participants   Most participants are eager to contribute, cooperate, and assist the total effort toward the group's objectives. However, there are some who occasionally cause problems, and one of them may be sitting at your next meeting. However, a little courtesy, tact, patience, and restraint on the part of the leader usually will ensure a successful meeting.

Meeting Tie-Up   Everyone who leaves a meeting should feel that something has been accomplished. That feeling can often be guaranteed if the last ten minutes of the session are handled properly. During that time the discussion should be summarized and key issues brought into focus. If adequate time has been given to the topics listed, and they are the type that call for a decision, a vote should be taken. Obviously not everyone can be satisfied, but most will be glad to see matters brought to a conclusion and decisions made.

It requires skill on the part of the leader not to *drive* for a decision, but to let the request for a vote or a decision come from the group. The leader has done a good job if the worst thing any of the participants say as they walk back to their desks is, "Well, I wasn't in complete agreement with the decision, but we *did* accomplish something."

Much else is involved in the conduct of a conference: the effective use of visual aids, report presentations, methods of handling debate, the use of consultants, how to handle the chairman of the board who has "just dropped in to listen quietly." But common sense, based on the principles cited, will usually provide workable techniques.

Step 3: The Postconference Period

The conference has been held, but it is not over. Its basic purpose was to hammer out another link in the chain of successful management. And the fastening of that new link to the others in the chain takes place in the postconference period.

Evaluation of the Meeting   It is now time for those who called the meeting to sit together for just five minutes to determine what the session accomplished, how the results or findings fit into overall company objectives or plans, and how the next meeting can be improved.

Distribution of the Minutes   A recapitulation of the meeting should be sent to each of the participants as quickly as possible. The form used should cover the topics discussed, votes taken, and decisions reached (see Figure 18–2). The advantages of distributing such a form are many. First, everyone receives the same summary of what took place. If anyone thinks he or she heard anything different from what is reported in the summary, then those views can be made known to the secretary immediately.

Next, there can be no confusion as to who was assigned to do what. Names are given and assignments spelled out in the "action items" section. This prevents Ms. Foreman from saying three weeks after the meeting, "Well, I didn't know *I* was supposed to do that. I remember there was a suggestion that I gather statistics, but I sure don't have them for tomorrow's meeting."

In addition, no confusion will exist on the decisions reached and the votes taken. They will be clearly stated in black and white. Here again, Ms. Cox can hardly say three weeks later, "Well, I don't remember the vote going *that* way; I thought we agreed to wait until the next meeting before a final vote was taken on that item."

Finally, the minutes become a matter of record. They can be referred to by those who were absent, and reviewed by those who were present.

This postconference period is as important as the other two. It helps tie the package together and completes the job that was begun when someone said, just five weeks ago, "Well, we ought to get some additional input on this, kick it around, and then decide which way to go."

There are those who feel that the structured approach of this three-step plan has a decided disadvantage. What happens if a participant has a brilliant idea he or she wishes to discuss, but which has not been included on the agenda (is not part of the preplanned structure)? Will that idea be lost forever?

Certainly not! All that is necessary is that the agenda carry an item "other business." The conference leader must then be sure that time is always saved to cover that point. In this way the advantages of both the structured and the unstructured meeting may be retained.

The conference decides which way to go—by common agreement. Voices are heard, ideas pursued, and personnel developed. A conference that is well run and democratically participated in is an outstanding communication vehicle.

The Use and Misuse of Meetings

Meetings can serve as one of the most useful communication tools in an organization. They bring about decision making through the democratic process; they build a team concept which engenders loyalty and commit-

FIGURE 18–2

Minutes of a meeting

CFC
California Foods Company

Minutes of Meeting

DATE: February 16, 19__

TO: Mr. R. T. Cahill, Production Manager

FROM: Mr. J. M. Kay, Vice President

SUBJ: Minutes of meeting
          February 15, __, 1:00 p.m., Lounge #2

Present: T. Caswell, L. Feinstein, F. Filtrip, F. Hokama,
          T. Hokama, T. Hokama, J. Jolie, M. Martin, P. Potter,
          L. Shapiro, T. Soromoko, S. Sugar

Summary of Discussion:
  Item one: Company-wide physical fitness program
  Item two: Employee participation in election campaigns
  Item three: Conversion of employee lounge #3 to a conference
               room

Decisions Reached:
  1. Physical fitness program continued to April meeting
  2. Employee participation in municipal elections not approved
  3. Conversion of lounge #3 approved

Action Items:

Item No.	Brief Description of Action Assignment or Task	Individual Responsible	Completion Date
1.	Investigation of physical fitness program in other companies.	M. Martin	April 5, 19__
2.	Legal ramifications of physical fitness program	S. Sugar	April 5, 19__
3.	Medical department input on physical fitness program	Dr. Kelly	April 5, 19__

ment; they provide a forum for the exposure of divergent ideas; and they give young personnel an opportunity to be seen and heard.

On the other hand, there are a few negative aspects (to be avoided) which have become increasingly apparent in meeting conduct.[5] Meetings should certainly not be called for the discussion of basic information, new procedures, or a change in regulations. On the whole, most items of this nature can be handled by a well-written announcement or bulletin. Of course there are some complex items which require a meeting where the detailed points are discussed, probed, and examined to insure that all those affected have a similar understanding of the data.

A second instance when meetings should not be called is the ploy of a manager avoiding decision-making responsibility by calling a meeting. These are usually concerned with relatively inconsequential items. "Shall we change the coffee break time?" "Shall we move the copy machine?" "Should plants be added to the office reception area?" "Shall we permit personal phone calls . . . and how to collect for them?" All such items should be settled by a manager making a decision. If the meeting is called for such trivial items, $500 to $1,000 worth of time will be expended. Even more important, it will send a signal to other managers that holding meetings for minor purposes is acceptable.

Then there is the manager who calls a meeting simply to "cover himself." If the decision doesn't work out in practice, he is the first to say, "But it wasn't my decision; I only followed the recommendations of the people who attended the meeting of May 10!" If a manager has the authority and responsibility for making decisions in instances that have been designated, then calling a meeting to "cover" himself is completely unacceptable.

Of course, the best way for an organization to avoid holding unnecessary meetings is to have a brief statement titled "Meeting Policies for the Baxter Corporation." When these are endorsed and *followed* by top management, they become a "way of life" for meeting conduct.

QUESTIONS FOR STUDY

1. How does an interview as an "exchange" differ from an interview as a question-and-answer session?
2. On what basis should participants be selected for attendance at a meeting?

[5]For further details, see Norman B. Sigband, "The Uses of Meetings," *Nation's Business,* February, 1987, p. 28R.

3. What is an orientation interview? Discuss three business situations in which it would be used.

4. Discuss the pros and cons of writing out an ordered series of questions to be used in an interview.

5. List four specific purposes for interviews and then briefly describe the procedure followed by your organization for each.

6. What type of interview would be held each week by engineering personnel who come together to discuss "Progress and Problems on X Project"? Explain.

7. Why is planning so vital for the interviewee in a selection interview?

8. Do you agree that the manager has responsibility to counsel an employee on the latter's personal problems (financial, drug abuse, health habits)? Explain.

9. Why is an appraisal interview difficult for a manager discussing the performance of an employee with whom he has maintained a friendship for 25 years?

10. How would you go about securing a relatively unbiased and objective series of comments from an employee in an exit interview?

11. What is the value, for both the interviewer and interviewee, in writing out critical questions prior to the interview?

12. What is a "crucial juncture" in an interview? Give an example.

13. Is there ever an instance when the manager should call a meeting to "cover" himself?

14. How would you define a meeting?

15. Of the several steps recommended to the conference leader for the period *before* the meeting, which do you feel is most important and why?

16. Why is it sometimes a good idea for the regular conference leader to choose another person (such as a younger, or very quiet and shy individual) to lead in the former's place? Explain.

17. What are the advantages or disadvantages of having notes for the meeting taken on a flip chart in front of the group instead of by a designated "secretary" who uses a note pad?

EXERCISES

18. Assume that you manage a large production facility. Employee turnover is low, but still common. Invent details as to what kind of business you conduct, then develop a set of questions to be asked of exiting employees. For each question, indicate in writing what information you hope to gain by the query.

19. Exchange with another student some of the graded assignments you have received in this course. Study your colleague's work and then conduct an appraisal interview with him or her.

20. Sit in, as an observer, on a meeting of a campus group or some other organization. Afterwards, evaluate the effectiveness of meeting participants in achieving their apparent goals. If the group members show interest in your evaluation, share it with them in a tactful way.

21. Recall an interview situation in which you felt uncomfortable. Analyze your discomfort. Who or what caused it? Then list several ways in which the interview could be restructured or reconsidered to reduce such discomfort.

22. You have noted that a group that you belong to (such as a student group) seems to waste considerable time in meetings. The group has several of the classic problems: lack of preparation, the wrong people in attendance, and little or no follow-up after the meetings. For such a group, prepare a policy statement on meetings and conferences.

23. Some people see meetings as their opportunity to set up a soap box and hold court. The meeting is not to be a replication of Sunday morning in London's Hyde Park. Sometimes, however, a meeting chairperson must verbally restrain one individual so the group can move forward and solve the problem at hand. Be prepared. Develop a list of ten optional statements (increasing in lack of tact) to derail the nonstop talker and keep the meeting on track.

24. The membership of your student organization has been on a steady decline, and the executive committee of the group has decided to meet in two weeks to discuss, "What Is Wrong with Our Group." In reviewing good meeting procedures, you feel that the topic is too big and will not lead to profitable discussion. Defining the appropriate problem is crucial if a solution is to be found. With this in mind, develop three alternative "titles" for the coming meeting that will aid the committee in accomplishing beneficial results.

25. Recently you were promoted to the position of manager of parts promotion for the Amco Tractor Co. In ten days you are to conduct your first interview with a prospective employee. You will be on your own, and the decision will be your responsibility alone.

    Because the firm has had some previous problems concerning fair employment practices, the company has a procedure for you to follow. Managers who are going through the interviewing process for the first time must submit potential questions in writing to the personnel office for approval. In a memo to Jane Jackson in the personnel office, list twelve questions you may ask the prospective employee. The interviewee is a recent college graduate from Belmore College. She has a double major in marketing and technology. (In preparing your materials you may want to review the legal implications of interviewing noted in Chapter 20.)

26. You're an assistant manager at Beta Video Productions. You find yourself conducting a sales meeting at which no one seems to have much to say.

Although you're reluctant to be an overly dominant meeting leader, you're afraid that if you stop talking, an embarrassing silence will fall. Consider your dilemma. Then list four ways to get others to participate freely in the meeting. List your suggestions in the order in which you would try them.

27. The head of your academic department has decided it would be beneficial for someone in the department to hold exit interviews with a sample of students graduating each year. Exit interviews don't just happen, and if they are to be beneficial, they must be more than gripe sessions. Assume you are assistant to the department head and you have been asked to outline policies, procedures, and implementation requisites for exit interviews. Place your materials in memo form and be thorough in your analysis and statement of procedures.

28. The business department at your college is going to host a group of business people for one day on campus. The conference is scheduled for two months from now. You have been placed in charge of one session in the entire conference. You are to make all the presession arrangements for a roundtable discussion between students and the business representatives on ''What Business Wants in Today's Business Student.''

The head of the business department has asked you to prepare a memo that outlines the actions needed to get the session organized. Be very precise in detailing your presession responsibilities.

29. You are the director of personnel at Federated Utilities. You're concerned about the high turnover rate among employees (less than eighteen months' service per employee, on the average). You prepare for an extensive series of exit interviews by drawing up questions you hope will get to the heart of the matter. You want to avoid leading questions, such as ''Did you want more money?'' Of course employees want more money. List at least six questions you could use in such exit interviews.

30. Draw up a set of meeting policies for an organization of which you are a member.

Legal Considerations

EMPLOYEE COMMUNICATION AND THE LAW

The most common audience for managers is the employee audience. The manager's freedom to communicate is limited in personnel matters, conditions and circumstances of employment, and labor relations.

Evolving from civil rights activities of the 1960s, laws and regulations were instituted that directly affect employment practices of many public and private organizations. The government directed its agencies to institute nondiscriminatory hiring, promotion, and retention procedures. It also directed most private firms doing business with the government to do likewise. The following acts contain the central legislation to date in these areas:

- Equal Pay Act 1963
- Civil Rights Act 1964, Title VII
- Age Discrimination Act 1967
- Equal Employment Opportunities Act 1972
- Vocational Rehabilitation Act 1973

By these acts, employers are generally prohibited from discriminating with regard to compensation and other aspects of employment or potential employment on the basis of race, creed, color, sex, national origin, handicap, or age. Recent court interpretations of these acts has extended that list to include sexual practice.

For managers, therefore, it is important in all kinds of employee-related communications to avoid mentioning explicit or implicit consideration of decisions premised upon the factors listed here. This prohibition includes handwritten notes, as in the following case. Roger Henry, Supervisor of Administrative Services at Fashion Frames' Midwest office in Evanston, Illinois, knows his company's regulations with regard to discrimination. He also values his frank, honest relationship with his subordinates. When a job announcement at a sister store in New Mexico is circulated among his employees, Ms. Joan Alred, in Accounts Receivable, expresses interest in the position. Henry, though he finds Alred's work record quite satisfactory, passes her over for someone else. In an effort to soothe her disappointment, he makes a serious mistake. He "explains" in terms that are clearly discriminatory:

"As you are married and have children starting school this fall, I didn't recommend you for this position; also, I understand that it could be difficult for your husband to find employment in Albuquerque—but I'm keeping you in mind for an advancement."

Putting the best construction on Henry's words, he was trying to be honest about his evaluation process. He sincerely felt that Joan Alred wouldn't have the time necessary to devote to this new, demanding job.

But his written words, as viewed by the Equal Employment Opportunity Commission, seemed clearly discriminatory. Ms. Alred apparently was not being judged on her performance but instead on her sex and circumstances. In such situations, employees frequently sue not only for the position they sought but also for backpay and punitive damages. When written records such as Roger Henry's handwritten note exist, employees usually win their cases.

LABOR COMMUNICATIONS

It is illegal for employers to threaten employees (e.g., "I'll fire you if you join the union.") Over the long history of labor relations law, the thrust of legislation is that the company (including its agents) may not intimidate employees over how they might vote on establishing a union. The employer does, however, have the right to communicate with employees on the issue. Companies do often ask their managers to intervene when a union tries to organize. But the written and spoken messages of the company cannot threaten the individual employee nor offer a benefit for a vote. The company's communications during such periods are governed by strict (and changing) regulation from the National Labor Relations Board.

INTERVIEWING CANDIDATES

In spite of the employer's desire to know as much about potential employees as possible, many interview questions are prohibited by law. For example, the employer cannot explicitly ask, "Do you intend to have children?" "Will you submit a photo with your application?" "What is your religious affiliation?" or "Where were your parents born?" These and other questions bearing upon race, religion, political preference, national origin, age, and sexual practice are ruled out of bounds by the Equal Employment Opportunity Commission.

AFFIRMATIVE ACTION

Affirmative action plans developed since the Civil Rights Act of 1966 call for 1) reviewing how the firm currently employs females and minorities, 2) comparing the numbers of people in various ethnic and sexual categories in the firm to the numbers available in the recruiting area, 3) establishing goals to correct inequities, 4) developing plans to accomplish the goals, and 5) auditing the flow of applicants and reporting periodically to the government. Communication concerning hiring and promotion of employees, especially where affirmative action is involved, must be done with the utmost care. To blatantly justify hiring an employee simply due to race or sex is as discriminatory as firing an employee on similar grounds. Employees passed over for the position may file reverse discrimination suits in such cases.

The most prominent job discrimination case in recent years is Ford Motor Company's $13 million damage settlement with the Equal Employment Opportunity Commission, which accused Ford of discriminating against minorities and women in hiring and advancement programs. In an investigation that spanned the period 1973 to 1980, the Commission investigated employee complaints of discrimination. Ford agreed to divide the $13 million among 14,000 persons allegedly discriminated against, and to spend an additional 10 million to recruit and train minority-group and women workers.

Part Five

Career
Communication

19 Career Planning

The search for a satisfying career begins by finding yourself.

One of the cruelest ironies of business life is the fact that hard-working students and employees often slack off just when they should be giving their best: when planning their careers and seeking a job. Some feel that their years in college or experience in previous positions have earned them the next step on the ladder to business success. Others are simply weary and pale at the thought of preparing résumés and letters or getting ready for interviews.

Both attitudes do a disservice to your future. No matter what each of us deserves, what we get is often a matter of what we make happen. Your career probably will not fall into your lap but instead will be shaped by calls you make, letters you write, and interviews you participate in. If those activities sound burdensome, especially at the end of a strenuous college experience, dig deep to find the energy for these crucial communication activities. Without them, the best academic or business preparation can be wasted.

Learning to plan your career through appropriate communication techniques pays dividends throughout your work life. Many employed people you know are happy with their positions and find each working day an enjoyable adventure. But many others are not happy, and there are some who thoroughly dislike their assignments. In addition there are people who have no strong feelings one way or another about their daily labors but who are neither challenged by their jobs nor working at their full potential. Often they are earning far less than they should be.

Too many people in our society remain in jobs for too many years—unhappy and dissatisfied, giving themselves and their families ulcers, bad tempers, and neuroses. The competent and hardworking person who is unhappy with his or her position or is insufficiently challenged should have absolutely no hesitation in attempting to find a new one.

The search for a different job may have useful results. The job hunter may learn that his or her current assignment is about the best available in the present job market. If so, he or she may well accept the job, the level, and the salary and thus overcome the urge to "do better." Or the individual may find a more satisfying or satisfactory job.

What we have to say in these two chapters will apply equally to the person seeking a first position as well as to the individual who is eager for self-improvement by securing a new job.

SOURCES FOR FINDING JOBS

There are a variety of different sources for the job seeker, several of which will be reviewed here.

College Placement Office

For the college or university student, there is probably no agency as effective, as well prepared, and as inexpensive as the school placement bureau or career services office. College placement officers are experienced in various phases of personnel testing, counseling, and evaluation. They are also usually well acquainted with the personnel directors and companies' personnel needs in that geographical area. Because of this background, placement directors can often make suggestions concerning job opportunities that may have never occurred to the student job seeker. However, their primary function is to match employers' needs with students' abilities.

Career placement offices usually host corporate recruiters who visit the campus to search for competent personnel. Recruiters select dates prior to campus visitations. The placement office then schedules prospective graduates for interviews with recruiters. Recruiters will usually interview a student once or twice on campus. Those who "pass" are then scheduled for subsequent interviews at company offices.

A wise student will take full advantage of the resources of his or her school placement service. This may include testing, evaluation, and reference materials such as annual reports, company history brochures, and company product bulletins. Many schools now maintain libraries of videotapes of corporate personnel reviewing their firms' policies, views, philosophies, and broad plans in reference to new personnel. Viewing such a tape before being interviewed can prove extremely valuable.

Employment Agencies and Placement Services

Employment agencies are also good sources for positions. Many now specialize in specific technical fields: engineering, business, computers, and so on. Agencies often act as intermediaries bringing the prospect together with the firm looking for individual skills. Fees are charged by these agencies for their services. At times the payment is made by the employing company; at other times it is absorbed by the employee. The percentage may vary from agency to agency, but it is often based on the new employee's first year's salary.

Obviously it is in the employment agency's best interest to place an applicant at the highest salary possible. At times, however, in an effort to make the "match" as quickly as possible, the agency may place you with a firm that can't or won't use you to your best advantage.

Many agencies will also offer to write your résumé based on their "years of experience." This, of course, entails an *additional fee*. Be wary. No one should be able to write a better résumé for you than you. The material in this book should give you all the information and examples you need to be an outstanding résumé writer. The reason you should prepare your own résumé has little to do with rugged independence. In an interview situation, you must respond to questions based on the words of your résumé. More than one job seeker with a slick agency-prepared résumé has stumbled badly over interview gaffes like these:

> *Mr. Wilkins, I see on your résumé that you have extensive experience as a nautical safety specialist.*
>
> *I . . . uh . . . that is, well, I was really a lifeguard for two summers.*

Too often, a résumé prepared by someone other than the job applicant is filled with overstatements, half-statements, and general "hype" that only subverts the job seeker's effort to establish credibility with interviewers.

The job seeker should be very careful when dealing with an employment agency, making sure to receive satisfactory answers to the following questions: What is the fee? Who is responsible for payment? What arrangements are made on the fee if the employer and employee agree after the first month that the "match" is not a good one? Are there counseling fees? Interview fees?

What all this says is, employment agencies serve a valuable function. But use them with care and caution and sign absolutely nothing before carefully reading the document and having *all* questions answered. And be sure to ask questions. As in every field, there are some employment agencies whose ethics and integrity leave much to be desired.[1]

[1]G. L. Solomon, "The $3,000 Resumé and Other Career Counseling Tales," *Working Woman,* November 1983.

Executive Search Firms

There are many different levels and types of executive search firms. Some specialize in specific job or administrative levels and others handle placement in executive positions that pay well into the six-figure category.

These organizations are often used by individuals who have some years of experience. It may be a manager or executive who presently has a job but is trying to improve his or her position or is unemployed. Like employment agencies, executive placement services usually charge a fee. Many keep in very close touch with corporations for the purpose of being made aware of existing openings. This permits the search firm to immediately call one of its clients whose attributes seem to match the company's job description.

Professional Associations

Local, state, and national organizations usually have their own placement services. Professional and semi-professional associations of personnel in accounting, advertising, engineering, health care, office management, computers, computer programming, marketing, finance, real estate, and most other business-related areas maintain flourishing placement services. In addition, they usually have speakers from corporations at their monthly meetings who can provide good leads. And of course, the members themselves are often aware of openings.

Individuals who are in the job market or about to enter it should join and attend the meetings of their professional society.

Instructors and Friends

Most college instructors who are active as authorities or consultants in their field have many contacts in companies that work or manufacture in their areas of specialization. Get acquainted with these professors; let them know you're in the job market. If you have distinguished yourself in their class or in your school, they will usually be happy to recommend you. The same is true of your own personal friends of even friends of your parents. Sometimes a phone call will do wonders when made on your behalf by a respected individual.

Advertisements

This is an obvious area: checking personnel ads in newspapers, magazines, and professional journals. Responding to an ad necessitates writing and mailing a résumé. Selecting the right ad to reply to is a task in itself, which will be discussed later in this chapter. The other side of the coin is to place an ad yourself indicating your availability.

STEPS PRECEDING THE JOB SEARCH

As with any important assignment, the job search should be preceded by careful planning, reading, and self-analysis. To assist you in determining the kind of job you want and to review others' ideas on careers, career planning, and the job search, you will find it helpful to spend several evenings doing some reading. A few suggestions are listed at the end of this chapter.

Of particular interest in Richard N. Bolles' *What Color Is Your Parachute?* is a listing of some three hundred different reference sources on careers and career planning. There are titles concerned with vocational planning, general books on job hunting, and books specifically for women, minority members, handicapped people, executives, and those interested in jobs in government and the military as well as those looking for volunteer opportunities. Specialized books are also listed for setting up your own business, selling, and a dozen other areas. In addition to this, a computer search of articles on jobs, résumés, and careers will generate dozens of titles of journal articles for just the past four years.

Obviously you can become mired down in reading about careers and opportunities and never get to the job search. That would be a terrible error. However, it is helpful for almost everyone in the job market to do *some* reading and determine whether or not his or her philosophy needs some change in direction.

Self-Analysis

After reading, one should move into the exercise of self-analysis to determine what he or she has to offer the prospective employer. What professional attributes do I possess? What are my specific capabilities? How expert am I in finance? Accounting? Do I enjoy working with others or not? How fluent am I in French? Can I handle business programs on the computer? Do I like to assume responsibilities? What is my level of initiative? Do I work well with others? How effectively do I supervise others or take orders from others? What are my strengths? What are my weaknesses?

One of the best ways to get to know yourself in preparation for interviewing is to write out, then talk out, your answers to the following questions.

Ten Windows to Who You Are and What You Want

1. How would you describe your personality?
2. What kind of people do you enjoy working with?
3. List three work-related activities you take pleasure in and three work-related activities you dislike.

4. Are you motivated more by praise or criticism? Why?
5. How much of your personal life are you willing to give in commitment to a job?
6. Do you seek work that contributes in an overt way to the development and well being of our society?
7. How important is money to you? What aspects of your life are you willing to compromise or sacrifice for financial gain?
8. How quickly do you want to "climb the ladder" within a company?
9. How patient are you with repetitive tasks? To what degree do you require variety and excitement in your job?
10. Where do you want to find yourself in ten years? How do you plan to get there?

In addition to this self-analysis, you should also visit the campus counseling center and career and placement offices. The personnel in these offices can usually give you excellent counsel and advice on your areas of competence, the future potential of many fields, salary levels, and related information.

The more you learn about a job in an interview and the more you know about your own desires and capabilities, the more easily you can determine whether or not this position is one you can work in most efficiently and enjoyably.

This self-analysis should include your written plans for the future. And these might well be headed "Long Term and Short Term." But keep in mind that there are only twenty-four hours in the day, and your planning, therefore, should include separate sections to cover career, personal, family, recreational, financial, and other concerns that are vital to you. The point is, if you don't know where you want to go, you won't get there! Or you may arrive somewhere, but not at the time in your life or at the level you desire.

What Do Employers Look for in Employees?

Corporations make an investment when they hire an individual, and it is not illogical that they expect to secure a fair ROI (return on investment). It is therefore understandable that they will look for specific qualities or assets. Here are some of the attributes that are important. How do you measure up?

Loyalty Employers will look at your length of employment in previous jobs, what you have to say about previous supervisors, companies, and teachers, and other evidence of your ability to follow through.

Cooperativeness How well do you get along with others? Do you work well with colleagues, especially under difficult situations? Do you handle stress well, especially in group work?

Industriousness and Commitment   Are you a hard worker? An employer tries to measure this by looking at accomplishments, grades, part-time work assignments while attending school, the quality of the application letter, and other items.

Ability to Communicate   In the modern world the ability to communicate effectively in writing and speaking is critical. Have you served as an officer in an organization? Have any of your writings been published? How well do you come across in the interview? Do you enjoy speaking before groups?

Wide Interests   Do you have interests in art, music, world affairs, books? Will you be able to carry on intelligent conversations with clients in social as well as business settings?

Ambition and Drive   How far do you want to go? Applicants who wish to move to management and executive positions are sought. Companies know that "hard drivers" who wish to go to the top will surely benefit the organization as a result of their own efforts and ambition. In addition, if an employee wants to secure an advanced degree while working, that in itself is evidence of his or her ambition.

Organization and Punctuality   Your organization and planning skills are evident in your short- and long-term career plans, the quality of your résumé, and the level of preparation made for the interview.

Good Physical and Mental Health   Because employee health problems cause loss in production and increased insurance costs, firms prefer employees who do not have such problems. Of course, a physically handicapped individual does not fall into this category. Most physically handicapped persons, when matched with the correct task, are extremely productive.

Good Appearance   Firms want you to look good—not necessarily attractive, but neat and well groomed, as evidenced by your clothes, hair, posture, and, most important, smile.

Researching the Job and the Job Market

Perhaps the first area to be checked is the specific job. If your abilities permit you to apply in two or more areas, which specific type of job has the best potential in the years ahead? Should you concentrate on computers or inventory control or cost accounting or auditing or personnel management if you have ability and knowledge in each of these areas? Of course, opportunities that become available within the company in the years ahead will also determine your career path. But you can help shape your future by making specific choices early in your career.

The second area to check is the job market itself. Examine the classified ad section of local as well as out-of-town newspapers; read the job-opportunities section of your professional journals; examine the list of jobs available at your college placement office; have interviews with company recruiters who visit your school; read the job-opportunity bulletins sent out by government agencies and corporations; take suggestions from your college professors, friends, and associates; check out such books as *The College Placement Annual* and others listed at the end of this chapter. Finally, and sometimes most effectively, send out letters of application to top-level firms and take advantage of the resulting interviews.

What about the companies in which employment is available? This is a third area to research. What are the firms' futures? What are their objectives? Do they or will they participate in space-age technology? What are their earning records? Their plans for expansion? Diversification? What do the records reflect in financial and personnel growth? Is there a possibility that the firms will merge or be "taken over"? What facts can be gained from their annual reports? What do knowledgeable people think about a particular firm? Does the company have a reputation for retaining its personnel for long periods or is there frequent change and turnover? Check *The Wall Street Journal,* the *Fortune 500* list, *Dun's Review,* and individual company annual reports, which you will find in most good libraries.

Because your future success is intimately associated with that of your employer, you should make every effort to take a position with a firm that seems to have a bright and dependable future.

Job Advertisements   If you are not already familiar with advertisements that list openings, begin reading them immediately. You will find announcements in your professional journals, the classified sections of major urban newspapers, and in *The Wall Street Journal* and *Barrons.* In addition, the sports or financial sections of major newspapers will often carry large ads (3 by 4 inches, 4 by 5 inches), known as display ads, listing professional job openings. This type of ad is also found in financial newspapers such as *The Wall Street Journal.*

Read job ads critically. In almost every case, recognize that spending time answering the top ad on this page would be wasted effort on your part. An ad of this type has been put in to attract individuals who will work on a commission basis only, or to secure names for an employment agency, or to build someone's mailing list, or for a number of other reasons that should not be relevant to you.

The ad that you should reply to, big or small, is the same one that other ambitious, intelligent people will find attractive. The ads on this page are typical of those found in the classified columns. The display ad usually lists advanced qualifications, higher salary, ability to handle responsibility, and several years' experience.[2]

Examine your own qualifications and attempt to match those listed in the ad. Choose only ads that are appropriate. If the ad calls for "10–12 years' experience as a corporate controller" and you are a 22-year-old recent graduate, there is little point in wasting your time or theirs by responding.

PERSONAL JOB APPLICATIONS

The value of the time-honored letter of application is still very high. Probably 50 percent of professional jobs are secured as the result of the cover letter and résumé sent out by someone who is looking for a first-time job or by someone who is presently employed but is making an effort toward self-improvement.

A recent survey of 500 corporate chief personnel officers indicated their preferences in personal résumés.[3] They stated that they preferred that an applicant's initial contact with the firm be made in writing. A résumé of one or two pages was the desired length; work experience, special aptitudes, health status, and willingness to relocate were indicated as vital. Respondents also stated they wanted to know specifically how an applicant's qualifications fitted the job. A list of three references and their titles was also listed as desirable. And overall qualities such as neatness, tone, correctness, good grammar, and appearance were vital. The ability to communicate was rated as the most important job-related skill (along with computer knowledge) by both students and recruiters in a 1984 survey.[4] The interpretation of "ability to communicate" involved writing skills as well as speaking ability at the interview and in front of groups.

One résumé-related problem that has arisen recently involves validity of content. In just the past six years or so, a number of articles have appeared concerning phony résumés. Personnel directors and recruiters increasingly

---

[2]P. S. Rooney, "Teaching the Job Search: Yet Another Approach," *ABCA Bulletin*, March 1982. This article gives hints on how to interpret job advertisements and job descriptions.

[3]B. Wells, N. Spinks, J. Hargrave, "A Survey of Chief Personnel Officers in the 500 Largest Corporations in the U.S. to Determine Their Preferences in Job Application Letters and Personal Résumés," *ABCA Bulletin*, June 1981.

[4]John Penrose, "A Discrepancy Analysis of the Job-Getting Process and a Study of Resume Techniques," *Journal of Business Communication*, Summer, 1984.

report that "facts" in some résumés are false and statements concerning education and experience are very often open to question.[5,6,7,8,9] What this means to you is obvious. In writing your cover letter and résumé, remember to be as specific as possible. List not only such information as degrees received, places of employment, and military service, but be sure to add specific dates, addresses, names of individuals, and other items that will not only lend credibility to what you've said but are also easily verifiable.

Types of Applications   Keep in mind that the job search letter is a type of sales letter: instead of selling a product or a service, you are selling yourself in a quiet yet forceful manner.[10] Naturally, there is always an internal struggle on the writer's part about how to sound acceptably modest and at the same time impress the potential employer with personal achievements. The line is a fine one, but it can be achieved with care, concern, and attention to the details of good writing.

Basically, there are two types of applications: the *solicited* letter, in which you are replying to an advertisement or an announcement by a firm, government agency, or institution; and the *unsolicited* letter, in which you send an inquiry to one or more firms, asking about job openings and requesting an interview.

If you reply to an ad or announcement, you know an opening exists but you will encounter competition. An interesting and inviting ad that prompts you to write will probably also bring letters from fifty to a hundred other applicants. You don't face this level of competition when you mail an unsolicited letter. But on the other hand, the company may have no immediate opening for you. That should not be a major deterrent, however. Large industrial corporations usually have dozens of persons working in manage-

---

[5]J. Davidson, "Paper Tigers Come in More Resumes than One," *ABA Banking Journal,* April 1984.

[6]R. P. Vecchio, "The Problem of Phony Resumes: How to Spot a Ringer Among the Applicants," *Personnel,* March–April 1984.

[7]S. Spang, "Business Besieged by Bogus Resumes," *Business and Society Review,* Winter 1984.

[8]J. Gallant and L. Haber, "DP Managers Say False Resumes Common," *Computerworld,* October 17, 1983.

[9]J. Davidson, "How to Spot a Phony Resume," *Supervisory Management,* May 1983.

[10]D. Watkins, "Sales Letters and Application Letters: Drawing the Parallel," *ABCA Bulletin,* June 1983.

ment, finance, engineering, accounting, and marketing. If an opening does not exist at the time your unsolicited letter is received, there will surely be one shortly and many corporations are quite willing to hire you immediately for the opening that is certain to appear in the near future.[11]

The formats for both solicited and unsolicited letters are as follows:

One-part: Brief presentation of all necessary facts in a letter.

Two-part: Introductory and summarizing cover letter accompanied by a résumé.

Job brochure: A booklet containing a few pages outlining in detail education, experience, membership in organizations, honors, awards, copies of letters of reference, and samples of work. This is usually used by an executive with a good deal of experience.

Let us now look at the attributes and makeup of job-seeking letters and then return to examples of the complete message presented in various forms.

LETTER ORGANIZATION

The job letter, like the sales letter, attempts to sell. The latter attempts to sell a product or service, but in the job letter, the writer attempts to "sell" the best possible picture of himself or herself.

Like the sales message, the application letter can be divided into several sections: First it attempts to *arouse the reader's interest* in the job seeker, then *describes the background* that makes the applicant eligible for the job, *continues with proof* for the statements made by citing degrees, places of former employment, and references, and concludes with a *request for an interview* (or the sale itself).

Obviously the amount of detail and the general approach differ depending on whether the letter is a cover (or covering) letter to a résumé, or an application letter for a job not accompanied by a résumé.

Arousing Interest

Prospective employers are not usually impressed with cute or clever openings, nor are they intrigued with the stereotyped "this is in reply to your ad" approach. Avoid openings such as the following, which revolve around the writer and are dull:

---

[11]In the Wells, Spinks, and Hargrave survey noted previously, 89 percent of the respondents agreed strongly or moderately that "letters of application are welcomed even though there are no job openings at present."

On June 5 I shall receive my degree from Central College and then will be ready to take a professional position with your firm.

This is in reply to your ad which appeared in the June 27 issue of the Times.

After many years of study and application, I have reached my goal and am now available to consider the position you have available.

The openings below are concisely worded, give the reader a quick overview of the applicant's qualifications, and indicate how the company can benefit from the applicant's abilities. The employer's attention is arrested when the applicant indicates major attributes and how they will help the company. This is the time for the writer to use the *you* attitude sincerely and effectively.

Your recent advertisement for a college graduate with a degree in marketing and part-time business experience seems to fit my qualifications.

A college degree in accounting, a CPA certificate, and three years' experience working directly under a corporate controller should certainly qualify me for the position you described in yesterday's Sunday Sun.

Ability to type, take dictation, speak intelligently to customers, clients, or patients, come up with an original idea occasionally, and be pleasant and good-humored are surely the attributes you'd like in the "Guy or Gal Friday" for whom you advertised. I have these qualities plus a good many others. Here are some details.

The three openings immediately preceding have merit; they are fresh, original, and indicate how the applicant's abilities will help the firm. (For some jobs, such as advertising and copywriting positions, it might be advisable to inject a real attention-getting statement, an intriguing sentence, or a startling and clever paragraph.) The opening statement also affords a good opportunity to give your reader a capsule account of your primary selling points: experience, education, special abilities, and the like.

Describing Your Abilities

In the one-part letter of application, clear and specific statements should be made describing your education, experience, leadership abilities, and awards. In the two-part letter, these accomplishments are alluded to rather generally in the cover letter and specifically listed in the résumé.

The description should be written to match the job's requirements or the ad's demands. If experience is emphasized in the job description and you possess it, this should be treated in some detail. If education is vital or leadership qualities important, then they should be emphasized. The sample letters displayed in Figures 19–1 and 19–2 illustrate several different methods for handling these situations.

FIGURE 19-1
One-part letter-résumé

This is a well-written and well-organized letter. The writer has made a strong effort to make reading and understanding easy through the use of topic headings, short paragraphs, and clear writing.

4150 North Wescott Lane
Kalamazoo, MI   49008
June 27, 19__

Personnel Director
Brunswick Corporation
One Brunswick Square
Skokie, IL   60203

Dear Director:

My college background, two years of part-time experience as an accounting clerk, three years' work in corporate training, and a keen desire to work in the field of human resource development qualify me to fill the position described in the <u>Midwest Accounting Journal</u>.

Your ad, which called for an "Associate Director of Training, is exactly what I had in mind.

<u>Experience</u>

During my last two years in college and for two summers I worked as an accounting clerk for Price Waterhouse. After graduation from the School of Business of Western Michigan University, I secured employment in the Management Training Department of Michigan Central Electronics Corporation. In this capacity, I am responsible for scheduling and coordinating various training programs for middle mangement-level employees.

I am still with Michigan and would not leave except for the limited opportunities for advancement in the training area which currently exist here.

<u>Education</u>

In 19__ I received my bachelor of science degree from the School of Business of Western Michigan University. My major area of study was marketing, with a minor in finance. I also served as teaching assistant in finance at Western Michigan.

Next year I hope to enroll in an evening Masters Program in Organizational Design and Development.

<u>Personal Data</u>

I am 26 years old, in excellent health, and very active in outdoor sports. I am an active member of the Academy of Management, the Finance Association, and the American Society for Training and Development (ASTD).

<u>References</u>

You may wish to check my background with any or all of the following individuals:

Dr. J. Bowman   Robert Kelbourne, Manager
School of Business   Price Waterhouse
Western Michigan University   234 S. Michigan Blvd.
Kalamazoo, MI 49008   Chicago, IL 60604

                                     Roberta Clark, Senior Accountant
Joan T. Morrison,   Price Waterhouse
Vice President   234 S. Michigan Blvd.
Human Resources Department   Chicago, IL 60604
Central Electronics Corporation
Industry Square
Milwaukee, WI 53203

Because of my background, I am sure I can do an outstanding job for Brunswick. I am familiar with your fine products and am eager to join your team. Please call me at 301/421-4211 so that an interview can be arranged. I have much more to tell you; I'm sure you have many questions to ask.

                    Sincerely yours,

                    Marilyn Berman

                    Marilyn Berman

FIGURE 19–2
One-part letter-résumé

This one-part letter is somewhat unusual in that it is concerned primarily with experience. That is quite acceptable for an applicant in this age category and with this quantity of experience

1020 W. Sunset Drive
Burbank, CA 91509
August 18, 19___

Director of Operations
Elton Electronics Organization
2000 Phoenix Square
Phoenix, AZ 80550

Dear Sir:

According to the <u>Phoenix Sun</u>, Elton Electronics is rapidly expanding as a result of being selected as a subcontractor for the DOD X-51 Missile System. Although I have been employed by Lockheed California for several years, I would be very interested in applying my electronics knowledge in your firm. This would permit me to move to Arizona where I have family and friends.

I have detailed below some of my assignments, which will provide an introduction to my background.

ELECTRONICS ENGINEER
From 1970 to 1974 I was employed by Motorola in Chicago as an electronics engineer with special application to mobile car telephones. In this capacity I helped develop a new monitoring system for which a patent was issued to the company.

MANAGER, ELECTRONIC TRANSMISSION SYSTEMS
In 1974 I moved to California, where I secured employment with a division of Hughes Aircraft. In just eight months I was made manager of a radar development group which worked on the Seascope, a sophisti-cated onboard system presently used by U.S. Naval vessels. I left Hughes in 1978 to accept an invitation from IBM in New York.

ENGINEER, AIR TO AIR GUIDANCE SYSTEMS
From 1978 to 1981 I was at IBM involved with management information systems as they applied to guidance controls. My responsibilities included supervising several technicians and six engineers. Our program was successfully completed and manufacturing begun. Several applications of the original work were spun off and applied to related projects.

SENIOR ENGINEER, ADVANCED PRODUCTS
In 1981 I accepted an offer from the Lockheed California Company and moved to California. As a senior engineer, I supervise a department charged with specific project development on highly classified work.

In all the positions listed above, 1970 to the present, evaluations of my competence, work habits, and personal attributes have been either "excellent" or "superior."

EDUCATION
I received both undergraduate and graduate degrees in Electronic Engineering from the University of Illinois. Attendance at numerous seminars has permitted me to keep abreast of my field.

From time to time I have also taught in evening divisions of universities in a conscious effort to keep up-to-date, rather than to supplement my income.

PUBLICATIONS
Since 1979 I have published five papers in various publications. In addition, I have appeared as a speaker in the annual conventions of the Western States Aeronautical Engineers Association in 1982, 1985, and 1988.

REFERENCES
These will be furnished in detail on request.

PERSONAL
I am 42 years old, in excellent health, a U.S. citizen, and happily married. I enjoy outdoor sports, especially skiing.

I shall be happy to fly to Phoenix for an interview or meet with you if you are in the Southern California area. I am eager to move to Phoenix and associate myself with a firm of your high caliber.

Sincerely yours,

Marcus Clark

Marcus Clark

When your résumé accompanies the job search letter, use the letter to pique the reader's interest through highlights of your academic or work experience. In short, give the reader something to look for when he or she turns to your résumé. Here is such a highlight statement from a brief job search letter.

> *Ms. Victors, you may find particular interest in my internship with IBM during the summer of 19___ . As described more fully in my résumé, that position certainly gave me "hands-on" experience in computer marketing.*

When Ms. Victors turns to the résumé, she will not be perusing it to see what catches her eye. Instead, she will be *looking* for something—in this case, the IBM experience. When she finds it, she will experience a double satisfaction: first, the pleasure of simply finding what she was looking for; and second, the pleasure of recognizing the applicant's accomplishments. When a reader feels satisfaction, the writer has achieved an important goal.

Proving Your Statements

In the one-part application letter, your references, degrees, and former employers (all proof of your abilities) may be indicated specifically, but in the cover letter of a two-part application, they are only referred to, leaving them for the résumé or data sheet.

In listing degrees it is wise to indicate specific areas of study. When noting previous employment, a brief description of duties and responsibilities should appear so that the prospective employer has some idea of what you can do. And the same thing is true of any activities that illustrate leadership qualities: offices held, meetings conducted, articles written, conferences attended. The applicant should remember to list volunteer work in religious, civic, or charitable organizations. Human resource managers report they are looking for individuals with volunteer experience. Such background indicates the use of valuable skills that are easily transferable to the job market.[12]

Getting the Interview—the Request for Action

In both the cover letter for the résumé and the one-part letter of application, the final statements are usually concerned with making arrangements for the job interview. This should *not* be a simple "If you are interested, please call me" or "If you have any questions, I shall be pleased to answer them."

Your request for an interview should be emphatic and positive, and should clearly state that you want the interview so that you can tell the pro-

---

[12]M. Zippo and H. Z. Levine, "Volunteer Experience: A Plus on Any Resume," *Personnel,* September/October 1984.

spective employer about your attributes in greater detail than appear in the letter and résumé. Perhaps an implied statement can be made indicating that what has been said in the letter is only part of the story (as it can only be) and that the interview is desired to expand, add, and clarify details.

> *May I have an interview so that we can discuss in greater detail my education, experience, and other qualifications for the position? I can be reached . . .*

> *I would appreciate an opportunity to meet with you so that I can explain more completely how my experience, education, ability to work hard and take responsibility all qualify me for the job. Please call or write . . .*

> *When can we get together? The sooner the better so that I can give you a more complete picture of how a degree in accounting, six years of responsible work as assistant to the controller, and a desire to work very hard where opportunity is unlimited can be put to use by the Cantrel Corporation.*

THE ONE-PART JOB APPLICATION

Although the cover letter and résumé are most popular and effective in the modern job market, there are some individuals who prefer the simple letter of application (see Figures 19–1 and 19–2).

The one-part letter usually is general in nature and somewhat brief. For the individual who lacks some qualifications for the job but is eager to secure an interview, this type of letter may have some merit. The *lack* of qualifications may not be as apparent in the one-part letter as it might be on the résumé or elsewhere in the two-part letter.

KEY POINTS TO REMEMBER

Several very interesting facts were determined concerning all types of application letters and résumé in the survey of Fortune 500 personnel directors mentioned earlier:

- The initial contact by the job applicant should be in writing.
- Letters of application are highly desirable even though there are no job openings at present in the company.
- A satisfactory tone, good grammar, proper spelling, typing (not handwriting), and neatness are absolutely essential attributes of the application letter-résumé.
- A one- or two-page résumé is much more desirable than a three-page résumé.

- Three references should be listed. The types of persons listed are of major importance to the personnel directors in the company.[13]
- Previous work experience and/or special aptitudes are of major importance in the résumé.
- The traditional order of listing information in a résumé is preferred over all other methods.

Perhaps the most important factor in seeking a full-time job or in making a career change is to go about the task optimistically and systematically. There are positions available out there, and if you use the correct procedure, you will be successful. But it is absolutely vital to determine what you want and what you have to offer. Next, what does the market want? Once these facts are known, it is then essential to match all the factors involved. Be careful not to shoot too high or too low.

Approach the task as you would a campaign. Don't be content with responding to one ad or applying to one company. If you use an unsolicited résumé approach, select ten to twenty prospective companies and drop letters to all in the mail simultaneously. If you are answering ads, respond to the ten you have carefully selected. In that way, if you receive five invitations for interviews, you can schedule them all within a few days, select the best job, and make a commitment.

If you send out only one letter and wait a week for a reply, and then another letter and wait a week, you may stretch your job search out to three months.

Above all, *work* at finding the job that will challenge and reward you to your satisfaction. The positions are out there. Companies are always looking for hard-working qualified individuals. You *can* secure what you want and are qualified for, if you expend the effort in a logical and well-organized manner.

SELECTED BIBLIOGRAPHY

Books About Job-Seeking

D. Berliner, *Want a Job? Get Some Experience. Want Experience? Get a Job,* New York: American Management Association, 1978.

J. R. Birsner, *Jobhunting for the 40+ Executive,* Facts on File, 1985.

Richard N. Bolles, *What Color Is Your Parachute?* Berkeley, CA: Ten Speed Press, 1981.

---

[13]In the survey referred to in the Wells *et al* study (see footnote 3), personnel directors were found to place major importance on the types of persons listed as references.

D. P. Campbell, *If You Don't Know Where You're Going, You'll Probably End Up Somewhere Else*, Niles, IL: Argus Communications, 1974.

Marvin J. Cetron, *Jobs for the Future*, New York: McGraw-Hill, 1984.

R. J. Gerberg, *The Professional Job Changing System*, Parsippany, NJ: Performance Dynamics, 1980.

D. R. German, J. W. German, *How to Find a Job When Jobs Are Hard to Find*, New York: American Management Association, 1981.

Mary Healey, *The Job-winning Resume Kit*, Westbury, NY: Caddylak Publications, 1985.

G. Howes, *Career Tomorrow*, Times Mirror, New York: 1979. Describes career tracks, forecasts future demand, and suggests ideas for reaching career goals.

Barbara Karchin, *Job Search Strategies*, Hinsdale, IL: Continuing Education Systems, 1985.

C. G. Moore, *The Career Game*, National Institute of Career Planning, 1976.

D. B. Peskin, *Sacked*, New York: American Management Association, 1979.

R. J. Rinella, C. C. Robbins, *Career Power*, New York: American Management Association, 1980.

P. I. Robbins, *Successful Midlife Career Change*, New York: American Management Association, 1978.

H. L. Rust, *Job Search*, New York: American Management Association, 1979.

J. Shingleton and R. Bao, *College to Career: Finding Yourself in the Job Market*, New York: McGraw-Hill, 1977.

Books About Occupations and Careers

Career Planning Handbooks: A Guide to Career Fields and Opportunities, U.S. Civil Service Commission, U.S. Government Printing Office, Washington, DC.

Dictionary of Occupational Titles, U.S. Department of Labor, U.S. Government Printing Office, Washington, DC. Describes skills and characteristics for 23,000 occupations.

Occupational Outlook Handbook, U.S. Bureau of Labor Statistics, U.S. Government Printing Office, Washington, DC. Lists employment opportunities in various fields.

Career Information Service, Box 51, Madison Square Station, New York, NY.

Career, Career Inc., 15 W. 45th Street, New York, NY. Lists employment opportunities in leading organizations.

Directories and Guides

College Placement Annual, College Placement Council, 35 East Elizabeth Street, Bethlehem, PA. Contains a listing of almost 2000 organizations, their addresses, contacts, and related information.

College Placement Directory, Industrial Research Service, Dover, NH. Some 1500 business firms are described, with their addresses, types of graduates desired, etc. Like the *Annual,* it also has an occupational and geographical index.

Foreign Operations, Foreign Operations, Inc. New Haven, CT. Lists overseas employment opportunities.

Dun and Bradstreet Middle Market Directory. Lists names, addresses, and phones of about 23,000 firms.

Dun and Bradstreet Million Dollar Directory. Similar to above but for firms of over $1 million net worth.

Fortune Magazine's Directory of Largest Corporations. Published in four parts.

Poor's Register of Directors and Executives; U.S. and Canada. Standard and Poor's Corporation, 345 Hudson Street, New York, NY. Lists 27,000 firms, addresses, principal products, and key officers.

Thomas' Register of American Manufacturers, Thomas Publishing, 461 Eighth Avenue, New York, NY.

QUESTIONS FOR STUDY

1. No rigid set of rules can be given to determine when to quit a job. What personal signals will tell you when it is time to look for a new position?
2. Discuss the place of persuasion in a job letter. In particular, show how the job letter is organized to fulfill needs perceived by the employer.
3. What is an unsolicited employment letter? How does it differ from a solicited employment letter?
4. Why is it important to know your own goals and abilities before beginning the job search?
5. Comment on the pros and cons of using the one-part job application letter.

6. Which source of job placements is usually best for applicants just grad-uating from college? Why?
7. What should be highlighted in the letter accompanying your résumé?
8. What is a "job brochure" and who would logically use it?
9. What is often a problem in using a résumé prepared for you by someone else?
10. Good application letters lead to action on the part of the employer. What specific action should be requested in an application letter?
11. Who might want to use a one-part job application instead of the two-part process?
12. If you are using the unsolicited application letter approach, should you send out one letter at a time and wait for a response or use some other procedure? Explain.
13. How can writers of application letters avoid inappropriate boasting while trying to "sell" themselves to a prospective employer?
14. What is an executive search firm?
15. What are four questions that should guide your own evaluation of what you have to offer a prospective employer?

EXERCISES

16. Talk to at least five recent job applicants to determine what interview questions they found most difficult to answer. List those questions, then write out your own response to each.
17. Visit an employment agency to inquire about their fees and policies. Write a "trip report" detailing what the agency does for an applicant, what the obligations of the applicant are, and any other pertinent information.
18. Prove it! List at least five elements of proof you could cite in your appli-cation letter and résumé to support the contention that you are qualified for the job you want.
19. Read the job ads critically. For the profession you want to join, obtain three employment notices. Select ads that differ in the way they describe the job and its responsibilities and compensation. Critically analyze each ad. Clearly identify which job of the three is best for you and why.
20. What are the advantages of using the free placement bureau on the col-lege campus? Write to the director of one campus placement bureau and ask him or her to identify the primary benefits of using the on-campus service. Your instructor will coordinate this assignment so each student writes to a different director.
21. The admissions office of your college has advertised the position of "recruitment counselor" in the campus newspaper. The ad specifies that

the graduating student must do a considerable amount of traveling to recruit students for your college. The position requires many on-campus public relations activities. Résumés are to be sent to Dr. Margaret West-lund, Director of Admissions.

You have a fine résumé, but you know that for this sales-oriented job you had best develop a good cover letter. Develop a four-paragraph letter in which each paragraph accomplishes one purpose of the job letter. Be prepared to discuss how you accomplished the various goals of the "sales" letter in this application.

22. You want to contact an employment agency for help in securing your first full-time job. However, you are unsure how such agencies work—especially when it comes to the payment of fees. Using the telephone book for a major metropolitan area, identify at least three employment agencies. Write to each of them to discover how they handle fees for their clients. Keep writing to agencies until you obtain at least one answer. Be prepared to discuss in class the topic of fees for clients of employment agencies.

23. The job market climate sometimes changes rapidly. This can be discouraging for a college student who spends years preparing for a particular profession and then, at graduation time, finds that the market for her or his vocation has turned sour. However, with some planning and careful observation, you can avoid such problems and stay on top of the employment market.

Identify a specific job in the profession you want to pursue. In correct bibliographical form, list the following:

- Two books published within the past two years that provide you with information relative to your specific job hunt.
- Two articles published in bulletins or journals (published within the past year) that provide specific projections for your profession.
- Two items from newspapers or current periodicals (published within the past six months) that provide a current update on the prospects of your profession.

Premised upon your research, do the following in a short report:

- Describe the job outlook for the profession you want to enter.
- Explain how the outlook will influence your job hunt strategy.

24. Interview a personnel director of a corporation. What does he or she want to see in effective job application letters and résumés? What mistakes are often made by job applicants? What "tricks of the trade" can he or she tell you about the job application process? Write up the results of your interview for your instructor.

25. Revise each of the following one-part application letters (only the letter body appears). In your revision, strive to be clear, enthusiastic, specific, and thorough. You will no doubt want to add details and topics not supplied in these flawed samples.

a. As you may have read in the newspaper, Western University will be holding its graduation for business majors on June 7, 19__ . I am one of those graduating (major in Finance) and, of course, I'm trying to find a job. That's what this letter is about.

I would describe myself as hard-working, intelligent, and sociable. Once I take on a task you can be sure it will be done on time and in a competent fashion. My past job experiences and university work have proven that.

The job I'm particularly interested in is the one you advertised last week in the classified section. You didn't mention much about the benefits in the advertisement, so please send me information on that topic as soon as possible.

If you want me to come in for an interview, please keep in mind that I can't come on Mondays, Tuesdays, or Thursdays due to classes that I'm finishing up at Western. I understand that you hire a lot of Western graduates and I hope you'll hire me.

b. It has come to my attention that you seek an entry-level employee recently matriculated from a major university with a business-related degree.

Without presuming to know your specific requirements, I can with some assurance say that I am such a person. Barring unforeseen complications in my current classwork, I shall be granted the undergraduate degree in Marketing from Bingham State University on the seventh of June, 19__ . While my extensive academic references summarize my academic career in some detail, I may mention here that my grade point average qualified me for the Dean's list all but one semester (the lapse due to what I still consider a blatant case of professorial incompetence).

As you may surmise from this correspondence, I believe I can bring a certain lustre and panache to your organization—the touch of class, if you will, that distinguishes true corporate enterprise from mere business.

Should you wish to speak personally before concluding our arrangements for this position, I shall make every effort to find a place for you on my calendar. You may contact me directly at 290-3923 or leave a message with my mother at 382-3894.

20 Résumés and Employment Interviews

The prospective employer's primary question is "What can you contribute to my organization?"

What is the most important business document you've ever written? When asked that question, Roger Wyse—a remarkably successful young aerospace manager—didn't name a particular memo, letter, proposal, or report. "The document that has meant the most in my career rise," Wyse says, "has been my résumé."

This short document sums up "you" in a page or two. Because it is so vital to your job-seeking and job-changing efforts, the résumé deserves your best effort. The résumé also has uses over and beyond the job search. It can be used as a substantiating document when you submit an article or a paper for publication, when you file for office, or when you apply for credit. People who ask you to lead or serve on a committee or give a speech or be a member of a panel will find your résumé helpful.

The résumé should be looked upon as something that grows with the individual. It should be written early in your career and then revised and updated as your career progresses, your goals change, and your background becomes richer. The style, format, and layout of résumés change with the times, and yours should change also.

This chapter will first discuss résumé, followed by the cover letter to the résumé, the combined cover letter and résumé, the job interview situation, and finally job-related letters of various types. Examine all the materials carefully and use them, when needed, as a basis for your own efforts. Although you would not want to *copy* a cover letter, résumé, or job acceptance letter, you can derive ideas from the samples shown. They should assist you in "building" your own job-related communications—both résumés and solicited and unsolicited letters of application.

Looking at résumés first forces us to summarize our major strengths and weaknesses as they apply to the job search. Once we have listed our attributes under specific headings such as experience, education, personal attributes, volunteer work, references, honors, and so forth, we can see which areas may be emphasized and which must be handled with care.

Making up the résumé *before* the cover letter is like preparing an outline *prior* to writing a report or essay. It tells us what to emphasize in what depth and in which order in the cover letter.

THE RÉSUMÉ

The résumé should be prepared so that it can stand alone, without a cover letter. In some situations in which a résumé is needed—prior to giving a speech or when you are asked to serve on a committee, for instance—not all the items of information on the résumé may apply. But their presence does not detract from the effect of the résumé.

Length

Perhaps the best answer to the question of length is the one Abraham Lincoln supposedly gave when asked, "How long should a thoroughbred horse's legs be?" to which he replied, "Long enough to reach the ground." So too with the résumé: long enough to cover the subject and no longer. A common modern admonition is to keep the résumé to one page. This is good advice if all the facts needed will fit easily on a single page. But to omit important and persuasive information just to adhere to this limit is foolish. If a prospective employer is going to make an investment of thousands of dollars in an employee, he or she won't mind reading a second page. As a matter of fact, more details are better than fewer. And if you choose to list three or four impressive references, it is almost impossible to keep your résumé to one page. Thus, prepare your résumé first, including all information necessary. Check it carefully for clarity, conciseness, completeness, and attractiveness. Use the number of pages the result requires. If you should encounter a rigid one-page requirement from an association, a group you are addressing, or even a prospective employer, and your résumé is somewhat longer than a page, have it typed on a large sheet of paper (17" × 22") and then reduce it so it fits comfortably on an $8\frac{1}{2}$" × 11" sheet of paper. Most modern office copiers are capable of reducing (or enlarging) materials a significant percentage. Once reduced, the items are still perfectly legible and balanced nicely on the page.

Content

Most résumés cover the following areas, although not always in this precise order:

- Name, address, and phone number
- Career objective(s)
- Major qualifications
- Education
- Experience
- Awards, honors, organizations
- Personal data
- References

Career Objective(s)   In your career objective, you may wish to specify both your short-term and long-range goals. Be careful to do so tactfully so that you do not sound brash or insensitive.

An immediate association with a firm as a junior accountant. Eventually I hope to become a vice president of finance where I can make a significant contribution to the growth of a progressive organization.

Note the strong use of the "you" attitude above. The applicant says he or she wishes to contribute to the firm; the statement does not say, "I expect to increase *my* knowledge," or "I'm looking for a firm that will reward *me* very well financially for my efforts."

It is proper and acceptable to indicate that you wish to rise to "vice-president, operations," or "a controller's position," or "a top management position in a high-tech organization." Most prospective employers are delighted to hire ambitious people. They know that a young person who wishes to become a vice president of marketing will probably work hard to attain that goal and, in the process, carry the firm forward as he or she ascends.

A word of caution is in order, however. Be sure that the career objective section is worded in such a way that attaining your goals will also be beneficial to the organization (you-attitude).

Major Qualifications[1]   This also is a brief (two- to four-line) statement. In essence it is a short summary of your major selling points. Don't trumpet your qualifications but do list them; no one else will do it for you.

A degree in accounting, two years of part-time plus one year of full-time experience with a major accounting firm, and a recently acquired CPA certificate.

---

[1]See also K. L. Hutchinson, "Personnel Administrators' Preferences for Résumé Content: A Survey and Review of Empirically Based Conclusions," *Journal of Business Communication*, Fall 1984.

Collegiate background in marketing, on-the-job consumer research experi-
ence, creative abilities in problem-solving, and proven ability to work with oth-
ers are some of the qualifications I can offer your firm.

Education and Experience   These two sections will doubtless take up most of the space in your résumé. How you handle them is critical because they are vital to "selling" you to a potential employer. If your major selling point is education, list that first after the "major qualifications" heading. If experience is your long suit, then that should be first. In both education and experience, list your most recent school and job first, and then work backward chronologically. An exception is to list first a job or education that ties in closely with the position for which you are applying.

In listing experience, describe the positions with an eye to easy readability as well as visual attractiveness. A good format might look something like this:

> **Baxter and Robinson, Certified Public Accountants**
> 101 South Webster Avenue
> Eugene, Oregon 97401
> Dates: January 19___–May 19___ (Part-time)
> Duties: Worked with T. L. Baxter, CPA, as an assistant.
>   Primary involvement was with corporate tax
>   returns and audits.

> **Western Lumber Corporation**
> 1540 West Franklin Boulevard
> Eugene, Oregon 97402
> Dates: June 19___–Present
> Duties: Senior Accountant in charge of accounts payable,
>   receivable, and all tax matters. A staff of five report
>   directly to me.

If you have held a variety of part- and full-time jobs while attending college and several of them have no association with your present field, it is probably best to list them as a group:

> Date: 19___–___
> Several part- and full-time jobs were held
> concurrently with my attendance at college. The
> income paid for all educational expenses.

In listing education, you should again start with the most recent and work backward. There is little point in listing secondary education unless it is directly related to the field. Note colleges, universities, degrees and dates received, and major and minor field(s) of study. Whether or not courses should be listed is debatable. In the fields of accounting and finance, such a list serves a good purpose. Avoid meaningless designations like "Accounting 421 or Finance 250," however. It is more helpful to be informative—"Cost Accounting; Advanced and Corporate Finance," for example. If you have attended seminars, executive programs, and other special training sessions associated with your field, list those also. Again, be aware of readability. Use white space and indentations to separate schools and internal listings.

In both experience and education, be certain to note special attainments. If you are fluent in another language, if you were promoted to manager within a year, if you were self-supporting throughout your college career, or if the spotlight shone on you in any special way at school or at work, say so! If you feel that the listing section of the résumé is not the right place, slide it adroitly into the cover letter. But do say it, with modesty and discretion, of course.

Honors, Awards, and Associations   This section, usually brief, lists educational, work, and civic honors and awards. You should also note professional association memberships, published papers, and presentations made at professional meetings.

Personal Data   Very brief statements regarding age, health, marital status, recreational preferences, and travel can be made here.

References   Many prefer simply to note "References will be furnished on request," a frequent practice of individuals who presently hold jobs but are looking for a change. The reason is obvious: although firms do not usually get in touch with a reference before checking with the applicant, some do. It is very embarrassing to have your boss asked about your qualifications when you don't want it known you are in the job market! Even a note like "Please do not contact prior to an interview with me," can be overlooked or ignored.

If you have no reason *not* to list references, do so. An impressive series of names and titles can only be of value to you. A basic rule is to list a minimum of three and a maximum of four references: two work-related, one academic, and one personal. Prospective employers rely primarily on what a work reference has to say about you. To a lesser extent, academic references are perceived as reliable.

RÉSUMÉS WITHOUT COVER LETTERS

There are many occasions on which you can use a résumé without a cover letter. You may see an attractive advertisement in your professional journal or your newspaper that lists a phone number rather than a post office box. You call and chat with the appropriate person, who suggests, "Well, let's get together. If Wednesday at three is good for you, please come in, and bring a copy of your résumé." Or you may be asked by a city official to serve on "The 19__ City Transportation Committee" and to send a copy of your résumé for the public record. Because you need a résumé quite often, you should have a quantity on file. As you gain experience and background, you will probably rewrite your résumé several times, adding sections for Publications, Political Offices Held, Major Presentations Made, and other categories.

Figures 20–1 through 20–3 are examples of résumés without cover letters.

THE COVERING LETTER TO THE RÉSUMÉ

The cover letter to the résumé should almost always change according to the advertisement being answered or company being applied to. If an ad places heavy emphasis on experience, the cover letter should focus on that. If "excellent interpersonal skills" are called for, the cover letter should emphasize that. In other words, determine what attribute the prospective employer feels is vital, search your own abilities to see if you can match it, and then focus on that as a key sales point. When your reader finishes your letter, there should be no doubt about your superior abilities in one or two specific areas.

In addition to emphasizing your primary "selling point," the cover letter should arouse interest, reflect enthusiasm, and motivate the reader to reach eagerly for your résumé. Write your letter from the reader's point of view. Explain how your education, your experience, your background, and your enthusiasm will benefit the organization to which you are applying.[2]

Makeup of the Cover Letter

Although there are no rules about content, a good cover letter usually consists of a minimum of five brief paragraphs, each of which attempts to accomplish a specific objective.

The *first* paragraph may well summarize your major attributes and how you can help the organization:

Two years of part-time accounting experience, a bachelor of science degree in the same field, and a desire to work hard make me feel I can make a significant contribution to your firm in the job you advertised.

The *second* paragraph should emphasize your key attribute or selling point:

My experience as the assistant controller of a major corporation for four years and the owner of a twelve-employee CPA firm for three years qualify me for the position you described. In my work experience I was responsible . . .

[2]See D. M. Watkins, "Creating 'What I Can Do for You' Emphasis in Application Letters," *ABCA Bulletin,* December 1980.

FIGURE 20–1

Sample résumé

```
                        TODD  G.  LAMBERT
                         P.O.  BOX  770
                      Georgetown  University
                      Washington,  DC   20057
                         (202)  944-4712

CAREER  OBJECTIVE
     Begin  as  an  entry  level  management  trainee  and  advance
through  experience  and  education  to  a  leadership  position  of  a
major  financial  unit  within  the  company.

MAJOR  QUALIFICATIONS

     *Prepared  by  my  degree  in  finance  and  extensive  experience  in
managing  accounts  receivable  to  assume  management  role  with
strong  growth  potential.
     *Experienced  in  leading  and  motivating  groups,  as  demon-
strated  by  successful  leadership  positions  in  college  and  previ-
ous  employment.

EDUCATION

     Degrees
     Candidate  for  B.S.  in  Finance,  Georgetown  University.   Degree
expected  May,  19__
       Pertinent  Courses
     Business  Financial  Management
     Advanced  Financial  Management
     Managerial  Communications
     Management  and  Organizational  Behavior

     Cumulative  G.P.A.  3.74  on  a  4-point  scale

ACTIVITIES  AND  AWARDS

     Dean's  List  Fall  19__,  Fall  19__  -  Spring  19__
     Georgetown  Intramural  Champion—Football
     Georgetown  Intramural  Champion—Softball
     Teller,  Student  Federal  Credit  Union,  Spring  19__  -  Present
     Member,  Student  Investment  Alliance,  19__  -  Present
```

WORK EXPERIENCE

<u>Manager-Accounts Receivable</u>, Industrial Protection Products, Summer 19__ - 19__

Handled all accounts receivable transactions. Operated extensive computer accounts and arranged for payments, which included personal visits to customers. Assisted in the reviews of company payment plans. Administered and reviewed credit applications of new customers.

<u>Lumber Worker</u>, Doyle Lumber Company, Summer 19__.

Assisted in the completion of customer orders. Personally served 12-30 customers daily.

PERSONAL

Interests include guitar, skiing, water skiing, and Boston sports teams.

REFERENCES

Furnished upon request.

FIGURE 20–2

Sample résumé

RAMON A. RODRIGUEZ
1717 West Park Lane
Austin, Texas 78701
(512) 221-2242

JOB OBJECTIVE

A position with a large corporation in the area of finance with special attention to acquisitions and mergers. A long-range position of finance director is desired.

MAJOR QUALIFICATIONS

Bachelor and Master of Business Administration degrees in corporate finance and three years' experience with petroleum corporations in engineering and financial management.

EDUCATION

University of Texas, MBA Degree, June 19__
Courses included corporate financial management, financial accounting, long-range corporate planning, strategy, policy, mergers and acquisitions, and related topics. In-depth research carried through on "Major Corporate Takeovers, 19__ to 19__."

University of Texas at Austin, Bachelors Degree, June 19__
Major area of study was Petroleum Engineering, Internship with Mobil Corporation plus scholarship for junior and senior years, Degree awarded, June 19__.

EXPERIENCE

Baker Corporation, 19__ to 19__
   Field engineer primarily charged with liaison to various corporate field units on drilling operations: bit selection, core drilling, sand use, etc.

Mobil Corporation, 19__ to 19__
   Division of Financial Management. Responsibility for audit and controls of all foreign expenditure, foreign payroll of U.S. citizens, and foreign tax analysis. Supervised staff of eight personnel.

MILITARY

U.S. Army, Administrative Officer, Pershing General Hospital
   Active Duty, 19__ to 19__. In charge of purchases, travel, and dependent allocation for all enlisted and officer personnel.

PERSONAL BACKGROUND

Ongoing interest in national and international business affairs, music, and outdoor sports. Have traveled extensively in Europe and the Near East. Married, no children; age 28; health, excellent; height, 6'; weight, 190. Free to relocate.

REFERENCES

Available on request.

FIGURE 20–3

Sample résumé (no cover letter)

Mary C. Van Geem
4141 South Viceroy Ave.
Philadelphia, PA 19102
(215) 768-7113

QUALIFICATIONS

Six valuable years of experience in the retail grocery business, with both a small privately owned chain and a large corporate chain. Started at bottom level of the industry and advanced to the highest nonmanagement position. Direct, first-hand knowledge of all phases of the grocery business, including marketing, ordering, stocking, merchandising, customer relations, and overall store management. Formal education in mass communications, advertising, and broadcast sales was obtained concurrently with work experience.

PERSONAL DATA

AGE: 24
MARITAL STATUS: Single
HEIGHT: 5'4"
WEIGHT: 119 lbs.
HEALTH: Excellent
CITIZENSHIP: U.S.A.

EDUCATION

Franklin Junior College (Philadelphia)
September 19__ - June 19__
Associate of Arts Degree—General Education
Satisfied all lower-division requirements in preparation for upper-division courses on university level.

University of Pennslyvania
September 19__ - June 19__
Bachelor of Arts Degree—Communications Studies.
Communications major; stressed theoretical analysis of mass- and interpersonal- communications techniques; advertising, public relations, and a particular emphasis on the print and broadcast media.

Radio Advertising Sales Workshop (Philadelphia)
Graduated—August 19__
Course dealt with all aspects of modern commercial broadcasting including sales presentations, marketing research, prospecting, merchandising, copywriting, and competitive advertising media.

EMPLOYMENT EXPERIENCES

BEN FRANKLIN MARKETS, INC.

July 19__ - Present
June 19__ - Present Assistant Manager
Primary responsibilities include
supervising night personnel and effectively
serving customers on a personal basis at
second largest store in chain.

July 19__ -June 19__ Journeyman Grocery Clerk
Primary responsibilities included
stocking store merchandise and effectively dealing
with customers on a personal basis in a
retail situation.

HI-TOP FOOD MARKETS

July 19__ - August 19__

June 19__ -August 19__ Assistant Store Manager
Responsibilities included writing and transmitting
merchandise orders, managing store personnel on
second shift.

June 19__ -June 19__ Apprentice Clerk (Buena Park)
Advanced from first-stage apprentice
clerk to the highest nonmanagerial position in one
year (the fastest time possible). Turned
down promotion into management in order to
complete education. Responsibilities
included learning all phases of marketing
operation and management of customers.

PERSONAL CHARACTERISTICS

Effectively communicates with customers and all levels of management.

Dedicated professional with a strong desire to excel in challenging and rewarding field.

Good planner and organizer; knows the value of proper research and preparation.

REFERENCES

Excellent references available upon request.

The *third* paragraph should give your second-level selling point. For many people, this is experience or personal attributes. Or it might be education:

> *My experience has been complemented by a four-year program in business, with accounting as a major, at the University of Illinois. After completion of this rigorous course of study, I supplemented it with graduate-level courses in taxation and corporate law. The attached résumé lists . . .*

The *fourth* paragraph should give some indication of your personality and perhaps your goals and aspirations:

> *Because I have always enjoyed working with people, and seem to have an ability to motivate them, I feel I can do an excellent job in the area you described. My selection as both Supervisor of the Month and Salesperson of the Month at Federal Stores indicates that I . . .*

The *fifth* paragraph, sometimes referred to as the action paragraph, functions to secure action or a response:

> *I feel it would be mutually beneficial if we could meet for an interview. At that time I can tell you in greater detail about my education and experience and how they can be put to work for your firm. At the same time, I can add details in supplementary areas in which you are interested. I can be reached at (201) 564–2888 and will be happy to come in at a time convenient for you.*

The cover letter could have more or fewer than five paragraphs. But the five areas covered above should appear as a minimum. On the other hand, the cover letter should never be more than one page.

Most important—the cover letter should carry a strong *you* attitude throughout. The emphasis should be on the contribution *you* can make to the organization.[3] See Figures 20–4 and 20–5 for examples of effective cover letters.

COMBINING THE COVER LETTER AND RÉSUMÉ

We have examined résumés and cover letters separately. Now we consider them together.

Both documents should appear on high quality bond paper. An off-white or light beige stock is desirable. A top quality typewriter or, at the least, a letter-quality computer printer should be used. Where appropriate, boldface type may be used, and ''bullets'' are acceptable to note key items. If the résumé has been printed, an effort should be made to match the typing in the cover letter with that in the résumé. Spacing, white areas, and margins should contribute to the attractiveness and clarity of the pages. And the con-

[3]See ''A Checklist for the Job Letter Writer,'' on pages 498 and 506.

FIGURE 20–4

Sample cover letter to a résumé

2105 West Lexington Avenue
Norman, OK 73003
April 15, 19__
(405) 456-6543

Ms. Roberta Peterson, Personnel Director
Western Refining Corporation
One Oklahoma Square
Oklahoma City, OK 73101

Dear Ms. Peterson:

1 This application is in response to the request you made to me in our campus discussion earlier this month. You may recall that I told you that with my degree in accounting (to be awarded next month), my two years of part-time experience in the field, and my strong desire to be affiliated with WRC, I know I can make significant contributions to the firm in the years ahead.

2 My undergraduate work in accounting at the University of Oklahoma was concentrated in taxation, which was the area you and I discussed. In addition, I have taken several seminars sponsored by the Oklahoma Accounting Association in the same field. This educational background plus my courses and experience with computers certainly equip me to be an asset to your financial management department.

3 During my last two years of college, I worked part-time and summers for Meister and Feister, CPAs, in a variety of accounting assignments. This gave me the experience and confidence I need to handle competently the assignments I will encounter at WRC.

4 Although I will pursue my MBA on a part-time evening basis, I am eager to enter the wonderful world of accounting now. It is a discipline that I have always enjoyed and found challenging since my first course in bookkeeping in high school. I enjoy being part of a team and I know "Teamwork" is a key word at Western Refining Corporation.

5 I look forward to having a formal interview with you, Ms. Peterson. I am sure you have questions. In turn I want to add to the details you will find on the attached resume. Please let me know when it will be convenient for us to meet. I can be reached at the phone number listed above.

Sincerely yours,

Suzanne Garro

Suzanne Garro

enc

1 Summary paragraph   **3** Experience paragraph   **5** Request for action paragraph

2 Education paragraph   **4** Discussion and personal paragraph

FIGURE 20–5
Sample cover letter to a résumé

5800 W. Franklin Boulevard
Indianapolis, IN 46204
September 10, 19__
(317) 101-2410

Ms. Glenda Owens
Personnel Director
Elliot Systems, Inc.
1500 Kellogg Square
Indianapolis, IN 46201

Dear Ms. Owens:

I enjoyed meeting your Western Region manager, Paul Kane, at the Computer World meeting last week. He suggested that I contact you to express my interest in joining Elliot Systems, Inc.

With my degrees in Decision Systems from Indiana University, extensive work experience in computer applications, and a stong desire to take on professional challenges, I feel I can make a strong contribution to your company. Given your reputation in the field, I'm also aware of how much you have to offer me.

As manager of information systems for my present organization, I am responsible for inventory control, billing, payroll, taxation, and a dozen other areas which I have converted from tons of paper to efficient computer printouts. I find directing a staff of twelve to be enjoyable, challenging, and rewarding.

As for my education, in some respects it began (rather than ended) with my degree in Decision Systems from Indiana University. I have gone on to a Masters Degree (secured earlier this year) and seminars in management information systems. As a matter of fact, I have even crossed the educational desk and next week will begin teaching an evening course in computer technology at the local community college.

I am eager to meet with you to discuss employment possibilities. You can contact me at the address and phone number above. I look forward to hearing from you.

Sincerely,

Stanton Murphy

Stanton Murphy

enc.

tent should be checked and rechecked for accuracy in spelling, grammar, and punctuation. The letter and résumé should be perfect.

As we have seen, it is quite possible to write a résumé that will prove useful in many situations. However, a separate cover letter should be written for each situation, whether it is a response to an advertisement or a completely unsolicited effort.

Examine Figures 20–6 through 20–8 carefully, noting styles and approaches.

A CHECKLIST FOR THE JOB LETTER WRITER

After you have finished your cover letter and résumé, check them carefully for the following attributes:

Attractive   When the prospective employer reads your letter and résumé, you want him or her to say, "This is obviously a well-organized, conscientious individual. The letter has excellent balance, logical organization, and easy readability. Care was taken in its preparation."

Accurate   Personnel directors, without exception, expect college graduates' letters and résumés to be error-free. All that is required to achieve that is careful editing. As one employment supervisor has stated,

> *There are few more important letters an individual will ever write than the job application letter. It should be perfect. We can understand when a letter from a shop supervisor exhibits an error or two, but not when the message comes from a college-trained man or woman. After all, if he or she is careless in a letter, what can we expect in his or her handling of our ledgers?*

So check your letter carefully, and make sure it is clear, concise, complete, and correct.

Reader-Oriented   Have you attempted to point out how the *company* will benefit from your skill, service, and ambition? The personnel director is not particularly concerned with how the firm will give *you* experience, provide *you* with interesting and challenging situations, and offer *you* promotions and pay increases. He or she is interested in learning how your education, experience, and travels can be used in the advancement and progress of the firm.

> *My degree in accounting and two years of part-time experience with Merril and Maxwell, CPAs, should prove of value to your company.*

> *If your company can use a professionally trained advertising person who has loads of energy and ambition, plus three years' experience, I'm the one who can make a contribution to your firm's progress.*

FIGURE 20–6a

Cover letter (see next page for accompanying résumé)

1011 Fourth Street
Santa Monica, CA 90403
July 14, 19__
(213) 394-2163

Box 242, Terminal Annex
The Wall Street Journal
Los Angeles, CA 90067

Dear Personnel Director:

Your very attractive advertisement in yesterday's The Wall Street Journal seemed made to order for me. Your needs are for an assistant manager for your Vienna subsidiary. The individual you want should have "thorough background in financial management, good marketing skills, and some fluency in German." I feel that I score at the top in all three areas.

My experience and educational background have given me excellent training in financial management and marketing. For two years, as an employee of a well-known PR firm, I was almost totally involved in marketing entertainers. As for financial management, that was my MBA area of concentration.

My fluency in German is first-rate. For two years I attended graduate classes at the University of Heidelberg. From 1986 to the present I have compiled, summarized, and translated materials from German for researchers at the well-known "think tank," The Rand Corporation.

In addition to this, I have served as a lecturer in the School of Business at the University of Southern California. In this capacity I was in daily contact with dozens of individuals and found that I related very well with all of them. This ability, plus my complete understanding of German work habits, culture, and values, will permit me to do an outstanding job for your organization.

The attached résumé will provide some facts for you. However, I'm sure you want to learn more about me as an individual. I certainly want to know more about your organization. Please call me at (213) 394-2163 so we may arrange a time for an interview to be held at your convenience.

Sincerely yours,

Bonnie Swihart

Bonnie Swihart

enc

Note how smoothly the second and third paragraphs cover
both education and experience.

FIGURE 20–6b

Résumé accompanying cover letter in Figure 20–6a

BONNIE JEAN SWIHART
1011 Fourth Street, Apt. 115
Santa Monica, CA 90403
(213) 394-2163 (Home)
(213) 743-7061 (Work)

EDUCATION

MBA, University of Southern California
May, 1988
Emphasis: International Business
Fellowship award, 1986-1987.

MA, University of California at Los Angeles
December, 1982
German Language and Literature
Teaching Associate for German 1, 2 and 3.

University of Heidelberg, West Germany
September, 1975 to May, 1977
Graduate studies in German language and literature at the
Germanische Fakultaet and the Dolmetscher Institut.

BA, Scripps College, Claremont, CA
June, 1975
Major: German

EXPERIENCE

University of Southern California
May, 1987 to present
Instructor for Business Communications,
School of Business Administration
Prepared and administered all coursework for undergraduate
class designed to develop skills in public speaking and writing for
business purposes.

International Business Machines
July to August, 1988
Representative for the Olympic Message System, introduced at
the 1988 Olympic Games. Assisted the West German Olympic
Delegation in the use of the Olympic Message System.

The Rand Corporation, Santa Monica, CA
February, 1984 to present
Researcher for Dr. Michael Mihalka and Mr. Alex Alexiev.
Responsible for compiling, summarizing, and translating material
for research projects. Topics include: German and British national
security policy in the 1930's; East German involvement in Third
World countries; German occupation of Soviet territories during
World War II.Translations of texts from German into
English. Private tutorial in German for seven Rand analysts.

Hanson & Schwam, Public Relations, Los Angeles, CA
August, 1984 to June, 1985
Administrative Assistant to the Vice President, Corporate Division.
Performed all activities relating to the service of corporate clients
in the entertainment industry.

BONNIE JEAN SWIHART

EXPERIENCE
(cont'd)

R. W. Thom & Co., Beverly Hills, CA
April, 1983 to August, 1984
Personal Lines Underwriter for the insurance agency. Managed all personal insurance accounts for the agency; responsible for all duties related to coverage of homeowner's, auto, and personal liability insurance.

Department of Germanic Languages, University of Los Angeles
September, 1981 to December, 1982
Teaching Associate, German 1, 2 and 3. Performed all duties of teaching and grading language courses designed to develop speaking, reading, and writing skills in German.

Bishop Amat High School, La Puente, CA
September, 1978 to June, 1981
Teacher of German, English, and business courses. Prepared, administered and evaluated all coursework. Business courses taught: Business Law, Business Procedures, and Typing.

AWARDS

California State Scholarship, 1973-1975

Scholarship to the University of California Summer Program at the Eberhard-Karls Universitaet Tuebingen, West Germany, 1982.

Fellowship, University of Southern California, Graduate School of Business Administration, 1986 to 1987.

LANGUAGES

German; fully fluent.

English; native language, two years of teaching and tutorial.

French; reading, three years.

ORGANIZATIONS Foreign Trade Association of Southern California
Member, USC Professional Business Women's Association

REFERENCES

Dr. Michael Mihalka, Political Science Department, The Rand Corporation.

Mr. David Wisely, V.P., Corporate Division, Hanson & Schwam Public Relations.

Prof. Norman Sigband, Business Communications Department, University of Southern California.

FIGURE 20–7a
Cover letter

```
                                    5151 W. Wabash Avenue
                                    Boston, MA  02104
                                    August 4, 19__
                                    (617) 468-8642


    Box 101, Museum Annex
    Boston Globe
    Globe Square
    Boston, MA  02101

    Dear Sir:

    This morning's Boston Globe carried your ad for "an office manager to
    supervise a staff of 12 of a growing consumer financial corporation."
    My previous experience as an office manager for an export firm,
    knowledge of office procedures and equipment, and a college education
    in business and administrative management are all qualities that
    should serve you well.

    In 19__ I dropped out of college because of financial pressure and
    took the position of office manager with an exporter of electronic
    components.  For three years I built the office practices and proce-
    dures of this growing organization.  In addition to carrying out the
    usual duties that go with the job, I installed a computer system for
    billing, inventory, and payroll as well as word processing.

    In 19__ I left the export firm and returned to the University.  Just
    one year later I received my Bachelor's Degree and have since taken a
    job with a major retail electronics firm in its consumer education,
    adjustment, and sales department.

    My educational background includes work in administrative management,
    computer science, and a dozen seminars in office automation, word
    processing, office management, and related areas.

    My background in administration, consumer behavior, and research
    seems to dovetail very well with your requirements.  I know I can do
    the kind of job for you that will consistently show up in your asset
    column.  I look forward to an interview with you where I can cite in
    much more detail how my qualifications will benefit your organiza-
    tion.  Please call me at the phone number noted above so we may
    arrange a time for an interview.

                                    Sincerely yours,

                                    Ito Tanaka

                                    Ito Tanaka
```

FIGURE 20–7b

Résumé accompanying cover letter in Figure 20–7a

ITO TANAKA
5151 W. Wabash Avenue
Boston, MA 02104
(617) 468-8642

career objectives

To secure a position as office manager where my skills can help advance the organization. My long-range plan is to rise to an officer position in the area of finance or consumer relations.

major qualifications

Several years' experience in office management, educational background in finance and consumer education, and a desire to work hard as a conscientious team member.

experience

Electronic Exports, Inc.
1000 W. Western Avenue
Boston, MA 02102
 Dates: Jan. 19__ to June 19__
 Duties: In charge of staff with responsibility for billing, payroll, and all overseas documentation. Established a computer system and word processing, hired and trained specialized personnel, and proved out system to working efficiency

Marston and Kelly, Electronics
5222 N. Franklin Avenue
Boston, MA 02102
 Dates: Jan. 19__ to Oct. 19__
 Duties: In charge of consumer sales, education, and adjustment department. Created all form and guide sales adjustment, and acknowledgment letters. Established an on-going consumer contact system and completed research for a direct mail campaign.

French and French Shoe Outlet
1000 W. Main Street
Newton Highlands, MA 02109
 Dates: Feb. 19__ to Oct. 19__
 Duties: Floor clerk in women's shoe department. Leading sales figures for any clerk in 19__.

education	Boston University Schcol of Business Bachelor Degree, 19__

Major Courses

Marketing I and II	Computer Sciences I and II
Consumer Behavior	Management Communication
Advertising	Financial Management
Administrative Management I and II	International Trade

Seminars, 19__ to 19__

Topic Areas

Word Processing Methods	Computer Billing
Office Management	Export-Import Documentation
Personnel Management	Management Communication
Financial Management	Others

honors, awards, organizations	Blue Key (Business School Honors Organization) President, Administrative Management Ass'n., Boston Chapter, 19__ Employee of the Month, City of Boston, May 19__ American Finance Ass'n. Boston Chamber of Commerce Toastmasters
references	Available on request

FIGURE 20–8

Cover letter

4721 Wilshire Blvd.
Los Angeles, CA 90027
October 19, 19___

Search Committee
Director of Management Education
Bridge 100A
School of Business Administration
University of Southern California
Los Angeles, CA 90089-1421.AA/EOE

Dear Committee Members:

I am applying for the position of Associate Dean/Executive Director of Management Education based on lengthy experience, significant educational background, and the recommendation of Dr. Norman Sigband, with whom I have worked. I have more than thirteen years' experience working in university communities. This background is complemented by seven years as a management development practitioner in business and industry. I am confident that my experience, energy, and style make me an excellent candidate for the position:

● Proven ability to successfully direct a multi-faceted management development organization currently in a growth mode.

● Academic credentials appropriate to a high-level representative of the University of Southern California.

● A talent and track record for innovation and creativity within existing organizational structures.

● Sensitivity to change that maintains "leading edge" curricula.

● A confident, diplomatic style that moves easily among various cultures and levels of management.

I am currently applying my talents as an internal consultant in management development with Southern California Edison, the leading electric utility in the country. My responsibilities at Edison include the "marketing" and "sales" of training and development services to fifteen line organizations.

I look forward to meeting with you in the near future.

Yours truly,

Linda Williams

Linda Williams, Ph.D.

Specific   The letter that generalizes about what the applicant has done in the past and can do in the future usually makes little impact on the reader. We live in a world of specialization; in professional areas especially, employers like to know precisely what the job seeker can do for them.

It isn't enough to indicate that your degree is in business administration; what specific area? There is too much left to the imagination with, "I held a management position for two years with Croxton and Croxton."

"I was the office manager of Croxton and Croxton's Southfield division," or "personnel assistant in charge of training" is better. On the other hand, the applicant must be careful not to give the reader the impression (unless he or she sincerely means to) that he or she would only be happy doing inventory control or could do only payroll accounting. There is certainly a middle ground that should be indicated.

Enthusiastic and Personal   Your cover letter should reflect your enthusiasm and your personality. There is nothing deadlier than a flat recitation of facts, figures, dates, and company and school names. Make sure your letter comes alive. There's nothing wrong with stating, "I really enjoy working with people," or "All my life I've dreamed of the day when I could assume responsibility as Joe Martin, CPA." Let the real you shine through your letter with a well-placed phrase or two.

Original and Honest   Never copy a paragraph—and certainly not a complete letter—from another source. Anyone can find examples of clever letters in texts, paperbacks, and a dozen other sources. Use them for *ideas* if you wish, but be aware that personnel directors have read them all many times over. Honesty is critical. Stretching the truth, inventing a job, or falsely claiming to have taken a course of instruction will only return eventually to haunt you. Use good judgment to avoid a nasty surprise—termination—after the first month of employment, when letters of confirmation begin to roll in.

THE JOB INTERVIEW[4]

The letter of application rarely results in a job offer; we hope, however, that through the letter we can secure an interview. That is the way it should be written—with the objective of securing an interview, not a job.

A job is offered only after we have sold ourselves at the interview. As much time and care should be spent on that phase as on the preparation, planning, and writing of the letter. The half hour spent talking to the prospective employer is vital. We must give evidence of a pleasant personality,

[4]See also J. J. Phillips, "Ten Ways to Improve the Effectiveness of Your Campus Interview," *SAM Advanced Management Journal,* Autumn 1982.

ability to communicate, knowledge of our area, our objectives, the information we have about the company, our level of courtesy, and familiarity with topics of professional, political, and cultural interest. This requires preparation.

New York Life Insurance Company issued an excellent booklet titled "Making the Most of Your Job Interview." It begins with the statement:

> *The employment interview is one of the most important events in a person's experience, because the 20 or 30 minutes spent with an interviewer may determine the entire future course of one's life.*
>
> *Yet interviewers are continually amazed at the number of applicants who drift into job interviews without any apparent preparation and only the vaguest idea of what they are going to say. Their manner says, "Well, here we are." And that's often the end of it, in more ways than one.*

Others, although they undoubtedly do not intend to do so, create an impression of indifference by acting too casually. At the other extreme, applicants work themselves into such a state of mind that when they arrive they are in nervous fright, able to answer only in monosyllables. These marks of inexperience can be avoided by knowing what is expected of you and by making a few preparations before the interview.

Preparing for the Interview

To prepare for your job interview, think of twenty or so questions the interviewer is likely to ask and rehearse how you will answer them. Examine the following list of typical questions asked by personnel recruiters. How would you answer them?

What are your future vocational plans?

In what school activities have you participated? Why? Which did you enjoy most?

In what type of position are you most interested?

Why do you think you might like to work for our company?

What jobs have you held? How were they obtained and why did you leave?

What courses did you like best? Least? Why?

Why did you choose your particular field of work?

What percentage of your college expenses did you earn? How?

How did you spend your vacation while in school?

What do you know about our company?

Do you feel that you have received a good general training?

What qualifications do you have that make you feel that you will be successful in your field?

What extracurricular offices have you held?

What are your ideas on salary?

If you were starting college all over again, what courses would you take?

How much money do you hope to earn at 30? 35?

Do you think your extracurricular activities were worth the time you devoted to them? Why?

What do you think determines a person's progress in a good company?

What personal characteristics are necessary for success in your chosen field?

Why do you think you would like this particular type of job?

Do you prefer working with others or by yourself?

Are you primarily interested in making money or do you feel that service to humanity is your prime concern?

Can you take instructions without feeling upset?

What kind of boss do you prefer?

How did previous employers treat you?

What have you learned from some of the jobs you have held?

Can you get recommendations from previous employers?

What interests you about our product or service?

Have you ever changed your major field of interest while in college? Why?

When did you choose your college major?

Do you feel you have done the best scholastic work of which you are capable?

How did you happen to go to college?

What do you know about opportunities in the field in which you are trained?

Which of your college years was the most difficult?

Did you enjoy your four years at your university?

What job in our company would you choose if you were entirely free to do so?

What types of books have you read?

Have you plans for graduate work?

What types of people seem to rub you the wrong way?

Have you ever tutored an underclassman?

What jobs have you enjoyed the most? The least? Why?

What are your special abilities?

What job in our company do you want to work toward?

Would you prefer a large or small company? Why?

What have you done which shows initiative and willingness to work?

Do you like routine work? Do you like regular hours?

What size city do you prefer? What is your major weakness?

Define cooperation! Do you demand attention?

Do you have an analytical mind? Are you eager to please?

Do you like to travel? How about overtime work?

What kind of work interests you?

What are the disadvantages of your chosen field?

Are you interested in research?

Even a quick survey of the questions above shows how important preparation is. Try to answer the first three questions now. How well did you do?

"Tell me about yourself," is the type of question designed to get you to talk. What you say and how you say it will give the interviewer a measure of your personality, your perception of yourself, and others' perceptions of you.

Questions regarding what kind of job you seek point out the importance of selecting a major area or two for which you feel qualified. The applicant who says, "I just want a job" or "I can do anything," makes the interviewer think, "That person can probably do nothing." So determine what you can do and want to do. Then assemble all the facts that substantiate your choice: education, experience, personal attributes, goals, desires, and so forth.

"What do you know about our company?" is a favorite question, designed to test your interest in the firm and desire to become affiliated with it. If you show considerable knowledge of the company, the interviewer will assume your desire to join it is considerable too. You should have information on the company's products, plant locations, number of employees, financial past and present, its growth picture, its past and present position in the market, and a dozen other factors. These background data can be secured from sources such as the following:

The company's annual report and 10K

Thomas' Register of American Manufacturers

Government booklets (for federal departments, bureaus, and divisions)

AN ILLEGAL DISCRIMINATORY ACT [1]

Pressure from women's interest groups and the recent guidelines set down by the EEOC (Equal Employment Opportunity Commission) have increased attention to the subject of sexual harassment. The guidelines prohibit sexual harassment in the workplace and place the responsibility for dealing with it with the employer.

In the past, sexual involvement in the workplace was a personal matter and the employer was not accountable to anyone because of it. Discrimination against sex, race, religion, etc. has been prohibited and illegal since 1964 by Title VII of the Civil Rights Act. However, the discrimination cases involved were primarily discriminatory employment practices in the areas of hiring, firing and promoting of individuals. With the new guidelines and interpretations, harassment is defined as another form of sex discrimination and the employer is now liable for acts of sexual harassment by supervisors and other employees.

A DEFINITION OF TERMS

The term *sexual harassment* has a variety of interpretations. To some people it connotes unwanted sexual advances, to others suggestive language or the telling of an off-color joke. Regardless of how individuals understand sexual harassment, the EEOC has defined the subject in rather broad and vague terms.

Learn the names of the company president and chairman, and find out about recent acquisitions, mergers, or take-over efforts. In short, "do your homework" before the interview.

The remaining questions also indicate the need for thoughtful preparation. Take care not to ramble or make political hay if asked about foreign policy, national affairs, or your profession. Make your comments concise—and in good taste. If you are asked about instructors or former employers, remember that the interview is not the place for disparaging others. But be frank and honest in all replies. A statement that is not true may trip you up sooner or later.

Obviously, dressing neatly, having good posture, and speaking clearly, correctly, and completely are all crucial in the interview. Ask yourself, "How do I come across in interviews?" Do you talk too much? Too little? Are you a good listener? How good is your eye contact?[5] You certainly know *what* to do. If you don't do it, figure out how to change.

Plan to find an opportunity during the interview to tell about your major achievements or important qualities.

---

[5]K. G. Rasmussen, Jr., "Nonverbal Behavior, Verbal Behavior, Résumé Credentials, and Selection Interview Outcomes," *Journals of Applied Psychology*, November 1984.

The new and final guidelines (November 1, 1980) state, "Unwelcome sexual advances, requests for sexual favors and other verbal or physical conduct of a sexual nature constitute sexual harassment when (1) submission to such conduct is made either explicitly or implicitly a term or condition of an individual's employment, (2) submission to or rejection of such conduct by an individual is used as the basis for employment decisions affecting such individual, or (3) such conduct has the purpose or effect of unreasonably interfering with an individual's work performance or creating an intimidating, hostile or offensive working environment."

In applying these guidelines, the EEOC can now hold the employer responsible for sexual harassment in the workplace. This means the employer can be held responsible for the conduct of the supervisors, other employees and even non-employees where the employer knows or should have known of the conduct of the employees or non-employees. To comply with the guidelines, the employer is responsible for informing all supervisors that sexual harassment is an illegal discriminatory act and as such cannot be tolerated or allowed in the workplace.

To avoid liability for cases of sexual harassment, the best remedy is to take immediate action to stop it.

¹An Illegal Discriminatory Act" from *Leader Letter,* Second Quarter 1981, Vol. 6, No. 2. Copyright © 1981 by Rexnord, Inc. Reprinted by permission.

My job in the bookstore helped me to pay almost 80 percent of my college expenses.

My knowledge of Spanish is good enough for me to carry on correspondence and routine business activities with your Latin American accounts.

I received a General Bank and Trust Company scholarship as a freshman, and held it, on the basis of grades, for all four years.

You should also plan to ask several carefully worded questions. These may concern opportunities within the firm, compensation in addition to the base salary (hospitalization, annuity funds, tuition-refund plans, stock option programs, profit sharing), plans for company expansion and diversification, job duties, travel requirements, advancement policies, and so forth.

Can you tell me what a typical day would be like?

What are the major responsibilities of this position?

Can you explain the typical career pattern of someone entering in this position?

Can I progress at my own speed or is it structured?

How frequently do you relocate professional employees?

Does this firm recommend taking evening classes during the first year?

What is the firm's policy with regard to paying for educational tuition and fees?

How often are performance reviews given?

Is it possible to transfer from one division to another?

Does this firm promote from within the ranks?

How much responsibility is given after one year?

How much exposure and contact with management is there?

What is the average age of middle management, top management?

What are the commonly experienced satisfactions and frustrations of this job?

Is it possible to move through the training program faster than average?

How much freedom is given and how much discipline is required of new employees?

The answers to these questions may determine which job you choose. Furthermore, this two-way discussion gives you an opportunity to relax as the interviewer speaks. And it may open up important new avenues for discussion. But be extremely tactful in framing your questions.

Quite obviously you would not say, "What are the vacation privileges?" (The interviewer may say to himself, "he doesn't have the job yet and he already wants to go on vacation.") However, the question is important, so think it through. You'll probably come up with, "Can you tell me about the firm's employee benefit package?" The same is true of advancement. It's a reasonable topic, but don't ask, "When do I get promoted?" How about, "On the basis of hard work and merit, does the firm have specific policies on advancement?"

Be prepared to deal with a job offer during the interview. If you aren't prepared to accept it at that moment, don't stall or accept it with some mental reservation. Say directly that you have other interviews scheduled and that you want to defer a decision, for the benefit of the company as well as yourself. Interviewers are usually reasonable people; they will accept an honest approach.

The Interviewer's Point of View

The interviewer is looking for the most qualified person for the job. How that is determined is largely a function of his or her own perceptions, values, and training. Some interviewers use a *structured* format, almost following a checklist of questions. In fact, some interviewers score answers, adding up the points at the end of the interview!

Others use an *unstructured* approach, in which topics and subjects change rapidly according to the interests of each party. The interviewer is as interested in learning about the interviewee's personality, attitude, and values as much as about experience and education.

The somewhat unusual *stress* interview is designed to keep the interviewee under a degree of tension through relentlessly pointed, barbed, personal, and even somewhat antagonistic questions. The goal is to see how the interviewee responds under stressful conditions. One personnel director, who uses a free flow of ideas, has said that her questions are designed to determine the following:

How the applicant feels about the job for which he is applying. Is the area vital? Challenging? Fun?

How he feels about people.

How he feels about himself. His level of confidence. Competence.

What he feels are his major strengths. Weaknesses.

What are some of his personal values?[6]

Keep in mind that the interview is a vital step in the job-seeking process. Expend lavish amounts of time to prepare for it. Role-playing the interview situation with a qualified person is a good idea. Because of its importance in your future, the interview deserves your full attention, careful preparation, and maximum effort.

THE FOLLOW-UP LETTER TO THE INTERVIEW

You would not normally send a follow-up letter as a result of an initial, brief, exploratory interview. However, if you have been interviewed at length and you are very much interested in the position, you might well send a follow-up note. Very few persons take the time or make the effort to do this. When the interviewer receives such a letter, you can be sure he or she will be impressed.

The written follow-up to the interview (see Figure 20–9) should be concise, sincere, and courteous. Its purpose is to thank the interviewer for the time and effort expended in talking to you and to review briefly your own qualifications. Perhaps the most important quality of the letter is honesty. If it contains obviously insincere statements or overly enthusiastic praise, it will surely fail. It should be mailed the same day or the day following the interview.

---

[6]Cindie Pridy, Manager of Employment, Star Kist Foods, Inc., March 6, 1985 (personal communication).

```
                                          May 27, 19__

        Dear Mr. Cates:

        Thank you very much for the time you spent with me this morning.
        I found your discussion of the Fairmont Company most interesting,
        and the opening you described was very challenging.

        You will recall that I received my commerce degree from California
        State last year, acquired a CPA certificate a few months ago, and
        have been employed for one year as a junior accountant with
        Continental Aerospace Company.

        I would certainly like an opportunity to work more extensively in
        an electronic data processing position such as the one you
        described.  I do hope you will call me at 826-4622 for further
        discussion.

                                          Sincerely yours,

                                          Roy Yakamoto

                                          Roy Yakamoto
```

Declining a Job Offer

At some time you may find yourself in the enviable position of having more than one job offer. Don't be tempted to call the interviewer's secretary and state, "Please tell Mr. Martin that I can't take the junior accountant's job after all, but I sure appreciate his asking me." Instead, write a carefully worded, courteous note (see Figure 20–10). It can build goodwill, while a telephone message will not. And in addition, a note may pay important dividends for the future.

Letters of Resignation

Although it is always difficult to resign from a position, it is wise to do so tactfully and courteously. Setting down the facts in a letter tends to keep the record straight. In addition, it is a good idea to have such a letter in your file in the firm in the event a reference on you is requested of that company some years later. Such a letter may also assist those in the company who may not know you, but who must deal with a request for information on you. In a potentially difficult situation, as in the case in Figure 20–11, a direct factual approach is usually the best.

FIGURE 20–10

Letter declining a job offer

2208 W. Morse Avenue
Chicago, Illinois 60645

June 27, 19__

Dear Mr. Berman:

Thank you most sincerely for the time you and Ms. Cannon spent
with me during our discussions during the past two weeks.

I was certainly impressed with the operations of your organization and the potential opportunities the company affords its
employees. However, the position does require rather extensive travel, and as I indicated, this is something I would
like to avoid.

On that basis, I have accepted a position with a local firm in
the same capacity we discussed.

I know you will understand my position and accept my sincere
appreciation for your courtesy.

Sincerely yours,

Iris Anderson

FIGURE 20–11
Letter of resignation

September 15, 19__

Dear Mr. Kelly:

Doing marketing research for the past two years under your direction has been a rewarding, enjoyable, and challenging experience.

I found all my academic background put to good use and the freedom to innovate (which you encouraged) a delightful situation.

Recently, however, I have been asked to head up the marketing division of a consumer products company. The opportunity is really too good to turn down. I can only hope that I will do as good a job with that firm as you do here.

On that basis, I would like to suggest that I leave at the end of the first week in October. If you feel that time is not convenient, I am sure alternative arrangements can be made.

Sincerely yours,

Manuel Ortega

Manuel Ortega

QUESTIONS FOR STUDY

1. Would you compare an individual's résumé to a Polaroid picture or an oil painting? Discuss your answer.
2. Why are extremely thorough, multi-page résumés often less successful than one page summary résumés?
3. Should you contact references you have included on your résumé? What information about them should appear on the résumé?
4. In what general ways do résumés differ for a student just out of college and a manager fifteen years into his or her career?
5. To what degree should your résumé be correct in grammar, mechanics, spelling, and use of margins? Why?
6. What is a "justified" margin?
7. What are the basic requirements of a good follow-up letter that you may send after being interviewed?
8. Computerized dating services attempt to "match" your characteristics with those of another person. In what ways is your cover letter to a prospective employer similar to the computerized dating service?
9. Why should cover letters and résumés be specific? Give two examples of specific details that you might include in a cover letter.
10. How can a job applicant prepare for a job interview? Be specific.
11. Discuss key differences between the structured and unstructured job interview.
12. If a résumé should be able to stand alone, without a cover letter, why might you send both a cover letter and a résumé to a prospective employer?
13. Why should a job offer be rejected in writing?
14. Why should the recent college graduate present a mix of references to a potential employer? Why wouldn't it be a good idea to list six professors?
15. What purpose do the following publications serve in the job search: *Moody's Manuals*, *Poor's Register*, and *Thomas' Register*?

EXERCISES

16. Many books offer guidance, much of it conflicting, on how to produce a winning résumé. Find a recent book that describes résumés different in style and content from those described in this text. Discuss in writing the advantages or disadvantages of these alternate styles.
17. The résumé is closely identified with the job search. However, the résumé can serve purposes that have nothing to do with seeking employment.
    (a) Identify the profession you plan to enter.

(b) For that profession, describe two situations in which it would be beneficial to have an up-to-date résumé.

18. Ask two or three of your classmates to form a mock interview panel. In advance, tell them the job for which you are applying. They should interview you for twenty to thirty minutes, using interview questions contained in this chapter in addition to their own. After the interview, complete the following tasks:

(a) Write down your own assessment of your performance. What did you do well? What needed improvement? Which questions were especially easy or difficult?

(b) Ask each of the panel members to list three things you did well and three things you should work on.

(c) Listen as an "unseen observer" as the panel discusses your interview and decides whether to offer you the job. After you have heard what they have to say, write down the points that seemed especially important to the panel in reaching its decision.

19. Distribute your résumé to at least five people. Ask them to circle two or three items on the résumé that they would use as the basis for interview questions. After you have collected your résumés, draw some conclusions about the success with which you designed your résumé with interviews in mind. In what specific ways can you highlight material you want your interviewer to ask you about?

20. Stating the career objective in specific and realistic terms is often one of the more difficult parts of the résumé to construct.

(a) Write a career objective that addresses only your short-term goal.

(b) Write a career objective that combines both your short- and long-term goals.

21. The résumé should be an honest representation of your abilities and qualifications. However, if one of your personal characteristics is a liability, you should not list it on the résumé. Give some examples of items that a person might leave off of a résumé but be willing to address in an interview.

22. Imagine that you have just been interviewed for a job. Write the following letters:

(a) A thank-you letter for the interview

(b) A letter accepting a job offer

(c) A letter declining a job offer

23. The chapter discusses an ongoing controversy in the business communication literature—the length of a résumé.

Prepare two résumés for yourself, one of them one page long and the other two pages. Submit both résumés, along with your critical analysis of each. Your analysis should clearly state which résumé you will use in your actual job search. Specifically address the issue of résumé length.

24. College bulletin boards, daily newspapers, and the Yellow Pages regularly advertise résumé preparation services. Call two or three such services to learn what, in addition to typing, they offer their clients. Specifically, inquire about what they claim to do for you that you cannot do for yourself. Write down their claims and your response to those claims. End your analysis by indicating whether or not you would use a résumé preparation service. Submit this paper to your instructor as a completed memo.

25. It is vital that an interviewee be well prepared before the employment interview. The chapter indicates a variety of sources of materials for obtaining information needed for the interview.
    (a) Name a specific organization with which you might reasonably interview.
    (b) Name a job you might consider in the organization.
    (c) List three specific questions you would probably ask the interviewer.
    (d) Cite at least five places where you could secure information about the organization; briefly indicate the kinds of information listed in each.

26. During the past several years a number of articles have appeared in the press about dishonest résumés. Evidently some people take more than literary freedom with what they include in their résumés. Some résumés contain incorrect information about colleges attended, degrees earned, positions held, employment responsibilities, and the like.

    As a résumé writer who wants to be completely honest, what can you do in your résumé and cover letter that will suggest that all facts presented are valid and verifiable?

27. Revise each of the following unsatisfactory letter bodies, using the checklist in this chapter.

    A thank-you letter:

    Just a note to say thanks. Let me know if anything comes of our discussion. I sure hope you'll see fit to hire me. You can call me day or night at 862–6832.

    A letter declining a job offer:

    I'm very sorry to tell you that I cannot accept the offer made to me in your recent letter.
    Thank you, however, for considering me for the position.

    A letter of resignation:

    Effective May 5, 19___ , I resign. My desk and files will be cleaned out by 5 P.M. on that date. I request that all necessary forms be sent to me immediately.

Part Six

1717 Covington Dr.
Revere, MA 32233

August 1, 19__

Farnsworth Corporation
Office and Stationery Supplies
2100 S. Hampton Drive
Chicago, IL 60024

Dear Sir:

Please send me the following supplies:

computer paper

Farnsworth Corporation
Office and Stationery Supplies
2100 S. Hampton Drive

August 7, 19__

Mr. Henry Wineman
1717 Covington Dr.
Revere, MA 32233

Dear Mr. Wineman:

Thank you for your order of August 1, 19__. It will be
shipped to you immediately, to arrive no later than August 15
C.O.D. Total charges due at that time will be $283.33.

We appreciate your confidence in our products and look forward
to serving you.

Sincerely,

Robert Kevin
Vice President

Business Correspondence

21 Principles of the Business Letter

Companies don't do business with companies; people do business with people. Make your writing sound like people talking.

Every company, big or small, communicates to dozens of different publics. These publics are all *external* to the firm: suppliers, dealers, manufacturers, customers, vendors, prospective purchasers, regulatory bureaus, government agencies, community groups, educational institutions, and on and on. Of the many types of written or printed external communications, such as newspaper and magazines advertisements, direct mail pieces, telegrams, reports, and letters, it is certainly letters that are used most frequently. When a record is required or facts must be stated—prices quoted, offers made, or deliveries promised—a letter is needed.

Our modern world of computer and electronic communications has made a striking difference in our use of business letters. Many external messages are now being sent from computer to computer to computer printer to recipient, instead of being dictated, typed, and then mailed to the recipient. The computer-generated letter completed Monday afternoon in New York may be received the next morning in California. And if the companies involved have an electronic link, the communication can be received far more quickly. Electronic typewriters and printers are turning out hundreds of letters, all with the same content but with individualized addresses and salutations. In the best examples, there is no clue in the letter itself that it is, in fact, part of a mass mailing.

Even though the transmission of the business letter is changing, the essential act of sending a message from one person to another remains the same. Since one person still is communicating with another, it is important to be aware of and practice the basic principles of business communication.

THE BUSINESS LETTER AND THE COMPANY IMAGE

In many firms the business letter is the primary means of external communication. There are several reasons: a letter establishes a tangible record that can be used for later reference; distances can be spanned quickly at relatively low cost; the time spent traveling to another person's office and carrying through a discussion can be eliminated; and routine business matters can be completed efficiently with the help of letter guides and forms.

For example, consider a large insurance company with thousands of policyowners and hundreds of agents from coast to coast. Questions about premiums, cancellations, medical bills, changes in beneficiaries, overpayments, hospitalization benefits, past-due accounts, conversions, reinstatements, and a thousand and one other situations arise each day. Letters flow into the home (or central) office from a variety of sources. And replies must go out, all on the company's stationery and written by hundreds of different employees, all contributing to the company's image.

When policyowner Mrs. Baxter of Three Forks, South Dakota, reads the letter she receives at her farm home, she forms a mental picture of the company; so too does Mr. Smythe as he sits in his apartment on the forty-fifth floor of a Chicago condominium; and so does the corporate officer who is considering the purchase of major policies for his or her company. Each person—young or old, rich or poor, from the policyowner to the corporate officer, from the community member to the secretary of the state insurance commission—builds an image of the company on the basis of the letter he or she reads.

If the letter is curt, the company appears abrupt; if the letter is hackneyed, stereotyped, and dull, the company appears backward and stodgy; if the letter is discourteous or tactless, the company appears high-handed; if the letter is unattractive and sloppy, the company appears careless and negligent. On the other hand, if the letter is clear and concise, the firm seems well organized and competent; if the letter is courteous and friendly, the company seems concerned and helpful; if the letter is attractive and neat, the company seems efficient and accurate. And so it goes. Regardless of who wrote the letter, the message will reflect the image of the company.

The managements of many companies have set up training programs to improve the letter-writing abilities of their personnel. Some major corporations have departments whose primary function is to evaluate company correspondence and train employees in letterwriting. One large insurance firm holds classes, reviews correspondence, issues bulletins, and at frequent intervals reminds its employees of the importance of effective correspondence.

Other strategies are possible. Some companies engage outside consultants to evaluate and train, and many firms subscribe to letter-improvement bulletins sent out periodically by companies specializing in this service.

Most firms today are aware of the importance of good company correspondence, and are doing something about raising their standards or keeping them high.

MECHANICS

Training programs for correspondents and management personnel usually place little emphasis on the form and mechanics of the business letter because they are considered the responsibility of the typist. However, the manager should have some familiarity with the topic. For that reason, Appendix B contains suggestions.

The mechanics and form of the business letter vary considerably from one company to another. One firm requires that its employees use block form; another prefers modified block. One organization recommends identifying initials of dictator and typist, and another company omits them entirely. The "correct" form is the one the firm requires. Many companies publish their own correspondence manuals and guides, which indicate company preference in letter layout, use of abbreviations, address style, signatures, and so on.

PRINCIPLES OF COMMUNICATION

Although the mechanics of a business letter should be correct, an error in typing or letter layout will cost nearly as much goodwill as a tactless or sarcastic statement. Thus it is knowledge of the *principles* of business writing that is most important.

Tone

In written communications, tone is the total impression made by the words, topics, and level of formality used in the message. After reading a letter, a person may say, "The tone of Acme's message was extremely friendly," or "tactful," or "impersonal," or "very positive." Our impression of tone seems to depend on our reactions to the words used, the phrasing of sentences, and the order of ideas. The impression we form of a letter's tone—friendly, formal, courteous, high-pressured—tends to be extended to the company as a whole.

Naturalness   There was a time when a good deal of attention was given to eliminating stiffness in business letters: hackneyed phrases, obsolete and archaic references, and pompous statements. In modern business practice the number of letters that contain such expressions is relatively small. If you do sometimes use hackneyed expressions, drop them for more natural ones. It is doubtful that you use the following, or other such expressions, in speaking; why use them in writing?

As in the above	Enclosed please find
According to our records	Esteemed order
Advise	Hand you
As indicated	Hand you herewith
As per	Hereby acknowledge
At hand	Hoping to hear
At early date	In accordance with

The use of one or two of these in a piece of writing is certainly not bad; but a letter filled with them conveys an impression of an impersonal and unfriendly company. Compare the two letters in Figure 21–1. Notice that the messages are similar but the tone is not. What would your feelings be toward the companies that mailed them? The longer letter required a little thought and probably cost the company more in typing time than the first. But it is surely worth the investment: it reflects sincerity, warmth, and a natural tone that builds goodwill. The shorter one creates the impression of a company that is unfriendly and hardly concerned with going out of its way to satisfy a customer.

Some years ago Connecticut Life Insurance Company published a booklet for its employees titled *Speak When You Write*. Its eighteen pages were filled with suggestions on how to inject a natural, friendly tone into communications so that goodwill for the company would increase. The key perhaps is in the title—which, of course, should not be taken too literally. If we did "write as we speak," our written communications would probably be wordy and repetitious. What is really meant is to write as *you sound* when you talk. This way your written communications will reflect the natural, friendly spontaneity of your spoken words.

Courtesy   In this hurried world, we sometimes overlook an opportunity to extend a little courtesy to those with whom we communicate. Letters often conclude with a phrase such as "Your merchandise was shipped on January 14." Why not add a "Thank you very much," or "Your business is always appreciated," or "We were happy we could ship this equipment immediately, as you requested"? When *thank you, please, I appreciated,* or similar expressions are used in a letter—and used sincerely—they help create goodwill.

Positive Language   Certain words and phrases evoke an unfavorable mental reaction, which we may associate with the phenomenon, like a product or

FIGURE 21–1

An unfriendly business letter and a friendly business letter

Farnsworth Corporation

Office and Stationery Supplies

2100 S. Hampton Drive

Chicago, Illinois 60024

August 7, 19___

Mr. Henry Wineman
1717 Covington Dr.
Revere, MA 32233

Dear Mr. Wineman:

Per our conversation Thursday last, this is to acknowledge receipt of your order dated August 1, 19___. In accordance with mutually agreed upon credit arrangements, we will expect your C.O.D. payment in the amount of $283.33 upon your receipt of merchandise.

We advise that said shipment should reach you on or before August 15. In the event of problems in this regard, do not hesitate to contact us.

Respectfully yours,

Robert Kevin

Robert Kevin

Because of the hackneyed phrases and the cold, formal tone, the reader may feel that the writer is totally unconcerned with the former's welfare.

August 7, 19___

Mr. Henry Wineman
1717 Covington Dr.
Revere, MA 32233

Dear Mr. Wineman:

Thank you for your order of August 1, 19___. It will be shipped to you immediately, to arrive no later than August 15 C.O.D. Total charges due at that time will be $283.33.

We appreciate your confidence in our products and look forward to serving you.

Sincerely,

Robert Kevin

Robert Kevin
Vice President

The use of personal pronouns and courtesy promote a feeling of personal concern.

service, to which the words refer. Thus a department store does not put up a sign saying, "Complaint Department," because it would stimulate an unpleasant association. "Adjustment Bureau" or "Customer Service Department," on the other hand, makes the customer anticipate a positive experience.

What would be a customer's reaction to an order form with the statement, "To avoid errors and mistakes in shipping, complete the order form as directed"? The immediate "picture reaction" to this sentence is obvious. The customer sees the order delayed or lost and anticipates being billed for merchandise never received—it would be safer to tear up the order form and do business elsewhere. That is why the messages on most order forms aim to stimulate a favorable reaction, a positive picture. Toward that end they may state, "Please complete the order form as requested for accurate and rapid shipment of merchandise." What is it about those two statements that triggers different reactions? It is the words themselves. Certain words and phrases in our culture, used in a specific context, induce unfavorable (negative) mental associations, while others evoke positive responses.

Negative: *We hope you won't be dissatisfied with the new All-American line.*
Positive: *We are sure you will be satisfied with the new All-American line.*

Under most conditions, it is wise to avoid words that evoke a negative response. Words such as *trouble, dissatisfaction, complaint, hope, if, neglect, errors,* and *negligence* usually result in unfavorable mental associations for the product or service under discussion.

However, a negative tone is not always undesirable. It can be used for shock value when it is followed by a positive solution. This device is frequently used in advertising:

Negative problem: *Have you provided for your advancing years?*
Positive solution: *Let us show you how enjoyable your retirement can be with Parker Protection.*

The negative tone, when used in this way, helps sell many products: insurance, health items, and safety and personal hygiene products. But the negative tone must always be handled with care, for negative symbols are more likely to be remembered (and associated with a product) than pleasant, positive ones. This may be why more and more insurance today is *not* sold as "death benefits or protection from disaster"—all negative—but for "living comfort, peace of mind, and security"—all positive.

Tact   In communication, tact is certainly abstract and, therefore, difficult to define. The person in the street might say that "tact is saying the right thing at the right time in the right way." But when you are trying to write a tactful letter, what is the right thing to say? When is the right time? What is the right way? It is clear that the standard definition of tact is not an adequate guide.

Like so many factors in communication, tact is intimately involved with words, their use, and their interpretation. If we say, "You failed to include the order form," or "We were surprised you did not understand the directions," or "We received your letter in which you claimed we did not ship," we are certainly being tactless. Is it because of the *denotations* of the key words, "You failed," "We were surprised," or "You claimed," or their *connotations*? Here we see an excellent example of how important the personal interpretation of words can be. Words can assume special connotations in specific contexts and result in statements that are interpreted as tactless and discourteous.

The solution to the problem is to avoid words or phrases that may antagonize or embarrass. Pointing out another's error can be done so that the other person will not lose face if you choose the rights words.

Tactless: *We received your letter in which you claim we did not send . . .*
Better: *Thank you for your letter concerning our shipment of December 3.*

The *You* Attitude

Perhaps there is no quality in business writing that has received more attention than the *you* attitude. We discuss it, write about it, and lecture on it. Yet it seems an elusive and difficult concept to understand and use.

Because of our nature and the society in which we live, our interests, activities, and goals usually center on ourselves. Most of us are impatient when *our* problems, *our* situations, *our* purchases are not examined from *our* point of view. We usually analyze and communicate about the situations in which we are involved from *our* position and with *our* perceptions. It is easy to forget that the other person may have a position, feelings, and reactions. Our decisions and actions seem logical to us. But do we ask ourselves how logical our actions are from the other person's viewpoint?

A *you* attitude consists of viewing a situation from the other person's point of view. It requires sensitivity, an appreciation of others, and respect. And this interest must be sincere, for if it is not, the other person will be aware that it is false and resent it.

The use of the *you* attitude is most important when a difference of opinion exists. At such times it is vital to appreciate the other person's point of view, to be sensitive to his or her needs, and to communicate your appreciation of the situation.

Of course, the *you* attitude is not synonymous with *agreement.* It is possible to communicate a strong *you* attitude while disagreeing with the other person. The secretary who wants a new $1000 typewriter is more willing to accept a *no* if his or her employer first shows an understanding of *why* the secretary wants a new machine.

The letters in Figure 21–2 and 21–3 illustrate the difference between a *you* attitude and a *we* or *I* attitude. In 21–2, Mr. Moreau is clearly concerned with his own profits and accomplishments. In 21–3 however, he shows how his shop is there for Ms. March's convenience.

If a business letter has a sincere and effective *you* attitude, it needs little else, for the *you* attitude ensures that all other principles will be followed. It will be courteous, friendly, natural, and carefully organized. The writing will be clear, concise, and correct.

Effective Composition[1]

Completeness   When facts or ideas have been inadvertently omitted from a business letter, we tend to brush this off with, "Oh, I forgot all about *that.*" The result, however, is that the recipient must write again, and we in turn must reply again. Perhaps no great harm is done in one isolated case, but if 10 percent of the letters a firm sends out are not complete, and the company mails approximately three thousand letters a week, the cost can be staggering. Not only is there the writing, typing, and mailing of unnecessary letters (at a cost of about $9.75 each), but the loss of goodwill and, quite possibly, a customer.

In other situations, the results are more difficult to measure. If, for example, Company Z writes to firms A, B, and C for information concerning cost, shipping dates, and guarantees on plastic widgets and receives complete replies from firms A and B but not from C, will Z write back to C? Not unless C's prices were significantly lower. Z will probably choose between A and B.

From time to time our letters will not cover everything the recipient wants. However, we should be certain we don't omit important facts through carelessness. The key to writing complete letters is simple: Organize the facts at hand before you write.

Good Organization   Before even the simplest letter is written, the writer should know precisely what topics will be covered. Some writers make notes in the margin or at the bottom of the letter to which they are replying. Others make notes on a piece of scratch paper or draw up an outline of their reply. Still others prefer to outline mentally. The method doesn't matter, as long as the writer has a guide to writing or dictating the reply letter. By checking the guide against the inquiry letter, the writer can ensure that the reply will be complete.

Conciseness   The recipient of a business letter must read it all because it involves a business transaction. It can be irritating if it rambles on and on, with unending paragraphs, meaningless phrases, and unnecessary words.

---

[1]Although principles of effective composition were reviewed in chapter 9, they are touched upon in this chapter also, with special attention to business letters.

FIGURE 21–2

"We"-centered letter—focusing too much on the writer's needs

Viva la France
Gourmet Specialties

29 Wilshire Blvd.
Los Angeles, CA 93828
(213) 798-8382

Ms. Wendy March
Owner
Wendy's Kitchen
3029 Reardon Dr.
Beverly Hills, CA 92833

Dear Ms. March:

We are happy to announce the grand opening of Viva la France Gourmet Specialities, the single finest source for gourmet culinary items on the West Coast.

Our European-trained staff has painstakingly assembled a chef's paradise of hard-to-find spices, herbs, cooking implements, and recipe guides. Their efforts are directed by Pierre Raudanne, who for seven years was head chef at L'Oeuf in Paris. Mssr. Raudanne was trained at Cordon Bleu and has written more than twenty articles on French cooking and cuisine for international magazines.

At our grand opening, we will feature discount prices on many items, including the "French Starter Pack" of sauce recipes and spices. The owners, Mssrs. Goban and Fourier, will be on hand to lead the festivities.

We are proud to be the first and best source for gourmet items in Southern California.

Sincerely,

Francoise Moreau

Francoise Moreau
Manager

FIGURE 21–3

You-attitude letter—reader-oriented (compare with Figure 21–2)

Viva la France
Gourmet Specialties

29 Wilshire Blvd.
Los Angeles, CA 93828
(213) 798-8382

Ms. Wendy March
Owner
Wendy's Kitchen
3029 Reardon Dr.
Beverly Hills, CA 92833

Dear Ms. March:

You may have been driving to San Francisco or waiting weeks for delivery of your gourmet culinary needs. If so, celebrate with us the grand opening of Viva la France Gourmet Specialities, the single finest source for gourmet culinary items on the West Coast.

To meet your needs, our European-trained staff has painstakingly assembled a chef's paradise of hard-to-find spices, herbs, cooking implements, and recipe guides. Your expert-in-residence is Pierre Raudanne, who for seven years was head chef at L'Oeuf in Paris. Trained at Cordon Bleu and author of more than twenty articles on French cooking, Mssr. Raudanne looks forward to answering your every question about French cuisine.

To welcome you to a new, convenient source for gourmet items, we will offer discount prices at our grand opening on many items, including the "French Starter Pack" of sauce recipes and spices. The owners, Mssrs. Goban and Fourier, will be on hand to greet you.

You can look with confidence to Viva la France as your first and best source for gourmet items in Southern California.

Sincerely,

Francoise Moreau
Manager

Note that the tone throughout this letter seems to suggest, "We are interested in *your* welfare."

Overall length is no sure guide to conciseness. A letter covering a third of a page may be short but wordy. On the other hand, a three-page letter may be concise. We should strive to write business letters that do not waste words, letters in which every phrase, every clause, every statement says only what needs to be said.

> *Wordy:*   *I would ask your involvement in making a request to Mr. Bevins that, in anticipation of our meeting, he take the time to make a review of all records of sales for the fiscal year 1987.*
>
> *Revised:*   *Please ask Mr. Bevins to review the 1987 sales figures prior to our meeting.*

Notice how the meaning becomes clearer, understanding easier, and impact greater when unnecessary words have been dropped and phrases made shorter.

Clarity   Much confusion has been caused by unclear business communication. The sentence that can be interpreted in two different ways or can't be understood at all is most disturbing. How should the reader interpret this statement: "If the safety bracket for the 333 Press has been completed, send it at once"? What should be shipped? The press? The bracket? Both?

Everything you write, whether a six-line memo or a three-page letter, should be checked for clarity. If there is the slightest doubt about its clarity, you should revise it.

Precision   Statements can be clear, unified, and coherent yet not accurate and precise. If you mean "thoroughly examined," you should not say "looked over"; if you mean "A proportional stratified sample was taken," you should not write "A survey was made."

Because business communication is often the basis for making decisions, precision and accuracy in diction (word choice) are very important. One or two carelessly chosen words may convey a meaning far from the one desired.

> *Vague:*   *Sales of the Kenwood Lumber Company have gone up during the past two or three years.*
>
> *Precise:*   *Sales of the Kenwood Lumber Company increased by 4 percent in 1989 and 8 percent in 1988 over the gross sales figures of 1987.*

Accuracy   It is a strange quirk of human nature that causes most people to notice that something is awry. An error in grammar or punctuation in a letter will be immediately apparent to the reader. Focusing on the error, voluntarily or not, he or she will necessarily give less attention to the content of the message or the letter. Some of its impact is lost.

And because letters are often all the recipient knows of a company, errors in basic English diminish his or her opinion of the firm. Management must be certain, therefore, that its correspondents have mastered not only tact, courtesy, clarity, and precision, but also the basic principles of good English. And the author of every piece of written communication should proofread it carefully before it is placed in a communication channel.

Attractiveness   The final principle of effective composition has little to do with effective statement of ideas, but everything to do with communication—for communication depends as much on the nonverbal message as it does on the verbal one. Your ideas may be brilliant, your statements clear, tactful, concise, accurate, and grammatical—but if they are thrown together haphazardly on the paper, with no form or balance, the recipient may not even read them; if he or she does, it will be with prejudice. The careless erasure, the negligent strikeover, the jammed margin, the enormous, heavy, forty-two line block paragraph, the message poorly spaced and placed badly on the page—these all reflect poorly on the company sending the letter or on the manager who signs it.

Although the mechanical aspects of the business letter (such as typing, style, and format) are secretarial tasks, the manager should have some familiarity with them (see Appendix B). It is the manager's responsibility to see that letters going out over his or her name meet standards of attractiveness.

QUESTIONS FOR STUDY

1. What items are mandatory in a company's letterhead? What items are optional?
2. Do you agree or disagree with this statement? "Only secretaries care about the format details of a business letter. Everyone else just wants the message." Justify your answer.
3. What is the *you* attitude? In what specific ways can it be achieved?
4. The technology of writing letters has changed dramatically in the last twenty years. Describe at least three major changes.
5. How do you define *clarity* in business communication? What helps create it? What destroys it?
6. Why is the *you* attitude important in business communication?
7. It is suggested that the letter writer prepare the materials in a "natural tone." Why would an executive not duplicate precisely what he or she says in what he or she writes?
8. What's worse—a mechanical error or an error concerning the connotation of the message? Explain why there is a difference in these types of errors.

9. What is the difference between "write as you speak" and "write as you sound"?
10. What is the difference between conciseness and brevity?
11. Do people really react to words? Explain.
12. Is it ever appropriate to project a negative tone in business correspondence?
13. What does "losing face" have to do with tact?
14. Submit to your instructor a form letter or personal letter received at your home or office. Circle all words or phrases you would designate as "hackneyed."
15. Discuss the relationship between completeness and effective outlining of business letters.

EXERCISES

16. The *you* attitude is easy to understand and often difficult to implement. For each of the following situations, write a first sentence for the letter clearly reflecting the *you* attitude.
    (a) A letter to a company that repaired your photocopy machine. Within three hours after the job was done, it broke down again; it's the fifth time this has happened.
    (b) A letter to the General Electric Company requesting a copy of its annual report.
    (c) A letter to the mayor asking if a street near campus can be closed on homecoming night for the annual bonfire.
17. Convert each of these *we*-centered statements to *you* statements.
    (a) I want your account so that I can demonstrate how experienced I am in property management.
    (b) My new store will open on May 17. Come see my fabulous collection of designer furniture, all personally selected by me to reflect the latest trends in contemporary interior decoration.
    (c) I appreciate the hospitality I received during my recent visit to the corporate offices of Henderson, Kay, and Co.
    (d) I am writing to provide notification that, according to my records, the September payment has not been received. I need that payment so that I can, in turn, make my own payments.
18. Convert each of the following statements from a negative tone to a positive tone.
    (a) You failed to obey the detailed instructions we provided with your glider kit.
    (b) We assume that you will not find fault with your Grass-All mower.

(c) This company has no reason to doubt that our relationship will be free from unnecessary hassles and disappointments.

(d) Please do not neglect to watch for unintentional errors when reviewing the manuscript.

19. Which of the popular business letter styles do your friends and acquaintances prefer? Conduct your own survey by showing two or more different formats of the same letter to those surveyed. When they have made their choice, ask them to explain their preference. Sum up those reasons in a short statistical and interpretive report on the survey.

20. Gather at least four of your old reports or term papers. From them, glean a list of hackneyed expressions you have a tendency to use. Beside each hackneyed phrase, write down a more adequate alternative.

21. Tone has a lot to do with word choice. Some words reflect a positive tone, while others reflect a negative tone. Illustrate the extreme by setting up a dozen matched pairs of words or phrases; one list will be positive, the other negative. For example:

Negative Tone	*Positive Tone*
cheap	inexpensive

22. Hackneyed expressions will date you and will generally not reflect favorably upon you. Even though you feel you have written a good letter, the use of these terms may ruin your credibility before the reader gets past the first paragraph. The following are sentences that do not belong in any business person's correspondence. Revise appropriately.

(a) As per your request, here is the summary of the *Marketing Research* article you wanted.

(b) Hoping to hear from you in the near future, best wishes.

(c) At your earliest convenience will you please return the draft memo so that it can be polished and distributed.

(d) According to our records you have not returned *Communicating In Business* to the company library; may we hear from you at your earliest convenience?

(e) Regarding your recent promotion, permit me to say how pleased Jane and I are for you; you deserved it and we wish you every success.

23. Find an advertisement that, in your opinion, exemplifies the appropriate use of the *you* perspective. Write an evaluation in which you suggest how this perspective influences those reading and viewing the ad.

24. Rewrite the following letter body so that it reflects the principles of tact discussed in this chapter. (These sentences are being sent to students who have not qualified for scholarship aid.)

This will inform you that you have failed to qualify for scholarship aid for the coming academic term. Only students who demonstrated the ability to score 780 or higher on the Standard Qualification Index were considered for awards. If you have complaints about this decision, it is our duty to inform you of your right to appeal this negative response to the Complaint Committee of the Scholarship Board.

25. Drawing upon recent experience, clearly describe a situation in which you used language that resulted in a response you certainly did not anticipate. In other words, the connotation was inappropriate. Then indicate what you could have done to avoid the situation.

26. Incomplete letters create problems at both the sender's end and the receiver's end of the communication. The problem can be remedied if the initiator of the communication takes special effort to ensure that all of the necessary information is included.

    You receive a telephone call that is summarized as follows:

    Robert Walberg of the International Association of Business Communicators wants to know if the hotel has one large meeting room (for 50 people), hotel rooms (35 singles), and banquet facilities for 50 people. Need this for the day and night of Wednesday, February 17, 19___ .

    You are to respond to this request as assistant manager of the Magnolia Hotel. Indicate on a separate sheet of paper the process you would go through to ensure you provide R. Walberg with complete information.

27. A university has a policy that freshmen must live on campus, in approved university housing, or with their parents or guardians. Susan Murphy lives in the town in which the university is located and resides with her parents. She receives the following letter (in part) from the university housing office:

    Dear Miss Murphy:

    As you are residing in unapproved housing you are in violation of Section 1-c of the university housing regulations. See Mr. Pat Herman of our office before October 10, 19___ , or your registration will be cancelled.

    The letter has no *you* orientation, and the computer or personnel in the housing office have erred. However, now Sue is hopping mad. How could the letter be written with more tact and not pronounce her guilty before hearing about the situation? Prepare a tactful letter that will not make innocent people angry with the organization.

28. For each of the following vague statements, write a brief paragraph discussing the problems that might ensue if these messages were actually sent.

(a) (from a vice president to a unit manager) I received your memo, and agree that we need to hire necessary help. Please proceed to do so.

(b) (from one employee to another) You and I are supposed to prepare something for next week's meeting. Let's get together sometime this week.

(c) (from an accountant to a manager) Monthly cash balances show some irregularities.

(d) (from a company president to vice presidents) I'll be on vacation for three weeks. Handle matters as best you can until I return.

22 Inquiries, Requests, and Orders

The right words are the greatest motivators of all.

The most common business letters of all (and often the most overlooked) are inquiries, requests, orders, claims, and collection letters. Too often these brief communications misfire because the writer has looked upon them as "just routine." He or she has forgotten to be concise, complete, courteous, and reader-oriented.

In fact, the routine letters of business are among the most important. Even the most simple business transaction usually requires requests for information, confirmation of orders, communications with regulatory agencies, and dozens of other routine written messages. These are the stitches that hold the fabric of business together.

MAKING INQUIRIES AND REQUESTS

Essentially, an **inquiry** asks for information. A **request** goes further; it asks for someone's services as a speaker, for endorsement of a product, for a free sample—in short, it requires action beyond a simple written reply.

Before you begin to write a letter of inquiry or request, determine exactly what your purpose is—what information or action you want. Keep in mind that you and the recipient of your letter are both busy. Make an outline, including all important points, both pro and con.

Your inquiry may be simple and brief: Who is the distributor in our area? How quickly can a carload be shipped? Is a discount available? Or your inquiry may be complex and difficult: What would be involved in air conditioning our offices? What kind of market is there for our product on the West Coast? What does the Affirmative Action Program mean to us? Regardless of the nature of the inquiry, the principle is the same—be complete, clear, and courteous. And get to the point immediately, particularly when the problem is complex. Your first sentence or two should state the subject, so that from the very beginning the receiver can identify the problem; he or she will not have to wade through extraneous greetings and references. Responses will probably be more specific and direct if you ask in the same manner. Figure 22–1 shows examples of a poorly written and a well-written letter of inquiry. Notice that both letters request information, but the effective letter will elicit exactly what Mr. Owens needs to know.

The effective letter of inquiry has several attributes:

1. Reason for inquiry in the first or second sentence.
2. Explanation of circumstances, if necessary.
3. The inquiry itself, with specific questions listed.
4. Indication of the date by which a reply is needed.
5. Assurance that information will be considered confidential (if applicable).

Note that the well-written letter in Figure 22–1 meets these criteria, enabling the reader to reply intelligently and to take action. Every letter of inquiry should aim to elicit an intelligent and complete reply.

The letter of inquiry should make it easy for the recipient to reply. It can do this by listing questions in an orderly fashion and by limiting itself to essentials. It is unrealistic to ask so many questions that replying to the letter would require an unreasonable expenditure of time or money. If a problem is very complex, abstract, or detailed, it may be necessary to set up an interview or a conference to discuss it. Finally, the writer may even wish to assist the recipient by including a self-addressed envelope.

Request letters follow the same pattern as inquiry letters. Because they are asking for action rather than just an answer, it is even more important that they be clear, and they should be written far in advance of the proposed date of action.

RESPONDING TO INQUIRIES AND REQUESTS: SAYING "YES"

When a major corporation places a double-page spread in a national magazine, it is not unusual for the advertisement to bring in one to two thousand inquiry letters: Where can I buy your television set? Is the model pictured in the lower left-hand corner available in walnut? What are the dimensions of the set pictured in the upper center of the page? What is the address of the dealer nearest my home?

All inquiries should be answered because each one represents a potential sale. It would not be practical to answer each individually, so standard replies are prepared. These may be form letters, brochures, pamphlets, or

FIGURE 22–1

A poorly written letter of inquiry and a well-written letter of inquiry

Heavenly Mattress Corporation

383 Timber Drive
Portland, OR 20393
(493) 298-3831

Ms. Wilma Rudens
Vice President, Sales
Bennington Enterprises
989 Fifth Steet
Seattle, WA 60843

Dear Ms. Rudens:

Because you market a line of steel bed frames, you are probably familiar with the Wendex frame. We have had bad luck with that frame. In fact, more than half of the complaints and returns we have had on our mattresses from our six discount warehouses have been due to frame collapses, not mattress flaws.

Needless to say, we want to do something about this problem, and so are writing to you since you are the major competitor, we understand, to the Wendex line.

Thank you for answering our questions as soon as possible.

Sincerely,

Ralph Owens

Ralph Owens
Quality Control Supervisor

Request is vague
and incomplete.

Heavenly Mattress Corporation

383 Timber Drive
Portland, OR 20393
(493) 298-3831

Dear Ms. Rudens:

I am writing to ask your help with an expensive problem faced by this company: collapsing bed frames.

Since 1985, we have supplied Wendex Model #203 steel frames with our twin, full, double, queen, and king size mattress sets. Much to our dismay, 16 percent of these frames are returned to us for replacement within 24 months (our warranty period).

Therefore, we are looking for a more satisfactory frame. Specifically, we would appreciate your response to three questions:

1. Do you sell a frame comparable in price to the Wendex #203 but more stable in design and construction?

2. If so, is that frame available for all common mattress sizes?

3. Can you deliver in quantities of 100 frames directly to our six discount warehouses (addresses and map attached)? Please include an estimate of delivery costs.

We are eager to find a frame that matches the high quality we build into our mattress sets. Thank you for your early reply.

Sincerely,

Ralph Owens

Ralph Owens
Quality Control Supervisor

Specific questions help the reader make a definite response, and they help the receiver make a specific reply. Assurance of confidence is often important.

even post cards. The form is relatively unimportant, provided the inquiry is answered completely and as quickly as possible. Further, and perhaps most important, the reply—in whatever form—should express thanks for the inquiry and interest in serving the inquirer.

Nonroutine Replies

There are, however, many letters of inquiry or request which cannot be adequately answered with a printed form or pamphlet. A purchasing agent wants to know if a modification to an existing model is possible; a sales manager would like a price consideration on a quantity purchase; and a bookkeeper's inquiry concerns the handling of depreciation under unusual conditions. Such queries require individual replies.

When you can answer an inquiry or grant a request, do so near the beginning of your letter. Don't leave the recipient in suspense. The letter in Figure 22–2 follows a general organizational pattern:

1. An introductory statement acknowledging the inquiry.
2. The grant itself.
3. A list of the necessary information or reference to the source where it may be found.
4. A constructive suggestion, if possible.
5. A sales appeal (if applicable).
6. A friendly close.

Reply Promptly   Regardless of whether your reply to an inquiry or request is favorable or unfavorable, it is vital that the inquiry be answered promptly. When questions come in concerning products or services, make every effort to reply within twenty-four hours. If you can tell inquirers "yes," so much the better, but do not make them wait several days to receive a "no, we're sorry." If you communicate your decision immediately, they can then attempt further action. Or, if you cannot meet their wishes, they can turn elsewhere.

Of course, an immediate answer should be sent to every letter you receive, but in the case of an inquiry it is especially vital that a reply go out at once.

RESPONDING TO INQUIRIES AND REQUESTS: SAYING "NO"

We all prefer to say "yes" to inquiries and requests made of us, whether they come from clients or coworkers. They are pleased when we accommodate their wishes—and, frankly, we like to be thought of as "good guys" who please others.

FIGURE 22–2

Individualized answer to an inquiry or request

SP *SYSTEMS PLANNING CORPORATION*
11394 N.W. 23rd Street   Washington D.C. 20071

May 19, 19___

Ms. Donna Hayworth
Manager of Training
Energy Electronics Corp.
101 Sutter Street
San Francisco, CA 94150

Dear Ms. Hayworth:

We received your letter of May 15 in which you inquired about the recent training program conducted for our office personnel. I am happy to give you the information you requested.

The training was done by Communication Services, located here in New York. We selected middle-management people whose job responsibilities require that they write a good many business letters and reports. The class was limited to 16 members and met for two hours each Tuesday afternoon, on company time. Twelve such sessions were held. Communication Services provided the instructor, text, and all handout material. Home assignments were given to the participants, and these were evaluated by the instructor and returned to the students.

We found the program to be very valuable. Our employees enjoyed it and came away with many valuable ideas, which are clearly evident in their day-to-day writing assignments. We have scheduled a second class for this fall, and we know it will be as profitable as the one we just concluded.

If you wish any other information in this area, I shall be very happy to cooperate with you.

Yours truly,

Cathleen Campbell

Cathleen Campbell
Training Director

---

1 Present a positive answer as quickly as possible.
Note how specific the reply is.

No manager, however, succeeds for long without the ability to say "no" firmly and politely. At times, you probably have to say "no" to inquiries that touch upon sensitive company information. At other times, you'll have to say "no" to requests, however earnest, for favors that you cannot or will not grant.

How does it feel to say "no"—and what does it say to others about you? In his best-selling book, *When I Say No I Feel Guilty,*[1] psychologist Pete Smith discusses the necessary ability to say "no" with a clear conscience. Your refusal of an inquiry or request, while perhaps disappointing to others, does not brand you as a social or business outcast. Much better, Smith contends, to say "no" politely and honestly rather than to invent white lies—excuses that, sooner or later, will be unraveled.

Here's a case in point. Mike Farring manages Victory Outdoor Signs, Inc., and supervises a large fleet of flatbed trucks. Marjorie Wilkes, director of a local charity, writes to Farring with the request shown in Figure 22–3.

Put yourself in Farring's shoes. On the one hand, he feels that the charity does important work. On the other hand, his trucks must be available every day in June, the busy season, if the company is to meet its contracts. Farring decides to say "no." But should he invent an excuse—"insurance reasons," perhaps, or "broken-down trucks"?

Such excuses would lead Farring directly into trouble. If he refuses the request on insurance grounds, Ms. Wilkes may well offer to pay for a supplemental policy during the days of the Festival. Then what is Farring to say? If he refuses on the grounds of mechanical problems with the trucks, Ms. Wilkes may round up volunteer mechanics to fix the problem. Then what?

Farring decides to tell the truth politely and honestly. His letter is shown in Figure 22–4.

You may ask, "But shouldn't he *solve* Ms. Wilkes' problem? Shouldn't he volunteer to rent three trucks for her?" Frankly, no. While he can choose to become involved in the Children's Charities project, *he is under no such obligation* merely because he has received a request.

But, while Farring recognizes his freedom not to fulfill Ms. Wilkes' wishes, he also knows that feelings are involved. She has made a sincere, well-intentioned request and does deserve courtesy and, where possible, an explanation of the refusal. By appreciating the feeling involved, Farring can be sure that Ms. Wilkes will not consider him a blackguard. Nor will she spread damaging rumors about his company's lack of civic involvement. Although Farring probably cannot prevent momentary disappointment on her part, he can at least buffer that disappointment by a courteous, explanatory response.

[1]Peter Smith, *When I Say No I Feel Guilty,* New York: McGraw-Hill, 1979.

FIGURE 22–3

Request eliciting negative reply

CHILDREN'S CHARITIES
302 Broad Street   Boise, Idaho 30234

March 11, 19__

Mr. Mike Farring
Manager
Victory Outdoor Signs, Inc.
293 Seventh St.
Boise, ID 30231

Dear Mr. Farring:

A client of yours, Brad Jenning, suggested that I contact you to
request a favor--a very worthwhile one.

Children's Charities wants to participate in the city's Summer
Festival parade this June. We're seeking three flatbed trucks
we can convert to floats for the parade. Mr. Jenning pointed
out to me that your trucks would be ideal for this purpose.

Thank you, Mr. Farring, for considering this request. All of us
at Children's Charities hope for your favorable response, and
eagerly await your answer.

Sincerely,

Marjorie Wilkes

Marjorie Wilkes
Director

FIGURE 22–4
Brief refusal letter

VICTORY OUTDOOR SIGN
293 SEVENTH STREET
BOISE, IDAHO 30231

March 14, 19__

Ms. Marjorie Wilkes
Director
Children's Charities
302 Broad St.
Boise, ID 30234

Dear Ms. Wilkes:

We at Victory Outdoor Signs, Inc., have admired the fine work of Children's Charities at the annual Summer Festival parade for many years.

As it happens, Ms. Wilkes, we've already made contractual commitments during June for the equipment you request. We are, of course, obligated to fulfill those commitments to our customers as well as to our many employees who will be needed to complete our contracts. Not to do so would result in a hardship on both groups.

Thank you for thinking of us, however. We send you and your coworkers our best wishes for another successful Summer Festival.

Sincerely,

Mike Farring

Mike Farring
Manager

In summary, remind yourself that just as others have the right to make requests of you, so you have the right—often the necessity—to turn down those requests in a polite and, if possible, constructive way. In usual business practice you'll soften the disappointment by

1. providing a rational explanation (not an invented excuse);
2. suggesting possible alternatives; and
3. expressing empathy in such a way that good will is retained.

The best guide for finding the right words in saying "no" is to place yourself solidly in the other person's shoes. What would he or she feel? What explanation would be helpful without undercutting your refusal? What alternatives might be offered? By considering the other person's feelings, you will choose words that communicate your message without creating barriers to future business and communication. See Figure 22–5 for a letter of refusal that succeeds in doing so.

PLACING ORDERS

Because of the volume of orders, modern firms usually place orders using printed order blanks or purchase order forms rather than individual letters; the former is more efficient and less costly. Whether you use a form or a letter, you must be certain to include most (or all) of the following data:

1. Catalog number
2. Quantity
3. Description of merchandise (model number, size, color)
4. Unit price; total price
5. Precise identification of purchasing unit or purchaser
6. Shipping address
7. Shipping method (e.g., UPS, air express, truck)
8. Payment method (COD, open account, check enclosed, etc.)
9. Delivery date desired
10. Miscellaneous information that may be included:
    (a) Order number
    (b) Date of order
    (c) Salesperson's name
    (d) Information on substitutions
    (e) Instructions for "back order"

The business person or consumer who writes a letter to place an order should be sure that it includes as much of the above data as possible. The objective is to receive the merchandise and not a reply requesting additional information.

FIGURE 22–5

Refusing a request

Amex Electronics, Inc.
402 Digital Street
Houston, TX 30244

AMEX

Ms. Roberta Venk
Manager
Alpha Acoustic Design
303 Freedom Trail
Boston, MA 02933

Dear Ms. Venk:

Thank you for your inquiry concerning technical specifications and design drawings for
the Amex Hi-Load Switch (#508).

1 While the technical details of the switch itself are proprietary (Patent #1092929), I am
happy to send along service schematics and user bulletins issued by our technical staff.
I trust these will be of use to you in your efforts to adapt the Hi-Load Switch to your
amplifier application.

2 We also maintain a user "hot-line" for product questions, and would be pleased to
answer your specific questions as they develop. Feel free to call us during business
hours at (800) 398-2391.

Thank you for your choice of Amex products.

Sincerely,

Cynthia Morgan

Cynthia Morgan
Technical Sales

---

1 The refusal is implied.

2 Constructive suggestions are usually appreciated.

RESPONDING TO ORDERS

In sending an order to your company, many—perhaps most—clients feel that they have done you a favor. They look to you not only for prompt delivery of the order, but also for good will and gratitude. In this way orders provide an opportunity for salesmanship leading to future business. Whether acknowledging orders, handling problem cases, or even refusing orders, your communications with clients can make or break future business relations.

Acknowledging Orders That Can Be Shipped

Most business transactions between buyer and seller are routine. Merchandise is ordered on Monday and delivered on Wednesday. These are often stock items and few, if any, problems ever arise. If a portion of the order is not delivered on Wednesday, it will probably be sent out the following week.

However, when products are manufactured on the basis of special instructions, or are to be delivered within a limited period of time, it is usually wise for the seller to acknowledge that the order has been received. This permits a formal understanding between buyer and seller so that possible problems at a future date may be avoided. If the buyer requests a Black and Johnson Cutter, Model 304, to be delivered within 30 days, and he receives an acknowledgment of the facts of the purchase from the seller, he may then assume that understanding exists. However, if he receives an acknowledgment from the seller indicating that a Model 403 cutter is being prepared for shipment, he can wire and correct the error immediately. Had the wrong cutter been shipped, both parties would have suffered. A simple acknowledgment has added to the efficiency of operations of the companies.

Many acknowledgments can be made by means of a form or guide letter; some cannot. This distinction lies largely in whether the buyer is a steady customer or a new one.

Steady Customers   Firms that acknowledge orders from steady customers usually use post cards, form letters, or duplicate invoices. The post card contains only a brief message indicating that the order has been received, is being processed, and will be shipped shortly. Usually, the ordered items are not listed for customer verification.

The form letter usually functions like the post card. However, it seems slightly more courteous because it travels in a stamped envelope. Completing these in a word-processing center is relatively inexpensive and rapid.

The most efficient and least expensive means of acknowledgment is the duplicate invoice, which is sent to the buyer. It is typed at the same time as the invoice (along with other needed copies). This duplicate fulfills three functions. It informs the buyer that the order is being processed; it is an expression of courtesy and consideration; and it permits the buyer to check the specific details of the order.

Every now and then a personal letter of acknowledgment should be sent to steady customers as an expression of pleasure in the business relationship (see Figure 22–6). Good customers like to know that they are not just taken for granted. Such a letter tells customers that they have not become mere account numbers to the seller. This kind of unnecessary act helps build goodwill.

New Customers   Although it is impossible to respond personally to every order from steady customers, it is necessary to do so to the first order of new customers. We want them to know that we truly appreciate adding their names to our customer list. This message also gives us an opportunity to delineate procedures and to clarify sale and payment terms.

This letter can effectively be made up as a guide letter and individually typed when the need arises. The readers should feel the red carpet has been rolled out for them, but the letter should not be so effusive as to sound insincere.

New customers are primarily concerned with their orders; the order should therefore be mentioned first. Then other details may be given on the company's services, policies, and practices. For further verification of the order, a duplicate of the invoice may accompany the letter. The letter in Figure 22–7 is a good example of a new-customer acknowledgment.

Acknowledging Orders When There Is a Problem

Not every order can be filled completely and efficiently. There are times when all the merchandise requested is not in stock, when the order isn't clear, or when the credit status of the customer is questionable.

Incomplete Orders   Sometimes orders are either incomplete, indefinite, or not clear. It is usually unwise to guess at what the customer means, for if the wrong merchandise is shipped it will be returned, and ill will and expense will result. Either an individually typed letter (see Figure 22–8) can be used, or a form letter with fill-in spaces can be prepared by the word-processing center. Notice in the letter the tactful and positive approach in Figure 22–8. The writer did not say, "You neglected," or "You forgot to list." She simply indicated the oversight and as soon as the correct information was received, the merchandise would be shipped.

Merchandise Not Handled   A customer may request merchandise not handled by the seller. Such an order may come in separately, or it may be one item in a large order.

FIGURE 22–6

Personal letter of acknowledgment to a steady customer

Cross Timing Devices
1225 Lehigh Avenue   Boulder, Colorado 80396

May 4, 19__

Mr. R. Stephan
Vice President
Brunswick Corp.
One Brunswick Plaza
Skokie, IL 60077

Dear Mr. Stephan:

This is just a short note to tell you that your order of April
28 has been received and is being filled according to your usual
instructions.

Your purchases, which have been made so regularly during the
past year, are always appreciated. Of course, we haven't written you an individual letter for each of the orders, but we want
you to know that we will always make every effort to supply you
with quality merchandise at the lowest possible prices.

If you have any special needs that we can fill, please give us
an opportunity to assist you. We appreciate your confidence in
us and shall try to earn it for many years to come.

Yours truly,

Emma Bartelli

Emma Bartelli

FIGURE 22–7

Letter to a new customer

Hobby Supplies, Inc.
492 Jason Street
New York, NY 10939
(202) 183-3923

June 1, 19__

Mr. Thomas Williams
Manager
The Hobbyist
30 Cactus Drive
Palm Springs, CA 70939

Dear Mr. Williams:

We want to welcome you to the Hobby Supplies family of satisfied customers. At Hobby Supplies, we pride ourselves on immediate response to customer needs, including any problems or emergencies that may arise. Count on us to give you our best.

As specified in your credit contract, we will supply merchandise to you, to a credit limit of $10,000, provided payment is made within 30 days of receipt. If you pay within ten days of billing, a 3 percent cash rebate will be applied to your account. (Many of our customers accrue hundreds of dollars of savings through such prompt payment.)

Jeff Thomas, your area representative, will call on you next Thursday to introduce himself and acquaint you with the full line at Hobby Supplies. His 24-hour message number is (202) 383-5935.

Thank you for your first order to Hobby Supplies. We are confident that you will be pleased with our products, prices, and service.

Sincerely,

Constance Yesterly

Constance Yesterly
Sales Director

FIGURE 22–8

Acknowledging an incomplete order

Western Home Products
878 Sheridan Road
Miami, Florida 33541

March 20, 19__

Mr. Ken Conway
Conway's Home Center
1515 W. Portland Ave.
College Park, MD   20740

Dear Mr. Conway:

Thank you very much for your order of March 17, #204, which arrived today. All the merchandise that you requested is in stock and will be shipped via Florida Freight Lines.

You may recall that you listed four dozen American Beauty two-quart cooking containers. However, you did not indicate whether you prefer these with the copper or the stainless steel bottoms. If you will check your preference on the enclosed airmail card, your order will be processed and shipped immediately.

I am also enclosing a flyer on our new outdoor grill line. If you wish to order a quantity of these fast-moving items, you can so indicate on the same card.

Sincerely,

Brenda Banks

Brenda Banks
Customer Service

What to do about this request? If we suggest a source of supply, we will create goodwill with the customer. However, there are some practical dangers inherent in this procedure. The source of supply will probably make every effort to satisfy the customer, and it may be that we will lose the customer to the very source we suggested. On the other hand, business ethics almost demand that we make such recommendations.

A letter handling such a situation might follow the general outline suggested by the letter in Figure 22–9. When the merchandise requested by a customer is only related to the usual items handled and does not compete directly with an item in stock, it is a good deal easier to make a recommendation, as in Figure 22–10. In some instances, a firm will obtain the item (which it does not handle) from a supplier and forward it to its customer. This is a matter of courtesy, as usually no profit is made, but this way a third party (who might be a competitor) is not introduced into the transaction.

REFUSING ORDERS

For a variety of different reasons, orders must sometimes be refused, even when the merchandise is in stock and available for immediate shipment. A few such cases are as follows:

1. The buyer is a poor credit risk.
2. The buyer has exceeded his credit limit.
3. Company regulations concerning a franchise or distributorship agreements would be violated.
4. Filling the order might be contrary to government regulations.
5. Filling the order would be unprofitable because of the limited quantity ordered, distances to be shipped, or modifications requested.
6. Only a limited supply is in stock, and this must be retained for steady accounts.

All of these cases should be handled tactfully, positively, and with a strong sales orientation. Figures 22–11 and 22–12 show two acknowledgment situations that can arise. The message communicated in each of these order refusals is conciliatory, rather than confrontive or offensive. The author says, in effect, "Look, we're very much interested in doing business with you. We appreciate your order. But we need to restructure the order to make it work for both of us. Let's try doing it this way . . ."

The client, therefore, has no reason to feel insulted. He or she faces the reality that the company has necessary standards for business practice, and is pleased to know that the company wants to make some arrangement work—if not now, then in the future.

FIGURE 22–9

Acknowledging an order for merchandise not handled

WILSHIRE OFFICE PRODUCTS
388 Marine Drive
Los Angeles, California 90099

January 10, 19__

Mr. Calvin Hart, Manager
Prime Time Corp.
Six North Forenbain Blvd.
Milwaukee, WI 52313

Dear Mr. Hart:

We have received your Order #202, dated January 7; all the merchandise, with one exception, will be on its way to you by this afternoon.

Although we handle all types of office supplies, we have never stocked the Arco Filing Cabinet. This is recognized an an excellent unit; however, our customers' needs at this level have always been fulfilled by the Apex Line, which we do stock. We can fill your order for Apex products immediately.

However, your request specifically lists your preference for the Arco. These may be purchased from the Dearborn Office Furniture Corporation, located in Chicago.

It has been a pleasure doing business with you, and we know that you will be satisfied for many years to come with the consistently high quality of merchandise we handle and the competitive prices we offer. Please call collect if you would like to purchase the Apex items.

Sincerely,

Cliff Van Art

Cliff Van Art
Sales Manager

FIGURE 22–10

Recommending a source for merchandise not carried

Quality Auto-Parts

1500 West Fulton Street   Philadelphia, Pennsylvania 19102   (215) 650-0550

February 5, 19__

Ms. F. W. Flynn
Ass't. Sales Manager
Powers Pontiac
150 S. Main Drive
Santa Monica, CA   90401

Dear Ms. Flynn:

Thank you for your recent note inquiring whether we handle auto-mobile seat covers as well as our usual line of automobile accessories.

As you may know, we stock over 5000 parts for cars. We have considered putting in a line of seat covers, safety belts, and so on, but have not as yet.

Through our own experience, we have found that the Los Angeles Auto Seat Company is an excellent firm. The quality of their merchandise is high and their prices competitive. I recommend that you get in touch with them. Ask specifically for Mr. Kameron, who has always given us excellent service.

Enclosed you will find our latest parts catalog. Check through it; we know you will find many items of interest.

Cordially yours,

Tom Jackson

Tom Jackson
Ass't. Sales Manager

FIGURE 22–11
Refusing an order on the basis of poor credit risk

General Market Products, Inc.
2693 Container Drive
Huntington Park, CA 82033
(392) 298-3838

Mr. George Taylor
Manager
Taylor Mini-Marts, Inc.
1093 St. Louis Avenue
San Diego, CA 30293

Dear Mr. Taylor:

Thank you for applying for credit purchases from General Market Products.

1 Our credit agency, TRW, advises us that you qualify for a cash payment account at this time. If you have questions about specific reasons for their evaluation, plese contact them directly at (800) 828-3267.

2 As a cash customer, you will receive a 2 percent discount on all purchases. After a period of six months as a cash customer (or as soon as you clarify your credit status with TRW), we will be most happy to review your application for credit purchases.

Thank you for looking to General Market Products to serve your needs.

Sincerely,

Victoria Buenasto

Victoria Buenasto
Credit Manager

1 A direct, courteous explanation.

2 A positive comment listing advantages.

FIGURE 22–12

Refusing an order on the basis of violating regulations

Cross Timing Devices
1225 Lehigh Avenue   Boulder, Colorado 80396

May 25, 19__

Mr. Fred Franklin
Franklin's Jewel Box
1010 So. Martin Drive
Washington, DC 20319

Dear Mr. Franklin:

We were happy to receive your request to stock our new Precision
Watch Line.

Some months ago we visited Washington and at that time selected
twelve jewelry outlets to handle the Precision Watch. Unfortunately, we did not get in touch with you. However, we did assure each of the twelve dealers that Washington would have a
maximum of one dozen franchises. In all fairness to these outlets, therefore, and in conformity with our agreement, we can
open no others at this time.

If, however, one of these twelve does not wish to retain the
franchise, we will get in touch with you immediately to determine your availability.

We certainly appreciate your interest in the Precision Line. We
have enclosed our new catalog in the hope that you will find
other non-franchise items of interest to you.

Sincerely yours,

Steven Andrews

Steven Andrews
Manager

QUESTIONS FOR STUDY

1. In what ways does routine correspondence with new customers often differ from such correspondence to established customers.
2. Why are routine business letters often produced carelessly?
3. In what ways can the writer of an inquiry letter make it easy for the recipient to respond?
4. What opportunities for salesmanship exist in responding to orders?
5. Why is negative language inappropriate in responding to incomplete orders?
6. Discuss reasons why orders must sometimes be refused.
7. Why is clarity so important in inquiries, requests, and orders?
8. For receiving orders, why have many organizations created forms when there is a letter called the order letter?
9. Under what circumstances is it appropriate to explicitly list what it is you want in your letter of request?
10. What purpose is served by including a "due date" in an inquiry letter?
11. In what types of inquiry letters would you assure the reader of confidentiality? Cite three examples.
12. What can the writer of the inquiry letter do to help the recipient respond in a complete manner?
13. Replies to letters of inquiry are frequently compared to sales letters. In what ways are they similar? Different?
14. Are there some legal factors which one should be aware of in replies to inquiries? Explain.

EXERCISES

15. Assume you're planning a trip to Europe with college friends. You have to get a passport—and in a hurry. Write a letter, as if to your local passport office, emphasizing your need for quick service. Try to build a persuasive message that not only tells your reader what you want, but motivates him or her to help you attain it.
16. A professor last semester gave you a much lower grade than you expected or, you believe, deserved. Unfortunately, he has now left your college. Write a letter to the chair of his department inquiring what steps you can take to have your grade reviewed.
17. Visit or call three personnel directors. Determine from them if they have made changes in the last few years in their replies to requests for evaluations of previously employed individuals. Have these changes been due in some respects to legal responsibilities and recent court cases? Be as specific as possible in your report on this topic.

18. Secure three actual refusal letters from three different companies. These may refuse orders, credit, or job applicants. Report on the organization of each letter as to the placement of the refusal statement(s), the explanation, and the goodwill portion. Indicate strong and weak points of each according to your perception.

19. In the role of an office manager, write brief letters of refusal to each of these requests:

    (a) Our organization wishes to use your company cafeteria on May 6 from 2:00 to 5:30 P.M. for our "Feed the Homeless" project.

    (b) I understand that few of your secretaries practice shorthand anymore. As a retired teacher of shorthand, I will be happy to teach your people this invaluable skill. My fees are quite reasonable.

    (c) The Eagle Troop would like to spend a day with your employees, matched one-on-one, to observe the goings-on of actual business. We'll have approximately 140 youngsters on hand, most in their early teens.

20. In one of the business periodicals you read an ad concerning executive desk blotters. You can order them in a variety of sizes and colors of leather and with or without accessories such as letter openers, ink wells, and pencil holders. You want a blotter in green leather, about 30" by 20", and you have no need for any accessories. Order the item. Incidentally, the order form has been misplaced, so you will have to send a letter to the Barry Office Company, Box 3, Jefferson City, MO 65101.

21. You are chairman of your school's Business Awareness Week. One of the activities during the week will be a series of speakers who will have different perspectives on business.

    You are to write a letter of request to each individual. In some ways the letters can be the same, but they will have to be individualized also. The following is a list of the people you are going to ask to speak. Write the basic request letter.

    Ms. Elizabeth McRoy, President, Onyx Inc. is one of your state's largest employers.

    Dr. Raymond Jennings, Director, Consumer Affairs Office, and assistant to the governor of your state.

    Mr. Dennis Anthony, executive director of your city's Chamber of Commerce.

    Mrs. Deloris Rayfield, who is active in community affairs and an outspoken critic of businesses and current business practices.

    Mr. Harold Dykum, author of the book, "Businesses Rip You Off."

    Dr. Patricia Malcomb, business professor who teaches business ethics at another college in your region.

In making your request you should also recognize that you have no funds to offer honorariums to these individuals; you can cover none of the expenses associated with their coming.

22. An item college graduates often need is a transcript of their college work. You work in the Registrar's office and you see the hodgepodge of letters that arrive daily requesting transcripts. More than half the letters provide insufficient information to allow the desired response. In an attempt to make the process more efficient, you suggest that graduating seniors be given several order blanks for transcripts along with their diplomas. The Registrar says, "Fine idea; please develop the form."

    In developing the form, keep in mind that (1) postage rates change periodically, (2) some transcripts are needed for personal use and some are sent to potential employers, and (3) you must ensure, because of privacy laws, that the request is valid.

23. You have received an advertisement for briefcases. The ad neglects to mention specific colors, referring simply to "a full range of popular shades." It happens that you want a light tan briefcase. Order the briefcase, making sure that the dealer does not send you the wrong shade of brown.

24. Write brief, constructive refusal letters to the following orders:
    (a) Please send thirteen cases of Comstock Lubricant, your catalog #20301, no later than February 3. As a new company, we have not yet completed our banking arrangements, and therefore will appreciate credit arrangements for the next 60 days or so.
    (b) We think your line of graduation jewelry will please our students. Before we order, however, we'd like to see actual samples. Please send several 18-karat class rings, bracelets, and chains for our inspection. We'll then let you know about the order.
    (c) You don't mention in your catalog if you sell on consignment. We assume, therefore, that you do. Please send 140 lamps and lighting accessories (see list attached) by May 6. This order must arrive in time for the grand opening of Western Lighting Showroom. We have high hopes for the success of our venture, and count on your merchandise to make the grand opening a smash.

LEGAL CONSIDERATIONS

TERMS AND TITLES OF LAWS AND REGULATIONS OF IMPORTANCE TO THE MANAGER-COMMUNICATOR

Term or Title	Explanation
Agency	This area of law has evolved from common law and, in the context of the business or other organization, establishes that the principal (*e.g.*, the employer) can employ people to act on the principal's behalf; establishes a communication link between the company and the manager.
Antitrust Acts	Legislation that has been passed concerning restraint of trade.
Contract	An agreement between two or more persons which will be recognized under the law.
Decertification	A procedure available to union memberships that permits them to eliminate their collective agreement with their union.
Defamation	Injury to an individual's person or character through communication of false information.
EEOC	Equal Employment Opportunity Commission; can establish and monitor regulations concerning employer's hiring, promoting, training, and retirement practices.
EPA	Environmental Protection Agency; can establish and monitor regulations concerning organization's "communication" via odor, noise, and sight.
Equal Protection of the Laws	The constitutional principle that says people shall not be treated unfairly by reason of race, sex, creed, or national origin.
ERISA	Employer Retirement Income Security Act; stipulates that employer shall communicate retirement program to employees in understandable language.

Term or Title	Explanation
Exempt (exempt employee)	Employee exempt from overtime pay—generally a manager.
FTC	Federal Trade Commission; is granted authority to provide consumers with protection against "unfair methods of competition." This can include how companies use language to communicate with customers.
Garnishment	A legal proceeding wherein a creditor is permitted to hold property or some wages of debt for satisfaction of a debt.
Libel	A defamatory communication without legal justification.
NLRB	National Labor Relations Board; can establish regulations concerning labor practices—regulations include communication activities.
Non-exempt (nonexempt employee)	Employee not exempt from overtime—generally an employee paid by the hour and subject to overtime compensation, not a manager or supervisor.
SEC	Securities and Exchange Commission; created to oversee and regulate stock exchanges and those dealing with them. SEC can create rules and regulations on the relationship (communication) between the owner, manager, and other parties.
Subpoena	Order of the court to appear and testify; *subpoena duces tecum,* to appear with specific documentation.
Sunshine Laws	Laws enacted to permit greater scrutiny—to let the "sun" shine in. Governments, as part of sunshine legislation, have been forced to open files and meetings to individuals and to the public. Therefore, this legislation has influenced communication.
UCC	Uniform Commercial Code; suggested language for uniform laws among the various states in such areas as contracts, sales, and letters of credit.
UCCC	Uniform Consumer Credit Code; drafted federal legislation published for adoption by the states. Grants rights to consumer and regulates creditor.
Warranty	An assurance or guarantee that may be communicated explicitly or implicitly about a good; a kind of contract.

23

Claim, Credit, and Collection Letters

Effective communication: the basis for credit relationships.

Claim, credit, and collection letters can be treated together because of their marked similarities. All three types are concerned with money—claims for it, credit purchases without it, and collection of it. And all three are written against the backdrop of the law. In the case of claims, legal action is often around the next corner if the claim is not satisfactorily handled. In matters of credit communication, the law (in particular, the Fair Credit Billing Act of 1974 and the Fair Credit Reporting Act of 1970) prescribes what information must be communicated and when. Finally, in the case of collection letters, the law provides both protection for the debtor (especially in the Fair Debt Collection Practices Act of 1978) and means by which the creditor can collect what is due.

In this chapter, we will examine each of these forms in turn. Although they are not the most pleasant business communications to compose, they are among the most important—and, often, the most difficult. One initial word of caution: in all matters related to credit and collection law, seek the specific advice of a competent business attorney before delivering your correspondence to its recipient. The sample letters in this chapter may be relied upon as a **guide to style,** but **should not** be used as a **legal guide,** especially because credit and collection law changes frequently.

CLAIMS

Business transactions do not always run smoothly. Regardless of how careful or efficient business organizations are, things will go wrong from time to time. Merchandise may be shipped to a wrong address or arrive in less than perfect condition; badly needed articles may be delayed; quality may not be at the level expected.

When such situations arise, a claim letter is usually sent. And because most people in industry recognize that errors do take place, the letter—if it is reasonably and properly written—will bring the desired adjustment. Claims must be handled efficiently, for in one year's time the amount of money involved can reach a very significant level. One Los Angeles firm, for instance, found that many of its vital dollars were being drained away because of poor claim procedures. A management consulting firm found that in one year the company had submitted some $60,000 in claims to suppliers, shippers, and dealers. However, for that time period it had received only $8000 in adjustments. Investigation disclosed that the claims entered had been incomplete and inaccurate and follow-ups almost nonexistent. The poor ratio of adjustments received to claims entered was the fault not of the firms to whom the requests were submitted, but of the company itself.

In an attempt to improve the adjustment record, a brief training program was given to those persons concerned with claims. Once they began writing complete, clear, and specific claim letters, the dollar amount of adjustments rose dramatically. In the year following the initial survey, adjustments received increased an estimated $30,000 as a result of improved communication.

There are various levels of claim problems. If a transaction does not go precisely as we have requested and it is a matter of correcting a very understandable situation, we make a *routine* claim. If, however, the situation has several facets and there is a question as to who is responsible, we enter a *nonroutine* claim.

Routine Claim Letters

Routine claim letters are usually associated with relatively minor problems. When the wrong quantity, size, color, or model has been shipped or an error has been made in pricing, discount privileges, or other routine matters, all that is necessary is a clear, specific, concise claim letter listing the facts of the situation. Note in Figure 23–1 that the writer says clearly that, except for three watches, the delivery was satisfactory. He does not say, "You mispacked the watches," (personal statement criticizing an individual), but "Due to mispacking." He mentions the demand for the product and assumes his claim is completely valid and will be taken care of immediately (positive tone).

Because mistakes do happen in order filling, shipping, and billing, some firms have form letters for routine claims, with blank spaces to be completed.

Nonroutine Claim Letters

Often when an error occurs, the facts are not always clear-cut and obvious. The buyer may feel that $140 is due because the damage took place prior to receipt of the merchandise. The seller, however, contends that it left the

FIGURE 23–1

Routine claim letter

RANDALL FINE WATCHES
47 Main Street
Phoenix, AZ 60302
(313) 698-3819

September 18, 19__

Ms. Linda Ortiz
Customer Relations
Grenell Watch Company
80 West Sixth Street
Cincinnati, OH 67032

Dear Ms. Ortiz:

Thank you for delivering our order of August 1 in time for our
"Back to School" watch sale.

Three watches included in the shipment, however, were damaged in
transit, apparently because of mispacking. The boxes for these
watches were not taped shut (your usual practice), and during
shipment, the watches fell to the bottom of the shipping container.

I've enclosed the damaged watches. You will note the abrasions
on the bands and faces.

We will appreciate replacement of these watches by UPS one-day
service so we can fill standing orders in a timely way. Please
call immediately if you anticipate a delay.

Sincerely,

Tim Watson

Tim Watson
Owner

premises in perfect condition. Or perhaps the buyer maintains that a case of merchandise was not received, although the seller insists that it was. Situations like these require nonroutine claim letters. They are nonroutine because there is a difference of opinion as to who is at fault. Sometimes the adjustments are in favor of the seller; sometimes they favor the buyer. One thing is certain: the seller does not relish receiving a claim letter nor does the buyer like to write one.

The claim letter should be so well written that it will result in a specific answer. Buyers hope that answer will be a "yes, we will credit your account." If, however, buyers cannot secure an affirmative reply, they should strive for one that suggests a compromise. And if they can secure neither, then they should look for an answer that says "no." Of course, the "no" is not very satisfactory, but at least it tells them where they stand. They may now take their business elsewhere if they are unhappy or accept the "no." Obviously a follow-up to a "no" will depend on the strength and size of the claim. However, the claimant should make every effort to avoid eliciting a reply that conveys no definite answer. Such a response is merely a brush-off or a delaying action. It goes something like this:

> We will look into it; may we suggest that you do the same. Please be assured that this will be settled to our mutual satisfaction. Now let me call your attention to a special we are running . . .

This type of letter is no better than none at all. Time has been wasted, and as the days and weeks go by without an adjustment, the strength and immediacy of the claim decline.

However, claim letters can be written so that they will result in a definite answer. The following outline should be generally followed in the composition of an effective claim letter:

1. An introductory statement referring precisely and specifically to the transaction.
2. A specific description of the loss or damage incurred.
3. A specific statement of the adjustment desired.
4. A statement which will motivate favorable action.
5. A friendly close.

When buyers are certain that their claim is correct from every point of view, and that the adjustment they are requesting is honest in every respect, then they should check their letter to be sure that the tone is positive (not accusing), the statements specific, and the details precise. On the other hand, if they are not sure who is at fault or how the damage or loss occurred, they can only honestly request that both parties do what is necessary to reach an equitable solution.

If the buyer's letter reflects a tone of uncertainty, the recipient will very probably seize upon that tone to delay making an adjustment. In the following examples the revised phrases have a much more positive tone:

Original: *We believe the damage took place . . .*
Revised: *The damage took place . . .*

Original: *We think you did not include . . .*
Revised: *. . . was not included.*

Just as the tone should be positive, so too should the statements of loss or damage be specific and precise. Note the contrast between the original and revised versions of the sentences below:

Original: *We suffered a considerable loss.*
Revised: *Our loss was $58.12.*

Original: *The damage was quite extensive and we believe that . . .*
Revised: *The damage amounted to $114.52.*

Sometimes the writer, in an effort to be courteous, will not be as positive and as specific as possible, lest his or her statements be interpreted as pushy. It is important to be courteous, but uncertainty or vagueness may give the adjustor an opportunity to send a response that will result in delay and unnecessary correspondence. When the claim letter is outlined as suggested, when its tone is positive and its statements specific, the reply usually will be favorable.

Notice in Figure 23–2 how precisely the writer presents the facts and how positive the tone of the letter is. It is apparent that the writer is certain the recipient will not question the claim. The contrasting letter in Figure 23–3, however, enables the reader to send back an equivocal reply. It offers many opportunities for the recipient to legitimately delay taking specific action. The *probably* will surely result in a letter asking for further investigation. Then too the writer did not indicate whether the table had been left with its protective wrappings on while stored, and she certainly neglected to point out what adjustment she would consider equitable. Should the table be replaced or refinished? And finally, she made no reference to former business associations that might help motivate a favorable response. Thus when she receives a reply that only suggests further investigation, she will have no one to blame but herself.

Claims at the Consumer Level

What about typical consumers who have purchased a faulty television set or automatic washer? We frequently hear them complaining, but when asked what they have done about the situation, they respond with, "How can I fight a giant corporation like . . . ?" They suffer (and lose money) in silence.

FIGURE 23–2
A well-organized claim letter

Hank's Hardware
300 Main Street
West Point, Virginia 23181

May 15, 19__

Ms. Roberta Fox, Sales Manager
Summer Fun Furniture Co.
101 So. Felly Drive
Chicago, IL 60604

Dear Ms. Fox:

On March 15 we received our order #207 from you. You may recall that this included a large quantity of lawn furniture, barbecue accessories, and outdoor cookware.

If you will check our original purchase order, you will find that we requested six dozen sets of your Patio Grill Sets. Three dozen were to be sent in the regular style at $2.50 each and the remainder in the deluxe at $3.50 per set.

We have just started to display this merchandise and we have found that you inadvertently sent us five dozen of the regular and only one dozen of the deluxe. However, we have been billed according to our original purchase order.

Although we are aware that claims are to be submitted within ten days of receipt of merchandise and almost five weeks have now gone by, we nevertheless feel that you will understand our position in this case and credit our account for the $24.00 which is due.

Inasmuch as this is the first claim of this nature that we have submitted in some three years of satisfactory business relations with you, we know you will handle it as we request. In the future we shall check the markings on each package to avoid such a situation.

Sincerely yours,

Frank Fale

Frank Fale
Vice President

The writer has been so specific that the reader must take positive or negative action.

FIGURE 23–3

A poorly written claim letter

Kalamazoo Plastics
Industrial Park, No. 10
Kalamazoo, Michigan 49001

July 10, 19___

Mr. William Wolf, Vice President
Wolf Bros. Furniture
101 Star Street
Glenview, IL 60625

Dear Mr. Wolf:

On March 28 your truck delivered the Empire Conference Table which we ordered
February 2.

Because our executive office facilities were not yet completely decorated at the time of
delivery (as we had hoped they would be), the table was stored in our warehouse. Two
days ago the painting and decorating of the conference room was completed and the
table was brought in. It was at that time we noticed a deep scratch running across the
top of the table.

You may be sure we were very upset, for we feel that the damage probably occurred
prior to our receiving this piece of furniture. We do hope that you will want to make
the proper adjustment in this case and we look forward to hearing from you at your
convenience.

Yours truly,

Kimberly Lally

Kimberly Lally

The claim is so vague that the recipient could hardly make an
adjustment even if he were so inclined. Note also that a specific
adjustment is not requested, nor is a due date for action given.

The truth is that they *can* enter successful claims against major companies. They *should* complain; if their letters are written as suggested here, they will probably receive the satisfaction to which they are entitled. But they must keep in mind that major corporations receive dozens of claim letters each day, of which perhaps 50 percent are legitimate. If they will write their letters specifically, courteously, and accurately and enclose necessary substantiating data (such as bills) chances are very good that they will receive the adjustments they deserve. Certainly it would be foolish for a major corporation to pay a television star $300,000 a week and then not take care of a faulty $40 relay switch in an automatic washer. Companies want to build goodwill; quality products and friendly service will help achieve that goal. When consumers have difficulty, it is just as important for them to write excellent claim letters as it is for the wholesaler. The letter shown in Figure 23–4, like other good claim letters, is specific, precise, and positive. Under ordinary conditions, it should result in favorable action.

One of the key factors is to be restrained and tactful in describing the situation and requesting an adjustment. To bluntly accuse the recipient of your letter of intentionally causing you a loss can only result in hard feelings and unfriendly relations. Every claim letter should be based on the premise that the error was completely inadvertent. No one likes being accused, and when a claim letter is unreasonable in its comments and its requests become demands, the effect on the recipient is likely to be negative.

MAKING ADJUSTMENTS: CLAIM GRANTED

The number of items most modern firms handle is greater than a generation ago; billing procedures are more complex; inventory controls are more difficult; handling and shipping of merchandise require more attention; as a matter of fact, the current process of getting goods from source to consumer requires many more steps than it did in the past. Because there are more factors involved, there are greater possibilities for error. Most business people recognize that errors do occur, so their claims or adjustments are tempered with patience.

Intelligent managers are aware that a claim or a complaint can bring attention to an internal area needing improvement or change. In addition, they accept most claims as legitimate and fair. Furthermore, managers recognize that the people who submit claims are customers, and it is upon their business that the seller's firm stands. Thus it is important to handle claims and complaints quickly and courteously so that the seller is perceived as fair. But sellers must not gain the reputation for being too soft and accepting any claim, or too severe and refusing all.

Most claims are legitimate, and it is on this basis that firms usually establish a fairly generous adjustment policy. If there is a question as to the fault, companies usually give the benefit of the doubt to the buyer. Their future

FIGURE 23–4

Claim letter from a consumer

91 Dennison Drive
Dallas, TX   60603
December 2, 19__

Mr. Todd Wilson
Customer Relations
Apex Computers, Inc.
2393 Gelson Avenue
San Jose, CA   90393

Dear Mr. Wilson:

We have a problem with our Apex SuperPro computer, and we need
your help in solving it.

We purchased our Apex (Serial #28393829) from Flash Electronics,
28 Victor St., Dallas, on September 7, 19__. After approximately one hour of normal use, stray characters began appearing
on the screen ("garbage," our dealer called them). He said the
extra characters were caused by overheating within the computer,
and installed a small fan at no cost to us.

We didn't have occasion to use the computer for periods of time
longer than one hour for about ten days thereafter. But when we
did, the stray characters again began appearing on the screen.

We called our dealer, only to discover that he had gone out of
business.

Our Apex computer is still under warranty, and we want the problem resolved as quickly as possible. Please contact us as soon
as possible with instructions on how to proceed. If you have
another dealer or authorized service center within reasonable
driving distance, we are willing to drop off the computer for
repair.

Thank you for giving this matter your early attention.

Sincerely,

Barbara and William Underwood

Barbara and William Underwood

Note that the tone is courteous and understanding, while the
facts presented are clear, specific, and complete.

business is involved, along with the profits that go with that business. Certainly there will be some claims having no merit; the seller may accept these and make adjustments, but individuals or firms that make such requests too frequently are eventually recognized and dealt with properly.

An adjustment policy is often governed by whatever is accepted in the trade. For example, furniture manufacturers from coast to coast have agreed on a standard return privilege; and appliance manufacturers have set down an industrywide repair policy. This practice results in advantages to the seller in an adjustment situation.

The way in which the adjustment is made can build or erode goodwill. An adjustment given grudgingly usually will do more harm than one that is refused but carefully and courteously explained.

Buyer at Fault

Not infrequently in business, buyers submit unjustified claims. Someone has run a machine over its rated capacity and now requests a replacement; a customer returns furniture after the ten-day return period has passed or orders merchandise at a special price long after the last date announced for the sale. When these claims are granted, it is purely for the purpose of building goodwill.

When the buyer is at fault and the claim granted, it is usually wise to structure the letter so that an explanation precedes the favorable adjustment (see Figure 23–5). We stated earlier that good news should be given immediately in a business letter. This is not true, however, when granting a claim in which the buyer is at fault. If the adjustment letter immediately grants a claim, the buyer may not read further to learn that he or she was at fault. And even when he or she does read the entire letter, the psychological impact of the explanation may be lost. A courteous, straightforward explanation before the grant is made should point out that the buyer was at fault. In most cases the following organization is recommended:

1. A statement referring to the specific transaction.
2. A statement explaining tactfully and discreetly how the buyer is at fault. Take care to avoid causing him or her to "lose face."
3. A statement granting the claim graciously.
4. A sales appeal, if appropriate.
5. A friendly close.

Perhaps equal in importance with the organization is the tone. It should be direct, courteous, and open-handed.

> **Poor:**   *While the circumstances of this breakdown are suspicious at best, we are giving you the benefit of the doubt in making an adjustment.*
>
> **Revised:** *We are pleased to make the adjustment under these circumstances.*

FIGURE 23–5

Granting a claim—buyer at fault

All-Company

203 Sperry Road   Madison, Wisconsin 16303

July 10, 19__

Mr. Meyer Milton
Plant Manager
Summer and Summer Co.
14 S. Lansing Blvd.
Ann Arbor, MI 48109

Dear Mr. Milton:

We received your letter of July 5 in which you requested that we pick up the American 1/3 h.p. motor and replace it with a 3/4 h.p. unit.

We were sorry to learn that the 1/3 h.p. motor which we sold you on June 15 did not prove satisfactory. In your letter, however, you indicated that it was used to power a Jackson-Smith Industrial Saw, model #208. We checked this with our chief engineer because we are always desirous of furnishing our customers with the best and most efficient materials available.

He found that the manufacturer of this saw recommends that a 3/4 to 1 h.p. unit be used with this particular model. Apparently this was overlooked by the people in your shop and our 1/3 h.p. unit was used. Of course, we realize that incidents such as this occur and we are sending out the larger motor you requested. However, for your satisfaction and the most efficient operation of equipment in the future, we strongly suggest that the manufacturer's recommendations be checked and followed.

The new motor should be delivered to your warehouse no later than August 10; at that time our driver can pick up the original unit. If we can assist you in any way in the future, Mr. Milton, please call on us.

Sincerely,

Frank Ferragamo

Frank Ferragamo
Vice President

The customer is tactfully told he is at fault *before* the grant is made. If the grant were made first, he might stop reading and thus never become aware of his error.

Poor:	*In our view, your demands are clearly without foundation. But to put an end to the matter, we are granting your claim and crediting your account in the amount you requested.*
Revised:	*We understand your side of the story in this unfortunate incident, and have credited your account as you request.*

Seller at Fault

When the buyer at fault requests an adjustment, the seller may grant the claim, refuse it, or offer a compromise. When the seller is at fault, however, there is no alternative: the claim must be granted.

Before Receiving a Claim   At times the seller is not aware that a mistake has been made until a claim is made. But when the seller determines shortly after a shipment that something is wrong, he or she should attempt to correct the error before the buyer asks for an adjustment. The seller may discover that a particular lot of merchandise has not been manufactured properly after the merchandise is on its way to the customer. Or the seller may receive a justified complaint from only one of several buyers. In any of these situations, all other buyers who have been shipped faulty merchandise should be notified and offered a proper adjustment. The seller who makes an adjustment before receiving claims and complaints will secure an amount of goodwill no advertising can purchase. Adjustments made under these circumstances are the mark of a reliable house, and the reputation gained by such action proves invaluable.

Answering Claims   The letter granting a claim when the seller is at fault is a difficult one to write. The seller must indicate that an error has been made, but in such a way that buyers will not lose confidence and take their business elsewhere.

What makes this such a difficult assignment is the fact that people act like people. Although most of us will readily admit that we make errors, we cannot understand how those from whom we purchase can make such "dumb and completely inexplicable mistakes." Thus when a seller does make an error, we often enter a claim, accept the adjustment, and then take our business elsewhere. This reaction holds true for many consumers; however, at the wholesale level the business person usually recognizes that mistakes do happen and will accept the adjustment in good faith.

What is the proper order of points in the letter where the seller is at fault and grants the claim? If the message opens with a grant, the item of major interest, the reader may never continue to the explanation of how the situation occurred. To reverse the order is always problematic, however. After all, the buyer is primarily interested in whether he is going to receive a credit of

$52 and is not very much concerned with the fact that your computers suddenly went out of kilter. Probably the situation and prospective reader should determine the order of your letter.

Indeed, there is a question as to whether an explanation should be included at all. A detailed discussion of what went wrong and why may only compound the situation and erase what little confidence the customer has in us. Perhaps the best thing to do is to open by saying that we made a mistake, are making an adjustment, and will do our best to see that a similar case does not arise in the future.

The following is a good organizational pattern for an adjustment letter when the seller is at fault:

1. An opening referring to the situation and making a grant.
2. An explanation of how the incident occurred, if such an explanation sounds reasonable. If it will only magnify a careless error, it should be omitted.
3. An attempt to regain the customer's confidence.
4. A sales appeal, if it seems appropriate.
5. A friendly close.

In the letter in Figure 23–6, several possible explanations are alluded to that will probably help make the entire situation more understandable to the buyer.

Third Party at Fault

In most transactions between buyer and seller, a third party is involved: a shipper, carrier, broker, or storage agent. It may be that the loss or damage involved in the claim took place while the merchandise was in the hands of a third party. In such a situation, the seller will normally reply with a courteous letter and extend assistance to the buyer. If some of the seller's accounts are small retail merchants, he or she may even offer to process the claim for them (see Figure 23–7). Naturally, it is costly for the seller to get involved in a claim in which he or she has no legal responsibility. However, the goodwill that may accrue in such circumstances will be well worth the effort expended.

Other Adjustment Situations

There are times when both parties are at fault; in other cases the fault is not known; and sometimes the problem is the result of a misunderstanding. Each of these situations, and other comparable ones, must be handled on its own merits and in conformity with the adjustment policy of the seller.

FIGURE 23–6

Granting a claim—seller at fault

Benson Mirrors, Inc.

509 W. Ninth Avenue
Tucson, AZ 60832

September 6, 19__

Ms. Vera Olin
8723 Sunset Drive
Tucson, AZ 60834

Dear Ms. Olin:

1 While we never enjoy hearing that a valued customer has experienced problems, we do thank you for your letter of September 4. The problem you describe--a Benson mirror losing its silvering-- is rare indeed. We will replace the mirror in question at no cost, and we hope no inconvenience, to you.

To help us understand and correct this unusual occurrence, we would appreciate your answers to three questions:

    1. Was the mirror in contact with solvent or solvent fumes, including nail-polish remover?

    2. Was the mirror exposed to hot afternoon sun over a prolonged period of time?

    3. Was the mirror exposed to sustained moisture?

2 Your answers to these questions will help us make sure that Benson mirrors remain the finest on the market.

Please call us at your convenience to make arrangements for installation of your new mirror.

Sincerely,

Brett Felson

Brett Felson
Sales Manager

1 It's often wise to get in step with the writer (appreciate *his* or *her* perceptions and verbalize them).

2 It's usually wiser to end on a reference to a positive future than to a negative past.

FIGURE 23–7
Granting a claim—third party at fault

EKKO
ELECTRIC COMPANY
404 N. Fourth Street
Bellville, California 91602

September 15, 19__

Mr. Roger Canterbury
Canterbury Corp.
15 So. Foremost Street
Claremont, CA 91711

Dear Mr. Canterbury:

We were extremely sorry to hear that several of the lamps included in order #705, which we shipped via Rapid Freight Lines, did not arrive in satisfactory condition.

As you know, this carrier, like all others, inspects merchandise before accepting it. We have their receipt indicating that this order was turned over to them in excellent condition.

For this reason you will probably want to get in touch with Rapid Freight as quickly as possible and enter a claim for the four damaged lamps. I have enclosed two blank copies of Interstate Commerce Commission Form 202, which you can complete and forward to the carrier.

If I can assist you in any other way, Mr. Canterbury, please let me know and I will be happy to cooperate.

Sincerely,

Hedda Hill

Hedda Hill
Manager

This tactful statement sets the record straight on where the fault lies.

Regardless of the circumstances, all such adjustment letters should carry a strong sales and goodwill message (see Figure 23–8). Sometimes a claim can be adjusted through the expedient of "educating" the customer. This may be done through courteous instructions for handling the product (see Figure 23–9).

UNFAVORABLE RESPONSES: CLAIM NOT GRANTED

As suggested in our discussion of inquiries and requests, saying "no" is never easy. Yet we sometimes must turn down claims and demands. The task is made more difficult when the person we must refuse is someone whose goodwill we value highly: a spouse, a child, a brother, a friend, a customer, a subordinate, or an associate. Nobody enjoys being told "no."

We recognize that, but we also recognize that it is possible to refuse a request in a manner that will maintain goodwill and arouse a minimum of antagonism. The "no" letter does not soft-pedal the facts. As shown in Figures 23–10 and 23–11, the explanation and refusal are presented as courteously and tactfully as possible. In both of these letters the explanation is complete and accurate. After each implied refusal, a positive offer or suggestion is made. Notice that there are no statements that might arouse negative or unpleasant associations. Once the refusal is made, even if only by implication, it is not referred to again, and there are no abject apologies.

The reason for the refusal is given, the refusal is tactfully implied, and a suggestion is made by the writer in a way that makes it apparent the reader would be ill-advised not to accept it. Thus the organization for a communication (a letter, an interview, or a telephone conversation) that contains an unfavorable reply follows this basic plan:

1. An introductory statement acknowledging the reader's problem or need.
2. An explanation of the situation making the refusal necessary.
3. The refusal, implied or expressly stated.
4. A constructive suggestion.
5. A sales appeal, if applicable.
6. A friendly close.

CREDIT COMMUNICATIONS

Our purses and wallets bulge with plastic credit cards that can be used to finance almost everything from gasoline to the quarterly tax payments due our state and federal governments.

Around us we see credit-financed skyscrapers going up like mushrooms, factories expanding in all directions, and companies spawning plant

FIGURE 23-8

Making an adjustment graciously

Bakers
Fashions
Inc.
102 Main Street
Racine, Wisconsin 53467

October 10, 19__

Mr. Kermit Dayton
Dayton Family Shoes
100 S. Main Street
Doraville, GA 30340

Dear Mr. Dayton:

You're correct. Your order #506 did call for six dozen Women's
Casual Line footwear. Why we sent you sixteen dozen (and billed
you for this number) is a mystery we can't solve.

You may return them, of course. As a matter of fact, we will be
happy to pick them up when we deliver your latest order which is
scheduled to arrive in your store one week from today.

May I suggest, however, that you seriously consider retaining
the extra ten dozen. This line is moving far beyond our expectations, and we think you will find this merchandise a satisfactory sales item. Our advertising on this item is now in full
swing, and a double-page spread will appear in the June issue of
the Women's Shopping Guide. We know that this, plus the high
quality of this footwear, will help increase your sales.'

Naturally, we will save shipping and bookkeeping costs if you
elect to retain all the original shipment. For your cooperation, we would like to have you deduct 5 percent from the bill
which covers this merchandise. Please call me collect, extension 205, and let me know if this proposal is satisfactory to
you.

Yours truly,

Wendy Ward

Wendy Ward
Vice President

Excellent *you*-attitude opening.   Soft-sell sales appeal may prove effective.

FIGURE 23-9
An "educational" claim adjustment

Nathan Polishes, Inc.

698 Pirate Cove Drive
Wilmington, VT 60832

December 7, 19__

Mr. Peter Marshall
Owner
Marshall Antiques
77 Coast Highway
Lefton, SC 38922

Dear Mr. Marshall:

We were sorry to hear from you that our #7900 finish stripper did not meet your expectations. We enclose a refund.

You mentioned in your letter that the stripper was applied to furniture "out behind your shop." It is possible that outdoor temperature and moisture conditions reduced the effectiveness of the stripper. (You'll note on the application instructions packaged with the stripper that it "should not be applied when temperature falls below 55 degrees F. or when humidity exceeds 70 percent.")

Because our #7900 regularly is rated by independent laboratories as the best stripper on the market, we trust you'll give it another try. For our part, we'll test the partially used can you returned to make sure it meets our high standards.

Sincerely,

Brenda Nelson

Brenda Nelson
Products Manager

The friendly tone of this explanation should build goodwill.

FIGURE 23–10
Claim not granted

Wilmette Department Store
1900 E. Lake Avenue   Wilmette, Arkansas 72203

April 19, 19__

Mrs. Bernice Hardy
2025 South Robins Drive
Wilmette, AR   72203

Dear Mrs. Hardy:

When we received your letter of April 15 and the package containing our Beach Fun bathing suit, we were, of course, concerned to learn that your daughter did not find the suit satisfactory and wished to exchange it for a different model. Under
ordinary circumstances we do everything possible to please our
customers in the matter of adjustments, for we recognize how
important you and thousands of other purchasers of our product
are to the Beach Fun Company.

The bathing suit presents a problem, however, for in keeping
with the statutes of this state, garments of this type may not
be restocked after they have been sold. I am sure that you were
not aware of this regulation, but because of it you will understand why we are not sending out the model you requested in
exchange.

The suit you sent to us is being returned along with the addresses of several dealers who handle the Beach Fun line in your
city. We know that you will find all the latest styles and
fashions in beach wear on display in our dealers' stores.

Cordially yours,

Merle Maxwell

Merle Maxwell
Customer Service

FIGURE 23–11

Claim not granted

FOREMAN'S FINE FURNITURE
1933 Cally Road
Lewistown, West Virginia 04321

December 7, 19__

Mr. Sam Stark
Stark Fashion Furniture
201 Center Street
Long Beach, CA 90810

Dear Mr. Stark:

We received your letter of December 3 concerning your request for credit to your account of $28.50. You may be sure we want you to receive the full benefit of the discounts due you.

As you are probably aware, the discount policy throughout the furniture field permits a 2 percent reduction when bills are paid within ten days of date of invoice. The amount, which represents our saving in billing and handling, is passed on to our customers.

We checked your July and August orders (with which this $28.50 discount is concerned) and found that they were inadvertently paid 18 (#209), 16 (#402), and 22 (#991) days after the discount period. This oversight in handling bills payable sometimes occurs and has certainly happened to us. Nevertheless, you will understand that in all fairness to our other accounts, as well as to our own position in this case, we cannot agree to your request.

We think you will feel as we do that this action is equitable; however, if some special circumstances are involved in your case, we will be very happy to review the facts.

I have enclosed our new brochure on the Patio Aluminum line of outdoor furniture. Our preferred customers may take a 10 percent discount from the prices listed, from now through the end of the month. Why not indicate your needs on the enclosed order form and return it so that we can ship you a quantity of this high quality, excellent-markup line of furniture.

Sincerely yours,

Fred Feldman

Fred Feldman
Credit Mgr.

This letter does not accuse,
"*you* did not pay," or "*you* overlooked."
The statements concerning the faults
are very impersonal.

The writer closes on a positive note
rather than a negative one.

additions daily. Credit enables businesses to carry inventories much larger than their cash resources ordinarily would permit; they are thus in a position to make many more sales. Although estimates vary, about 65 percent of retail sales and 85 percent of wholesale and manufacturers' sales are conducted on credit.

What is credit? Credit is an estimate of the ability and the desire of the individual or company to pay debts at a later date. This ability and desire are usually weighed by the credit manager on a careful analysis of the classic C's: capital, character, conditions, and capacity.

The Role of the Credit Manager

Even the most honest individual may not always be able to meet his or her obligations. An oversight, a difficult business situation, or hard times may cause delay in paying bills. The credit manager must watch every step of the credit process to ensure maximum benefits to the company as well as to the credit user.

The manner in which managers administer has a profound effect on the progress of the firm. If credit is granted too liberally, company resources can be overextended. However, if a conservative viewpoint prevails, competitors will secure the rejected accounts. In such instances, sales may not advance or may even decline appreciably.

Management recognizes the need for a thorough, progressive, carefully administered and controlled credit system. In it, the credit manager plays the dominant role—often through letters and reports. The purposes for which letters are written include:

1. Acknowledging requests for credit.
2. Acknowledging receipt of credit data.
3. Requesting credit information from applicants' references.
4. Sending credit information in response to requests from other credit managers.
5. Granting credit.
6. Refusing credit.

Acknowledging a Request for Credit

Companies often encourage their customers to open charge accounts or credit accounts. The customer who enjoys a credit line with a firm will usually fulfill most needs through that company. Furthermore, the mechanics of a sale are often simpler when credit rather than cash is used.

When a customer asks that a credit account be opened, the acknowledgment should be swift and courteous. Note the optimistic and positive tone in Figure 23–12. For example, the statement "We will be happy to fill

FIGURE 23–12

Acknowledging a request for credit

Dear Mr. Phelps:

Thank you for your interest in a credit account at Foster Wholesale Plumbing. Please fill out the enclosed credit application and return it to me as soon as possible.

In the meantime, we will be happy to fill your cash orders at a 2 percent discount. I have enclosed our current catalog, with several pages marked for your special attention.

Again, our thanks for your interest in a business relationship with Foster Wholesale Plumbing.

Acknowledgment and directions

No Commitment-- positive or negative-- is made.

your cash orders at a 2 percent discount . . ." is much better than "After your credit rating is approved . . ."

Acknowledging Receipt of Credit Information

Sometimes fifteen to thirty days may be required to secure the information needed to make a decision. In such cases it may be wise to let the applicant know that the request for credit is being processed (see Figure 23–13). Such a letter is especially necessary if it is obvious that an unusual delay will be encountered.

Requesting Credit Information

When you request information on an individual or a company that has applied for credit, you are basically sending out an inquiry letter. A vital requirement of such a letter is that it be easy to answer. To achieve this, the letter can be reduced to a few courteous statements with room provided for fill-ins, or else a complete form can be attached to a brief cover letter (see Figure 23–14).

Many organizations also use credit-rating services or credit bureaus to determine whether the applicant should be approved.

FIGURE 23–13

Acknowledging receipt of credit information

Dear Mr. Phelps:

Thank you for returning your completed credit application so promptly. We have begun our evaluation process and, as promised, will contact you with our response no later than December 17.

Our area representative, Jeff Fields, would like to stop by your store to introduce himself and to acquaint you with several exciting promotions we're conducting. He will call first to arrange a convenient time for you.

We look forward to serving your needs for wholesale plumbing items.

Supplying Credit Information

Frequently credit managers are asked to send information on their accounts to other places of business. Usually this requires little more than completing and signing a form. At other times the request is broad, and the respondent is asked to send background credit data. Usually a brief letter, such as the one in Figure 23–15, will prove satisfactory. When it is necessary to return a negative evaluation, care should be exercised in the choice of words. Statements should be qualified and opinions stated tactfully. Legal considerations suggest the use of discretion. Some companies, in sending out replies of this nature, omit the name of the firm on which the evaluation is made. A reference, instead, is made to the date of the inquiry.

Granting Credit

It is always easy to tell people, "Yes, you can have what you asked for." But the credit letter should also attempt to build sales and goodwill. In addition to granting credit, the letter should also set down the terms of credit in a clear and specific manner to ensure prompt and correct payment and to avoid misunderstandings (and ill will) at a later time concerning due dates, discount

FIGURE 23–14

Requesting credit information on a consumer application

September 5, 19__

Ms. Sally Frame
Credit Manager
Holbrooke and Holbrooke   CREDIT APPLICANT:
141 South Marquette Dr.   Mr. Robert Forester
Studio City, CA 91604

Dear Ms. Frame:

The above-named individual has applied for a retail credit account with us.

Your comments on his financial responsibility, his credit reputation, and his payment record with you will prove very valuable to us.

The information you send will be kept confidential.

A stamped envelope is enclosed for your convenience. Thank you for your cooperation.

When did applicant have an account with you?
_____

What item(s) was purchased?_____
His high credit was $_____
His payments were_____ _____ _____
                      prompt   slow   delinquent
Does he have an open account with you now? _____ _____
                                            Yes   No

Other Comments:_____
_____

FIGURE 23–15
Supplying credit information

Dear Ms. Johnson:

As you requested, we are supplying confidential credit information on National Yacht Design, Inc.

Account Status:	Active, paid to date, since 1979
Credit Limit:	$10,000
Payment Record:	80 percent of payments within 30 days, 10 percent within 60 days, 10 percent within 90 days

Please contact us if we can be of help in any way.

privileges, and related factors. The letter in Figure 23–16 follows the usual pattern in letters of this nature:

1. A friendly opening.
2. The credit grant (this may be part of the opening).
3. A clear and specific statement concerning company credit policies and practices (or reference to a booklet describing these in detail).
4. A friendly close.

If possible, these letters should be individually typed and signed. It isn't necessary to make each one different; they can be typed from a guide letter, but the use of the recipient's name and some personal reference is wise. (See Chapter 4 for a discussion of guide letters.)

Refusing Credit

It is always difficult to say "no" to people, especially when an evaluation of the applicant's personal character is involved. The organizational pattern for

FIGURE 23–16

Granting credit to a commercial applicant

Dear Mr. Phelps:

Welcome to the Foster Wholesale Plumbing list of preferred credit customers.

A positive
opening

Your account number is 39823, with a present credit ceiling of $5000. We look forward
to raising that limit as our business relationship grows.

Details of
billing are
presented

You will find credit order forms enclosed, pre-printed with your account number and
delivery address. Please check these with care. If you wish to make changes, call our
order hot-line, at (800) 323-3829.

Our sincere thanks for doing business with Foster Wholesale Plumbing. We will do our
best to meet your needs.

this type of letter is similar to that of all refusal correspondence. The key is to explain the reason for the negative action before denying the request for credit.

At times the credit manager will find that the information received on a consumer is so negative that to explain or mention it as a basis for the refusal might very well arouse antagonism. After all, how can you point out that you've checked and found an applicant to have a consistently delinquent account and, therefore, to be an overall poor risk? In such instances it is wisest not to explain but simply to refuse tactfully. This will save face for the applicant and perhaps serve to retain his or her goodwill. A refusal letter to a consumer requires extra tact, for a private individual may not be as understanding or as objective about a refusal as a company accountant or executive.

Refusing the Commercial Credit Applicant With business clients, the usual refusal pattern is followed almost invariably. However, it is important to project a sincere *you* attitude. You must explain your refusal and yet retain their goodwill. Just one or two poorly chosen words can turn your explanation into a lecture and be perceived as antagonistic.

Examine the letter in Figure 23–17. It offers a brief explanation of the refusal, a suggestion on how the business relationship can still be maintained, and hope that credit will be granted in the future.

The credit letter is vital. It must be well-written, for the applicant we refuse today may be a most desirable credit account in five years. Thus it is essential to secure and maintain his or her goodwill.

COLLECTION LETTERS

Collecting from Retail and Wholesale or Commercial Accounts

Consumer accounts that become delinquent require different types of communications from those used for the wholesale or commercial account. The collection letter sent to the "good risk" will certainly be different in content from the one sent to the "poor risk." Because time is short and work loads heavy, companies formulate standard collection letters, which can be adapted to different situations. Perhaps that is why collection letters are not particularly successful; they lack the individual, personal approach. Yet how

---

FIGURE 23–17

Refusing a commercial credit applicant

At times the explanation for refusal is such that the applicant will only be embarrassed by the facts. However, by stating what *can* be done you also indicate what *cannot* be done.

Dear Ms. Thompson:

Thank you for applying for a credit account with XYZ Landscape Products.

Your credit information was carefully evaluated by the Commercial Credit unit at TRW. Based on their report, we cannot extend the credit you request at this time. If you wish to know details of their evaluation, please contact them directly at (800) 613-2812.

We hope you will continue to take advantage of the 2 percent discount given on cash sales. Certainly we will be pleased to reconsider a credit application when your credit circumstances have changed.

Thank you for looking to XYZ Landscape Products for the best buys in plants and plant supplies.

can we possibly send personal, individually typed letters to each of our 5700 delinquent retail or wholesale accounts, who owe us anywhere from $2 to $2000 each? We compromise. We begin with a form letter and follow this with a more personal approach for difficult accounts.

Credit and collection procedures for consumer accounts differ from those used for industrial, commercial, or manufacturing accounts. Naturally, our approach with Mrs. Johnson, who earns $20,000 a year, will be different from our treatment of National Automotive Parts Company with annual sales of $10 million. And yet they have common factors: they both may be classified as good risks; they are both delinquent in their payments; and they are both customers whose sales and goodwill we wish to retain.

Classification of Risks

From our earlier discussion you will recall that, before granting credit, a company evaluates an applicant in four major areas:

Capital or financial position

Character, based on personal and business history

The conditions that currently exist in this business or industry

The capacity of the firm to do business successfully

After the information is weighed, the account may be classified as a good, fair, or poor risk. Upon further evaluation, the classification is broken down into "good risk—good pay" or "good risk—poor pay," or "poor risk—fair pay," or whatever is considered appropriate. An account that is a good risk but slow to part with money may be classified as a "good risk—poor pay." On the other hand, the new business person who owes for fixtures, merchandise, equipment, and vehicles may make every effort to pay bills within the discount period so that his or her credit reputation will improve. Such an account is classified as a "fair risk—good pay."

Steps in the Collection Series

Most corporations, in dealing with delinquent accounts, divide their collection procedure into three steps: form reminders, personal letters, and, finally, collection agencies or court action.

The Reminder   Shortly after a bill has become past due, most firms send out a reminder. The assumption is that the account merely has been overlooked.

One form of reminder is a colored sticker pasted on a duplicate invoice, bearing a message such as "Please," "Past Due—Please Remit Today," "This

Bill Is Now Due and Payable," "Perhaps You've Overlooked," or "Don't Forget Us." Sometimes a rubber stamp is used. Reminders are also printed on cards, small sheets of stationery, and even rolls of tape (in different colors to indicate different levels of urgency), which can be cut off and attached to the invoice.

Some firms have found that the most effective type of reminder is a short, sincere note written on the face of the invoice. When this is signed by the company president, treasurer, or controller, the delinquents are likely to feel the personal touch very strongly. They will surely react most favorably to this type of appeal.

The Personal Letter   Sometimes it is necessary to send more than a reminder. A personal letter (or two or three) usually will produce payment or explanation. People will generally respond when they are treated like people, rather than like computer cards.

The Collection Agency or Legal Action   If a series of personal letters to a debtor does not result in payment, it will finally be necessary to turn the account over to an agency or legal firm for collection. This should be only a last resort because it is good neither for the debtor nor for the creditor.

Variables in Collection Letters

Before a collection letter is sent, we should know whether the account has been classified as a good, fair, or poor risk and what further evaluations have been made. On the basis of our classification, several factors in our collection actions will vary:

Tone of the Letter   The tone of the letter sent to the poor risk will surely be more insistent and less lenient than that of the letter sent to the good risk; *because* he or she is a poor risk, we know that funds are not usually readily available. A more severe, insistent, and demanding tone is used in this instance.

> *Poor risk:*
> *We have now sent you two reminders and a letter. We have received no response concerning your delinquent account. Legal action will be started within fourteen days of the date of this letter if payment of this past-due balance of $547.85 is not received.*
> *Good risk:*
> *For over ten years you have paid your accounts promptly and taken advantage of the discount privilege. That is why your present past-due balance of $480.00 disturbs us. We know there must be a reason. John Campbell of our office will be in your area on March 5 and will stop by to see you. I'm sure arrangements can be worked out.*

Type of Appeal   The type of appeal may vary. Some types of appeals (see the discussion below) are more adaptable to the good risk than to the poor risk. An appeal to fear or self-interest may be wiser with the poor risk than an appeal to pride.

Number of Letters   Normally more letters are sent to the good risk than to the poor risk before drastic action is instituted. Where the good risk may receive from four to seven letters, the poor risk may get two to four. The poor risk may well be delinquent to several firms and subject to many pressures. If we insist on sending seven letters before taking action, it may be too late to recover anything.

Time Between Letters   The person who has been in business for twenty years, has adequate capital, and whom we've classified as a good risk will certainly be given *more time between* collection letters than the poor risk.

Time Before Action   Time before action may vary according to type of risk. The poor risk's account will be turned over to a collection agency or lawyer more quickly than the good risk's delinquent bill. Here again, if we are too lenient with the poor risk, we may find ourselves arranging a court date only to find that the delinquent has paid off as much as possible—and has, perhaps, left town.

Appeals Used to Motivate Payment

Individuals or companies do not owe money to a creditor because they want to. They have trouble, and probably owe several creditors besides you. They have to choose what to do with their limited funds. They can choose to pay the other debts, to buy more merchandise for their business, to increase advertising in order to build up sales . . . or to pay you.

Where should they place their limited funds to achieve maximum effectiveness? A simple appeal, "Send it to me," may not be very effective when weighed against the demands they are receiving from others. You must show them why they should pay you now—why it is to their benefit to do so. This is where the collection correspondent can employ the *you* attitude very effectively.

Appeals vary in strength, but they are all designed to make debtors want to pay their bills or to send along an explanation of why they can't pay at present and what their plans are. The appeal may be to ethics and fair play, or to maintaining a good credit reputation, or to self-interest, or to the saving of time and trouble, or to status, or to fear of court action, or to a combination of these motives.

Collection letters frequently use more than one of the appeals listed previously. However, the effective letter (or series of letters) emphasizes the benefits to the debtor of paying the bill. The letters in Figures 23–18 and 23–19

FIGURE 23–18

Typical collection letter

Dear Mr. Donnelson:

Your account is overdue, with a current amount due of $285.

We request immediate payment. Won't you take a moment right now to write a check for $285 and mail it in the enclosed envelope?

Your payment must be received no later than January 16 to avoid additional fees and possible legal action against you. Thank you in advance for paying $285 today.

An appeal to self-interest and avoidance of future trouble.

FIGURE 23–19

Collection letters using various appeals

Fair play

Dear Ms. Tumkosit:

It has now been _____ days since your account for $_____ has been marked "Past Due." We are puzzled and can only assume that you have inadvertently overlooked this bill.

We certainly did "the right thing" in filling your requests promptly for quality furniture at competitive prices. They say "Turn about is fair play"; therefore won't you do the right thing and pay this bill today?

I've enclosed a stamped envelope for your convenience. Please return it with your check for $_____.

Reputation

Dear Ms. Tumkosit:

The head of our accounting department has just been in to see me about your delinquent account of $_____.

I must say I was surprised; there must be a very good reason for your nonpayment. Why don't you pick up a pen and jot a note on the reverse side of this letter telling me what the problem is? We want to help in any way we can.

For some time you have been one of our valued customers and you have enjoyed a fine credit reputation. Surely we both want that credit rating of yours retained. Won't you help me to help you by sending me a check today or an explanation for the nonpayment of your bill for $_____?

Action/ Reputation

Dear Ms. Tumkosit:

We are at a loss to understand why you have taken no action to pay or reduce your bill of $_____, which is now _____ days past due.

We have written you several times and have received no response. You can appreciate our position, for we must now think of turning your account over to the National Furniture Wholesalers Association for collection.

We do want to avoid this for it means that your name is published and distributed industrywide as a delinquent account. Obviously such an announcement does your credit rating almost irreparable damage.

We have no recourse except to forward your name to the Association within 15 days or by _____, 19__. Won't you help us to avoid such action by mailing us your check for $_____, or a substantial part of this sum, prior to the date indicated?

Legal action

Dear Ms. Tumkosit:

After several reminders and letters concerning your past-due bill of $_____, we are now forced to consider taking drastic steps to collect. This means turning your account over to our attorneys for court action.

This will not be desirable for either party. For you it means the payment of not only the sum due but court costs of no inconsiderable amount. In addition, there are the time and trouble involved.

Why not save yourself all this difficulty by sending us your check for $_____? If we do not hear from you by _____, your account will be turned over to McAlister, Kelley, and McAlister for legal action.

are typical of those sent out to collect from past-due accounts. The different appeals are clear. Notice that few, if any, collection letters bother with a sales appeal unless the letter is the first or second in a series. The primary purpose is to secure money due, and any discussion that clouds that central message usually is eliminated.

Collection Form Letters

However, for large corporations it is almost impossible, from the point of view of cost, to send personal letters to all delinquent accounts. Furthermore, they are usually not necessary, for a short, courteous form letter will motivate most persons to forward part or all of the sum due or an explanation for nonpayment. Therefore, most companies have form collection letters.

Whether in a form letter or an individually typed letter, the collection message should always do the following:

1. Be courteous and restrained. Insults, accusations, and sarcastic comments serve no useful purpose. They may be construed as harrassment, which is illegal.
2. List specific dates when payment is due or when more drastic action will be taken—and stick to these dates.
3. List the precise amount due in every letter from the first three-line reminder to the last carefully worded appeal.
4. Include a *you* attitude, which clearly shows the debtor how he or she will gain from making the payment requested.

It is not very practical to write one series of collection letters to be used for all types of risks. The tone, number of letters, and other factors will differ depending on the account. For that reason it is usually wise to make up three different series, one each for good, fair, and poor risks.

The letters may be preprinted and provided with blank spaces, which can be filled in with the proper dates and amounts due. Or guide letters can be written and then bound into a folder and used as models for individually typed messages. The latter method is more effective because of the personal tone and better appearance of the letters, but they are more expensive to process. Today, however, most word-processing centers can easily, quickly, and inexpensively "call up" a previously recorded letter. Names, dates, and amounts can be added or changed, and the final letter can be printed at the touch of a key. The result is a personal yet inexpensive letter.

Unusual Collection Letters

There is something to be said for the imaginative collection letter. At best, collecting money is a difficult task. Sometimes the right proportions of humor, fact, and appeals to common sense—all cast in relation to the reader—work very well. Notice in the letter in Figure 23–20 that the level of language, the style of humor, and the type of appeal would be appreciated by most people.

Unusual collection letters may have a boomerang effect, though. The debtor may not take seriously the cute, clever, or funny collection letter, especially if several creditors are bringing pressure at the same time. If one of the creditors finds the situation humorous, perhaps that creditor is a logical choice for delayed payment.

FIGURE 23–20
Imaginative collection letter

Dear Ms. Conway:

We're risking a 25-cent stamp on you.

We believe that, with a well-intentioned nudge, you'll take a moment right now to write your check for your overdue account balance: $126.32.

We picture you, in fact, putting that check in the enclosed envelope, licking the stamp, and mailing them today!

In short, we know you're a valued customer well worth the risk of the 25-cent stamp.

(P.S.   The amount is $126.32 . . . today!)

QUESTIONS FOR STUDY

1. Sellers often feel a mixture of anxiety and anger when trying to collect overdue debts. Discuss whether these feelings should be expressed in collection communications. If so, what form should they take?
2. On what basis are risk categories assigned to various customers?
3. Should a business person always give a detailed written description of precise reasons why credit was denied?
4. "The customer is always right." What shortcomings do you see in this policy as a way of dealing with claims in which the buyer was at fault?
5. Discuss ways in which delinquent debtors can be motivated to pay.
6. Is it every advantageous for a seller to become involved in adjustments where a third party was at fault? Explain your answer.
7. What is the difference between a routine claim letter and one that is nonroutine?
8. Why are accusations inappropriate for the claim letter?
9. In writing the claim letter, why should the writer have a definite idea of what she or he wants before writing the letter?
10. In what way(s) is a collection letter like a sales letter?
11. There are three common steps that most firms divide their collection procedures into in dealing with delinquent accounts; what are the steps and why is this sequence followed?
12. In what way does the tone of the collection letter sent to the poor risk differ from the tone of that sent to the good risk?
13. Are there any problems in sending cute and clever collection letters to delinquent accounts? Why or why not?
14. Who is more likely to accept your refusal of credit—the consumer credit applicant or the corporate controller? Why? How does this influence your communications?
15. When a person or organization finds there will be a delay before an applicant's request for credit can be replied to, what should be communicated to the individual making the request, if anything?
16. What are the standard classifications of credit risks; why are the categories important; how do they influence communications?

EXERCISES

17. Saying "no" to someone's request for credit can cause disappointment. Describe specific ways you can lessen that disappointment in your credit communications.
18. You can assume that your reader will feel pleasure when you say "yes" to his or her request for credit. What other messages in your letter can be conveyed to advantage at this time of good feelings?

19. Mr. Henderson bought an expensive television from you two years ago on a three-year credit agreement. The television, now beyond its warranty, has broken. By telephone, Henderson has angrily told you that he won't make any more payments until you provide him "with a brand new TV to replace this lemon." Describe the collection steps you would take. Write out at least three of the collection letters for various stages of the collection process.

20. In working through your in-basket, you handle the following claims. Write two adjustments, two refusals, and two requests for additional information in processing the following six items:

   (a) Ms. Marta Owens requests a full refund for her toaster purchased nine months ago (your warranty was for sixty days). She has enclosed a piece of burnt toast and tells you "to pick up your toaster anytime after giving me my money back."

   (b) Brentwood Leather insists on a 15 percent rebate on the commercial stitching machine they purchased last month. The machine went on sale at your store nine days after they paid full price. As a steady customer, they think they deserve the sale price.

   (c) Victor Ortiz encloses an electric razor purchased from you three weeks ago. He simply states that it does not run and he wants his money refunded. It appears to you that the razor has been dropped into water, but you cannot be sure.

   (d) Queen Lake Bakery writes to complain that your model #293 mixer is not strong enough to mix bread dough. They purchased nine mixers from you last month and want to return all nine for a complete refund. They ask you how you wish them to send the mixers.

   (e) Frank Collins writes to demand a refund for a fishing reel he purchased five months ago (under sixty-day warranty). He claims that the connection holding the reel to the fishing rod was defective. A large fish on his line yanked the whole reel out to sea. Naturally Collins has not included the reel. It lies "about 400 feet down in the ocean," he estimates.

   (f) Pacific Packing claims that your plastic carpet protectors are sticky to the touch when temperatures rise above 90 degrees. They have purchased $3800 worth of protectors in the last two months and want to know what you plan to do about their problem.

21. Illustrate how word processing can speed up and personalize the collection-letter series. Why will this system be better than the old form letter?

22. Your company manufactures all kinds of stickers—from mailing labels to holiday stickers. Westmont Furs sometimes has a bill-collecting problem and wants you to develop a message that can be placed on a small sticker. In turn, the sticker will be attached to the past-due bill and sent to the customer. Generally one must be cautious in using gimmicks, but in this case Westmont thinks the idea is most appropriate. Design at least three stickers for Westmont from which they can select one to use.

23. As the new owner-manager of Louie's Furniture, you are attempting to build business and establish a loyal clientele. You took over the established business from a previous owner, and you retained some of that owner's customers. However, you have altered the product line in the store and are upgrading the lines you carry.

    You note that during the six months you have operated the store about 90 percent of your business is cash. You recognize that people who have charge accounts are more likely to visit and make purchases at a store than those who do not. In an attempt to build a loyal clientele, you want to send a letter to all customers who (a) have made a cash purchase in excess of $100 or (b) have made three or more purchases regardless of the amount spent in the past year.

    Develop a letter you can send to these people encouraging them to open a charge account today at Louie's Furniture.

24. As manager of Jack and Jill's Clothing in Carbonville, a university town, you have a segmented market: the established local population and the more transient college student. Your clothing line appeals to both, and your sales during the year are almost evenly divided between these two groups.

    For the local, established customer group, almost all of the steady customers have charge accounts with you (your own charge system) and you rarely have any problem in collecting the amount due. Because of your success, a few years ago you started to let apparently credit-worthy college students also open charge accounts with you. It has been a disaster. Your accountant told you to take immediate action to remedy the accounts receivable. Finally, you had to write off those losses, and at the same time you established the policy of no credit to nonresident college students.

    In your store you have brochures available to people who want to apply for credit. Rather frequently a nonresident college student will submit one of the brochures requesting credit. Develop a form response that you can send to the students making this request. You know you have to keep credit available to members of the established community, or you run the danger of driving those people away.

25. Write a three-part series of collection letters to Olney Electrical Supply, a company that purchased $2782 worth of office furniture on credit from your company. They agreed to pay $182 each month for 24 months. Forty days have passed since the sale and you have not received any payment.

26. Today has not been your day.
    (a) The side chair you ordered for your office arrived; however, instead of being trimmed in green leather as ordered, it was in red.
    (b) At home, you discover that the custom-made shirts you ordered with your initials monogrammed arrived—JRW; the only problem is, your initials are RJW.

(c) For years you have ordered items from the MAIL-IT catalog and have always been satisfied. But, today the white caulking substitute (a product to improve the look of bathroom tile caulking) arrived and you feel that the advertisement in the MAIL-IT brochure misrepresented the product.

For each of the above situations, write a claim letter. Keep in mind that you want to be fair and firm and also indicate what kind of settlement will be satisfactory to you.

27. Choose a brand of automobile. Assume a breakdown has occurred and you cannot get satisfactory service from your local dealer. Write a claim letter to the automobile factory representative. Describe your problem clearly, as well as the steps you have already taken to resolve the problem. Make your request clear and specific.

28. In the role of a factory customer representative, respond favorably to the claim letter described in Problem 27. Do so without compromising the integrity of your dealerships.

29. Again in the role of a factory customer representative, respond negatively to the claim letter described in Problem 27. Explain the grounds for your refusal. Offer the customer constructive alternatives to resolve the problem.

LEGAL CONSIDERATIONS

CREDIT, COLLECTION, AND THE LAW

Debtors are viewed as disadvantaged and, therefore, particularly vulnerable by the law. As such, they are protected against unfair pressure or manipulative tactics from those to whom they owe money.

The Truth-in-Lending Act of 1969 (Title I of the Consumer Credit Protection Act) ensures that people gaining credit are fully and accurately informed of the details of their credit agreement. Regulation Z directs advertisers of credit to specify the terms clearly and conspicuously. The Truth-in-Lending Act also outlines garnishment procedures. For instance, an employer cannot fire an employee because wages have been garnished for any single debt.

The Equal Credit Opportunity Act of 1974 (Title VII of the Consumer Credit Protection Act) prohibits discrimination in the granting of credit on the basis of marital status, color, race, sex, national origin, or age. The law requires that any refusal of credit be in writing. Previously common questions concerning plans for children are prohibited. Married women seeking their own credit can no longer be asked to gain the co-signature of their spouse. As an extension of this act, auto dealers, real estate brokers, and others who arrange for credit must comply with the same federal antidiscrimination rules that apply to lenders.

The Fair Credit Billing Act of 1974 ensures speedy attention to the customers' complaints about bills. The act requires the credit grantor to communicate certain kinds of information to clients on a regular basis. The bill must be sent at least fourteen days prior to the payment due date so that the client can avoid a finance charge. When the client inquires in writing about a bill within sixty days of receiving it, the creditor has thirty days to acknowledge it.

The Fair Debt Collection Practices Act of 1978 (Title VIII of the Consumer Credit Protection Act) prohibits unreasonable means of collecting debts. The false suggestion or implication of a lawsuit cannot be made. In specified situations, the creditor may be prohibited from contacting the debtor's employer or telephoning the debtor or relatives.

This act was passed because of unscrupulous actions on the part of some creditors and their agents. Communications regarding debt may not be initiated in a harassing manner, and the communications must not create false impressions or cause the recipient to become physically ill. To settle Federal Trade Commission charges that they illegally harassed debtors, Universal Collection Bureau, Inc., and six of its affiliated companies agreed to pay $90,000 in civil penalties. The firms were accused of falsely representing that customers who did not pay debts would be arrested, of using obscene language on the phone, and of telling other persons that the consumer was in debt.

Sales, Goodwill, and Other Letters

24

Every letter you write should be a sales letter.

Companies use many methods of persuading the public to buy their products. You are doubtless familiar with most of them: radio and TV commercials, letters, brochures, pamphlets, newspaper and magazine advertisements, bulletins, and billboards. For our purposes, we will focus on the sales letter. It is a "rifle" type of approach to the customer because it is directed at particular individuals. We select a target group—pediatricians, say, or business executives, or accountants, or registered nurses—and aim at them. This differs from the TV approach, in which we "shotgun" at thousands of viewers in the hope that an appreciable percentage of them will prove to be prospects for our product.

ADVANTAGES OF DIRECT MAIL[1]

Doing business by direct mail advertising has proved to be effective, inexpensive, and profitable. Compared with radio, television, or newspaper advertising, direct mail has a number of advantages.

1. **Timing** You control when your advertising reaches the public rather than waiting for the publication date of a magazine or newspaper.

---

[1]See the following articles for more information on direct mail: L. Janus, "Time Tested Rules for Writing Direct Mail Copy," *Publishing Trade*, Sept/Oct. 1984. L. Brock, "Cutting Sales Call Cost Through Direct Mail," *Direct Marketing*, Mar. 1983. W. Coddington, "Using Promotions to Build Mailing Lists," *Sales and Marketing Management*, Nov. 12, 1984. L. Janus, "Custom Design Envelopes to Boost Response," *Publishing Trade*, May/June 1984. J. Bivins, "The Sale is in the Mail," *Chain Store Age Executive*, Mar. 1984. G. Bailey, "Direct Hit," *Canadian Business*, Feb. 1984. W. Cohen, "These Examples Demonstrate the Power of Direct Marketing," *Marketing News*, Feb. 17, 1984. "Time-Tested Tactics for the Outer Envelope," *Direct Marketing*, Aug. 1987, pp. 83–84. "Developing Literature that Sells as Well as Tells," *Direct Marketing*, March 1987, pp. 122–23. "Sales Pitches in Software," *Venture*, March 1987, p. 11.

2. **Flexibility**   You are not limited to the graphic preferences of a particular publication, but instead can create advertising as imaginative as your abilities permit.
3. **Competition**   Your promotional appeal, if opened and read, receives less competition than it would if placed on a page with other ads.
4. **Individualization**   A message received by mail can be personalized and customized in a way that mass advertising through media cannot.
5. **Reply Packages**   You can enclose all the reader needs to respond favorably to your appeal: order form, envelope, postage, and perhaps even a pencil or pen.

There are other advantages: a sales letter will frequently penetrate (to the president's desk, for example) where other advertising media may not; it can be directed to widely separated geographic areas for much less money than it costs to send sales representatives; it can introduce a product prior to the personal call; and it can accomplish a dozen other tasks quickly, selectively, and inexpensively.

MAIL ORDER CATALOG SALES

Perhaps the fastest growing segment of sales by mail in the past few years has been as a result of catalog sales.

In 1986 the U.S. Postal Service distributed 11.8 *billion* catalogs from which Americans ordered $30 *billion* in merchandise. That figure rose to $33 *billion* in 1987. Not too many years ago that figure was in the millions—not billions.

There are many reasons for this almost unbelievable growth. However, chief among these are:

1. The high number of women who work during the day and thus have less time to shop.
2. The availability of toll-free telephone numbers which make ordering merchandise easy, inexpensive, and convenient. (Perhaps we should abolish the term "mail order" and use "phone order" instead.)
3. Improved systems to track orders and inventory.
4. The availability today of almost everything by mail order, from garden tools to gargoyles.
5. The wide distribution and acceptance of credit cards.
6. The consistent high quality of most of the merchandise available and the excellent standards of delivery, exchange, and refunds maintained by most firms.

However, the future of catalog sales has some clouds on the horizon. There is a good possibility that the U.S. Postal Commission may raise third class rates 15 to 30 percent. And more and more catalogs are offering the same or very similar merchandise. This factor causes many catalog recipients to discard their catalogs without reading them. Nevertheless, the future has much to offer those who are innovative and creative and desire to enter the catalog sales area of sales communication.

Catalog Merchandise

L. L. Beane of Maine, one of the leaders in the field, totaled almost 370 million dollars in 1986 catalog sales. In just the October–December 1987 period the figure was over 300 million dollars! And that merchandise was shipped in 3.5 million packages!

What can the shopper buy through catalogs? The answer is almost anything—food, clothing, toys, furniture, electronics, and on and on. One firm specializes in paperweights, another in music boxes, a third in English muffins, and even one in carousel horses.

Each year fans of Neiman-Marcus wait for the sumptuous December catalog which lists unusual "his and her" items. It began in 1960 with the offer of a his and her Beechcraft airplane. In 1987 there was a $7,500 his-her opportunity to join a circus for a day of clowning or tightrope walking. In the interim, the store has sold ermine bathrobes, Chinese junks, ostriches, submarines, and mummy cases. And believe it or or not, most items sold. In fact, in 1986 the store sold over 100 California spangled cats (a new breed) at $1,400 each.

Catalog Changes

In the last few years, catalogs have become so popular that they are now being placed in bookstore magazine racks where they sell as rapidly as many of the popular magazines. In addition, some merchandisers are now selling advertising space in their catalogs to non-competitive firms.

Catalog sales have come a long way since 1872 when Aaron Montgomery Ward sent out a flimsy sheet of parchment-like paper in which he offered silk fans, honey soap, parasols, cashmere suits, and handkerchiefs.[2]

WRITING THE SALES LETTER

Writing the letter that sells a product or service can be an exciting adventure. To do a good job requires vivid imagination, skill in the concepts of written communication, and the sales ability to create desire through words.

---

[2]This material on catalog sales is based on an article which appeared in the *Los Angeles Times*, November 30, 1987, Part IV, p. 5.

Writers must possess the **imagination** to project themselves into the readers' position and recognize their hopes, needs, and desires. This is not easy, for our world revolves around *our* needs, *our* hopes, *our* desires. Sales-letter writers must *become* the people they are attempting to sell; they must see, appreciate, understand, and feel the readers' needs.

Imagination is also necessary to recognize new needs, new uses, and new reasons for the product. And imagination is needed to select the words that will build a compelling picture of the product in the readers' mind.

Skill in composition is required in every written communication, but especially in the sales letter. The organization of the letter must be logical and smooth. Persuasive points must be constructed unobtrusively from the introduction to the final statement, which motivates the purchase of the product or service. The sentences must be so clear that they flow effortlessly from one idea to another. Never should readers be required to stop and reread to understand a statement.

The word choice must be accurate and precise so that it evokes the exact response desired. There should never be a question about possible interpretations. The words should be selected so that they will elicit only one response. And the total composition must be concise. Modern readers do not have the time, patience, or inclination to read through three pages if the message can be contained in one.

Sales correspondents must combine imaginative abilities with communication skills to **build desire;** their words must persuade readers. It can't be just a "white or blue blouse." It must be a "highly styled, classic blouse, fashioned in luxurious silk and available in Wedgwood Blue or Snow White." It can't be "a modern office desk." A better picture is achieved if we say, "Contemporary styling in rich oiled walnut or burnished rosewood to enhance your present office decor and provide your staff with an efficient, convenient, and attractive work area."

Initial Steps

There are several steps sales writers must carry through before writing letters:

1. Conduct a product analysis.
2. Complete a market analysis.
3. Review the needs of the prospect.
4. Select the attribute(s) of the product that will fulfill the need.
5. Plan the presentation.

Product Analysis   Sales-letter writers must know their product intimately and thoroughly if they hope to sell it. They must know how it is made, what its components are, where the raw materials came from, what research has gone into it, what it will do, how it will do it, and a dozen other factors. They must also know a good deal about competing products. Only then will they be qualified to do a good job of selling. Such detailed information not only permits them to talk knowledgeably about the product or service, but it also adds two vital selling factors to their presentations: (1) sincerity and belief in the product, and (2) the ability to anticipate almost any question or objection the prospect might raise.

A product analysis may be conducted in many ways. Sales writers may visit the manufacturer and interview those engaged in making the product. They may gather information about quality and sources of raw materials, production techniques, quality control standards, method of operation, performance levels, design and appearance, distinguishing features, repair and service facilities, and prices and terms.

These are just some of the areas about which information can be secured. The areas examined can be used as headings on a chart and the data entered under each head. When the writers are finished, they possess an excellent resource chart from which to draw information for sales letters and promotion pieces.

Market Analysis[3] Today most companies bring out new products only after sophisticated market analysis. Sales writers do not make the market analysis themselves, but they need to know what the analysts have discovered.

Thousands—sometimes hundreds of thousands—of dollars are invested in producing a product. It would be unwise to spend these huge sums without first determining whether or not a profitable market exists. Such market analysis will determine:

The potential number of buyers

The present sales and acceptance of competitive products

The present buying habits and geographical concentrations of potential buyers

The likes, drives, and status symbols of potential buyers

What the potential buyer wants in the product

The buyer's buying power

The conditions and terms under which the buyer will act

The short- and long-range selling potential of the product

Any possible tie-in with other products

---

[3]The *Journal of Marketing Research* and the *Journal of Marketing* are both excellent sources for research studies. The *Journal of Consumer Research* presents much valuable information on consumer response to persuasive communications.

Answers to these questions and others may be secured from a variety of sources. Company records, earlier market studies on similar products, government statistics on buying habits, and journal articles that discuss the future sales potential in various fields are only some of the easily available *secondary* sources. *Primary* sources of information are also extremely valuable. Interviews with and questionnaire surveys of a sample of potential buyers are frequently used. Also valuable is unobtrusive observation, at the very moment of selection, of just how or why a buyer decides to purchase one product instead of another. Discussion with people who have had years of experience in the field—manufacturers, advertising executives, and sales representatives—is also helpful.

Needs of the Buyer   The market analysis should indicate which group or groups in the population can be expected to become buyers. These specific groups must be examined under the magnifying glass, so to speak, to determine their needs and drives, along with what appeals should be used to motivate them.

Psychologists say that most daily activities revolve around our efforts to fulfill our needs. These needs are usually divided into three categories: physical, social, and egoistic. In modern society our physical needs—food, shelter, warmth, and so on—are usually met, and thus we concentrate on our social and egoistic needs. Our social needs include our desire to give and receive affection, to affiliate with others and be affiliated with, and to take care of others and be taken care of (nurturance).

Unlike the social needs, which concern our relationship with others, the egoistic needs involve our relationship with ourselves. These needs may be filled by achieving recognition for something we have done, acquiring status symbols such as expensive cars or luxurious homes, occupying a position of authority, and so on. Most of us have the following egoistic needs:

Love	Efficiency	Approval from others
Security	A position of authority	Respect
Social distinction	More time	Prestige
Comfort	Good health	Good food
Pleasure	Warmth	

Specialists in consumer motivation have produced various lists of human drives or motives which include from fifty to several hundred items. Of course, many of these wants are offshoots of those listed above and overlap each other.[4] All of these wants must be taken into account, for *consumers*

---

[4]Vance Packard, in several of his popular books (*The Hidden Persuaders, The Status Seekers, The Pyramid Builders, The Waste Makers*), discusses the buying drives of the American consumer.

usually buy on the basis of the need that the product will fulfill rather than the product itself.

The buyer of an expensive automobile may be purchasing prestige and respect rather than transportation; a person may want from a mink coat status and position rather than comfort and warmth; in owning a foreign sports car, instead of simple transportation, a person may be looking for individuality, nonconformity, and distinctiveness; a teen-ager may be purchasing beauty and popularity rather than just cosmetics, soap, or clothes.

And so on. In the time-worn phrase: "Sell the sizzle—not the steak."

Major Appeal   In selling, it is necessary to select one or two outstanding attributes of the product or service offered—the *major appeal*—and emphasize these in the sales message. The characteristics chosen will help fulfill the real or imagined needs of the prospect.

This is necessary for two reasons. First, customers don't have the time or inclination to examine and weigh ten or fifteen wonderful attributes of the product. They ask, "Why is it better than the other cars, typewriters, shavers, or television sets on the market? Give me a short, quick answer, and I'll decide for myself whether to purchase your product."

Second, the seller is interested in showing how his or her product surpasses competing items. When the seller emphasizes one or two product attributes absent from competing products, attention is drawn to so-called superior features rather than to common attributes. This major appeal is always based on the needs of the prospect.

Let's see how this works in practice. We have just been asked to sell prospects on the idea of coming to our appliance store to purchase the new Arctic Refrigerator-Freezer for $695. We are to mail out 50,000 letters to greater Chicago area prospects to try to induce them to come to our downtown location.

Our refrigerator-freezer has many outstanding attributes, but our prospects are not interested in all of them. And furthermore, their needs vary. Some of them live in $180,000 to $350,000 homes in upper-class suburbs, while others live in densely populated neighborhoods. Their incomes vary from $12,000 per year to $150,000. The sizes of families range from two to ten. These people are all excellent prospects, but their needs and buying motives vary. We must therefore try to adapt our appeals to our prospects' needs.

In one letter (directed to upper-income areas), our major appeal may be an automatic ice cube maker, contemporary styling, or a new temperature-controlled butter keeper or vegetable crisper. To another group (perhaps suburban or rural), we emphasize the frost-free freezer. For the low-income group, we may focus on price, installment buying, time-payment plans, and trade-in deals. And in the letter sent to neighborhoods with large families, we may underscore Arctic's storage capacity, and efficiency. Of course, the refrigerator-freezer and its price never change, but the major appeal does.

Look through newspapers and magazines and note how the advertisements for the same car, the same soap, the same cigarette, and a thousand other items change from one publication to another. The various messages appeal to the needs of the various buying segments. The same variation appears in sales letters.

The major appeal for a sales letter must be based on market analysis and market segmentation. In selling to consumers, appeals may be based on emotion—status, prestige, beauty, securing an attractive mate, and so on. In letters sent to wholesalers, the central appeal is more practical—emphasizing profits, business efficiency, and rapid turnover.

Parts of the Sales Letter

Many of those who work in sales communication feel that the most effective sales letter has four parts:

Interest   Because of the tremendous competition for the attention of the prospect, the sales letter must almost instantly secure the reader's attention and hold it.

Description   Once interest has been secured, we must explain how the product or service will fulfill the prospect's needs and result in benefits.

Proof   Because the marketplace gives the prospect an opportunity to select from competing products and services, we must prove that ours is superior and should be selected.

Action   And because the payoff for both seller and buyer is in the sale, we must request the action that will complete the transaction.

Thus we should check every sales communication we write for IDPA: Interest, Description, Proof, and Action.

Arousing Interest   Following are some of the devices, ideas, and plans used to awaken a prospect's interest. How clever, tricky, or unusual they should be depends on who the reader is and the nature of the product or service.

The sales correspondent should avoid the attention-catching idea that is a tasteless gimmick. And it shouldn't be so unusual that the reader's interest focuses on the attention-catching device rather than on the item to be sold.

Sample of the Product   Although this can be a rather costly way of attracting attention, it is one of the most effective. Who can discard a sample swatch of cloth, slice of plastic, piece of metal, or square of rubber without first carefully examining it? Some companies have even had their letters printed on a sample of their product (wood, plastic, cardboard).

When prospective buyers can see, feel, bend, tear, taste, or smell the actual item, they are more likely to go back to the sales letter accompanying the sample, and read it carefully.

Photographs or Sketches   Some items are too big or bulky or in some way not adaptable for a sample. A good photograph permits the prospect to see the product and integrate it into the word picture that is described in a letter.

Gadgets and Gimmicks   Various plastic, paper, metal, cardboard, and wooden figures are used successfully. They may be reproductions of the product or some related item that ties in with the product or service offered. These may be attached to the letter, be a part of the message, or be a separate item altogether. Sometimes they are clipped or pasted to the letter. They may pop up or out or fold down.

Every large city has several agencies which specialize in the sale of advertising novelties and stickers of this type.

Different Openings to Attract Attention   Unusual messages, type sizes, and word arrangements can be used to attract attention:

1. Unusual offer

    Let me send you six weeks of Sports Fisherman for free.

    A genuine ruby can be yours—absolutely free—for responding to this letter.

2. Surprising statement

    Most cookware lasts only 18 months.

    Housewives control more money than America's twenty richest people.

3. Inside address opening

    Just How Often
    Have You Said "No"
    When You Should Have Said "Yes"?

4. Vital facts about the product

    What drinking water passes the American Medical Association test for purity? Only one . . .

5. Story opening

    In 1879, Erich Andrews' first ride down Slippery Jack Mountain was accidental. A mining cart got away from him and slid more than 2000 feet down the snow-covered hillside. Erich would laugh today to see thousands of avid skiers taking the same route . . .

6. Reference to prospect's problem

> *Face it: you don't have time to jump in the car, wait in line, then search for change every time you need a photocopy.*

Notice in several of these openings that the reference is personal: *you*. This approach immediately involves the reader and can be accomplished with most openings.

Openings of sales letters should be positive, so designed as to awaken in the prospect favorable associations with the product or service. And they should always be pertinent and concerned with the sales item. Readers are usually irritated to find that their interest has been awakened by a device that has nothing to do with the product.

Describing the Product or Service   Now that we have aroused the prospect's interest, we must describe the product carefully and show how its purchase will be beneficial. Not only must we describe the product so the reader can almost see and feel it, but we must do this in such a way that he or she *desires* it. In our description we answer the questions of, "What does it look like?" and "How is it made?"

> *The Torata-1000 laptop computer weighs a mere six pounds. It slides easily into a standard briefcase or its own carrying case. Powered by battery, the T-1000 goes anywhere—airplane, train, car, or park, with many hours of use before a few minutes of quick, easy recharging. The tilt-up screen features a full 24 lines of text in crisp, clear detail. All external components are formed from impact-resistant plastene, the same material used for jet cockpits.*

Although we shouldn't inundate the reader with details, there should be enough so that he or she can visualize the product or service. And the details should add strength to the central appeal. If the letter is accompanied by an enclosure, brochure, or pamphlet, the details, sketches, and pictures can go into that. If not, they must be carefully selected and presented in the letter.

But even as the prospect reads, silent questions are asked: "What will it do for me?" "How will I benefit?" And these questions must be answered early in the letter if we are to hold the reader's attention: how the product or service will provide profit, prestige, comfort, security, love, beauty, economy, health, or some other desired factor to the potential buyer.

> *Working at the computer would be ever so much easier if it weren't for the noise, the smoke, the clutter, the interruptions—in short, if it weren't at the office.*
>
> *Bring the computer home—the Torata-1000 laptop computer. Or take it with you to the library or park. Relax under a tree as you propose a merger. Spread a blanket on the sand to finish an important report. The Torata-1000 helps you escape the hassle factors and get down to work.*

In describing the product and explaining the benefits, be specific, positive, and detailed in reference to the primary selling appeal. It isn't necessary to describe the product first and then show the benefits. The order can be reversed, or the two steps can be integrated.

Proving Your Point   Americans are skeptical: "Sounds great, but I don't believe it will do all that. Prove it!" And prove it we must if we expect the prospect to make the purchase.

The type of proof we select will depend in large part on who the prospect is and the nature of the product. Where one person will be impressed by a testimonial from a movie star, another will only shrug. Some of the common types of proof follow:

Samples   Carefully examine the enclosed swatches of cloth—cloth that is used to tailor America's finest suits. Note the silklike quality of the Italian sharkskin, the beauty of the English tweeds, the design of the American worsted silks, and the attractiveness of the smartly styled gabardines. Each can be hand-tailored to . . .

Guarantee   And you will be happy to know that your National Stove is backed by a full 5-year guarantee on parts and service. Plus, it has the National Homemakers' Seal of Approval.

Free Trial   Therefore, with no obligation or risk on your part, we will be happy to send you the next six issues of *National Affairs.* After you have read a few copies of this vital national news magazine . . .

Names of Previous Purchasers   After your firm has received its Executive Conference Table, you will find it as useful and as attractive as have International Harvester, General Motors, Western Electric, and many other American corporations.

Testimonials   "There can be no doubt," said Martel plant superintendent Bill Peterson in a recent letter to us, "that Kelley Safety Equipment is directly responsible for our safest year on record."

"The National Briefcase," wrote Mr. Harry Berg of Hughes Aircraft, "has carried a multitude of papers and books for me and looks as attractive and impressive today as the day I purchased it almost ten years ago."

"Outside" Agency Records   Conclusive tests conducted by the chemistry department of Central Illinois University during the winter of 19__ indicated that every one of the Teltax cans of paint examined contained. . . . These samples of Teltax were purchased at random throughout Illinois, Michigan, and Indiana. Surely . . .

The United States Testing Company, Inc., carefully evaluated each of our new lines and found . . .

Money-Back Guarantee   We are so sure you will find the new Arctic Frozen Fruit line so tasty, delicious, and satisfactory that we promise to refund *double* the price you have paid for any item which does not meet with your complete satisfaction. All you need do is . . .

The proof in the sales letter should be restrained, specific, and well documented. It should overcome any doubts the prospect has, and it should convince people that the product or service will be of value.

Although proof is normally placed after the description, it need not be. Sometimes the proof can be so startling and dramatic as to serve the twofold purpose of arousing interest and convincing the prospect to make the purchase.

Dear Mr. Bertonelli:

You're considering the purchase of a Selway Solar Heater, and you're in good company. The system has already been installed at the corporate headquarters of IBM, Wang, Prudential, Santa Fe, TRW, Zenith, Standard Oil, and General Electric.

Action for Sales   We have aroused the interest of our prospects through a well-written opening; we have made them want to possess the product or service through our description of it; and we have proved to them that it will give full value. Now they must take the most important step of all—they must buy it. But most people hesitate. According to Henry Hoke, editor of a periodical in the field of direct mail, the two big barriers to action are inertia and the competition for the reader's money.

For this reason, the "buy" section of the sales letter should use an appeal sufficiently strong to move prospects to action (see Figure 24–1). And, we hope, immediate action. The longer they delay, the less likely they are to act favorably.

The action need not be the purchase of a product. It may simply involve "purchasing" the next step. It may be sending for a brochure, agreeing to see a sales representative, accepting a demonstration, or setting up an appointment.

The type and tone of the approach to use in the action section will depend on the prospect. Sometimes incentives are offered to potential buyers so that they will act quickly (see Figure 24–2):

Premiums	Special deals for a limited time
Special prices	Limited availability

FIGURE 24–1

Letter that gets action

HAIBAB CARPET OUTLET
17 RAILWAY CENTER
OAKLAND, CA 89182

January 7, 19___

Ms. Virginia Fellows
Box 889
San Francisco, CA   92039

Dear Ms. Fellows:

We like to let our regular customers know about special sales
before our ads hit the newspapers.

Beginning January 12, at 8:00 a.m., we will feature a 24-hour 30
percent off sale on all wall-to-wall carpeting, including the
newest designer patterns and tufted wools. We have over 900
colors and patterns to choose from, at truly incredible savings.

Who's invited? Only a select handful of our best customers--
including you-- as well as San Francisco's finest interior designers and office space architects. To make your shopping even
more pleasant, we're hosting a champagne brunch buffet.

Where? The one stop for carpet bargains: 17 Railway Center,
just behind the Broadway department store on Market Street.

We look forward to greeting you, one of our favorite customers,
on January 12.

Sincerely,

Mora Haibab

Mora Haibab
Owner

FIGURE 24–2

Action letter with incentive

EKKO

ELECTRIC COMPANY
404 N. Fourth Street
Bellville, California   91602

April 16, 198_

Mr. Pat Harper
Harper's Home Center
4040 W. Walnut Grove
Philadelphia, PA 19174

Dear Mr. Harper:

1 A full 22 percent margin when you sell a set of Palmer Patio Lights at the nationally advertised price of $6.95 per unit!

2 Palmer Patio Lights consist of a string of eight colored lights wired at 5-foot intervals and attached to a heavy-duty outdoor extension cord 40 feet long. There are three styles from which to choose, and you will find your customers buying one of each as they change the motif of their outdoor gatherings. The Party Line is especially popular, with the Oriental Occasion and the Hawaiian Luau running close behind.

3 All units are approved by the Underwriters' Laboratories and sold with a money-back guarantee. You can order them in dozen lots, either in cartons of four sets of each of the three lines or packed twelve of a type to a carton.

4 The enclosed folder describes the Palmer Patio Lights in more detail, lists prices, and tells you how you can get three free sets for yourself when you order before June 1. Order today; you'll be happy you did.

Sincerely yours,

Kelly Kanowski

Kelly Kanowski
Vice-President

---

1 Attention-catching opening

2 Product description

3 Proof

4 Incentive to order

It also helps to set prospects in motion if you tell them what to do and how to do it.

"Cut out the coupon"

"Sign and mail"

"Check box, sign, and mail"

"Include a quarter, add your signature, and mail"

COVER LETTER AND ENCLOSURE

Sales letters usually cover one page, although in some cases a sales letter of several pages has proved very successful. However, most experts, when faced with the need for a rather long, involved presentation, prefer to use a variation of the one-page sales letter.

This usually consists of a letter accompanied by a brochure, a pamphlet, or a flyer. Prospects do not object to reading through an attractively laid out and well-written enclosure if it is concerned with a product they are seriously considering buying. They do, however, object to wading through six typed pages of a sales letter. That is why most people in direct mail prefer the cover letter and enclosure to the detailed sales letter.

Authorities in direct mail seem to feel that the cover letter should take one of two forms:

1. A very general letter designed to arouse interest and motivate the reader to turn to the enclosure (see Figure 24–3).
2. A short sales letter following the IDPA formula—interest, description, proof, and action (see Figure 24–4). Each section is so brief that the letter must be supplemented by the enclosure.

The design, color, layout, and copy of the enclosure can be as imaginative as the writer wishes. Naturally decisions will always be governed by the prospect group and budgetary concerns. The enclosure directed to a business person will be more conservative than that sent to a teenager. But with modern high-speed printing devices, which reproduce photographs and color artwork with remarkable fidelity, the only limitations on the sales writer are money and imagination.

MAILING LISTS

The best sales letter will not sell if it does not reach a potential buyer. It is for this reason that special attention is always given to the mailing list. The competent sales writer reviews his or her list of names periodically.

FIGURE 24–3

Cover letter arousing interest

Closet Systems, Inc.
2891 Trent Avenue
Cambridge, MA 28392

Mr. Tom Briggs
3892 Emerson Place
Cambridge, MA   28393

Dear Mr. Briggs:

Go ahead--it will take just a few seconds to throw away the attached brochure. And a minute or two to eventually take out the
trash.

Or you could take the next three minutes to read it with care.

What do you have to gain? Freedom from clutter, wrinkled
clothes, misplaced belts, lost ties. Hours of new-found time
each month--time made possible by a new, organized approach to
personal living.

But the choice is yours. We hope you'll read on.

Sincerely,

Rachel Barker

Rachel Barker
Director

FIGURE 24-4

Cover letter incorporating the four parts—interest, description, proof, and action

---

Western Home Products
878 Sheridan Road
Miami, Florida 33541

May 7, 19__

Dr. Bruce Miller
155 W. Beverly Drive
Glenview, IL 60025

Dear Dr. Miller:

ENJOY--

Cool days and pleasant nights during the warmest, most uncomfortable weather Chicago has to offer.

Yes, that's what an Arctic Central Air-Conditioning System can give you at an amazingly low price.

The unit occupies very little space in your yard and may be placed behind shrubs or bushes. Its operation is whisper-quiet, thoroughly efficient, and almost completely maintenance-free.

Cool, refreshing air flows through the present ductwork in your home and provides comfortable days and restful nights.

Our expert engineers will make a scientific survey to determine the exact size unit your home requires. Then with no fuss, muss, or bother to you, the Arctic System will be installed in one afternoon.

You may be sure you will be as satisfied as the 9400 Chicagoland homeowners who purchased a unit last year. The Arctic System has also been approved by the American Home Builders' Association, and carries our five-year guarantee on parts and services.

Examine the enclosed brochure and then return the postal card to us. One of our expert engineers will stop by to see you--no obligation, of course--to show you how easy and inexpensive it is to own an Arctic Air-Conditioning System.

Sincerely yours,

Phil Phorest

Phil Phorest
Sales Manager

1. Is each name spelled correctly?
2. Is every person a good prospect for the product or service?
3. Do all persons listed have several common attributes?
4. If the list is long, has it been divided—by geographical location, economic level, and ethnic characteristics, for instance? When this is done, different appeals can be used in different sales letters selling the same product.
5. Have all the names of people who have moved, died, or expressed no interest in the product been removed?
6. Have names of new accounts, customers, and prospects been added?

Most firms develop their own mailing lists, usually made up of the names of customers. A list of this type has much to recommend it. These people have already established a friendly relationship with you, and they are willing to buy through the mail.

But every firm wants expanded sales and therefore seeks new names for its list. One way of obtaining them is from a mailing-list firm. Thousands of different lists are available, covering almost every conceivable category—clock manufacturers, blacksmiths, sculptors, female World War II veterans, compact-car dealers, and bell collectors, to name a few. College students are subdivided into a dozen categories—male, female, in universities or in community colleges, at denominational or public schools, by major fields, and by ethnic group. If the mailing-list firm does not have a list in some field, it will compile one.

It is worth paying more to a firm that keeps its lists up to date. There is no point in buying a list of names of people who have moved, died, or changed jobs.

But it isn't always necessary to buy a list. Company records are another excellent source; lists may be rented or borrowed from other merchants; and organizations—professional, social, or business—will sometimes provide membership lists. Public rosters also offer good sources: tax rolls, vital statistics listings, auto registrations, and voters' lists. And hundreds of different directories are available—not only telephone and city directories but directories of lawyers, doctors, manufacturers of aircraft components or auto parts or rugs, shippers, clothing dealers, building contractors, and a hundred and one other categories of professions and businesses. These provide names, addresses, and vital facts of business operations. For a list of directories and other reference sources, see Chapter 7.

Businesses can compile mailing lists by offering a premium or a prize that requires that the prospect complete a card with his or her name and address. Thus, there are many ways to complete, design, or obtain mailing lists.

GOODWILL LETTERS

The goodwill letter is somewhat similar to the sales letter, but instead of selling a product or a service it sells friendliness, sincerity, and good relationships. It is the letter that doesn't *have* to be sent but *is*. It is the business letter whose purpose is to build good will—not to sell, inquire, or adjust.

Many business people think this kind of letter is nonsense, but they are wrong. It is human nature to want to be appreciated.

For a goodwill letter to be successful, it must be sincere. There is no place in it for a strong sales pitch. On occasion one may wish to sell the idea of resuming business relations when an association has been broken off. Usually the recipient will feel irritated if the apparent goodwill letter turns out to have the ulterior purpose of trying to make a sale.

Some business firms feel they are sending out goodwill letters when they mail form letters addressed to "Dear Customer," or "Dear Occupant." They are like those people who say they don't have time to write personal letters, and instead buy ready-made greeting cards which they spend a great deal of time on signing and mailing.

How much more effective is the short, sincere, individually written letter, whether it comes from a company or from a private person!

Use of the Goodwill Letter

Business people find numerous situations in which to use goodwill letters. The two major categories are:

1. Letters that extend good wishes or thanks. These are usually sent to steady customers and are sometimes mailed in conjunction with a national holiday.
2. Letters that attempt to build good will with accounts who have terminated or cut down their business relations.

To the Steady Customer   Steady customers are often taken for granted; they become account numbers. We give them special attention only when they interrupt their relationship with us. By that time, it is probably too late. The best time to thank them is when their orders are coming in consistently.

To the New Customer   Perhaps your sales representative has been working for some time to get an account. That first order has just been shipped. Let the new customer know that not only the salesperson but the company president appreciates it (see Figures 24–5 and 24–6).

FIGURE 24–5
Goodwill letter

ROYAL BLUE POOLS

31 West Plains Drive
Dubuque, Iowa 38928

Mr. Samuel Nolan
3829 S. Bend Road
Hinton, Iowa 38908

Dear Mr. Nolan:

1 We're writing to thank you for the opportunity to build your new pool, and to wish you many enjoyable years of carefree swimming.

2 Over the years, Royal Blue Pools has built a reputation for craftsmanship and value by giving customers what they deserve: the best possible workmanship for the best possible price. As a result, more than half of our business is now by word of mouth, as satisfied customers tell their friends and neighbors they got a square deal at Royal Blue Pools.

Remember that we're here to answer any questions you have as you learn to use your new pool. Call on us at any time. And again, thank you for trusting your pool project to Royal Blue Pools.

Sincerely,

Brad Ashmont

Brad Ashmont
Marketing Director

1 A sincere opening

2 The writer points out benefits to the reader.

FIGURE 24–6

Goodwill letter to a new customer

Vermont
Office Supply
Company

114 N. Vermont Avenue   San Diego, California 80061

March 10, 19__

Mrs. B. Melton, President
Melton Office Supplies
500 East Grant Avenue
Burbank, CA 95014

Dear Mrs. Melton:

Welcome to Vermont Office Supply. We are delighted to have you as one of our customers, and you may be sure we will do everything possible to merit your business and goodwill.

Our activities have always revolved around the wishes and demands of our customers. You come first. If you have some special desires or requests on shipments, merchandise, account payments, or product modifications, let us know. We will work with you.

Each month our sales representative will bring you window fliers and display materials. Our salesperson also will be happy to make arrangements for you to obtain our special counter and floor display cases. And then there are traveling demonstration units that can be scheduled for your place of business.

All in all, Mrs. Melton, we are delighted to welcome you, and we want you to know that we will work with you . . . from president to stock clerk. Just tell us how, and we'll jump into action.

Sincerely yours,

Betty Clayton

Betty Clayton
Vice President

1 It's usually good to let customers know what they may expect in the way of assistance.

2 Note the personal tone achieved by including the customer's name in the body of the letter.

To the **Absent** Customer   Wide-awake businesses survey their accounts periodically. When they do, they are likely to find a number of inactive customers. Some were excellent accounts, others mediocre. But they all added to the company's profit margin. A goodwill letter seeks to re-establish the business relationship.

To the "**Incomplete**" Customer   A surprising number of accounts may purchase only part of their needs from you. This may be because they aren't aware of how extensive your line is, or because they are satisfied with another source of supply.

If you can get all or almost all of their business, your sales will rise appreciably while the increase in the cost of selling will be only minimal. You want to make better customers of them.

Evaluation

A goodwill letter program may not produce immediate, tangible results. It requires a long-range point of view.

Check the goodwill letter before it goes out. Does it carry a personal pen-and-ink signature? If it is processed, does it look neat and attractive? Is the letter always sent by first class mail? Does it have a friendly tone and a *you* attitude? And above all, is it honest and sincere?

MISCELLANEOUS LETTER SITUATIONS

Letters may serve a variety of purposes in addition to those we have just discussed: to tell someone that he or she has received a promotion, to send a congratulatory message, to comment on a job well done, and to convey condolence and sympathy. For most of these situations (and hundreds of others), greeting card companies have developed mass-produced messages. But how well do they achieve their objectives?

Mrs. Eileen Martinson was elected president of the 900-member Belleville City Cancer Prevention Association three days ago. Today she received seven "congratulations on your election" cards. Two are cute, two are clever, and three extol her virtues to the sky. Each is signed by a good friend. She notes that on the cards price codes indicate they cost from 75 to 95 cents each. Mrs. Martinson also received the brief note shown in Figure 24–7. Which of the eight messages will she most likely remember? Chances are it will be the note from Betty Anderson. And Mrs. Anderson undoubtedly spent less time

FIGURE 24–7

Personal letter of congratulations

```
Dear Martha:

The "old gang" at Western Electric read with pride (but not
surprise) about your election to the Henryville City Council.
Our sincere congratulations!

During your years with us, you consistently demonstrated the
difference that commitment and hard work can make.  We're sure
you'll bring that same energy to your new civic responsibili-
ties.

We're proud of you, Martha, and hope to see you soon.
```

and effort on her message than did the others who had to visit card shops and make selections.

Congratulatory Letters

Because of the hundreds of situations that call for congratulatory letters, it is difficult to select examples. They should all follow the same basic principles: They should be brief, deal with the primary topic only, and carry a positive, conversational tone.

Letters of Condolence

The letter of condolence is difficult to write. One person may be grateful for a brief, sincere note; another would appreciate a longer message. Perhaps the best advice is to remember to whom you are writing and write from the heart (see Figure 24–8).

FIGURE 24–8
Condolence letter

Dear Bob:

I learned of Pauline's tragic accident late last night. My
thoughts and prayers are with you.

She brightened the lives of all who knew her. I particularly
recall her comment before dinner when we got together for
Christmas Eve last year: "Let's live the best we can today.
That's the best we can do."

Call on me at any time, Bob. I'll be in touch soon.

My very best wishes,

Richard Pilson

QUESTIONS FOR STUDY

1. Discuss reasons why people often fail to even open direct mail advertising. How, in your view, can such resistance be overcome?
2. Evaluate the effect of direct mail advertisements that are addressed to "Occupant" or "Head of Household." What alternatives does a direct mailer have?
3. The best communications seem sincere. List at least five ways in which a writer can achieve the elusive quality of sincerity.
4. Discuss the relation between the reader's needs and the appeals included in sales letters.
5. Agree or disagree with this statement: "You establish the appeals for a product primarily premised upon the product and not the people to whom you hope to sell the product." Justify your stance.
6. What single guideline matters most in composing condolence letters?
7. List the major advantages of direct mail advertising. In your opinion, which advantage is most important?
8. What are the key disadvantages to direct mail advertising?

9. In most cases, where should the "action step" be placed in an effective sales letter?

10. Agree or disagree with the following statement: "The ethical communicator will not use language in the sales letter that arouses the receiver's emotions." Justify your stance.

11. In what way can goodwill letters be categorized as sales letters?

12. Explain how sincerity is linked to the success of a sales letter.

13. What are the categories of customers that can conceivably receive a company's goodwill letter?

14. What is an "incomplete" customer?

15. Do gadgets and gimmicks really arouse interest? Explain.

EXERCISES

16. You want to market a new line of matched luggage. Develop a list of at least six reader needs. For each, determine what qualities in the luggage to emphasize in your sales appeal. Use your list in writing a direct mail letter.

17. As manager of a growing computer firm, you're always on the lookout to hire bright talent. Write a congratulatory letter to an old college roommate for the publication of her book, "Understanding Computer Networks." Indicate (with some subtlety) that you would like to discuss job possibilities with her. Conclude your letter by trying to arrange a meeting.

18. As director of promotion for your service fraternity, you want to notify various civic clubs, social agencies, retiree groups, etc., that your organization will donate time to assist them in their community activities. Explain how you can develop a mailing list so you can send an informative letter to these organizations.

19. Your company has moved to an industrial park that contains 23 other businesses. Write a goodwill letter letting those companies know who you are and what you do.

20. Write the opening paragraph of a sales letter (not the entire letter) for each of the following items advertised by direct mail:
    (a) A new computer magazine
    (b) A set of gourmet kitchen knives
    (c) A subscription to a book club
    (d) A time-sharing arrangement for condominium rentals in vacation areas
    (e) A watch that needs batteries only once every five years
    (f) A set of encyclopedias directed toward the junior high and high school levels

21. Enclosures can help get the message across; enclosures will also potentially run the cost of your mailing up because they may increase the weight. Your college wants to send a first-class letter to the top merit scholars in your state. The letter will include a one-page communication from the college president and an enclosure. Write the president's letter and select the enclosure. Keep the total weight of the mailing to under one ounce. If your college does not have an appropriate item to use as an enclosure, design your own.

22. Identify a product that has been on the market for less than six months. Following the suggestions presented in the chapter, briefly analyze the market for this product. Finally, decide whether the product will survive or fail in the marketplace. Explain your rationale in some detail.

23. *From backpacks to briefcases.* Trends change, and the Albright Company has determined that whereas college students have been "packing" backpacks for a number of years, the trend is going to shift from that means of lugging things around campus to the briefcase. In line with this market analysis, Albright has developed an attractive briefcase, which is very lightweight, sturdy, and virtually mar-proof. It is expandable, so it can carry almost everything students have carried in their backpacks. Also the case is a neat item for simply carrying some paper, pencils, and one text.

    Albright does not sell its products in retail outlets but via mail. And its customers have traditionally been "older"—several years removed from the college-age population. Therefore the direct-mail approach will need to be carefully thought out as it targets the college market. Here are the problems, and you may work on all or some of them as assigned:

    (a) Analyze the product.
    (b) Analyze the market.
    (c) Specify the needs of the potential buyers.
    (d) Identify the major appeal.
    (e) Concerning the appeal, does it change by (1) male vs. female student; (2) graduate student vs. undergraduate student; (3) major—liberal arts vs. business?
    (f) What are two different ways the Albright Company can go about developing reliable mailing lists? Keep in mind that college students are traditionally very transient.
    (g) What can be enclosed with the letter? How can the enclosure be designed to appeal to women, men, and people of different races?
    (h) Should some gimmick be used, and how will college students relate to a gimmick? Name a potential gimmick and determine if it should be used. Test the gimmick on some students to see if it will help or hinder the sales letter.
    (i) Write a letter that you feel would be successful in getting orders from college students.

24. As a key wordsmith within your business organization, you've been selected to lead a one-day seminar on effective sales writing for company writers. What topics would you cover? In which order? What "recipes" would you offer (or would you offer recipes at all)? Create a one-page description (as if for circulation to employees) of your seminar.

25. A former college roommate, now graduated, writes to you with "an idea that just can't fail." He has access to men's and women's belts at good prices. He wants you to join him in a direct mail effort to sell the product. Write a letter to your former roommate in which you objectively analyze both the pros and cons of the idea. (Feel free to make up any financial information you require.)

Legal Considerations

PRODUCTS, PROMOTION, AND THE LAW

The claims companies make for their products and services have legal consequences. To limit the company's liabilities in such communications, managers must first understand the uses and abuses of letterhead stationery. Messages on letterhead should involve business matters only. Discussions of an individual's personal, political, or religious activities or preferences should not appear on company stationery. The letterhead signifies the organization's concurrence with the message regardless of any statement to the contrary. In other words, the letterhead establishes the "agency" relationship between the writer and the company. To avoid exposure to the company and potential legal entanglements, many executives keep personal stationery at the office.

To reinforce the agency relationship, many writers add the company name beneath their personal signature. Note, however, that omitting the company name does not dissolve the agency relationship when the message is written on letterhead.

Contracts can occur in ordinary memos, letters, and even college catalogs, as construed by many state laws. A contract relates some kind of promise that the law will recognize. That "promise" can be stated in sales language, as in the promotional promise to "service what we sell." It is not always necessary for the person to whom the offer is made to communicate in return. If, for example, a bank offers "$1000 for information leading to the arrest of the person who robbed the bank . . . ," the person claiming the reward need not have accepted the contract in advance.

Warranties communicate that the product or service will do certain things. The language of such warranties must be in simple, easily understood language, according to a 1975 law. The law does not require that products come with warranties. But for items costing more than $15 and accompanied by warranty, the language and terms of the warranty must meet specified criteria, such as specifying whether the warranty is "full" or "limited." If under full warranty, the product must be repaired or replaced by the seller within a reasonable time without charge if there is a defect. A limited warranty describes what the seller does and does not promise to do, and must be conspicuously displayed so that buyers are not misled.

The Fair Packaging and Labeling Act of 1966 permits the FTC and the Food and Drug Administration to specify what kinds of language can be used on packages, and to develop standards for package sizes. Also known as the Truth-in-Packaging Act, this legislation has gone far toward ensuring that labels accurately describe the product contained within the package.

Major Federal Legislation, Executive Orders, and Supreme Court Decisions Relating to Managerial Communications

Item	Action	Approx. Date	Manager-Communication Implication(s)
1	Sherman Act	1890	Prohibits businesses from conspiring or communicating to restrain trade.
2	Clayton Act	1914	Prohibits price-discrimination practices, tying contracts, and exclusive dealing contracts. It is important that company communications do not imply such entanglements.
3	Federal Trade Commission Act Amended, Wheeler-Lea Act, and subsequently amended	1914 1938	Prohibits unfair trade, establishes FTC; establishes regulations concerning false advertising; regulates language used in describing products.
4	National Labor Relations Act (Wagner Act)	1935	Directs business to communicate with unionized employees over wages, pay rates, working hours, and conditions of employment; business felt it limited their right to speak regarding unionization. Creates NLRB.
5	Fair Labor Standards Act Equal Pay Act	1938 1963	Established the 40-hour week; Act has been amended many times; the equal pay stipulation makes it illegal to pay women less than men doing the same work with equivalent skills; communications are to reflect such.
6	Labor-Management Relations Act (Taft-Hartley Act)	1947	Permits businesses greater speech rights: Sec. 8C, "that expressing of any views, argument, or the dissemination thereof, whether in written, printed, graphic, or visual form, shall not constitute or be evidence of an unfair labor practice . . . if such expression contains no threat of reprisal or force or promise of benefit."
7	Civil Rights Act, Title VII Amended by the Equal Employment Opportunity Act	1964 1972	Prohibits discrimination in employment, hiring, upgrading, pay, and benefits on the basis of race, color, religion, national origin, and sex; creates EEOC, which can establish regulations for affirmative action programs for government vendors.
8	Freedom of Information Act	1966	Permits individuals to have greater access to government files; as amended in 1974, allows for speedier access. Allows competitors to have access to what firms report to the government.
9	Fair Packaging and Labeling Act (Truth-in-Packaging Act)	1966	Permits the FTC and the Food and Drug Administration to establish standards for regulating what language can be used on packages; also promotes the voluntary development of standards for package sizes.

Item	Action	Approx. Date	Manager-Communication Implication(s)
10	Executive Order 11375 (L. B. Johnson)	1967	CEO should issue a written statement declaring the organization will not discriminate on the basis of race, creed, or national origin plus physical handicap. The EEO policy must be communicated to recruiters, subcontractors, unions, and employees.
11	Age Discrimination in Employment Act	1967	Prohibits discrimination against persons between 40 and 69 in hiring, discharge, retirement, pay, and conditions of employment. Communications should not refer to employee's or potential employee's age.
12	Consumer Credit Protection Act (CCPA)	1968	The original legislation, periodically amended, dealt with unscrupulous practices on the part of creditors.
	Truth-in-Lending Act (part of CCPA)	1969	Concerns complete disclosure of credit terms; also specifies that careful and clear wording shall be used in lending agreement.
13	Clean Air Act[1] (Amends 1967 Air Quality Act)	1970	Empowers Environmental Protection Agency (EPA) to set air quality standards to protect public health.
14	Fair Credit Reporting Act (FCRA)	1970	Protects credit standing and reputation of individual; businesses are to be correct in communicating credit information and are to correct errors.
15	39 U.S. Code (Concerning U.S. Mails)	1971	Sets restrictions on mailing of sexually oriented advertisements in the mail; establishes procedures for people to not receive such by having name removed from certain mailing lists. It is communicator's responsibility to not communicate with those requesting to be eliminated from list.
16	Noise Control Act[1]	1972	Empowers EPA to establish noise emission standards.
17	Warranty Legislation; UCC-Sec. 2:312–18 (periodically amended)	1972	The uniform Common Code is *not* federal legislation, but is an attempt to gain common statutes among the states. This particular section establishes seller's responsibilities for express or implied warranties.
18	Vocational Rehabilitation Act	1973	Stipulates equal opportunity for handicapped; communications shall not reflect discrimination on this basis.
19	Family Education Rights and Privacy Act	1974	Permits parents and students over 18 to have access to their files held by public schools and colleges; the legislation has altered the use and nature of recommendation letters.

Item	Action	Approx. Date	Manager-Communication Implication(s)
20	Privacy Act	1974	Concerns governmental information and how individuals can update information in government files; for managers in governmental agencies, limits their exchange of information among agencies.
21	Fair Credit Billing Act	1974	Establishes methods by which creditor must communicate with customer; establishes time limits for various kinds of communication creditor may send to customers.
22	Employer Retirement Income Security Act (ERISA)	1974	Stipulates that each employee must receive retirement fund information in easily understood language.
23	Equal Credit Opportunity Act	1974	Eliminates discrimination in credit on basis of standard discriminatory acts; also requires creditor to state in writing why credit was denied.
24	The Consumer Product Warranty Act and Federal Trade Commission Improvement Act (Magnuson-Moss Warranty Act)	1975	Establishes that warranties must use language that is free of ambiguous terms, exemptions, and disclaimers.
25	Fair Debt Collection Practices Act	1978	Places limits on methods and substance of communication from creditor to debtor.
26	U.S. Copyright Law (Amendment of 1909 Law)	1978	Protects publishers for a limited amount of time from others publishing their materials; the new statutes limit the use of photocopying and prohibit the reproduction of consumable items.
27	U.S. Supreme Court First National Bank of Boston et al. vs. Bellotti, Etc. et al.	1978	Banks can communicate to public via advertising and executive speech, for example, on a referendum issue. Establishes that corporations can communicate.
28	U.S. Supreme Court Consolidated. Edison Company of New York, Inc. vs. Public Service Commission of New York	1980	Establishes right for public utility company to communicate to customers with bill insert on controversial issue; company need not grant envelope space to opposing groups.
29	U.S. Supreme Court Central Hudson Gas & Electric Corp. vs. Public Service Commission of New York	1980	Establishes right for a public utility to communicate a point of view that is not consistent with a national goal.
30	Job Training Partnership Act	1982	Establishes government/private sector programs for job training; sets forth employee rights of trainees.
31	Comprehensive Immigration Reform and Control Act	1986	Sets forth communication rights and communication channels for immigrants.
32	Competitive Equality Banking Act	1987	Extends description of depositor rights and reasonable expectations in business relations with banks.

[1]Noise and smoke communicate noverbally. Since the early 1970s there have been various federal and state bills designed to regulate these potentially harmful nonverbal communications—smog, noise, and waste disposal.

Cases

Cases

The cases in this section have all been adapted from real-life situations, although the names used are fictitious. As you read them, you will probably say to yourself, "I saw a similar situation when I worked at the Blank Company three years ago."

The cases reflect interpersonal and organizational communication situations. In some instances, you will recognize potential problems that are just beginning to emerge; in other situations, problems will be in sharp focus.

Among the major objectives of studying these cases is to improve your abilities to analyze, solve problems, and make decisions. What do you see as the problem in the case as compared to your colleague's perception? What action do you suggest? How would you handle the interview? The report? The directive?

Don't look for a "textbook" solution. In most instances there is no one right answer. That is because the cases are very brief, and there are many variables (the people, companies, situations, economic conditions, and so forth) that are not given. The value is not in finding one answer, but in your analysis and the recognition that your colleagues may perceive the situation very differently from the way you do.

The point to keep in mind is that there may be more than one answer to a problem. And it is quite possible that the "correct" answer may not be yours. Thus, you should develop abilities for careful analysis and an appreciation for different perceptions so that your decision making may be completed logically.

HOW TO USE THE CASES

Each case has the potential for an almost infinite number of communication exercises. You will probably want to design your own. The following are possibilities:

Group Analysis and Discussion

Groups of four to five people may wish to analyze and discuss the case. Each group may then have its spokesperson tell the other groups the important points identified and the solutions reached by his or her group members.

Each paragraph in the cases is numbered to facilitate reference and identification in group discussions.

Written Exercises

Your instructor or group leader may request:

Reports	Proposals
Letters	Written Case Analyses
Memos	Summaries

Any one of these can be drawn from the case. Individuals named in the case may address letters or memos to each other, request a report, or issue a proposal.

Oral Exercises

Your instructor or group leader may request that you and one or more of your colleagues hold an interview or meeting or give an oral report.

In these situations you will probably be asked to participate in a role-playing situation and assume the identity of someone described in a case.

It is important that when the exercise has been concluded, an unbiased individual(s) gives you constructive feedback on the content and delivery of your presentation. In the case of interview role plays, you probably should ask one person to act as an "observer." (See the Observer Evaluation Checklist on pages C–42 and C–43.)

In all situations, whether you are holding a discussion, conducting an interview, or writing a report, assume the case is a real-life incident and you are the involved manager or employee.

Case 1
The Mark Teller Case

1. Mark Teller has been with the Pembroke Company for nine months, but he hasn't done as well as you expected. Prior to coming to Pembroke, he had a rather successful career as a salesman for three different firms, one in recreational and school equipment, one in commercial real estate, and one in printing.

2. He is thirty-six years old, married for the second time (now separated), and evidently likes to live well. He is a bit overweight, jovial, and apparently always in good spirits. He is well liked by his fellow workers, usually insists on picking up the tab, and is always good for a lively joke.

3. He has participated in several sales-training programs, both on his own and under company sponsorship. Mark invariably takes a very active part, knows the answers, and contributes materially to the success of such meetings. He has a fine grasp of sales principles, reads extensively in the professional sales journals, and has undoubtedly retained much of what he learned about marketing at the University of Michigan, which he attended for almost three years.

4. Despite all of this, the sales in his territory have been declining—not seriously, but steadily. This worries you for two reasons: (1) His areas have excellent potential, and sales should be twice what he now has because of a boom in industrial and retail business firms, and (2) Mark's record is far less than you expected. Of course, this is a blow to your own ego, for you confidently told your partner that, in your judgment, Teller was a "real comer." This statement is now beginning to bounce back on you.

5. In an effort to find some answers, you have gone out on the road with Mark on several occasions. He is always greeted by industrial accounts as a long-lost brother. There is much good-natured ribbing, back slapping, and coffee drinking. Mark's supply of jokes is inexhaustible, and his faculty for remembering names is remarkable.

6. He is a fluent and easy talker, and you envy his steady line of chatter. He is never at a loss for an answer, a word, or a phrase.

7. You have made several stops among Mark's prospects and everyone feels he's a great guy. Mr. Kelly said, "Without Mark, I'd be a flop; he keeps me supplied with jokes." Goren feels he's a good man, but "he has a hell of a time giving me the information I want. He changes his quotes and prices from day to day."

8. Only Ms. Kimball has complained directly about Teller. Kimball has been a major customer and should be a good long-term account. She recently said, "I feel business is business, and there is a limit to horsing around. Teller could get his calls done here in fifteen minutes if he knew what he was doing. He wastes his time and ours."

9. Back at the office, you check Mark's files and you find that many of the problems in his transactions have arisen purely as a result of his carelessness and negligence in making notations, reporting, and entering quotes.

10. The ironic thing about this is that Mark seems to have every attribute that makes for a good salesman, and yet his sales are declining. There is a special sales-training program scheduled for July by the San Diego Sales Association. Maybe we should send him to that.

11. What are the major problems? What communication barriers exist? What action should be taken now? What should have been done in the past? By whom?

ASSIGNMENTS

1. Group Discussion

Break into small groups and discuss the case. Your first step should be to review the situation. The purpose of this review is to determine that all participants in each group have a similar perception of the incidents described in the case.

Next, analyze the case. What is the major problem? The contributing problems? What specific communication barriers are evident? Who is responsible? How can the major and minor problems be solved? What action should be taken now?

After ten to fifteen minutes of private discussion among the members of each group, open the case to the entire class. Do this by having the spokespersons of four or five groups report those groups' findings to the class. Permit class members to respond or ask questions, after each spokesperson reports.

2. Interview Role Play

Break into groups of three. Have one person play the boss; one, Mark Teller; and one, the observer (see the Observer Evaluation Checklist). Act out a five- to eight-minute interview between the boss and Mark Teller in

which an attempt is made to resolve the situation described. At the conclusion of the interview, have the observer report his or her reactions.

Change roles and repeat the role playing to get another person's approach to the same problem.

3. Memos

(a) Assume you are the boss. Write a memo to Mark Teller in which you attempt to alleviate or correct the situation described.

(b) Assume you are the boss. Write a memo to your partner describing the situation and the action you intend to take to solve the problem(s).

√4. Letter

Assume you are the boss. Write a goodwill letter to Ms. Kimball. Make any logical assumptions you feel are valid.

she's about to take her business elsewhere

Case 2
The Jim Cantonelli Case

1. For some time, Southern California Utilities Director of Finance Bob Baker had been looking for a competent individual to take over Section Two, Employee Disbursements. Unfortunately, Ken Carpenter, who headed up Section Two for three years, was leaving to take over a family business in the Midwest. Baker had thought about Marty Martin, who had been one of Ken's assistants for two years. However, Baker wondered about Martin, inasmuch as the latter was attending an MBA program at night, trying to

pay for a Porsche, and leading a very active social life.

2. Baker also talked to Jim Cantonelli, about whom he had always received very favorable reports. Cantonelli had been in Section One (Accounts Payable) for three years and had done a good job programming many routine functions on the computer. Although Baker and Jim had a favorable initial chat, Jim seemed reluctant to pursue the discussion.

3. Before 1981, Jim worked for an aerospace firm, and before that, at an electronics corporation. He had completed an engineering/computer education in Europe to what would equal our junior college level. However, he could not continue because he was called up for army service.

4. Jim has proven to be one of the hardest working and most conscientious employees in the Finance Division of Southern California Utilities. He has never complained about assignments, has frequently stayed after hours and worked Saturdays "on his own." No job has proved too difficult for him. He has completed not only regular tasks, but also extra ones willingly. And there were dozens of "extra ones" in 1987 when the new IBM equipment was installed.

5. His relationship with other company employees is minimal. He rarely participates in employee affairs and doesn't trade chitchat to any great degree with fellow workers. Nevertheless, he seems respected, if not well liked, by his associates.

6. When he was approached about becoming the chief of Section Two, he was reluctant. He noted his slight foreign accent, his lack of formal education in this country, and the trouble he now has in writing up his weekly reports. But when Baker pointed out, in three discussions, the extra compensation he would receive, his new job title, his experience in computers, the seniority level he was in, and the confidence Baker and other offi-cers had in him, he accepted. Jim did have some misgivings, but Baker overrode them.

7. During the first two months of Section Two's operations under Jim, all seemed to go quite well, although Baker understood that Jim had two or three rather severe arguments with Marty Martin. Baker also suggested to Jim that it wasn't necessary for him to stay late so many nights, that if he would just let his subordinates take over on assignments, they would probably fulfill them to his complete satisfaction. It was true that payroll activities worked in a very cyclical way, but no one should work until midnight night after night.

8. Last month Marty Martin left his position. He told Baker it was for a better job in industry. However, others have indicated that he left because of utter frustration in never being permitted by Jim to handle a complete assignment, or to take over full responsibility for a major project.

9. When Baker questioned Jim about this, he said, "That guy has school and women on his mind; besides, he's about as slow and lazy as every other worker in this unit." Of course, he backed up after a few minutes, probably because Baker appeared so surprised by his remark.

10. In the last few weeks, Baker has visited Jim's area almost every day. Jim usually appears agitated, and seems to be "going like sixty," obviously upset. In the past three weeks, Baker has received several informal complaints from the personnel of Jim's section. Jim himself seems more upset than ever, perhaps because of several computer-related problems and comments concerning errors. And of major importance is the quality (or lack of it) of the work produced by his section. There have been several kickbacks, and Baker's vice president has let Baker know that he isn't overjoyed with the operation of Section Two. The heads of other sections with whom

Jim must work have also complained (rather quietly) about Jim's grouchiness and lack of cooperation.

11. Two weeks ago, Jane Albermarle, who worked under Jim, quit, saying, "I can't work with that nut, Cantonelli." Yesterday, Bob Carter and Art Phillips, both excellent employees, caught Baker on the way out of his office and asked for transfers to Section Three. When Baker questioned them, Carter and Phillips said something about people in Section Three being in their car pool. However, a couple of others who work under Jim said, "I guess he's OK. All bosses are the same. He's new and nervous . . . but he should settle down."

12. It's obvious Baker must do something about Jim Cantonelli. But today when Baker questioned him in general terms, Jim said that he's just about got everything under control, "and in another month, if I can get these idiot employees to do a day's work, we'll be running as smooth as silk."

13. But Baker is upset and so is management. Perhaps that seminar next month at the State University on "New Techniques in Computer Payroll Methods" sponsored by the Western Finance Officers Association might be just the thing for Jim. The registration fee is nominal, and it might be the answer.

14. What are the communication problems between Baker and Cantonelli? Between Cantonelli and his people? What do you think should have been done in the past? What should be done now?

ASSIGNMENTS

1. Group Discussion

Break into groups of four or five and discuss the case. Your first step should be to review the situation presented in order to determine that all participants in each group have a similar perception of the incidents described.

Next, proceed to analyze the case. What is the major problem? The contributing problems? What specific communication barriers are evident? Who is responsible? How can the major and minor problems be solved? What action should be taken now?

After ten to fifteen minutes of discussion by the groups within themselves, open the case to the entire class. Do this by having the spokespersons of four or five groups report their groups' findings to the class. Permit class members to respond or ask questions, or both, after each representative speaks.

2. Interview Role Play

(a) Break into groups of three. Have one person play Mr. Baker; one, Jim Cantonelli; and one, the observer (see the Observer Evaluation Checklist). Act out a five- to eight-minute interview between Mr. Baker and Jim Cantonelli (after paragraph 13) in which an attempt is made to alleviate or correct the situation described. At the conclusion of the interview, have the observer report his or her reactions.

(b) Change roles and repeat the role playing to see another person's approach to the same problem.

(c) Break into groups of three. Have one person play Bob Baker; one, Art Phillips; and one, the observer (see paragraph 11). Repeat as above.

3. Report

Assume you are an outsider who has just reviewed the situation existing under Mr. Baker. Submit a report to *Mr. Baker's boss* on your findings, conclusions, and recommendations. Remember that you are an unbiased and objective consultant.

4. Memos

(a) Assume you are Bob Carter. Send a memo to Mr. Baker through your boss, Jim Cantonelli, in which you request a transfer to Section Three (see paragraph 11).

(b) Assume you are the vice president to whom Bob Baker reports. Send a memo to Bob Baker concerning the situation in Section Three (see paragraph 10).

5. Letters

(a) As the director of training of Jim Cantonelli's company, send a letter of inquiry to the Western Finance Officers Association asking for details (content, fee, prerequisites, length) of the seminar "New Techniques in Computer Payroll Methods" (see paragraph 13).

(b) As the personnel director of Jim Cantonelli's company, send a letter to Marty Martin inviting him to an exit interview with you at his convenience (see paragraph 8).

Case 3
The St. Paul
Hospital Case

1. You serve as administrator of a large urban hospital. 'Large," in fact, is hardly the word: 520 beds, 400 nurses, 320 staff members, and a host of resident and consulting physicians. Every day, you tell yourself, is an adventure in organizational management and interpersonal relations. Most days go quite well.

2. And then there are days like yesterday. You talked for more than two hours with an ad hoc delegation from the data processing unit at the hospital. The issue is wages, and tempers are rising.

3. Vernon, supervisor of data processing, seemed ready for war: "Nurses had a 10 percent raise two months ago, and orderlies got about the same last month. You, the administrator, received a big raise at the beginning of the year. Now it's our turn in data processing."

4. You couldn't deny his facts. But you had said "no" to the raise demands and would continue to say "no." You had reasons, not all of which you wanted to explain to the employees in data processing. For one thing, their work over the past year had been mediocre at best. They lacked the team spirit that characterized other work units, especially the nurses' units. Petty squabbles always seemed to pop up in the data processing group, with key employees going for days without speaking to one another.

5. Consequently, the unit ran perpetually late on important assignments. When data runs did finally appear in your office, they were a mess: disorganized, poorly packaged, and often incomplete. Your staff had a standing joke about "here comes chaos" when the office mail arrived from data processing. The Admissions and Records unit seemed to have better luck, for some reason. Maybe data processing simply played favorites when it came to giving adequate service.

6. The data processing employees made no effort to hide their anger over your "no" answer. When you mentioned to Betty Kendell, one of the section heads in data processing, that the last printout on physician

associations and hours contained some serious omissions, she looked you in the eye and said, "You get exactly what you pay for." Actually, you don't think you are getting your money's worth now. How could you think of a raise for data processing personnel?

7. You had another reason for saying "no." Two years ago you talked the hospital's Board of Trustees into a major capital investment in computing equipment on the promise that you would hold to a pre-agreed pattern of wage increases in the data processing unit. You have kept your word so far, and you aren't about to lose face and faith with the Board now.

8. Today you got your first indication of what Betty meant by her comment, "You get exactly what you pay for." The monthly order for surgical supplies can't go out on time because a mysterious bug has hung up the computer-controlled inventory analysis. At the same time, one of the unit's three minicomputers has failed completely. Admittedly, it had a sporadic history of breakdowns—but how ironic that it should fail today.

9. The problem of supplies is serious. Without an accurate inventory, next month's order would almost be made up "in the dark." To under-order may cause serious medical problems. If too much is ordered, some items may become outdated and have to be discarded. In addition, certain levels of specific items must always be on hand to satisfy review boards, disaster control agencies, and so forth.

10. The problem is so serious that you put off telephone calls for an entire hour to think through the situation. Today's bugs and inconveniences might well turn into tomorrow's disasters if you don't act soon. The data processing unit has responsibility for patient and employee files, hospital financial data— some of it quite sensitive—and even payroll.

Standard diagnostic routines costing thousands of dollars are stored on computer tape in the data processing unit. Hardware worth half a million dollars also would be easy prey for vandalism. Although most of the employees in data processing were angry over your refusal of the raise, you didn't think your rank-and-file workers were seriously scheming to subvert the hospital and its work. At least not yet.

11. However, someone in the unit was letting errors slip into key programs—slight, untraceable, innocent-looking errors in just the right spot to crash important programs. You didn't suspect Betty or Vernon, certainly. They had been with the hospital for years, through good days and bad. They were angry, but they had too much integrity to endanger patient health care, the hospital's reputation, or internal organization by fouling up records and supplies.

12. Probably the culprit was one of the dozen or so new employees brought aboard in the rush of growth during the past eighteen months. You tried to picture the type: someone with just enough knowledge of the system to be dangerous, and too little loyalty to the hospital to care. At least you hoped it was an isolated computer vandal, rather than the work of the entire unit.

13. The key question was what to do. Should you involve Vernon, Betty, and other senior employees? Will they work with you or simply "play dumb"? Should you get tough and bring in hospital security right away, threatening criminal charges against the perpetrators? Should you reconsider the raise issue, or at least make appearances of reconsidering it while things cool down? Should you back down and recommend that the Board grant the percentage increase demanded by the data processing personnel? Should you hire a private investigator?

ASSIGNMENTS

1. Group Discussion

Choose three members of the class to play the role of the hospital administrator. One by one, ask them to "think out loud" about the situation, letting the rest of the group listen to their thoughts. These thoughts need not be strictly analytical or structured. No answers are necessary.

After the three presentations, open the forum to general group discussion. Assign a secretary to keep notes on majority and minority positions within the group. When discussion begins to fade, bring the issue to a head: what can the group agree on for a course of action?

2. Interview Role Play

(a) Divide the entire class into pairs, one person playing the role of the hospital administrator and one person playing the role of Vernon, head of the data processing unit. The purpose of the interview is to find out what Vernon knows about the situation, and perhaps to solicit his help. Be ready to report to the class on useful ways you discovered to break down barriers of suspicion, anger, and secrecy.

(b) Break into groups of five or six. Let one person play the role of the administrator and the others, the roles of new employees in the data processing unit. The purpose of this meeting is to make sure each employee knows the seriousness of computer vandalism at the hospital and to seek out any leads and information that may be useful in

resolving the situation. After the session, be ready to discuss ways to avoid accusation and hostility.

3. Presentation

Develop an 8 to 10 minute presentation on the problems in data processing, with your recommendations for solutions. Include at least one visual aid (for example, a visual representation of the work slow-down). Deliver the presentation to an assembled group of classmates playing the role of the Hospital Board.

4. Meeting

Assume that you have just delivered the presentation described above. Join with at least four other classmates, representing Hospital Board members and officials, in a meeting intended to review your presentation and reach consensus on a course of action.

After the meeting has reached its goals, stop to consider the communication that has taken place among meeting members. What alliances were formed among members? Were such unions permanent throughout the meeting? What role did emotions play? What proved to be decisive points in the meeting? Which speakers were dominant?

5. Memos

(a) In the administrator's role, write a memo to Vernon, head of data processing. Recap the suspicious events described in the case, and take steps in the memo to involve Vernon in resolving the problem.

(b) Again in the role of the administrator, write a memo to Betty in data processing. Invite her to a meeting with you to discuss the meaning of her comment, "You get exactly what you pay for." In the memo, briefly express your concern about the situation in her unit.

6. Letters

   (a) In the capacity of a private investigator, write a letter to the hospital administrator offering your services to find a quick answer to the vandalism problems in data processing. The hospital administrator had talked to you by telephone and invited your letter of proposal.

   (b) In the capacity of Vernon, head of data processing, write a letter to the hospital administrator. Describe how your unit wants to handle its own problems, without outside review or interference. Be thorough and specific to create credibility for your plans.

7. Reports

   (a) The Chairman of the Hospital Board has caught wind of the problems in data processing. He requests from you, the hospital administrator, a written report to the Board on the situation and your recommendations for solving the problem.

   (b) Assume the culprit or culprits have been discovered. As a staff member working directly for the hospital administrator, write a brief report summarizing the situation for the Hospital Board. Recommend any action you deem appropriate.

Case 4
Hostile Takeover

1. Susan Underwood, a senior manager in charge of company publications, first read of the takeover attempt in *The Wall Street Journal*. She saw her shares of company stock soar, then plummet, as news broke, pro and con, about the takeover. Her emotions rose and fell as well. After sixteen years with Lever Electronics, she felt considerable loyalty to the goals, methods, and overall culture of the company. It had been her home.

2. She feared that a takeover, even if it didn't cost her job, might change her work environment drastically. Would she be told to manage in a new way? Would she be given an impossible workload? Would her authority be ripped away from her by putting her in a subordinate reporting position, no matter what her title? At 41, Susan wasn't eager for a job change.

3. H. Richard Galloway, financier, was indeed in the process of taking over Lever Electronics through a carefully staged program of buying company stock. He now owned enough to sway board decisions, and soon would control the board completely. Lever Electronics seemed powerless against Galloway's invasion, as stockholders one by one sold out to his inflated offers for company stock.

4. Galloway's announced goal was to "trim" Lever Electronics of its cash-rich, asset-rich business base—in short, to mortgage it to the hilt. He would carry away the proceeds from new loans, sales, and stock offerings as his booty for a successful takeover. In fact, he stood to make more than $30 million from the twelve-week business venture.

5. On the very day that Galloway successfully installed his own person as chair-

man of the board, Susan Underwood began receiving new instructions for company publications. The first came in a terse memo from Galloway himself:

"Design and submit a program of communications reassuring company employees that, while changes will take place, every effort will be made to assure their positions, with some adjustments in compensation made necessary by our transition period."

Susan was being asked—told—to "sell" the takeover through the publications she managed.

6. Since she was in large part responsible for assigning all and writing many of the articles in the company magazine and newsletter, Susan felt an ethical and professional dilemma. Could she in good conscience ask her coworkers to trust new management that might well prove untrustworthy? How should she use the bond of trust that had developed over the years between her and her readers?

ASSIGNMENTS

1. Group Discussion

With class members playing the roles of company employees, enact an off-site meeting of "old" company employees. They can speak freely and off the record about their concerns.

After the discussion, decide what makes the difference between a general "gripe" session and a meeting that leads to constructive action. Once you have decided how the group can settle upon action goals, re-enact the meeting, this time re-directing discussion toward a goal of some sort—something employees can do about their situation.

2. Interview Role Play

A student should take on the role of Susan as she interviews Galloway about his plans for the company. The interview ostensibly serves the purpose of gathering information for articles; its hidden agenda, however, is for Susan to feel out Galloway's real motives and plans.

3. Memos

(a) Write a memo from Susan to one of her staff writers, instructing the writer to prepare some articles, in keeping with Galloway's directive. Go on to instruct the writer how the article should be researched. Bear in mind Susan's strong ethical commitment to telling her readers the truth.

(b) Write a memo from Susan to Galloway. In the memo, develop some means of finding out more about his plans for the company. You could, for example, ask a series of direct questions. Or you could request a meeting, with suggestions for agenda items. If you deem it wise, you might take the bull by the horns and write a frank memo expressing your personal ambivalence and misgivings.

4. Report

Draw up the report requested by Galloway. Show what communications employees will receive, how such messages will be written, and where they will appear. In your report, cover as many employee subgroups as possible.

5. Proposal

Draw up a relative short proposal to circulate, privately, among Lever employees. The proposal should show a practical way by which employees themselves could take over ownership of the company and forestall Galloway's takeover. Remember that good proposals demonstrate not only solutions but also a clear understanding and exposition of the problems.

6. Letters

  (a) On behalf of employees, write an open letter to Galloway. Express the personal and professional concerns of employees. Ask for a meeting or series of meetings in which these concerns can be discussed directly with the new CEO.

  (b) In the role of Galloway, write an open letter to employees. Before beginning your letter, decide whether you are going to "play it tough" or give in to employee requests for meetings, reassurances, and compromises.

Case 5
The Brooks-Martinez Case

1. Joe Green has been in charge of the drafting department of the Belleville plant for about eighteen months. He has always enjoyed his job, the security of the position, the elimination of traveling, and the friends he had in Belleville.

2. However, Joe did encounter a problem recently when one of the five forepersons under him resigned. Green's superior, Mr. O'Brien, asked Green to designate a replacement. This was not an easy task for Green because the individual who he thought was most competent, Georgia Brooks, was an employee with whom he had a good many differences of opinion. Another employee in the same unit, Carlos Martinez, was also considered very seriously by Green. However, Carlos has had a series of absences, and because of a strong accent, he sometimes has difficulty making himself understood. But he is a very competent employee and has excellent training. Both Georgia Brooks and Carlos Martinez are leadpersons (a position just below foreperson) in their groups.

3. Green knew that if he chose Georgia, some people would say that he was forced into it by his superior because of Georgia's competence. If Green did *not* select her, he would be accused of being jealous of Georgia's ability.

4. If he selected Carlos, it would appear that he was just avoiding the competition Georgia might give him. If he did *not* choose Carlos, there was sure to be talk of discrimination on his part, and accusations of bias from the Hispanic work force.

5. Green discussed this whole affair with his supervisor, Mr. O'Brien, who listened very carefully to Green, examined all aspects of the situation with him, but would not commit himself. "You must work with this person," he said, "and you're the only one who can make the decision."

6. After a good deal of thought, some soul-searching, and a few sleepless nights, Joe Green had Georgia Brooks designated as the foreperson.

7. It's been about two months since Georgia has been on the job, and things have gone from bad to worse. Green now feels his decision was not wise, but he's sure that had he selected Carlos, things would not have turned out any better.

8. Carlos has not worked well since Georgia's appointment; comments have

drifted back to Joe Green and Mr. O'Brien in the cafeteria and elsewhere about prejudice against Hispanics, and production and efficiency in the total work force seem to have declined.

9. Although Green thought Georgia Brooks would really begin to work with him, the situation between Green and Brooks is now worse than ever. Because things aren't going too well (errors in production, confusion in priorities, work pile-up, etc.), Brooks has accused Green of trying to make her look bad. Her appointment, she insists, was against Green's recommendation and was forced on him because of Brooks' competence.

10. Brooks has also changed Green's orders on certain procedures on at least two occasions, causing confusion in the unit. Brooks claimed it was to speed things up and avoid red tape.

11. Mr. O'Brien has tried to counsel Joe Green on a couple of occasions. He has even suggested that Green stop riding Brooks. And at that suggestion, Green almost exploded. But more and more, Mr. O'Brien seems to be upset with Green . . . and vice versa.

12. Green has hesitated to ask another supervisor to take Brooks. First of all, there don't seem to be any openings elsewhere in the plant; second, it will cause Green to lose a great deal of face; and of even more importance, everyone has heard of the problem and would prefer not to get involved.

13. "This dissension as well as the low morale in your unit must end and productivity must increase. And as a matter of fact, the company's internal auditing team has selected the Belleville Plant for total review next month," Mr. O'Brien tells Green. Then he goes on, "And I want your section humming smoothly in two weeks or else!"

14. Green wonders what he can or should do. Just a few weeks ago he was

delighted with his job. Now he's miserable. He'd like to quit himself, but he's got nine years with the company, a wife, and three children.

15. What communication problems brought all this on? Who was at fault? Green? Brooks? O'Brien? What plan of action do you suggest for Green? What should be done with Carlos?

ASSIGNMENTS

1. Group Discussion

Break into groups of four or five and discuss the case. Your first step should be to review the situation presented in order to determine that all participants in each group have a similar perception of the incidents described.

Next, proceed to analyze the case. What is the major problem? The contributing problems? What specific communication barriers are evident? Who is responsible? How can the major and minor problems be solved? What action should be taken now?

After ten to fifteen minutes of discussion by the groups within themselves, open the case to the entire class. Do this by having the spokespersons of four or five groups report their groups' findings to the class. Permit class members to respond or ask questions after each speaks.

2. Interview Role Play

(a) Break into groups of three. Have one person play Joe Green; one, Georgia Brooks; and one, the observer (see the Observer Evaluation Checklist). Act out a five- to eight-minute interview between Georgia Brooks and Joe

Green (after paragraph 14). After the interview, have the observer report his or her reactions.

Change rolls and repeat the role playing to get another approach to the same problem.

(b) Break into groups of three. Have one individual play Joe Green; one, Carlos Martinez; and one, the observer. Hold the interview with Carlos *after* Georgia Brooks has been appointed foreperson (after paragraph 6). Repeat as above.

3. Memos

(a) In the capacity of Supervisor Joe Green, send a memo to Georgia Brooks appointing her foreperson. Add any special instructions you feel are necessary.

(b) In the capacity of Supervisor Joe Green, send Carlos Martinez a memo thanking him for his interest in the opening for foreperson, the discussion you had with him regarding the job, and the fact that Georgia Brooks has been designated for the position.

(c) In the capacity of Vice President O'Brien, send a memo to Joe Green noting the production and morale decline in Green's unit, and the fact that the company's internal auditing team will be visiting the plant next week (after paragraph 13).

4. Letter

In the capacity of Vice President O'Brien, send a letter of congratulations to Georgia Brooks on her appointment as foreperson of Section Three (after paragraph 6).

5. Meeting

Break into groups of six. In the capacity of Joe Green, call a meeting of your five forepersons to prepare for the visit next week of the company's internal auditing committee. The committee will want to check productivity, morale, housekeeping (cleanliness), attitudes, safety, training, and related factors.

Hold the meeting for twenty minutes. At the conclusion of the meeting, spend fifteen minutes evaluating the conduct of the meeting leader, participants, progress, visual aids, and related factors.

Case 6
When East Doesn't Meet West

1. Bob Markoff is an entrepreneur-professional businessperson. He is alert, progressive, conscientious, and honest. All these qualities paid off for him. Five years ago he purchased Crown Drugs. At that time it was owned and operated by Joe Crown who served as pharmacist, clerk, manager, bookkeeper, and in just about every other necessary capacity in a small operation. Each day for 20 years, Joe opened and closed his 3000 square foot operation. Then with a good offer from Markoff, he sold out.

2. Markoff, with a Doctor of Pharmacy degree, four years of chain store experience, and great expectations, had big plans for Crown Drugs. Now, just three years after the store's purchase, it was really a different operation. Bob knocked down the side walls and expanded the store's area fourfold; closed off and refurbished the pharmacy section giving it a very professional air; purchased $10,000 worth of new display fixtures; and

expanded the over-the-counter areas significantly. Patient records were computerized, marketing and sales promotion efforts increased, and all customer services expanded.

3. Sales at Crown Drugs have climbed steadily and the profit margin has kept up. Obviously this is no longer a "one-man" operation. Bob has four store clerks now, one of whom is part-time. Chances are good that he will need at least two more full-time clerks for the Thanksgiving/Christmas period, perhaps even as permanent employees. The most dramatic improvement has come in the pharmacy section. Bob has visited all the physicians in the area and is now well known among them. He has addressed a dozen community groups on everything from "New Medications for the Cardiac Patient" to "Drugs and the Teenager." He has cooperated in a dozen different ways with church and local fundraising groups. And the result has been more prescriptions filled in the last year than Joe Crown filled in five.

4. But all is not sweetness and light at Crown Drugs. There are problems in the pharmacy which don't have to do with sales, inventory, or dispensing. There are people problems *behind* the counter, not in front of it.

5. John Webster and Don Chui are both full-time, experienced registered pharmacists. John is outgoing, popular with the individuals who bring prescriptions in to be filled, excellent on the telephone with doctors and their staffs, and a competent employee. Don Chui is quite different. He is extremely knowledgeable and will always come up with an answer when John cannot. However, Don is quiet, reserved, and would prefer not to get involved with customer relations and counseling or phone calls, especially when a physician's prescription must be questioned. But Don is a genius when it comes to technical matters.

6. On the surface, these two should make a great team, but they do not! They seem to bicker constantly. Because Bob Markoff has not only been spending more time on community affairs but also searching for a possible second store location, he isn't around to arbitrate between Webster and Chui.

7. Webster feels that Chui doesn't do his share of the work at the counter, with customers, or on the phone. Chui, on the other hand, says he does much more work than Webster because he fills most of the incoming prescriptions. Furthermore, says Chui, because he (Chui) is quiet and polite, Webster plays the "big boss" and orders him around as well as the clerks. The fact is, Chui continues, Webster is not as knowledgeable as he should be on patients' questions about some of the new drugs, is not fully aware of obvious drug problems and trends, and on the whole, "is a big bag of wind."

8. The result of all this bickering is that the clerks are confused, neither Webster nor Chui speaks to each other except for essential discussions, customers sense a tense and charged atmosphere, and quite a few sales have been lost.

9. Chui had a brief discussion with Bob Markoff just a few minutes ago as the latter was leaving the store on his way to inspect a possible new store location. Chui complained (for the tenth time) about Webster and said that he (Chui) would probably have to leave at the end of the month.

10. As far as Markoff is concerned, that would be disastrous. It is imperative, he feels, that both Webster and Chui stay on. They are both good employees and should constitute an excellent team. But all they are doing now is losing sales for Crown Drugs.

11. Bob Markoff is in the middle of his expansion effort and would hate to make changes at this time. He's got to turn this

around, and he's sure that neither money nor fear of termination will prove to be effective motivating factors with Webster or Chui. Thus he's left with communication to solve his dilemma.

12. What specifically should Markoff do with Don Chui and John Webster? Be precise in your recommendations as to the place, type of statements to be used, and the near-term objectives. But also, be practical and not "blue sky."

ASSIGNMENTS

1. Group Discussion

Break into groups of five or six individuals and analyze the case. What action should Mr. Markoff follow with Don Chui and John Webster? Do you suggest training? Counseling? Termination? Discussion? Be very specific in your suggestions.

Have one spokesperson from each group offer suggestions. Invite comments on the suggested course of action.

2. Interview Role Play

(a) Have one student take the role of Don Chui and another the role of Bob Markoff. Carry through an interview. Markoff's purpose is to solve the problem in the case.

Have a third student act as the observer (using the Observer Evaluation Checklist). The observer should offer constructive criticism after the interview.

(b) Conduct the role play above with different students—except have one student in the role of John Webster, one as Bob Markoff, and one as the observer.

(c) Have a neutral individual (perhaps the president of the local pharmacists' association) interview both Chui and Webster (together) in an effort to solve the problem. Have several students act as observers/evaluators of the interview. A student should role play the pharmacy association president.

3. Memos

(a) As Bob Markoff, write a memo to Don Chui in which you attempt to motivate him to work more cooperatively with John Webster.

(b) As Bob Markoff, write a memo to Don Chui in which you attempt to change his mind about leaving the organization at the end of the month.

4. Letter

(a) Write a letter to a customer who complained to you (Bob Markoff) because she received two different opinions (one from Chui and one from Webster) concerning how to take one specific medication.

(b) As Bob Markoff, write a good will letter to a physician who has just set up practice in the neighborhood. You will, of course, point out that Crown Drugs will be happy to fill his prescriptions as well as take care of the various pharmaceutical-related needs in his practice.

(c) A new chain of convalescent care facilities has recently begun operations in your city. Write a letter to the head administrator offering to fill all pharmaceutical needs for all his facilities. You can offer very competitive prices, delivery service 18 hours each day, and patient records. Offer any other services which you feel are reasonable.

(d) Write a letter to all patients now on your mailing list. Offer them free and accurate blood pressure tests during the week of June 21–28.

Case 7
The Frank Farmer Case

1. Frank Farmer has worked for Martin Management and Realty Corporation for almost three years. He began in 1982, worked for one year, and left to sell for a Ford agency. In 1986, he returned and has been with you ever since. For almost a year now you have used him to supervise and promote building-management accounts. He has proved quite successful.

2. His job involves calling on the owners of the buildings your firm manages and keeping them up to date. And his primary responsibility is bringing in new management accounts. With the people, companies, corporations, and partnerships of those buildings you already have, Frank's job is essentially to build goodwill so the account may be retained. He answers questions, discusses major repairs, rentals, vacancy rates, and reports of Martin's management procedures for the properties.

3. Frank is capable and competent, and he is punctual and cooperates quite well with you (Clem Martin, one of the company partners) and the other sales personnel. However, he is far from being a dynamic, persuasive salesman. As a matter of fact, when new legislation, tax structure, and other legal details are instituted, Frank asks you to go out with him on the first day to help with explanations. He says, self-consciously, "I can hardly keep all the new facts, figures, and details straight in my mind, let alone explain them to someone else. I always seem to ball things up."

4. Frank has attended several sales-training and tax programs in real estate. However, they do not seem to have made much impression on him, nor have they altered his sales record appreciably.

5. Frank is thirty-eight years old, married for the second time, and has four children at home, two of whom are from his previous marriage. As far as you know his home life is satisfactory, although you've heard his wife drinks a good bit. Certainly her conduct at the last Christmas party would bear that out.

6. Accounts on whom he calls have few comments on Frank. They say he does a good job, although he doesn't seem to keep everyone informed about new programs, rates, etc. One woman calls him moody, and two people have mentioned his generally unenthusiastic manner. Several say he is "definitely OK."

7. Last week Frank told you that "old man" Farrell had been giving him a hard time. This disturbs you because Tom Farrell is one of Martin's very good accounts. He owns three apartment buildings (thirty-two, forty-eight, and sixty-four units) and a block of stores in a suburb of Chicago, which you manage. It is true that he is somewhat eccentric, but he is along in years and has very definite ideas. Besides that, he is an officer in one of the local service organizations and has a good deal of influence around town.

8. You ask Frank what the trouble is, and he tells you that Farrell always requests special service, complains about too many expenditures for repairs and maintenance on his buildings, and "is about as unreasonable as Allan Allenby of the Allenby Park Apartments."

9. Of course you're upset by this. You know Frank had some trouble with Farrell,

but his comment on Allan Allenby is news to you. After all, Allenby has six 48-unit buildings in his Park Apartment Complex and it's probably the sweetest building-management deal Martin Realty has. In any event, you go out to visit Farrell next day on the pretext of bringing him some good news from your tax accountant.

10. Farrell is certainly angry with Frank. He maintains Frank is a smart alec, isn't watching all angles for Farrell the way he should, and permits needless expenditures. You check all this out and find Frank is in the clear and that Farrell is just angry and being somewhat unreasonable. It's obvious that it all comes down to a personality conflict between him and Frank. Of course, it makes no difference who is right or wrong; Farrell is still the customer . . . and the customer is always right. It's obvious that all it will take is a few words for the whole thing between Frank and Farrell to really explode. However, by the time you leave, Farrell is happy and is talking to you about taking over the management of his two large units in Barrington on January 1, which one of your competitors now handles.

11. The next day you make it a point to sit down with Frank and discuss the tremendous importance of the Farrell account to Martin Realty. He listens carefully and courteously and agrees with you, but after about ten minutes he says, "Yeah, yeah, I've got the picture. I'll really watch my step on all the accounts." At that point he stands up, gives you a slap on the back, and walks out. You sit there quite frustrated and somewhat irritated.

12. Just two weeks later, Frank stops in your office on the way home. You chat about several things, compliment him on bringing in the new Fairmont Apartments account (24 one- and two-bedroom units), and then Frank, with a forced air of nonchalance, says,

"By the way, I lost the Farrell account today. The old man told me to come back when it's a zero day in July." You looked amazed and he says, "Well, we had it out, and I told him off."

13. Of course you're stunned by the news, but your eight salesmen are gathering for your regular Tuesday meeting, and this is no time to talk to Frank. You tell him you want to seem him immediately after the meeting, but you're not sure what you should do at that time.

14. What major problems do you recognize? In what order of priority have you listed them? Where have breakdowns in communication taken place? What specific communication problems do you recognize and on whose part? What should be done at this moment?

ASSIGNMENTS

1. Group Discussion

Break into groups of four or five and discuss the case. Your first step should be to review the situation presented in order to determine that all participants in each group have a similar perception of the incidents described.

Next, proceed to analyze the case. What is the major problem? What are the contributing problems? What specific communication barriers are evident? Who is responsible? How can the major and minor problems be solved? What action should be taken now?

After ten to fifteen minutes of discussion by the groups within themselves, open the case to the entire class. Do this by having the spokespersons of four or five groups report their groups' findings to the class. Permit class members to respond or ask questions after each speaks.

2. Interview Role Play

(a) Break into groups of three. Have one person play Frank Farmer; one, Clem Martin; and one, the observer (see the Observer Evaluation Checklist). Act out a five- to eight-minute interview between Frank Farmer and Clem Martin (after paragraph 13). At the conclusion of the interview, have the observer report his or her reactions.

Change roles and repeat the role playing to get another approach to the problem.

(b) Break into groups of three. Have one person play Clem Martin; one, Farrell; and one, the observer (see the Observer Evaluation Checklist). Act out the interview between Clem Martin and Farrell (after paragraph 9). After the interview have the observer report his or her reactions.

Change roles and repeat to get another approach on the problem.

3. Memos

In the capacity of Clem Martin, send Frank Farmer a memo indicating the importance of the Farrell account to Martin Management and Realty Company and the need for Frank to build goodwill with all accounts (after paragraph 11).

4. Letter

In the capacity of Clem Martin, send a good will letter to each of the 188 accounts for which Martin Management and Realty Company manages properties. The letters are to be dated January 2, 19___, and will be typed on automatic typewriters with personalized salutations (names of individuals) and pen-and-ink signatures.

Case 8
The "No Bias Here" Case

1. Lara Tanfani has worked as a pharmacist for Full Care Hospitals, Inc., for six years. This is an extensive chain in the Midwest, all owned by a very large corporation.

2. Each of the 85 hospitals in the chain has from one to six full-time pharmacists assigned to it. There are eight supervising pharmacists, one for each of the eight districts. The chief pharmacist is an elderly, white-haired gentleman, Avram Hamurabia.

3. Mr. Hamurabia, whose background is Middle Eastern, is a stern taskmaster who has a major financial interest in the Full Care Hospital chain. He is a very hard worker, extremely knowledgeable about his field, active in any state or federal legislation involving health care, and thoroughly involved with all aspects of each of the 85 pharmacies.

4. Lara Tanfani has a doctorate in pharmacy and has worked in the field for 10 years. She was originally hired for her present job in Milwaukee before the hospital became part of the Full Care Hospitals organization. At the time, she was almost assured of becoming the head pharmacist at the hospital (Milwaukee Central Hospital) when Mr. Kramer retired from that position. However, Full Care took over Milwaukee Central six months after Lara took the job and when Kramer retired five months later, Mr. Hamurabia appointed John Lovejoy.

5. Lovejoy has since been promoted to the position of District Pharmacist and

another man took his place as head pharmacist at Milwaukee Central. Lara Tanfani was amazed each time she was passed over. When she asked for an appointment with Mr. Hamurabia it turned out to be a problem—he was never available. One day, against her usual quiet and courteous nature, she "marched in" and asked for an explanation.

6. "My reviews by my district supervisors have consistently been 'superior,' " she said. "I've published three articles in three years, all carrying my Full Care Hospitals affiliation," she continued, "And I know you've received a score of letters about me from grateful patients." Mr. Hamurabia fumbled and bumbled and implied that because several "lady" pharmacists had married and then resigned to start families, he was concerned. And furthermore, district pharmacists often worked nights, and "Women should not be out at night . . ."

7. Lara countered all these and finally asked directly, "We don't have one district or head hospital pharmacist who is a woman except those who held the position before Full Care Hospitals took over. Are you not going to place any women in supervising positions?"

8. "Heavens, yes," Mr. Hamurabia almost shouted (as he envisioned a court case on the horizon). "There is no bias here. I love women but things have just not worked out when we've had a woman in either a district or hospital supervisory capacity . . ." he finished weakly.

9. The fact of the matter is simply this: Mr. Hamurabia just doesn't feel women should be pharmacists and if they are, they surely can't function as managers. But no one has ever heard him say this directly and no two people together have ever heard him make an anti-feminist remark. He is very, *very* careful. But his actions in a dozen different ways prove the point. Almost never is a woman selected as Full Care Hospitals'

"Pharmacist of the Month." Nor are they often approved for company sponsored convention and conference attendance. Fewer and fewer women are recruited as openings occur, but overt comments from Mr. Hamurabia in speech or writing never appear—especially in a context where they can be quoted or cited by two or more individuals. It is even possible that Mr. Hamurabia's bias is so cultural and deep-seated that even *he* is unaware of it. But it surely bothers every woman who works under his direction.

10. Lara Tanfani's style may be reserved, but she is also a fighter. Besides, she has invested six years in Full Care Hospitals. She feels she (and other women) should receive rewards that are deserved. She must do something—not only for herself, but for all women professionals. But she also recognizes that communication is her only "weapon."

11. What specific action should Lara Tanfani take? Keep in mind that Mr. Hamurabia sits on the Board of Directors of Full Care Hospitals . . . and also remember to be practical.

ASSIGNMENTS

1. Group Discussion

Break into groups of five or six individuals and discuss this case with the objective of reaching a workable action plan. Have one spokesperson from each group offer the suggestions of his or her group for solving the problems in the case. Permit evaluations of the suggestions made.

2. Interview Role Play

Assume six months have passed since the events in Paragraph 8. No significant changes have taken place. Hold mock interviews (all students should participate) by having one student play the role of Mr. Hamurabia, one Lara Tanfani, and one the observer (see the Observer Evaluation Checklist). After each interview is concluded, carry through a feedback session (led by the observer) on the activities of the interview.

3. Memos

(a) As Lara Tanfani, write a memo to Mr. Hamurabia after Paragraph 4 questioning his decision to appoint John Lovejoy instead of you. You may wish to ask him for an alternative course of action.

(b) As Lara Tanfani, write a memo to Mr. Hamurabia after Paragraph 8 in which you make your feelings known. Remember, however, that tact is also necessary.

4. Report

Assume you are Lara Tanfani. Write a report on your situation—as objectively as possible—to the Director of the local office of Equal Opportunity with a copy to the Organization of Rights for Minorities. Assume that the time is six months *after* the events in Paragraph 8 and no changes have taken place concerning the appointments of women at the hospital.

5. Proposal

A mediator from the Office of Equal Opportunity has requested that you (Lara Tanfani) write a proposal to Full Care Hospitals on the recruitment, retention, evaluation, and advancement of women personnel to be considered as policy for the future. Complete such a proposal.

Case 9
The High-Tech Communication Case

1. Bob Brownell received his MBA from Stanford's Graduate School of Business three years ago and immediately took a job with Arrow Electronics. The position was exactly what he wanted, for his responsibilities were primarily in planning, futures, strategy, and financial management. The experience and salary he received were all outstanding.

2. Early this year, however, Arrow merged with a giant aerospace corporation that already had an entire department devoted to planning. Bob was welcomed into it by the department head; however, it was obvious that he would now be "low man on the totem pole." That position was not his style and besides, he had always detested being a "little fish in a big pond."

3. One month after the merger, Bob submitted his resignation to the aerospace firm and accepted an exciting job offer from Spartan Space Systems. This 15-year-old company was in some measure a collection of consultants that worked for and with NASA, various divisions of DOD (Department of Defense), the Rand Corporation (a "think tank") and other commercial and governmental organizations concerned with satellite placement, space stations, and various top secret space projects.

4. It was made clear to Bob by the Executive VP, Wes Webster, that Bob would be indispensible to Unit #5 because of his overall business and strategic knowledge and background. The first day on the job for Bob was primarily given over to orientation with the benefits officer plus introductions at headquarters. On the second day, Bob was brought over to the Unit 5 area which occupied the third floor of the annex building. "Unit 5,"

said Wes, "is made up of about 24 personnel. They are all engineers: aeronautics, space, physical science, computers, electronics, and mathematics. I would guess that more than half have Ph.D's. They really don't have a director or head because they don't want one, although Mary Ann Kinsey is the administrative manager. However, she seems to act in an administrative capacity only and handles all the routine paper work; budgets, payroll, requisitions, travel, etc."

5. "But whom am I to work with?" asked Bob.

6. "Well, I guess you'll have to work that through," answered Wes. "They have split themselves into five teams, and I'll introduce you to the present team leaders. But even that is difficult for they often rotate the job of leader among the team members."

7. "That's crazy," said Bob. "I never heard of such a loose organizational structure."

8. "I agree," said Wes, "but they all work on 'Star Wars' type projects and what they're doing seems to be eminently satisfactory to Washington. We just received an approval to fund their entire project for this year and next without question. And let me tell you, we won't question that!"

9. "But there must be one person—even an unofficial leader—that I could work with at least to set some goals and objectives," Bob said in a rather exasperated manner.

10. "No, I really don't know of any one," stated Wes. "But they are all very nice people and I know they will cooperate with you. All I can say is that two aspects are vital for you to work on: planning and financial management. The only problem we had with a DOD audit three months ago centered on that department. Their complaint was that lack of planning was the cause for duplication of effort by three different teams in Unit 5. That caused unnecessary expenditures of funds

and the duplication of tests ordered from outside agencies."

11. "But certainly I won't be in charge of Unit 5 to bring about needed changes—or will I?" asked Bob.

12. "Oh, heavens no," answered Wes. "If we suddenly brought an outsider into that group as chief, they would probably all walk out. And what's worse, our competitors would hire them all in two hours."

13. Bob has now spent two months in Unit 5 and the only progress he seems to have made is to consider visiting a psychiatrist. He has tried to set up both short- and long-term goals plus budgets, but he's not been successful. The personnel of Unit 5, however, are courteous and cooperative. They meet, go to lunch, and have coffee with Bob but their conversations are always so complex that Bob goes away befuddled. He has tried to call a meeting of the entire Unit but half can't attend because they are in Washington, D.C., on their way there, or on their way back. If it's not trips to Washington then it's conferences at MIT or Cal Tech. Ms. Kinsey is no help.

14. "I gave up long ago," she told Bob. "I just sit in my office and process requisitions and vouchers. Once every month I distribute their paychecks, and if I didn't do that, half the checks would sit on my desk until their spouses called me. Why not try to work with each team?" she suggested.

15. "I have," said Bob, "but many of the people serve on two or three teams and in some cases, the teams have integrating projects. I just don't know. I've worked with matrix organizations in the past, but this one doesn't fit any pattern I've ever encountered in either theory or practice." All the men and women of Unit 5 are courteous, friendly, and even seem to respect Bob. It's a relationship he would like to continue and he knows that if he attempts to impose plans or goals (and he is aware he isn't knowledgeable enough in

Unit 5's area to do that) or budgets, the personnel of Unit 5 would ignore every one of them.

16. At this point Bob is in a quandary. He likes the company, the pay is excellent, and the assignment a challenge. But how to accomplish his objectives is beyond him. Perhaps you have some suggestions.

ASSIGNMENTS

1. Group Discussion

Break into groups of five or six individuals and discuss this case with the objective of reaching a workable action plan. Have one spokesperson from each group offer suggestions for solving the problems in the case. Permit evaluations of the suggestions made.

2. Interview Role Play

Hold an interview between Bob Brownell and one of the team leaders. The objective is to secure counsel and suggestions from the team leader on how Bob may better succeed in his objectives of playing a leadership role (insofar as planning and finance are concerned) for Unit 5. Have one student play Bob Brownell, one the team leader, and one the observer (see the Observer Evaluation Checklist).

3. Memos

As Bob Brownell, write a memo to each of the five team leaders announcing a meeting for a week from this Friday at 1:00 P.M. Attendance is required for each of the five leaders.

The tentative agenda includes several items concerning compensation and benefits as well as planning to include due dates for the next quarter.

4. Report

As Bob Brownell, write a quarterly report to your boss on the activities and personnel of Unit 5. Assume you have now been employed by Spartan Space Systems for eight months.

5. Meeting

Hold a meeting of all team leaders and assistant leaders (a total of 10 personnel). Design a system that will eliminate duplication of effort among the five teams.

Case 10
The Sun Fresh Case[1]

1. Bill Hillman is the Operations Manager of the Sun Fresh Food chain located in the Midwest. This is a strong organization, founded in 1966 and now made up of 82 stores in Illinois and Wisconsin. Most of the stores cluster around the greater Chicago area.

2. The chain has had its ups and downs over the years, but some of its greatest changes have taken place since 1985.

3. In that year, a very large Eastern food manufacturer, Jackson and Trent, purchased Sun Fresh, supplied funds, and gave the green light to "expansion." Up to that date, everyone seemed to know everyone else at Sun Fresh. Of course, Sun Fresh only had

---

[1] In conjunction with this case, you may wish to view the film by Norman B. Sigband, "Communication: The Company Grapevine," AIMS Media, 26 min., color. It is based on the Sun Fresh Case and should be shown *after* the case has been discussed and a role play exercise completed. It is available from: AIMS-Media, 6901 Woodley Av., Van Nuys, CA, 91406.

thirty-eight stores at that time, and promotions and changes in personnel always occurred from "within." As a matter of fact, this has always been a well-known company policy and practice: advancements and promotions from within.

4. However, in 1987 the company opened twenty-two new stores and the chain (or Bill Hillman) just couldn't find enough competent store managers in Sun Fresh to take over. The company had to go "outside" and as a result about sixteen of the new store managers came from other firms in the area or simply as a result of recruiting: newspaper ads, recommendations from friends in the food industry, etc.

5. Bill Hillman doesn't seem to be concerned one way or another about this source for new managers. However, he is slowly becoming aware that his "old-line" employees resent this deeply. As he travels around with Rob, a company officer, he notes that store managers and even district supervisors comment on the "new policy." Bill and top management have talked about putting out a bulletin or having all district and store managers in for a two-day meeting to explain growth, company goals, policies, and new directions. However, it was agreed that a printed bulletin wouldn't "do the job," and Bill felt strongly that it would be extremely costly to hold such a meeting even if time were available . . . which it isn't. Largely due to his strong feelings, such a companywide meeting of store managers was not held.

6. The comments Rob and Bill receive are biting and rise above the "humor" level and give clear indication of fear and antagonism. "So the brass is sweeping all us old hands out, I see." "It looks like my sixteen years with Sun Fresh will soon be tossed in the trash can." "Now that we've helped make the firm, it looks like our usefulness has come

to an end and we're being replaced." These are the types of statements that are heard.

7. Of course, Rob and Bill try to dispel and counter these individual comments, for replacement of seasoned employees is not a company policy at all. But it is evident that the managers don't really believe the statements from top management. On top of this, four store managers have been replaced since the first of July. They had each been promoted from within and had been with Sun Fresh (prior to promotion) for many years. But Jane Kelly left Sun Fresh to join a family-owned business, Ferris and Martinez proved incompetent, and the other one asked to be relieved when he complained that the responsibility was too much for him. Purely by chance "outsiders" replaced each of the four.

8. These four cases are frequently cited to Bill Hillman (and certainly to many others) as clear evidence of the "new policy." Bill has also noted a lack of enthusiasm and evidence, perhaps, of poor morale in the stores. There just doesn't seem to be the old banter, good-humored kidding, and "let's set another sales record this week" attitude which always seemed to exist in the past. This is obvious among the store managers, produce and meat department supervisors, and almost everywhere else in the company. Sales are also down and employee pilferage is up (on a percentage basis) throughout the chain.

9. Today Bill encountered the most serious problem. Three store managers, including Hugh at Oakdale, are leaving Sun Fresh as of September 1 and are going to work for the competing chain, SavMor, or themselves. Bill has spent two hours with two district supervisors, and they told him that the three are among the very best store managers in Sun Fresh. They are seasoned veterans, and they each said, in so many words, "As long as the company is going to bounce us in the near

future, we might as well leave while we have an opportunity to make a good connection." In addition, three department supervisors, such as Joanne, produce manager at Oakdale, have also resigned.

10. The employees' perceptions about bringing in outsiders is not accurate. But Bill realizes he must—somehow or other—communicate the truth to all the Sun Fresh employees. And yet he just can't send out a bulletin and say, "We aren't replacing our old-line employees," for that is just about what everyone will then believe.

11. What communication problems exist? Between whom? What barriers exist? What channels of communication are being used? Why? What should have been done in the past? What should be done now?

ASSIGNMENTS

1. Group Discussion

Break into groups of four or five and discuss the case. Your first step should be to review the situation presented in order to determine that all participants in each group have a similar perception of the incidents described.

Next, proceed to analyze the case. What is the major problem? The contributing problems? What specific communication barriers are evident? Who is responsible? How can the major and minor problems be solved? What action should be taken now?

After ten to fifteen minutes of discussion by the groups within themselves, open the case to the entire class. Do this by having the spokespersons of four or five groups report their groups' findings to the class. Permit class members to respond or ask questions, or both, after each representative speaks.

2. Interview Role Play

(a) Break into groups of three. Have one person play Bill Hillman; one, the store manager, Hugh Purcell, who has indicated he will leave Sun Fresh as of September 1 (see paragraph 9); and one, the observer (see the Observer Evaluation Checklist). Act out a five- to eight-minute interview between Bill Hillman and Store Manager Hugh Purcell (after paragraph 10). At the conclusion of the interview, have the observer report his or her reactions.

Change roles and repeat the role playing to get another approach to the problem.

(b) Break into groups of three. Have one individual play Bill Hillman; one, District Supervisor Mark Webster who has ten Sun Fresh stores under his supervision; and one, the observer (see the Observer Evaluation Checklist). Act out a five- to eight-minute interview between Bill Hillman and District Supervisor Mark Webster (after paragraph 10). At the conclusion of the interview, have the observer report his or her reactions.

Change roles and repeat the role playing to get another approach to the problem.

3. Memos

(a) In the capacity of Bill Hillman, send a memo to the editor of the Sun Fresh employee monthly magazine, *Sun Up*. Ask him to run a story: "Promotion Opportunities to Store Manager Positions Now Available." Enclose with your memo a copy of page 4 of the Sun Fresh Policy Manual, which states eligibility requirements for the job.

(b) In the capacity of Bill Hillman, send a memo to each of the store managers who has indicated his or her desire to resign as of September 1 (see paragraph 9). Attempt to have each call you for an interview during which you will attempt to retain the individual as a Sun Fresh Manager.

4. Report

Send a report to corporate president, Clara Campbell, who has requested a review of the personnel problems you are encountering in the area.

Make any reasonable assumptions you feel are necessary (personnel, sales, turnover, construction, training, etc.).

5. Oral Report

After you have completed the written report, give an oral presentation to the firm's board of directors based on the material in the report. Be prepared to answer questions from the board members.

Ask your colleagues for constructive criticism at the end of your oral report.

6. Meeting

In the capacity of Bill Hillman, call a meeting of the eight Sun Fresh district supervisors. Your purpose is to discuss and determine which method of communication should be used to eliminate the rumors (after paragraph 10) and improve employee morale.

Hold a ten-minute evaluation of the meeting form, content, leader, and participants.

Case 11
When the Marriage Doesn't Work

1. It was early in the year when Fairbanks Engineering took over the Westmont Corporation. Both firms had been well established in Boston for over 30 years. However, when Mr. Westmont reached 70, he felt that as long as he had no children or other family to leave the business to, he would simply look for a friendly take-over bid, take the money, and take off.

2. Fairbanks, with some 480 employees (as compared to Westmont's 190) seemed a good choice. The merger was completed and although Mr. Westmont did not come out with a "golden parachute," what he did receive was certainly sterling silver.

3. The two firms, from a consultant's point of view, seemed to be perfectly suited for integration that would achieve a "whole much greater than the sum of the parts." In an examination of the technical and professional aspects, it was obvious that where Fairbanks was weak, Westmont was strong; where Westmont lacked depth, Fairbanks more than compensated. Fairbanks also had a strong client base where Westmont did not. So, the Westmont offices were closed and the personnel moved to the Fairbanks building. Some "outside" tenants were displaced and all Westmont employees who elected to stay were integrated into Fairbanks' various departments.

4. Problems arose—not unexpectedly—from the beginning. Perhaps they would not have arisen had the Westmont Corporation remained an independent operation. But that did not make sense to President Bob Fairbanks because there were skills among Westmont personnel that were crucial for

Fairbanks to integrate among its own teams immediately.

5. What happened is quite simple. As staff were assigned within Fairbanks, the feeling arose among Westmont personnel that "we are being downgraded." Individuals who had been supervisors at Westmont (word processing, records, drawings retention, legal, etc.) felt they were now put in subordinate positions at Fairbanks. The grapevine grew, discontent rose. This perception was not accurate but who can argue with people's perceptions? What is true to them is true to them.

6. The same feeling began to rise among the professional Westmont personnel. Engineers, design experts, and others frequently said they were given the routine, uninteresting, and problem assignments; that all the best projects were allocated to Fairbanks people. Again this was not true. However, relations and communications between the two camps grew more and more strained. Interactions declined, cooperation broke down, hostility and resentment increased.

7. The top management at Fairbanks was not unaware of all this. And as a consequence, they made efforts to alleviate and even eliminate the problem. Salary levels were coordinated and if anything, Westmont people fared much better than Fairbanks personnel on increases and bonuses. As a matter of fact, several "influentials" among Westmont personnel were given sizable increases. Social events designed to bring together Fairbanks and Westmont personnel were attempted: picnics, circus nights, the "Fairbanks Family Autumn Party," baseball games, and on and on. But nothing seemed to work. It finally reached the point where the employee lunchroom was divided—with Fairbanks employees sitting at one group of tables and Westmont people at others.

8. Bob Fairbanks, his brother John, and their two vice presidents have just held a meeting. The status report is not good. Projects are behind schedule because of lack of cooperation (or communication) among personnel; problems on jobs have arisen which may be due to negligence if not outright intent; and productivity and profits have declined. "I wish I hadn't ever *heard* of Westmont," Bob shouted as he slapped a report onto the conference table. "In fact, if it weren't for the possibility of 135 unlawful termination lawsuits, I'd fire all the Westmont personnel *today*!"

9. But of course that is no solution. How would you improve internal interpersonal communication and relations?

ASSIGNMENTS

1. Group Discussion

Break into groups of five or six individuals and discuss this case with the objective of reaching a workable action plan. Have one spokesperson from each group offer suggestions for solving the problems in this case. Permit evaluations of the suggestions made.

2. Interview Role Play

(a) As President Bob Fairbanks, hold an interview with the senior Westmont person now working for Fairbanks. Your objectives are 1) to find out what's bothering the former Westmont personnel and 2) to determine what steps Fairbanks should take to make the Westmont personnel happy.

(b) Have one student play Bob Fairbanks, one the former senior Westmont employee and one the observer (see the Observer Evaluation Checklist). Offer your constructive suggestions to the role players after the interview.

3. Memos

(a) In the role of John Fairbanks, Director of Human Resources, write a memo to all personnel announcing the merger and asking for cooperation from all personnel.
(b) Acting in the same capacity as memo problem (a), write a memo to all personnel as you view the situation after Paragraph 6. Your objectives are to improve morale and increase productivity.

4. Letter

As Bob Fairbanks, write a letter announcing the merger to all personnel (Fairbanks and Westmont) immediately after the merger. The letter is to be sent to each employee's home.

5. Report

As an outside consultant, assume you have made a thorough study of this case and its problems. Write a report for the Fairbanks Board of Directors including 1) the present situation as you see it and 2) the recommendations you offer for the year ahead.

Case 12
The Juan Ramirez Case

1. Juan Ramirez received his MBA from Northwestern University just five years ago. For four of those years he worked in the Man-agement Division of Arthur Andersen and Company. However, it appeared to him that there was little possibility of his becoming a junior partner in the forseeable future (if ever). Thus he began to look for a new job with a salary in the $65,000 to $90,000 category.

2. What he found paid in the middle of that range but also carried heavy responsibility. It was with Century Health Center in the capacity of Administrative Director.

3. Century Health Center is a seven story modern office-medical building. As an organization, it has existed for 17 years, growing in personnel and its physical facility. Two years ago, the organization moved into this new building.

4. The modern facility is occupied by about 50 physicians plus their accompanying staffs of nurses, office personnel, and clerks. The concept is really very clever and was more or less put together by Dr. Pearson who probably would have been an eminently successful Chief Executive Officer had he gone into business instead of medicine. But even in medicine he has enjoyed great financial success. He started Century Health in two offices and has moved it every few years to larger quarters as medical services were expanded. Now, he wants Juan to run the administration so he can devote all his time to his ophthalmology practice.

5. Century Health Center is limited to five specialized areas: internal medicine, ophthalmology, radiology, orthopedics, and obstetrics/gynecology. In addition, the building has a lab (owned by Dr. Pearson), an emergency care unit, and radiology, pharmacy, and dispensing ophthalmic facilities. Each of the medical groups has its own floor in the building and each of the groups is broken into sub-units in its own office complexes. Most of the M.D.'s are limited partners in the financial operations of the building.

6. Juan, after being interviewed by four different committees of M.D.'s, was finally hired, but he was never able to get a specific job description. Dr. Pearson said, after Juan accepted the position, "There's plenty to do—why don't you just get started and then write your own job description."

7. "For example," he continued, "when offices are vacated, you must negotiate leases with new tenants; see that rents come in on time; handle all building repairs and maintenance; hire and supervise custodial, security, and parking personnel; control costs; purchase necessary non-medical supplies; secure all building insurance; take care of building inspections and taxes; plus everything else necessary to run Century—but most important, see that there is a profit for the partners at the end of the year.

8. It's taken eight months for Juan to set up systems, establish routines, and install a new computer billing system for the medical offices and sub-groups that wished to utilize this central financial service. Obviously, they paid for the service, which now adds income for Century. Juan has worked seven days a week accomplishing all this, and he is elated that Dr. Pearson appreciates his efforts. Income has risen, costs have been cut, and services improved. Both the interior and exterior of the building look excellent and patients are pleased with the overall sense of professionalism.

9. But Juan has a problem with the physicians. He feels he is a well-educated professional and deserves the same treatment from the physicians which he accords them. But it seems like most of them don't see him that way. They seldom address him as Mr. Ramirez, although he is always expected to refer to them as "Doctor." During the course of the day he is as frequently addressed as "Ramon" or "Jose" as he is "Juan." Seldom do the doctors use the prepared forms to request sup-

plies or report problems. Messages are usually incomplete sentences scribbled on a scrap of paper: "Broken faucet in 405," "Where are those folders we req'd 6 months ago? Dr. M." "No light in closet, Rm. 506," "What happen. air cond. yesterday?" or "How come your hot shot computer broke down again?" These notes are bad enough but all too often it's a comment made to Juan in the corridor, the parking lot, or a cryptic phone call. Of course when the message comes from a nurse or office manager, it's much more courteous. But that's changing also as the staff members overhear the doctors' communications with Juan.

10. Of course the physicians are very busy, but that's no excuse for not being courteous. Juan is looked upon, he feels, as just another "hand" or perhaps just one step above the custodians. But it is even possible Juan has permitted or even shaped this perception of himself on the part of the physicians. In a phrase, "he don't get respect," and it bothers him.

11. Certainly Juan can't buy or demand a change in the physicians' perception of him. His only alternative is to communicate in some way to change that perception.

12. What do you suggest he do at Century Health Center, or do you feel he should simply send out a new résumé?

ASSIGNMENTS

1. Group Discussion

Break into groups of five or six individuals and discuss this case with the objective of reaching a workable action plan. Have one spokesperson from each group offer suggestions for solving the problems in this case. Permit evaluations of the suggestions made.

2. Interview Role Play

As Juan Ramirez, carry through an interview with Dr. Pearson (after Paragraph 10) in which you (Juan Ramirez) try to secure Dr. Pearson's cooperation in changing the perceptions, attitudes, and actions of the health professionals at the Century Health Center. Have one student play Dr. Pearson, another Juan Ramirez, and a third, the observer (see the Observer Evaluation Checklist).

At the conclusion of the interview, seek feedback on the level of success of the interview.

3. Memo

   (a) As Juan Ramirez, write a memo to all health care professionals at Century Health Center in which you attempt to set up ground rules for communications with you and/or your staff members concerning building matters. The memo is to be sent out two weeks after you (Juan Ramirez) have assumed the position.
   (b) Send out a second memo attempting to accomplish the same objectives after Paragraph 10.

4. Letter

Send a letter to Dr. Pearson (after Paragraph 10) in which you indicate that if the situation (concerning Century Health Center's professionals' relations with you) doesn't improve within 30 days, you will be forced to terminate your employment 60 days later.

5. Meeting

Have one student play Juan Ramirez and five others physicians from Century Health Center. One of the physicians is Dr. Pearson. This is a meeting Juan Ramirez has called ostensibly to discuss changes in building regulations, forthcoming maintenance and painting schedules, etc. However, Mr. Ramirez has a hidden agenda point: changing the attitudes and actions of the health care professionals (including nurses, technicians, clerks, etc.) toward him and his staff.

All other students in the class should act as observers and offer evaluations on the level of success of the meeting. (See Observer Evaluation Checklist.)

6. Proposal

As an outside consultant, write a proposal that contains your recommendations on solving the problems which exist between Juan Ramirez and his staff and the health care professionals at Century.

Case 13
The Jackson Yard Case

   1. Although it is always difficult to handle theft and pilferage problems at service centers, the situation at Jackson Yard is really a difficult one. It isn't only the service center superintendent, Bob Roberts; it's the whole picture.

   2. Jackson Yard is located in the center of what the newspapers refer to as a culturally deprived and economically depressed area. Housing is far from excellent, the population density is great, the income level is low, and the crime rate is astronomical. The yard has had an unusually high incidence of theft and vandalism. Special Agent Mark Foster has told you, the vice president and director of

personnel of Commerce, Inc., that it is partially Bob Roberts' fault.

3. Foster has been out to see Roberts several times for a variety of reasons. For example, early this year one of the trucks parked just outside the yard had a good deal of equipment taken from it. Foster checked it out and suggested to Roberts that trucks should always be pulled into the yard and the gates kept locked at all times. Of course taking these precautions takes time and effort, and many drivers prefer not to bother.

4. Apparently the trucks were looked upon as an easy mark by some of the neighborhood vandals because four similar thefts took place in March and April. Foster went out there each time and evidently saw Roberts on every trip. And somewhere along the line Foster must have pulled the wrong switch.

5. Roberts called you, very irritated, with a few things to say. He wanted you to know that he had more to do than play Sherlock Holmes for every twenty-five-dollar ladder in the yard; that he had a half-million dollars' worth of expensive equipment to watch, forty-four vehicles, a staff of thirty-five people, a plant worth $800,000, and "I damn well am not going to spend all my time patrolling in the hope of catching some two-bit punk in the act of stealing a fifty-cent roll of twine."

6. Furthermore, said Roberts, just because Foster has a tin badge is no reason he can tell Roberts, who has worked for Commerce "more years than Foster is old," how to run his yard!

7. You immediately called Foster in and tried to get his perception of the situation. He was amazed that Roberts had called and was very surprised at the yard superintendent's reaction. "I had no idea my suggestions upset him," said Foster.

8. "Well, what did you expect?" you asked. "Well, not anything, but I think it is his job to maintain the security of all Commerce property, and he's not doing his job if he doesn't do that," answered Foster.

9. But that was three weeks ago. There have been developments since then. The story isn't yet clear, but it began when a gang of young boys—more for kicks than anything else—improvised some type of makeshift ladder and dropped one of the boys over the seven-foot chain-link and barbed-wire fence. He managed to toss a number of items over the fence and get back over. This happened three times in two weeks. Nothing very valuable was ever taken and, as a matter of fact, several of the items were left outside the fence. Some, like wire unrolled from spools, were damaged; others, like tools and insulators, were not.

10. Each time Special Agent Foster went out and talked to the local police and, of course, to Mr. Roberts. About ten days ago, however, Roberts must have come back to the yard on a late Saturday afternoon when there was almost no activity.

11. He waited in hiding until a tall boy about sixteen got inside the yard, picked up a number of items, and ran toward the fence. He caught the youngster near the fence, and they struggled. The six-foot 180-pound young man pushed Roberts hard, and Roberts fell. He was more angry than hurt and lashed at the boy with what might have been a tool handle. A superficial cut on the youngster's head resulted in an immediate and heavy flow of blood.

12. By this time the boys in the gang on the other side of the fence were shouting, throwing rocks, and stopping cars. In no time at all there were about a hundred area residents, most of whom were from ethnic minority groups, shouting at Roberts. He refused to let the boy go and turned him over to the

police. They both got into the squad car, the boy's head still streaming blood, and roared away. However, the crowd had gotten ugly and almost succeeded in tipping over the squad car just before four other police cars came on the scene.

13. At the police station Roberts insisted that the case be pushed to the limit. Three local pastors and the neighborhood councilman were involved. If something isn't done soon, it will surely turn into a major newspaper case of the Minority Community vs. Commerce. Roberts insists, however, that he was assaulted and wants justice. Special Agent Foster talked to him at length, but all he kept telling Foster was "First you tell me to do your job, and when I do, you want me to back away."

14. What communication problems exist? Between and among whom? What should have been done in the past? What should be done now?

ASSIGNMENTS

1. Group Discussion

Break into groups of four or five and discuss the case. Your first step should be to review the situation presented in order to determine that all participants in each group have a similar perception of the incidents described.

Next proceed to analyze the case. What is the major problem? The contributing problems? What specific communication barriers are evident? Who is responsible? How can the major and minor problems be solved? What action should be taken now?

After ten to fifteen minutes of discussion by the groups within themselves, open the case to the entire class. Do this by having the spokespersons of four or five groups report their groups' findings to the class. Permit class members to respond or ask questions, or both, after each representative speaks.

2. Interview Role Play

(a) Break into groups of three. Have one person play the director of personnel; one, Bob Roberts; and one, the observer (see the Observer Evaluation Checklist). Act out a five- to eight-minute interview between the director of personnel and Bob Roberts (after paragraph 13). At the conclusion of the interview, have the observer report his or her reactions.

Change roles and repeat the role playing to get another person's approach to the same problem.

(b) Break into groups of three. Have one person play the director of personnel; one, Special Agent Foster; and one, the observer (see paragraphs 7 and 8). Repeat as above.

(c) Break into groups of three. Have one person play the director of personnel; one, the director of the neighborhood Council; and one, the observer (after paragraph 13). Repeat as above.

3. Report

The president of Commerce has requested a report from you (the director of personnel) regarding the entire incident. Of course he will expect your recommendations.

4. Memos

(a) Commerce has six service centers in addition to Jackson Yard. As the director of security at Commerce, send a

memo to each of the six yard super-
intendents concerning security. You
wish to avoid another Jackson Yard
incident.

(b) As the director of personnel, send a
memo to your director of public
affairs concerning the Jackson Yard
incident. You would like to avoid any
unfavorable publicity in the media.

5. Letter

Assume the Jackson Yard incident has been
settled to everyone's satisfaction. As the president of Commerce, you feel it would be wise
to send a message to the director of the Neighborhood Council, Calvin Farnsworth. Write
such a letter.

6. Interview with the Press

Break into groups of ten. Have one person
play the role of the director of public affairs for
Commerce; one, an observer; and the other
eight, newspaper and TV reporters. The
director of public affairs should make a two-
to three-minute prepared statement to the
reporters and then answer questions for five
minutes. At the conclusion of the press conference, have the observer report his or her
reactions. Because of legal implications, the
observer should be especially sensitive to the
director's word choice, as well as to nonverbal
communication.

Select a different director of public affairs
and repeat the exercise.

7. Oral Report

As the director of personnel, give an oral
report to the Commerce board of directors on
the Jackson Yard incident. Indicate what steps
management has taken to prevent a similar

incident from arising. Entertain a question
period.

Case 14
The Broken Team Case

1. Harry Ross was chief of Section Five
of Southwest Telephone (in Abilene, Texas)
for about six years. The section was often
cited as an outstanding example of high productivity, morale, and competence. Because
of its makeup, Section Five, which included a
half dozen Hispanics, several blacks, and a
few Orientals, among others, was called "The
Internationals." About six months ago Harry
Ross retired, and Marty Hayworth was
brought in by top management from the
Brownsville office of Southwest Telephone to
take his place.

2. It was not really a very popular promotion, for almost everyone in the section
assumed that Ramon Vargas, who had been
in Section Five for nine years (and was next to
Harry Ross in years of service) would be
made section chief. As a result, there were
several unhappy people in the section. As for
Vargas, he became a changed man. Formerly
good natured, happy, and cooperative, he
became moody and reticent.

3. Marty thought things would change,
and they finally did after about four months,
but only slightly. Some of the 26 people in the
section seemed to be happier and more cooperative. However, Manuel Rodriguez and
Roberto Mendoza remained very truculent.
And both of them, plus Ramon Vargas,
seemed to spend almost all their time
together.

4. Again and again, when there was a
hook-up job to complete, a major wiring job to

carry through, or a storm damage problem to take over, they asked to go out together. Their work was excellent and, insofar as the customer was concerned, courteous, and eminently satisfactory.

5. Two months ago, Vargas' transfer to the Dallas office came through, and he and his family moved to that city. Marty, who was beginning to reflect the strain of having a rather unhappy section, thought that surely the climate and tone would now improve, but another incident intervened.

6. Marty carried through performance appraisals a week after Vargas left. Being conscientious, Marty carefully read the letter accompanying the blank appraisal forms. It was from the Senior Vice President of Southwest Telephone and it emphasized again and again the need for accuracy. "If the individual is outstanding in the various categories, say so; if satisfactory, say so; if unsatisfactory, for heaven's sake—in all fairness to our 21,000 other employees—say so!"

7. Marty thought, hesitated, meditated, and worried. He finally rated five employees as "not satisfactory" and seven as "satisfactory." Three were rated "superior" and the rest were "excellent."

8. The next morning, immediately after the forms were distributed, he was greeted by an extremely angry group of men.

9. "Why do you say we are "technically competent and excellent" and then you rate us "unsatisfactory" or "satisfactory" only? You know what that will do to our future promotions much less our percentage salary increase?"

10. This was only one of the more polite comments Marty received. The others were much more vitriolic, pointed, and even profane. In every case, Marty spent time with each individual who complained. He explained that the overall rating was due to "poor attitude," "lack of cooperation," and in some cases to actual "insubordination to a supervisor."

11. Of course not one person walked out of Marty's office convinced. And as Marty expected, he received a call that afternoon from Division Manager Brewster asking, "What the hell is going on in Section Five? A revolution?" Marty tried to explain, and even cited the vice president's letter. However, Brewster merely grunted and finally responded, "Yeah, yeah, Marty. I understand all that, but you know we can't get the job done with unhappy employees, and you've got a hell of a lot of unhappy guys down there. We both know what a reputation Section Five had under Harry Ross. And we both know what's happened to Section Five's production record under you."

12. Two weeks have passed since Brewster's call, and now Marty is faced with still another problem. He must appoint a new foreman for Section Five to begin work Monday morning.

13. It's pretty well agreed that the choice must be Roberto Mendoza or William Washington. Of course Roberto is supported by the Hispanics while William is strongly championed by the blacks. Interestingly enough, both candidates have been in the section and the company an equal number of years. They also both fit the foreman's job description in about the same way, with similar job evaluations and appraisals.

14. Marty is in a quandary. If he selects Roberto, the blacks will accuse him of discrimination. If he chooses William, the Hispanics will shout "favoritism." In desperation, Marty calls Division Manager Brewster and asks for guidance.

15. Brewster listens patiently for 15 minutes while Marty summarizes the strengths and weaknesses of both Roberto and William. Then Marty asks, "What do you think I should do, Mr. Brewster?"

16. Brewster replies, "Look, Marty, I agree you've got a problem. But you're the one who must work with the new foreman, so you've got to make the choice. But you'll have my support, Marty. Just be sure you select the right guy. I'll talk to you in a day or two . . ." And he hangs up.

17. Marty really doesn't know what to do. And no amount of turning, tossing, and perspiring during the long night has helped. However, it's now 8:45 A.M., and he knows that Brewster's office needs his selection by 9:30.

18. What do you see as the problems in this case? Who should Marty choose as foreman? What can he do about the section's low morale, high absenteeism, and declining productivity? What steps should be taken by Marty Hayworth and by Division Manager Brewster, to build Section Five into a productive team?

ASSIGNMENTS

1. Group Discussion

Divide into groups of not more than ten. By means of group discussion and analysis, settle upon an order of precipitating events for the problems that now plague Marty. Which events were within his control? Which were not? What steps could have been taken to improve the situation in Section Five? When should they have been taken? Why weren't they? How could upper management now assist Marty?

When you have reached conclusions for these and other questions of your own, compare your results with those of other groups.

2. Interview Role Playing

As Marty, interview a classmate playing the role of Roberto. Plan a series of questions that will help you evaluate his potential as a foreman.

Then interview William in similar fashion. Choose between the two for the job of foreman, and explain your choice to the class. Mention specific aspects of the interview that influenced your decision. (These interviews can be made into group experiences by extending the interview panel to two, three, or more members.)

3. Presentation

Your manager asks you, Marty, to make a presentation to upper management. He wants you to sum up affairs in Section Five since you took charge. "Don't worry," the division manager tells you. "The other section heads are doing the same thing." Develop a presentation (approximately 10 minutes long, or as specified by your instructor) that is both accurate and positive in tone. Deliver it to an audience of at least six members. Answer questions after the presentation.

4. Meeting

In the role of Marty, use your class as an assembled meeting of workers. You will conduct the meeting. Listen to their complaints and feelings. Explain your recent actions and future plans for the section. Pay particular attention to the comments about the controversial evaluations you recently issued. Try to steer the meeting away from hostility and mutiny and toward understanding and teamwork.

5. Memos

(a) In the role of Division Manager Brewster, write a memo to file documenting what you perceive to be Marty's leadership failures in Section Five.

(b) As Marty, you've made your choice between Roberto and William. Write a memo to be distributed among section employees. Reveal your choice in the memo and provide any explanations or other appropriate details.

6. Letters

(a) In the role of William, you feel that you have been passed over unjustly for the foreman job. Write a letter to the local Affirmative Action coordinator asking what steps you can take to ensure your full consideration in this and future supervisory openings.

(b) As Marty, you remember Harry Ross very well. When he left the company, he offered "lots of free advice whenever you ask for it." Write a letter to Harry in which you ask for his advice regarding the worsening situation in Section Five. Do not let your language become so negative that Harry loses confidence in you.

7. Report

Because you lead a section with substantial interracial and intercultural mixing, a corporate vice president picks you for the "honor" of writing up a short report on ways to manage effectively in such mixed situations. Draw together five suggestions for managers of interracial/intercultural work units. Structure the five suggestions into a report to managers throughout the company. You may conclude with special recommendations if you wish.

Introduction to Cases 15 and 16

The two cases that follow are designed primarily for interview role plays.

In each instance, the case has a Part A and a Part B. Part A is written from the perception of one individual; Part B is written from the perception of another person.

To obtain the greatest value from the exercise, the individual playing the role described in A should read only the A portion of the case prior to the interview. The person playing the role described in B should read only the B portion. The observer to the interview should read both portions A and B.

The purpose is to reflect a real-life situation. In most instances one party in an interview is never quite sure what the other party's perception is, although it can be imagined. However, in our case, we have both parties' perceptions described.

Remember—if you are asked to play the role of A, *do not* read portion B. If you play B, you *should not* read A's role prior to the interview.

Case 15
The Zenith Computer Company Case

Viewpoint A
Carla Kaufman, *Senior Engineer*

You have been employed by Zenith for ten years. It's been a good place to work, but you should have left years ago with Art and Smitty. You didn't, however. They set up their consulting firm without you, have done extremely well, and now have a staff of almost seventy people with posh offices in Newberry City. But that is water under the bridge . . .

Here at Zenith you worked with Jack Jerletti for several years and really liked the guy. You and your husband and Jack and his wife often had dinner together; you played tennis with him a few times; you pulled him out of several severe problem situations at work; you supported him a dozen times against the brass; and then he recommended that that kid, Al Armour, rather than you, take his (Jack's) job when Jack was promoted. You just don't understand it. Or maybe you do . . .

After all, both Jack and Al had attended Michigan Technical Institute and they often went to alumni affairs together. And of course, Al was always laughing at Jack's jokes, buttering him up, offering to run section meetings for him, and in a dozen different ways ingratiating himself with Jack. In a way, Al practically bought the promotion, but the kid had no administrative background, whereas you ran a department for five years when you were with General Motors.

Well, you were plenty burned after the promotion was announced. As a matter of fact, for a couple of weeks you barely spoke to anyone because you were afraid you would bite someone's head off.

But it's over and done and you're now doing the best you can. After all, the compensation for the job doesn't pay for all the extra time that's put in plus the grief. So you've decided, "The hell with it." You'll do your best, work your hours, not take the job home with you, and let Al Armour have the fun of playing Big Boss. But you can't see how someone like Al, with relatively little background or experience, can be successful. Technically he's well qualified, but administratively—oh

no! And that pompous, know-it-all, I'm-the-boss attitude he's developed in the past few months really gripes you. But he is the boss . . .

Right now you're on your way to see Al Armour. Unfortunately, you got tied up and it's 2:20. Your appointment was for 2:00 but you just couldn't get away from that problem with the production people. You don't think Al will mind because he said it involved a technical problem on the current project. In any event, you want to try to leave early so you won't be too late for the regularly scheduled 2:30 Thursday meeting with the proposal-writing team.

Viewpoint B

Al Armour, *Department Chief*

You have worked for Zenith for six years and have enjoyed your assignment tremendously. Well, "tremendously" up until four months ago when you were promoted. Since that time there have been problems—not because of your knowledge, your subordinates, your superiors, or the work itself, but because of one person: Carla Kaufman.

Your section had been run by Jack Jerletti for almost three years. Jack was in his late forties, a dedicated and very competent professional, and well liked by everyone. You worked closely with Jack, as did Carla Kaufman. Sometimes you or Carla ran the section meetings even when Jack was present. Most people in the section probably looked upon you and Carla as Jack's primary assistants. Of course you never did this "extra work" with the expectation of taking Jack's job; you just did it. Besides, Carla was in the section at least three to four years longer than you, was Jack's age or slightly older (you are 32), and often referred to herself as the section straw boss.

In any event, about five months ago Jack Jerletti was informed of his promotion and his move (which he had requested) to the Zenith installation in Arizona.

He (Jack) and his boss (Vice-President Connors) took you to lunch, then took Carla, and then you again. At the second lunch session, you were asked to take Jack's position. You pointed out your age, Carla's seniority in the section, and your own ambivalence. You liked engineering, you had almost no experience in administration, and you weren't "sure." But the title and the money were both tempting. You accepted the offer.

For three weeks after Jack left, Carla spoke to no one and certainly not to you. She did her work and, as usual, did it well. But two months ago, Carla changed. She came out of her shell but not in a way that was helpful.

At meetings she speaks up—frequently in very distinct disagreement with you. She frequently counsels younger personnel on project problems (really your responsibility), she overstays break time, she frequently disappears for an hour or two and you have no knowledge where she is (although she sometimes tells you later she attended—by invitation—a meeting called by another section), she arrives at your meetings late, and often gets up noisily and leaves early. In short, she obviously resents your leadership, is opposed to it, and is attempting to either play your role unofficially or make it so difficult for you that you will eventually turn the job over to her. One thing is certain: your personnel are confused, your decisions are frequently questioned, morale is down, and you almost wish you hadn't said "yes" four months ago.

In any event, you finally decided to have a talk with Carla. You set the appointment up for 2:00 today (it is now 2:20 and she still has not arrived). When she asked you the purpose, you didn't know how to say, "To get this behavior of yours straightened out," so you said something about "the technical electrical problems on the current project." However, your primary purpose is for both of you to understand who is boss. On the other hand, Carla is very well qualified in the areas your section is working in and you're not sure you can afford to lose her. But keeping her under these conditions. . . .

ASSIGNMENTS

1. Interview Role Play

Break into groups of three. Have one individual play Al Armour, department chief; one, Carla Kaufman, senior engineer; and one, the observer (see the Observer Evaluation Checklist).

After "Carla Kaufman" has read viewpoint A, "Al Armour" viewpoint B, and the observer both A and B, hold a ten- to twelve-minute interview in which the major problem between Carla and Al is discussed. After the interview, have the observer report his or her reactions.

Change roles and repeat to secure another approach to the problem.

2. Group Discussion

After your entire group has role played and/or read the case (viewpoints A and B), have a group discussion.

Break into groups of four or five and discuss the case. Your first step should be to review the situation presented to determine that all participants in each group have a similar perception of the incidents described.

Next, proceed to analyze the case. What is the major problem? The contributing problems? What specific communication barriers are evident? Who is responsible? How can the major and minor problems be solved? What action should be taken now?

After ten to fifteen minutes of discussion within the groups, open the case to the entire class. Do this by having the spokespersons of four or five groups report their groups' findings to the class. Permit class members to respond and/or ask questions after each representative speaks.

Case 16
The McKelvey Lumber Company Case

Viewpoint A

Martin McKelvey, *President*

Two years ago, at the age of twenty-six, you became head of the largest company in Bakersville, California: McKelvey Lumber and Construction. Of course, the situation that placed you in that spot was a surprise. No one had expected Ronald McKelvey, your father, to have a fatal heart attack at age fifty-three . . . but he did.

At the time, it took your mother almost ten days to find where you were in Europe (at a ski resort) and another few days for you to get home. And just fourteen days after your dad's death, you were head of a multimillion-dollar company and several dozen employees.

The first year was really rough. After all, you had spent most of your life in school. And as a matter of fact, when the instructors at the University of California at Davis became "chicken" and demanded that you complete

papers and take exams, you just told them what they could to with their degree, the school, and the nonsense. That's when you hit Dad for a few thousand and took off for Europe.

But is wasn't as if you did not know the business. After all, you spent several weeks each summer with the crews. There were two summers when you were a junior and senior in high school and two summers after that. Of course, your work was very basic: record-keeping, inventory routines, and some back-breaking labor.

But now you're in charge and running things! And you like that. However, you are worried. Sales have dropped dramatically this year and some of your best employees have quit. But, of course, that isn't your fault. Everyone knows what's happened to commercial and residential construction, mortgage rates, etc. However, other businessmen in Bakersville indicate that sales are excellent.

Something else that bothers you is the attitude a lot of people have toward the McKelvey Company. You don't think it's personal, of course. However, people are always telling you what a great person your dad was; how much everyone respected him; what a marvelous businessman he was; how much he contributed to the town of Bakersville, and on and on. Of course, they usually add, rather quickly, "And you're so much like him . . ."

Dad was an unusual person. Everyone did like him and he liked everyone. Well, almost everyone. He had had some hard feelings toward Mr. Davis of American International Bank. Mr. McKelvey had begun doing business with the bank, but when he needed a substantial loan, he was refused. The small loans he secured, he felt, were never handled well, and he always felt the bank (or Mr. Davis—now long gone) took advantage of him financially. Finally, he shifted everything over to Fidelity Bank, and that's where the McKelvey Company has been for the last fifteen years.

Come to think of it, you agreed to see Helen Hopkins, new branch manager, Bakersville branch, American International Bank, at 11:00 A.M. today. She sounded nice enough on the phone, but you're wary, especially after what your dad had to say about this outfit. Fortunately the business is very solid; Dad left an enormous liquid surplus, and you could have your choice of banks. However, Fidelity Bank has proved very satisfactory, although at times you wonder if the outfit isn't so big that it doesn't have time for a small-town business. Of course there is nothing that one bank offers that another does not except service.

In any event, your secretary just buzzed you to say Ms. Hopkins was waiting.

Viewpoint B

Helen Hopkins

Manager Bakersville Branch,
American International Bank

You have been with American International Bank for seventeen years and really like the organization. Of course, it's been a struggle getting your own branch, but it finally came through. As a matter of fact, you are the only woman branch manager among the bank's twenty-three branches.

You began with the bank while still attending college and slowly worked your way up. You graduated with a degree in finance, earned some sixteen years ago, from your state university.

Just six months ago you were transferred from Highpoint to take over this branch. So far you've done quite well making some

changes within the branch, revising a few procedures, and just getting a handle on the employees, the town, and business opportunities in Bakersville for the bank.

In the last two months you've been making sales calls, attending Rotary, and in general doing some external public relations. You must admit, however, there has been no great rush of business from Fidelity and First Federal Bank to American International. Not that you expected a stampede, but you did think you could get accounts much more easily. You were successful with the major drug store, the Ford Agency, and the Campbell Real Estate Office, but not with fifteen other firms.

It just seems that every business is tied in not only financially but socially with its present bank . . . and not terribly eager to make a change to American International.

One that you have really had your eye on is McKelvey Lumber Company. Not only would it be a plum because of its volume, but the firm has all kinds of connections with other accounts: contractors, builders, homeowners who wish to remodel, and so on. But McKelvey wouldn't even return your calls until last Monday.

On the other hand, you're not very optimistic about getting the account. Old Ron McKelvey, you understand, was a tight-fisted, penny-pinching, conniving guy. You're well aware that he threatened to bring a lawsuit against American International seventeen or eighteen years ago unless he got what he wanted . . . but didn't deserve. One reason old Dan Davis left the bank sixteen years ago was because McKelvey had pushed him into a corner.

As for that spoiled son of his who took over a highly profitable, going business after the old man's death . . . you have really heard some stories about him.

Apparently this Martin McKelvey, with whom you have an appointment shortly, never worked a day in his life, and wouldn't be able to find a clerk's job if he hadn't been born into the right family.

He's the same kid who got bounced out of college, drove around Europe in a Porsche for a year, and was now making every mistake in the book while running a multimillion-dollar company.

But whether or not Martin McKelvey is a spoiled twenty-eight year old is immaterial. The account would be a real prize and would surely impress the brass at the bank if you could land it.

Well, here goes; Martin McKelvey's secretary has just said, "He will see you now."

ASSIGNMENTS

1. Interview Role Play

Break into groups of three. Have one individual play Helen Hopkins, manager, Bakersville Branch, American International Bank; one, Martin McKelvey, president, McKelvey Lumber Company; and one, the observer (see the Observer Evaluation Checklist).

After "Martin McKelvey" has read viewpoint A, "Helen Hopkins" viewpoint B, and the observer both A and B, hold a ten- to twelve-minute interview. Helen Hopkins' primary purpose is to have Martin McKelvey switch all his financial affairs from Fidelity Bank to American International. After the interview, have the observer report his or her reactions.

Change roles and repeat to get another approach to the situation.

2. Letters

(a) In the capacity of Helen Hopkins, send out a goodwill letter to the merchants in Bakersville who are not now with American International, and attempt to persuade them to switch their commercial accounts to your organization.

You have all the usual check services, a loan department, computer facilities for their payrolls, afterhours banking, a safe-deposit department, plus many other services. These are all available at slight extra charges.

(b) As Helen Hopkins, send out a "Welcome to Our Bank" letter to new commercial accounts such as the Ford Agency, Farrell's Drugs, and Campbell's Real Estate Company. These have recently opened accounts with American International.

3. Group Discussion

After your entire group has role played and/or read the case (viewpoints A and B), have a group discussion.

Break into groups of four or five and discuss the case. Your first step should be a review of the situation presented in order to determine that all participants in each group have a similar perception of the incidents described.

Next proceed to analyze the case. What is the major problem? What are the contributing problems? What specific communication barriers are evident? Who is responsible? How can the major and minor problems be solved? What action should be taken now?

After ten to fifteen minutes of discussion by the groups within themselves, open the case to the entire class. Do this by having the spokespersons of four or five groups report their groups' findings to the class. Permit class members to respond and/or ask questions after each representative speaks.

Observer Evaluation Checklist

1. How conducive was the interview climate to a free exchange? Was it friendly? Relaxed? Hostile? Tense?

   _____

   _____

   _____

   _____

2. Who talked the most? Was that appropriate?

   _____

   _____

   _____

   _____

3. How effectively did each listen? For facts? For feelings?

   _____

   _____

   _____

   _____

4. Did the interviewer cover strengths (positive tone) before discussing weaknesses (negative tone)?

   _____

   _____

   _____

5. Was agreement reached for solving problems? Were action items established?

   _____

   _____

   _____

   _____

6. If conflict was involved, was there a specific effort made to resolve it? How? Win/Lose? Win/Win? Negotiation?

_____

_____

_____

_____

7. Did both parties prepare for the interview?

_____

_____

_____

_____

8. Were crucial junctures recognized? When?

_____

_____

_____

_____

9. Which of the following techniques did the interviewer use?
   _____ Open-end questions   _____ Negative/positive word choice
   _____ Closed-end questions   _____ Praise
   _____ Loaded questions   _____ Silence
   _____ Listening   _____ Tact

10. At the conclusion of the discussion, did the interviewer summarize agreements and action items to the satisfaction of both parties?

_____

_____

_____

_____

11. Do you feel the interview accomplished its purpose? Comment.

_____

_____

_____

The instructor may wish to reproduce this form for observers when cases are used for role play.

The New York Times INDEX 1945
The New York Times INDEX 1945
The New York Times INDEX 1946
The New York Times INDEX 1946
INDEX 1947
INDEX 1947
The New York Times INDEX 1956
INDEX 1957
INDEX 1958
INDEX 1959

Part Eight

Readings

What Communication Means

Peter Drucker

Communication in management has long been a central concern of students and practitioners in all institutions—business, the military, public administration, hospital administration, university administration and research administration. In no other area have intelligent men and women worked harder or with greater dedication than psychologists, human relations experts, managers and management students have worked on improving communications in our major institutions. The trickle of books on communications has become a raging torrent. A recent bibliography prepared for a graduate seminar on communications ran to 97 pages: a recent anthology contained articles by 49 different contributors.

Yet "communications" has proved as elusive as the unicorn. Each of those 49 contributors has a different theory of communications which is incompatible with all the others. The noise level has gone up so fast that no one can really listen any more to all that babble about communications. But there is clearly less and less "communicating." The so-called communications gap within institutions and between groups in society has been widening steadily—to the point where it threatens to become an unbridgeable gulf of total misunderstanding.

In the meantime, there is an "information explosion." Every professional and every executive suddenly has access to data in inexhaustible abundance. But what must be done to make this cornucopia of data add up to

Abridged and adapted from Chapter 38 in *Management: Tasks, Responsibilities, Practices* by Peter F. Drucker. Copyright © 1974 by Peter F. Drucker. Reprinted by permission of Harper & Row, Publishers, Inc., and Heinemann Professional Publishing.

information, let alone to knowledge? The one thing clear so far is that no one really has an answer. Despite "information theory" and "data processing," no one yet has actually seen, let alone used, an "information system," or a "data base." The one thing we do know, however, is that the abundance of information changes the communications problem and makes it both more urgent and even less tractable.

There is a tendency today to give up on communications. In the psychology of management, for instance, the latest fashion is the T-group, with its "sensitivity training." The avowed aim is not communications, but "self-awareness." T-groups focus on the "I'll" and not on the "Thou." A decade or two ago the rhetoric stressed "empathy"; now it stresses "doing one's thing." However needed self-knowledge may be, communication is needed at least as much (if indeed self-knowledge is possible without action on others—that is, without communications). So whether or not T-groups are sound psychology and effective psychotherapy, their popularity attests to the failure of attempts at communications.

A good deal has been learned about information and communications. However, most of it has not come from the work on communications to which so much time and energy has been devoted. It has been the by-product of work in a large number of seemingly unrelated fields, from learning theory to genetics and electronic engineering. Equally there is a lot of experience—though mostly of failure—in a good many practical situations in all kinds of institutions. Although communications may never be understood, there is now some knowledge about communications in organizations—or "managerial communications."

This knowledge leads to some surprising conclusions for managers—for instance, that the traditional downward communication in companies and other organizations does not and cannot work; that the human relations approach of "listening" to subordinates does not work, either; that more and better information does not solve, but worsens, the communications problem; that almost no computer today is being used properly. The honest, sincere efforts which have been made to "communicate" in management have no validity. To understand why this is so requires an understanding of the knowledge and experience which have been gained by study of psychology and perception.

Mastery of communications, even in organizations, is still far away. But at least we increasingly know what does not work and, sometimes, why it does not work. Indeed most of today's brave attempts at communication in organizations—whether business, trade unions, government agencies, or universities—are based on assumptions that have been proved to be invalid, and therefore these efforts cannot have results. But now, perhaps, what might work can be anticipated. The four fundamentals of communication have been learned, mostly through doing the wrong things—that communication is *perception*, that it is *expectation*, that it is *involvement* and that it is *not* information. Information presupposes functioning communications, but they are totally different things.

An old riddle asked by the mystics of many religions—the Zen Buddhists, the Sufis of Islam, or the Rabbis of the Talmud—goes: "Is there a sound in the forest if a tree crashes down and no one is around to hear it?" The right answer is "no." There are sound waves. But there is no sound unless someone perceives it. Sound is created by *perception*. Sound is "communication." This may seem trite; after all, the mystics of old, too, always answered that there is no sound unless someone can hear it. Yet the implications are great.

First, it is the recipient who communicates. The so-called "communicator" only "utters." Unless there is someone who hears,

there is no communication, only noise. The communicator cannot "communicate"; he can only make it possible, or impossible, for a recipient—or rather "percipient"—to perceive.

Perception, moreover, is not logic. It is experience, and always part of a "total picture." The gestures, the tone of voice, the whole environment, not to mention the cultural and social relations, cannot be dissociated from the spoken language. In fact, without them the spoken word has no meaning and cannot communicate. The same words—for example, "I enjoyed meeting you"—will be heard as having a wide variety of meanings. Whether they are heard as warmth or as icy cold, as endearment or as rejection, depends on their setting—say, the tone of the voice or the occasion. By themselves, without being part of the total configuration, the words have no meaning at all. To paraphrase an old saying, "one cannot communicate a word; the whole man always comes with it."

But men can only perceive what they are capable of perceiving. Just as the human ear does not hear sounds above a certain pitch, so human perception does not perceive what is beyond its range of perception. A man may hear physically, or see visually, but if he cannot accept what he hears or sees, it cannot become communication. The teachers of rhetoric have known this for a very long time—though the practitioners of communications tend to forget it again and again. In Plato's *Phaedrus* Socrates points out that one has to talk to people in terms of their own experience, to use carpenters' metaphors when talking to carpenters, and so on. One can only communicate in the recipient's language or altogether in his terms. And the terms have to be experience-based. It therefore does very little good to try to explain terms to people. They will not be able to receive them if they are not terms of their own experience.

The connection between experience, perception, and concept formation—that is, understanding—is infinitely subtler and richer than any earlier philosopher imagined. But one fact is proven. Percept and concept in the learner, whether child or adult, are not separate. We cannot perceive unless we also conceive. But we also cannot form concepts unless we can perceive. To communicate a concept is impossible unless the recipient can perceive it, that is, unless it is within his perceptions.

There is a very old saying among writers: "Difficulties with a sentence always mean confused thinking. It is not the sentence that needs straightening out, it is the thought behind it." In writing, people attempt, of course, to communicate with themselves. An "unclear sentence" is one that exceeds the writer's own capacity for perception. Working on the sentence—that is, working on what is normally called communications—cannot solve the problem. The writer has to work on his own concepts first to be able to understand what he is trying to say—and only then can he write the sentence.

In communicating, whatever the medium, the first question has to be: "is this communication within the recipient's range of perception? Can he receive it?" The most important limitations on perception are usually cultural and emotional rather than physical. That fanatics are not convinced by rational arguments has been known for thousands of years. But it is not argument that is lacking. Fanatics do not have the ability to perceive communication which goes beyond their range of emotions. To conceive them, their emotions would have to be altered. In other words, no one is "in touch with reality," if that means complete openness to evidence. The distinction between sanity and paranoia does not lie in the ability to perceive, but in

the ability to learn, in the ability to change emotions on the basis of experience. . . .

There is an old story about the blind men and the elephant, in which every one of them, upon encountering this strange beast, feels part of the elephant's anatomy, his leg, his trunk, his hide, and reports an entirely different conclusion, each one held tenaciously. This is simply a story of the human condition. And there is no possibility of communication until this is understood and until he who has felt the hide of the elephant goes over to him who has felt the leg and feels the leg himself. There is no possibility of communications, without first knowing what the recipient, the true "communicator," can see—and why.

Men perceive, as a rule, what they expect to perceive. They see largely what they expect to see, and hear largely what they expect to hear. That the unexpected may be resented is not the important thing—though most of the work on communications in business or government thinks this is so. What is truly important is that the unexpected is usually not received at all. It is neither seen nor heard, but ignored. Or it is misunderstood—that is, mis-seen as the expected or mis-heard as the expected.

The human mind attempts to fit impressions and stimuli into a frame of expectations. It resists vigorously any attempts to make it "change its mind"—to perceive what it does not expect to perceive, or not to perceive what it expects to perceive. . . . A gradual change, in which the mind is supposedly led by small, incremental steps to realize that what is perceived is not expected, will not work. It will rather reinforce the expectations and make it even more certain that what will be perceived is what the recipient expects to perceive.

Before we can communicate, we must therefore know what the recipient expects to see and to hear. Only then can we know whether communication can utilize his expectations—and what they are—or whether there is need for the "shock of alienation," for an "awakening" that forces the recipient to realize that the unexpected is happening.

Communication, in fact, always makes demands. It always demands that the recipient become somebody, do something, believe something. It always appeals to motivation. If, in other words, communication fits in with the aspirations, the values, the purposes of the recipient, it is powerful. If it goes against his aspirations, his values, his motivations, it is likely not to be received at all, or at best, to be resisted. Of course, at its most powerful, communication brings about "conversion"— a change of personality, of values, beliefs, aspirations. But this is the rare event, and one against which the basic psychological forces of every human being are strongly organized.

All through history, the problem has been how to glean a little information out of communications—that is, out of relationships between people, based on perception. All through history, the problem has been to isolate the information content from an abundance of perception. Now, all of a sudden, there is the capacity to provide information, both because of the conceptual work on "data processing" and "data storage"—especially, of course, because of the computer and its tremendous capacity to store, manipulate and transmit data.

Now, there is the opposite problem from the one mankind has always been struggling with, the problem of handling information *per se*, devoid of any communication content.

The requirements for effective information are the opposite of those for effective communication. Information is, for instance, always specific. We perceive a "configuration" in communications, but we convey specific individual data in the information process. Information is, above all, a principle of economy. The fewer data needed, the better the information. And an overload of information—anything much beyond what is truly needed—leads to a complete information blackout.

At the same time, information presupposes communication. Information is always encoded. To be received, let alone to be used, the code must be known and understood by the recipient. This requires prior agreement or communication. At the very least, the recipient has to know what the data relate to. Are the figures on a piece of computer tape the height of mountain tops or the cash balances of banks? In either case, the recipient has to know what mountains or banks are, to get any information out of the data.

Communications, finally, may not be dependent on information. Indeed, the most perfect communications may be purely "shared experiences," which are not based on any logic. Perception has primacy rather than information. . . .

For centuries managers have attempted communication "downwards." This cannot work, no matter how hard and how intelligently they try. It cannot work, first, because it focuses on what the manager wants to say. It assumes, in other words, that the utterer "communicates"—when in fact, communication is the act of the recipient. The emphasis has been put on the emitter, the manager, the administrator or the commander, to make him capable of being a "better communicator." But all that can be communicated downwards are commands, that is, pre-arranged signals. Nothing connected with understanding, let alone with motivation, can be communicated downwards. This requires communication upward, from those who perceive to those who want to reach their perception.

This does not mean that managers should

stop working on clarity in what they say or write. Far from it. But it does mean that *how* they say something can come only after they have learned *what* to say. And this cannot be found out by "talking to." "Letters to the Employees," no matter how well done, will be a waste unless the writer knows what employees can perceive, expect to perceive and want to do. They are a waste unless they are based on the recipient's rather than the emitter's perception.

But "listening" does not work either. The theory of Elton Mayo was that instead of starting out with what "we," that is, the executive, wants to "get across," the executive should start out by finding out what subordinates want to know, are interested in, are (in other words) receptive to. To this day, this human relations prescription of "listening," though rarely practiced, remains the classic formula. Of course, "listening" is a prerequisite to communication. But it is not adequate, and it cannot work by itself. Perhaps the reason why it is not being used widely, despite the popularity of the slogan, is precisely that, where tried, it has failed.

"Listening" first assumes that the superior will understand what he is being told. It assumes, in other words, that the subordinates can communicate. It is hard to see, however, why the subordinate should be able to do what his superior cannot do. There is no reason for assuming he can, or to believe that "listening" results any less in misunderstanding and communications failure than does talking. In addition, the theory of "listening" does not take into account that communications is involvement. It does not bring out the subordinate's preferences and desires, his values and aspirations. It may explain the reasons for misunderstanding. But it does not lay down a basis for understanding.

Again, "listening" is not wrong, any more than the futility of downward communications furnishes any argument against

attempts to write well, to say things clearly and simply, and to speak the language of those addressed rather than one's own jargon. Indeed, the realization that communications have to be upwards (or rather that they have to start with the recipient, rather than the emitter), which underlies the concept of "listening," is absolutely sound and vital. But listening is only the starting point.

More and better information does not solve the communications problem, does not bridge the communications gap. On the contrary, the more the information, the greater is the need for functioning and effective communication. In the first place, the more impersonal and formal the information process is, the more it will depend on prior agreement on meaning and application, that is, on communications. In the second place, the more effective the information process, the more impersonal and formal will it become, the more it will separate human beings and thereby require separate, but also much greater efforts, to re-establish the human relationship, the relationship of communication. The effectiveness of the information process will depend increasingly on the ability to communicate; in the absence of effective communication—as today—the "information revolution" cannot really produce information. All it can produce is data.

Perhaps more important, the test of an information system will increasingly be the degree to which, by freeing human beings from concern with information, it frees them for work on communications. The test of the computer, in particular, should increasingly be how much time it gives executives and professionals on all levels for direct, personal, face-to-face relationships with other people. It is fashionable today to measure the "utilization" of a computer by the number of hours it runs during one day. But this is not even a measurement of the computer's efficiency. It is purely a measurement of input. The only measurement of output is the degree to which availability of information enables human beings **not** to control—not to spend time trying to get a little information on what happened yesterday. . . .

The "information explosion" is the most impelling reason to go to work on communications. The frightening communications gap all around us—between management and workers; between business and government; between faculty and students, and between both of them and university administrations; between producers and consumers, and so on—may well reflect in some measure the tremendous increase in information without a commensurate increase in communications.

In terms of traditional organization communications we thus have to start upwards. Downward communications cannot work and do not work. They come *after* upward communications have been successfully established. They are reaction rather than action; response rather than initiative. Nor is it enough to "listen." The upward communications must first be focused on something that both recipient and emitter can perceive, focused on something that is common to both of them. And second, they must be focused on the motivation of the intended recipient. They must, from the beginning, be informed by his values, beliefs, and aspirations.

One example—but only an example—is found in the promising results in one organization. Here communication started with the demand by the superior that the subordinate think through and present to the superior his own conclusions as to what major contributions to the organization—or the unit within the organization—the subordinate should be expected to provide and should be held accountable for. What the subordinate then comes up with is rarely what the superior expects. The first aim of the exercise is precisely to bring out this divergence in perception between superior and subordinate. But the perception is focused, and focused on something that is real to both parties. To realize that they see the same reality differently is in itself already true communication.

Second, in this approach, the intended recipient of communication—in this case the subordinate—is given access to experience which enables him to understand. He is given access to the reality of decision-making, the problems of priorities, the choice between what one likes to do and what the situation demands, and above all, the responsibility for a decision. He may not see the situation in the same way the superior does—in fact, he rarely will or even should. But he may gain an understanding of the complexity of the superior's situation, and above all of the fact that the complexity is not of the superior's making, but is inherent in the situation itself.

Finally, the communication, even if it consists of a "no" to the subordinate's conclusions, is firmly focused on his aspirations, values and motivation. It starts out with the question: "what would you *want* to do?" It may then end up with the command: "this is what I tell you to do." But at least it forces the superior to realize that he is over-riding the desires of the subordinate. It forces him to explain, if not to try to persuade. At least, he knows that he has a problem—and so does the subordinate.

A similar approach has worked in another organizational situation in which communication has been traditionally absent: the performance appraisal, and especially the appraisal interview. Performance appraisal is today standard in large organizations (except in Japan where promotion and pay go by seniority, so that performance appraisal would serve little purpose). Most people want to know "where they stand." Indeed, one of the most common complaints of employees in organizations is that they are not being appraised and are not being told whether they do well or poorly.

The appraisal forms may be filled out. But the appraisal interview in which the appraiser is expected to discuss his performance with a man is almost never done at all. The exceptions are a few organizations in which performance appraisals are considered a communications tool rather than a rating device. This means specifically that the performance appraisal starts out with the question, "what has this man done well?" It then asks: "and what, therefore, should he be able to do well?" And then it asks: "and what would he have to learn or to acquire to be able to get the most from his capacities and achievements?"

This, first, focuses on specific achievements. It focuses on things which the employee himself is likely to perceive clearly and gladly. It also focuses on his own aspirations, values and desires. Weaknesses are seen as limitations to what the employee himself can do well and wants to do, rather than as defects. The proper conclusion from this approach to appraisal is not the question: "what should the employee do?", but "what should the organization and I, his boss, do?" A proper conclusion is not: "what does this communicate to the employee?" It is: "what does this communicate to both of us, subordinate *and* superior?"

Perhaps these small examples illustrate conclusions pointed to by past experience with communications—which is largely an experience of failure—and past work in learning, memory, perception and motivation. The start of communications in organization must be to get the intended recipient to try to communicate himself. This requires a focus on the impersonal but common tasks, as well as on the recipient himself. It also requires the experience of responsibility. Perception presupposes experience. Communication within an organization therefore presupposes that the members of the organization have the

foundation of experience to receive and perceive. The artist can convey this experience in symbolical form: he can communicate what his readers or viewers have never experienced. But ordinary managers, administrators, and professors are not likely to be artists. The recipients must, therefore, have actual experience themselves and directly, rather than through the vicarious symbols.

The traditional defence of paternalism has always been "it's a complex world; it needs the expert, the man who knows best." But paternalism really can only work in a simple world. When people can understand what Papa does, because they share his experiences and his perception, then Papa can actually make the decisions for them. In a complex world there is need for a shared experience in the decisions, or there is no common perception, no communications, and therefore neither acceptance of the decisions, nor ability to carry them out. The ability to understand presupposes prior communication. It presupposes agreement on meaning.

There will be no managerial communication or any kind of communication, in sum, if it is conceived as going from the "I" to the "Thou." Communication only works from one member of "us" to another.

How to Organize Your Thoughts for Better Communication

Sherry Sweetnam

Do you want to analyze the way you communicate and the way you think and organize your thoughts? Study your writing. It will tell you whether you are reader-sensitive or whether you are communicating strictly from your own point of view.

This example shows communication strictly from the writer's point of view:

The Personnel Department
is pleased to announce that
MARY R. NAKOVEY
formerly special assistant to the director
executive director of human resources
and associate executive director
Department of Manpower Planning
has joined the firm
as manager of personnel.

What's the problem with this business announcement? *It wastes time.* The big news is the new personnel manager; so why not say it up front? Instead, the writer forces you to wade through 30 words to get to the main point. Stalling the main point causes frustration, annoyance, and tension in the reader and creates negative feelings toward the writer and the information.

Many of us fail to get to the point when we communicate—both orally and in writing. There are logical explanations as to why we organize our thoughts like this. They are:

1. We're trying to impress. Often, we're so concerned about building our credibility and establishing our importance that we show off when we write. But showing off turns most people off. Readers don't care how great a person, department, or unit is. The reader's business concerns are: What's new? How is this going to affect me?

2. We're trying to figure out what we think. Writing helps us clarify thought. It is an excellent tool for moving through the thinking process itself. However, writers need to edit their work so that their key information is not buried in the maze of the process itself.

3. We're not clear about what is important to our readers. In writing sheerly from our own point of view, we lose sight of the reader's concerns and interests. It's fine to write this way in the initial drafts, but the final draft should be reshaped with the reader's interests in mind.

4. We tend to organize information chronologically rather than psychologically. Most of us are natural storytellers. ("Guess what happened on the subway today!" "Let me tell you what happened in yesterday's marketing meeting.") As storytellers, we naturally slip into a system of ordering information chronologically. There's nothing wrong with using the story format in the appropriate environment. The "right" organization to use always depends on who is reading the report and what their needs are.

5. We were trained to write that way in school. We learned to put the summary, conclusion, the last word, the bottom line, at the end of our school compositions and reports. We memorized and religiously followed the academic formula: (1) introduction, (2) body, (3) conclusion. And we continue to use it.

There's nothing wrong with organizing our communications that way *if* we have a captive audience, *if* we are so interesting no one can put our writing down, and *if* people have a lot of time. But that is rarely true in business. Most people are very busy with their own agendas and don't have time to wade through a lot of words to get to the point. When we bury our key points we lose credibility because we are not being sensitive to our reader's interests and time constraints.

POSITIONING YOUR THOUGHTS

Effective business communication organizes thought in the opposite way. The rule is to get to your point up front; then give the background and details. That is why executive summaries are so popular. After getting the nuggets up front, the reader can decide whether he or she wants to continue reading.

The most critical ideas should be in the most powerful of the three positions on the page—the beginning, middle, or end.

The beginning. The most powerful position is the first 50 words of a memo, letter, report, or proposal. Since the opening paragraph is key, that's where you want to load your most important ideas.

The middle. This is no-man's land—the weakest position on a page. It may or may not get read, depending on whether you've been able to hold your reader's interest up front.

The end. This is the second strongest position (assuming the reader gets to it). Why? Because it is the last thing that the reader will read. Therefore, it has greater impact than what was in no-man's land.

HOW TO FRONTLOAD WRITING

Frontloading means placing your key idea first. To do this, first go through your writing with a pencil and underline the key ideas in sentences and paragraphs. Then rearrange those key phrases and ideas so that they appear at the beginning of the memo, paragraph, or sentence.

Consider, for example, the difference in impact between these titles:

Subject: Statistical Data Due Dates
vs.
Subject: Due Dates for Statistical Data

The phrase *statistical data* is not the critical information in the title. It doesn't hook the reader because it doesn't answer such critical questions as: What do I have to do? Why is it important that I read this? The phrase *due date* is urgent; therefore, it needs to be frontloaded.

Frontloading Letters

Here is an example of how writers backload key information in a letter. The key information is italicized and appears at the end of the letter.

> Due to a processing error, your June payroll deduction, credited to your account on January 24, 1986, was inadvertently priced at $33.15145. The correct price for this transaction should have been $36.4214. *We have corrected this problem and adjusted your account accordingly.*

The last sentence should be repositioned so that it becomes the first sentence. The result could possibly read, "We have adjusted your account because we made an error in our calculations."

Why does this work? Because it is written from the reader's point of view. When it comes to problems and solutions, what most readers and customers want to know is: Have you solved the problem? If the news is good, then don't bury it! As a rule, give your reader the good news first instead of striking a negative note at the outset.

Frontloading Action Requests

The following is an example of a request for action. Notice that the request is buried in the second paragraph:

> Steve, I have been searching the lower Minneapolis area for over three months for qualified candidates with a strong knowledge of AVS to support the chemical data system. I have been unsuccessful. As a result, the project is in jeopardy.
>
> Therefore, *I am requesting your support to obtain the necessary approvals* required to begin reviewing candidates from outside the lower Minneapolis area.

By repositioning the request at the beginning of the piece, it would become a far more powerful communication.

Why don't we state requests up front? Because we don't want to appear too bold or too aggressive. In fact, however, stating your request up front is considered by many to be direct, forthright, and nonmanipulative. It is also good business because it gets to the point quickly. Again, there's no waste of time.

Frontloading to Persuade

Writing to persuade someone about an idea, service, or product is trickier than writing to inform or request action. You must decide how interested your reader is in what you're trying to persuade him of. If your reader is interested, then state your idea up front. For example, you might start out by writing: "I recommend that we buy XYZ computer."

However, if your reader isn't so interested, backload your recommendation and frontload the benefits of your idea or product so the reader will be sold.

TOUGH MESSAGES: THE THREE EXCEPTIONS TO FRONTLOADING

There are three situations in which frontloading your key idea doesn't work:

1. *When you have to say "no."* When you have to tell someone "no," it makes much more sense to begin with a positive tone or a kiss. Then you can ease into the bad news or the kick in the second paragraph. In this way, the *no* isn't such a blow.
2. *When your reader is not interested in buying your new idea, service, or product.* When you have to convince someone of your ideas, then it makes sense to frontload the benefits and advantages and conclude with your recommendations.

3. *When you know your reader doesn't want to comply with your request.* The best thing to do in this instance is to ease into your request or suggestions.

WHY RETHINK?

One of the best ways to achieve force and interest in your writing is to frontload ideas. This means frontloading in all your writing—your titles; all types of memos, letters and reports; and at the sentence and paragraph level. Frontloading will grab your reader's interest and get your memos read. The inner voice of your reader will be saying, "Here's a writer who knows what's important and doesn't waste my time."

A fringe benefit of reorganizing your written communications is that you will find yourself getting to the point more often when you're speaking to people. Frontloading is a mental exercise that trains you to get to the point in all of your communications.

The Business of Listening
John L. DiGaetani

Listening is a rare skill, the most often used yet least understood and researched of the communicating processes. We do it all day long, usually without even thinking about it, yet we do not always do it well. William Ford Keefe, in his perceptive book *Listen, Management!*, reports the findings of several studies that conclude that most executives spend between 45 and 63 percent of their day listening.[1] Given the amount of time listening demands in so many business situations, it is crucial that it be done well. But how can we tell if we are good listeners? How can we tell when we need to improve those listening skills? What can be done to improve them?

Listening is so rare a skill because it is difficult. But why? One reason is that people are usually absorbed in their own lives and activities and really listening to someone else becomes boring and painful for them. Only when the other person is through and we can start talking do most of us enjoy the conversation. But the fact that so many people look upon listening as something irksome to be endured before the interesting part begins indicates the scarcity of really good listeners and the rarity of the skill they have mastered.

Of course, some people in business do become very good listeners. Does this mean they have simply learned to "suffer and be still," to cancel out their own interests while others talk? Or have they turned their office into that of a psychiatrist, with the result that they see some of their workers on a weekly basis? In business such passive, self-effacing approaches to listening would be unproductive at best. This is because the business person who listens well must achieve two very significant things: he must "hear" what his speaker is really saying and then take action based on what was heard. Let's look at some areas of the business world in which good listening can prove beneficial.

Management.   Douglas McGregor's *The Human Side of Enterprise* contrasts two kinds of managers, X-Theory and Y-Theory. The X-Theory is the old-fashioned manager who is sure that he knows best and that his workers are in general shirkers who have to be prodded, even forced, to do an honest day's work. But the newer and more progressive Y-Theory manager feels that he has a lot to learn from his workers and that if he treats them respectfully and maturely they will re-

spond in kind.[2] In modern business the cynical X-Theory manager is fast being retired in favor of the supportive Y-Theory manager, because workers are most productive and happier under the latter. And a good Y-Theory executive or manager is a good listener.

To listen to what an employee is saying is helping the business and company to operate more equitably and to benefit from that particular employee's viewpoint. Such a system depends upon a manager's being sensitive enough to hear exactly what is being said. If an employee feels he has a better way of organizing his day, doing his work, or reorganizing the division of work, management should listen, and listen well. Many labor relations problems come down to X-Theory managers and poor listening.

Finance.   What does the customer want you, the investment counselor, to do with his money? How sensitive are you to what the customer knows about the stock, commodities, and bond markets, and what he wants in his portfolio? Can you help him capitalize on current market trends and appreciate his investments? Do you know what he wants you to do? Does he himself know what his options are for optimum growth? If a financial manager does not listen carefully to his clients and hear what they are saying, they will take their portfolios to another firm.

Banking.   When is it wiser to grant or deny a loan request? What is the best savings account for a prospective customer? Will that same customer be a good loan risk? How much credit can be extended to him? These questions face the banking industry every day and intelligent listening can help to resolve these questions wisely.

Accounting.   The C.P.A. auditor has to listen carefully and critically to understand the nature of the books he is to investigate. There are, of course, many different systems of keeping books, and the wise auditor can understand and investigate all of them. This involves communicating with the keeper of the books, and from the accountant's point of view this means critical listening for accurate solutions to problems in accountancy. In tax accounting as well, the expert tax man knows how to listen to his client's description of his finances to find the best tax deductions for him.

Personnel.   The area where listening is most important is probably in personnel work, for it is here that human problems are most likely to get aired. Why does an employee want a transfer? Why does someone else really want to work for the firm? Why do some managers retain loyal employees in their departments while others go through them as quickly as they are found? Here the counseling qualities of listening are most important in understanding and diagnosing problems of human relations in business. Sigmund Freud was the first counselor to lay as the basis of his therapy the accurate and critical listening of the therapist.

Marketing.   Advertising agencies that survive the rigors of Madison Avenue competition have learned that contracts won't be renewed unless they can give the client exactly what he wants. When an advertising campaign is designed, it must be based on an accurate understanding of what a company wants for its product in terms of image presented and audience intended.

Sales.   Here, too, the perceptive listener has the edge. When customers ask about a product, a good salesperson can tell whether they are interested in a good bargain, a status item, or something in between. Does the customer for a new TV want "only the one on

special" or "one that will last" or "a nice piece of furniture"? Whatever the television has to offer can be highlighted to appeal to a particular customer's expectation of the product. Again, the shrewd salesperson listens between the lines when the customer asks to see a certain product and lets him sell himself.

The effects of really good listening can be dramatic. These effects include the satisfied customer who will come back, the contented employee who will stay with the company, the manager who has the trust of his staff, and the salesman who tops his quota. Good listeners are valued highly by the people they work with because to listen to someone else, as Carl Rogers has pointed out, gives that person validity. It suggests that that person is worth something and worth hearing, that both what he says and what he is are important.[3]

But listening, in addition to being important, is a complex process involving several skills. There are basically two types of listening.

Social Listening.   This is the kind of listening people do when they are in a bar chatting with friends, in a classroom before the class begins, or in a barber shop. There people listen to be pleasant, to pass some time, to be agreeable, because they have nothing else particularly important to do. They listen, but they also let their minds wander.

Critical Listening.   This kind of listening is more difficult and demands longer periods of concentration. It requires both serious attention and critical hearing, both concentration and penetration, both memory and knowledge. Attending a lecture, a concert, or a debate requires this kind of listening if substantial communication is to occur.

But the two categories listed above are really too neat to describe the complexities of the human brain, for it is so powerful it can entertain many thoughts and impressions at the same time. Think of the many thoughts that go through a student's mind during a typically interesting college class—what the professor is saying, what he or she is wearing, what went on last weekend, what the plans are for the coming weekend. As a result of the immense powers of the brain, shifting from critical to social listening is the norm, though better students are more capable of prolonged critical listening.

Good listening requires a series of skills: concentration, the ability to focus the brain's attention; a desire to understand the other person's point of view; an awareness of what is meant, often distinguished from what is being said; and, judgment about how to act on this information.

But before going into various specific qualities of a really good listener, it would be helpful to know the different types of poor listeners and the attitudes and behaviors that typify them.

POOR LISTENERS

There are variants of unproductive behavior in listening skills. The major types of poor listeners are:

The Fidgeter.   His or her body language and gestures clearly indicate that he is not interested and, in fact, is interested in few things that don't immediately relate to himself. The fidgeter often views listening as an imposition, as being a patsy, and sees talking as the way to gain power over others.

The Aggressive Listener.   He tries so hard to be a good listener that he intimidates people with his stares and intensity.

The Pseudointellectual.   He listens only for ideas and is deaf to the emotions behind them. As a result, he is often bored by most people's conversation because he doesn't hear a fifth of what they are saying. He is also quick with solutions when people bring up problems, while the speaker really wants someone to talk to and can think of the solution himself. The pseudointellectual, when told that someone has a headache, will often insensitively say "take aspirin," which implies of course that the speaker was too stupid to think of that himself.

The Overly Passive Listener.   He has nothing to contribute to the conversation and will nod agreement with anything the other person says, probably out of a sense of fear. This person fails to communicate any sincerity because he is comfortable only as a passive rather than an active listener.

The Inaccurate Listener.   If someone mentions federally funded medical insurance, he hears "communism." If someone mentions being busy, he fears rejection. He can't hear what people are actually saying because of his distorted listening.

Now that we know the traps to avoid, especially if we recognize ourselves as one of the many types of poor listeners, we can proceed to positive suggestions.

KEYS TO GOOD LISTENING

Learn to Tolerate Silence.   One sure sign of a good listener is that he or she is not afraid of silence. Most people have a horrible fear of silence or are embarrassed by it, so they either chatter or encourage others to chatter to kill the awful sound of silence. But is it so awful? Paul Simon and Art Garfunkel heard a lot in it, and Mozart himself once said that the most profound music is silence. The psychiatrist Dominick Barbara said, "Silence has a particular healing and is curative in certain intimate situations.''[4]

In conversation silence often has the effect of putting the ball in the other person's court and letting him start the conversational game. Will he, first of all, interpret this behavior as pressure to talk? Or will he tempt the other person into talking by remaining silent? If he does start the conversational ball rolling, what kind of ball will he bat to the other person?

Look and Listen Hard.   As we talk we reveal ourselves and the listener can have the joy of observing what others reveal. But with that joy comes a real power, provided the listener is observant enough. Have you ever really listened, carefully and observantly, to the way people talk? Do they seem nervous or comfortable? If nervous, when? When do they look at you, and when do they break eye contact? Does she break eye contact with you when she tells you to type a letter? If so, why? Does he break eye contact with you when he says that he really needs and deserves a raise? Why?

The careful listener is not passive but has real power. He can indirectly sway the direction of the conversation, and he is free to observe minutely. To observe other people carefully while they speak is a real opportunity for understanding them—provided, of course, that the right person is doing the observing. Look hard, and hear hard, for facial expressions, gestures, bodily movements, body language in general, use of eye contact—especially when and where these all occur.

Know Your Power as a Listener.   The listener has real power and responsibility in any speaking situation. A poor listener can destroy the speaker's desire to talk or his confidence in his ability to communicate. In a classroom situation, poor listening behavior can undermine a teacher's desire to teach. In a debate, an obviously hostile audience can intimidate speakers, though greater speakers can be encouraged by the same sight. Know your power as a listener and use it to your advantage.

Ask Questions.   Don't ask questions just to be polite but rather to clarify what's going on. Don't be afraid to admit you don't know something. If you're not sure you understand some directions, ask for them again.

Reflect Feelings.   When someone mentions a particular reaction or emotional response, repeat it so he knows you understood it. It also implies that you are being sympathetic to his point of view, or at least understanding it. Thus, when he explains why he can't work with someone, state the reasons again for him. Restate or rephrase things and ask the speaker to correct you if necessary. Not only does this help you get things straight, but it also lets the speaker know that you are hearing what he is saying and are interested in it.

Let Your Body Give Positive and Reinforcing Messages.   Julius Fast has written an influential book on the importance of body language, a new science call kinesics. You may say you are interested in something, but your body may prove you're bored stiff.[5] Make sure your body reflects an understanding and interest in a problem. Don't fidget or keep distant from your speaker; turn off the telephone, keep eye contact, and let your posture indicate you are listening sympathetically.

Know Your Own Emotional Biases and Try to Correct for Them.   One of the biggest barriers to effective listening is emotional biases; these are, by definition, attitudes and prejudices within us that distort what we hear. Do we think of some groups of workers as lazy, dishonest, or neurotic and power-hungry? These are the kinds of emotional filters that cloud the issues and damage the powers of an otherwise perceptive listener. When you hear of a communist country, do you think totalitarian? When you hear of government offices, do you think of bureaucratic inefficiencies? When you hear about large American companies, do you think either of super-efficiency or super-exploitation? In either case you have become the victim of your emotional filters, and your biases are hanging out and exposing you.

To be completely free of emotional filters is impossible since we are all a product of contemporary American culture and share at least some of its blind spots. The most we can hope for is awareness, an awareness of our own emotional biases so we can be warned that they might be working against our ability to honestly and sincerely *hear what has been said and nothing else.*

Avoid Judging. Your speaker is going to clam up if he feels that you are judging and evaluating everything he says. That you are, if you are, should not be communicated to him. A good listener creates a warm, nonjudgmental atmosphere to encourage the speaker to talk. If someone is complaining about not getting a raise, keep quiet even though you may know that there was good reason why he was not given a raise. You may want to explain this at the end, or very briefly during the course of the conversation; but if you want him to open up to you, avoid judging or even explaining. Also avoid ''Why?'' questions since these questions make people defensive. Why do you hate your supervisor? Why don't you get along with your coworkers? Why can't you do your job properly? These are the kinds of ''Why?'' questions that indicate insensitivity.

Once you have heard, carefully and accurately, what the speaker is saying, you may

be in a position to act on it. If you are in this position, be someone who hears and then takes necessary action and avoid the reputation of being a do-nothing.

On the basis of what you have heard, promise only what you know you can deliver. If you have to disappoint a person, explain why you can not do what was asked. Stress, however, the positive and do it promptly. Afterwards, inform the speaker and all other parties concerned of the action you are taking and, if relevant, why you are. Avoid office rumors, if you are the manager, by making decisions promptly and keeping people informed. Acting promptly will communicate efficiency and will discourage repeated visits to a manager's office. Remember, a manager is not a psychiatrist.

The main trouble spot for most listeners is their own anger. Someone attacks you verbally, and you get very defensive. A speaker expresses racial, ethnic, or sexual slurs that may apply to you. The speaker can also be arrogant, domineering or presumptuous. And the speaker can inadvertently hit upon your own sore nerve.

Another major trouble spot for a good listener is the speaker's anger. Be solicitous if this should happen. Allow some cooling off by diverting attention from the immediate source of anger or by delaying the conversation; then end such a session by stressing positive action that is possible.

HANDLING POOR LISTENERS

How can you behave when you are around poor listeners and have to do business with them? How do you act when you have to deal with someone who you are sure is a poor listener? Do you have an employer who will only hear what he or she wants to hear? When you mention raise, does he hear inflation? When you mention vacation, does he think bum? Life would be much simpler if all the people we did business with were good listeners, but since this is sadly not the case, how does one handle poor listeners?

One way is to know what their emotional blind spots and biases are and talk to them in a way that avoids them. This is a way of making sure that they hear what you are saying—in other words, making sure that you can communicate with them. Another way is to ask them to repeat what you have said. Or, you can repeat yourself several times. For giving direction to an employee who is a faulty listener, writing can be the best way because it gives him something permanent he can refer to repeatedly.

Given the amount of time it demands, listening is clearly a business activity too easily dismissed. It has been called the missing link in communication, and that appellation is certainly just. Given its magnitude of importance, good listening is clearly a skill worth acquiring, and the good listener is clearly at a business advantage. Listening is much more than a passive way of receiving information. In any encounter, the listener shares with the speaker a large percentage of the responsibility for the success of that encounter.

REFERENCES

[1]William Ford Keefe, *Listen, Management!* (New York: McGraw-Hill, 1971): 10.

[2]Douglas McGregor, *The Human Side of Enterprise* (New York: McGraw-Hill, 1960): 15–25 ff.

[3]Carl Rogers, *Carl Rogers on Encounter Groups* (New York: Harrow Books, 1970): 50.

[4]Dominick A. Barbara, *How to Make People Listen to You* (Springfield, Ill.: Charles C. Thomas, 1971): 29.

[5]Julius Fast, *Body Language* (New York: Pocket Books, 1971): 2–5.

The Information Society
The Royal Bank of Canada

One would have to be very much cut off from the world not to have heard that we in the developed countries are caught up in the information revolution. We have been told again and again that, because a new age is bursting upon us, we had better adjust to conditions of living that are radically different from those of the past. The message has more immediacy to those whose work has been changed by the latest wave of technology than to others to whom the world looks much the same as it did 20 years ago. But it seems that, whatever our circumstances, most of us are at least a little puzzled as to what is actually going on.

First of all, are we really in a revolution? The word is defined as a "turning upside down" or a "great reversal of conditions"—is that what is happening, or are we merely experiencing a vast acceleration of the age-old evolutionary process which, by its very speed, gives the impression of a massive structural shift?

There can be no doubt about the speed-up. A paper published by the Science Council of Canada in 1982 says that the pace of technological advance in the past few years has only been matched by its absorption into the marketplace at a rate seven to ten times faster than any previous technology. Nor can we discount the magnitude of the change: The same paper notes that since 1968, the power of computers has increased 10,000 times while the price of each unit of performance has decreased 100,000 times. Stanford University economist Edward Steinmuller says that if the airlines had changed as much as computer-related technology, an airplane would now be carrying half a million passengers at 20 million miles an hour for less than a cent apiece.

Many more spectacular statistics are quoted to show that the recent developments in electronics are of a revolutionary nature. But the story is perhaps more clearly told in terms of real events.

Revolutions overthrow the established order, and no business was more firmly established a few years ago than the Swiss watchmaking industry. But the advent of the inexpensive and accurate quartz watch made in Japan caused the loss of tens of thousands of jobs and the bankruptcy of hundreds of watch companies in Switzerland before the industry recovered to find a niche for itself in the prestige market. The upheaval was symbolic of the move out of the age of industry and into the age of electronics. The world's finest mechanical devices were replaced by tiny crystals and batteries with no moving parts.

Many other familiar institutions have been jolted by microelectronic technology. The American television networks had never known a decline in viewership until video games and recorders successfully challenged their dominance of the home screen. The traditional service station is giving way to self-service outlets offering lower prices because of computerized pumps which record purchases of gasoline at a central cash desk. The neighborhood hamburger stand has been supplanted by chain operations which use computerized systems to speed through orders and control inventory.

The time-honored institution of banking hours has been effectively abolished by electronic terminals which offer round-the-clock service. The Post Office has been challenged by the private transfer of letters and documents via word processors—electronic mail. Word processors also threaten to bury the office typewriter, just as the electronic calculator has buried the mechanical adding machine. In a reversal of form, the old institution nostalgically known as the penny arcade has been revived by electronic games.

So we can assume that there has been a revolution of sorts. It has been brought about mainly by the development of microchips. These little bits of silicon can be made to count, to memorize functions, to recognize symbols and to respond to instructions. They have made possible such wonders as the telephone that answers itself and the cash register that "knows" what to charge for a bunch of grapes and can tell by reading those mysterious stripes on the sides of packages whether a can contains tomato or chicken soup.

The chips have an incredible ability to store information. They can squeeze the contents of books by at least 10,000 times. Using a combination of microchip and laser technology, all the words in the 435 kilometres of book shelves in the Library of Congress in Washington could be contained on one wall of a large living room. And the capacity of microchips is expanding all the time.

When most people hear the word "information," they are inclined to think of television news and documentary programs. The fact that we are the best informed—or at least the most massively informed—society in history is an important feature of the information age. But the prophets of this age have much more than public information in mind when they say that our lives are coming to be ruled by information. It might be basically defined as "something told," and telling things to one another has become one of the leading preoccupations of a modern economy.

To an ever-increasing extent, things are told through a combination of microchip and telecommunications technology which is best described in a word adapted from French: "informatics." At the same time as the capacity of domestic communications systems has been expanded thousands of times by the replacement of copper wires with microwave links and silicon-based fibres, satellites have extended the range of instantaneous communications around the globe.

The ability to move information regardless of distance and time and to store it for future use has transformed many of the standard ways of doing things. For example, investment money in a country no longer need be directed to domestic stock and bond markets. Through informatics, it can seek the best return anywhere in the world, around the clock.

The fact that microchips can store and manipulate information has aided this process. If a broker in Vancouver wants to find the latest price of a stock in Hong Kong, he can call it up at any given time on a video display terminal. The microprocessor in the machine will draw on its memory to calculate the price-earnings ratio and yield as well.

Machines today not only tell things to people, they tell things to each other. Computer-to-computer communication has become common in industrial plants. A few years ago, a tradesman would guide a machine tool by hand through a series of motions dictated by a hand-drawn blueprint. Now, the instructions formerly carried on the blueprint are developed by a computer and fed to another computer which operates the machine. Those instructions are information—"something told."

The exchange of information among computers has caused a kind of population explosion. They multiply the amount of information available by mating different sets of facts to breed new facts. Their capacity for comparing and combining disparate pieces of data has opened new horizons for research into any number of subjects. The question at the heart of all scientific inquiry—"what if?"—can be endlessly explored by matching facts and figures with one another until a proposition is proved or otherwise.

Because more and more information is being produced, it is taking up more and more of the energies of the society. A study done by Shirley Serafini and Michel Andrieu for the Federal Department of Communications in 1980 found that information workers then comprised at least 40 per cent of the Canadian labour force, compared with 29 percent in 1951. They included as information workers all those who produce it (such as engineers and surveyors), process it (such as clerks and managers), distribute it (such as teachers and journalists), and run the technical system (such as machine operators and printers). Their criteria hold some surprises for those who think of information in traditional terms: for instance, optometrists are classified as information producers because, when you think of it, the results of eye tests are information. Judges are considered information processors because they must analyze the evidence presented to them by lawyers, who produce information by gathering facts and legal precedents.

According to management sage Peter Drucker, information has become "the central capital, the cost centre, and the central resource of the economy." With the fading of the industrial age, in which most workers were concerned with producing goods, the number of information workers is bound to rise in inverse proportion to the number of workers directly engaged in goods production. There will be relatively fewer machinists in industrial plants and relatively more software specialists working at preparing computerized diagrams. Even in raw materials production such as mining and logging, fewer miners and lumberjacks will be employed, as microchips are incorporated into the machinery used.

The loss of employment to automation is one of the great fears that haunt the information economy. Some prophets of doom use what they call the "horse analogy" to forecast that machines will devastate the present labour force. They argue that micro-electronics will have the same impact on human labour as the internal combustion engine had on horses; and that there is no more reason to believe that displaced workers will find employment in the new industries that are emerging from the change than that horses would have found work in the automobile industry in the 1920s. Actual experience has proved far less dramatic. In the decade or so since informatics exploded on the Canadian economy, employment has not collapsed, even though we have gone through an extremely severe international recession.

Despite shifts in the traditional pattern of employment—shifts of a kind which we have often seen before, such as when households stopped heating with coal—the economies of the developed countries have shown considerable resilience in the face of the technological onslaught. As long ago as 1980, a long time in terms of technological advance, 400,000 computers in the United States were said to be doing the jobs of 5 *trillion* people without throwing masses out of work. Productivity reaps its own rewards in international competitiveness and hence jobs for the workers of competitive nations. Japan has very low unemployment by western standards, yet it is known as the most productive nation of all.

As for Canada, it has no choice but to increase its productivity through technological advance if it is to maintain its place as a trading nation. Fortunately, Canadians have been rather quick to adopt informatic technology. Canadian companies are among the world leaders in satellite communications, digital switching, word processing, and computerized civil engineering. While export oriented "high-tech" industries such as these promise fresh job opportunities for Canadians, we are learning new and more efficient ways of doing old things with micro-technology. A more productive and competitive economy will be a more prosperous economy for all Canadians in the long run.

The real danger lies in viewing technological advance as a kind of occult force with a life of its own which is beyond the control of its human creators. With computers now programming and manufacturing other computers, and with artificial intelligence built into many machines, we could easily fall prey to what Canadian communications scholar Harold Adams Innis termed the "superstition of science." It is natural to summon up a Kafkaesque vision of armies of computers taking over the world at the bidding of a few power-crazed individuals. Stretch the imagination a little further, and you have computers and robots which defy their human masters and take over power on their own.

And indeed they do have the power to dehumanize life if their use is not controlled and firmly steered towards human betterment. Sociologists already worry about the anti-social effects on the young of computer games. They are still more worried that a class of "electronic hermits" will arise when it becomes possible, through videotext systems, to work, shop, bank, and entertain yourself without ever leaving your own doorstep. What will that do to the social intercourse which is so essential to the wellbeing of the community? Educators complain that computer-guided learning systems "program" the students and not vice-versa, leaving no opportunity for critical or intuitive thought.

Because the machines give the impression of "thinking" at stunning speed, there is a temptation to confuse the information they contain with knowledge. "Where is the knowledge we have lost in information?" T. S.

Eliot wrote many years before the computer ever entered the scene. The answer is that information only becomes knowledge when it is sorted out, organized into a conclusion, and checked for accuracy.

Much of the so-called information in computers is false, biased, incomplete or garbled. An over-reliance on computerized information helps to explain some of the classic blunders in budgeting and decision-making that so often make the news. The facts and figures in the machine must be subjected to the cool scrutiny of human logic and experience. When using them, we should keep in mind the occupational slogan of computer specialists: "Garbage in, garbage out."

We should never make the mistake of believing that these machines can do our thinking for us. Despite all the talk about "smart" computers, they do not have intelligence because they do not have ideas. Rather, they are aids to human thought which can take on repetitive, laborious and time-consuming mental tasks while men and women are left free to use their minds to do what they do most usefully. The magic of the mind lies in its imaginative side—its intuition, originality and individuality. Machines do not have these qualities. They do not have the faculty of synthesizing facts and knowledge into that precious thing called wisdom. They have no critical instincts. They cannot exercise judgment. They cannot come together in discussions to produce intellectual results that are greater than each party to the discussion could achieve alone.

What they *can* do is provide the undigested raw materials of intellectual endeavour in a quick and convenient fashion. In the process, they are capable of helping us greatly in our striving towards the highest aspirations of mankind. The accessibility of these raw materials can help make our society more democratic and fair by giving everybody more

of a voice in decision-making. It can help make it into a society which seeks wisdom through life-long learning. It can bring us as close as we have ever come to forming the ideal society of which the Greek philosophers dreamed.

But to gain wisdom through technology, we must ourselves treat it wisely. We must not read too much into it or expect too much out of it; above all, we must not expect it to do our own real mental work. The great French critic of the technological age, Jacques Ellul, has written that we each have a choice between allowing ourselves to develop robot minds or becoming people who are able to use technology without being used or assimilated or dominated by it. The servant could indeed become the master if we, as a society, give way to our fears about it or regard it as a force we cannot handle. If, on the other hand, we think of what to do with it with human values first in mind, it can be made to serve us magnificently. This is what it is meant to do; whether it does or not is entirely up to us.

Let a Data Base Get You the Facts
Changing Times

Want to put a wealth of information at your fingertips? By subscribing to an on-line data base service, you can get continually updated news, stock quotes, sports scores and weather forecasts on your computer screen. You can replace outdated reference books with an on-line text of a 21-volume, regularly updated encyclopedia or get a list of all the articles available on a topic you're researching.

Some on-line services also let you play video games with other subscribers, exchange messages nationwide, bank at home, shop by computer and make travel reservations.

The big hitch is the cost. It's not unusual to spend $25 or more a month using even the lowest-priced service. Each minute you spend using a data base will cost at least 10 cents and probably closer to 40 cents, not counting such additional costs as a subscription or start-up fee, a charge for each data search and separate charges for the phone calls that connect your computer with the data base.

You also need a modem to connect your computer to your telephone, and communications software to help your computer receive the information. You might also need an interface card, a line cord or both to connect your modem with the computer. Some data base services charge extra for the manual you need to use them. These add-ons could cost less than $300 or more than $1,000 depending on your preferences and computer.

WHAT'S A DATA BASE?

Think of a data base as a computerized library—a collection of up-to-date information that's organized so that different users can get at it for their own purposes. You can even create your own data base—of accounting records, recipes or whatever you want; a variety of software programs are available to help you set up that sort of thing.

On-line services make data bases stored on large, central computers accessible from a computer in your home or office. Some of the largest services, such as DIALOG and Bibliographic Research Services (BRS), were designed with research specialists in mind and are marketed primarily to businesses, professionals and educational institutions. They

tend to be too expensive for individuals, but their fees may be substantially discounted in off hours.

On-line data bases can be classified into three types.

▶ *Reference* data bases direct you to articles, books and other sources of information on a given topic. They allow you to search for listings using key words, dates and authors' names. You can also crossreference by designating, for example, Iran, Iraq, war and 1984 to receive a list of recent news stories on that topic. Summaries or abstracts of the sources cited are often available on-line, and for an additional charge some services will send you a printed copy of the full text. DIALOG Information Services charges $5 to $12 per full-text copy.

▶ *Full-text* data bases put the complete text of news stories, articles and other material right on the computer screen. Among the relatively few full-text data bases available are several from LEXIS, NEXIS, Dow Jones News/Retrieval (DJNR) and NewsNet.

▶ *Source* data bases provide data ranging from stock market quotes to information on physical and chemical properties of, for instance, plastics. Listings of export trade opportunities and airline schedules fall into this category.

In addition to data bases, there are interactive services that permit you not only to retrieve data but also to add your own. They supplement the collection of data bases on The Source, CompuServe and DJNR. These include financial transactions, such as home banking, and communication with other subscribers.

Data bases and interactive home services are available in some places through the new videotex services, such as the Viewtron system in southern Florida and Keycom in Chicago. Videotex generally provides better graphics, more local news and lower subscription fees than nationwide on-line data bases, but it requires a special terminal or software.

Viewtron, instead of transmitting data to a home computer, uses the AT&T-made Sceptre terminal, which costs $600 to $900 and lacks the versatility of a computer because it can only be used for videotex. Keycom uses a $50 software program that enables a home computer to receive videotex graphics. IBM recently introduced similar software, called PC/videotex, priced at $220 for the PCjr and $250 for the PC and PC/XT. In the future more videotex services will be for home computers rather than special terminals, blurring the already hazy distinction between videotex and on-line services.

FOR FUN OR PRACTICAL USE

Different on-line service are geared toward different needs:

Business and Professional Research

Several data bases have been designed for just this purpose, including LEXIS for lawyers, MEDLARS for medical specialists, Data Resources, Inc. (DRI) and DJNR for business-people, and BRS for specialists in a variety of fields. The off-hour services on some of these are geared toward individuals conducting research for their own business, term paper or other purpose. For researching tax rules, the IRS has put 66 of its publications on-line, available to BRS and CompuServe subscribers.

Investing

You don't have to be a professional broker to use financial data bases that track the value of your portfolio and quickly identify stock trends. Investment data bases provide current and past stock price quotes, individual company data and information on economic trends. E. F. Hutton clients don't have to subscribe to one of the on-line data base services to review their accounts and receive research reports on-line. They can subscribe directly to Hutton-line. Trade*Plus, based in Palo Alto, Cal., works with discount brokers and lets you buy and sell on-line, as does Ticker-screen, which is available through Max Ule & Co. in New York and CompuServe.

Banking

CompuServe has several banks on its line that let you check your account and pay your bills directly from a home computer. Most banks charge $8 to $10 a month for this service, and you still have to pay the regular bank service charges and on-line service fees. Some banks let you handle your account on-line without subscribing to one of the on-line services. Bank of America in California and Citibank in New York offer home banking directly to their customers, and several other banks are going on-line. PRONTO, a home-banking system designed by Chemical Bank, includes on-line stock, and option trading through Trade*Plus and is available to customers of nine major banks nationwide.

Travel Planning

You can make airline, hotel, car rental and other travel reservations through Firstworld Travel Service, accessible 24 hours a day through The Source and CompuServe. The Source also offers Mobil Guide, which indexes hotels and restaurants in the U.S. and Canada by location, price range and facilities.

The Official Airline Guide on Compu-Serve and DJNR includes nationwide schedules updated weekly and fares updated daily.

Through CompuServe you can also get the State Department's advice about travel to a foreign destination or, for a trip in the U.S. or abroad, arrange to exchange your home for a vacation home in the spot of your choice.

Entertainment

Whether it's a classic like chess or backgammon or a shoot-'em-up battle against space aliens, you can play it on CompuServe or The Source. CompuServe lets you play directly against other subscribers anywhere in the country, and three of the 40 games The Source offers are interactive.

If you're a sports fan, check out the news, commentary, scores, schedules and predictions for football and other sports, which are available on a number of data bases. And the movie reviews on The Source, DJNR and CompuServe include each week's new releases, the top 50 current films and a look at what's coming.

Shopping

Comp-U-Store, the largest on-line shopping service, is available to CompuServe, DJNR, and The Source subscribers and offers about 60,000 items ranging from mattresses to videocassette recorders. Indexing by brand name and price helps you locate what you're looking for, and the prices are frequently lower than you can find at local discount stores.

Communicating

Geographical and social barriers break down when subscribers become acquainted by computer by telling jokes or exchanging information—personal or practical. CompuServe users who happen to be on-line at the same time can send each other messages directly, as can subscribers to The Source. Groups can confer at prearranged times with those services, too.

Using electronic bulletin boards, you can also put ads or messages into a computer memory directed either to a specific person or to members of a special interest group (SIG) centered around a hobby or job. On CompuServe's medical SIG, doctors who exchanged early warnings on the dangers of Zomax, a prescription painkiller, helped get the drug pulled from the market. Job openings and résumés receive a nationwide audience on an employment bulletin board maintained by The Source.

TOUGH TO CHOOSE

It's difficult to select which one you want among the 350 or so on-line services, which offer at least 2,400 data bases. The same information might show up on several different data bases, and you might find the same data bases on different on-line services. Choosing among them can be tricky because you have to consider not only differences in format but also whether a service includes a full data base or only selected parts of it.

You can get help from the Cuadra Associates' *Directory of Online Databases,* found in many libraries. It lists data bases by producer and subject, and describes each one and tells which on-line services offer it. An annual subscription is $75, or order a single issue of this quarterly publication for $40 from Cuadra Associates, 2001 Wilshire Blvd.; Suite 305, Santa Monica, CA 90403.

Comparing costs can be even more confusing. Each service has its own method of computing hourly costs and miscellaneous charges. Some charge a start-up fee, others have a monthly minimum, and some services give new subscribers a few hours of free time.

You pay an hourly fee for the time you spend tapping into the service's central computer. Included in that fee or billed separately is a telecommunications charge, which covers the cost of transporting data from the central computer over a communications network. A phone call to the nearest node of this communications network connects you with the central computer.

In most major metropolitan areas you can access such services as DJNR, The Source and CompuServe with a local phone call. (There's a 25-cent access charge to call CompuServe.) But if you aren't within local reach of a communications network, you might have to pay long-distance charges for time spent on-line or make your own arrangements with a communications service, such as Telenet or Tymnet. Even with a local call, you might be charged message units.

Another major cost factor is the amount of time it takes to find what you want on an on-line data base. A service with relatively high hourly fees can sometimes be a better bargain than one with lower fees if its keyword index and instructions help you quickly find what you're looking for. Both CompuServe and The Source are making efforts to standardize the way information is presented in the data bases and to provide manuals that are written more clearly. CompuServe wants to make its commands more consistent and put more instructions on-line so users don't have to rely so much on the manuals. BRS is trying to make its manuals more comprehensible but says its users are pleased with the on-line instructions.

You can get cost tips and other information, including listings of free data bases from government sources, from the *Data Base Informer,* a monthly newsletter. It costs $48 a year and is published by Information USA, 12400 Beall Mountain Rd., Potomac, MD 20854.

For general information about going on-line, see *The Complete Handbook of Personal Computer Communications* by Alfred Glossbrenner (St. Martin's; $14.95 paperback).

Before you choose a data base service, try to get hands-on experience with at least a few. At some computer stores you can try The Source on a limited basis, and investment software from Dow Jones comes with trial hours on DJNR. Many university libraries that subscribe to data bases will perform a search while you watch; you'll get charged the hourly fee. Even better, find a friend or a user's group with an on-line service that you can try out, and pay the hourly fee.

Breaking the Barriers: Overcoming Four Communication Obstacles

L. W. Fernald, Jr.

Management communication problems exist just about everywhere. The results can usually be measured in terms of low morale, high turnover, low productivity, and a less than desirable bottom line. Good communication is hampered by four types of barriers: intrapersonal, interpersonal, organizational and technological.

Intrapersonal Barriers.   The two main intrapersonal barriers are selective-perception and individual differences in communication skills. Selective-perception is the complex re-

"Breaking the Barriers" by Dr. L. W. Fernald, Jr. from *Management World,* September/October 1986. Copyright © 1986 by Administrative Management Society. Reprinted by permission of AMS, Trevose, PA 19047.

lationship that exists between perception and communication. Be aware that meanings lie in people, not in the words they use.

An example: Office manager Peggy Ruhl was very upset after she checked on an important project she had given to one of her best workers, Charlie Drake. The project should have been finished, but, to Peggy's dismay, the project not only wasn't finished, it had not been started!

This was due to *the way* Peggy had assigned the job to Charlie. She told him to "Get on this as soon as you can," meaning, in her mind, "in four or five minutes." To Charlie, it meant "after I finish the job I'm presently working on."

Individual differences result from people's various strengths and weaknesses. For example, some people cannot express themselves verbally but are able to write well. Others are good speakers but poor listeners. Some people read slowly or have difficulty understanding what they have read. Thus, the comprehension level of company bulletins, employee handbooks, magazines and training manuals is often above that of their intended audience. There can be no communication without understanding.

Interpersonal Barriers.   Four interpersonal factors which can create barriers to communication are climate, trust, credibility and sender-receiver similarity.

The climate or relationship between managers and employees largely depends upon how they treat each other. A negative climate can lead to restricted communication, manipulation of information, distrust and antagonism.

Trust is essential. Distrust between a manager and employee increases defensiveness and decreases open expression.

Credibility is established by the person receiving information. At the individual level, an employee's perceptions of his or her su-pervisor's credibility are directly related to that employee's satisfaction with the supervision. At the group level, highly credible work units or departments experience greater communication openness, information accuracy, and higher within-group interaction rates.

Finally, sender-receiver similarity affects communication. The more similar two people are, the better they communicate.

Organizational Barriers.   Eight organizational factors can become barriers to communication: status, hierarchy, condensation, closure, expectation, association, group size, and spatial constraints.

Employees usually prefer to communicate with individuals of higher status for two reasons: it gains them peer group recognition and prestige, and it is a means of increasing one's chances of getting what he or she needs.

Large chains of command can hamper communication. The more levels a message must pass through, the longer it takes to reach its destination and the less likely it is to be accurate.

Often, word-of-mouth messages get distorted when passed from one person to another. What is repeated will be shorter and less detailed than what was received. In addition, the longer the period between the time a message is received and the time it is relayed, and the larger the number of people involved in its transmission, the more likely it is to be distorted.

Also, people often bias communications to conform to their own attitudes and expectations. A manager might say, "Stop what you are doing!" The employee may interpret the message to mean he or she did something wrong.

Events or outcomes that have occurred together in the past are often associated with one another at a later date. For example, if past errors were attributable to a certain individual, that person is likely to be blamed for similar errors in the future, often without justification.

Work group size also affects communications. Interpersonal communication becomes increasingly difficult as the size of a work group increases, partly because the number of possible communication channels increases dramatically.

Physical distance also affects communication. Arranging for people to share common facilities (copying machines, elevators, eating areas, desks) is a common method of encouraging communication. Separated facilities, physical distance, closed doors, walls, indirect lines of communication, and different working hours are devices which will usually discourage communication.

Technological Barriers. Finally, there are technological barriers involving meanings, nonverbal cues, channel effectiveness and information overload.

The meaning of a message is determined by prior experiences, personal needs and social background. Suppose a manager tells an employee, ''You must improve on your absenteeism as it has been excessive. Otherwise, you'll be disciplined.'' What does the manager mean by ''improve on your absenteeism'' or ''excessive''? What discipline does the manager have in mind?

Nonverbal cues play a key role. Only about seven percent of the content of a typical message is transmitted verbally. The remaining 93 percent is transmitted by tone of voice (38 percent) and facial expression (55 percent).

Be aware of the channel effectiveness factor, especially written and oral channels. Written channels are best for transmitting lengthy and detailed material. Oral channels are suited for communications that require translation and elaboration when rapid trans-

mission of information and immediate feedback are desired. Oral channels are also preferred for handling sensitive or confidential matters involving employees.

Information overload is another hamperer of communications. It is partly a product of the knowledge explosion of our times. Stress from resulting confusion and overwork is often signaled by increases in error frequency, interdepartmental friction, anger, aggression, or other more serious forms of personal distress. The consequences of such pressures are increased absenteeism and employee turnover.

Numerous techniques are available for improving communication, such as developing sensitivity, promoting two-way communication, using understandable, repetitive language, and protecting credibility.

The best way to improve communication is to be sensitive to employee needs and feelings. Most managers think they are sensitive, but studies show that they are neither as perceptive nor as sensitive as they believe. Knowing the various forms of nonverbal communication cues can help increase sensitivity.

Another approach is two-way communiation. By allowing employees to speak freely, managers will get more accurate information. Most managers, however, do not like to hear unfavorable reports, and employees tend to screen their comments. Some executives try to overcome such resistance by telling their staff that they want accurate reporting—bad news as well as good must be communicated. However, if they become angry upon hearing bad news, employees will again edit their reports.

Technical terminology and multisyllabic words may be impressive, but they can also be misunderstood by the listener. A supervisor talking to staff workers must communicate appropriately; so too must the executive making a report to the board of directors. Communication must always be clear and understandable. Use repetitive language! Sometimes a message will not be fully grasped the first time. Convey information gradually, building the essence of the message.

The Third Dimension

Dale O. Ferrier

The speech, strangely enough, was a dismal failure. The speaker had impressive credentials and good material. The manager of a multimillion dollar division of one of the largest corporations in America, he had a long track record of success and a military bearing that commanded respect and attention. His speech was filled with "meaty" statements, many of which were quotes in newspapers the next day. But his presentation was a disaster. All the little things went wrong. He made the common mistake of overlooking details which may appear insignificant but can be crucial to the success of a speech.

Following is a baker's dozen of suggestions to help you deliver more effective speeches in your management role:

Approach the Lectern with Confidence.   The audience begins to assess you long before you say your first word. Therefore, the way you act during the introduction, the time it takes you to get to your feet and the way you approach the lectern all go into the mosaic of opinion the audience is creating in its collective mind.

Ideally, the speaker should be filled with eager anticipation. You should appear alert and interested while you are being introduced, then jump to your feet and walk

From *The Toastmaster* January 1981. Copyright © 1981 by Dale O. Ferrier. Reprinted by permission of the author.

briskly to the lectern. You will thus create the impression that you know what you are going to say, that it is worth listening to and that you are ready to get started.

Be Dressed for the Occasion.   Second only to what you say and the way you say it is how you look. Obviously your attire should fit the occasion. Sports coats for the men and pantsuits for the women are going to be glaringly out of place at a black tie affair. However, a tuxedo or long dress will not be as wrong at a more casual event. Therefore, if you err let it be toward the formal rather than the casual side.

Also, be sure your clothes are clean, carefully and tastefully put together and look freshly pressed. Wrinkled trousers, a torn hem or a run in a stocking may distract the audience and undermine your confidence.

Build a Visual Bridge to the Audience.   Except in very special circumstances, a speaker cannot reach out and make physical contact with the audience. That limitation makes the visual bridge to the audience especially important.

Don't speak with closed or half-closed eyes. It shuts out the audience and invites their attention to stray. Don't let your notes or text trap you into looking down too often. It breaks your visual contact with the audience and thus reduces the impact of your speech.

Also, don't be afraid to establish direct eye contact with individuals in your audience. Eye contact is warm and personal. It communicates. The speaker who stares at a spot on the wall just above the listeners' heads takes on a glassy-eyed, detached look and appears to be talking *at* the audience rather than *to* it.

Start Barehanded.   Every performer knows the importance of showmanship, and every speaker is a performer to some degree. I believe most audiences prepare to be bored when they see the speaker take out a manuscript or a large sheaf of notes and start arranging them on the lectern. No matter what your management credentials are, at that point you look like a rank amateur.

If you must use notes or a text, put them on the lectern ahead of time and use them as sparingly as possible. Most competent, professional managers know their field so well that, except for statistics and financial notes, they should be comfortable with only the briefest notes—perhaps just a few key words on one side of a single 3 × 5 card.

Make Friends with Your Notes. If you must use notes, there are several ways to make them friends instead of adversaries. You must be able to see them clearly and to know at once where you are in your notes as well as what they mean. If you rehearse your talk several times, you should be comfortable speaking from an outline of key words.

If your notes are very long or detailed, use color codes to help you find your place with only a glance. Write the main points of your outline in black. Use green for illustrations, blue for quotations and write important statistics or other numbers in red. Put your notes on 3 × 5 cards, using only one side. They are inconspicuous and easy to handle.

Have an ear for tempo. Just as the tempo of a musical presentation is important to its enjoyment, so is the tempo of a talk. If you speak too fast, you will seem nervous and frantic. If you speak too slowly, you will seem sluggish and unsure of yourself. A good speaker develops an ear for tempo and tries to achieve a pace that is comfortable for the audience. Once the tempo is under the speaker's control, it can be varied to add emphasis and drama to what is being said.

An excellent way to train your ear to evaluate the tempo of your speech is to listen to yourself. Get in the habit of tape recording

every talk at least once before you give it and, if possible, record the actual performance. Then, listen to yourself frequently and think about the effect the tempo is having on the speech. Experiment! Try a passage faster or slower and note the effect. Soon you will train your ear, as a good musician does, to hear the tempo and use it to improve your speaking style.

Put the Playthings Away. Nervous energy will seek an outlet—often an activity extraneous to the job of delivering a good speech. Don't let the rattling of keys in one pocket or the jingling of coins in another spoil a good talk. Use your glasses for reading or looking at the audience. Don't wave them around or point with them or chew on them. Channel that energy into meaningful activity. Use it to make a powerful, enthusiastic, exciting talk. Let it make your stance, gestures and delivery spontaneous and energetic.

Be Heard. Your speech may rival the "Gettysburg Address," "The Sermon on the Mount" and Washington's "Farewell Address" all rolled into one but if the audience does not hear it, you may as well have stayed home.

If you are speaking without a microphone, watch the people in the back of the room. If they don't laugh when they're supposed to, if you keep losing their attention, or they seem to be straining to hear, you need to increase your volume.

If you are using a microphone, try to get to the room a minute or two early to check the volume level with the sound man. If people seem to be having trouble hearing or the sound system acts up during your speech, stop and get it straightened out before you go on.

Remember the most basic rule of all when you are using a microphone: Keep it between you and the audience. If it is a hand mike, as you move around, always hold it between your mouth and your audience. If it is a stationary mike, when you turn your head you need to move in a slight arc around the mike so that it stays between you and your listeners. Microphones are notoriously temperamental, so it is always a good idea to check them out before you depend on them.

Be Seen.   Being seen by the audience is second only in importance to being heard. If the lectern is too tall and you can't adjust it, you might have to step out from behind it in order to be seen. A hidden voice from behind the lectern is not going to build much rapport with the audience. Also, check the location of stage lights. If they are behind you, they create an annoying silhouette that prevents the audience from seeing your face.

Be Still.   Purposeful movement that has meaning and contributes to a speech is a good thing, but aimless movement is a distraction. Don't bounce on your toes. Don't rock back and forth or side to side. Don't wander around the platform without a reason. Keep your energy under control and make it work for you.

Keep Your Window Open.   A person's face has been called the window of the soul, so keep your window open. Don't give your talk with a deadpan face. That's like tying one hand behind your back. Allow your face to be full of life and interest. Let the full range of emotions in your speech register on your face. It is a contact point with the audience that will help you communicate more effectively.

Have Fun.   A speaker who dreads giving a talk will soon have the audience sharing that feeling. If you pick a subject you are interested in and knowledgeable about and if you prepare the speech well and rehearse it sufficiently, you should be able to look forward to

giving it. If you can relax and have fun delivering your speech, chances are the audience will also have fun with you.

Stop Too Soon.   The old vaudeville comic used to say, "Leave 'em wanting more." That's a good idea for a speaker, too. If your audience begins to fidget before you finish your speech, you probably have too much material for the time allowed. Don't try to cover too much ground in one speech. The master speaker, Bill Gove, says you should not try to make more than two or three points in one speech. He prefers only one point, well developed. Save your best illustration, story or joke until last and leave the audience wishing you would continue. It's a good way to get invited back.

Every great artist—whether he or she is a painter, sculptor, or chef—will admit that the difference between good enough and great is subtle. These elements of effective speechmaking can also make a big difference. In the words of the song writer: "Little things mean a lot." So don't take these details for granted. Let them be your friends—not gremlins bent on your downfall—and your speech will be a resounding success.

Careers in the Communication Field
Peter B. Clarke

Business communication has become an essential tool for everyone engaged in business, industry, medical and educational adminis-

Reprinted with permission of The Free Press, a Division of Macmillan, Inc. from *The Standard Handbook of Business Communication* by David E. Gootnick and Margaret Mary Gootnick. Copyright © 1984 by The Free Press.

tration, government . . . in short, anyone who is part of an organization of people working toward a common purpose.

American business, industry, and government are continually changing in response to the conditions they find themselves in. People working in these organizations must be informed about those conditions and about how to react to them. In general, this is done by maintaining a constant flow of information between people and between organizations. Working or being in business or government means, in fact, being part of this flow of information.

Some information about what is going on takes the form of numerical data: engineering and accounting data are examples. But words convey all the rest through writing and speaking. And someone must eventually digest and convert numerical data to written or oral form so that management can use it.

Communication, then, is how business does business. Memos, letters, reports, meetings, manuals, procedures, proposals, sales literature, videotapes, films, magazine articles, speeches, advertising—the forms of communication are as varied as the information they carry and the activities of the people who use them.

Everyone in business and government communicates to some degree or other. It may be as little as the single annual report a supervisor makes on the status of a department in a factory. Or it may be as much as someone can turn out who does nothing but write full time.

In this chapter, I am going to discuss some of the things a communicator can do for an organization, for there are indeed careers in communication in business, industry, and government. The focus of my attention will be on the many and varied careers of writers within organizational settings. In addition, I will discuss how one can learn to become a business communicator and even a business

communication educator. Throughout this book, the subject of careers in communication will be thoroughly discussed with numerous references to the careers presented in this chapter. Furthermore, many different jobs involving oral, interpersonal, and organizational, as well as technological, communication skills will be addressed.

Business-writing careers can be personally and materially rewarding, and they can lead as far up the ladder as one's ability permits. The activities of a writer can often spread over many areas, bringing him or her into contact with more of the operations of an organization than most people usually see early in their careers.

But just as important, perhaps more so, is the personal satisfaction in writing. It is one of the few jobs that must be done alone, and that yields something you can look at and say, "I did that." Despite whatever supervision you receive and despite how many people contribute material to what you write, eventually you alone at your typewriter must do the job. There is an independence in writing that is rarely found today, an opportunity to "be on your own" that is immensely challenging and rewarding.

What follows is hardly a complete description of the opportunities for careers in business communication. The jobs vary widely from organization to organization depending on what each organization does.

TECHNICAL COMMUNICATION

One kind of communication career is technical communication. This might start with turning out manuals, but the job goes well beyond that. Parts manuals that generally show drawings of something and list the parts that go into it are a simple but essential form of technical communication. So are the service manuals that accompany products to show

how to operate and maintain them. These are more complex and often present a real challenge to a writer to simply and directly describe complex operations.

There are other kinds of technical communication than manuals, such as special bulletins to customers and to company personnel. There are communications to people in the field, failure analysis reports, and procedure manuals for quality assurance and zero defect programs. Organizations often videotape procedures to show processes in action, and someone has to script these.

Safety is a primary concern to any organization, especially when manufacturing is involved, and there is a constant need for safety procedures and rules, and for audiovisual materials to teach these rules and procedures. Companies also call on communicators for safety contests, awards, displays, and the like.

Writing procedures is a specialized type of technical communication, and some writers find themselves spending all or most of their time preparing them. Gathering the material for writing procedures can give valuable insights into how an organization works and present opportunities to make real contributions to it.

Proposals are another type of technical communication. Usually, they are detailed explanations of why an organization is qualified to handle a project and how it expects to go about it, should it get the job or be given the responsibility. Proposals are extremely important; an organization's well-being may depend on them.

Whatever goes on in an organization must be communicated to its management and customers. This is accomplished through written and oral reports. Depending on what is being reported, and to whom, such reports can range from single-page memos to elaborate multimedia presentations. Some examples are personnel reports, feasibility studies,

research reports, progress reports, and corporate quarterly and annual reports. There are many more. Someone has to organize and put all of these into final form.

Technical communication also presents opportunities for writing and editing speeches and articles. Executives may ask people to "ghostwrite" articles and speeches for them. This may mean writing the article or speech from scratch, or it may require just editing and polishing. In either case, it brings the communicator into close contact with management. There are also numerous opportunities to write original articles, and there is a ready market for them in the many magazines published for business and industry. As well as giving the writer recognition in an organization, such articles can be financially rewarding.

TRAINING AND EDUCATION

Many organizations, especially larger ones, carry on extensive training programs for their employees. These organizations need people to plan courses, to interview consultants and employees, and to write course outlines and descriptions, text materials, audiovisual aids, programmed instruction materials, videotaped courses, and "how-to-teach" materials. There is a constant need for skilled communicators in this area. Often companies describe these training activities as industrial education, training and development, or management development.

MARKETING AND PUBLIC RELATIONS

One of the biggest, but at the same time most amorphous, areas of communication in business and industry deals with marketing, sales promotion, and public relations. Career opportunities abound in both business and government, and in the advertising and public relations agencies that serve them. Such communication is distinguished by one common attribute: it involves selling products and services.

This may mean preparing sales training materials such as films, videotapes, sales letters, manuals, etc. It may also mean creating sales materials, the tools salespeople use. These may be brochures, or they may be audiovisual materials: sound-slide presentations, motion pictures, videotapes, or the familiar flip charts. Such communication is often called *sales promotion,* and it is an essential part of any company's sales effort. People in an organization may write its sales literature and sales presentations, or an advertising agency or outside company that specializes in such work may do them.

Another type of communication to support sales is advertising. For industrial products this usually takes the form of advertisements in trade and business magazines. For consumer products, advertising makes use of newspapers, magazines, radio, television, and usually represents a much bigger outlay of money. Advertising is generally prepared by advertising agencies, and advertising copywriters do the writing. Anyone can practice this specialized kind of writing, provided they have the creativity and talent to do it. It's a hard field to break into, but it can pay very, very well for those who are successful. There are also companies who do all their own advertising and need copywriters in the same way advertising agencies do.

Advertisements, especially printed ones, often circulate inside and outside a company separately from their appearance in magazines and newspapers. This is called *merchandising* advertising, making sure customers and company personnel see the ads. Someone has to write the supporting material that accompanies this kind of advertising.

Whether industrial- or consumer-oriented, most companies support their prod-ucts and services with direct mail, basically letters and literature sent directly to customers and prospects. You've received direct mail: subscription offers from magazines, offers to sell you insurance, books, and just about anything else you might be persuaded to buy. For some companies, direct mail may be their only way of selling. Whether it is or not, it is nevertheless an important form of promoting sales, and all of it must be written. Like advertising copy, direct mail is a pretty specialized kind of writing. However, for those who have a knack for it, and who have gained the experience needed to do it, direct mail writing is a needed and well-paid job.

Advertising and public relations overlap and blend into each other, partly because their functions differ from organization to organization. This is especially true of public relations, a line of work no one has ever been able to define satisfactorily.

In its most familiar form, public relations can be preparing press releases, the announcements sent to news media about developments in a company or its products or services. These announcements are designed to provide material for the media to print or broadcast.

Public relations usually, however, calls for a wide range of communicating jobs. Often, management may ask public relations to prepare a speech for someone to give, or to handle special or "problem" correspondence. Frequently, it is the public relations department that fulfills the requests for information that continually come in to any organization.

The annual report is often a public relations function. This is an important publication, since it usually represents a company's major contact with its stockholders and the financial community. Quarterly and annual reports and other similar corporate publications are sometimes prepared internally, sometimes by outside firms specializing in such design and writing, sometimes by an advertising agency. In any publicly held company, stockholder relations is a most important function, and contact with stockholders is made almost exclusively in writing—by the company's regular reports, by special publications, and by correspondence.

Public relations work may involve setting up meetings for different groups of people. This can mean choosing the location and making the physical arrangements, but it also can mean preparing the meeting program or agenda and writing or assisting with the presentations to be made at the meeting. At conventions and trade shows, public relations may assume the responsibility for arranging for the design and construction of an exhibit and for shipping it, erecting it, running it during the show, dismantling and then returning it when the show is over.

Also, public relations may be called on to ghostwrite or edit articles for general, business, and technical magazines.

EMPLOYEE COMMUNICATIONS

In most organizations, the employee communications function comes under industrial relations. Sometimes the task of preparing material for employees is called corporate or organizational communications. Whatever the name, it is a vital part of smoothly running a company, of keeping employees interested and motivated to do a good job.

The most basic kind of employee communications is a company magazine or newspaper. Some of these are quite sophisticated and in large organizations have circulations that are the envy of commercially published magazines. Writing and editing the company magazine is important and respected work, and many successful careers have been built doing this.

Other employee communications are reports to employees, safety and morale campaigns, directives to employees, and employee education and training. All of these require writing, though they may be oral or audiovisual in their final form.

MAGAZINES, BOOKS, TELEVISION, AND MOTION PICTURES

There are also the businesses of publishing magazines and books and producing films and television programs. All publishers and producers require writers and editors. If this type of journalism is appealing, there are many opportunities available for those willing to serve their apprenticeships.

BUSINESS COMMUNICATION

You can see that there is a wide range of communication jobs in business, industry, and government: jobs in technical communication, training and education, marketing and public relations, employee communications, magazine and book publishing, and entertainment.

We have only looked briefly at some of the areas of communications that exist, and must admit that we have barely scratched the surface.

For instance, there are communications and management consultants, working either on a free-lance basis or for consulting firms. Writers and teachers who are experienced in business communications frequently find excellent positions as consultants.

Another operation that makes use of communication specialists is a bureau of business research. These are numerous and are usually attached to universities.

Communication jobs exist everywhere in business, industry, government, education—in short, everywhere people communicate with each other.

LEARNING TO BE A COMMUNICATOR

There are two keys to preparing for a career in communication. The first is practice. The second is education.

No one was ever born knowing how to communicate. Writing and speaking are like golf or tennis in one respect: The more you practice, the better you get at it. You can be taught *about* writing and speaking, but you must teach yourself *to* write and speak. You do this by writing and speaking and by submitting what you do to experts who can critique what you have done.

The other key, education, is essential. The minimum is a bachelor's degree—a master's degree is better. Some universities now offer undergraduate and graduate programs in technical or business communications, and these have proved to be successful and effective.

LEARNING TO TEACH COMMUNICATORS

Should you wish to teach business communication, you will of course need at least a master's degree to teach in a community college. To teach in a university requires an earned doctorate. The usual procedure is to pursue a Ph.D., DBA, or Ed.D., following one of the usual tracks toward the degree, but doing the dissertation in the area of business communication.

What the rest of this chapter recommends is admittedly an ideal. If you are considering working toward an advanced degree or counseling a student who is interested in our field, this is the kind of educational foundation that will prepare a person to teach business communication, do research in it, or both. Naturally, the requirements set by the school granting the degree will be the prime governing factor in determining the program,

but many universities are displaying a great deal of flexibility today in meeting their graduate students' needs. These recommendations, then, are a guide.

First, we assume a thorough grounding in the fundamentals of oral and written communication upon completion of undergraduate work—a reasonable assumption for anyone who does not assiduously avoid all courses having to do with writing or speaking.

THE MASTER'S DEGREE

Basically, a master's degree should prepare one for a management position in corporate communications. Thus, we recommend an MBA with a concentration in business communication. Whether the student enters the business world after completing the MBA or goes on to a doctorate, this program will provide a solid background.

Ideally, it would be good if the program allowed eighteen hours in business communication courses and six hours in electives and required coursework. Since this ideal is unlikely to be achieved, we suggest that, within the requirements of the department granting the degree, the student complete the core program, take as many business communication courses as is practical, and complete the requirements with interdisciplinary electives.

CORE PROGRAM

Accounting
Economics
Electronic data processing
Financial management
Marketing management
Statistics
Electives

BUSINESS COMMUNICATION

Theory of communication
Administrative communication
Organizational communication
Seminar(s) in business communication

INTERDISCIPLINARY ELECTIVES

Economics
Education
Journalism
Linguistics
Management
Marketing
Mass communication
Psychology
Speech and dramatic arts

Communication and the Law

Richard B. Sypher

The cry for clear communication in business is nearly universal. We are exhorted on all sides by professionals extolling the benefits of clear and comprehensive communicating in establishing efficient and profitable enterprises. Yet, because of the sophisticated legal world we inhabit, effective communication needs to be undertaken cautiously. The executive's zeal to communicate should not override the need to protect the company's legal position.

PRIVILEGED COMMUNICATION

In the American legal system, a party in a lawsuit may obtain a wide range of information from his opponent prior to the trial of the case. The Federal Rules of Civil Procedure provide for discovery of "any matter, *not privileged*, which is relevant to the subject matter involved in the pending action, including the existence, description, nature, custody, condition, and location of any books, documents, or other tangible things," so long as the information "appears reasonably calculated to lead to the discovery of admissible evidence." Also, through depositions of executives, opposing lawyers are able to probe for conversational and other oral communications that may have taken place. In fact, most lawsuits these days involve companies and individuals in the production of mammoth amounts of information, both through requests for the production of documents and through extensive depositions of prospective witnesses.

Some documents and conversations, however, need not be disclosed. These so-called privileged communications are those that transpire within the attorney-client relationship. They are protected from compulsory disclosure primarily in order to encourage clients to communicate freely with their attorneys and to promote voluntary compliance with the law. Our legal system, which encourages business people to seek attorneys' advice, could not advance that goal if clients feared that their confidential communications with their lawyers would be disclosed to others. As one court described this policy:

> In a society as complicated in structure as ours and governed by laws as complex and detailed as those imposed upon us, expert legal advice is essential. To the furnishing of such advice the fullest freedom and honesty of communication to pertinent facts is a prerequisite. To

"Communication and the Law" by Richard B. Sypher from *The Handbook of Executive Communication* by John L. DiGaetani. Copyright © 1986 by Dow Jones-Irwin. Reprinted by permission.

induce clients to make such communications, the privilege to prevent their later disclosure is said by courts and commentators to be a necessity. The social good derived from the proper performance of the functions of lawyers acting for their clients is believed to outweigh the harm that may come from the suppression of the evidence in specific cases.

United States v. *United Shoe Machinery Corp.*, 89 F. Supp. 357, 358 (D. Mass. 1950).

Not all attorney-client communications are thus privileged, however. The alert executive is thus well advised to be aware of exactly what sorts of legal communications may be protected by this privilege. The rule protects only those communications made in confidence by a client to an attorney for the purpose of obtaining legal advice.

What Is a "Communication"?

For purposes of the attorney-client privilege, a communication can be either oral or written (or even gestural, as in a nod or shake of the head in response to a question) so long as it is conveyed by the client to the attorney. An attorney's perceptions are not privileged; nor are documents given to the attorney for safekeeping. Because it is difficult if not impossible to separate a client's communications from the attorney's response, the attorney-client privilege also protects any communication of the attorney to the client that would implicitly disclose the content of the client's communications. As one court put it, "Ordinarily the compelled disclosure of an attorney's communications or advice to the client will effectively reveal the substance of the client's confidential communication to the attorney. To prevent this result, the privilege normally extends both to the substance of the client's communication as well as the attorney's ad-

vice in response thereto." *In re Fischel*, 557 F.2d 209, 211 (9th Cir. 1977).

What Is Meant by "in Confidence"?

The key distinction here is between the confidential *form* in which the information is conveyed and the confidential *nature* of the information itself. It is not necessary that the information be confidential, only that it was communicated in confidence. Such confidentiality must be intentional on the client's part, but if the communication is overheard or not carefully protected, the privilege may be lost. In a recent case, for example, a plaintiff's attorney found documents in the defendant's garbage. The documents, despite their confidentiality, were not protected by the attorney-client privilege. The court found that the intent of the defendants to maintain their confidentiality was belied by the lack of precautions they took with regard to them. *Suburban Sew 'N' Sweep Inc.* v. *Swiss Bernina Inc.*, 91 F.R.D. 254 (N.D. Ill. 1981).

By its very nature, confidentiality implies privacy and secrecy. Thus if others are present when the information is divulged, the communication will not be protected—unless the other persons are functionally vital to the parties. The presence of secretaries and other associates will not destroy the privilege, but the presence of adverse or neutral parties will.

What Is Meant by "to an Attorney"?

To be protected by the attorney-client privilege, the communication must be made to an attorney, namely, to a licensed lawyer acting in that capacity. In other words, not only must the parties to the communication bear the relationship of attorney and client, but the attorney must have been consulted by the client for the purpose of obtaining legal advice. The privilege applies equally to corporate counsel who provide regular legal advice within their companies and to outside counsel retained by a company for a particular purpose.

When an attorney acts in any capacity other than that of providing legal services or advice, nothing communicated to him is privileged. Attorneys frequently serve as business advisors, negotiators, agents, and personal friends of their clients. Unless the attorney is acting as a lawyer, however, communications involving the attorney are not privileged merely because he happens to be one.

What Is Meant by "by a Client"?

A client may be potential as well as already retained, corporate as well as individual. In the landmark case of *Upjohn Co.* v. *United States,* 449 U.S. 383 (1981), the United States Supreme Court clarified the corporate problem of determining which persons within a corporation could be deemed to represent the corporation for privilege purposes. Before *Upjohn,* communications had not been privileged if the employee communication was insufficiently identifiable with the corporate client.

The Confusion Before Upjohn. Before the *Upjohn* decision, the primary standard to evaluate a company employee's status as company representative in order to qualify for the attorney-client privilege concerned whether the employee was a member of the company's "control group," that is, whether the employee was empowered to substantially determine corporate behavior after receiving legal advice. Courts also considered the subject matter of the communication, including most importantly whether the employee was authorized to communicate the matter within the description of his or her normal duties.

The Upjohn Decision. In *Upjohn,* the company had instructed its attorneys, including both in-house and outside counsel, to investigate payments to foreign officials. A wide spectrum of Upjohn's employees had been questioned, and their responses were incorporated in the attorneys' notes and memoranda. When the Internal Revenue Service sought access to these papers, the company refused to comply on the ground of attorney-client privilege. Upjohn also refused to permit its employees to be deposed concerning the foreign payments.

The Supreme Court found that the communications were covered by the attorney-client privilege because: (a) they had been made to the company's counsel acting in that capacity; (b) they had been made at the direction of corporate officers; (c) they were made in order to gain legal advice and concerned matters within the normal scope of the employees' duties; (d) they were made in the awareness that their responses to the attorneys' questions were intended to produce legal advice for Upjohn. Although the Supreme Court in *Upjohn* explicitly declined to enunciate a general rule, these elements now seem necessary for employees' communications to come under the umbrella of the attorney-client privilege.

What Is Meant by "for the Purpose of Obtaining Legal Advice"?

A client's communication to an attorney is not privileged unless it is made in order to secure the attorney's legal advice. If the attorney is consulted merely to investigate facts and recommend business decisions, there is no protection under the attorney-client privilege, since the work involved could be performed by nonlawyers.

The legal advice sought can, however, be implied, so that even if the communications are themselves routine, they may be protected if they are part of an overall plan to keep the attorney apprised of facts—so long as their ultimate purpose is to gain the attorney's legal advice. Background data, however, are generally not protected.

Waiver of the Privilege

Assuming that all the constituent elements of the attorney-client privilege are satisfied, the privilege may still not be available where the client has disclosed the communication to third parties, whether voluntarily or through lack of sufficient precaution. Involuntary disclosures, such as those made through the loss or theft of confidential documents, are not protected, thus imposing on those who would invoke the privilege the burden of being cautious.

Protecting the Privilege

Because the attorney-client privilege may protect confidential documents from disclosure during litigation, a company is well-advised to incorporate communications systems that will preserve it. As a minimal precaution, legal personnel should be clearly identified in all table of organization, directories, and interoffice correspondence. Legal matters should be clearly identified as such and filed accordingly. Memoranda incorporating legal opinions—even when combined with business judgments and recommendations— should probably be characterized and identified as legal documents.

All such legal memoranda, as well as any documents or correspondence involving legal advice, should be distributed only to responsible executives or others who have a real need to be informed of their contents. Widespread distribution of legal memoranda can become the grounds for destroying whatever attorney-client privilege may be inherently available in them. Similarly, such documents should not ordinarily be distributed outside the company.

COMMUNICATION WITH EMPLOYEES

Companies should give a good deal of thought to the implications of establishing any policies regarding communications with their employees. On the one hand, it is obviously good employer-employee relations to communicate the company's policies with regard to such matters as hiring, termination, fringe benefits, and job security. On the other hand, because of the peculiar nature of employer-employee relations in the law, certain communications to employees may bind the company to contractual obligations it had no intention to make. For this reason, an employer should probably limit communication concerning the employer-employee relationship and the terms of the employment to those matters that the employer is willing potentially to be bound by.

Such considerations become particularly important in the context of discharging an employee. It is, of course, to management's advantage to retain the option of discharging employees at its own will. Traditionally, this has indeed been management's prerogative. It is still the case, despite union organization and the development of employment contracts for executives, that most American workers are employed for indefinite terms. This means that the employee may seek work elsewhere and resign his employment at any time; it also means that a company may terminate an employee at any time with or without cause relating to the employee's conduct on the job.

Such freedom of termination is not complete. Some federal and state statutes restrict an employer's ability to terminate at will. For example, the Taft-Hartley Act protects employees from being discharged for engaging in union activities. The Civil Rights Act similarly protects employees from discharge because of their age, race, color, religion, sex, or national origin. The Consumer Credit Protection Act prohibits an employer from discharging an employee because his wages are garnisheed. Nevertheless, most employees may be discharged at will, unless the employer has by representation in a contract made termination dependent upon particular acts or procedures.

In an effort to communicate effectively with employees, many companies produce and circulate personnel manuals. In some instances, these manuals articulate the employment policies followed by the company. If the company follows this course, however, it may find itself subject to a claim that the personnel manual constitutes an extension of an employment contract and binds the company to the terms stated therein. This method has in fact been adopted by courts in several U.S. jurisdictions to compromise the freedom of discharge in the usual employment arrangement. In 1980, for example, a California court determined that a discharged employee had an implied contract right to job security derived from a set of regulations, circulated by the employer, that dealt with discharge procedures. *Cleary* v. *American Airlines, Inc.*, 11 Cal. App.3d 443, 163, Cal. Rptr. 722 (1980).

In the same year, two employees sued Blue Cross and Blue Shield for breach of contract, alleging they had been fired without cause. Although they had no individual written contracts, the court sustained their suit, modifying the implied at-will employment relationship by inferring contractual obligations from provisions in the employee policy manual that provided a good cause standard for terminations and established procedural guidelines:

> We hold that employer statements of policy, such as the Blue Cross Supervisory Manual and Guidelines, can give rise to contractual rights in employees without evidence that the parties mutually agreed that the policy statements would create contractual rights in the employee, and, hence, although the statement of policy is signed by neither party, can be unilaterally amended by the employer without notice to the employee and contains no reference to a specific employee, his job description, or compensation and although no reference was made to the policy statement in pre-employment interviews and the employee does not learn of its existence until after his hiring.

Touissant v. *Blue Cross and Blue Shield*, 408 Mich. 579, 292 N.W.2d 880 (1980).

The *Touissant* court noted that an employer could protect himself from such contractual obligations by having each employee sign a written contract explicitly providing that the employment is at-will.

The legal concept underlying these cases is illustrated by a 1983 Minnesota case where the court held that an employer was bound by the terms of a procedure contained in an employee manual that is issued after the plaintiff was employed. The court based this conclusion on the concept that a personnel manual becomes part of an employee's contract if it meets the standards generally applied to contract formation. The court reasoned as follows:

> Generally speaking, a promise of employment on particular terms of unspecified duration, if in form an offer, and if accepted by the employee, may create a binding unilateral contract. The offer must be definite in form and must be communicated to the offeree. Whether a proposal is meant to be an offer or unilateral contract is determined by the outward manifestations of the parties, not by their subjective intentions. . . .
> [W]here an at-will employee retains em-

ployment with knowledge of new or changed conditions, the new or changed conditions may become a contractual obligation. In this manner, an original employment contract may be modified or replaced by a subsequent unilateral contract. The employee's retention of employment constitutes acceptance of the offer of a unilateral contract; by continuing to stay on the job, although free to leave, the employee supplies the necessary consideration for the offer.

Pine River State Bank v. *Mettile*, 333 N.W.2d 622, 626–27 (Minn. 1983).

The court was careful to point out that circulating the handbook was sufficient communication of the offer. The court recognized that writing separate contracts for individual employees would create enormous costs for the employer.

Such cases have raised serious questions concerning the desirability, until recently simply assumed, of communicating company policies to employees through policy manuals. Indeed, the implications of the cases are so broad that it is questionable whether an employer any longer can safely circulate handbooks, manuals, or other statements of company policy concerning discharge without creating contractual duties subject to a discharged employee's lawsuit. At the very least, it is clear that the greater the information disseminated to employees, the more likely the employer is binding himself to contractual obligations. Thus, an employer must decide whether the preservation of managerial discretion as to employee discharge is more or less important than the dissemination of information to employees.

The wave of recent court decision limiting the employer's freedom of discharge suggests that employers should take care even before an employee is with the company to insure

that recruiters and other hiring personnel do not make statements that may later provide a basis for a lawsuit against the company for wrongful discharge. Even oral representations made by recruiters eager to hire an attractive employee may later become the legitimate predicate for such a suit. Thus it seems advisable for hiring personnel to avoid overstating the prospects of the job, since an employee (and later, a court) may interpret such glowing promises as obligations of job security. Any language giving rise to expectations of continuous or permanent employment can return to haunt its maker.

Written employment applications should similarly be carefully drafted. A company may even wish to include in such an application a direct statement, to be acknowledged by the applicant, that the employment is to be considered terminable by the employer without cause. Indeed, such direct, up-front disclosure of the company's freedom to discharge at will may advance the cause of employee relations by avoiding the creation of unrealistic expectations on the part of the employee. An employment application may also include disclaimers of any oral representation made or thought to have been made by recruiters or others. In one case, the company avoided a suit for wrongful discharge on the basis of this disclaimer in the employment application, which had been signed by the employee:

I agree to conform to the rules and regulations of Sears, Roebuck & Co., and my employment and compensation can be terminated without cause, and with or without notice, at any time at the option of either the company or myself. I understand that no store manager or representative of Sears, Roebuck & Co., other than the president or vice president of the company, has any authority to enter into any agreement for employment for any specified period of time, or to make any agreement contrary to the foregoing.

Novosel v. *Sears, Roebuck & Co.* 495 F. Supp. 344 (E.D. Mich. 1980).

The desirability of personnel manuals is based on the concept of effective management communication. In the light of recent court decisions, however, such written personnel manuals must be carefully drafted with the understanding that they should never offer or promise more than the company intends to be bound by.

Recognizing that written policy manuals may be considered enforceable contractual obligations, employers should attempt to minimize this possibility. For example, such manuals or brochures should explicitly state that they are not contracts and that they give rise to no contractual obligations. A statement at the outset of a personnel manual that the company reserves its right to change the terms of the personnel manual would be another useful way to minimize liability. It could resemble the statement quoted above from the employment application. Stated negatively, companies should probably avoid phrases promising security or other terms that could be construed as benefits not intended by the employer.

General Motors, for example, took pains to avoid the possibility that its personnel manual would be interpreted as a contract between the company and its employees. At the beginning of the handbook, General Motors printed the following statement in italics, outlined by a red border:

The contents of the handbook are presented as a matter of information only. While General Motors believes wholeheartedly in the plans, policies, and procedures described here, they are not conditions of employment. General Motors reserves the right to modify, revoke, suspend, terminate, or change any or all such plan, policies, or procedures, in whole or in part, at any time, with or without notice. The language used in this handbook is not intended to create, nor is it to be construed to constitute, a contract between General Motors and any one or all employees.

Kari v. *General Motors Corp.*, 79 Mich. App. 93, 261 N.W.2d 222 (1977), *rev'd* 402 Mich. 926, 282 N.W.2d 925 (1978).

Furthermore, most companies have regular procedures for evaluating their employees, many of which are committed to writing. If a company uses such evaluation forms, evaluators should make sure that they do not include in any such form an implied promise of promotion or even of retention of the employee, unless that company wishes to be so committed. For example, if the company desires to discharge an employee who has received nothing but glowing comments and evaluations, it is unlikely that a court will be sympathetic if the employee later sues for wrongful discharge. Supervisors need to be careful not to use such evaluation forms simply to avoid friction among employees or to justify an automatic raise.

In fact, straightforward job evaluations not only shed light on employee problems at an early stage, but can also avoid the later impression that an employee has been performing better than he or she actually has. In short, performance appraisals should conform to the truth of the situation. They should be objective, based on first hand observation, clearly and openly expressed, and subject to a procedure for review. If communication is clear and honest with regard to employee evaluations, litigation may be avoided.

Communicate:
The Power of One-on-One

Robert W. Goddard

Informed employees make for a more productive workforce. Because of this, managers agree that employees should be well informed about their job, department and company.

This is especially true in today's workplace. In 1982, the Public Agenda Foundation interviewed a random sample of 845 employees nationwide to better understand the fundamental changes in job values transforming the workplace. The study also isolated the factors that improve employee productivity.

The employees were asked to rate 46 job qualities on a scale of importance. Their responses indicate they desire connectedness that goes beyond the external rewards of work. "Working with people who treat me with respect" was considered a very important job value by 88 percent of the participants; "Working for people who listen if you have ideas about how to do things better" was considered very important by 83 percent; and "Feeling well-informed about what is going on" by 78 percent.

Unfortunately, these needs are not being met very well, according to surveys. In a recent four-year study of employees' perspectives on their jobs and companies, the Opinion Research Corp. discovered growing dissatisfaction with organizational communications.

More than 50 percent of the 30,000 managers, professionals, and clerical personnel surveyed said that management is losing

touch with employees. Sixty percent believed their companies are not doing a good job of keeping them informed about company matters. The majority give supervisors an unfavorable rating on providing them with the information they need to do a good job. Fewer than 30 percent of the employees and less than half of the managers in the study feel their companies are willing to listen to their problems.

Adding fuel to the fire, management consultants Towers, Perrin, Forster & Crosby polled 10,000 U.S. and Canadian employees on their current and preferred sources of organizational information. The 1984 findings indicate that many organizations are misusing or underusing their most effective communication channels (*see chart*).

ONE-ON-ONE

Apparently, most of us rate personalized, face-to-face communication as the most preferred (and, by inference, most credible) source of organizational information, with internal print media a strong, but less effective, alternative. Interestingly, mass meetings and audio-visual programs rank low, despite the common management belief that the bigger the audience the more effective the communication. Thus, the believability of a source has little to do with its size, cost, or accessibility, and the best communication is a trusted person-to-person communication.

To understand how difficult and dangerous the communication process can be, consider the perceptual problem. Management expert Peter Drucker and others correctly point out that "downward" communication does not work, primarily because it focuses on what *we* want to say rather than on what

Sources of organizational information			
Preferred Rank	Source	Major Source For	Current Rank
1	Immediate supervisor	92.3%	1
2	Small group meetings	63.0%	3
3	Top executives	55.5%	10
4	Annual employee business report	45.8%	8
5	Employee booklets	41.2%	5
6	Orientation program	41.1%	11
7	Local employee publication	40.4%	7
8	General employee publication	38.5%	6
9	Bulletin board(s)	37.1%	4
10	Upward communication programs	33.8%	15
11	Mass meetings	30.3%	9
12	Audio-visual programs	23.2%	14
13	Union	20.4%	12
14	Grapevine	10.5%	2
15	Mass media	8.8%	13

the audience needs and wants to know. It ignores the fact that the recipient's perceptions control the outcome of the communication process. If we continually focus on the message without regard for how it is being received, we unintentionally create a huge problem for everyone.

Drucker argues that downward communication can work only *after* it has been informed and shaped by upward communication. In other words, downward communication is a response to the values, beliefs, and aspirations of those who are receiving the message. If management ignores or does not understand these principles, downward communication will not connect with its audience in a way that fosters shared perceptions of reality.

With this in mind, let's look at how managers can improve their employee communications.

Possibly the greatest need that people have at work is the need to understand work's meaning and their role in the scheme of things. In North America, we are our work. This helps explain why our need for information on the job and for human reaction and interaction are so intense. They are gut-level requirements.

Some fascinating work conducted a few years ago by Texas Instruments indicates that employees have certain job needs, and they follow a predictable pattern. In the beginning, they have a consuming need for job mastery. This is followed by the need to know the rules of the organization. Once that is satisfied, they want some evidence, no matter how skimpy or tentative, that they are appreciated, they are members in good standing of the organization, and they are, in fact, loved. Only when people attain this level of satisfaction on the job are they ready to give their allegiance, talents, and energy with little or no reservation.

CONSISTENT AND CREDIBLE

Everything you do and say transmits a message about you and what you value. Perhaps the most dangerous communication trap faced by managers is the naive belief that only words communicate. The truth is that words probably communicate least of all. Policy, personal mannerisms and style, decisions, significant and insignificant, departmental and corporate actions all speak volumes about the manager and the organization. When words and actions have little relationship to one another, we create a disordered and deranged situation that confounds people's ability to understand things around them. That's why consistency is important.

This means establishing credibility and trust with the employee, and recognizing the employee's humanity, personal rights, and dignity. We must be open and honest in our communications in our daily transactions with our associates and work group.

Perhaps most of all we must recognize and serve the human needs of our employees with some expression of love and concern. This could involve intense listening, a pat on the back, or having the guts to say, "I'm sorry." The possibilities are endless.

FILLING ROLES

In the emerging world of knowledge work, information is the raw material people need to perform their jobs. Managers must be planners, counselors, coaches, psychologists, and even philosophers. They must be able to define work, review progress, and function as a pressure valve. They must manage compromise and conflict, balance the needs of a number of intelligent and articulate followers, and turn frustration and hostility into problem-solving energy.

To begin in these roles, sit down with employees and determine if they know why they are on the payroll, if they truly understand the work group's goal, and if they are aware of what the group's priorities are. Periodically review such matters as goals and priorities with your employees, and keep them posted on their individual and collective progress in meeting those goals.

Serve as a pressure buffer between the organization and the individual, and maintain a reasonable work climate for your people. Be alert for what comes from others, and accommodate that input. Pay close attention to the tasks of employee development and performance review. Be prepared to take all the personal risks and the occasional pain that accompany close involvement with other human beings.

A few years ago a large midwestern company asked its self-described "highly motivated" people to assess their supervisors' behavior. The responses are enlightening:

- easy to talk to even when under pressure;
- tries to see merit in your ideas, even if they conflict with his or her own;
- tries to help people understand company objectives;
- tries to give people all the information they want;
- has consistently high expectations of subordinates;
- tries to encourage people to reach out in new directions;
- takes your mistakes in stride, so long as you learn from them;
- tries mainly to correct mistakes and avoid them in the future; and
- expects superior performance and gives credit when you do it.

Managers must maintain lines of communication with all layers of a work group. They may also encourage feedback on employee concerns and perceptions of company and departmental goals, strategy, and performance. We need a reliable system for checking the quality of the information we are getting.

The system should include a genuine open-door policy; regular staff meetings to impart information and resolve problems; active solicitation of complaints and suggestions for improvement, meaningful participation of employees in decisions affecting their work; regular feedback on their performance; and constant recognition of achievement. Dropping in on people—or "management by walking around"—should be integral to the process.

Managers should have the training and skill necessary to orient new employees about the organization and jobs, to instruct them in specific job functions, and to resolve individual conflict.

Employees also should understand the importance of their roles in acting as surro-gate communicators for us and in providing us with accurate reports of what people are saying and thinking.

Good communication, after all, is shared perceptions which do not come painlessly. They are normally the product of dialogue and experience. Communication media cannot accomplish this kind of human interchange. They can reinforce it, enlarge it, interpret it, but they can't supplant it. However, this is what many organizations are trying to do in their communications programs, and it simply isn't working.

Business-communications consultant Stanley Peterfreund has found that the average employee has little information about his or her company. Peterfreund also found that employees who *feel* better informed have consistently more favorable attitudes about virtually every phase of their worklives than those who consider themselves uninformed.

Brief Guide to Usage

In preparing a speech, writing a report, or composing a letter, all of us, from time to time, have to stop and check on the correctness of a punctuation mark, the spelling of a word, or the grammar of a sentence.

The sections that follow may be used as a quick reference guide. There are many excellent texts and handbooks available that offer a more comprehensive discussion of the areas of diction and grammar.

PUNCTUATION

Use a Comma:

1. To set off an introductory phrase or subordinate clause from the independent statement.

    When I entered the crowded assembly hall, I immediately noted the presence of armed guards in the gallery overlooking the stage.

2. Before the coordinating conjunction (*and, or, but, for, yet,* or *nor*) linking two independent clauses. If the independent clauses are very short, the comma may be omitted.

    Key management personnel in the organization should be carefully selected, and all managers should be informed of their responsibilities.

    Barry shouted and Betsy turned.

3. To set off nonrestrictive (or nonessential) phrases or clauses.

    Dr. John Kelly, who taught philosophy for 25 years, received frequent commendation from students and faculty.

    The present chairman of the board, as you may or may not know, began as a stockboy with this firm 41 years ago.

4. To set off phrases or words in apposition.

    Mrs. Spear, fashion director for Century Clothes, was elected president of the Designers' Association.

5. To set off a name directly addressed.

    If you will write me at your earliest convenience, Mr. Barclay, I'll arrange a tour for your group.

6. To set off a mild interjection.

    Oh, I didn't want you to purchase a new one.

7. To separate adjectives in a series when they modify the same noun.

   They were young, promising, enthusiastic athletes.

8. To separate words or short phrases in a series.

   The sofa was clean and uncluttered, inexpensive but not cheap, and colorful but not garish.

9. To set off a quotation from the reference source in a sentence.

   "I shall arrive in Los Angeles before midnight," said Mrs. Kelley.

10. To indicate the omission of a word or words (usually a verbal form).

    Buckingham Way has been renamed Washington Street; Devonshire Place, Adams Avenue; and Kavenaugh Way, Jefferson Street.

11. To avoid confusion in interpretation or to assist in reading a sentence correctly.

    That that is, is; that that is not, is not.

Use a Semicolon:

1. Between coordinate, independent clauses not joined by a conjunction.

   Mrs. Spear submitted her monthly report; it was accepted without comment.

2. Before a conjunctive adverb (*hence, however, therefore, consequently, inasmuch as*) joining two coordinate clauses.

   The girls enjoyed their vacation; however, their funds were badly depleted by the end of the second week.

3. Before a coordinating conjunction joining two independent clauses if the clauses are very long or have commas in them.

   When the race, which has been held every year since 1925, was scheduled, we had 22 contestants; but 5 additional entrants paid their fees to the official registrar, who immediately issued a verified certificate.

Use a Colon:

1. To introduce a list, a statement, a question, a series of statements, a quotation, and in some cases, a word.

   Each person should bring the following equipment: one sleeping bag, hiking boots, rainwear, a small shovel, and heavy outdoor clothes.

2. Before or after a specific illustration of a general statement.

   In the first week he broke a turning rod, dropped a glass test kit, and tore a rubber protection sheet: he was an extremely negligent worker.

   Winter arrived with a sudden fury: the temperature dropped to 15° below zero, six inches of snow fell, and the wind howled violently.

3. Following the salutation in a business letter.

   Dear Mr. Anderson:

Use a Dash:

1. To set off—and emphasize—parenthetical material.

   Rolsted—you know he had worked for us since the 1950s—retired in June.

2. To indicate when the idea in a sentence has been broken off abruptly.

   Do you believe that—

3. To indicate a sudden change in thought within a sentence.

   Do you believe that—no, I'm sure you would never accept it.

4. To precede a summarizing statement at the end of a sentence.

   Magazines were everywhere, the record player was on, clothes were tossed helter-skelter, food disappeared like magic, laughter filled the air—the kids were home for the weekend.

Use Parentheses:

1. To enclose ideas not directly related to the main thought of the sentence.

   Compton's periodic reports (following the format recommended by the National Trade Council) were submitted by all department managers.

2. To enclose a numerical designation of a verbal statement. This is sometimes found in legal documentation.

   The escrow deposit of five hundred dollars ($500.00) will not be refunded except through court order.

Use Brackets:

1. To enclose an explanatory comment within a quotation or to insert a correction into quoted material.

   In her article on political upsets, Sarah stated, "Martin was defeated in the election of 1956 [he was defeated in 1952], and this marked the end of 36 years of Democratic treasurers in Wade County."

Use Italics (Designated in Typing by Underlining):

1. To indicate the titles of books, plays, journals, long financial documents and reports, movies, and newspapers.

   We read *Theories of Management* before seeing the film *Listening: A Key to Problem Solving*.

One article in the *Los Angeles Times* referred to the E.P.A. report, *Hazardous Waste Removal Techniques.*

2. To identify foreign words and phrases.

We simply could not say *adieu* as the French said it.

3. To give words and phrases special emphasis.

On the contrary, I instructed you *not* to reveal the ingredients of our product before testing was completed.

4. To call attention to words as words.

Your letter uses *I* more often than *you* and *me.*

Use Quotation Marks:

1. To enclose direct quotations.

Sally said, "People don't change; their basic characteristics remain the same throughout their lives."

"I don't agree," said Marty.

2. At the beginning of each paragraph and the end of the last paragraph in a quoted passage.

3. To enclose a quotation within a quotation. The initial quotation is enclosed in double quotation marks; the quotation within that in single; and a quote within that one in double.

Stevenson said, "If we are to live in peace, we must, as the Israeli representative has indicated, 'Appreciate the dignity of all people at all times.' "

The professor said, "All groups have the same pleasure values, although Carter disagrees with this when he says, 'Entertainment values are not the same for all age groups; a "trip" to some is attractive; to others, repulsive.' "

4. To enclose titles of articles, chapters in a book, or any part of a whole unit such as an opera, play, book, or magazine.

Thomas Carton wrote the article, "The Problems of International Finance," which recently appeared in *The Financial Quarterly.*

5. To enclose a question mark or exclamation point if it refers to the quotation. Place the quotation mark or exclamation point outside the last quotation mark if it applies to the statement as a whole.

Dr. Martin asked, "Isn't that their usual performance?"

Did Dr. Jameson say, "The students completed work at a very high level"?

Did you say, "Will all of them receive their degrees in June"?

Dr. Meloan asked, "Did you write the article, 'Communication and Decision Making'?"

Kelly replied, "No, I did not, but I did submit one to *The Journal of Communication* titled, 'Is There a Relationship Between War and Words?' "

Special Note

In using marks of punctuation with quotations or quoted words or statements, remember:

1. That commas and periods are almost invariably placed *within* quotation marks.
2. That semicolons and colons are almost invariably placed *outside* quotation marks.
3. That question marks, exclamation points, and dashes are placed *within* the quotation marks when they apply to the quoted material, *outside* when they refer to the whole statement.

Use a Hyphen:

1. To divide a word at the end of a line.
2. To form compound nouns, verbs, and adjectives.

    Mrs. Lyons was my mother-in-law.

    He got angry when he saw that I had double-spaced the letter.

    He is not a well-known artist.

Use an Ellipsis:

1. To indicate the omission of a part of a sentence. Use three periods if the omission is within the sentence. If the omission is at the end of the sentence, use four periods.

    The transaction was completed . . . and provided for Garson to receive the car plus miscellaneous items. . . .

Use an Exclamation Point:

After statements of very strong or sudden emotion.

    "I will not!" he almost shouted.

    Stop that noise!

(See also the section on quotation marks for placement of this mark.)

Use a Question Mark:

1. After a direct, but not an indirect, question.

    Have you completed your analysis of the Compton Company case?

    He asked if we were coming.

2. A question mark is not followed by a comma, period, or semicolon when used in a quotation.

   Glenn said, "Will you drive or shall I?"

(See also the section on quotation marks for placement of this mark.)

Use a Period:

1. After a complete declarative or imperative sentence.

   Effective communication is a vital management tool.
2. To indicate an abbreviation.

   He worked for Kingston, Inc. for over ten years.

Use an Apostrophe:

1. To indicate the omission of one or more letters in a contraction or one or more digits in a numeral.

   He hasn't been home since he graduated in '70.
2. To indicate the plural of letters, figures, or words. (Usage varies. The apostrophe is often omitted where there is no chance of confusion.)

   Betsy received three A's and two B's on her report card.

   His essay contained one sentence with three *and*'s in it (or *ands*).

   Her *l*'s always looked like *t*'s.

   She belongs to the Gay '90's (or '90s).
3. To form the possessive case of nouns.

   The three boys' jackets were red.

   He purchased a dollar's worth of candy.

   That was my aunt's coat.

   The men's tools were left behind.

Notes

If the word in question already ends in *s*, add only an apostrophe; if it does not, add *'s*.

The girl's coat was green.   The girls' coats were green.

On the whole it is best to avoid the use of possessives with inanimate objects; e.g., *sink's top, lamp's cord,* or *chair's leg. Sink top, lamp cord,* and *chair leg* are standard.

Additional Uses of the Apostrophe to Indicate Possession

1. If two or more persons or objects own one item, possession is indicated on the last named only. If the writer wishes to indicate individual possession, an apostrophe is used with each name or object.

   Robin and Shelley's car. (Robin and Shelley own one car in partnership.)

   Robin and Shelley's cars. (Robin and Shelley own more than one car in partnership.

   Robin's and Shelley's cars. (Robin and Shelley each own one or more cars individually.)

2. In compound words, an apostrophe is added to the secondary or last word to indicate possession.

   My brother-in-law's car was damaged in the accident (singular possessive).

   My brothers-in-law's cars were all parked in front of the house (plural possessive).

3. Certain phrases involving time that seem to express possession use the apostrophe.

   A month's pay was granted.

   Three hours' time is not adequate for the job.

   His dream was to take four weeks' vacation in Hawaii. (Or *a four-week vacation.*)

4. The apostrophe is used to indicate possession with indefinite pronouns.

   One's thoughts are sometimes private.

   Anybody's ideas are acceptable in this brainstorming session.

5. Where an appositive is used, possession is indicated on it, rather than the basic word.

   That is Mr. Carson, the janitor's, responsibility.

6. Possession is indicated on the *junior* or *senior.*

   Martin Kelly, Jr.'s, coat was a plaid.

   Thomas Kale, Sr.'s, store was sold.

7. When one-syllable words, especially names, end in s, and possession is to be indicated, an 's should be added. If the basic word has more than one syllable and ends in s, usage varies. Either 's or simply an apostrophe can be added.

   Mr. Jones's car is new.

   Charles' (or Charles's) coat is lost.

8. Pronouns in the possessive case do *not* use the apostrophe to indicate ownership; such words are already possessive.

   The radio is hers.

   The chair is yours, but the table is ours.

Its surface was scratched, but it's (this is a contraction of *it is,* not the possessive pronoun) really of no great importance.

PRONOUNS

Pronouns take the place of nouns and permit us to avoid constant repetition.

1. Pronouns agree in person, number, and gender with the word to which they refer (antecedent).

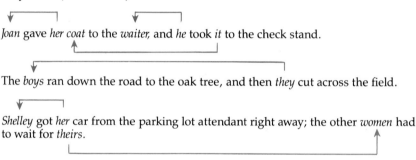

Joan gave *her coat* to the *waiter,* and *he* took *it* to the check stand.

The *boys* ran down the road to the oak tree, and then *they* cut across the field.

Shelley got *her* car from the parking lot attendant right away; the other *women* had to wait for *theirs.*

2. Use a singular pronoun for antecedents connected by *or* or *nor.* Note that the pronoun refers to one or the other antecedent singly, not to both collectively.

   Shelley or Betsy will give you her key if you arrive before noon.

   A rake or a hoe will serve no purpose if its handle is broken.

   Neither Mr. Carleton nor Mr. Frank will give you his advice without an assurance of confidence.

3. The pronoun should be plural if the antecedents are connected by *and.*

   The car and the train blew their horns simultaneously.

   Barnes and Blackwell gave their briefcases to the messenger.

4. When two antecedents are simply different names for the same person, the pronoun is singular.

   The professor and conference leader received a scroll for his efforts.

5. When two antecedents refer to different persons, the pronoun is plural.

   Usually the second reference is preceded by *the.*

   The professor and the conference leader received scrolls for their efforts.

6. When two or more antecedents are closely associated by usage or practice, a singular pronoun is used.

   Tea and toast has its place in a convalescent's diet.

7. Antecedent nouns take either a singular or plural pronoun, according to the sense of the sentence or the idea to be conveyed.

The jury reached its verdict (one verdict coming from one jury).

The jury put on their hats and coats and left for home.

8. The words that follow, when used as antecedents, should take singular pronouns. More and more frequently, however, many of them are being interpreted as plural.

anybody	someone	nobody
neither	none	any
either	everyone	one
each	somebody	another
everybody		

Neither of the men paid *his* bill.

Everybody in the room has *his* or *her* own opinion.

None of the girls had *her* paper completed. (*or*) None of the girls had *their* papers completed.

Note that the sentences above really say, *Neither one of the men; Every single body in the room; Not one of the girls.*

Personal Pronouns

The choice between *I* and *me, she* and *her, they* and *them* sometimes causes confusion. Each of the following explanations includes the standard grammar rule as well as a short-cut method. To begin, let us review the pronouns in the objective and subjective cases.

	SINGULAR	PLURAL
Subjective or nominative case	*I, you, he, she, it*	*we, you, they*
Objective case	*me, you, him her, it*	*us, you, them*

Nominative Case

1. A pronoun takes the nominative or subjective case when it serves as the subject of a sentence or a clause.

Betty, Dorothy, and I (not *me*) have made arrangements for the party.

Short-cut method: Would you say, "*I* have made arrangements" or "*me* have made arrangements"? Certainly you would choose the former.

Mr. Kelly and I (not *me*) were selected.

Short-cut method: Would you say, "*I* was selected," or "*me* was selected"? Certainly you would choose "*I* was selected."

2. A pronoun completing the meaning of a connective verb or predicate complement (*am, is, are, was, were, be, been,* or *will be*) should be in the nominative case.

> It was *he* who was selected.

> I believe it is *she* who should receive the award.

3. When the pronoun is the subject of an implied verb, the nominative or subjective case should be used.

> He is quicker than I (not *me*).

> Short-cut method: Would you say, "He is quicker than *me* am quick," or "He is quicker than *I* am quick"?

> He did more for the church than they (not *them*).

> Short-cut method: Would you say, "He did more for the church than *they* did for the church" or "He did more for the church than *them* did for the church"?

Objective Case

A pronoun in the objective case is chosen when it is the object of a verb or a preposition or when it serves as an indirect object.

> He mailed the books to Bob, John, and me (not *I*).

> Short-cut method: Would you say, "He mailed the books to *I*" or "He mailed the books to *me*"? Certainly, it is the second.

> He called Miss Johnson, Miss Short, and me (not *I*).

> Short-cut method: Would you say, "He called *I*" or "He called *me*"? Obviously, the second sounds better.

Relative Pronouns

Some of the more frequently used relative pronouns are *who, whom, which, what* and *that*. The two that are often confused are *who* and *whom*. However, informal usage seems to be accepting *who* for *whom* more and more.

Subjective Case—*Who*

Who, like personal pronouns in the subjective case, is used as the subject of a sentence or a clause.

> Miss Costello is a girl who (not *whom*) I am sure will do well.

> Short-cut method: Would you say, "I am sure *she* will do well" or "I am sure *her* will do well"? Certainly "*she* will do well" sounds better than "*her* will do well." Inasmuch as *she* and *who* are both in the same case, the sentence must be "Miss Costello is a girl *who* I am sure will do well."

Objective Case—*Whom*

Whom, like the personal pronouns in the objective case, is used as the object of the verb or preposition or an indirect object.

The soldier whom (not *who*) she loved has been sent overseas.

Short-cut method: Would you say, "She loved *he*" or "she loved *him*"? Obviously "she loved *him*" sounds better than "she loved *he*." Because *whom* and *him* are both in the same case, the sentence must be "The soldier *whom* she loved has been sent overseas."

Miss Colgate is the girl to whom (not *who*) we gave the award.

Short-cut method: Would you say, "We gave the award to *she*" or "we gave the award to *her*"? Because *her* and *whom* are both in the objective case, the sentence must be "Miss Colgate is the girl to *whom* we gave the award."

Whoever and Whomever

Whoever is in the subjective case and *whomever* is the objective case. Their use follows the same principles as for *who* and *whom*.

The company will award contracts to whomever (not *whoever*) they find acceptable.

Short-cut method: Would you prefer "They find *they* acceptable" or "they find *them* acceptable"? The second choice is better and because *them* and *whomever* are in the same case, the sentence must be "The company will award contracts to *whomever* they find acceptable."

Mrs. Taylor, Miss Jones, and whoever (not *whomever*) else is selected will vacation in England.

Short-cut method: Would you say, "*She* is selected" or "*her* is selected"? Certainly it would be "*she* is selected" and because *she* and *whoever* are in the same case, the sentence must be "Mrs. Taylor, Miss Jones, and *whoever* else is selected will vacation in England."

PLURALS

Form the plural of most nouns by adding -*s*:

report   reports   page   pages

Mr. and Mrs. Brown   the Browns

editor-in-chief   editors-in-chief

Nouns ending in -*f* or -*fe* change their final letters to -*ve* before adding the -s:

leaf   leaves   life   lives

Nouns ending in -*y* after a consonant change their final letter to an -*i* before adding -*es*:

lady   ladies   buddy   buddies

Nouns ending in -*o* form their plural by adding -*es*. In some cases, such nouns add only -*s*. Check a dictionary when in doubt.

hero   heroes   veto   vetoes

solo   solos   memo   memos

auto   autos   zero   zeros/zeroes

Some nouns form irregular plurals:

ox   oxen   child   children

goose   geese   thesis   theses

alga   algae   fungus   fungi

Lower case letters and abbreviations form the plural by adding an apostrophe, then an -s:

c's   R.F.P.'s

When the practice causes no confusion, the plural of such letters and abbreviations often omits the apostrophe:

three Bs   the VIPs

CAPITALIZATION

1. Capitalize the first letter in the opening word in a sentence, a direct quotation, or each line of verse.

    He was an outstanding student.

    Mr. Boynton said, "Effective communication is the executive's primary management tool."

    My heart leaps up when I behold
       A rainbow in the sky:
    So was it when my life began;
    So it is now I am a man:
    So be it when I shall grow old,
       Or let me die!

2. Titles that precede names are capitalized.

    Senator Birmingham   Aunt Anna
    President Adams   Commissioner Baxter

3. Names of national groups, races, languages, or similar designations are capitalized.

    French   Israelis   Canadians   English

4. Names of holidays, days of the week, holy days, and months of the year begin with a capital letter.

    Veterans' Day   Rosh Hashanah
    Wednesday   June
    Good Friday

5. Capitalize the first letter in words which designate names of historical periods, treaties, laws, government departments, conferences, commissions, and so on.

    Renaissance   United States Supreme Court
    Clayton Act   Bill of Rights

6. Capitalize the first letter in words which refer to names, national or international organizations, or documents.

   House of Representatives
   Drug Council of the International Medical Association
   World Council of Churches

7. Capitalize the first letter of a noun referring to a deity, a Bible, or other religious reference sources.

   The Bible, the Koran, and the Torah   Allah
   the Congregation of the Missions   God, Lord, and the Almighty
   Capitalize pronouns referring to a deity only in biblical extracts or to avoid ambiguity.

   God in His mercy

8. The first letter of each important word is capitalized in titles of magazines, books, essays, plays, and so on. Short prepositions, articles, and adverbs in such titles are not, except as first word.

   Journal of Business Communication   *The Taming of the Shrew*
   An Analysis of Government Taxation   *My Fair Lady*
   The Decline and Fall of the Roman Empire

9. Capitalize a general term that is part of a name: Santa Fe Railroad.

   Southern College of Arts and Sciences   Baptist Church
   New Horizons Psychedelic Temple   Hudson River

10. Although words which refer to directions are not capitalized, words derived from directional terms are. Names of geographical areas or directional terms that refer to parts of a nation or the world are also capitalized.

    a path directly northwest of the tower

    Far East   Wild West   Orient   a Southerner

MODIFICATION

Placement of words *matters* in effective business writing. Readers can be misled when a word or group of words accidentally stands in an incorrect relation to the word it describes (or "modifies").

   Unclear: Considering a low-risk investment, the municipal bonds appealed to Frank.

The modifying phrase *considering a low-risk investment* should stand near "Frank," the word it modifies.

   Clear: Frank, who considered making a low-risk investment, favored municipal bonds.

Such "dangling" or "misplaced" modifiers can occur at the beginning, end, or interior parts of a sentence:

Unclear: Besides offering sales bonuses, a company car was part of the deal described by the manager.

Unclear: The cake was delivered to the office decorated with candles.

Unclear: Sarah promised in May to review my performance.

Notice how each of these unclear statements can be clarified by proper placement of modifying words:

Clear: Besides offering sales bonuses, the manager included a company car in the deal.

Clear: The cake, decorated with candles, was delivered to the office.

Clear: In May, Sarah promised to review my performance.

or

Sarah promised to review my performance in May.

EXPRESSING NUMBERS

Should numbers be expressed in figures or words in written communication? To help solve this question, a number of general rules have been established.

1. When several numbers are used in one sentence and they are all above ten, use figures. If they are below ten, write them out. If a sentence begins with a number, write it out. However, it is usually wiser to revise the sentence.

    We shipped 75 chairs, 90 tables, 32 lamps, and 32 pictures.

    You have requested two rugs, three TV sets, and eight area rugs.

    Seventy-five chairs, 90 tables, 32 lamps, and 32 pictures were shipped on December 3.

    On December 3 we shipped 75 chairs, 90 tables, 32 lamps, and 32 pictures.

2. When some numbers above ten and some below are used in one sentence, follow one pattern for consistency. Round numbers over ten are usually written out.

    He owned three shares of AT&T, seven shares of Sears, and fifty-five shares of Zenith.

    The Scouts consumed 8 pies, 7 chickens, 8 quarts of milk, and 32 bottles of soda.

    He made two great throws, one of sixty feet and the other of fifty-five.

3. When two numbers are used in different contexts in the same sentence, one should be written out and the other indicated in numerals.

    The thirty-man team canvassed more than 50,000 homes.

4. When one number immediately follows another, express the smaller in words, the larger in numerals.

He purchased five 59-cent notebooks for use in his spring quarter classes.

5. Place a comma between two unrelated numbers when they immediately follow each other.

In 1975, 95 supersonic aircraft were available for commercial use.

Dates

1. Write out the month when expressing a date.

June 27, 1979

27 June 1979

It is strongly recommended that numerals for both month and day not be used. Although American custom is to place the month first and then the day, the reverse is true in many countries of the world.

1–4–78   Preferred: January 4, 1978

3/7/78   Preferred: March 7, 1978 or 7 March 1978

2. Only use *nd, rd, st,* or *th* with the day of the month when that day precedes the month or stands by itself.

She became engaged on the 4th of January.

In your order of the 2nd, you did not list the colors desired.

Your shipment of the 1st was lost in transit.

Please mail your check by March 28.

Addresses

1. Street numbers should always be expressed as numerals except one, which should be written out.

One East Wilshire   2157 South Topeka Avenue

10 North Roscomare Road

2. Use words for streets from one to ten inclusive; use numerals after ten. The letters *nd, rd, st,* or *th* may be used with numerals.

2115 West Fifth Avenue   210 North 19th Street

3. When a number is used as a street name, use a dash to separate it from the street number only if a street direction is not included.

210–10th Street   205 North 41st Street

Amounts of Money

1. All sums of money, domestic or foreign, should be presented in figures.

   Johnson paid $155.60 for the merchandise.

   It is difficult for me to convert £275 into dollars.

2. For sums of less than a dollar, follow the figure with the word *cents* or the cent sign (¢); an alternative is to use the dollar sign with a decimal point.

   It cost 25 cents.   It wasn't worth 65¢.   Tom paid $.75 for the ball.

3. When expressing even or round sums of money, omit the decimal and zeros.

   His payment was $275.

4. In legal statements the numerals should be enclosed by parentheses and the sum written out.

   A firm offer for the car of seven hundred forty dollars ($740) is hereby made.

Decimals and Fractions

1. When a decimal fraction begins with a zero, do not place a zero before the decimal. If the decimal fraction begins with a whole number—precede the decimal with a zero.

   .04683   0.1746

2. Simple fractions are written out. When whole numbers and fractions make up one unit, a decimal is used only for fractions in decimal notation.

   It took him one half hour.

   It was 25.5 feet long.

   It was 25½ feet long.

Miscellaneous Quantities, Units, and Measurements

1. Distance: Use numbers unless the amount is less than a mile.

   We were one third of a mile from the house.

   It is 9 miles to Kingston and 350 miles from there to Prampton.

2. Financial quotations: Use numerals.

   IBM stock hit 56⅞ this afternoon.

3. Arithmetical expressions: Use numerals.

   Multiply 70 by 44 and you will have the area of the house in square feet.

4. Measurement: Use numerals.

   He quickly found that 15 kilometers did not equal 16 yards.

5. Specific numbers: Use numerals.

The engine number was 4638147.   Write for Training Manual 255.

6. Time: Use numerals except when the word *o'clock* is used.

The plane leaves at 7:17 P.M.   He is due to arrive at ten o'clock.

7. Dimensions: Use numerals with either × or *by.*

The room measured 10 × 15 ft.

The trim size of the annual report was 8½ by 11 in.

8. Age: Use numerals except where approximations are used.

She became 21 and got engaged on the same day.

I would say that he's about seventy years old.

For your information, Bob is exactly 3 years and 6 months old today.

9. Government units: Write out such expressions as congressional units or districts.

He served in the Eighty-seventh Congress and represented the Tenth Congressional District of the state.

10. Book or magazine references: Major units or divisions are indicated by Roman numerals; minor units by Arabic numbers.

He found the reference in Volume XX, number 4, of the *Journal of Communication.*

You will find Figure 4 next to Table 7 on page 83 of Section 4.

WORDS FREQUENTLY CONFUSED

Accede: to comply with
Exceed: to go beyond

Accent: to stress or emphasize; a regional manner of speaking.
Ascent: a rising or going up.
Assent: to agree; agreement.

Accept: to receive, to give an affirmative answer to.
Except: to exclude; to leave out; to omit.

Access: admittance or admission.
Excess: surplus or more than necessary.

Accidentally:
Incidentally: in both cases, the *-ly* ending is added to the adjective forms, *accidental* and *incidental,* and not the noun forms, *accident* and *incident.*

Ad: abbreviation for advertisement.
Add: to join; to unite; to sum.

Adapt: to accustom oneself to a situation.
Adept: proficient or competent in performing a task.
Adopt: to take by choice; to put into practice.

Advice: counsel; a recommendation (noun).
Advise: to suggest; to recommend (verb).

Affect: to influence (verb).
Effect: result or consequence (noun).
Effect: to bring about (verb).

Aggravate: to increase; to intensify; to make more severe.
Irritate: to exasperate or bother.

Allot: to distribute.
A lot: much or many.

All ready: prepared.
Already: previously.

All right: completely right.
Alright: an incorrect usage of *all right*.

Allusion: a reference to something familiar.
Illusion: an *image* of an object; a false impression.
Delusion: a false belief.

Almost: nearly; only a little less than.
Most: an informal use of *almost*; correctly, it means greatest in quantity or the majority of.

Altar: a place to worship or pray.
Alter: to change.

Altogether: completely or thoroughly.
All together: in a group; in unison.

Alumnus (sing.): male graduate.
Alumni (pl.)
Alumna (sing.): female graduate.
Alumnae (pl.)

Among: refers to three or more.
Between: refers to two only.

Amount: quantity without reference to individual units.
Number: a total of counted units.

Anxious: upset; concerned about a serious occurrence.
Eager: very desirous; anticipating a favorable event.

Anyone: any person in general.
Any one: a specific person or item.

Assay: to evaluate.
Essay: to try to attempt.
Essay: a literary composition.

Balance: as an accounting term, an amount owed or a difference between debit and credit sums.
Remainder: that which is left over; a surplus.

Bank on: informal expression for "rely on."

Bazaar: an establishment that sells merchandise.
Bizarre: eccentric in style or mode.

Being as, being that: should not be used for *since* or *because*.

Beside: by the side of.
Besides: in addition to.

Biannually: two times a year (also, *semiannually*).
Biennially: every two years.

Borne: past participle of *bear* (to carry, to produce).
Born: brought into existence.

Breach: an opening; an infraction of a law; a broken promise.
Breech: part of a firearm.

Calculate: to determine by mathematical process. Dialect for "think" or "expect."

Callous: not sympathetic; hardened.
Callus: hardened area of skin.

Can: refers to ability or capability.
May: refers to permission.

Canvas: a coarse type of cloth.
Canvass: to solicit; survey.

Cannon: large gun.
Canon: a law; church official.

Capital: a seat of government; money invested; a form of a letter.
Capitol: a government building.

Carat: unit of weight generally applied to gem stones.
Caret: mark showing omission.
Carrot: vegetable.
Karat: unit for measuring the purity of gold.

Cease: to halt or stop.
Seize: to grasp or take possession.

Censer: an incense pot.
Censor: a critic.
Sensor: an electronic device.
Censure: to find fault with or to blame.
Criticize: to evaluate; to examine.

Cereal: any grain.
Serial: arranged in successive order.

Choir: organized group of singers.
Quire: measure of paper.

Cite: to quote from a source.
Sight: act of seeing; object or scene observed.
Site: a place, such as "building site."

Coarse: composed of large particles; unrefined.
Course: a direction of progress or series of studies.

Collision: a clashing of objects.
Collusion: a conspiracy or fraud.

Command: to direct or order; an order.
Commend: to praise or laud.

Complacent: satisfied, smug.
Complaisant: obliging.

Complement: that which completes or supplements.
Compliment: flattery or praise.

Complexioned: refers to skin coloring or appearance.
Complected: dialect for "complexioned."

Confidant: one who may be confided in.
Confident: positive or sure.

Consensus of opinion: redundant; *consensus* means "general opinion."

Contact: meeting of surfaces. Frequently misused as a verb to mean "to ask," "to call," "to consult," or "to inform."

Continual: taking place in close succession; frequently repeated.
Continuous: no break or letup.

Council: an assembly of persons.
Counsel: to advise; advice; an attorney.
Consul: a resident representative of a foreign state.
Councillor: a member of a council.
Counselor: a lawyer or adviser.

Core: a center.
Corps: a body of troops; a group of persons in association.
Corpse: a dead body.

Credible: believable or acceptable.
Creditable: praiseworthy or meritorious.
Credulous: gullible.

Critic: one who evaluates.
Critique: an analytical examination of.
Criticism: an evaluation.

Currant: fruit.
Current: timely; motion of air or water.

Data:
Criteria:
Phenomena: The plural forms of *datum, criterion,* and *phenomenon. Data* is sometimes used as a singular, collective noun.

Deal: informal use for a business transaction; use instead *sale, agreement, plan.*

Deceased: dead.
Diseased: infected.

Decent: correct; proper.
Descent: going from high to low.
Dissent: disagreement.

Decree: a proclamation of law.
Degree: difference in grade; an academic award.

Defer: to delay or put off.
Differ: to disagree.

Deference: respect.
Difference: unlikeness.

Depot: a storehouse for merchandise or goods.
Station: a place for passengers; a regular stopping place.

Deprecate: to express disapproval of.
Depreciate: to lessen in value because of use and/or time; to belittle.

Desert: a reward or punishment.
Desert: to abandon.
Desert: a barren geographical area.
Dessert: a course at the end of a meal.

Device: a mechanism.
Devise: to formulate a plan.

Different from:
Different than: either may be used, although American usage prefers "different from."
Differ from: to stand apart because of unlikeness.
Differ with: to disagree.

Disapprove: not to accept.
Disprove: to prove wrong.

Disburse: to make payments; to allot.
Disperse: to scatter.

Discomfit: to frustrate; to disconcert (verb).
Discomfort: distress; not comfortable (noun).

Discreet: prudent; good judgment in conduct.
Discrete: separate entity; individual.

Disinterested: neutral; not biased.
Uninterested: not concerned with; lacking interest.

Disorganized: disordered.
Unorganized: not organized or planned.

Dual: double or two.
Duel: a contest between two antagonists.

Dying: in the process of losing life or function.
Dyeing: changing the color of.

Each other: refers to two.
One another: refers to more than two.

Either:
Neither: refers to one or the other of two. With *either* use *or;* with *neither* use *nor.*

Elicit: to draw forth, usually a comment.
Illicit: unlawful; illegal.

Eligible: acceptable; approved.
Illegible: impossible to read or decipher.

Elusive: difficult to catch.
Illusive: deceptive.

Emerge: to come out.
Immerge: to plunge into; immerse.

Emigrate: to travel out of one country to live in another.
Immigrate: to come into a country.
Migrate: to travel from place to place periodically.

Eminent: outstanding; prominent.
Imminent: impending, very near, or threatening.
Immanent: inherent.

Enthuse: a colloquialism meaning "to show enthusiasm."

Envelope: container for a communication.
Envelop: to surround; cover over or enfold.

Erotic: sexually arousing.
Erratic: unpredictable, irregular.
Exotic: foreign.
Esoteric: of interest only to a select few.

Exceptional: much better than average; superior.
Exceptionable: likely to cause objection; objectionable.

Expansive: capable of extension or expansion.
Expensive: costly.

Expect: informal use of *suppose* or *think.*

Extant: living or in existence.
Extent: an area or a measure.

Extinct: no longer living or existing.
Distinct: clear, sharply defined.

Facet: a small surface of a cut gem stone; aspect of an object or situation.
Faucet: a spigot.

Facilitate: to make easier.
Felicitate: to greet or congratulate.

Faint: to lose consciousness (verb); feeble, weak (adjective).
Feint: to pretend or simulate; a deceptive movement.

Farther: refers to geographical or linear distance.
Further: more; in addition to.

Fate: destiny.
Fête: to honor or celebrate (verb); a party (noun).
Feat: an act of unusual skill.

Faze: to disturb, discomfit, daunt.

Fiancé: the man to whom a woman is engaged to be married.
Fiancés (pl.):
Fiancée: the woman to whom a man is engaged to be married.
Fiancées (pl.):

Flair: natural ability.
Flare: a signal rocket; a blazing up of a fire.

Formally: according to convention.
Formerly: previously.

Freeze: to turn solid because of low temperatures.
Frieze: ornamentation along the top edge of a wall, sometimes on hung fabric.

Genius: unusual and outstanding ability.
Genus: a grouping or classification, usually on a biological basis.

Grisly: ghastly; horrible; very bad.
Grizzly: a subspecies of bear.

Hale: free from defect; healthy.
Hail: precipitation that has frozen.
Hail: to greet or call out.

Healthful: giving or contributing to health.
Healthy: having health.

Hoard: to collect and keep; a hidden supply.
Horde: a huge crowd.

Holey: having perforations or holes.
Holy: sacred, saintly.
Wholly: entirely; completely.

Human: pertaining to man.
Humane: kindly, considerate.

Immunity: safety from infection; exemption from regulation.
Impunity: freedom or exemption from punishment.

Imply: to hint at or to allude to in speaking or writing.
Infer: to draw a conclusion from what has been said or written.

In: indicates location within.
Into: indicates movement to a location within.

Incite: to stir up.
Insight: keen understanding; intuition.

Incredible: extraordinary; unbelievable.
Incredulous: skeptical; not believing.

Indignant: angry.
Indigenous: native to an area or country.
Indigent: needy; poor.

Individual: refers to a single item.
Party: a festive occasion; legal reference to a group or single person.

Ingenious: clever, resourceful.
Ingenuous: frank, honest, free from guile.

In regards to: incorrect; use *in regard to* or *as regards*.

Inside of: informal use for *within* as "inside of five minutes."
Outside of: informal use for *except* or *besides* as "outside of those three members. . . ."

Irregardless: nonstandard for *regardless*.

Its: a possessive singular pronoun.
It's: a contraction for *it is*.

Later: refers to time; the comparative form of *late*.
Latter: refers to the second named of two.

Lean: to rest at an angle.
Lien: a legal encumberance.

Learn: to acquire knowledge.
Teach: to impart knowledge.

Less: smaller quantity than, without reference to units.
Fewer: a smaller total of units.

Let: to permit.
Leave: to go away from; to abandon.

Lie, lay, lain: to recline.
Lay, laid, laid: to place.

Likely: probable.
Liable: legally responsible.
Apt: quick to learn; inclined; relevant.

Load: a burden; a pack.
Lode: a vein of ore.

Loath: reluctant; unwilling.
Loathe: to hate; to despise; to detest.

Locate: informal for *settle;* "to make one's residence."

Lose: to cease having.
Loose: not fastened or attached; to set free.

Magnate: a tycoon; important official.
Magnet: a device that attracts iron.

Marital: used in reference to marriage.
Marshal: an official; to arrange.
Martial: pertaining to military affairs.

Maybe: perhaps (adverb).
May be: indicates possibility (verb).

Medal: a badge of honor.
Mettle: spirit or temperament.
Metal: a mineral substance.
Meddle: to interfere.

Miner: an underground laborer or worker.
Minor: one who has not attained legal age; of little importance.

Moral: a principle, maxim, or lesson (noun); ethical (adjective).
Morale: a state of mind or psychological outlook (noun).

Nice: pleasant, agreeable; finely drawn, subtle, as in "nice distinction."

Notable: distinguished.
Notorious: unfavorably known.

Observance: following or respecting a custom or regulation.
Observation: act of seeing; casual remark.

Off of: informal use of *off.*

Oral: by word of mouth.
Verbal: communication in words whether oral or written.

Ordinance: a local law.
Ordnance: military weapons; munition.

Overdo: to do in excess.
Overdue: past due.

Peak: top of a hill or mountain; topmost point.
Peek: a quick look through a small opening.

Peal: sound of a bell.
Peel: to strip off.

Pedal: a foot lever.
Peddle: to sell.

Percent: should be used after a numeral (*20 percent*).
Percentage: for quantity or where numerals are not used (a larger *percentage*).

Persecute: to subject to harsh or unjust treatment.
Prosecute: to bring legal action against.

Personal: private; not public or general.
Personnel: the staff of an organization.

Plaintiff: the complaining party in a lawsuit.
Plaintive: sorrowful; mournful.

Plane: to make smooth; a tool; a surface.
Plain: area of level or treeless country; obvious, undecorated.

Practical: not theoretical; useful, pragmatic.
Practicable: can be put into practice (not used in reference to people).

Precedence: priority.
Precedents: cases that have already occurred.

Proceed: to begin; to move; to advance.
Precede: to go before.

Principal: of primary importance (adjective); head of a school; original sum; chief or official.
Principle: a fundamental truth.

Provided: on condition; supplied.
Providing: supplying.

Quite: almost; entirely; positively.
Quiet: without noise.

Real: actual, tangible; also slang for *very* or *extremely.*

Recent: newly created or developed; near past in time.
Resent: to feel indignant.

Respectfully: with respect or deference.
Respectively: in order named.

Resume: to begin again.
Résumé: a summing up.

Right along: informal for *without interruption* or *continuously.*

Rise: to move upward; to ascend (rise, rose, risen).
Raise: to elevate; pick up (raise, raised, raised).

Root: part of a plant.
Rout: to defeat.
Route: a traveler's plan.

Salvage: to save (verb); material saved from a fire, shipwreck, etc. (noun).
Selvage: edge of cloth.

Sit: to be seated.
Set: to put in position (set, set, set).

Shear: to cut.
Sheer: thin; steep; altogether.

Sometime: at one time or another.
Sometimes: occasionally.

Spoonfuls, carfuls, shovelfuls: the plural forms of *spoonful, carful, shovelful*.

Stationary: not moving; fixed.
Stationery: writing paper or writing materials.

Statue: a carved or molded three-dimensional reproduction.
Stature: height of a person; reputation.
Statute: a law.

Straight: direct; uninterrupted; not crooked.
Strait: narrow strip connecting two bodies of water; a distressing situation.

Than: used in comparison (conjunction): "Joe is taller than Tom."
Then: relating to time (adverb): "First he ran; then he jumped."

Their: belonging to them (possessive of *they*).
There: in that place (adverb).
They're: a contraction of the two words *they are*.

To: preposition: "to the store."
Too: adverb: "too cold."
Two: number: "two apples."

Toward:
Towards: identical in meaning and used interchangeably; *toward* is preferred.

Veracity: truthfulness.
Voracity: ravenousness; greed.

Vice: wickedness.
Vise: a clamp.

Waive: to give up; relinquish.
Wave: swell of water; a gesture.

Ways: procedures; also slang for distance.

Weather: climate or atmosphere.
Whether: an alternative.

Who's: a contraction of the two words *who is*.
Whose: possessive of *who*.

Your: a pronoun.
You're: a contraction of the two words *you are*.

TWO HUNDRED FREQUENTLY MISSPELLED WORDS*

About twenty years ago a researcher in the field of English made the claim that 95 percent of the spelling errors made by educated people occur in just 100 words. Our language has undergone many changes in the past two decades, but many of the same words *do* continue to plague us. The list below contains the 100 words in question as well as 100 others that often give trouble.

absence	bicycle	dilemma	hemorrhage
absorption	brilliant	dilettante	holiday
accede	bulletin	disappear	hosiery
accessible	calendar	disappoint	hypocrisy
accommodate	campaign	disbursement	illegible
accumulate	canceled	discrepancy	immigrant
achieve	canvass	discriminate	incidentally
acoustics	category	dissatisfied	indelible
acquittal	ceiling	dissipate	independent
advantageous	cemetery	drunkenness	indispensable
affiliated	changeable	ecstasy	inimitable
aggressive	clientele	eligible	inoculate
alignment	collateral	embarrassing	insistent
all right	committee	endorsement	intermediary
aluminum	comparative	envelop (verb)	irresistible
analyze	competitor	exaggerate	irritable
anoint	concede	exceed	jewelry
apostrophe	connoisseur	exhaust	judgment
apparent	connotation	exhilaration	judicial
appropriate	conscience	existence	khaki
argument	consensus	extraordinary	kindergarten
asphalt	convenient	fallacy	labeling
assistant	convertible	familiar	legitimate
asterisk	coolly	flexible	leisure
athletics	corroborate	fluctuation	license
auditor	criticism	forty	likable
bachelor	definitely	gesture	litigation
balloon	description	grammar	loneliness
bankruptcy	desirable	gratuity	loose
believable	despair	grievous	maintenance
benefited	development	haphazard	mathematics

*This list was compiled by J. Douglas Andrews, Chairman, Department of Business Communication, Graduate School of Business Administration, University of Southern California.

mediocre
minimum
misspelling
necessary
necessity
negligence
negotiable
newsstand
nickel
noticeable
occurrence
omission
opponent
oscillate
pageant
panicky
parallel
paralyze
pastime

peaceable
penicillin
permanent
perseverance
persistent
personnel
persuade
physician
plagiarism
plebian
possesses
potato
precede
predictable
preferred
privilege
procedure
proceed
professor

pronunciation
psychology
pursue
questionnaire
receive
recommend
repetition
rescind
rhythmical
ridiculous
sacrilegious
salable
secretary
seize
separate
sergeant
sheriff
stationary
stationery

succeed
suddenness
superintendent
supersede
surgeon
surprise
tangible
tariff
technique
tenant
tranquilizer
truly
tyrannize
unanimous
until
vacillate
vacuum
vicious
weird

Business Letter Style and Format

THE SECTIONS OF THE BUSINESS LETTER

The business letter is usually divided into six major parts: the heading, which includes the letterhead and the date; the inside address; the salutation; the body; the complimentary close; and the signature.

The Heading

The heading of the business letter contains the letterhead and the date. The former is given a good deal of attention by most firms because it contributes to the company image.

The date should not be typed as 1/4/9_ or 1-4-9_ even in intracompany memos. Many persons feel that this exhibits a distinct lack of courtesy. A more important reason for avoiding this method is to eliminate the possibility of misinterpretation. Although most North Americans would read 4/7/9_ as April 7, 199_ , most Europeans and Latin Americans would read it as July 4, 199_ .

The date should be written out using either of the following methods:

January 4, 19___   4 January 19___

The Inside Address

The inside address should be sufficiently complete to ensure accurate and rapid delivery of the letter. The information in the inside address should duplicate the address on the envelope.

The data for the inside address are usually drawn from the letterhead of the piece of correspondence being answered. Exact company designations and titles (as they appear in the letterhead) should be followed for the inside address.

The recipient's name in the inside address should be preceded by his or her title—*Ms., Mr., Mrs., Dr., General, Reverend,* etc. If the individual occupies a supervisory office, both the title and the area of responsibility can be indicated.

Dr. Lester Jameson, Director
Medical Research Department
Cicero Clinics
3148 North Cicero Avenue
Chicago, IL   60606

If the initials that designate degrees have the same meaning as the person's title, one or the other should be omitted.

INCORRECT   CORRECT
Dr. Robert Clock, M.D.   Dr. Robert Clock
                                  Robert Clock, M.D.

Dr. Roberta Mann, Ph.D.   Dr. Roberta Mann
                                  Roberta Mann, Ph.D.

Words in the inside address, such as *street, north,* and *avenue,* should not be abbreviated unless the company specifically requires such action. On the whole, the use of abbreviations should not be encouraged for the inside address.

Street numbers should always be written in numerals with the exception of *one.* Street names should be written out from First to Tenth streets. After that, numerals should be used. The zip code should follow the state. The following examples illustrate these recommendations.

Dr. Alberta Fine, Director   Ms. Joan Star, Manager
Conrad Research Center   Personnel Department
Conrad General Hospital   Foods, Inc.
1007 West 63rd Street   One East 95th Street
Los Angeles, CA   90024   Cincinnati, OH   45216

Reverend Peter Jackson   John T. Kasper, Ph.D.
Lutheran Central Church   Department of Management
7 South Ninth Avenue   Illinois State University
New York, NY   10010   Springfield, IL   62704

Rabbi Herman Schaalman   Thomas L. Lamp, M.D.
Temple Emanuel   Allerton Medical Center
5959 North Sheridan Road   17 North Bolton Avenue
Chicago, IL   60626   Columbus, OH   43227

The Salutation

Every effort should be made to use the recipient's name in the greeting or salutation. People respond more actively and sincerely to their names than to *Dear Occupant, Dear Friend, Dear Sir,* or *Dear Purchasing Agent.*

Many firms have expended large sums of money to have a personally typed inside address and/or salutation added to thousands of form letters before mailing. It is felt (usually with reason) that the form letter receives a much better reaction from the reader because of the added personal touch.

When individual letters are typed and the name of the recipient is not known, it is customary to use *Dear Sir* or *Dear Madam* in the singular, and *Gentlemen* or *Ladies* in the plural. *My Dear Sirs, Dear Sirs,* and *Mesdames* are all considered obsolete. Today, in an effort not to use one sex designation over another, neutral titles are strongly suggested by most office managers. *Dear Director, Dear Supervisor, Dear Owner* are all preferable to *Dear Sir* or *Dear Madam.*

Many individuals, in an effort to add a more friendly and informal tone to their letters, and to give some significance to the opening, use a "salutation phrase" instead of a salutation. These might be *Thank you, Mrs. Klay; We were happy, Mr. Conway; Enclosed, Mrs. Finer, you will find; Your order, Ms. Fay, was sent.* These phrases appear, in the letter, in place of the salutation.

These are certainly different and do attract attention. Some authorities argue that they may be too different and therefore resented by the recipient. However, they can be used with certain readers very effectively. And in sales writing they may well serve a very useful purpose.

The Body

Any discussion of the "body" of the letter must be concerned with the type of letter (sales, credit, collection, etc.) under consideration. From the point of view of appearance and format, however, the body should be attractively centered, broken into relatively short paragraphs, and surrounded by plenty of white space.

The Complimentary Close

The standard forms used in most letters are *Yours truly, Truly yours, Sincerely, Sincerely yours, Yours sincerely,* and to a lesser extent, *Cordially* or *Cordially yours.* As in the case of the salutation, attempts have been made to make the complimentary close more meaningful and personal. Some companies close their letters with phrases such as *Buy Arctic Freezers Today, See Your Arctic Dealer, Arctic for Quality, Arctic Is Yours Truly, Soft Glo for the Best in Lighting,* or *Truly a Fine Product.*

When such phrases are chosen with care and discretion, they often produce excellent results. However, the letter writer should not reach too far for an interesting close. What may seem clever to the writer might be interpreted by the reader as much too cute. Some firms compose a close, use it on all letters for two weeks, and then switch to a new one. In effect most persons will not see the same one repeated under this system.

The Signature

This section of the letter is handled in a variety of ways. In most firms the signature has three or four parts, with the trend toward the latter number. The four-part signature includes the name of the company, the signature of the writer, and his or her typed name and title. If the signature has only three parts, the name of the company (in the letterhead) is omitted. (See the signatures at the right.)

Sometimes one will find initials placed immediately below the signature. This is done when the secretary signs the writer's name and adds his or her own initials. However, this practice is often interpreted by the reader in a rather poor light. The reader may be irritated that the writer apparently could not find fifteen seconds to sign the letter, but had a secretary do it. This is understandable, so every effort should be made by the writer to sign every letter.

Of course it is possible that the writer could have dictated the letter in the morning and then have left on a business trip. In such case, the writer obviously would not have been available to sign the letter when it was ready for a signature. However, the fact is that most people resent what the initials below a signature imply.

Yours truly,
CAIN PRODUCTS CO.

John Kingley

John Kingley
Sales Manager

Sincerely Yours,

Robert Black

Robert Black
Superintendent

Truly yours,
LOOP LAMP COMPANY

William Key

William Key, Manager

Sincerely yours,
BAINE INC.

Roberta Baine

Partner

OTHER MECHANICAL FACTORS OF BUSINESS LETTERS

The Attention Line

Frequently we find that one person in a company with which we are doing business gives us excellent service. Thus, in order to have Kelly handle our requests, we send our communications to his *attention*. If we send the letter directly to him, and he has left the company, it is very possible that the envelope will be *returned* to us or *forwarded* to him. However, if the letter is sent to his *attention* and he has left the company, the communication will normally be opened and processed by his successor. When a recipient's name is not known, you may address the letter to the department or position (e.g., Attention: Service Department).

The position of the attention line varies, although it usually appears in one of the following places:

Belmont Steel Company
1122 West Ninth Street
Belmont, Indiana   60397

Dear Mr. Keelton: Attention of Mr. Keelton, Teasurer

Belmont Steel Company
1122 West Ninth Street
Belmont, Indiana   60397

Attention of Mr. Keelton, Treasurer

Dear Mr. Keelton:

Belmont Steel Company
1122 West Ninth Street
Belmont, Indiana   60397

                         Attention of Mr. Keelton, Treasurer

Dear Mr. Keelton:

Many firms use an abbreviation for *attention, Attn:* or *Att.*

The Subject Line

The subject line is another device used to speed handling or retrieval of correspondence from files. In addition, it can eliminate much of the first paragraph if it is worded carefully. Its position, like the attention line's, varies according to company preference.

Kelvyn Clock Company
1515 West Granby Street
Springfield, CA   92077

Ladies and Gentlemen: Subject: Your order #2136

Betsy B. Ice Cream
1000 West Nevada Avenue
Boulder, CO   80303

                                        Subject: Your invoice #201
                                              January 7, 19___

Ladies and Gentlemen:

This *subject* line, like a *file number* or *in reply refer to file number* _____ , can save time and increase office efficiency.

Identifying Initials

For many years it was customary to place the dictator's and typist's initials in the lower left-hand section of the business letter. In recent years the trend seems to be toward omitting them.

But many firms still follow the practice, especially when all letters from a department are signed by one individual even though any one of several people may have done the dictating. In this instance, the dictator's initials are used and, of course, do not match the signature of the department head. The initials identify the person who actually wrote the letter.

Some of the accepted variations in handling identifying initials are shown below. Note that both a slash mark and a colon are acceptable separators.

JS/rt   MRL:AO   LT/MR   TTA:bm

Enclosure Line

The enclosure notation is usually placed immediately below the identifying initials and indicates that some item such as a check, invoice, or reprint has been included in the envelope along with the letter.

Either the word *Enclosure* or the abbreviation *Enc* is used. For only one enclosure, no numeral is used; for more than one, the number is indicated. Some firms and most federal government agencies identify each enclosure so that when one is withdrawn, it can be easily identified.

BM:rt   LSM/rd
Enc   Enclosures 3

GM/tl   LM:ML
Enc 3   Enclosure
    1. Birth certificate
    2. Visa
    3. Letter of reference

Carbon Copies or Photocopies

Obviously if a letter is sent to Mr. Robert Blackstone, a copy of that letter should ordinarily not be forwarded to anyone else; the contents of a business letter are a private matter between the writer and addressee. It is easy to understand how offended Mr. Blackstone might become if another person indicated, through a comment or a note, that he was aware of information that had been contained in a letter sent by Acme Products to Blackstone.

To avoid such a situation, and because it is also a matter of ethics, we tell Mr. Blackstone that a copy of this letter addressed to him was sent to Mr. Clayton. The device of *cc:* (carbon copy) or *c:* (copy) is used. Even though photocopies have now largely taken the place of carbon paper, the abbreviation *cc* or the simple word *copy* is more common than *pc* or *xc* (photocopy or Xerox copy).

```
DM/ts                          LT/sa
cc: Mr. Clayton                copy: Mr. Clayton
                                     Credit Department
```

Firms sometimes employ the initials *bc* or *bcc* which stands for *blind copy* or blind carbon copy. This is typed only on the copy and not on the original letter and tells the reader of the carbon copy that Mr. Blackstone is not aware that a copy has been sent to a second party.

Letterhead

The letterhead that shouts at us with oversize pictures of the product, unattractive sketches of the plant, or "call us day or night" statements does not convey the best image of the company. However, the trend in letterhead designs today is toward simplicity and clean-cut type faces that reflect dignity and good taste. Pictures of products or office buildings or factories, if included, are usually small and very well executed, so they will not detract from the overall letterhead "message" or from the letter itself.

There are many specialists and advertising agencies to assist business people in designing a new letterhead or revising one. And this revision is necessary, for styles in letterheads change as does the company image. Certainly outmoded type styles or a picture of a 25-year-old car or office machine in the letterhead design will not contribute to a favorable impression of the company. *Printer's Ink* magazine had this to say about the letterhead design and the message it conveys:

> *In addition to identifying the sender, letterheads convey, both liminally and subliminally, an image of the company. The great mass of mail sent out by the average company gives its letterhead a significant role to perform in its sales-promotion and public-relations programs.*

Many of the large paper corporations will also assist in letterhead revision. Their staff artists will draw up a new letterhead or send out letterhead kits that contain sample designs of letterheads and different grades and colors of stationery, graph paper, and directions for a "do-it-yourself" approach.

In addition to being attractive, meaningful, and in good taste, the letterhead should answer the questions *who, where,* and *what.* The *who,* of course, is the name of the company, presented exactly as the firm wishes to be identified. This includes the precise abbreviations ("Corp." or "Inc.") and designations ("Furniture Manufacturers" or "Manufacturers of Furniture").

The *where* includes street address, city, state, zip code number, telephone number, cable address, and other items of this nature.

The *what* tells the reader the nature of the company's operations. It is disconcerting to receive a letter from the R. T. Cronin Corporation at 102 East Adams Street in Los Angeles and not be able to determine whether the firm manufactures kitchen appliances or conducts national surveys. See Figure B–1 for arrangement of a typical business letter.

Many firms are also using the empty space along the bottom of the page. A listing of the cities in which the company has outlets or plants, small pictures of the firm's products, or even the company address can be included. The type should be small and distinct, and the layout in balance with the information at the top of the stationery.

PUNCTUATION

The terms *open* or *closed* punctuation refer to end-of-line punctuation in the salutation and complimentary close. Much correspondence today uses open punctuation, for it saves typing time and therefore money. (See Figures B–2 and B–3.)

LETTER PLACEMENT AND FORMAT

The appearance of the letter adds to the reader's image of the organization. Certainly a twelve-line letter jammed at the top or bottom of the page contributes little to a good impression. A similar reader reaction results when the letter or report has two heavy block paragraphs on each page with one 34 lines long and the other 44!

On the other hand, a well-balanced page with plenty of white space, attractive and adequate margins on all four sides, and typing that is centered provides a visual appearance that is positive. These factors contribute to the type of image most firms wish to convey.

Several different letter formats can be used. The most popular today are *full block, modified block,* and *modified block with indented paragraphs.* (See Figures B–4 through B–7.)

FIGURE B–1

A typical business letter

(1)

SCHOOL OF HOTEL MANAGEMENT
Midwestern University   Ann Arbor, Michigan 48109   (313) 654-2819

August 3, 19___

(2)

Ms. Elaine Cane, Editor
Gourmet Times
1500 East Pine Street
San Francisco, CA 94111

(3)

Dear Ms. Cane:

(4)

Your December issue of Gourmet Times was absolutely outstanding. The content, layout, four-color photography, and a dozen other details were completed in a most professional manner. In fact, it was all done so well, we want to request a favor of you.

As you probably know, the Division of Hotel Management at this University enjoys an excellent reputation. In addition to our usual classes and degree program in Hotel Management, we conduct two seminars each year for Chefs de Cuisine. Each of these seminars is four weeks in length.

The participants in this program receive notebooks of materials. These are reference papers, readings, and a variety of materials which supplement the presentations and demonstrations. We would like to purchase 200 of your last two issues of Gourmet Times to include in the notebooks.

In addition we would appreciate your participating in each seminar as a guest lecturer for a three-hour period. Of course we would be happy to provide first-class air fare, necessary accommodations, and a modest honorarium of $800 for each presentation.

Please call me collect, Ms. Cane, so we may discuss this, and if at all possible, select dates that you find convenient.

(5)

Cordially yours,

(6)

Raphael Peterson

Raphael Peterson, Ph.D.,
Associate Dean

RP/bp

(7)

Enclosure: Sales Brochure, Chefs de Cuisine Seminars

(1) Heading	(4) Body	(6) Signature
(2) Inside address	(5) Complimentary close	(7) Enclosure line
(3) Salutation		

FIGURE B–2

Open punctuation

```
      Mr. Robert T. Scott
      Morrell and Company
      1515 West Ohio Street
      St. Louis, MO   63125

      Dear Mr. Scott

      _____
      _____
      _____


                                    Yours very truly
```

FIGURE B–3

Mixed punctuation

```
      Mr. Robert T. Scott
      Morrell and Company
      1515 West Ohio Street
      St. Louis, MO   63125

      Dear Mr. Scott:

      _____
      _____
      _____


                                    Yours very truly,
```

FIGURE B–4

Heading on blank stationery

```
                                    4130 South Nelson Drive
                                    Dallas, TX   75240
                                    April 28, 19__

      Mr. Frank Fellway
      Personnel Director
      Compton and Compton, Inc.
      1000 North Point Drive
      Dallas, TX   75242

      Dear Mr. Fellway:
```

FIGURE B–5
Full block form

Lyons Laundry Supply   4880 West Markham Avenue   Oklahoma City Oklahoma 73127   (405) 949-3000

December 3, 19__

Ms. Eleanor Lang
Christ Community Hospital
1200 West Piedmont Ave.
Oklahoma City, OK 73128

Dear Ms. Lang:

Thank you for your inquiry of November 28 concerning the uniforms of your cafeteria and security personnel. Yes, we can certainly handle your request.

If it meets with your schedule, we can arrange to pick up all soiled linen on Monday and Thursday or Tuesday and Friday. All items picked up on Monday will be returned on Thursday; those picked up on Thursday will be returned on Monday. This rapid turnaround service permits you to operate with a minimum number of uniforms in your inventory.

All uniforms are washed in mild detergents, which lengthens the life of your linens. Minor tears or holes are repaired free of charge and areas of heavy stain are carefully hand-scrubbed.

You will find our prices are extremely competitive: 35 cents for each shirt, jacket, skirt, or trouser unit. This includes washing and ironing and applies to 100 units or more per pickup. If less than 100 units are picked up, the price is 50 cents each.

We now service Manor Community Hospital, all branches of Franklin Savings and Loan, The Health-Mor Retirement Homes, and many others. We guarantee your complete satisfaction. Please call or visit our installation today, Ms. Lang, and we can begin service tomorrow.

Sincerely yours,

Joan Lyons
Sales Manager

JL/rm

FIGURE B–6
Modified block form

CHATEAU BABY TOYS, INC.
Palos, New Mexico   88032

                                        October 12, 19__

Ms. Toby Wren, Senior Buyer
Gale's Department Stores
One North Hampden Road
New York, NY   10024

Dear Ms. Wren:

Although it will require overtime scheduling on our part, we
will certainly fill the special order you called in yesterday.
Of course we are delighted that our new Charming Toddler Line
has been received so favorably by your customers.

As you requested, we will ship Order 2150 to your Lincoln Warehouse, and Order 2151 to your Market Terminal. Both shipments
will arrive on October 24. Billing will be on our usual terms
plus $450 for the additional labor charge we will incur. As you
recall, we agreed on this sum (45 hours at $10.00 per hour) in
our telephone conversation of October 11.

It is always a pleasure to do business with you. I am especially happy we were able to fulfill this emergency request.

                                   Cordially yours,

                                   Fern Maple

                                   Fern Maple
                                   Production Manager

FM/mm

cc: Mgr., Gale Lincoln Warehouse
      Mgr., Gale Market Terminal

FIGURE B–7

Modified block with indented paragraphs

Quality Auto-Parts

1500 West Fulton Street   Philadelphia, Pennsylvania 19102   (215) 650-0550

May 15, 19__

Mr. John Baker, Mgr.
Ford Auto Service Center
100 West Conway Blvd.
Philadelphia, PA   19106

Dear Mr. Baker:

    Thank you for your interest in stocking our complete line of auto radio, stereo, and tape decks. Certainly the Clear Bell product has earned an excellent and well-deserved reputation.

    Because you indicated that you would like to stock some 200 units on a consignment basis, we were forced to get in touch with our headquarters. This was necessary because all our sales are on a strict COD basis. Inasmuch as your suggestion would be a departure from our usual terms and might cause problems with our other accounts, we feel it is not possible to comply with your request.

    We can, however, offer an alternative. We will ship the order with payment of one-half the total on a COD basis and the balance within 90 days. In both instances, our 2 percent discount will apply.

    We do want to work with you in every way possible, Mr. Baker. Please call us collect and all items will be shipped to you within 10 days.

Cordially yours,

Martin Cahill

Martin Cahill
Vice President, Sales

MC/bp

FOLDING A BUSINESS LETTER

One of the first ways we spot "junk" mail is by the off-center, slap-dash fold of the letter. Distinguish your business correspondence by folding letters precisely. Note that in folding both two-fold and three-fold letters, a tab is provided for the reader's convenience in opening the letter.

Two-fold way (for long envelopes)

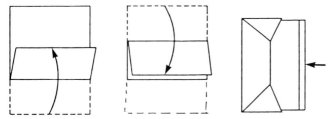

Three-fold way (for short envelopes)

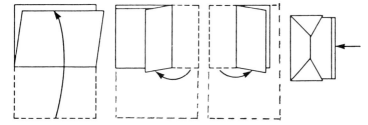

Envelope Conventions

The envelope's balanced, neat appearance influences your reader's attitudes toward your letter even before he or she has opened it:

```
Western Investors, Inc.
396 Branchaw Blvd.
Dallas, TX  59392




                          Ms. Brenda Victors, Manager
                          Cognetics, Inc.
                          33 Seventh St.
                          Dallas, TX  59392


                                             Personal
```

According to the 1982 National Zip Code Directory, the U.S. Post Office recommends the following placement of addresses (for easier reading by optical character recognition equipment):

Large envelopes (Number 10)

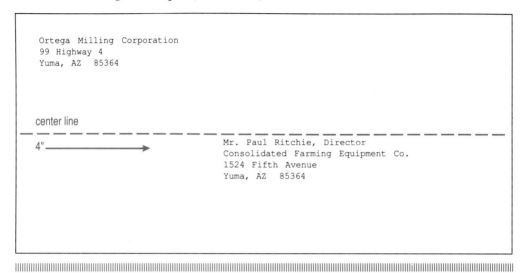

Small envelopes (Number 6¾)

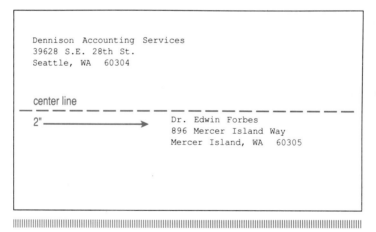

Use the following abbreviations for states (without a period that usually accompanies abbreviations):

AL	(Alabama)	LA	(Louisiana)	OK	(Oklahoma)
AK	(Alaska)	ME	(Maine)	OR	(Oregon)
AZ	(Arizona)	MD	(Maryland)	PA	(Pennsylvania)
AR	(Arkansas)	MA	(Massachusetts)	PR	(Puerto Rico)
CA	(California)	MI	(Michigan)	RI	(Rhode Island)
CO	(Colorado)	MN	(Minnesota)	SC	(South Carolina)
CT	(Connecticut)	MS	(Mississippi)	SD	(South Dakota)
DE	(Delaware)	MO	(Missouri)	TN	(Tennessee)
DC	(D.C.)	MT	(Montana)	TX	(Texas)
FL	(Florida)	NE	(Nebraska)	UT	(Utah)
GA	(Georgia)	NV	(Nevada)	VT	(Vermont)
HI	(Hawaii)	NH	(New Hampshire)	VA	(Virginia)
ID	(Idaho)	NJ	(New Jersey)	WA	(Washington)
IL	(Illinois)	NM	(New Mexico)	WV	(West Virginia)
IN	(Indiana)	NY	(New York)	WI	(Wisconsin)
IA	(Iowa)	NC	(North Carolina)	WY	(Wyoming)
KS	(Kansas)	ND	(North Dakota)		
KY	(Kentucky)	OH	(Ohio)		

ADDITIONAL INSTRUCTIONS ON ENVELOPES

Business communication texts usually recommend that instructions such as "Confidential," "Personal," or "Time-dated Materials" be placed to the left or the right of the address, and a bit below it:

```
Trevor Cosmetics, Inc.
702 Western St.
St. Louis, MO  70892




                        Ms. Betty Konway, Manager
                        Style-Setters  Salon
                        70 Billings Road
                        St. Louis, MO  70896


                                    Time-dated  Materials
```

The Post Office suggests that only instructions intended for the mail deliverer (such as "Special Delivery") be placed on the right of the envelope. Such instructions, the Post Office requests, should be placed four spaces below the stamp.

```
AVC  Audio  Corporation
602  Gentson  Lane
Houghton, PA    7023



Confidential                                           Special  Delivery


                      Technical  Service  Director
                      Frede  Computer  Products,  Inc.
                      30702  Hill  Drive
                      Boulder, CO    60982
```

Index and
Photo Credits

Index

Photo Credits

Pg. 31 (l)	Courtesy IBM
Pg. 31 (r)	Courtesy Santa Fe Southern Pacific Corp.
Pg. 32	Courtesy California Faculty Association
Pg. 34	Courtesy Hughes Aircraft Company
Pg. 36 (l)	Courtesy Xerox Corporation
Pg. 36 (r)	Courtesy Northrup
Pg. 40 (l)	Courtesy of IBM World Trade Europe Middle East Africa Corporation
Pg. 40 (r)	Courtesy University of Southern California
Pg. 72	Hirmer Fotoarchiv, Munich
Pg. 74	Historical Pictures Service, Chicago
Pg. 77	Reproduced with permission of AT&T
Pg. 79	Courtesy Apple Computer, Inc.
Pg. 86	Reproduced with permission of AT&T
Pp. 90, 99	Courtesy IBM
Pg. 100	Courtesy Apple Computer, Inc.
Pg. 178	"Hughesnews Readership Survey" from *Hughesnews,* September 23, 1983. Copyright © 1983 by Hughes Aircraft Company. Reprinted by permission.
Pg. 186	Letter from Simmons Market Research Bureau, Inc. Reprinted with permission.
Pg. 319 (tl)	Courtesy Delta Airlines, Inc.
Pg. 319 (tr)	Courtesy H&R Block, Inc.
Pg. 319 (b)	Copied with permission of American Greetings Corporation
Pg. 322	Courtesy Delta Airlines, Inc.
Pp. 323–24	Copied with permission of American Greetings Corporation
Pg. 325	Courtesy H&R Block, Inc.
Pg. 334	Courtesy Hewlett-Packard Company.
Pg. 382	Toastmasters International. Art by Jeff Koegel.
Ex. 1	Data courtesy of *Beverage World*, March, 1988. Reprinted by permission.
Ex. 6	Reproduced with permission, *High Technology* Magazine, February 1985. Copyright © 1985 by High Technology Publishing Corporation, 38 Commercial Wharf, Boston, MA 02110.
Ex. 9	Courtesy Verascad Corporation
Part Three	Milt and Joan Mann/Cameramann International, Ltd.
Part Seven	Robert George Gaylord

All other photos property of Scott, Foresman.